The Eastern International

OXFORD STUDIES IN INTERNATIONAL HISTORY
James J. Sheehan, series advisor

THE WILSONIAN MOMENT
Self-Determination and the International Origins of Anticolonial Nationalism
Erez Manela

IN WAR'S WAKE
Europe's Displaced Persons in the Postwar Order
Gerard Daniel Cohen

GROUNDS OF JUDGMENT
Extraterritoriality and Imperial Power in Nineteenth-Century China and Japan
Pär Kristoffer Cassel

THE ACADIAN DIASPORA
An Eighteenth-Century History
Christopher Hodson

GORDIAN KNOT
Apartheid and the Unmaking of the Liberal World Order
Ryan Irwin

THE GLOBAL OFFENSIVE
The United States, the Palestine Liberation Organization, and the Making of the Post–Cold War Order
Paul Thomas Chamberlin

MECCA OF REVOLUTION
Algeria, Decolonization, and the Third World Order
Jeffrey James Byrne

BEYOND THE ARAB COLD WAR
The International History of the Yemen Civil War 1962–68
Asher Orkaby

SHARING THE BURDEN
The Armenian Question, Humanitarian Intervention, and Anglo-American Visions of Global Order
Charlie Laderman

THE WAR LORDS AND THE DARDANELLES
How Grain and Globalization Led to Gallipoli
Nicholas A. Lambert

FEAR OF THE FAMILY
Guest Workers and Family Migration in the Federal Republic of Germany
Lauren Stokes

POLITICS OF UNCERTAINTY
The United States, the Baltic Question, and the Collapse of the Soviet Union
Una Bergmane

SUHARTO'S COLD WAR
Indonesia, Southeast Asia, and the World
Mattias Fibiger

THE EASTERN INTERNATIONAL
Arabs, Central Asians, and Jews in the Soviet Union's Anticolonial Empire
Masha Kirasirova

The Eastern International

Arabs, Central Asians, and Jews in the Soviet Union's Anticolonial Empire

MASHA KIRASIROVA

OXFORD
UNIVERSITY PRESS

Oxford University Press is a department of the University of Oxford. It furthers
the University's objective of excellence in research, scholarship, and education
by publishing worldwide. Oxford is a registered trade mark of Oxford University
Press in the UK and certain other countries.

Published in the United States of America by Oxford University Press
198 Madison Avenue, New York, NY 10016, United States of America.

© Oxford University Press 2024

All rights reserved. No part of this publication may be reproduced, stored in
a retrieval system, or transmitted, in any form or by any means, without the
prior permission in writing of Oxford University Press, or as expressly permitted
by law, by license, or under terms agreed with the appropriate reproduction
rights organization. Inquiries concerning reproduction outside the scope of the
above should be sent to the Rights Department, Oxford University Press, at the
address above.

You must not circulate this work in any other form
and you must impose this same condition on any acquirer.

Library of Congress Cataloging-in-Publication Data
Names: Kirasirova, Masha, author.
Title: The eastern international : Arabs, Central Asians, and Jews in the
Soviet Union's anticolonial empire / Masha Kirasirova.
Description: New York, NY : Oxford University Press, [2024] |
Series: Oxford studies in international history |
Includes bibliographical references and index.
Identifiers: LCCN 2023040826 (print) | LCCN 2023040827 (ebook) |
ISBN 9780197685693 (hardback) | ISBN 9780197685709 (paperback) |
ISBN 9780197685716 (epub) | ISBN 9780197685730
Subjects: LCSH: Soviet Union—Foreign relations—Middle East. |
Soviet Union—Foreign relations—Asia, Central. | Middle East—Foreign
relations—Soviet Union. | Asia, Central—Foreign relations—Soviet Union. |
Arabs—Soviet Union. | Central Asians—Soviet Union. | Jews—Soviet Union.
Classification: LCC DS63.2.R9 K53 2024 (print) | LCC DS63.2.R9 (ebook) |
DDC 327.4705—dc23/eng/20231205
LC record available at https://lccn.loc.gov/2023040826
LC ebook record available at https://lccn.loc.gov/2023040827

DOI: 10.1093/oso/9780197685693.001.0001

Contents

Acknowledgments vii

Introduction: The Eastern International in the Long Soviet Century 1

1. Anticolonial Dreams and the Territorialization of Soviet Power 23
2. A Bolshevik Laboratory for Revolution in the East 60
3. Arabization, Purges, and Terror 92
4. Muslim Tradition Forbids Reciting the Qur'an While Drunk 124
5. Decolonization and the Thaw 153
6. Scripting Central Asian Revolution for the Afro-Asian World 185
7. The Eastern International in an Age of Globalization 217
Conclusion 241

Notes 249
Bibliography 333
Index 363

Introduction

The Eastern International in the Long Soviet Century

On May 18, 1925, a few hundred students gathered in a lecture hall of the Communist University of the Toilers of the East (KUTV) housed in a repurposed mansion in the heart of Moscow.[1] This group, consisting of mostly men and a few women, came from across Eurasia. Most had come from non-Russian territories that had been conquered and incorporated into the imperial polity at different times: Siberia and East Asian parts of the Russian "East" that had been the dominion of the tsars since the sixteenth century and from the southwestern borderlands in the Caucasus and Central Asia that had been conquered in the eighteenth and nineteenth centuries. Some had traveled from as far away as China, Japan, South Africa, and the Americas; others came from more proximate Mongolia, Iran, Afghanistan, India, and Egypt and Palestine in the Eastern Mediterranean. Some were dressed in the clothes they had brought with them on these long journeys; others were already clad in their KUTV uniforms—overcoats inherited from demobilized Red Army fighters or suit jackets worn over soldiers' shirts or tunics. The diversity in dress and appearance demonstrated that the new Bolshevik state could attract a wide range of supporters and, potentially, change the world. As a group, the gathering also reflected the state's view of these particular individuals as "Easterners."

The meaning of this label, "Eastern," was the subject of the lecture anticipated that day from Joseph Stalin, another migrant from the imperial periphery who, despite his accented Russian, had risen to lead the revolutionary state and serve as its commissar of nationalities. When necessary, Stalin could also play the Asiatic card. As he told the Japanese foreign minister Matsuoka when he visited the Kremlin in April 1941 to negotiate the Non-Aggression Pact, "You are an Asiatic, so am I."[2] From the KUTV podium, he addressed the students as "comrades," boasting that they represent "no less than fifty nations and national groups of the East." Yet their composition pointed to a significant analytical duality:

The Eastern International. Masha Kirasirova, Oxford University Press. © Oxford University Press 2024.
DOI: 10.1093/oso/9780197685693.003.0001

One group consists of people who have come here from the Soviet East, from countries where the rule of the bourgeoisie no longer exists, where imperialist oppression (*gnet*) has been overthrown, and where the workers are in power. The second group consists of students who have come from colonial and dependent countries, from countries where capitalism still reigns, where imperialist oppression is still in full force, and where independence has still to be won by driving out the imperialists.[3]

It is possible that some of the students recognized themselves in this duality. Some may have even understood that it referred to the entrenchment of Soviet state borders after the civil war and the embrace by Soviet ruling elites of the "Socialism in One Country" thesis—the idea that the USSR should turn inward and focus on strengthening communism nationally rather than globally.

In other respects, however, Stalin's duality was blurry and unsettled. The world was changing rapidly, but the Sovietization of the domestic East was still incomplete. The idea of "workers" being "in power" was controversial in regions like the newly delimited Turkestan where a mostly ethnic Russian proletariat, who were also technically colonial settlers, struggled with local inhabitants over how to achieve decolonization equitably and peacefully. The very fact that Stalin insisted that the domestic East was "liberated" suggests that he may have been worried that someone might mistake it for an occupied zone. In colonized regions of the foreign East, the anti-imperialist struggle would entail identifying and isolating parts of the national bourgeoisie that were compromising the interests of the proletariat. This was no easy task, as communists and nationalist revolutionaries would discover. Furthermore, this dynamic looked different in less developed countries like Morocco, in moderately underdeveloped countries like China and Egypt, and in more developed countries like India. The one thing that seemed clear was that this opportunity to live and study in Moscow required figuring out what it meant in the revolutionary movement to be acceptably "Eastern."

This book traces how the concept "East" (Vostok) was used by the world's first communist state and its mediators to project, channel, and contest power across Eurasia. These mediators—including some in Stalin's audience—used this concept to access the state's resources, engage in global conversation about decolonization, and win legitimacy for the Soviet Union as an anticolonial state power. Through much of the Soviet Union's existence they succeeded in this task because ideas of anticapitalism, antifascism, and freedom from colonial exploitation inspired so many worldwide. By contextualizing their stories within a global historical frame, this work shows how these Eastern mediators popularized critiques of capitalism, fascism, and colonialism through propaganda, education, cultural relations, and later, political and economic aid in international Eastern regions, even as they helped to conceal other inequalities and forms of exploitation, including those in the Soviet "domestic East." These conversations severed all analysis of Soviet anticolonial and imperial politics from other conversations about twentieth-century colonialism, anticolonialism, and postcolonialism.

The networked world of actors and institutions that made up the "Eastern International" sustained the myth of the Soviet Union as an anticolonial power. This network spans the lifetime of the Bolshevik/Soviet state, from the revolutionary transformation of empire during World War I through the Soviet collapse. Its history is traced here through chronological case studies. Taken together, these case studies enable a retelling of the story of the "Soviet century" with a new focus: the long-neglected regions and peoples participating in the wider effort to "build a world after empire."[4]

At the end of World War I, Soviet leaders—like their counterparts in reconfigured European empires, the League of Nations' protectorates in the Near East, and newly sovereign states such as Turkey—were grappling with the legacies of Ottoman, Russia, and Hapsburg collapse. The collapse of these empires would prove to be a contingent and interconnected process.[5] Most Soviet leaders well understood that the Russian and Ottoman empires had been linked by centuries of trade, temporary migration and pilgrimage, more permanent migrations of Muslim refugees fleeing the Russian conquest of the Caucasus and Central Asia, and even the education of important members of their respective political elites.[6]

Given the perceived dangers of imperial collapse, Lenin and Stalin attempted to neutralize nationalism by creating a new federative system that simultaneously promoted and coopted forms of nationhood.[7] The same dangers also motivated them to establish anti-imperialist credentials abroad. The latter effort involved repudiating all tsarist and Provisional Government debts, exposing and renouncing tsarist-era diplomatic treaties, creating opportunities for foreign communists by building new institutions such as the University for the Toilers of the East, and promoting their own postwar vision of peace. The fact that the USSR was left out of the Versailles Treaty, and the system of collective security it had created, pushed the Bolsheviks to continue to pursue an overlapping anti-imperial and anticolonial foreign policy conducted on an inter-state level by the Ministry of Foreign Affairs and through transregional communist networks by the Third International (Comintern). The intersection of these domestic and international priorities, as well as frictions between different institutions, could at times be rewarding and at other times risky for the various intermediaries that participated in building the first multiethnic state in world history to define itself as an anti-imperial state.

Historians have identified the impossibility of thinking outside of the categories of difference of their time, many of which cut deep into the intellectual and even theological traditions of the Russian and wider European imperial intellectual context, as a characteristic of political modernity.[8] In Russia, specifically, the proposition that state politics could be divided into "European" and "Eastern" or "Asiatic" components is a key imperial vestige and an enduring, resilient dimension of how Soviet leaders thought about statecraft. This division of Russia into Europe and Asia is at least as old as the early eighteenth century, when Peter the Great had tried to give Russia a more European appearance by building St. Petersburg as a "Venice of the North," requiring noblemen to wear European dress, changing his title from tsar to emperor (*imperator*), and renaming Russia as an empire (*imperiia*). This meant, geographer Mark Bassin writes, that "like Spain or England, the Netherlands or Portugal, ... Russia ... could be divided into two major components: a homeland or metropolis that belonged within European civilization, and a vast but foreign extra-European colonial periphery."[9] Cartographers and other experts who studied the imperial terrain would demarcate and distinguish these realms.[10] As a result, "Asiatic Russia" became an ever more commonplace term, used in the nineteenth and early twentieth centuries to underscore the abiding linkage between "Asiatic" and "Russian" spaces, variously defined.[11] Although the category "Asia" was more grounded in geography, it would often be used interchangeably with the "East" (Vostok), a more cultural category but one that connoted the same status of non-Western imperial dominions. Both categories were critical to the fashioning of Russian as an *imperiia*, and both played a role in its refashioning by the Bolsheviks as an anti-imperialist and anticolonial state.

Recognizing these imperial vestiges in Soviet history need not lead inevitably back to old debates about the classification of the Soviet Union as either an "empire" or a "modernizing state."[12] After the collapse of the USSR, as concerns about the "evil empire" waned, scholars were able to see empires in new ways—they could be seen as a context for later, modern, multiethnic and multinational states, or as variations on the question of state power, which in the case of Bolshevik state building were deeply ideological.[13] Earlier "totalitarian" models that treated the Soviet state as a monolithic entity with the capacity to bring about an atomized society through control and manipulation had rendered its differentiating dynamics invisible. Likewise, these dynamics were excluded in revisionist approaches that treated ideology as a cover for something else "really going on" that could be revealed through social history, or subjectivity studies that focus mostly on the individual. By foregrounding the roles of various intermediaries—their imperial contexts, networks, group identities, and interests—this book is inspired by approaches to empire as an intellectual problem that can be considered through the eyes of the historical actors grappling with its various meanings.

Debates over culture in eighteenth- and nineteenth-century Russia had only partially challenged the Eurocentrism of its imperial ideology and East-West divide. "Westernizers" argued that Russia wasn't European enough and that it needed to adopt more European technology and more liberal forms of government. Their opponents, the Slavophiles and Pan-Slavs, identified Europe with violence, pernicious individualism, and lust for profit. Yet, they continued to use West-East territorial distinctions to describe imperial space when they referred to nineteenth-century territorial conquests in East Asia, the Caucasus, and Central Asia.[14] A minority offshoot of the Slavophile movement called themselves *Vostochniki* (Asianists) and imagined a greater kinship with Asia, having come to admire China's unwavering conservatism and more robust form of autocracy.[15] Yet the majority saw the gulf separating Russia from the Occident as considerably less wide than the one separating it from the Orient.

Within the Asiatic or Eastern space of empire, one region acquired the status of Russia's paradigmatic colony. Turkestan, the region that became Soviet Central Asia, was the last large, densely populated Muslim-majority territory conquered by Russia in the context of imperial competition with Britain in the 1860s and 1870s. Neighboring Bukhara and Khiva were also subjugated at this time but left as protectorates until after 1917.[16] The Caucasus, which Russia conquered earlier in the nineteenth century following examples of European colonial expansion, were less densely populated and never consolidated under a coherent administrative system.[17] By contrast, Turkestan's special administrative status—it was ruled by a military-civilian administration under a governor-general who answered to the Ministry of War—and its significant exclusion of the native population from the imperial mainstream reinforced its attributes as a separate colonial territory within the empire.[18] Imperial officials had frequently used the word "colony" to describe this region,[19] so Soviet officials turned Tashkent into the premier showcase of Soviet decolonization and development of the East.[20] Although Soviet propagandists often elided Central Asia and the Caucasus (and sometimes other Muslim or Asian regions of the Soviet Union) when they spoke of the "domestic East," Central Asia's special status for Soviet legitimacy as an anticolonial state makes it the main focus of this book.

As the Bolsheviks considered what it meant to rule a territory that was once an empire with colonies in Asian and Eastern realms, they accepted the eighteenth-century delineation of Russia's Asiatic realms at the Urals; they codified *European* and *Asiatic* categories for territorial-administrative purposes; and they formed "Eastern" institutions that they hoped would achieve world revolution. Later, Soviet leaders vacillated between competing with "the West," as Khrushchev and Brezhnev did, and embracing Westernization, as Gorbachev and Yeltsin did, in trying to build a "common European home."

The profound and lasting power of this East-West divide is still evident in scholarship about Russia, conceptualized as it is along the lines of "Russia and the West" and "Russia and Asia," with the former attracting significantly more scholarly attention than the latter. The idea that Europe is the main shaper of world history and that Europeans alone are capable of initiating change has profoundly shaped the production of historical knowledge around the world. The Soviet intelligentsia based in Leningrad and Moscow have also historically viewed themselves and their location as Western or "Western-oriented." Their attitude toward the West has been described by historian Michael David-Fox as a "superiority-inferiority complex" and by Eleonory Gilburd as a "utopian" construction.[21] This attitude has fortified historical narratives throughout the second half of the twentieth century.[22] The Gorbachev- and Yeltsin-era "Westernization" and the proliferation of Russia's cultural relations with individual European countries further bolstered assumptions about the preeminence in Russia of European culture and civilization. These intelligentsia's assumptions have distorted studies of Soviet international cultural exchanges. For example, those who write about their perspectives tend to conflate the "abroad" (*zagranitsa*) with the "West" (*zapad*).[23]

By contrast, work on "Russia and Asia" has tended to focus on Russia's geopolitical "impact" in Asia or on assessing the cohesion of the Soviet multiethnic Eurasian state.[24] This subfield has emerged, in part, out of World War I and World War II German and later Cold War–era efforts to destabilize Russia and then the Soviet Union by fostering Soviet Muslims' potential to resist Sovietization.[25] More recently, scholars interested in non-Russian borderlands,[26] and scholars of nineteenth-century literature and culture, have revived an interest in imperial history as a way to engage in conversations with scholars of other empires, including on topics of orientalism and exoticism.[27]

Interest in integrating Russian, Central Asian, Global, and Middle Eastern Studies has grown not only in literary and cultural studies circles but also among historians.[28] This book builds on these efforts and contributes to them by reconstructing how Soviet and Middle Eastern intermediaries used these categories to access Soviet power and to channel it to various ends.

Geopolitics, Intellectual History, and Biography

The Eastern International approaches Soviet politics generated by the category of East as a quasi-imperial formation at the intersection of global geopolitics, intellectual history, and the everyday experiences of people who shaped, and whose lives were shaped by, the "Eastern" institutions of the revolutionary party-state.[29]

Geopolitics is useful in several ways. First, it overcomes the separation of Soviet international and domestic policy into distinct topics. The persistence of a Soviet connection between the domestic and foreign Easts cannot be explained through an analysis of international or bilateral state relations alone, or by an analysis of internally focused Soviet histories alone. Understanding it requires attention to the nexus of global/international and local/national history. It requires seeing how historical actors responded to events and concerns about security and political legitimacy by moving between multiple forms of belonging available to them. KUTV students might navigate the 1930s purges by using the logics of Soviet nation-making or by crossing Soviet domestic or international borders to escape them.[30] For example, Khalid Bakdash officially assumed an Arab rather than a Kurdish nationality to access privileges allocated to those of the titular "oppressed" nationalities, while Tawfiq Abdel Hafiz al-Hassan (Aimarov) had to prove himself in the Soviet republic of Georgia to be allowed to return to his home in Palestine. Students might invoke anticolonial nationalism to explain their motives for joining regional communist movements while accepting the nation-state internationalism that structured not only the League of Nations but also membership in the Comintern. At other times they might invoke anticolonial internationalism (with its cross-cutting identifications, such as "oppressed people of the world," "youth of the world," "toilers and laborers," or "the colonized") or other anticolonial quasi-national ideas such as "Arab unity." Attention to intermediaries allows for situating the "Eastern international" in its various relevant contexts and observing not only how it was envisioned but also how it was practiced, manipulated, and performed.

Second, an emphasis on the nexus of global and regional geopolitics eschews Cold War exceptionalism, which usually stresses either the novelty of the Soviet regime or its continuities with Russian autocracy. It reveals instead how the Soviet state's political objectives are comparable to those of other states: maintaining internal security, projecting power into neighboring regions to exclude rivals, promoting its foreign policy interests, and ensuring access to resources essential to its security.[31] This underscores the specific and distinctive characteristics of Soviet internationalism and the state's long-term reliance on domestic and foreign intermediaries, institutions, and tactics to project influence to the Indian Ocean through Central Asia and the Caucasus.[32] In the process, Soviet formations appear explicitly anticolonial and yet strangely colonial at the same time.

Finally, this book uses the concept of geopolitics to highlight how Soviet ideas about territory and politics contributed to the intellectual history of this concept. This contribution has been filtered out of scholarship in part because of the Bolsheviks' later hostility to the very idea. Historian Milan Hauner has shown that "German *geopolitik* became one of the most violently despised terms in the Soviet anti-imperialist vocabulary."[33] In fact, geopolitical thinking was more popular among the early Bolsheviks than has previously been appreciated.

The architects of the "Eastern International" related territory to politics on scales of thought that transcended national, regional, and continental geography. Soviet theorists and activists were commended on their *masshtabnost'*, or large-scale, thinking about politics.[34] Bolshevik activist Konstantin Troianovskii's idea of an "International of the East" (*Internatsional Vostoka*) captures nicely the *masshtabnost'* of Soviet thought about the East. Troianovskii coined the phrase in 1918 to refer to "a united anti-imperialist democratic front that could oppose the Western international of capital." His anti-Western internationalism was meant to compete with other contemporary internationalisms, both European and Asian.[35] It was implemented to make Moscow a hub of global anticolonial activism that rivaled other notable centers simultaneously developing in Istanbul, Tokyo, Paris, London, and Berlin, but also to connect those networks to Moscow and other regions of the Soviet Union.[36] Eventually such efforts succeeded in turning Tashkent (defined as the forefront of world revolution in the East) into the most developed city in Soviet Central Asia. Other parts of the domestic East also became important and developed hubs of what historian Brigitte Studer called the "transnational world of the Cominterians."[37] In most cases, these connections and hubs outlasted the Comintern and, in some cases, even the USSR.

This Soviet concept of the East envisioned and often facilitated connections and solidarities between different types of "peoples of the East"—another large-scale idea. By 1922, Mikhail Pavlovich, the head of the All-Russian Scientific Association of Oriental Studies (Vserossiiskaia Nauchnaia Assotsiatsiia Vostokovedeniia, VNAV), understood his Association's objective as studying the East "on a state scale" (*v gosudarstvennom masshtabe*); for Pavlovich, this meant a study of "the whole colonial world, a world of exploited peoples not only in Asia but in Africa and South America, a world, the exploitation of which, supports the power of capitalist societies of Europe and the United States."[38] This definition of the East sounds like what was later dubbed the "Global South." Institutions like KUTV and the Comintern convened people from these different regions to listen to Stalin's and others' thoughts about the East. They also supported their creative efforts—in the form of translations of Marxist-Leninist and literary texts and performative experiments. Literary scholar Katerina Clark has argued that ultimately they succeeded in including more Asian literary voices in what was a predecessor of the postcolonialist movement and canon in literature, and in what might have been realized as a globalized system of "world literature."[39]

For the political activists using party-state institutions to strengthen the anticolonial state, protect its anticolonial legitimacy, and support the circulation of people and ideas, borders were critical. They were imposed by real-world constraints of resources and geography. They were also authorized at the highest levels by the emerging Soviet domestic nationalities regime, the new international system, and perhaps most incontrovertibly, Stalin and his distinction between "domestic" and "foreign" Easts. This last border became vital for asserting the Soviet Union's anticolonial identity.

Like other borders, the one between the two Easts was unstable and contested. Among other problems it was simultaneously temporal and spatial. Its temporal dimensions conveyed Marxist theories of stages of development, which in the mid-1920s still included Marx's incoherent writings about the "Asian social order" and the "Asiatic mode of production" (AMP) that associated the East with static features of state ownership of property, state management of water and natural resources, and a ruling class of bureaucrats.[40] Such ideas, especially AMP, sat awkwardly with other Bolshevik visions of the East as located on a temporal continuum from backwardness to modernization. By the early 1930s, AMP was discarded for a more a unilinear historical model of the *piatichlenka* (the five stages of primitive-communism, slavery, feudalism, capitalism, and socialism).[41] This other model could more easily fold Asian subjects into Soviet-Marxist history and, eventually, enable them to access Soviet-style development.[42]

As for its spatial dimensions, the domestic and foreign border delineated the "domestic East" as predominantly the Muslim Soviet republics in Central Asia and the Caucasus and a "foreign East" that included South and East Asia, Africa, the Middle East, and sometimes other parts of the colonial world that might eventually decolonize within the framework of a global transition to communism. Its spatial dimensions drew upon ideas of "Asia" consistent with an imperial conception of Russian space, but it repurposed them for what historian Stephen Kotkin has called "a viable Marxist approach to geopolitics."[43] This included radical forms of "defensive" expansionism, justified by an elaborate Soviet mythology that Soviet Central Asia and the Caucasus had been liberated and then incorporated into the USSR through anti-imperial revolutions.[44] This mythology came to shape Soviet oriental studies as well as multiple dimensions of Soviet and post-Soviet Central Asian history and culture, including official national histories, literary traditions, and cinema.

For this story to be persuasive, the boundary between the two Easts had to remain porous. In the same 1925 speech, Stalin articulated a strategy for how it might be crossed or even eliminated. KUTV could remain as it was, "with one foot on Soviet soil and the other on the soil of the colonies and dependent countries." The domestic East could function as a magnet that attracted "the workers and peasants of the neighboring colonial and dependent countries to the liberation movement."[45] Beyond that, the porousness was for others to figure out, narrate, and enact.

The Intermediaries

Telling stories about the Russian empire and how it was overcome was critical to Soviet legitimacy. Hence, those who constructed these narratives had considerable agency to shape Soviet ideology and inform concrete policy decisions of the anticolonial state, as well as make choices about their own lives. The ability to "speak Bolshevik" about the East, to embody or perform the right kind of Easternness, and to successfully tailor their performances to different audiences brought opportunities.[46] It allowed intermediaries to accumulate power, widen their creative or academic platforms, channel resources to benefit themselves and their comrades, and support particular groups, both within and beyond Soviet borders.

This project was heavily male-dominated. Although the project to "liberate women" and its particular emphasis on "women of the East" was a key component of Soviet modernization, support for it remained limited. The interests of women were repeatedly sacrificed for those of class and national politics, or in response to pragmatic concerns about child homelessness, urban unemployment, or peasant patriarchal attitudes.[47] Recent studies of the post–World War II period that rely on oral histories have offered correctives to claims that Soviet rule radically transformed gender norms, underscoring the superficial penetration of Soviet gender and family norms in much of postwar Central Asia, even in the cities.[48] Foreign communists and leftist intellectuals, especially those who came into contact with the Soviet Union, also often included "the liberation of women" in party programs or addressed it in articles to signal their acceptance of the Soviet approach or general modernity. Yet the number of women in party leadership or in the leftist intellectual circles in the Arab world remained small. Those who wrote about their experiences often described these circles as sexually exploitative and unjust.[49] With some exceptions, advocacy for women's rights and other notions of gendered or sexual justice could easily be dismissed as "feminist" and "bourgeois," or as politically trivial. Its erasure is compounded by the male-dominated production and shaping of data.[50] The intersection of different patriarchies in multiple "Eastern International" contexts made this world profoundly dismissive of "personal" politics, such as sexual harassment, and thus dangerous for women. Whenever possible, this work highlights archival traces left by women in this male-dominated and masculinist world.

Yet male activists made significant sacrifices as well. Their work was risky in part because the notion of Eastern otherness so critical to the construction and defense of an image of the Soviet Union as an anticolonial state was so unstable. Official interpretations of Middle Eastern politics changed often. Likewise the story of Soviet domestic decolonization relied on ideological distinctions between colonizers, liberators, and the colonized that were periodically tweaked. Lowell Tillett has shown in his pioneering study of the changes in Soviet historiography about non-Russian nationalities that over time, these tweaks amounted to a kind of whitewashing of empire. This was especially evident in the official histories of Turkestan, which shifted from early 1920s narratives about Russian imperial power there as "colonial," to 1930s narratives about Russian colonialism as a "lesser evil" compared to the region's potential takeover by European powers, to postwar narratives of the region's progressive "annexation" because of allegedly beneficial ties with Russians.[51] This revision involved politicians, historians, writers, filmmakers, and even interior decorators of public spaces.[52] It required energy, talent, and a willingness to suppress alternative narratives, including those put forward by friends or even the authors themselves in earlier times. Telling these stories became more difficult over the course of the twentieth century, as more of the world decolonized and the Soviet Union encountered ever more complex challenges to its claims of being the world's first anticolonial state. Foregrounding how activists, students, intellectuals, and artists navigated these intricate challenges, this book explains the persistence of the two Easts, both as a boundary and as a relationship, and the stakes of its maintenance, since mistakes meant demotions, reprimands, and, occasionally, prison or even death.[53]

An obvious privilege enjoyed by these intermediaries in the Soviet context was their mobility. All of them moved between Moscow and Central Asia, and all of them traveled internationally to Israel/Palestine, Syria, Lebanon, Egypt, or elsewhere. These privileges gave them a stake in protecting narratives about Soviet domestic decolonization and anticolonialism abroad by repressing undesirable histories, cultures, and voices.[54] Similar to Black Americans who represented the United States abroad during the Cold War, a subset of privileged Soviet Central Asians could use their positionality, including their recognizably non-white features and bodies, to represent the Soviet Union to the decolonizing world.[55] As the United States, the Soviet "imperial edifice" was designed to give them a stake in "domesticating anti-colonialism."[56]

Arab communists and leftists also had stakes in the project. This did not mean they were Soviet "puppets" or "clients," as Western scholarship characterized them throughout much of the Cold War, which treated the so-named Third World as a backdrop to Soviet-American confrontation. More recent works on the global Cold War have illuminated the agency of Non-Aligned leaders and the extent to which such Third World engagements have shaped (mostly American) political and cultural history.[57] Recent histories of the Arab Left have also restored much of the agency of rank-and-file activists by highlighting how they translated, debated, and adjusted Soviet politics and Marxist literature in various Middle Eastern contexts.[58] This work on Arab leftists remains largely disconnected from studies of Soviet ideology and culture, including the role of domestic "Easterners" and how they have perpetuated certain assumptions at home and abroad.[59] This book is an attempt to bring them together.

Eurocentrism and Historical Exclusion of the East

Why have the Soviet Union's "Eastern" intermediaries been so overlooked? Some have suggested that the silence of postcolonial theory on anything related to Russia and the socialist world stems from the Soviet origins of postcolonial theory itself.[60] As historian Vera Tolz suggests in *Russia's Own Orients*, Edward Said's key definition of orientalism as a European system of knowledge meant to control colonial populations was commonplace in early Soviet scholarship. Tolz argues that Soviet critiques of Western orientalism likely reached Said via Egyptian Marxist sociologist Anwar Abdul-Malik, whom Said acknowledges in the preface to his book.[61] Abdul-Malik's 1963 article "Orientalism in Crisis" criticized Western orientalism for its racism and service to imperialism, but significantly its first reference is to the entry for *Vostokovedenie* (Orientology) in the Stalin-era second edition of the *Great Soviet Encyclopedia*. The entry states that "Bourgeois Orientology entirely subordinates the study of the East to the colonial politics of the imperialist powers."[62] Thus, Tolz argues, Said's work on orientalism was indebted—via Arab intellectuals' familiarity with Soviet critiques—to the critique of European oriental studies formulated by Sergei Ol'denburg and Nikolai Marr.[63]

Tolz's insight has inspired further studies of the relationship between Soviet internationalism and postcolonialism, including Rossen Djagalov's broader intellectual history of the largely unacknowledged ways that Soviet thought and experience contributed to Anglo-American postcolonial theory.[64] But what makes Tolz's argument so powerful for my purposes is simply that it shows a historical connection between late Russian imperial and early Soviet critiques of Western orientalism, 1960s Arab Marxists' critiques of colonialism, and later Western postcolonial theory.

The same historical connections that rendered postcolonial theory silent on anything related to Russia and the socialist world also contribute to the neglect of Western critiques of orientalism, including Said's, in Soviet and post-Soviet Russia.[65] They explain why the Russian conquest of Central Asia, a taboo topic in the Soviet Union, still attracts surprisingly little research.[66] As historians Su Lin Lewis and Carolien Stolte have argued, "The 'erasure' of Central Asia from global geography during the Soviet era has been termed a form of 'cartographical dismemberment'; the region disappeared almost entirely from the geographical imagination—eventually dissolving into the disciplinary cracks of Area Studies in the 1950s as an unlikely part of 'Eastern Europe' due to the geopolitical factions of the times."[67]

Another key byproduct of this history is the difficulty of thinking about Soviet Russia as an "empire" as opposed to a "modernizing" or an "anti-imperialist" and "anticolonial" state. This confusion stems in part from the effective use by Soviet mediators of categories such as the "East" to channel power. It reflects the success of the long-term workings of the Eastern International, fortified by a monopoly on sources and access to research about Soviet history, especially in Muslim regions. The network was able to control historical narratives about its past in domestic scholarship, public diplomacy, and even cinematic historical fiction. This control was accomplished through the silencing of alternative narratives and voices with threats of violence or demotion and the repression of hundreds of academic experts on the East.[68]

The history of violent repressions is not exclusively Soviet. Some of these silences persist in histories of the Arab and other Lefts, Arab communism, and international communism due to decades of political persecution of communists by colonial and, later, nationalist regimes; the destruction of communist party archives in Palestine, Syria, and Iraq; purges in Comintern-affiliated parties; and anxiety among communists about accusations that they, as communists, were "hirelings" of the Soviet Union or had engaged in "espionage" on its behalf.[69] These fears have made those whose lives came into contact with the Soviet Union reluctant to discuss their experiences. By considering the experiences of communists, intellectuals, and other actors in the transregional "Eastern International," this book interrogates these silences to challenge the universalizing tendencies of postcolonialism and link the history of Arab radicalism and the intellectual history of the Left with Soviet history.[70]

Further reinforcing these silences is the fact that so many Euro-American historians either accepted various Soviet claims, such as their elimination of religion, or were blinded by the Cold War and its effects on academic culture and popular representations.[71] In the West the rise of the "Three-World" ideology—a division of the world into a "free" First World that was modern, scientific, and rational; a "communist" Second World controlled by ideology and propaganda; and a "traditional" Third World characterized by overpopulation, religiosity, and economic backwardness—has delayed exploration of connections between the so-called Second and Third Worlds.[72] US government–funded area studies ahistorically divided Russia/USSR and the Middle East into two discrete and separate regions of study. Until recently, Soviet specialists were thoroughly trained in European history but not at all in the languages or history of the Middle East, let alone South Asia or Africa.[73] Specialists of the Middle East or Islamic world came to associate Islam narrowly with the Arabic-speaking world, ignoring Russia.[74] Meanwhile, scholars of postcolonial history focused more on the encounter with and resistance to Western Europe, ignoring other regional and historical connections. The work of bridging postcolonial, post-socialist, and "global" studies is a post–Cold War project in its early stages.[75]

This book aims to transcend these conceptual divides and to explain how they emerged. What did Soviet party-state support mean for anticolonial and anti-imperial activists embedded in its transregional "Eastern" field of power? What do the relationships between its various participants reveal? These questions usefully depart from tendencies in postcolonial studies to focus on texts produced by anticolonial thinkers and intellectuals, or on the final records of major international conferences (of the Comintern, the League of Anti-Imperialism, Afro-Asian events at Bandung, Cairo, and Delhi, the Tricontinental in Havana, and Non-Aligned events around the world). They show how the Soviet Eastern field of power attracted and empowered intellectuals, including those who participated in what historian Kris Manjapra has called the "transcolonial ecumene"—the far-flung, worldwide community of people committed to a single cause and engaged in discussions that generate a common discourse and an "economy of recognition."[76]

Historians who write global history have argued that it is possible to understand the myth of Western cultural superiority historically without reproducing its assumptions, especially the assumption that Europe was the only active shaper of world history.[77] This book takes a similar approach to Soviet history. After all, Soviet authorities shared with other Eurocentric thinkers certain entitlements: they could establish the criteria of facts and facticity and then change those criteria; they assumed that the Soviet Union was a vanguard, if not the realization, of a global ideal; and they believed that the Soviet Union and the Bolshevik revolution were key agents of historical change. Yet, one of the consequences of Soviet anticapitalist ideology and the long-term exceptionalist conceptualization of the Soviet state by Soviet and Western scholars alike is that Soviet history is not well integrated into global historical studies.[78] This is in part because so many theories of global integration rely on flows of capital and use metaphors of capitalism to understand connection and integration.

In an attempt to overcome the marginalization of "communist studies" from mainstream conversations about "global" history, this book uses transregional case studies that feature particular intermediaries to highlight socialist and anticolonial integration and friction. These case studies illuminate synchronic developments of the Eastern International, including developments that were subsequently and intentionally excluded or repressed. When possible, causation is connected to the global level.

The network's various accomplishments and disappointments challenge interpretations of the Soviet Union as just another "West," as articulated in critical 1980s anti-Western Islamist narratives, or as a "failure," as articulated in triumphalist Western accounts and more recent histories that rely on abstractions of socialist utopia.[79] Instead they expose complex post-imperial dynamics and contradictions of Soviet modernization theory, which were negotiated over time, and the fact that, although somewhat disappointed or disillusioned, people were still willing to give the Soviet Union another chance because of their opposition to imperialism, fascism, capitalism, or racism. The reasons for this willingness—which was eventually broken after the Soviet invasion of Afghanistan—require explanation.

Since it is impossible to study empirically these interactions across all the regions connected by the "Eastern International," this work focuses on a specific transregional set of actors and activities: those connecting Soviet Central Asia with the Eastern Mediterranean. This latter region of the former Ottoman empire was subdivided after World War I into the British and French mandatory entities of Syria, Lebanon, Jordan, and Palestine, which became independent and, in the case of Palestine, further partitioned into Israel/Palestine. Occasionally there are references to neighboring Egypt and Iraq. This region—referred to by people in this network as the "Arab world," the "Near East" or "Western Asia"—became one of the main theaters of the Cold War.[80] In the imperial period it was important as a "Holy Land" in which Russian imperial officials had created networks of schools and supported pilgrimage.[81] Yet in the interwar period its importance is less immediately apparent. After Orthodox interests lost their significance in 1917, and despite the "Arabist bias" among many of the European-trained Russian imperial orientalists who privileged Mediterranean (and hence largely Arab) regions of the Islamic world, the Arabic-speaking Eastern Mediterranean attracted less academic attention than Iran, Afghanistan, and Turkey.[82]

Nevertheless, the region held importance for early Bolshevik and Comarturnian officials, both as an object of study and as a space for political activism. In the geopolitical terms of the early interwar period, it was perceived to be the Achilles' heel of French and British colonial empires as a vital link between the European metropoles and more distant colonies in South and East Asia. Since the mid-nineteenth century it had been a destination for Russian Zionist migrants fleeing imperial legal restrictions on their geographical and social mobility, economic underdevelopment, and violent pogroms against their community. This migration produced a network of familial, social, and cultural connections between these Russian migrants in Palestine and Egypt, and members of the Bolshevik Left who rejected this option and instead joined one of the socialist parties in Russia. Eventually, most of those who joined the social democratic movement or one of the non-Bolshevik socialist Jewish parties either left or joined the apparatus of the party-state.[83]

The overrepresentation of Jews in the Bolshevik revolutionary movement and the early Soviet state has been well documented.[84] Yet connections between activists in early party-state institutions focused on the East, especially the Near East, and friends or relatives in Palestine seem especially dense.

Some researchers and administrators mention their relatives; others were lapsed Zionists themselves, having emigrated to Palestine, grown disillusioned, and then returned to Moscow. It is likely that such connections—and the very existence of the option of migration that could be explicitly rejected—informed their interest in the Near East and raised questions of cultural transformation, assimilation, and the conquest of backwardness.

These imperial legacies ensured that the Eastern Mediterranean was of enduring interest for those in the Comintern leadership seeking to "revolutionize the East." Indeed, many of those initially committed to spreading world revolution to this region came from Jewish families that had experienced some form of discrimination. In the 1930s most of these early Jewish activists were purged from positions of authority. Yet ironically, the base of outreach to the region they established in the interwar period was adapted and expanded. Its expansion was overseen by new intermediaries, mostly of Arab and Central Asian descent, but also some Jews who managed to officially register their nationalities as "Russians" and suppress information about their backgrounds. Together these intermediaries helped to reconfigure connections between the two Easts. Their stories challenge the common Cold War historical framings that emphasize the novelty of Soviet interests in the Arab world in the post–World War II period.[85]

This collective story recovers many repressed or discarded historical frameworks and contingencies. It brings together the institutional archives, cultures, and languages of the Comintern (1919–1943); the communist parties of the Soviet Union, Syria, Lebanon, Palestine, and Egypt; and KUTV; the Soviet Ministry of Foreign Affairs; institutions responsible for Soviet cultural diplomacy; the Soviet Afro-Asian Solidarity Committee; the Tashkent Afro-Asian Film Festival; and academic centers of oriental and international studies. The research—conducted in Moscow, Tashkent, Dushanbe, Damascus, Beirut, and Boston—required confronting vestiges of these official or officially sanctioned perspectives, especially in state censorship and archival restrictions. It involved identifying and working around key silences—of files of individuals and agencies that are still classified, of official narratives that mispresented certain efforts as new—and a fundamental Soviet-state perspective that was almost always Moscow-centric and assumed the *"global'nost'"* (global scope and resonance) of certain Soviet ideas and events, such as the Bolshevik revolution and faith in technocratic progress.

Chapter 1 begins by tracing the formation of the Eastern International as a blueprint for anticolonial and anti-imperialist revolution in the East as it was imagined in 1918 by the assimilated Jewish Bolshevik activist Konstantin Troianovskii, who became the first head the Comintern's Near East Section. Troianovskii's blueprint for revolution in the East, endorsed by Lenin and Stalin, was the Bolsheviks' initial response to the reconfiguration of the world order at the end of World War I. The collapse of the Ottoman and Hapsburg empires and British and French expansion into Arab territories created new possibilities for empire as well as challenges to the validity of imperial politics. Islamic universalism, Asianism, and efforts by Mongolian-speaking activists in Inner Asia to unite all the Mongol peoples under a banner of pan-Mongolism were just some examples of these new alternative internationalisms.[86] The "Eastern International" was the Bolsheviks' proposal for anticolonial liberation of the "East," but it also engaged with questions about Russia's identity that resembled those pondered by their imperial predecessors: did the future of Soviet Russia, now inextricably linked with world revolution, lie in Europe, or in Asia, or was it a more distinctly Eurasian trajectory? As head of the Near Eastern section of the Comintern in the early 1920s, Troianovskii "territorialized" this blueprint by helping to build a revolutionary network linking Moscow with "the Near East" (meaning Turkey, Iran, and the Arab world) through key outposts in Tashkent, Bukhara, and the seaports of Odessa and Batumi (in Georgia).

As party-state efforts in support of revolution in the "East" crystallized into a more permanent infrastructure, Soviet and Comintern officials created a "laboratory" for training Eastern revolutionaries from across Eurasia and occasionally from Africa and the Americas, which Chapter 2 explores. Between 1921 and 1938, Troianovskii and others trained thousands of students at the Communist University for the Toilers of the East (KUTV), including dozens sent by the communist parties of Egypt, Palestine, Syria-Lebanon, and Iraq. Students like Egyptian Hamdi Seliam and Palestinian Najati Sidqi were drawn to organized communism by an interest in Marxism, commitments to anticolonial nationalist politics, and the lure of seeing a new world.[87] In Moscow they were swept up in the excitement of urban life, the relatively accommodating cultural climate of the 1920s, and their encounters with various Soviet and Comintern authorities. In this period when new borders were being created—in the Soviet Union and the Eastern Mediterranean— distinctions of nationality, class, party affiliation, gender, and political interests could still blur, producing occasionally subversive meanings and effects.

In the 1930s, these boundaries hardened. The securitization of Soviet borders made the USSR an ever more hermetic place of cultural autarchy, and Soviet nation-makers placed greater emphasis on majoritarian ethnonationalism. In regions under the British and French mandates, anticolonial nationalist movements gained traction. And the boundaries between the Jewish and Arab communities in Palestine became more entrenched after violent clashes in 1929. Yet as records of Comintern purge trials show, KUTV continued to function as a "portal" of foreign and domestic ideas about the East. Namely, interpretations of domestic conflict between Russian colonial settlers and indigenous Muslims in Turkestan shaped interpretations of Comintern policy vis-à-vis Palestine, and foreign communists could be punished with exile to the domestic East. Ultimately, Chapter 3 shows how these dynamics led to the elimination of many high-ranking Jews employed at KUTV and in the Comintern, especially those with any connections to Palestine, Egypt, or Syria-Lebanon, paving the way for others to take their place as intermediaries of party-state activities in the East.

The outbreak of World War II turned Stalin's attention away from the Eastern Mediterranean, which remained a peripheral theater of the war compared to the Euro-American and Asian ones. Ironically, as Soviet interest in the East declined, interest in the Soviet Union as a symbol of antifascism, anti-Westernism, and antimaterialism grew for many left-leaning intellectuals, including some in Syria in Lebanon. Many of these intellectuals belonged to communist parties. Mostly, they were brought together by a collective quest for decolonization and a better world, in which the Soviet Union functioned as an anticolonial alternative to the West. In 1947, a delegation of Syrian and Lebanese leftists visited the Soviet Union and toured the domestic East on the invitation of a Soviet cultural diplomacy organization. Chapter 4 follows these visitors as they engaged with Russian, Jewish, and Central Asian intellectuals on cultural politics, socialist realism, and late Stalinist censorship. It concludes that these visitors' Eurocentric approach to the USSR, and a desire to protect it as a symbol of alternative modernity, required consciously overlooking various anticosmopolitan repressions happening across the Soviet Union, including those in the Soviet East.

The acceleration of political decolonization in the 1950s prompted Nikita Khrushchev to acknowledge Stalin's mistake in forsaking the East, which once again seemed to have world-historical political importance. As

Chapter 5 discusses, the expansion of Khrushchev-era investments in the Eastern Mediterranean still drew on Stalin's logics of differentiating and also connecting the two Easts despite widespread de-Stalinization. The notion that the domestic East could serve as a magnet or model for foreign Easterners was underscored by the role of Uzbek politician Nuriddin Mukhitdinov, who assumed many responsibilities for promoting Khrushchev's "East politics" at home and abroad. Part of this delegation of authority meant that Mukhitdinov and other Soviet Central Asians were able to leverage Moscow's concerns about the Afro-Asian world and Central Asia's historical connections to neighboring Turkic-, Persian-, and Arabic-speaking regions, including the tradition of early childhood education in Arabic, to direct resources to develop Soviet Central Asia.

As the momentum of global decolonization slowed, new challenges confronted the narrative of the Soviet Union as anticolonial and antiimperial. Right-wing coups cost Soviet leaders influence in Indonesia, Algeria, Ghana, and Mali. Nasser's defeat in the 1967 Arab-Israeli raised questions about Soviet commitments to Arab nationalism and opposition to Zionist colonialism. Meanwhile, the intensification of global competition between the USSR and China explicitly undermined Soviet legitimacy as a defender of worldwide anticolonial movements. Once again, these pressures activated connections between the two Easts.

The realization that film could reach greater audiences in the non-Western world than literature led Soviet cultural bureaucracies to invest in and promote Afro-Asian cinematic networks, as Chapter 6 narrates.[88] Yet telling stories about how the Soviet Union was decolonized proved more difficult for domestic Easterners than presenting non-white faces of the Soviet Union or acting out certain Muslim cultural codes. Tajik filmmaker Kamil Yarmatov struggled to craft a narrative about the Bolshevik revolution in the Soviet East that would appeal to domestic and foreign audiences. By 1968, the ideological constraints on historical interpretations of Central Asia's past had become so extensive that even the most talented and creative minds in Soviet screenwriting could not produce something that could be acknowledged as good work. At the 1968 Afro-Asian Film Festival, Yarmatov still managed to perform the role of a successful revolutionary Easterner for foreign audiences, but narratives about the domestic East as a model for the foreign East had lost their coherence. Soon Soviet and international filmmakers, as well as a new more disaffected generation of Soviet youth, moved on to more playful and subversive treatments of the Sovietization of Central Asia.

As the narrative threads connecting the two Easts unraveled, Soviet institutions continued to facilitate more emotive and less historically grounded linkages between the two, as Chapter 7 traces. In the early 1970s, despite the brutal repression of communists in Baʻathist Syria and Iraq, the Soviet Komsomol still invited Syrian and Iraqi youth to celebrate Arab-Soviet "friendship" in Tashkent and Dushanbe, against the same backdrop used for decades to host their communist victims. These linkages, as well as the general expansion of Soviet commitments in Asia and Africa, were fueled by proceeds of the 1973 oil revolution. The late 1980s collapse of the Soviet economy and institutions correlated with the explicit reversal of multiple assumptions underlying the Eastern International. Signs of institutional and material disintegration included the questioning of Soviet development and cultural politics by Central Asian and other Soviet intellectuals, the rebranding of the domestic East as a drain on Russian resources, the growing racism and resentment of domestic Eastern migrants in Moscow and St. Petersburg, and the requests from Soviet diplomats for bailouts from Gulf monarchies.

As post-Soviet Russia sets out to renegotiate the terms of the Soviet collapse—by asserting power in regions within its perceived sphere of influence, and by narrowing the scope of possible interpretations of Soviet history—the Eurasian connections created through the Eastern International will remain relevant for thinking about politics and culture. They will not only provide a historical basis for evaluating Russia's claims about its regional and international interests, but illuminate the blind spots of Russian, Middle Eastern, and postcolonial studies.

1
Anticolonial Dreams and the Territorialization of Soviet Power

On the eve of the Bolsheviks' seizure of power, Vladimir Lenin famously retorted to the proposal that Leon Trotsky take charge of foreign affairs: "What foreign affairs will we have now?"[1] At the time, the major Eurasian empires were collapsing politically and Bolsheviks anticipated that the entire world would soon be refashioned by revolution.[2] Lenin expected that the fragmentation of the world capitalist system would render international relations obsolete as the state form itself would "wither away" and yield a new global community, or "World Republic."[3] In *Imperialism: The Highest Stage of Capitalism* (1914) he argued that imperialism, contrary to assumptions about its essentially peaceful nature, was an inherently violent and exploitative division of the world. In the inevitable revolutionary crisis caused by these contradictions of capitalism, the state itself would disappear. Lenin expected that impending revolution in Germany and elsewhere would help Russia transcend its persistent problems by creating new opportunities for economic modernization, with assistance from the proletariat of these advanced industrial countries, thus repositioning Russia at the center of global social change.[4] Lenin's confidence in this vision and his economic determinism—and specifically his opposition to suggestions that the natural environment could control man's destiny—informed his consequential decision to sign the Treaty of Brest-Litovsk, which ceded significant formerly Russian imperial territory to the Germans.[5] Lenin explained that we wanted "to concede space . . . in order to win time."[6]

Not everyone in Lenin's circles shared his optimism about the demise of territorialized states. His concessions at Brest-Litovsk dismayed a number of Soviet negotiators.[7] The importance of territory was soon underscored by new challenges. As the Bolsheviks consolidated power in Petrograd and Moscow, revolts erupted around the empire. Anti-Bolshevik opposition was concentrated mostly on the edges of the former imperial space—the Baltics, Ukraine, Crimea, the Caucasus, Central Asia, Siberia, and the far north

The Eastern International. Masha Kirasirova, Oxford University Press. © Oxford University Press 2024.
DOI: 10.1093/oso/9780197685693.003.0002

of Russia—where anti-Red forces also drew support from British, French, Japanese, and American troops.[8] The ensuing civil war linked military outcomes in these borderland regions to the new regime's existential struggle for survival. The term "front" came to describe both military and intellectual endeavors, especially in propaganda addressed to people in the various peripheries.[9] The Russian civil war would determine new borders in the deserts, mountains, and plains of Soviet Eurasia, and it would shape the production of knowledge about them.[10] It would also reconfigure how Bolshevik leaders approached global politics and their projections for world revolution.

This chapter traces the Bolsheviks' messy and contentious early efforts to imagine and project world revolution to the colonized East. It follows the life and work of a little-known "Old Bolshevik" activist named Konstantin Troianovskii (1876–1951), who had been an architect of these early efforts. He was both a theoretician of how Soviet power might facilitate the spread of revolution to the East and an activist who published previously classified documents from the tsarist ministry of foreign affairs and then helped establish and run the Eastern Section of the Third Communist International (Comintern). Troianovskii was born in the Ukrainian village of Nosachiv, in the Kiev Governorate of the Russian empire that happened to be in the Pale of Settlement to which Jews had been legally restricted since the reign of Catherine the Great. His official autobiographical documents provide little information about his family other than that his father was a small tenant (*melkii arendator*). In a 1928 official questionnaire, Troianovskii listed his nationality as "Russian."[11] However, his granddaughter recalls that his parents had been Jewish.[12] As such, Troianovskii's life seems to represent the opportunities created by the Bolshevik revolution for Jews to achieve emancipation through assimilation.

Like other "Old Bolsheviks," Troianovskii's education included periods of study in Europe, imprisonment, and exile. He received a primary education at home until the age of fifteen, at which point he claimed his parents died and he moved to Odessa, one of the fastest-growing major cities in the Russian empire in the 1890s. Its public libraries and diverse population of Greeks, Italians, Jews, Ukrainians, Poles, Tatars, Armenians, Belarusians, Mordvinians, and Georgians, as well as foreign non-subjects, nurtured Troianovskii's curiosity about the world.[13] He was able to prepare for his university entrance exams while he supported himself as a private tutor, and in 1898 he relocated to study in Switzerland, a magnet for Russian students and antitsarist radicals as well as a node in a wider European network of Russian émigré communities.[14]

In Switzerland, Troianovskii studied philosophy in the University of Bern, supported by a university stipend and aid from local Russian student organizations. In 1900 he continued his studies of philosophy and political economy at the University of Berlin, attending additional lectures in Leipzig and Heidelberg while supporting himself through "physical and mental labor."[15] At Leipzig University he overlapped with the famous German geographer Friedrich Ratzel and likely encountered other ideas about geopolitics and political geography. After running into financial difficulties, Troianovskii returned to Russia in 1902. He was arrested after joining the social democratic revolutionary movement and spent three years in prison.[16] Upon release he was exiled from St. Petersburg and relocated to Moscow. There, he took part in the uprising of 1905, a general strike that turned into an armed insurrection by thousands of protestors against the imperial government.[17] For these activities he once again stood trial and, when released on bail, fled to back to Europe with the help of a relative of the underground Bolshevik Inessa Armand. After some time in Germany and France and the start of World War I, he returned to Switzerland, where he re-enrolled in the University of Bern, joined a group of revolutionary Maximalists, and married his landlord's daughter, Elena Stender, who would become his lifelong companion.[18] After the first 1917 Russian revolution that overthrew the monarchy he returned to Petrograd (St. Petersburg before 1914; Leningrad after 1924) on the same sealed train as Lenin, traveling through war-torn Europe under German protection.[19] In Petrograd he joined the last City Duma (parliament).

Troianovskii's trajectory after the second revolution of 1917 puts him at the center of many of the Bolsheviks' efforts to revolutionize the East. However, he was not Lenin's first choice for the job. As soon as the Bolsheviks overthrew the Provisional Government, Lenin and his comrades were confronted with some of the challenges of governance inherited from the old imperial state, including its strategic alliances and geopolitical vulnerabilities in the borderlands, especially along Russia's southern frontier (which they called the "East").[20] The survival of their revolutionary project depended on

Figure 1.1 Kostantin Troianovskii in Bern, date unknown. From Tatiana Matroshilina's Family Archive.

maintaining control over these borderlands, a task that required experts in politics and geography.

As committed institution-builders who were open in the early days to using the existing talents of would-be opponents or skeptics, Lenin and his circle turned to established academic orientalists for help in devising a coherent strategy in the "Eastern" front.[21] Before the 1917 revolutions, this group had been only somewhat cooperative with Russian imperial officials, who also occasionally sought their help. Many had openly objected to what they saw as the imperial government's arbitrary interference in the work of universities and the Academy of Science.[22] In the context of the revolutionary crisis, however, the future of the Academy itself seemed especially uncertain so its head, the Indologist Sergei Ol'denburg (1863–1934), agreed to meet with Lenin to discuss the shared interests of the Academy and the new government.[23] According to Lenin's personal secretary, at this meeting Lenin asked Ol'denburg to help with the recruitment of new cadres to work in the East. "Go to the masses (*v massy*)," he told Ol'denburg, "and tell them about the history of India, about all the centuries of exploitation of their many millions of people by the British. You will see how the masses of our proletariat react, and you will also be inspired to do new research, to produce new works of great academic importance."[24]

After the meeting, Ol'denberg demonstrated his readiness to cooperate with the new government by transferring the Committee for the Study of Central and Eastern Asia, which he headed, to the new Commissariat of Foreign Affairs (NKID). The Committee included prominent historian of Central Asia Vasilii Bartol'd, Turkologist Vasilii Radlov, and Indologist Fyodor Sherbatskii. As a result of this transfer, the NKID Eastern Section chief, Arsenii Voznesenskii, joined its leadership. Voznesenskii had studied in St. Petersburg University with Bartol'd. After graduating he joined the imperial Foreign Ministry and was one of the few to stay on to work in the revolutionary NKID. Under his leadership, however, the Committee did little to further any revolutionary strategy in Asia beyond translating a few documents, including Lenin's and Stalin's "Appeal to All Toiling Muslims of Russia and the East."[25] When Voznesenskii asked Bartol'd to help establish "normal relations between the Soviet government in Turkestan and its neighboring regions," he was asking for help with imagining a new relationship to a region of Central Asia that had been conquered by Russia in the nineteenth century and administered as a "colony." His former teacher replied that he could be of service to the NKID "only as a historian."[26] The academic specialists on Turkology, Iranology, Indology, and Arabic literature were as uninterested in the new state's foreign policy objectives as they had been in the imperial state's.[27] By the end of 1918, the Committee for the Study of Central and Eastern Asia was removed from the NKID and handed over to the Commissariat of the Enlightenment (Narkompros), a less prestigious agency headed by the intellectual Anatolii Lunacharskii and responsible for "cultural" affairs.[28]

Lenin's second directive to Ol'denberg, to bring orientalism to the masses, proved difficult to implement for other reasons. The economy had just collapsed, and procuring food for the cities became increasingly difficult. Under conditions of wartime communism, Petrograd University tried to organize popular scientific courses to "attract new elements" who, according to China scholar Vasilii Alekseev, "might not have had the desire to devote their student years to specializing in the study of difficult languages and cultures of the East."[29] It is difficult to imagine large audiences mobilized by an initiative that included six public lectures by Arabist Ignatii Krachkovskii on the renaissance of modern Arabic literature.[30] Other institutions also joined the effort, with few results. The Asiatic Museum opened its book collection to the general public; a new Museum of Eastern Art was inaugurated to educate the masses about the East with an exhibit that bore the highbrow Latin title *Ars Asiatica*; Maxim Gorky's world literature project sought to translate Eastern literature to "educate the Russian people about the Eastern soul," paying its employees with food and firewood rations.[31] It soon became clear that general conditions of poverty and hunger made it difficult to attract people in Moscow and Petrograd to such high-minded pursuits. Moreover, consistent with the tsarist academic system, which had long valorized erudition over outreach, many of the scholars in question were more interested in conducting their research than in popularizing it for a broader audience.[32]

Another group of activists would take up the mantle of "going to the masses" to raise consciousness and mobilize people for anticolonial revolution in the East. Many of the top Bolsheviks were themselves interested in anti-imperialist politics and the problem of the East. Besides Lenin, Nikolai Bukharin, Karl Radek, Platon Kerzhentsev, and Arsenii Voznesenskii had all published on the topic.[33] As the commissar of nationalities (Narkomnats), Stalin stressed the importance of the East in the Narkomnats journal *Zhizn' natsional'nostei* and tried to mobilize Muslim communists meeting in Moscow to "unite (*tesnee splotit'sia i ob"edinit'*) the revolutionary movement in the East with the revolution in the West into a single front against imperialist countries."[34]

Stalin's and Lenin's speeches in 1918 and 1919 envisioned many links between Russia's Muslims and neighboring Eurasian countries, both as potential threats to the regime and as potential assets.[35] On the one hand, the possibility of a two-front war simultaneously fought in Asia and Europe, in addition to Central Asia as a potential third front, revived earlier imperial security threats. The specter of a fourth front inside the empire, in the case of domestic ethnic upheaval, was another geostrategic trauma the Soviet Eurasian empire inherited from its tsarist predecessor.[36] On the other hand, Russia had ruled Muslims since the sixteenth century, and by the early twentieth century it had developed complex tools for governing and recruiting Muslim intermediaries.[37] The challenge was to find a new working relationship that would allay concerns about the perceived vulnerability of the empire that had preoccupied imperial officials.

Part of the challenge was to find the right categories for political mobilization. In the early 1918–1919 revolutionary period, Stalin believed in the existence of a Muslim world, an idea that had long been invested with meaning by Ottoman authorities and that became an object of intense political competition during World War I.[38] The war brought the Russian and Ottoman empires deeply together and politicized earlier modes of sectarian governance.[39] Ottoman and German propaganda encouraged *jihad* among Muslims within the Russian empire.[40] This risk was significant, since by the turn of the twentieth century Russia ruled over twenty million Muslims, six million more than the Ottoman empire. Such wartime interference seemed all the more dangerous when other wartime hardships and crises stressed the state's credibility and undermined public trust, including in Central Asia. Initially, after the revolution, Lenin and Stalin followed the tsarist and Provisional Government's patterns of working with Muslim leaders, organizing Muslim congresses, and issuing an "Appeal to the Muslims of Russia and the East." By 1919, however, Stalin shifted his strategy of political mobilization to the more amorphous categories "East" and the "peoples of the East." This move stripped religion of any state-sanctioned political meaning. It also diluted the category of Muslim by including non-Muslims "Easterners," such as Christians from Georgia and Armenia and Jews from Central Asia and the Caucasus. Such a conceptual expansion made it difficult to mobilize as "Easterners" for anything other than opposition to Western imperialism. Indeed, there were never calls for the extraterritorial autonomy of "Easterners."

Beyond Stalin, a number of key Bolshevik activists who led the effort to produce a new anticolonial politics and apply it in "the East" hailed from Jewish families in the Pale of Settlement and had participated in European debates about empire and "the Eastern question." The Russian Soviet Federative Socialist Republic's (RSFSR's) first diplomatic representative in Iran, Theodore Rothstein (1871–1953, Russian: *Fedor Rotshtein*), had published a book while working as a journalist in London in 1910 about British financial schemes and the subjugation of Egypt, including the process by which landed classes lost their lands to creditors. The English poet, anti-imperialist critic, and longtime Cairo resident Wilfrid Scawen Blunt wrote the book's foreword, which noted the critical geopolitical role that Egypt was likely to play in imperial affairs. Its location on the road to India made it especially important for "Continental Europe" as "the volume of its sea-borne trade comes to preponderate over ours."[41]

Similarly, Menshevik activist Mikhail Pavlovich (1871–1927), who worked for the Comintern and headed the All-Russian Scientific Association of Oriental Studies (VNAV) in the 1920s, had written articles while in Paris in 1910–1917 that analyzed the strengths and weakness of competitive European imperial railway projects in Africa and Asia. These railroads, he argued, allowed European powers to expand "from the sunburnt empty shores of the Red Sea to the great plains of central Africa, from the Indian Ocean to the fantastic regions of the great lakes which feed the grandiose arteries of the Nile, Congo, Zambezi."[42]

Yet it was Troianovskii who most clearly unified early Bolshevik efforts to imagine and enact "Eastern" revolution. After the Bolshevik takeover he and his wife relocated to Moscow, where Troianovskii spent several months at the NKID as head of its Indo-Arab Section, selecting and publishing secret documents from the imperial archives in 1918. For Troianovskii, this meant investigating the archives of the Imperial Ministry of Foreign Affairs "Asiatic Department" and the "Eastern Section" of the army's General Staff. This "Asiatic" or "Eastern" structure of governance had deep imperial roots. After Russia's victory in the 1768–1774 Russo-Ottoman War, Catherine the Great had reconfigured the Russian Imperial College of Foreign Affairs to include a Secret Office subdivided into sections of European and Asiatic affairs to oversee the expansion of the Russian consular network in Ottoman lands, a concession won in the war.[43] The Asiatic section had been preserved in the formal Foreign Ministry system established under Alexander I, with the Asiatic Department responsible for maintaining ties to Ottoman consulates and Orthodox churches. During Russia's expansion into the Caucasus and Central Asia in the nineteenth century it maintained contact with the imperial General Staff's Asiatic Department, staffed by military orientalists who were concerned about Russia's overreach in Asia.[44]

Troianovskii's initial focus in these archives had been on India, which he regarded as "the greatest target of [European] exploitation" and therefore the country most likely to become "the first citadel of Revolution on the Eastern continent (*vostochnom materike*)."[45] In keeping with Lenin's *What Is to Be Done?*, the preface to his publication of tsarist-era secret documents posed the following question: "How can we direct the cultural pan-Islamist movement and the Muslims' ambitions towards national unity?"[46]

Having surveyed the Russian Imperial Foreign Ministry's Persia and Central Asia Section and exposed its cross-border operations, Troianovskii set out to answer this question in a book-length synthesis of preconditions for revolution in India, Persia, and China.[47] The 1918 book with two titles—*The East in the Light of Revolution* and *The East and Revolution*—called for the creation of an "International of the East (*Internatsional Vostoka*), a united anti-imperialist democratic front that could oppose the Western international of capital."[48]

In imagining these preconditions, Troianovskii's approach drew on the arguments of late nineteenth- and early twentieth-century northern and central European thinkers who wrote in German and whose works Troianovskii likely encountered during his time in Europe and could read well, thanks to a childhood knowledge of Yiddish. Germany intellectual culture was popular in Russia. Germany had attracted many Russian imperial students, and the Imperial Academy of Science and the Russian Geographical Society had many German-trained scientists.[49] Many of the leading Bolsheviks, such as Karl Radek and Nikolai Bukharin, were avid readers in German as well as Russian, and they were familiar with the work of German political geographers. Troianovskii's main source of inspiration was Swedish historian Johan Rudolf Kjellén (1864–1922), who coined the term "geopolitics." As a

Figure 1.2a and b Covers of Troianovskii's *Siniaia kniga* (Blue Book, 1918) and *Vostok pri svete revoliutsii* (The East in the light of revolution, 1918).

student of the German geographer Friedrich Ratzel, Kjellén conceptualized international relations as a struggle of peoples and state organisms for existence and dominance.[50] Drawing on Kjellén's work, Troianovskii linked regional Eurasian dynamics to the global system by illuminating that system's weak spot: "the territories of the Turkish sultan . . . the geographical center of the world war."[51]

Troianovskii's faith in the transformative power of the revolution and its ability to direct "the cultural pan-Islamist movement" required a flexible approach to Islam, and for that he turned to the work of the Hungarian Jewish orientalist Ignaz Goldziher (1850–1921). In his "Lectures on Islam," Goldziher challenged earlier interpretations of the Islamic tradition as codified and immutable by emphasizing instead the dynamic influences of psychological and historical factors.[52] His argument about Islam's adaptability proved particularly useful to Troianovskii.

That Goldziher's ideas could be adapted to the purposes of rule over foreign Muslim territories had already been shown by the Austro-Hungarian colonial government of Bosnia-Herzegovina, but they may have appealed for other reasons as well.[53] Central European Jews like Goldziher had spent the nineteenth century struggling for political emancipation and social integration and were commonly designated as "Orientals." This made Goldziher particularly invested in formulating a response to European orientalists who viewed Islam and Judaism as stagnant Semitic religions incapable of development and lacking mythology. His insistence that Islam had the capacity to assimilate foreign ideas and adapt to changing circumstances could easily be read as an implicit hope for Judaism and the liberalization of the rigid Orthodox rabbinate of Hungary.[54] Russians and Bolsheviks were also orientalized by European scholars and statesmen, but the work likely resonated more for someone with a deeper sense of oppression, who understood what it meant to come from the legally restricted and economically underdeveloped Pale of Settlement.

Intellectually, Goldziher offered a useful starting point for seeing Islam as something that had already undergone multiple transformations, fragmentations, and reconfigurations and could therefore change, or be changed, again. Reflecting on the cultural and spatial geography that spanned Russia's southern frontier, Troianovskii suggested that the Bolshevik revolution could send cross-border "signals" to national and political movements in Persia, Turkey, and the Islamic regions of India and Egypt. These signals might come in the form of support for new borderland entities, such as the

Tatar-Bashkir Republic,[55] or of support for revolutionary movements in strategic locations, such as Persia.[56] Troianovskii argued, using particularly vivid geographical metaphors, that the Iranian plateau was an ideal "point of transfer (*peredatochnyi punkt*)" between the Muslim movement in Russia and the developing world, between "arctic Asia, tropical Asia, and India."[57] In another formulation, he described it as a "pooling area (*obshchii bassein*)" of progressive and democratic pan-Islamic movements from which "waves" could emanate to Asia Minor and European Turkey, Egypt, and the rest of North and Northeast Africa.[58] Troianovskii used a metaphor very similar to that of Pyotr Semyonov Tian-Shanskii, who also visualized the Russian Eurasian Empire as a "Continent-Ocean," stretching from "sea to sea."[59] The same metaphor of an international "ocean" would later appear in Comintern speeches about more cultural topics, such as the dream of a literary commons.[60] Yet Troianovskii was focused on territory and on how the revolution could "clear the ground (*raschistit' pochvy*) further to the East, to India, to China, to the strongholds (*tverd'iiu*) of imperialism in England, America, and Japan . . . [and ultimately serve as] a signal for a series of revolutions across the vast expanses of Asia."[61] Since the revolution would flow outward, Persia would become the "geopolitical center" and the Muslim regions of Russia the "cultural center" of the International of the East.[62]

The book's addendum outlined more specific economic and political steps to achieve anticolonial liberation. Countries had to renounce foreign debts; nationalize railroads, telegraphs, and other forms of communication; abolish monopolies and cancel foreign concessions and privileges; expel foreign military officers and instructors and form native militias; replace usury with small interest-free loans; implement progressive taxation; cancel customs duties for all imports and exports; and abolish the system of castes and estates.[63] Only then would the "overthrow of the foreign yoke" leave the working class as the only force capable of coming to power.[64] Once all private and bourgeois state property had been seized and transformed into public property, "full access and penetration of Asia [should be extended] to everyone who wanted to peacefully . . . exploit its inexhaustible resources and develop the productive forces of countries of the East."[65] As this occurred, Troianovskii posited, resorting to the Darwinism of Ratzel and Kjellén, free competition would replace monopolies and "natural selection of the most economically developed and most technically advanced rivals at the highest levels of social development."[66] This model would pave the way to the creation of a kind of "United States of Asia."[67]

Troianovskii's eclectic vision of anti-imperialist revolution also drew on critiques of Europe's moral authority that had emerged during World War I among anti-Western internationalists in East Asia and India. He cited poet and philosopher Rabindranath Tagore, a cult figure in the 1910s for Europeans, who had based his understanding of history on a dichotomy between the materialist West and the spiritual Orient.[68] Tagore contended that India was uniquely positioned to facilitate a fusion of East and West to make the world whole, but Troianovskii saw him more as a like-minded anti-imperialist who underscored the geopolitical importance of India.[69]

Troianovskii was also conscious of Russian imperial vestiges, including in the Russian-British competition over India. This competition had been a preoccupation in the nineteenth- and early twentieth-century political and military confrontation in Asia known as the Great Game, and even earlier during the Napoleonic wars. Illustrating the significance of imperial experience in this field, Russian imperial military orientalist Andrei Snesarev (1865–1937), who argued in 1906 that India was of primary importance to Russian Eurasia and that Russia must behave more aggressively in Central Asia, was recalled in 1919 to Moscow from the Western front against Poland, made director of the General Staff Academy, and given courses on the military geography of Central Asia.[70] Troianovskii's thinking about this competition over India, and the wider Muslim world, had been informed by German geopolitical thinkers who had made similar arguments that the path to the postcolonial world ran through India. For example, Karl Haushofer's arguments in the 1920s illustrated what some described as an "elective affinity" between Russian and German geopolitical thought.[71] Others saw in these arguments broader parallels between geostrategic ideas developed in the Soviet Union, in Germany, by English geographer Sir Halford John Mackinder, and even by exiled Eurasianists such as P. N. Savitskii.[72] As Troianovskii's trajectory shows, his arguments and Haushofer's were, in fact, tangibly connected. Haushofer regularly read *Novyi Vostok*, where Troianovskii published, and described the periodical in 1928 as "the masterpiece of geopolitical writing."[73]

Thus, while Troianovskii's elaboration of Bolsheviks' plans for leading Eastern Revolution referenced competing Asian universalisms such as pan-Islamism, pan-Mongolism, and Japanese imperialism, and cited their slogans, such as "Asia for Asians," his ultimate conceptualization of the role of territory and culture in international affairs reflected European ideas of his time.[74] These ideas had traveled far beyond Europe. Until 1922 even the American journal *Foreign Affairs* was the *Journal of Race Development*.

These conversations—about the duality of East and West, European racial categories,[75] Social Darwinism,[76] and concerns about India, Central Asia, and "the Eastern Question"[77]—were deeply inflected by legacies European and Russian imperial rule.

As evidenced by their approval of his book, most of the leading Bolsheviks in Moscow shared Troianovskii's worldview. His manuscript was recommended for publication to the All-Russian Central Executive Committee by Lev Kamenev and received positive reviews in the Soviet press.[78] Shortly after the book's publication, Troianovskii met separately with Lenin and Stalin, stating proudly on multiple occasions that both leaders extended their "moral support" to his project.[79]

In late 1918, Troianovskii's program for anticolonial revolution in the East became the charter for a new association he helped found, the Union for the Liberation of the East (Soiuz Osvobozhdeniia Vostoka, or SOV).[80] In part, the SOV intended to fulfill Lenin's mandate to bring the Orient to the masses. On the morning of its first meeting at the Polytechnic Museum in Moscow, the official newspaper of the Soviet government, *Izvestiia*, encouraged "everyone to respond [and help organize] this initiative," which the newspaper also described as "the International of the East (*Internatsional Vostoka*)."[81] In keeping with its lofty purpose and obvious support within high circles, the Union advertised an array of prominent speakers for its inaugural meeting, including Lev Kamenev, who spoke on the Balkans; the Secretary of the Commissariat for Muslims Affairs of Inner Russia, Ismail Firdevs, who spoke on "the regions of Islam"; representatives of the Turkestan Republic V. Troitsky and S. Iusupov, on Turkestan; and Vladimir Gurko-Kriazhin and Sultan Galiev, on "the other countries of Asia."[82] Subsequent meetings would feature speeches by renowned leaders of foreign communist parties, including Mustafa Suphi and Haidar Khan (nicknamed: Radjeb Bombi [the bomber]), as well as domestic celebrities such as the charismatic Commissar of the Enlightenment Anatolii Lunacharskii.[83]

Lunacharskii and Troianovskii got along well and had much in common. They were contemporaries, born one year apart in Ukraine, and both had left the Russian empire in their twenties to study in Zurich. They both returned to Russia in 1898, were arrested, and left again to study abroad, and both returned by sealed train in 1917 and joined the last Petrograd City Duma.

After 1917, both embraced the mandate of educating the masses about anti-imperialist politics. At the House of the Unions on December 8, 1918, Lunacharskii opined that socialism's approach to the East was to insist that the world's "more civilized peoples" have an obligation to assist the "more backward ones (*bolee otstalym*)" and to provide this assistance "without imposing European forms of civilization . . . but rather in a way that respects and values their indigenous culture (*samobytnost'*)."[84] This formulation sounds like a version of the "Red Man's Burden," common in 1920s Central Asia, but Lunacharskii's civilizing mission was broader in scope and ambition.[85] His statements about the East echoed sentiments he had articulated elsewhere about the proletariat and the intelligentsia, which he believed to be distinct social groups. Although the proletariat was capable in time of creating its own culture, the intelligentsia nonetheless had a role to play in the process because the proletariat could not start from nothing. It had to draw on the achievements of the "culture of the past" in order to produce its new culture.[86]

SOV members continued to institutionalize Troianovskii's vision of revolutionary politics for the East. Under the auspices of the SOV, instructors from the commissariats of Foreign Affairs, Nationalities, and the Enlightenment were recruited to teach propaganda courses about China, Japan, India, Persia, Turkey, the Caucasus, and the Islamic World (*Musul'manstvo*).[87] These courses were taught as "applied orientalism" at the Red Army's Military Academy and also at the Communist Academy, established in 1918 as a Marxist alternative to the Academy of Sciences.[88] Other SOV members participated in meetings with various party-state agencies interested in the East. One such meeting on November 30, presided over by Voznesenskii at the NKID Eastern Section, included colleagues from the Narkomnats, Commissariat for Muslim Affairs, and communists from India, China, Persia, Turkey, Turkestan, and Bukhara. At the meeting, SOV member Gurko-Kriazhin argued for a coordinated plan of action, echoing the SOV's charter with a call to establish an Eastern International of labor, to offset competing imperialist internationals such as the Japanese one, and to create a special Bolshevik organ that would react to global affairs by doing more than simply translating brochures.[89] The NKID agreed. In February 1919, Voznesenskii and his deputy commissar Lev Karakhan asked the highest executive authority of the RSFSR, the Sovnarkom, for 200,000 rubles to send agitators to China, Korea, India, and Iran and to produce more propaganda materials.[90] These types of organizational-propagandistic efforts would be

Figure 1.3a and b Troianovskii's SOV membership card (front and back).
GARF f. 539, op. 4, d. 2805, l. 26.

of the Revolutionary Military Council of the Turkestan Republic, *Red Front* (*Krasnii front*).[106]

The new branch of the SOV in Turkestan operated in a context of palpable weakening of the political order.[107] Breakdowns in food collection and distribution had aggravated the longer-term economic and social inequalities between locals and the relatively better-off Russian peasants who had settled in the region after its incorporation into the tsarist empire in the nineteenth century.[108] In the cities, Russian skilled workers, who enjoyed an elevated position relative to Central Asian peasants, used their status as worker-activists to monopolize access to food and other resources.[109] The work of government was dangerous. Troianovskii's wife recalled never knowing if he would return home alive since some Moscow emissaries had been killed.[110] To address the brewing crisis, Moscow dispatched a powerful new Turkestan Commission (*Turkkomissiia*), led by Shalva Eliava, which arrived in early 1919 with a staff of more than a hundred.[111] Member Georgi Safarov later remembered the situation they discovered as the residue of decades of Russian national privilege:

> The Russian working class in Turkestan, occupying a privileged position in the production process, and deprived of leadership, an agenda, a party, or a revolutionary tradition, ... proved incapable of withstanding the pressures of the national, predatory, and petit-bourgeois milieu [although his use of the word "*stikhiia*" connotes natural as well as social elements].[112]

Safarov's description hardly sounded like a front of Eastern revolution that Troianovskii had imagined. Yet Safarov, like others, remained hopeful that the specific dynamic in Turkestan—of a working class representing the interests of Russian colonizers and a national bourgeoise representing the interests of the national anticolonial revolution—could eventually be overcome to make Turkestan a model of revolution in the East.

Although its findings may have cast doubt upon his project, the arrival of the Turkestan Commission proved fortuitous for Troianovskii. Both Safarov and Elieva blamed the failures in Turkestan largely on the region's plenipotentiary commissar, Pyotr Kobozev, who had been sent by Stalin to "mobilize the natives" and "induct them in the new institutions of power."[113] Kobozev tried to attract local Muslims to the new institutions of the state by setting up a separate Bureau of Muslim Communist Organizations of Turkestan (Musburo) and by pressuring the Tashkent

Council to abandon its policy of Muslim exclusion.[114] This approach sparked resistance from many Tashkent Russian communists, who complained to Moscow about Kobozev.[115] One of the topics dominating the Fourth Congress of the Communist Party of Turkestan was the future of revolution in the East and Kobozev's proposed approach, which was that local communists should focus on their own territory and avoid involvement in the internal affairs of neighboring Afghanistan, Bukhara, or Khiva.[116] Kobozev voiced a similar critique in the local press, dismissing the SOV and attacking Troianovskii personally for his ignorance and arrogance in presuming to create a united anti-imperialist front.[117] Kobozev further suggested that in his delusions of grandeur, Troianovskii was aiming to split the Third International and create a Fourth "Eastern" International with a program that resembled the capitalist ones of Woodrow Wilson and the Berne International. It was Kobozev who pointed to Troianovskii's preference, expressed in *The East and Revolution*, for American-style imperialism. He saw this preference as implicit in his endorsement of the "United States of Asia" model and his unorthodox faith in market competition, which, Kobozev observed, "extracts its plunder more carefully and completely."[118] Troianovskii defended himself in the same newspaper, explaining that he was not an Americophile and that propagandizing the idea of Eastern revolution was consistent with the program of the Third International.[119]

This clash between two visions of anti-imperialism, both of which managed to attract interested local Muslims,[120] may have become ideologically perilous for Troianovskii if not for the intervention of the Elieva's Turkestan Commission, which was also following Lenin's mandate to convince the local population "that the Soviet people cannot be imperialists."[121] The Turkestan Commission's reorganization of the ruling structures in Turkestan undermined the Musburo, an institution about which Elieva, Valerian Kuybyshev, and especially Mikhail Frunze had been particularly skeptical.[122] Eliava insisted "categorically" that Kobozev be removed from the Turkestan Commission.[123] By August 1919, Kobozev had fled Tashkent upon hearing news of his planned arrest.[124] His critiques of Troianovskii were immediately delegitimized—an example of the many contingencies that shaped early Bolshevik institutions, including those that supported revolution across Eurasia. Troianovskii may have been lucky with the additional cover provided by his close friendship with the chairman of the Council of Peoples Commissars, Fayzulla Khodjaev (1896–1939), a Moscow-educated Bukharan whose political activities had also driven him into exile and with whom Troianovskii enjoyed conversing in French.[125] In 1919 in Tashkent, Khodjaev had formed a Young Bukharan Committee, a group that would tie its vision of the future to the Bolshevik projects of "liberating the East."[126] With the help of the Red Army in 1920, he would become the head of the Bukharan People's Soviet Republic.

The more significant contingency was that Troianovskii's exoneration in Turkestan unfolded against political backdrops of failed communist revolutions in Europe, specifically in Germany and Hungary, and the strengthening of the Red Army's position along the RSFSR's southern frontier. In 1919 the Red Army defeated Dutov's Cossack army, which reopened the Orenburg-Tashkent Railroad and resumed communications between Moscow and Tashkent. By early 1920 the Red Army's conquests in the Caucasus produced the new provisional Soviet republics of Azerbaijan and Georgia.[127] To seize the momentum to build an anti-imperialist front, activists in Moscow and Turkestan shifted their propaganda and organizational priorities to the "East."

Consequently, the pace of Bolshevik organizing intensified. In December 1919 the powerful Turkestan Commission formed a new Turkestan branch of the Council for International Propaganda in the East (Sovinterprop) to help "create a party organization for anti-imperialist propaganda with territorial sections."[128] The Turkestan branch was initially intended to serve as the "main base of revolutionary work," working with communist and revolutionary democratic parties in Iran, Turkey, Bukhara, India, Afghanistan, and China, as well as the Young Bukharan and Young Khivan parties.[129] Its secondary goal was to make the slogans of the Russian proletariat "more accessible and understandable to the workers of Persia, India, Bukhara, and others areas [of the East]."[130] The remnants of Troianovskii's SOV were merged into this new Sovinterprop organization.[131] In February 1920, Broido appointed the former SOV speaker Turkish revolutionary Mustafa Subhi to be its director,[132] and Troianovskii took over its publication section.[133] Meanwhile Eliava and Broido continued to travel around Turkestan recruiting cadres by giving speeches about the October revolution and the anti-imperialist struggle.[134]

Eventually, the Russian Communist Party (RCP) consolidated the Sovinterprop's personnel and responsibilities under the new Comintern Turkburo led by Safarov, M. N. Roy, and Grigorii Sokol'nikov.[135] This new

ANTICOLONIAL DREAMS 43

body projected tremendous confidence, asserting bureaucratic authority over "all institutions with information sections—possessing any intelligence (*agenturnye svedeniia*) and information both of a general and a secret nature related to the aforementioned regions, and the East in general (*Vostok v tselom*), including but not limited to Persia, Anatolia, Turkey, and Egypt."[136]

This confidence was strikingly reflected in the poster-sized watercolor diagrams of the Turkburo's various nodes and connections and the Sovinterprop's schema. The Turkburo's connected squares, circles, and rectangles in bright primary colors depict links between Comintern, the NKID, the Red Army, communist party representatives, and their "informers" in Tashkent, Baku, Irkutsk, Kushka [modern Serhetabat

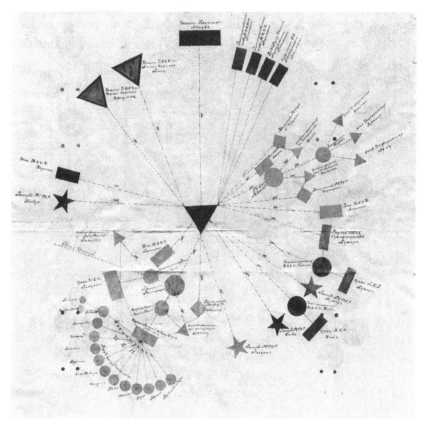

Figure 1.4 Turkburo (Turkestan Bureau of the Comintern). RGASPI f. 544, op. 4, d. 13, l. 34.

by the works of Soviet avant-garde artists. Its colors and shapes evoke the work of Kazimir Malevich and Wassily Kandinsky.[138] Indeed some Turkburo members actually belonged to the Moscow circle of visual artists interested in futurism, though it is unclear if one of them had produced either of the colorful Turkburo and Sovinterprop schemas.[139] Although the schemas visually abstracted geographical space, they ironically still aided the attempts to reterritorialize Soviet power by organizing links between places and making these links visible and systematic. In this sense of trying to project Russia's power across regions, "Eastern" revolutionaries collaborated with those who helped develop Soviet nationalities policies and integrate Russia's diverse populations after 1917.[140]

The excitement about the possibility of anticolonial revolution in the East—illustrated in a 1919 drawing by Aleksandr Rodchenko of a newsstand featuring the announcement of the revolution in Egypt (see Figure 1.6)—fueled the creation and recreation of new organizations, associations, and movements of key people across institutions and spaces. The creation of the Eastern International as a network during the Russian civil war was the work of building an anticolonial empire.

The story of the pinnacle of Bolshevik support for global anticolonialism is usually told through the published materials of two Comintern Congresses in 1920: the Second International Congress in Moscow and the Baku Congress of the Peoples of the East.[141] These accounts typically cite M. N. Roy's insistence before the Second Congress that the fate of the revolution in Europe "will depend greatly, if not entirely, on the course of the revolution in the East"[142] and Lenin's compromise with Roy at the Congress on the "Theses on the National and Colonial Question," which publicly signaled his respect for Roy as a representative of the colonized world. The ECCI then called for a follow-up Congress of the Peoples of the East in Baku, an event that seemed to some as "conducted with high levels of energy and a celebratory mood"[143] and to others as a disorganized and overwhelming "accumulation of white, black, brown, and yellow people, Asiatic costumes and astonishing weapons."[144] Reliance on the Comintern's published records, however, leads to narratives that conceal many of the negotiations and contingencies that shaped these decisions and their meanings.

For instance, both Troianovskii and Mikhail Pavlovich were sent to Baku to help organize the Congress of the Peoples of the East on behalf of the Comintern under the direction of Elena Stasova. Troianovskii worked around the clock, and just around the Congress's opening he fell ill with typhoid disease and then jaundice.[145] Thus, Pavlovich gets most the credit for articulating the Bolsheviks' vision for a post-imperial future and adapting their geopolitical metaphor to the cultural sphere, imagining "hundreds of millions of Asians" creating a "single common international ocean of poetry and knowledge of the toiling humanity."[146]

Of greater political significance was the extent to which the Comintern's message at Baku suffered from inadequate translation, although no translator could truly resolve its contradictions. These contradictions become especially visible when it comes to geopolitics. At Baku, Karl Radek assured Congress participants that "the Eastern policy of the Soviet government was no diplomatic maneuver and [that they were] not pushing the peoples of the East into the firing line so that the Russian Soviet Republic might gain some advantage by betraying them."[147] Yet a few months earlier, Radek had sent very different signals in anticipation of negotiations in London over a trade agreement between the RSFSR and Great Britain. He wrote in *Izvestiia* on May 28 that Russia was "ready for peace, compromise, and peaceful coexistence even with imperialist countries." If, however, Soviet Russia does not get peace, "it will strike in the weakest point [Central Asia and Asia Minor]."[148] In another article on July 10, he reiterated the threat.[149] Radek would not have been surprised to learn at Baku that Minister of Foreign Affairs Georgy Chicherin had already instructed Kamenev in London that "our politics in relation to England would determine the pace and intensity of our politics in the East."[150] Radek as well as members of the Commissariat of Foreign Affairs and the Red Army General Staff were all fond of Karl Haushofer's books about geopolitics in Asia.[151] Such geopolitical thinking undoubtedly shaped their approach to international relations, but it is unclear how much of Radek's suspicious denial was lost in translation at Baku.

Such double-dealing elicited different responses within the party-state. In 1920, Voznesenskii had tried to resign from the NKID, protesting to the Politburo that Soviet Russia had "no coherent Eastern policy." He also expressed concerns to M. N. Roy that Chicherin's interest in the East amounted to nothing more than a diplomatic bargaining chip.[152] For this, Chicherin had Voznesenskii barred from attending the Second Congress of the Comintern.[153] Chicherin also managed to convince the Politburo that "there was no one else [besides him] qualified to handle eastern affairs."[154] To an extent, these contradictions reflected early discrepancies between the Comintern and the NKID. After all, as the NKID wistfully admitted, the Comintern "did not have to make compromises in order to overcome Russia's political isolation in international relations."[155] Other disagreements were ideological and personal.

At Baku, triumphant Comintern rhetoric also helped conceal the territorial expansion of the Bolshevik state when a session was interrupted by an announcement of the "liberation" of Bukhara.

> Comrades, very important events have taken place in Bukhara.... After the October revolution, the emir of Bukhara sought happiness under the wing of the British imperialists.... The peoples of Bukhara have been freed at last—and so too, very soon, will the other peoples![156]

A round of the *Internationale* anthem following the announcement preempted any discussion.[157] Comintern chairman Grigory Zinoviev, who had urged Congress participants to declare "Holy War against the English and French robber-capitalists," was also clearly thinking geopolitically. Using Troianovskii's earlier metaphor, he claimed that if Persia was "the door" of Eastern revolution on its way to India, then "we must foment the Persian Revolution."[158]

Only later, behind closed doors, would the Comintern Executive Committee consider classified reports from Bukhara about such Red Army's "mistakes" as abuse, rape, robbery, and the theft of livestock and other food supplies. At least fifteen madrasas were turned into stables and barracks for soldiers, and some villages were completely destroyed, which sparked more rumors that the Russians had only come to the region to plunder.[159] The destruction was described using the term "*dogola*," which means to a state of nakedness and carries connotations of gendered violence against land and bodies. At the Baku Congress no discussions of these events were recorded. Most likely they never took place. The new Bukharan and Khorezm People's Soviet Republics formally concluded treaties with the RSFSR that emphasized sovereignty, independence, and the abrogation of all treaties and agreements with the former Russian government. Stalin described this special status as "the highest form of autonomy," motived by the "desire for the appearances of a genuine local revolution ... to serve as an example for the colonial East beyond Russia's borders."[160]

The survival of the party-state ultimately depended upon Bolshevik leaders' abilities to switch registers and tailor their message to different audiences. Propaganda statements addressing the Bukharan population stressed class conflict and depicted events as a popular uprising against despotic khans and mullahs.[161] Classified internal party correspondence, by contrast, used the language of geopolitics. For instance, the Turkestan Commission advocated surrounding Bukhara with Red Army garrisons to hasten the state's political degradation.[162] By June 1920, Frunze stressed the necessity of "immediate integration of Bukhara into the Soviet system" because its continued independence posed a direct military threat to Russia by keeping the hopes of counterrevolutionaries alive and making impossible the definitive pacification of Turkestan.[163]

The compromises in the international arena were driven by a combination of domestic and foreign concerns. The Bolsheviks, pressured by a deepening financial crisis exacerbated by the violence of the civil war and the policies of war communism, saw a lifeline in the 1921 Anglo-Soviet Trade Agreement. This agreement effectively ended the British blockade of the RSFSR and gave the Bolsheviks de facto recognition by the most powerful capitalist power in Europe.[164] In exchange, Britain insisted that the Russian government cease all propaganda that might threaten the British Empire, particularly in Asia.[165]

The immediate shift in the Comintern's priorities proved disappointing to those most invested in anticolonial revolution. At the Third Comintern Congress in 1921, Lenin still proclaimed that "the masses of toilers and peasants in the colonial countries ... will play a very great revolutionary role in the next phases of the world revolution," but M. N. Roy noted that both Trotsky and Zinovev had downplayed the significance of the East compared to the previous year.[166] The adjustment involved concessions that were tactical and theoretical. At the Third Comintern Congress, Lenin admitted, "In 1919 we said to ourselves: 'It is a question of months.' Now we say: 'It is a question of years.'"[167] In practice, Soviet leaders withdrew their support from the new revolutionary republic in the Iranian province of Gilan, which subsequently collapsed, sending a message to revolutionaries in neighboring regions about Soviet reluctance to extend support.[168] Roy was further concerned that the ECCI had moved to abolish the Comintern's Turkburo and the Tashkent branch of the NKID.[169] The Comintern Turkburo continued to function for another a year, ostensibly to help direct the communist parties of Bukhara and Khorezm and assist with their "cultural and economic development."[170] In practice, however, Bukharan communists complained that Turkburo officials were usually too busy to help.[171] The Turkburo continued to organize Kashgari revolutionaries living in exile in Soviet-controlled Ferghana, Zhetysu or Semirechye, Bukhara, and the Syr-Daria regions, and to "follow" events in Western China (Kashgar and Dzungaria), Afghanistan, India, Bukhara, Khorezm, and Iran.[172] Torn between their responsibilities to multiple party-state organizations and without sufficient resources,[173] most local members of the "internationalist" Comintern's Turkburo moved over to the "domestic" Turkburo of the Russian Communist Party, which became the Central Asia Bureau after its jurisdiction was extended to Bukhara and Khiva.[174] As part of this general reconfiguration, Troianovskii, Roy, and a number of other key organizers returned to Moscow to join the Comintern's Eastern Section.[175] This new organization was supposed to be responsible for "all communist propaganda in the Far, Middle, and Near East, supporting existing revolutionary parties, and creating new ones in places where they do not exist."[176] Presumably, in Moscow, such activities would be less visible to British agents and would be better coordinated with the diplomatic, economic, military, and intelligence interests of the emerging party-state.

The return to Moscow was difficult. Troianovskii's family had to travel in a locked freight car through regions experiencing a cholera outbreak and were unable to step outside for air or to buy food. In Moscow they were housed in a big room infested with rats and were awakened by their daughter's screams when one of the rats bit her finger.[177] In a 1934 autobiography, Troianovskii complained about having to return to Moscow with a "helpless" foreign wife and twin one-year-old daughters, while lacking money, housing, and food.[178] These were not unusual circumstances, however. His orientalist comrade Gurko-Kriazhin, who also relocated to Moscow from the Caucasus on Stalin's invitation around the same time, had to sell his possessions and work "like a convict," giving lectures and writing articles to survive.[179] What was unusual was that for Troianovskii, circumstances improved. His far-from-helpless German-speaking wife was hired as a secretary by Aleksandra Kollontai, and their children were placed in full-time daycare for Bolshevik elites, where they befriended Stalin's son Vasia.[180]

With newfound domestic stability, Troianovskii felt optimistic about his new position. Reflecting on his time in Central Asia, he acknowledged that the Baku Sovinterprop and the Tashkent Turkburo had failed to establish ties with revolutionary elements of the East or create a "special Eastern

Figure 1.7 Helen and Konstantin Troianovskii. From Tatiana Matroshilina's Family Archive.

literature corresponding to and growing out of [*otvechaiushchii*] the specific conditions of the East." He attributed these failures not to the complex struggles he witnessed over food, politics, or representation, or to the vestiges of Russian colonialism, as Georgy Safarov had, but rather to insufficient technical means to produce publications, a lack of experienced cadres, and "frequent changes in leadership and policy," which created openings for insidious personal and group influence. Troianovskii hoped these problems could be resolved in Moscow.[181]

Building an Eastern International from Moscow—with expanded technological capacity, a budget of millions of rubles, and the cooperation of communist parties of Europe and their colonies—meant that he had to broaden the imagined space of political action "to regions of Turkey, Mesopotamia, Algeria, Tunis, Morocco, India, and Afghanistan."[182] Expanding upon the Turkburo's connections to Anatolia and Iran through the Caucasus and Caspian and to northern India through Turkestan, Bukhara, and Afghanistan, the Moscow-centered Comintern could also be linked to the Arab parts of the Ottoman empire through the northern shores of the Mediterranean and to Southeast and Southwest India through "one of the centers in Europe."[183] In fact, Troianovskii even suggested that the center of anti-imperialist operations might be moved to one of the European capitals, where it could continue to work closely with the Third International and the RCP in Moscow. Of all the possible centers, such as London, Paris, or Berlin, where the Western Bureau of the Comintern was based, he had proposed Bern, Switzerland, perhaps thinking of his wife's extended family.[184] That this plan never materialized was just as well. Despite their hardships, Elena remained committed to the revolution until the end of her life, returning to Switzerland only once for a visit in the early 1930s.

The expansion of the imagined horizons of Eastern revolution brought new interest in regions beyond those immediately contiguous with the Russian empire, including the Arab world. While Troianovskii and other Bolsheviks had emphasized the strategic significance of Egypt in 1918–1920, other Arab territories of the former Ottoman empire fell mostly outside the scope of possible action envisioned by early party-state institutions.[185]

After 1920, the expanded geography of revolutionary spaces imagined by Cominternians reflected new access to the intelligence resources of the NKID and the OGPU and to information provided directly by regional communists. Through these resources the Cominternians became more aware of anticolonial protests in Iraq (1920) and Morocco (1920–1927) and of pressure building in Syria, Lebanon, and Palestine. They learned that in India, quite apart from Gandhi's efforts, violent protests by the Muslim Khalifat movement began with opposition to sanctions against the Caliph and spread to become the most serious protest against British rule since the Rebellion of 1857.[186] Evidence of the growing rejection of Western ways and "imperialism" also came from China, where the May 4th movement began as a student protest in Beijing against the transfer of German holdings to Japan and grew to involve nationwide strikes by industrial workers.

Addressing the developments specific to the Near East, the Comintern Eastern Section added "Arab countries (Syria, Mesopotamia, Arabia, Palestine, Egypt and others)" to its portfolio in 1921, perhaps in acknowledgment of the Covenant of the League of Nations, which had just established Mandates on these territories.[187] Despite the expansion of intelligence information and institutional coverage, however, individual bureaucrats remained poorly informed about "the question of the black-skinned peoples" (*vopros o chernokozhykh*) and still referred to the Arab world as a "*terra incognita*."[188] They could remain uninterested in specific contexts and simultaneously expand their institutional tracking of many regional movements because anticolonial protests could always be interpreted as symptoms of a larger crisis of imperialism imagined by Lenin, Stalin, and other Marxists as inevitable.

Deteriorating relations between the Soviet Union and Britain also helped project Soviet power in the Near East by removing obstacles imposed initially by the 1921 Trade Agreement on Soviet support for anti-imperialist movements in Asia. This shift was evident in the behavior of Soviet diplomats. In 1922, Commissar of Foreign Affairs Chicherin met with representatives of the Egyptian Khedive Abbas Hilmi, the nationalist leader Sa'ad Zaghlul, and the Sharif of Mecca Hussein at the Lausanne Conference. The Soviet Union had been invited to the Conference to participate in the renegotiation of restrictions on civilian passage through the Turkish Straits.[189] After a disappointing reconciliation between the West and the new Turkish government, Chicherin redirected his hope toward the Arab world as a possible partner for the Soviet state. Such an alliance, he hoped, could help challenge British predominance in Southwest Asia, overcome Soviet exclusion from the international diplomatic system, and strengthen ties with the "Muslim Near East."[190] On January 4, 1923, the Politburo agreed to support his proposal to establish diplomatic relations with the Kingdom of Hijaz. Soviet cooperation first with King Husayn of the Hejaz and later with Ibn Saud and Imam Yahya of Yemen expanded the bases for Soviet intelligence-gathering across the wider region that could serve the parallel, if sometimes contradictory, interests of the NKID and the Comintern.

While Chicherin was meeting with Arab leaders at Lausanne, Safarov and Karl Radek engaged in discussions about "the Eastern Question" with Egyptian socialist Husni al-'Arabi at the Fourth Comintern Congress in Moscow.[191] Al-'Arabi had arrived to advocate for the acceptance of the Egyptian Communist Party (ECP) into the Comintern, warning Moscow officials that "If we allow Egypt's zeal to dissipate without effect, its backwardness will be harmful to the revolution in the East and will delay it in the West."[192] Despite Comintern intelligence reports that characterized Egyptian communists as "ignorant of the basic principles of communism," Al-'Arabi's geopolitical arguments stressing Egypt's "geographical position as a bridge for British imperialism's expansion toward the Far East" proved effective and the Egyptians were accepted into the Comintern.[193] By the end of that year, Troianovskii had composed a set of "Theses of Action" for the ECP in which he referred to Egypt as "one of the most advanced countries of the East," the "capitalist nerve" of the British empire, and a potential "basis... for communist work not only in Arabia, but in the whole of the Near East, i.e. along the whole of the South and South East coast of the Mediterranean Sea."[194] These theses became a blueprint for establishing a non-diplomatic links between Soviet Russia and Egypt, a nominally independent state where Britain still retained control of foreign relations, communications, and the military. Soon similar links were forged with communists in other territories administered under a mandate system where the British and French empires were committing some of the most egregious acts of colonial brutality.[195]

Yet there was another deeper, more intimate connection between the Bolshevik revolution and the Arab world. The overrepresentation of Jews in the Soviet leadership was raised as an explicit concern in anti-Bolshevik propaganda and by the Bolsheviks themselves, including by Trotsky, who refused the post of commissar of internal affairs for fear of "providing our enemies with the additional weapon of my Jewishness."[196] Many of these Jewish Bolshevik leaders had been repeatedly confronted with imperial Russia's Jewish Question and the choices it generated, reinforced by violent expressions of anti-Semitism during the civil war. Beyond assimilation through Bolshevism, which seems to have been Troianovskii's choice, options for Russian Jews included emigration to the United States and Europe, which became a mass phenomenon in the 1880s; embracing Jewish nationalism in the forms of Zionist emigration to Palestine; staying in Russia and joining the Bund, a secular Jewish party formed in 1897 as the first social democratic political party in the Russian empire; and joining Poale-Zion, a trans-imperial, left-wing Jewish labor movement linked with the Second International (rival to the Comintern's Third) that formed after the Bund had rejected Zionism in 1901.[197]

By the time the Comintern started to make inroads to the British and French-controlled Eastern Mediterranean, tens of thousands of Russian Jews had already left the empire and settled in Palestine, where they were grappling with their new cultural and political realities. In 1919 the Palestinian section of the Poale Zion split further into a right-wing majority of those willing to merge with other local Jewish organizations and a smaller left-wing group. The latter group of about 100 activists eventually became the Palestine Communist Party (PCP) and sought the Comintern's support to help them overcome domestic political isolation.[198] Leading this left wing was Haim Auerbach (Abu Za'im), a former leader of a Poale Zionist cell in Ukraine who had relocated to Palestine in 1921.

Like that of all activists who dealt with the Comintern's Eastern Section, Auerbach's life was shaped by empire. For much of the Russian civil war, Poale Zionists, unlike the Bundists, were allied with the Bolsheviks in the hopes that support for the Russian Communist Party would eventually be rewarded with their acknowledgment as the legitimate party of the Jewish proletariat of the RSFSR, Ukraine, and Belorussia. However, the formation of the assimilationist Central Bureau of the Jewish Section (Evsektskiia) under the Central Committee of the Russian Communist Party clarified the early Bolshevik preference for dissolving and incorporating nationalist parties (including Jewish ones) into the Russian Communist Party. For Auerbach this was an unacceptable first step on the road to assimilation, and it prompted him to emigrate.[199] As a leader of a now "foreign" and territorialized Palestine Communist Party (PCP), Auerbach hoped to get the Comintern recognition that could not be extended to Poale Zion, as neither a domestic Jewish organization by the Russian Communist Party nor an international Jewish party by the Comintern.[200]

Auerbach's case to Comintern leaders used a language of geopolitics.[201] Echoing Troianovskii and other Comintern officials, he urged the Executive Committee (ECCI) in 1924 to consider Palestine's strategic location. First, its proximity to the Suez Canal, Persian Gulf trade routes, the Haifa-Baghdad railroad, and the British Cape Town–Cairo–Calcutta axis made it vitally important in the struggle against imperialism. Second, Palestine was part of an ethnographically and culturally unified region that Auerbach called "Western Asia" (*Peredneia Aziia*, literally "frontal" Asia). This region, he continued, had been artificially separated into Syria, Lebanon, Palestine, Mesopotamia (Iraq), Hejaz, and Transjordan, which were not independent states but French and British "puppets."[202] This wider geopolitical framework helped deflect attention from Auerbach's otherwise ambivalent take on his own Jewish community in Palestine. On the one hand, he suggested that this community was "created" by Britain and thus reactionary. On the other hand, it could play an integral "revolutionary" role in regional transformation by making Palestine "the most progressive land in the Near East."[203]

In the negotiations that followed, the PCP agreed to sever its ties to the secular Jewish Yiddish-oriented organization Verband and "finally get rid of its nationalist ideology."[204] It was then admitted into the Comintern, adopting the ECCI slogan of "territorialization." This acceptance overlapped with the beginning of the largest wave of Jewish immigration that Palestine had yet experienced.²⁰⁵ Many of the middle-class immigrants of this Fourth Aliya (1924–1926) brought new capital and expertise, setting off an economic boom in the Yishuv and unprecedented labor activism among Arabs. In this context, Moscow's disappointment with the PCP's efforts to establish a union of "Arabian and Jewish proletariat" was offset by reports about its "territorializing" initiatives, such as organizing neighboring communist parties in Syria and Lebanon (CPSL).²⁰⁶

By adopting the language of geopolitics, Arab and Jewish communist party leaders such as al-'Arabi, Auerbach, and Troianovskii presented themselves as willing mediators of the new expansionist, Soviet state-backed project of spreading world revolution in the East. As their statements suggest, early 1920s Comintern debates often presented territories in the East as lifelines for world revolution and, by extension, the new socialist state. In this respect, Troianovskii, al-'Arabi, and Auerbach echoed Ratzel's students in Germany, including Karl Haushofer, whose preoccupation with the idea that state survival depended on the acquisition of "living space" in the East would eventually influence Nazi foreign policy.²⁰⁷ In fact, Haushofer's books had remained so popular among the Bolsheviks that they had been translated into Russian without the author's permission and used in courses by Soviet military and foreign affairs experts.²⁰⁸ As historian Milan Hauner speculates, Haushofer's ideas of a Eurasian transcontinental bloc stretching "from the Rhine to the Amur and Yangste" may have caught Stalin's fancy and, if not his, then certainly Karl Radek's.²⁰⁹

This is ironic, since the German *Geopolitik* became one of the most violently despised terms in the Soviet anti-imperialist vocabulary after the German aggression of 1941, causing many of the Bolsheviks' early geopolitical arguments to be suppressed from official historical accounts of the Comintern and the revolution.²¹⁰ Yet in the 1920s, before the Comintern's turn toward an antifascist popular front, when its centralized structures were becoming increasingly subjected to the requirements of Soviet foreign policy, this was not yet the case. During this period, the language of geopolitics made for compelling and easily apprehended arguments among authorities of the overlapping Comintern and revolutionary state institutions.²¹¹

The Bolshevik desire to project revolution to the "East" attracted activists with very different understandings of revolution and its goals. Consequently, many of these early utopian schemes were disorganized, poorly staffed, and vulnerable to the wider political chaos of a disintegrating empire and a violent civil war.[212] Yet as the careers of Konstantin Troianovskii and other early Cominternians illustrate, these efforts were led by a dedicated circle of energetic men, many of whom had grown up in Jewish families subject to legal restrictions and discrimination in the former Russian empire. A number of these "old Bolsheviks" had spent decades before 1917 living in European capitals, participating in debates about imperialism, and engaging with ideas of political economy, geography, and the new geopolitical perspective on the relationship of space and political power. After relocating to Russia, they continued to work together in various configurations in the Commissariats of Foreign Affairs, Nationalities, Foreign Trade, and the Comintern and Profintern.

Of this group, Troianovskii stands out as a leading visionary and organizer of Bolshevik anticolonial revolution for the East. His vision of "an Eastern International" and its centrifugal revolutionary signals dispersed across Eurasia relied on geopolitical ideas and was endorsed by Lenin and Stalin. This endorsement allowed him to build a network connecting Moscow, Turkestan, the Caucasus, and many of Soviet Russia's Eurasian neighbors during a period when the state's international affairs were characterized largely by diplomatic isolation. His ideas and activism, which run like a thread through many of the early Bolshevik institutions created, dissolved, and recreated for the purpose of spreading Eastern revolution, reveal the eclectic and experimental nature of early engagement with the "East" as both an abstract object of Marxist thought and a concrete space of Soviet politics.

Troianovskii's work with the SOV, the Sovinterprop, the Turkburo, and the Comintern underscored that, although Lenin famously agreed to give up territory to buy time at Brest-Litovsk, high-level planning of world revolution and conversations about the future of the Soviet state were unfolding in explicitly geopolitical terms. In this regard, the Bolsheviks were participating in a global 1920s trend by which geography become "a unified worldwide discourse," with states explicitly concerned about the territorialization of politics.[213] Troianovskii's vision of the Eastern International specifically embodies a re-territorialization of the world that put greater emphasis on the regulation of space by states.[214] Significantly, the concept of "revolution in the East" could be used by different groups to promote divergent political objectives. Muslim communists in Turkestan and the Caucasus and leaders of the communist parties of Egypt, Palestine, and later Syria-Lebanon all used geopolitical language to emphasize their own significance and to argue for advantageous political outcomes. At the same time, the Party's Turkestan Commission could use geopolitical language to justify further restrictions on Turkestan's autonomy in the name of security. Ultimately, and unsurprising in hindsight however, such geopolitical arguments proved most adaptable to the interests of state power.

Alternative voices and narratives were silenced in part because concerns expressed on behalf of domestic or foreign Muslims could be treated as problems to be resolved with propaganda. NKID Commissar Chicherin had worried that the Politburo's redistribution of Central Asian territories might damage the Soviets' position in Turkey, Afghanistan, and Iran and "give the British the upper hand."[215] But this could be remedied by a shift in narrative rather than policy. This meant a constriction of the spatial and chronological parameters of Central Asian history and the suppression of comparisons with other regions or periods.[216] Any suggestion of continuities across the historical divide of 1917 were suppressed and channeled into the large academic, literary, and visual celebration of Soviet modernization. Comparisons between Soviet and European rule over "Eastern peoples" were disparaged or quickly rebutted by a new generation of Marxist orientalists.[217]

Ironically, this analytical and interpretive restriction occurred just as the party-state was expanding the range of intended and unintended inter-Asian encounters enabled by its new institutions. Within these new institutions, bureaucrats, activists, and intellectuals had to be persuaded to see the revolution from Moscow's ever-narrowing perspective. Some agreed to be persuaded because they were invested in the myth of the Bolshevik revolution as a global anticolonial event. Others simply sought the opportunities that these institutions afforded. To access these opportunities, domestic and foreign revolutionaries had to be willing to see this revolution from the perspective of the Soviet state, both in the foreign Easts and, even more importantly, in the USSR's domestic East.

The contradictions of the Soviet nationalities regime, anticolonial internationalism, and global trans-colonial solidarity remained unresolved and had to be concealed as the Eastern International was built. Sometimes this required accepting the territorializing logic of empires. For instance, the infrastructure built by the Soviet-backed Comintern inevitably normalized the territorial logic of European geopolitics in theory and practice. As part of Comintern's twenty-one conditions, new communist parties could only apply if they had accepted and conformed to the League of Nations categories, including its partition of the Middle East. The intersection of the territorial logic of European empire abroad and the Soviet state's creation of new domestic borders was rarely discussed. Nevertheless, it continued to shape the lives of Cominternians.

Troianovskii continued to engage with these questions, but over time he retreated from political activism into more scholarly pursuits. In 1921 he was formally purged from the Russian communist party, ostensibly for having failed to pay party dues, but he stayed in Moscow, supporting himself by editing the political-economic section of the VNAV journal, *Novyi Vostok* (New East), publishing a monograph about Egypt in 1925, and writing articles about Sudan, Iran, and Western China.[218] The head of VNAV, Pavlovich, continued to forward Troianovskii's reports to Lenin, Zinoviev, Stalin, Trotsky, Radek, Safarov, and other party-state officials interested in the East.[219] Later he worked as a librarian for the Communist Academy, and as a *referent* (researcher) for the State Planning Commission (Gosplan), a body established in 1921 and given authority to recommend a rational plan for the division of natural territory into functional units and a centralized economic plan.[220] He also worked at the Sovnarkom (1928–1929) and the Institute of Peoples of the USSR (1933–1936). For most of the 1940s he claimed to be unemployed, "working on a large theoretical work on the ethnics of socialist humanism" that was never published.[221] It is likely that this distance from high-stakes policy circles helped protect him during the deadlier purges of the 1930s. More likely, as his granddaughter speculated, he was spared because of his wife's valuable work as a German-language instructor and dialect coach in Moscow and her eventual work as a teacher of German at the Moscow State Institute of International Relations, which trained Soviet political, economic, and intellectual elites. It also trained many spies.[222]

The same contingencies that allowed Troianovskii to live out his old age likely explain why his name barely figures in the histories of Soviet orientalism or biographical dictionaries of orientalists.[223] Although he worked closely with "new" Marxist orientalists, led by his better-known colleague Mikhail Pavlovich, Troianovskii's omission reflects the vital but delicate nature of his specific contributions.[224] Being written out of this history was what allowed him to live until 1951, spending his time reading, writing, and drinking tea with his family, often wearing his Uzbek skullcap (*tubeteika*)—a reminder of his time in Turkestan and how it had shaped his life.[225]

2
A Bolshevik Laboratory for Revolution in the East

In November 1924, twenty-year old Muhammed Ahmed Said (Hamdi Salam; Russian: Hamdi Sel'iam, 1904–1966) arrived in Moscow to study at the Communist University for the Toilers of the East (KUTV). He was the son of poor peasants from outside Alexandria, Egypt, whose father did manual labor for a local landowner. His discovery of communism was facilitated, in part, by his landlord's son, who had had some exposure to some new ideas of anti-imperialist nationalism. Noticing Hamdi's inquisitiveness, he sent him to a local philanthropic school, *al-urwah al-wuthqa* (the strongest bond), named after the anti-British Muslim newspaper edited by Jamal al-Din al-Afghani and Muhammad Abduh. There, Hamdi's teachers, who were also activists in the Egyptian national movement, cultivated the young man's talent for poetry and elocution, taught him English, and exposed him to Bukharin's *ABC of Communism* (published in English in 1922), which inspired him to join the Egyptian Communist Party (ECP).[1] In 1924 he left for Moscow by way of Greece and Vienna, just barely escaping a deadly crackdown by the British secret police that decimated the Egyptian Communist Party.

Hamdi was a new type of international communist intermediary that emerged in the 1920s Moscow. As a foreign exchange student he and others in his cohort from Egypt and Palestine were entirely supported by the resources of the Comintern and the Soviet state. Their experiences within these institutions illuminate the dynamism of the early Soviet New Economic Policy (NEP) period, when the Communist Party retreated from the "War Communism" of extreme economic centralization during the civil war period and allowed for relative autonomy in the economic and cultural spheres while at the same time continuing to try to transform society, including "Easterners." These efforts produced opportunities for foreign students to participate in the experiment by shaping Soviet understanding of the region and exploiting uninformed assumptions and misunderstandings about it.

At KUTV, Hamdi's intelligence and aptitude for languages were immediately recognized by his classmates, who called him "the brains of the revolutionary Egyptian movement,"[2] and by KUTV administrators, who characterized him in official documents as an *"intelligent"* (a member of the intelligentsia).[3] Hamdi earned this reputation by throwing himself into study of the Russian language and using his knowledge of English and limited German to earn extra income translating Marxist texts into Arabic. One of his classmates, Palestinian student Najati Sidqi, whom Hamdi employed as an assistant, recalled these translation sessions as lively and chaotic:

> When [Hamdi] encountered a complex idea, or a complicated word with several possible meanings, he would become very agitated and try to enlist the help of [fellow Egyptian students] 'Aziz, Fahmi, Hassunah, and Zanberg. This would result in a mishmash of opinions leading to disagreements, until [another Egyptian] 'Umar would intervene with his opinion on the matter, aided by what knowledge he had of Marxist writings. As soon as they agreed on the meaning, Hamdi would turn back to me to dictate, often to find that I had gotten tired and left.[4]

This lively scene illustrates the excitement of the collaborative creation of a new revolutionary knowledge for the East. The work involved imagining, organizing, and naming key processes; translating foundational Marxist texts and ideas into Arabic; and gaining the trust of KUTV and Comintern authorities to do so. Translations such as these could not easily be verified by the ECCI and were thought to have the potential to affect international politics. Hamdi was able to gain the trust of Comintern leaders thanks to his unusual combination of intelligence, acceptable class background, and ability to navigate competing expectations at KUTV and figure out the role in which he had been cast. His energy and flexibility were especially important during the 1920s, when Soviet institutions were growing at a dizzying pace, and when the Bolshevik project to "revolutionize the East" was being re-centered in Moscow in response to various regional and global transformations. This chapter explores how these macro transformations intersected with and shaped the lives of KUTV students like Hamdi and, through them, the continued development of the Eastern International as an approach to politics and culture.

The expansion of the Eastern International networks in the 1920s, which helped to bring people like Hamdi to Moscow, were stimulated by the 1919

Treaty of Versailles and the alliances produced both for and against its new world order. Ruling elites in Russia, Germany, and colonized peoples around the world, including in the Arab territories of the former Ottoman empire, felt alienated by the treaty. For Soviet Russia, the fact that the contribution of hundreds of thousands of Russian citizens to the Allied effort in the Great War (through 1917) went unacknowledged and that Soviet Russia was officially excluded from the peace conference, which received delegations from Georgia, Azerbaijan, Armenia, and Ukraine, created several rationales for treating the result as illegitimate.[5] For Germany the harsh punitive measures imposed by the treaty also spurred a commitment by the ruling and middle classes to revise the peace settlement and helped fuel the rise of extreme nationalist parties.[6]

For those outside of Europe, the disappointment was perhaps even greater. Efforts by Britain, France, Italy, and Spain to extend their power into the ex-German territories in Africa and ex-Ottoman territories in Asia under the auspices of the League of Nations Mandate system triggered popular uprisings. Protests had already begun in 1918, when Tripolitanian peasants established a free republic independent of Italian Libya, and subsequently extended across North Africa to Egypt (1919), and then to Palestine and Iraq (1920). As more people under European colonial rule recognized that they had been betrayed by the Allies and that Wilson did not intend his doctrine of self-determination to apply to everyone, they looked for other sources of inspiration.[7] A shared opposition to the Versailles order became the basis for diplomatic relations established in 1924 between the Soviet Union and the Hejaz, led by Husein ibn Ali, sharif of Mecca, who refused to recognize the Paris peace settlement and the Mandate system.[8] It also became the basis for a massive expansion of Comintern networks that connected communists and anticolonial nationalists across Eurasia. This was not just a Wilsonian moment;[9] it was a Leninist moment too.

In the Eastern Mediterranean, political disappointments over European promises of independence were compounded by continued hardships of everyday life. During World War I, hunger and compulsory mass mobilization in the Bilad al-Sham—a region that today includes Lebanon, Syria, Palestine, and Jordan—displaced so many that the term *safarbarlik*, travel by land, became a popular way to describe wartime experience.[10] In the nineteenth century, Lebanon and Syria had experienced some of the highest emigration rates in the world, with many migrants seeking respite from economic troubles in the Americas.[11] In the 1920s, however, such opportunities became increasingly restricted by the isolationist American administrations of Harding and Coolidge.[12] This restriction occurred just as the Mandate countries were reincorporated into a recovering world trade system, a process augmented by the League of Nations' Open Door policy that expanded the late nineteenth-century idea of equal trade in China into a wider framework for promoting equalized trading opportunities beyond Asia.[13] Egypt fared better economically than other regions of the Eastern Mediterranean, despite an economic recession in 1920–1921, due mostly to cotton exports. The standard of living of poor peasants remained more or less steady until the sharp decline of agricultural wages in 1929, although the system offered few opportunities for upward mobility.[14]

Global migration reached new peaks in the 1920s, but Soviet Russia remained an unlikely destination.[15] On the face of it, the regime was ideologically welcoming to foreigners: in 1918 a Central Executive Committee decree invited foreigners to seek asylum in the Soviet Union from political or religious repression in their home countries, and the Constitution of the Russian Soviet Federative Socialist Republic (RSFSR) granted "the political rights of Russian citizens to foreigners living on the territory of the Russian Republic and to members of the working class or peasants not using the work of others."[16] But in reality, civil war, violence, famine, and epidemics made it an unattractive new home, and somewhere between one and two million emigrated.[17] Moreover, Soviet Russia had difficult visa requirements, compounded by limited consular representation abroad, and great discretion to expel foreigners.[18] As a result, only 80,000 immigrants were estimated to be living in Soviet Russia in 1928,[19] and the number of temporary visitors between 1917 and 1939 was estimated at around 100,000.[20]

While visitors from Europe and North America to the Soviet Union were the most numerous, it was people like Hamdi and his KUTV comrades, who arrived from the colonized world, who participated most actively in conversations about worldwide anticolonialism in the socialist capital. Visitors from the Eastern Mediterranean usually arrived after being initiated into one of the regional communist parties. Like Western visitors, their interests in Moscow varied.[21] Some expressed the desire to "merge" with the revolutionary masses or disillusionment with Wilsonian promises; others wanted to see the world, receive a free education, acquire professional skills, pursue new business opportunities, or escape the poverty of life under British and French Mandate rule. Some recalled that, after restrictions were placed on migration to the United States in the early 1920s, they simply opened up geography books to look for other wealthy destinations.[22] Soviet Russia may not have seemed particularly prosperous, but the opportunity was still enticing. Sometimes it was the only option for younger siblings of those who had already gone to the United States.

This chapter focuses on a subset of these visitors—students like Hamdi from the Eastern Mediterranean at KUTV. Their search for internationalist solutions to the problems of colonial modernity and economic hardship led them to become Comintern experts on the East or intermediaries able to direct some central resources as they connected Moscow to the external Asian periphery. The Comintern initially provided them with opportunity in the form of a small stipend to travel to Moscow and live there for the duration of their studies. These students usually undertook the journey alone, so as not to attract attention, following itineraries used by earlier pilgrims and merchants. Migrants had been traversing this Eurasian space for centuries, but new steamship and railway lines that connected the Russian and Ottoman worlds since the nineteenth century made this passage easier and faster.[23] Nevertheless, the students still had to be resourceful. The lengthy and clandestine nature of their travels at times made arrival in Moscow unpredictable. Some travelers ran out of the money initially given to them by the local communist parties and had to work to cover the cost of the remaining legs of the journey.[24] Others seemed to have set out for Moscow on their own initiative, seemingly without the approval of any communist party official, which attests to the KUTV's appeal. Arriving penniless, they petitioned the KUTV Rector for assistance, expecting the kind of beneficence allotted to religious pilgrims.[25] One student claimed to have lingered for days in a Moscow train station before finally being approached by a policeman, to whom he said the only word he knew in Russian: "Comintern."[26]

KUTV was a critical node of the new cultural front of revolutionary activities.[27] The Bolsheviks refocused on the "cultural front" in 1921 after their military and political victories in the civil war and Lenin's admission that world revolution was not as near as he initially believed. Historian Michael David-Fox argues that this cultural front was concentrated in new institutions of Bolshevik higher learning, which used terms such as enlightenment (*prosveshchenie*), education (*obrazovanie*), and upbringing (*vospitanie*) to connote a long-term effort to transform consciousness through tutelage and cognitive change.[28] Consistent with the Bolshevik revolutionaries' bifurcated East-West worldview, the Central Committee of the Russian Communist Party of the Bolsheviks (RKP(b)) established KUTV under the Commissariat of Nationalities (Narkomnats) in April 1921. It was to become the locus of the party-state's efforts to produce new "Eastern" men and women, a vanguard of domestic decolonization and the anticolonial front of world revolution, and a laboratory for Eastern culture.

In many ways the KUTV continued the work of Russia's imperial schools, preparing cadres to represent Russia's diplomatic and military interests in Central Asia, the Caucasus, and the foreign service.[29] Initially, the party created new "Eastern courses" at the Sverdlov University, a premier institution of Bolshevik training and thought founded in 1918. To head this initiative Stalin recalled to Moscow Grigorii Broido, Troianovskii's former superior from the Turkestan branch of the NKID.[30] Drawing on his Turkestan experiences, Broido created a curriculum that used Turkestan as a prototype for the East. Sverdlov's early Eastern courses focused on the history of Turkestan's revolutionary movement, the colonial politics of its bourgeoise, the construction of its soviets and of the party, and more-specialized courses on its ethnography, geography, cotton farming, and political economy.[31] Broido's efforts to integrate post-imperial space suffered from similar linguistic limitations as the late imperial initiatives that had trouble producing cadres to handle the linguistic complexity of imperial space. Instructors at Sverdlov could only teach in Russian and were unprepared for the specific challenges of the borderlands.

The solutions to these limitations seemed to lie with the new Communist University for the Toilers of the East, an institution formally created after a discussion of educational reforms at the Tenth Russian Communist Party Congress and by an All-Russian Central Executive Committee decree of April 21, 1921. Broido reflected on linguistic obstacles for training Easterners and on how they expected it might be overcome at KUTV, where he would become the first Rector, in the Narkomnats newspaper, *Zhizn' national'nostei*:

> The creative work of the party and Soviet organs in such republics must be wider and deeper than in any other region of mainland (*korennoi*) Russia.... Backwardness resulting from centuries of exploitation is the reason for the absence of these cadres.... Our goal is to create a cadre of native (*tyzemnye*) workers familiar with the economic needs, interests, everyday life, and psychology of the population.... They could form the brain

of the toilers (*mozg trudiashchikhsia*) of these borderlands, their communist intelligentsia.[32]

To fulfill this grandiose mission, Broido designed a more inclusive curriculum with an initial set of lecture-based courses offered in various languages (Dagestani, Azerbaijani, Farsi) and targeted to various language groups (e.g., Turkic and "international," which meant mostly English and French). Many of the courses were still focused on history—the history of human society, Russia, the class struggle in the West, and the revolutionary movement in Russia and the RKP(b). Others covered political economy, economic geography, soviet construction, orientalism (*vostokovedenie*), natural science, Russian language, and math.[33] KUTV's approach to "orientalism" differed from that of the Academy of Sciences because it emphasized contemporary politics over premodern texts, with modules on geography, patriarchal-clan systems, tribal conflicts, capitalist development, and revolutionary movements from the 1905–1917 period in Turkestan Bukhara, Afghanistan, and Khiva.[34]

Its first instructors included many of the activists who previously worked to promote Eastern revolution in Central Asia. For them, KUTV was the ultimate solution to the problem of cadres.[35] Troianovskii, who had joined its faculty in 1921, had also reassured his colleagues at the Comintern Near East Section that "for preparation of agitators, KUTV is enough."[36] M. N. Roy, who later took credit for advancing the idea of an Eastern University to Lenin and Chicherin, chose its first foreign students from among the Indian revolutionaries in Turkestan.[37] Broido continued to extol its potential to "chart untrodden paths . . . and tackle questions that had not yet been solved by Marxist theory."[38]

While some paths remained uncharted in 1921, debates about the "national and colonial question" were already taking form. Historians have characterized Bolshevik thought on this issue between 1917 and 1921 as a steady erosion of support for national self-determination in areas under Bolshevik control.[39] By December 1917, Stalin argued that the freedom of self-determination should be given only to the laboring classes and not to the bourgeoisie.[40] In 1919, Soviet diplomat Adolph Joffe voiced concerns about separatism in the "buffer republics."[41] And by the Tenth Party Congress,

Stalin was asserting that the only way to abolish national inequality was to establish the Soviet system.[42] In so doing, Stalin silenced any opposing ideas about needing to liberate the domestic East from legacies of Russian colonialism that had been articulated by Turkestan representative Georgi Safarov.[43]

Stalin's preferred method of integration and control of nationalist separatism in the borderlands was *korenizatsiia* (indigenization)—a strategy of training and promoting national elites into positions of leadership in the party, government, industry, and schools of each national territory. If *korenizatsiia* allowed Stalin to build what historian Terry Martin has called an "affirmative action empire,"[44] then KUTV became this empire's laboratory, as evidenced by its many reports that used ethnophilic language to celebrate the increasing national diversity of the student body.[45] Moreover, even as they celebrated KUTV's diversity, administrators remained conscious of underlying geopolitical space. These nationalities were still grouped into parent categories that were essentially territorial: the North Caucasus, the Volga Region, the Northern regions, Transcaucasia, Central Asia, the Near East, the Far East, and a "miscellaneous" category for Algerians, Indians, Jews, and Russians.[46] These territorial parent groups suggest that KUTV administrators approached their work of managing ethnic difference and building a new cultural front of Eastern revolution as statesmen concerned with geopolitics. This is underscored by the overlap of cadres in the KUTV administration, the All-Russian Scientific Association of Oriental Studies (Vserossiiskaia Nauchnaia Assotsiatsiia Vostokovedeniia, VNAV), and the Moscow Institute of Orientalism (MIV).[47] These three institutions were initially subordinated to the Narkomnats and were committed to producing knowledge useful to the new regime's state-building goals.[48] The experts they trained derived authority from the certifications and expertise acquired at these institutions; in the process they would interpret and expand Bolshevik power by translating it for new audiences.

How did these statesmen see or perceive the East? As VNAV leader Mikhail Pavlovich defined it in the first issue of *Novyi Vostok*, the East was "the whole colonial world, the world of exploited peoples not only of Asia, but also Africa and South America," in other words, "the world which sustained capitalist society in Europe and the United States."[49] This more abstract economic definition was then concretized for the territory Pavlovich referred to as "Modern Russia—Eurasia."[50] Like some of the other theorists of geopolitics and also the Eurasianist movement that would emerge in Europe in the 1920s, Pavlovich's emphasis on Russia's Eurasian location underscored its potential intermediary role in global politics. His use of the term "Eurasia" was unusual for a Bolshevik at this time, perhaps reflecting his background as a former Menshevik and a student of imperialism in Paris, as well as his more recent thinking about Soviet geopolitics as an instructor at the Soviet Military Academy, where he allegedly earned himself the nickname of "Red Imperialist."[51] He was also one of the organizers of the 1920 Baku Congress for the Peoples of the East. His definition had clearly informed KUTV's mandate to educate students from Russia's borderlands, including the émigrés living in exile in Central Asia and the Caucasus and others recruited by its "foreign sector," opened in 1922 and organized into seven language groups: Turkish, French, English, Chinese, Korean, Japanese, and Russian.[52] By 1924, around one-third of KUTV students were foreigners, mostly coming from such "countries of the colonized East" as Mongolia, Iran, Afghanistan, and Egypt, and some "oppressed minorities" from the West such as African American communists.[53]

However, imagining the East as an integrated Eurasian expanse became more difficult as new Soviet borders solidified. The USSR was created in 1922 with Transcaucasia as one of the founding four republics. This was followed by the 1924 delimitation of Central Asia and the adoption by Soviet elites of the "socialism in one country" thesis, which provoked questions about the extent of integration, especially between the domestic and foreign Easts.[54] Yet Stalin, who articulated this differentiation in his 1925 speech to a gathering of KUTV students, which undoubtedly included Hamdi, was forced to admit that the analytical distinction was unclear. The new republics of the Soviet East were still "developing and becoming consolidated as nations," Stalin admitted, and "they" were still separate from "our" metropolitan Russia both politically and temporally. The key connective space, KUTV, was expected "to draw (*priobshcheniia*) the workers and peasants of these republics into the work of building socialism in our country." The key connective process, industrialization, was expected to help "consolidate (*splocheniia*)" peasants' relations with the working class, "bring (*priblizheniia*) the Soviets closer to the masses and make them national in composition," while also "implanting" (*nasadit'*) national-Soviet statehood. The diversity of terms for the kinds of relationships that were supposed to be forged by and at KUTV suggests that the search for models of connection and integration of various groups marginalized by the colonial "West" was far from over.

Stalin's differentiation reprised Russian imperial boundaries in several ways. By implying that future decolonization of these regions would bring "them" to "us," Stalin was drawing on the late imperial cultural construct of a bounded "internal" or "native" Russia and its periphery.[55] The Soviet republics in this periphery were further expected to "attract the workers and peasants of the neighboring colonial and dependent countries to the liberation movement."[56] This description echoed imperial missionary efforts to bring *inorodtsy*, or non-Christian and non-Russian subjects of the empire, closer to the Russian people by converting them to the Orthodox faith.[57] This inward-focused model of "attraction," unlike Troianovskii's model of outward-moving revolutionary signals, reflected Stalin's more state-centered approach to difference in the Eastern and Western borderlands, one that accepted the principle of sovereignty that had grown out of the imperial context of Russian state formation.[58]

In his speech, Stalin tried to reassure KUTV students with his interpretation of international and domestic politics and its cultural implications. The world had entered a new era defined by a lull in the momentum of world revolution and temporary capitalist stabilization. Eventually, however, socialism would still produce a "universal" (*obshchechelovecheskaia*, literally: general-human) culture. The Bolsheviks' approach to the national question, exemplified by the delimitation of Central Asia, would also eventually prove superior to its alternatives. To Stalin, it already seemed more "just" than the League of Nations Mandates or the population exchanges between Bulgaria and Greece and Greece and Turkey. He was aware of his critics, who saw the 1924 partition of Central Asia—the contested and messy reorganization of Turkestan, Bukhara, and Khiva into new republics and autonomous regions along ethnic lines—as a colonial strategy of "divide and rule" that ignored local interests.[59] He also believed, more broadly, that the resolution of the national question could either accelerate or delay the fall of imperialism, and that his steps to transform the entire Soviet Union according to the national principle were taken in the right direction. As they all waited for revolution, it was especially important that KUTV students combat the "crusade conducted by the bourgeois press against our country."[60] This speech, like the doctrine of "Socialism in One Country," was not an abandonment of world revolution. Instead, it had everything to do with what Stephen Kotkin has called "imagining a viable Marxist approach to geopolitics."[61] Affirming this hope, in 1924 the Politburo of the Russian Communist Party increased the budget of the Comintern's Executive Committee as well as that of the Eastern Section by 33 percent.[62]

Comintern bureaucrats and Marxist orientalists, taking cues from Stalin's 1925 speech, began to adopt his bifurcated approach in their analysis of Eastern politics.[63] But for KUTV administrators, Stalin's instructions left many unresolved questions about how to organize the curriculum and student affairs. As the number of foreign students grew proportionally to the number of domestic students, the Comintern sought greater involvement in the university's activities. Within weeks of Stalin's speech, Broido found himself at odds with a number of Comintern Eastern Section officials over the university's curriculum, specifically the acculturation process for foreign Easterners.[64] One Comintern official took issue with the university's slogan, coined by KUTV administrator Vladimir Kuchumov: "First Sovietize the student, and only then Easternize him" (*Snachalo studenta osovetit', a uzh potom tol'ko ovostochit'*).[65] Comintern representative Moisei Rafes found his characterization "perhaps overly crude" (*mozhet byt' slishkom grubo*). To him, it recalled the Red Army political agitation formula for peasants that had come under attack a year earlier for being "ineffective": "First you de-peasantize the Red Army soldier, then only in the last three months re-peasantize him [*snovo ego okrestianet'*]." By de-peasantization, the army officials meant an eradication of peasant culture and autonomy by way of acculturating a solider into a dominant military culture; by re-peasantization, they meant the reintroduction of peasant culture before sending the veteran back to his village.[66] To Comintern officials this process of Sovietization seemed to go too far. Did KUTV officials really need to transfer foreign Easterners into the Russian Communist Party and require them to adhere to the particular Soviet form of party discipline?[67] How important was Russian-language training? Did Russian have to be the language of world revolution in the East? Perhaps, Rafes suggested, it made more sense to bring the KUTV curriculum "closer to the East" instead, thus shifting the burden onto KUTV to adapt more to the needs of foreign Easterners rather than the other way around.

Broido defended the status quo and reminded Rafes that, as an organ of the Central Committee, KUTV was under no obligation to follow the orders of, or even report to, the Comintern's Eastern Section, especially in matters of curriculum:

> Those insisting on maximal instruction of elements of orientalism (*vostokovedenie*) mean [by it] the study of the ancient history of the East. They represent a most ardent menshevism. The Comintern Eastern Section further disrupts KUTV work with its practical bias. It is interested only in

obtaining a worker quickly and is dominated by the pressures of the everyday. Meanwhile we are preparing a product that is more finished and polished.... This is possible only if we train [students] in the spirit of the Russian Communist Party.... For them the highest [aspiration] must be the RKP and the USSR.... The Eastern Section ... could not overthrow some central committee of a party in the East. But we might conduct such a mission with the help of KUTV students.[68]

The KUTV's importance rested on its capacity to change global geopolitics. On these matters, Rafes, a veteran of the Turkestan front of the revolutionary civil war, felt himself to be on solid ground. If the approach had worked in Turkestan, Khiva, and Bukhara, it could work elsewhere.

On the surface, Rafes's and Broido's disagreement concerned abstract notions of belonging to international communism as opposed to the Soviet Union and of the relationship of Bolshevik ideology to the idea of the "East."[69] Was the East something external to Bolshevik ideology that needed to be "approached"? Or was it something internal that could be socioculturally transformed? Were Easternization and Sovietization equally unstable processes that might converge under the leadership of the Russian Communist Party, or was one more stable than the other?

For Broido and Rafes this disagreement about the limits of integration and cultural assimilation had deeper personal roots as well. Both were former members of the Bund, a party formed in the Russian empire that debated Jewish assimilation and Jewish cultural rights for decades and eventually lost its assimilation-minded members to more universalist Russian or Polish Marxism and assimilation-opposed members to Hebrew-based nationalism in Palestine. Broido had left the Bund over a decade before Rafes, who remained the chairman of its Central Provisional Committee in Ukraine until 1919 and published a history of the Bund in 1923.[70] It is likely that Broido had grown more comfortable with the idea of assimilation into a "higher" Russian revolutionary culture, while perhaps Rafes remained concerned that eliminating national-cultural difference in party work meant erosion of his raison d'être, both as an official of the Comintern's Eastern Section and as a Jew.[71] As suggested by Stalin's comments at the Tenth Party Congress directed at Safarov, debates about political and cultural integration were taking place in other contexts, outside the Bund. However, as the exchange between Rafes, Broido, and many others involved in the Comintern's Eastern Section affairs shows, such conversations about assimilation, especially at

KUTV, often involved former members of the Bund or Poale Zion (Workers of Zion).

KUTV students were also left wondering about the ambiguities in Stalin's message.[72] One source of confusion may have been the fact that material conditions at KUTV blurred this particular boundary. Although foreign and domestic students lived separately, they often mingled in the dorms and in urban public spaces. Taking advantage of the university's location, a fifteen-minute walk away from the Kremlin, they strolled around downtown Moscow or congregated by the Pushkin statue in Strastnaia (now Pushkin) Square for poetry readings by Vladimir Mayakovsky.[73] The cold air often seemed preferable to uncomfortable living quarters. Because the university's growing enrollments had quickly outpaced its residential capacity, thirty students could find themselves having to share "a single large room furnished only with beds, just a couple of planks covered with straw mattresses and blankets; a few 'tables,' pieces of wood held together by studs; and some stools."[74] Others had to board with Orthodox nuns in the adjacent Strastnoi Convent, which had not been wholly liquidated as a religious establishment.[75] Najati Sidqi recalled about his period of study at KUTV (1925–1928) that some foreign students found their living conditions so uncomfortable that they chose to leave the country.[76]

The majority, however, seemed to appreciate the fact that they enjoyed food and material privileges, both relative to where they came from and to other Soviet students.[77] It is difficult to compare directly the experiences of foreign and domestic students.[78] But as material conditions deteriorated in late 1920s Moscow, with the arrival of millions of Russian peasants driven from the countryside by famine, collectivization, and the accelerated industrialization programs of the First Five-Year Plan, the KUTV administration was forced to evaluate its priorities.[79] Some foreign students complained they were being served stewed fruit with worms in it,[80] and others that the excessive starchiness of their diet, typical for Muscovites in the late 1920s, made "it necessary to continuously take purgatives."[81] One student even fled to "capitalist" Turkey, causing much embarrassment.[82] Considering these developments, KUTV administrators weighed their options: meet the needs of foreign sector students at a lower level, or give them what they wanted at the expense of Soviet sector students.[83]

Administrators repeatedly expressed sympathy for the foreigners.[84] At one point the KUTV foreign sector chief even asked the TsK if foreign students could be linked to the *Insnab*, a closed distribution system allocating special food privileges to foreigners.[85] Assimilation of foreigners at KUTV meant both that they were more tightly controlled by the NKVD than domestic students and that, in situations of scarcity, they were entitled to privileges unavailable to domestic students.[86]

Culturally, however, the differentiation of foreign and domestic Easterners at KUTV remained murky. As people from the former Russian empire, for whom official boundaries were not always clear or immediately important, many KUTV students seemed to want to enjoy the diverse cultural setting of 1920s Moscow without having to fit into one or another category or analytical box. Early 1920s student events at KUTV deliberately blurred national boundaries. A typical 1921 event, organized to celebrate the anniversary of the October Revolution, gave students opportunities to recite poems and stories, compete in "international" sports events, and perform a play culminating in all the different nationalities fusing together. This "Evening of Eastern Peoples," representing a "corner of the 'East'" (*ugolok "Vostoka"*) according to a writer in *Zhizn' natsional'nostei*, convened students of thirty-eight nationalities, including Russians, Armenians, Kyrgyz, Bashkirs, Japanese, Karelians, Chinese, Indians, Uzbeks, and Azerbaijanis.[87]

Activities of the KUTV cultural clubs for art, music, singing, and literary newspaper production attracted hundreds of foreign and domestic students on a daily basis and were designed to be inclusive.[88] For instance, the literary-newspaper club exposed students to world literature in an effort to create a global "proletarian" culture, and it trained students to create posters, newspapers, and a multi-lingual journal called *Zvezda Vostoka*.[89] The KUTV drama club was led in the mid-1920s by charismatic Turkish poet Nazim Hikmet who remained active in the post–World War II Afro-Asian Solidarity Movement. Under his guidance, the drama club brought together students of different nationalities to participate in performances on wide-ranging themes such as "European imperialists and colonial policy." These performances gave foreign and domestic students opportunities to work with prominent Soviet avant-garde directors, including Vsevolod Meyerhold, whose stylized performances with constructivist mise en scène and circus-style effects captured the energy and spirit of the revolution.[90] Meyerhold's actors' biomechanical exercises were showcased at a special event organized for international delegates to the Fourth Congress of the Comintern and the Second Congress of the Profintern in Moscow, where Hikmet also recited his poetry. At KUTV, Meyerhold attracted students from foreign and domestic Easts alike, as well as many other young Soviet artists, such as Sergei Eisenstein and some of the most distinguished comic actors of the USSR.

Hikmet had recruited Meyerhold to work with the KUTV club because of his stature in the revolutionary art scene but also because he seemed interested in "the East." Meyerhold believed that "every national theatre must be rooted in the life of its people, in its popular (*narodnye*) theatrical traditions, in folklore, and . . . be accessible to the broad-based working audiences of each people."[91] Hikmet also knew that Meyerhold's plays were spectacular, borrowing elements of pantomime, satire, and the grotesque, with sets designed by prominent contemporary artists such as Liubov Popova and Varvara Stepanova.[92] Under Meyerhold's direction, KUTV students enacted "mass scenes of colonial life in Turkestan, Caucasus, India, and China."[93]

Such performances seemed to capture the wider theatricality of the KUTV. The school dramas were personal and political, with participants sometimes feeling like authors of their own story and, at other times, as "showpieces" in a larger drama they did not always understand.[94] Hikmet enjoyed these theatrics, later recalling how much he loved going around Moscow in his KUTV uniform—a *budenovka* (the Red Army's signature peaked hat), footwraps, and his Red Army overcoat—and how much he enjoyed giving public poetry readings alongside Mayakovsky.[95] At KUTV, Sidqi also recalled meeting Hikmet at the drama club's rehearsal. He recalled one such play with students ridiculing the Turkish sultans by riding around on broomsticks and "saluting people left and right while other classmates would recite the sultan's anthem."[96] Such plays featured many of Meyerhold's strategies of pantomime and antics on stage, which were composed at his suggestion.[97]

The pleasure of mocking symbols of Ottoman and European oppression from a secure position afforded by the communist metropole and surrounded by people who accepted the inevitable collapse of capitalist imperialism made it easier for Hikmet, Sidqi, and Hamdi to embrace Soviet perspectives on the domestic East. In another fictionalized semi-autobiographical account of his time in Moscow, Hikmet recalled the beginning of one such KUTV performance, dedicated to the "revolution and the East":

> The students and their guests, all raucous, pushed elbowing their way into the hall. The most striking were not the Chinese, the Japanese, or even the Africans but [the people from] the Caucasus and Central Asia. It must have

been their clothing. In the city, they walked around in their local dress, sporting guns and daggers. The Central Asian young men were more handsome than the girls.[98]

This description celebrates diversity at KUTV but exoticizes and feminizes domestic Easterners. Hikmet's description may have echoed period Moscow newspapers that also portrayed domestic difference using highly clichéd and essentializing representations of each nation's place in the union.[99] It may have also been a little joke at the expense of Turkic Asians by a cosmopolitan intellectual from Salonica, with Circassian, Serbian, German, Polish, and elite Ottoman Turkish roots. Either way, the description subverts Stalin's prescription that domestic Easterners would "attract" foreigners because of some assumed Eastern commonality.[100] Clearly, the dynamics between students, including of attraction of foreign Easters to domestic Easters, were more complicated than official ideology prescribed.

The Arab Section, or "circle" as it was sometimes called, is a particularly interesting case study for thinking about KUTV experiments with cultural and ideological assimilation. In the 1920s the Comintern-affiliated Arab group at KUTV remained small.[101] By January 1930, only twenty-one "Arab" students from Palestine, Egypt, Syria/Lebanon, and North Africa had graduated out of a total of about 567 foreigners.[102] Despite its small size, the KUTV's Arab Section illustrates the complexities of their individual identities and group cohesion.

The designation "Arab" confounded Soviet categorization. Arabs could not be grouped with reference to any coherent Arab territory or existing nation-state. Thus early Soviet official documents referred to Arabs incongruously (and exceptionally) as a people rather than as a territory.[103] Additionally, under Ottoman rule, people in the Arab provinces were not grouped together as a nationality—as "Arabs"—but were divided according to their religions. Under the Mandate system new territories were carved up into separate British and French-controlled realms. Political ideas of Arabness that had started to develop in the late Ottoman empire were just beginning to be reimagined in the new post-Ottoman space as the basis of a secular anticolonial unity, but this work required sublimating other kinds of diversity in ways that were confusing and further undermined by European colonial manipulations of religious diversity.[104] For all these reasons, group coherence among KUTV "Arab" students seemed particularly weak.

In initially treating Arabs as yet another non-Soviet quasi-national group, KUTV officials expected them to exhibit and represent themselves and their identities.[105] One such KUTV requirement, to make a poster-like wall newspaper in Arabic and Russian, confused the students.[106] One student produced an illustration that none of his Egyptian and Palestinian comrades could recognize or understand. He explained that the field he drew represented "Arab lands" (*bilad al-'arab*) and that the red sun rising from the East symbolized freedom. His depiction of men in hats, tarbooshes (fezzes), and turbans running to and fro represented colonialists and different Arab reactionaries, fleeing from the rays of freedom. At KUTV, the fact that his Arab comrades couldn't recognize his scene as Arab provoked fruitful debate. They found his iconography, which seemed to recycle images from Soviet orientalist journals, humorous. This KUTV student environment was clearly more forgiving than, for example, Soviet cinema reviews, where Marxist orientalists criticized harshly "abstracted" (*uslovnyi*) and unrecognizable depictions of the East as useless phantasmagoria and decorative falsehoods.[107]

Literary exercises in national exhibition also sparked conversations about Arabness and cultural differences. One Egyptian student wrote an article that was ultimately rejected for publication in the group's newspaper. Its Palestinian editor explained to the author that the piece was rejected due to what he saw as a lack of taste. To express this idea, he used the Egyptian expression (*da kalam galiata*), which the Egyptian author found deeply offensive, as it suggested he was both lacking in taste and may have thought he was better than everybody else. Eventually other comrades had to make peace between the two by convincing the Palestinian to explain to the Egyptian that he did not know the real meaning of "galiata" and had misused it.[108] Nation-building activities in the KUTV curriculum sometimes highlighted regional and linguistic differences rather than Arab solidarities, but ultimately in the 1920s the university provided a relatively safe space to debate what it meant to be an Arab and to produce anticolonial Arab culture.

Integration into the KUTV institution was a deeply personal and individual process. In the 1920s, arriving students were initially met and settled in the Hotel Lux (today the Hotel Tsentral'naia on Tverskaia Street), which was reserved for high-level Comintern employees, NEPmen (businesspeople who took advantage of the opportunities afforded by the New Economic Policy), and foreigners.[109] Then they were interviewed by

Figure 2.1 KUTV Arab Circle Students with Soviet Orientalists (people identified in pen from left to right are Lutskii, Shami, Subotin, Ioske, Hamdi Selam, Roginskaia, Katz). RGASPI f. 495, op. 210, d. 74, l. 61.

employees of the Comintern's Eastern Section, sometimes with the help of a translator. These interviews illuminated personal connections between Eastern Section members and the region, especially Jews with connection to Palestine. For instance, Sidqi, who had been sent to the KUTV by the Palestine Communist Party (PCP) as proof of its success in attracting Arab workers, recalled being interviewed by the Deputy Head of the Near East Secretariat of the ECCI, Paltiel (Palia) Volkovich Kitaigorodskii. The administrator was another former Bundist from the outskirts of Kiev who had joined the RCB(b) in 1919, and was appointed as a *referent* (researcher and consultant) to the Comintern's Eastern Section due to his knowledge of French and "ancient languages, including ancient Hebrew."[110] During the interview, Kitaigorodskii shared with Sidqi that his brother still lived in Jerusalem and ran a store on Jaffa Street.[111] His admission of family ties to the Jewish community in Palestine may have been a test of Sidqi's ability to mediate different interests in the region, and it highlights the prominent role of Jewish transregional family ties in the work of the Comintern's Eastern Section.

After the creation of a special Cadre Department in 1932, literate students were also expected to write autobiographies in Arabic, French, Armenian, Russian, or any other language they knew, giving them more control over how they were represented but also documenting their possible mistakes for posterity.[112] However, in the 1920s, interviewers were still entrusted to gather information about students' families, social and economic class backgrounds, educations, occupations, and conversions to communism.[113] This information would then be used to assess their trustworthiness and potential for work either in Moscow or the Near East.

Some students Sovietized more than others. Hamdi Selam succeeded in this regard through a combination of resourcefulness and hard work. Like other comrades, he was briefly expelled from KUTV for "nationalism," an ironic charge levied against the editor in chief of the Arab national group's wall newspaper.[114] The charge raised questions about his suitability for party work in Egypt.[115] By that point, however, Hamdi's Russian language skills were good enough for him to gain admission to the medical faculty of Moscow State University (MGU). As an MGU student he continued to enjoy life in the socialist capital.[116] Avoiding some of the hardships of the First Five-Year Plan, he collected a medical student's stipend on top of a literary salary as a member of the Executive Committee of the Secretariat of the International Organization of Revolutionary Writers (MORP), a form of double-accounting for which he was later judged to be "unscrupulous."[117] More alarmingly, KUTV authorities received reports that he advised other foreign students on how to "game" the system to their own advantage. If a student wanted to return to Egypt but was prevented from doing so by the Comintern, Hamdi advised him to complain to the Norwegian embassy. If a student wanted to stay in Russia—a reasonable alternative to the almost inevitable prison sentences they faced as communists in French and British territories—he advised him to follow in his footsteps. "Create a scandal at KUTV and get kicked out," he reportedly advised. "Then you could be given a job and live well in the USSR . . . [and anyway] it was not worth it to return to work in the underground [in Egypt]."[118] For himself, he clearly preferred to stay and corrupt other students with drinking parties and debaucheries at his apartment.[119] For a while in the 1920s, Hamdi seemed to have the system figured out. He managed to get himself reinstated in the RKP(b) and was even invited back to the KUTV to teach Arabic.[120]

Part of Hamdi's and other KUTV students' success stemmed from their ability to navigate Soviet assumptions about Easternness, including the utilization of self-orientalizing language and the "rhetoric of backwardness" to defend themselves at party proceedings and win extra leniency.[121] But Hamdi's statement also emphasized his ability to transcend this backwardness with the help of his Soviet education. During a more consequential purge in 1936, when he was again expelled from the RKP(b) and was unable to return to Egypt, Hamdi presented himself in a letter to Georgi Dimitrov and Dmitri Manuil'skii as having managed to rise to the top of the Soviet system:

> During my entire time in the USSR . . . I struggled fiercely against the vestiges of that terrible backwardness that for centuries had been introduced into our blood and psyche. From the vague and amorphous fragments of knowledge that I received as a young boy in an antediluvian Egyptian madrasa, I have become a first-class academic researcher in one of the greatest institutions of the world, the Institute for Experimental Medicine.[122]

In his defense, he appealed to the Bolsheviks as good teachers by emphasizing the transformative—and what he hoped would be perceived as redemptive—role of Soviet education.

Unfortunately for Hamdi, it seemed that he had assimilated too well. Rhetorical flourishes could not spare him from a fate shared by thousands of Soviet people in the late 1930s, especially those with any foreign connections. He was abandoned by the ECCI in 1937,[123] arrested in 1938, and spent five years in a labor camp on trumped-up charges of working for the British through Zionist members of the PCP.[124] Hamdi managed to sustain himself during this difficult time by continuing to work as a doctor, a profession that made him useful in ways that helped spare his life.[125] After World War II he was released, allowed to return to work in Moscow, and eventually rehabilitated.[126]

In over forty years in the Soviet Union living under his KUTV alias, Hamdi had become a skillful mediator, for which he was rewarded with professional opportunities. In addition to working as a surgeon, he built a reputation as a writer and translator of Russian and Arabic, publishing journalistic articles about Soviet approaches to history in the Syrian journal *al-Tali'a* (*The Vanguard*), editing the Arabic section of the Publishing House of Foreign Literature,[127] working as an Arabic-language announcer for Moscow Radio,[128] and translating and dubbing Soviet films into Arabic.[129] For his more academic work, which included translations of the third and fourth volumes of al-Jabarti's chronicle, and Ibn Sina's *The Canon of Medicine* for the Institute of Peoples of Asia,[130] his colleagues at the Institute of Peoples of Asia and Africa acknowledged him as a "great Soviet orientalist" (*zamechatel'nyi Sovetskii vostokoved*) in the Institute's flagship journal.[131] Like other KUTV alumni, Hamdi taught Arabic to later generations of Moscow Arabists, including Vitaly Naumkin; he also produced Russian-language textbook for Arabs and created an 800,000-card catalog of translated Egyptian colloquial expressions for a dictionary of Egyptian colloquial Arabic.[132]

Yet throughout this long career, Hamdi continued to be viewed by his colleagues through a lens colored by Soviet assumptions about Easternness. In the same 1964 article in which he called Hamdi a "Russian Arab" (*rossiiskii arab*)—using the adjective *rossiiskii* instead of *russkii* to highlight Hamdi's civic belonging to the Russian state rather than his belonging to the Russian ethnic or linguistic community—Iranologist literary critic Joseph Braginskii objectified his colleague's physical features, comparing him to a supernatural creature from *The Arabian Nights*: "when you see this large head of the kindest of jinn from 1001 nights, there can be no doubt that doctor Seliam has remained an Arab in appearance. . . . The immensity of his activities is truly Eastern."[133] This description of Hamdi in the flagship orientalist journal as an exotic presence in Moscow suggests that Soviet orientalists continued to see the world as bifurcated into West and East and treat Easterners with disrespectful familiarity.[134] Nevertheless, Hamdi was able to navigate that world, live comfortably, and continue to teach these "experts" to better understand Arabic language and culture. As Broido predicted, he did so by employing his strangeness in ways that met the demands of the Soviet state, but also for his own benefit. In becoming a "familiar stranger," he followed a path that was uncharted by Marxist theory but paved by centuries of imperial politics and notions of difference.[135]

The constraints and opportunities created by the Soviet institutionalization of the revolution in the East continued to shape the lives of Hamdi and other KUTV students, or at least how they described themselves and spoke about politics and culture. Expectations and ideals of what the "East" meant entered their training, which involved continually having to evaluate themselves and others in terms of consistent political commitment, levels of energy, academic diligence, and treatment of others. Final assessments of these qualities were recorded in students' evaluations, compiled for review by the KUTV rector, and kept as background in their Comintern personal files. These assessments of character—if they were vain, selfish, wasteful, lazy, or exhibited an exaggerated interest in sex—had direct bearing on students' futures. They could determine if someone was to be expelled or tracked as a potential party organizer, propagandist, or theoretician.[136] All these evaluations were subjective and thus informed by the kinds of stereotypes expressed by Braginskii.

Although these self- and peer-evaluation exercises caused extreme stress, the playful atmosphere of 1920s KUTV "laboratory" setting, and the students' status as foreigners, gave them some leeway, even in the charged debates that ensued after the fallout between Stalin and Trotsky. This fallout occurred, in part, over foreign policy, when Stalin's misplaced faith in Chiang Kai-shek and his disastrous advice to Chinese communists to form a "revolutionary bloc" with the revolutionary bourgeoise ended in the massacre of hundreds of communists and labor activists in Shanghai.[137] Stalin had expected that Chiang would lead his army, and the communists, against the warlords and their imperialist paymasters to achieve an anti-imperialist revolution. In making his recommendation, Stalin had ignored Trotsky and Zinoviev's advice that China was ripe for socialist revolution and that the Guomindang under Chiang Kai-shek was fated to become an antisocialist dictatorship. His disregard of this advice left Stalin vulnerable in the massacre's aftermath. In part to avoid placing blame on Stalin, the Comintern's Sixth Congress (1928) reacted to Chiang Kai-shek's betrayal by shifting the global strategy vis-à-vis the colonized world away from a "united front" with social democratic and anticolonial nationalist parties in favor of an emphasis on class struggle.[138]

For Arab students at KUTV, however, the consequences for making interpretive mistakes seemed relatively light in the 1920s. When Sidqi was accused of Trotskyism for making an offhand statement in support of small landownership in Palestine, his Arab circle comrades reacted in ways that ranged from teasing to offering constructive advice on how to avoid the problem altogether. Following the accusation, Sidqi recalled the following scene:

> Hassunah approached me and said, "So, Mr. Mustafa, you want to create a commotion around yourself? Must you express your opinion? Would it not have been better if you had waited until you . . . return to your own country and then say whatever it is you wanted? Listen to me, apologize at the next session and say that you made a mistake. And it will be over!"[139]

Although the alternative of leaving Soviet Russia was not always real or even desirable, its existence allowed foreign students some flexibility in how they expressed their opinions. Similar leeway was allowed in matters related to religion. For instance, when one student was caught smuggling a prayer rug into KUTV, he defended himself by arguing that "Islam was a religion of socialism, and that prayer, in so far as it is a spiritual exercise, was not inconsistent with the idea of the breaking of bonds and doing away with exploitation."[140] One of his teachers had to help him correct the error of this thinking.[141] Similar correctives were offered to larger groups of students in lectures and discussions about the origins of religion (with a focus on Judaism, Christianity, and Islam) and its relationship to science and communism. These modules and antireligious "subbotniki" (Saturdays) were often led by Broido himself and went on past midnight.[142] Pedagogically, they drew on the 1920s antireligious campaigns, which involved orientalists, historians, and ethnographers from national republics who ventured to villages to lecture people about atheism. This suggests parallels between the education of foreign and domestic Easterners at KUTV and the wider state-building project across the Soviet Union.[143]

The use of socialist rituals and the creation of a new Communist everyday culture (*byt*) were taught to KUTV students and graduates not only through propaganda posters and lectures but also through everyday experiences with domestic Easterners in which religion was treated playfully and subversively. During a visit to Tashkent, Sidqi recalled how First Secretary of the TsK KP of Uzbekistan Akmal Ikramovich Ikramov offered him a cup of vodka and joked with him in Arabic, which Ikramov had learned as a child in a religious school.[144] Drink it, it's pure! (*Isqiniha sharaban tahuran!*), Ikramov said, using an iconoclastic reference a Qur'anic citation—"sharaban tahuran" (76:21), which describes the drinks that God will provide to believers in paradise.[145] By acknowledging their shared Muslim background in such a playful manner, this joke established a bond between the two men. By treating their shared Muslim background lightly, they modeled a way of being at once Soviet and culturally Eastern. Similar fusions of alcohol and traditional culture were later assimilated as "national" tradition through the use of "national" tea bowls in Muslim parts of Central Asia for drinking shots.[146] Such combination of alcohol and Islamic references would become more awkward in later postwar encounters between Soviet Central Asians and postwar Muslim visitors from the Arab world who may have been exposed to more puritanical attitudes toward drinking.

The cultural Sovietization of foreign Eastern students and their encounters with Soviet bureaucracies was a profoundly gendered process. The majority of students in KUTV's domestic and foreign sectors were young men.[147] In accordance with KUTV policies, most arrived, and also left, unmarried.[148] In theory, students were supposed to be "the Party's husbands and its creators,"[149] but in practice, as Broido complained, foreign recruitment remained disorganized. The cadres they got were not necessarily "the best local elements."[150]

Some students arrived married, while others were explicitly drawn to Moscow by expectations of free love.[151] Their relationships with Russian women seemed rife with misunderstandings. Sidqi recalled having to explain to one new arrival that swearing a threefold divorce oath at a Russian wife was not enough to dissolve a civil marriage.[152] Other students' files brim with complaints by spurned wives and girlfriends petitioning KUTV administrators for help after students left them, often for a Comintern assignment, pregnant or with young children.[153] Complaints were frequently reviewed by administrators whose own conduct was so reprehensible that they also stood accused of "degeneracy" (*bytovoe razlozhenie*) in everyday or domestic spheres.[154] Some women found the environment so difficult that they asked to be transferred to other universities.[155] Others had to rely on their comrades for protection.

There were fewer female students at KUTV from the Eastern Mediterranean than from other parts of Asia (e.g., China), and their experiences were shaped by their distinct regional and transregional contexts. For instance, the Jewish Egyptian communist Charlotte Rosenthal initially came to KUTV in 1922 with her husband, Yehiel Kosoi (party names: Avigdor; Constantine Weiss), who worked as a Comintern emissary and intelligence agent in Palestine, Egypt, Syria, and Lebanon throughout the 1920s.[156] A former Bundist, Avigdor took a circuitous route to the Comintern. From his birthplace in Dnepropetrovsk, Ukraine, in 1895, he first emigrated to the United States where he joined the left wing of Poale Zion. From there he traveled with a group of Jewish Americans to Palestine to fight with the Jewish Legion against the Ottoman Empire. After deserting he joined the local branch of the Poale Zionist Socialist Workers Party and then arrived in Moscow 1921 to negotiate its affiliation with the Comintern.

At the time, Comintern authorities were prioritizing Egypt, where the politics of anticolonialism seemed more straightforward than in Palestine. The eruption of violence between Arabs and Jews in Jerusalem on April 4,

1920, sparked criticism from Rafes and other Comintern authorities of "the Zionist enterprise in Palestine," while the first issue of *Novyi Vostok* ran a long article by Troianovskii about the future of Egyptian independence.[157] Avigdor agreed to redirect his energies to help organize communist party cells and the workers' movement in Egypt. It was there that he met Charlotte, the daughter of a founder of the Egyptian Socialist Party and a descendant of Ukrainian Jews who had emigrated to Ottoman Palestine in the middle of the nineteenth century. From Egypt, Avigdor began to advocate to Troianovskii in Moscow, by way of a South African comrade, for the ECP's admission to the Comintern.[158]

Charlotte's experience in Egypt, Palestine, and Moscow reveals the role of pre-revolutionary Jewish socialist networks in forging early Comintern contacts across the Eastern Mediterranean and in creating this transregional socialist space. For Charlotte these connections were personal.[159] She was first introduced to socialist ideas by her father, whose homes in Alexandria and Cairo became centers for labor activities and attracted workers—Jews, Italians, Greeks, and Egyptian—to learn about socialist theories and discuss the situation of the proletariat worldwide.[160] Charlotte's family was liberal enough to allow her to travel for work with Poale Zionists in Palestine, where she worked with Avigdor. With her father and peripatetic husband, she participated in strikes and protests in Alexandria and Tel Aviv, and she raised money for the International Committee for Russian Famine Relief after learning of the 1921 crisis in Russia.[161]

The demands of a transregional communist lifestyle and family inevitably conflicted. Her father was ousted from the Egyptian Communist Party, and somewhat fortuitously her marriage to Avigdor fell apart a few years before his arrest and eventual execution in the 1930s purges. She never had children. While British intelligence agents saw her role as significant—she had been deported from Palestine, imprisoned for her communist activities in Egypt, and was noted in one police report as the founder of the "women's section" of the ECP[162]—her Moscow comrades minimized her work and saw her more as a wife and daughter. Kitaigorodskii suggested that all she did was "follow her husband."[163] Another Jewish activist, Elie Teper (1893–1938, party name: Shami), also called Charlotte's work inconsequential and noted that she had made patronizing comments about Egyptian comrades and exhibited great-power chauvinism.[164] Charlotte was left to fend for herself, using her knowledge of Comintern languages—she was literate in German, French, English, and Yiddish; could speak Arabic and Italian; and eventually learned Russian—but she never once referred to herself in the surviving documents as a "woman of the East." While languages like Yiddish may have aided communication with some Comintern bureaucrats, it did not necessarily bring protection, especially in the 1930s. Like most of her Jewish comrades but very few Arab ones, she was arrested in 1937, sentenced to ten years in the camps, and rehabilitated in 1955.

Charlotte's experiences differed significantly from those of another female KUTV student from the predominantly Christian town of Antelias, near Beirut. Adal Ghassub (KUTV name: Alice Zarif, b. 1915) was educated at a local missionary school and was introduced to communism by her husband, whom she followed to Moscow.[165] There, her family support system broke down, as had Charlotte's, but the situation unfolded differently. Addressing her comrades in Arabic, Ghassub positioned herself as a woman of the East:

> It is unfortunate that I have reached the state of having to inform the Comintern about affairs between myself and my husband Jamil which reveal his bad ethics (*akhlaq*) and the foul customs and habits inherited from our corrupt system that we have not yet been able to overcome.
>
> These problems... involve a brutal beatings and insults, which Jamil has committed six times since we arrived in the Soviet Union. The [last] beating was so harsh that I almost lost consciousness....
>
> The reasons for this harsh treatment are that I spoke and laughed with our comrades, that sometimes he speaks to me on a subject and I answer him with something he does not want [to hear] and takes offense, or because it becomes clear to him that I am not his slave as seems obligatory, or as he wishes me to be [literally: he wishes me to be a prisoner] while he remains a free man.[166]

Ghassub's story was verified and acknowledged by Comintern authorities.[167] They officially reprimanded Jamil, warning him that there was no place at KUTV for such "non-comradely treatment of the family,"[168] while their comrades applied "social pressure."[169] The Comintern "trial" concluded with Jamil objecting to the "harassment" by his comrades about his personal affairs and asking to be allowed to return to his country so that he could "get back to doing Party work."[170] Not long after, the couple was sent back to Syria, leaving two weeks apart.

Ghassub's complaint and its outcome demonstrates the reconfiguration of official attitudes toward the family in the second half of the 1930s. The campaign to strengthen and stabilize the family made divorce more difficult and limited abortion, but it also emphasized male irresponsibility, especially in cases of nonpayment of alimony.[171]

The complaint also positioned Ghassub as a "woman of the East" in a way that differed from Charlotte. Although both were religious minorities in their milieux, Ghassub's Lebanese Christian background meant that, unlike Charlotte, who was Jewish, she could not in the Comintern context be accused of being a great-power chauvinist. Lingusitically it was harder for Ghassub to assimilate in interwar Moscow, unlike Charlotte, who spoke Yiddish, and whose ancestors had emigrated to Egypt from the former Russian empire. Like Hamdi, Ghassub could invoke the legacies of a "corrupt system" of colonialism, which she hoped her husband might be taught to overcome. Drawing on her training to become an organizer of women's communist cells in Lebanon, she advocated for herself as a woman trying to overcome the "backwardness" of her context and culture. Despite the availability of these ideological resources, the outcome of her case suggested the precarity of having to negotiate overlapping forms of patriarchal authority and the extent to which KUTV and the Comintern remained deeply unsupportive of women.[172]

Their cases could also be read in light of the contests over gendered hierarchies that were taking place simultaneously in Mandate Lebanon and Syria. There, activist groups were also contesting the status of women as second-class citizens in a colonial order that privileged men because they were better integrated into the French Mandatory state's institutions. As they challenged the gendered spatial boundaries of society and the city, these women contended with violence on the street, in cinemas, and in the press, especially after the suppression of the Syrian Revolt.[173] But even if KUTV extended the terrain of gendered conflict unfolding in the Eastern Mediterranean, it taught women like Ghassub to mobilize the civilizing mission of Soviet-backed communism against a more oppressive form of domestic paternalism.

The different outcomes for these two women underscores the role of cultural, linguistic, and gendered backgrounds in shaping how communists in the Arab Section saw themselves in relation to the Soviet-backed project of international communism. For a Christian Lebanese woman like Ghassub, it was easier to view herself and her husband from the party's perspective, as "backward," than it was for a Jewish communist from Egypt, like Charlotte, whose family ties—spanning Egypt, Palestine, and the former Russian empire—made it more difficult to use Easternness to her advantage.[174] As these few recorded women's experiences illustrate, access to Soviet state support remained profoundly gendered in terms of how "women of the East" were ideologically constructed, how they could use these constructs, and how they were treated as comrades, which was always inflected by other social, cultural, and biological factors and considerations.

KUTV offered students the opportunity to study in Moscow, the capital of international socialism and of the world's first anticolonial state. Because the university was founded in 1921—before the creation of the Soviet Union, the national-territorial delimitation of Central Asia, and the embrace of "socialism in one country"—its design reflected the more fluid spatial scales and logics of its time. It treated the southern borderlands of the former imperial state and the territories under European colonial rule as a porous space for potential Eastern revolution. This fluidity underscored that hopes for world revolution were never fully abandoned, even after the embrace of "socialism in one country." This institutionalization of early Soviet efforts to educate new Eastern men and women for a post-imperial world was reinforced by the Versailles system of collective security, which excluded Bolshevik leaders and anticolonial activists (including communists and occasionally nationalists). In the continued centering of the Eastern International in Moscow, the ambiguous and capacious category "East" proved useful to various parties and interests.

Despite their many ideological and political innovations, early Bolshevik activists remained captive to the centuries-old Eurocentric assumption— popular in both Russia and Europe and filtered through Hegel, Marx, and other European Marxists—of the binary division of the world, both spatially and culturally, along a West-East axis. Foreigners could use these assumptions, through self-orientalizing language in official contexts, to avoid having to speak about a topic, such as personal limitations or confusing family dynamics. Self-orientalizing language could help students avoid responsibility for ideological mistakes and thus create room for personal and intellectual maneuver. By emphasizing difference, it could also help activate students' privileged status as foreigners, as well as the mechanisms of affirmative action that were particularly robust for peoples assumed to be underdeveloped. Sometimes, it could also function as an implicit claim to having "expertise" in an area acknowledged by the authorities as academically underdeveloped and geopolitically critical.[175] This status of an "expert" on the East could lead to multiple paths of integration into Soviet life, including employment and publishing opportunities. It opened the doors of closed libraries, where a student could pursue research or creative projects,[176] enabled KUTV students and graduates to collaborate with Soviet scholars, and made it possible for them to otherwise inform or shape the Soviet Union's objectives in its different and interconnected Easts.

The imperial legacies that shaped this project varied. Besides invoking blatantly homogenizing assumptions about "the East," the idea of a communist laboratory for the creation of intermediaries for this East evoked the imperial-era legacy of missionary schools. Such schools operated within Russia but were also set up by Russia across the Eastern Mediterranean, as well as by American and European colonial powers across Asia and Africa.[177] Like them, KUTV also sought to provide a basic introduction to critical vocabulary and to teach the basics of communist spirituality and organization of social life, but was less concerned with high levels of achievements of literacy or full integration. Like them, KUTV used education to bring "other" people closer to the state, and it faced similar challenges of having to translate, communicate, and ultimately create new hierarchies of behaviors and norms. Most of KUTVs earliest teachers and students were also deeply shaped by their very recent experiences of empire, especially of the civil war in Turkestan, the limits of cultural assimilation, the politics of imperial parties such as the Bund and Poale Zion, and transregional family ties. These included ties of Jews migrating between Russia and Palestine but increasingly those of Arabs who acquired wives, girlfriends, and children in the USSR. The role of administrators highlighted the extent to which Russian imperial legacies informed the administration of international communism and support for anticolonialism in the East, both in the form of communist parties of the "foreign east" and in other Comintern-supported projects such as the League against Imperialism.

Unexpectedly for early Bolshevik planners, the 1920s turned out to be a decade of political and ideological border-making. In the Eastern Mediterranean, colonial governments experimented with drawing and redrawing borders and creating new proto-states.[178] Within these polities, a plethora of nationalist movements emerged in Egypt, Syria, and Palestine. These included a more ambiguous pan-Arab nationalism that grew out of late Ottoman cultural Arabism but came to be proposed, and then challenged, as a new type of political belonging (*qawmiyya*) across the Bilad al-Sham, Arabia, and Iraq.[179] A new federalist Soviet state that emerged after the Bolshevik victory in the civil war also tried to "resolve" the various oppositional national questions on its territories through national delimitation, including Turkestan's refashioning into new Central Asian republics. By 1925, Stalin acknowledged the ideological borders of the Soviet Union by embracing "socialism in one country" and articulating a new approach to Asia when he delineated the East into "domestic" and "foreign" components.

Interpretations of these delineations varied widely, but all parties seem to agree on one thing: a special relationship existed between the Soviet East, especially Turkestan, where most KUTV teachers and architects got their start, and other parts of Asia. Troianovskii imagined Turkestan as a beacon for revolutionary signals to other parts of Asia. Other veterans of the revolution in Central Asia, such as Broido and Safarov, hoped that Turkestan's struggles to decolonize would allow for communist control over both the kulak "colonizers" and the influential local "beys," and that this could become a model for other political movements in Asia.[180] Still, Comintern officials saw Turkestan as a training ground for foreign agents, such as Avigdor and Charlotte, and Arab communists, such as Sidqi and Bakdash, before sending them on assignment to Palestine, Syria, and Egypt. For their part, KUTV's foreign students occasionally looked upon Soviet easterners as an exotic presence. Their views differed from Stalin's who hypothesized that the domestic East could help "attract" foreigners to anticolonial movements and instructed everyone to fight the crusade conducted "against our country" by the bourgeois press, including critiques by Central Asian nationalists and émigrés in exile. Instead, their different real and imagined links and solidarities tuned KUTV into an ambiguous contact zone of different groups and interests loosely defined as "Eastern."

Among these groups, and mostly unacknowledged in official documents, were Jews from the former Russian empire. Their experiences, which occurred at a key intersection of Russia's imperial legacies and the revolutionary efforts to create an international anticolonial culture, undoubtedly attracted them to the kinds of questions being explored at KUTV. These questions included the limits of assimilation into the dominant, and not always welcoming, supra-national Russian Marxist culture, and the stakes of rejecting Zionist and socialist Zionist alternatives that involved emigration to Palestine. Their interest in the Near East was thus itself a product of the politics of empire, both of the late imperial treatment of the Russian Jewish minority and of the British empire's support for the Balfour Declaration.

The fact that conversations about nationalism and supra-national belonging were happening at KUTV was itself a legacy of empire. In the 1920s, Moscow replaced St. Petersburg as the metropole where "the peripheries largely negotiated their relations to each other."[181] Surveying the university, Stalin tried to conceal some of these imperialist overtones by drawing an analytical distinction between the two Easts. Yet even this act resembled earlier examples of "imperial thinking" about Soviet Russia's differentiated peripheries, now further differentiated as foreign and domestic. In practice, this analytical distinction proved difficult to work with. In the 1920s, state power was still weak compared to the 1930s, and new boundaries were still easier to ignore, reinterpret, or appropriate in creative ways. KUTV fed into the playful creativity of this period and was enlivened by Moscow's vibrant urban environment, which allowed foreign and domestic students to engage with prominent intellectuals who were also busy producing a new "culture of the future" with support from party officials interested in youth and civilizing-enlightenment projects.[182] Their experimentation with officially recognized and hierarchically distinct units, including the two Easts as well as other types of identity categories such as Arab, Egyptian, and other national categories, was inflected by changing domestic ideas about Soviet nationalities politics.[183] For such experiments, KUTV remained both a laboratory and a crossroads of people and ideas, connecting different spaces, races, and regimes responsible for building domestic empire and for promoting global anticolonialism abroad.

This decentralized network connected activists from Asia and Africa to anti-imperial communities in Paris, London, Brussels, and Berlin, but the excitement of being at KUTV—at the heart of a revolutionary new world—made Moscow a particularly attractive node. This attraction helped ensure that the Bolshevik category "East" remained a productive mode of communist power that stimulated and supported the translation of books and articles, and the production of art, literature, plays, and academic studies of political, economic, and literary transformation. To pursue these projects, KUTV graduates traveled across Eurasia empowered as intermediaries of the party-state to foster new linkages and extend Comintern or Soviet state support to new anticolonial activists, initiatives, and organizations. But because of the emphasis placed on the domestic East, the wider conversation about political, cultural, and intellectual decolonization was particularly circumspect about the status of Central Asian and Caucasian autonomies. Throughout most of the Soviet period, the willingness to see these peoples and places from the perspective of the party-state remained a litmus test for international communist party loyalty as well as for fellow travelers who considered themselves participants in a broader intellectual project of decolonization.

3
Arabization, Purges, and Terror

On a cold night in February 1933, two Palestinian Arabs boarded a train traveling from Moscow to Rostov-on-Don, over 650 miles southeast. Aimarov (b. 1908) and Kafri (b. 1908 or 1909) had been expelled from KUTV for "antiparty activities."[1] They were given one year to prove themselves worthy of readmission by working and participating in the party life of Rostsel'mash, a newly established factory that specialized in the production of agricultural machines.[2] When they arrived they were given privileged accommodations typically reserved for foreign specialists: housing in the foreigners' colony and access to the foreign workers' cafeteria.[3]

After just three days, Aimarov and Kafri wrote to their KUTV comrades to express disappointment in their new jobs. Instead of being "taught a trade," they claimed they were assigned to general menial tasks, which they described as "black work" (*chernaia rabota*), and then, after complaining to the factory administration, moved to a department of mechanical repairs.[4] "We do not want to break party discipline, but that has its limits," they threatened the following week.[5] Within two months they returned without permission to Moscow, telling a special KUTV Committee that they would not to go back to factory work "under any circumstances, even if their conditions were to substantially improve."[6] Instead they demanded that they would file a complaint with the higher-level Comintern International Control Commission against their teachers who, they claimed, were Jews secretly working "to break apart our Arab Party."[7]

Aimarov and Kafri's experiences were shaped by multiple currents of the Stalin Revolution. As foreigners arriving in Moscow in 1930 they were part of a growing stream of workers, tourists, and intellectuals drawn to the USSR by the lure of its accelerated industrialization at the start of a worldwide economic depression.[8] Across industrialized Europe and the United States, the depression brought unemployment, under-employment, and all the associated hardships.[9] Rural societies fared even worse. Peasants in rural areas of Hungary, Romania, India, and China who had nowhere to go faced starvation. In the Middle Eastern Mandate territories under

The Eastern International. Masha Kirasirova, Oxford University Press. © Oxford University Press 2024.
DOI: 10.1093/oso/9780197685693.003.0004

French and British control since the early 1920s—with the significant exception of the Jewish community in Palestine (Yishuv), which boomed due to an influx of wealthy European Jewish immigrants—the 1930s recession brought falling wages, rising unemployment, and languishing agriculture. As strikes multiplied, workers came to recognize their common grievances.[10] These pressures pushed some young people toward communism and the idea promoted by regional communist parties that the Soviet Union's rapid economic growth served as proof of communism's superiority over capitalism.[11]

Yet Kafri and Aimarov did not see themselves as belonging to the group of engineers at the factory's foreigners' colony who had been willing to relocate to the USSR (mostly from Europe and the United States) to contribute to the building of socialism.[12] They had tried to see themselves as students being "taught a trade," in line with broader expectations about the "proletarianization" of students in this period. This proletarianization meant, in part, the selective recruitment of students with proletarian backgrounds at Soviet universities and cultural establishments, and in part the reorganization of education to yield a maximum, immediate output of engineers, agricultural specialists, technicians, and skilled workers for the First Five-Year Plan.[13] At KUTV this policy translated into a requirement that all students undertake an internship (*praktika*) in a Soviet factory or a similar enterprise in Moscow, or in one of the national republics. For instance, in 1933 all first- and second-year students were expected to work on a construction site for the Moscow metro. There, they were expected to synthetize their academic learning with more practical training in the Russian language, agrarian-technological disciplines, and party construction by studying the mood (*nastroeniia*) of the metro-builders and their views on international politics. They were also to help the construction workers "elevate [their] culture" by paying attention to the cleanliness of their beds, clothes, and general hominess of their barracks.[14] Although this requirement was applied to domestic students, the blurring of domestic and foreign internationalisms at KUTV meant that some foreigners were also working in the metro.[15]

Aimarov and Kafri did not interpret their assignment to Rostsel'mash as an opportunity to "proletarianize." Nor did they see it as an opportunity to acquire training that could contribute to rural development in the Eastern Mediterranean by mechanizing agriculture and thus saving labor time and raising the productivity of poor peasants. The fact that they saw it as a form of internal exile, inflicted on them unjustly as a consequence of ethnicized

Arab-Jewish tensions, suggests the unusual entanglements of the domestic and foreign Easts that operated in the KUTV Arab Section since the late 1920s.

This story, unfolding in the middle of an official public campaign against anti-Semitism that began in December 1927 and reached its height between 1928 and the early 1930s, makes little sense from a purely internal Soviet or international perspective.[16] Understanding it requires seeing the intersection of nation-making projects in the Mandates and in the Soviet East. In the interwar Middle East, Zionism and majoritarian Arab national anticolonial movements strengthened mostly within the new borders and with reference to the idea of rights to a "national" home. In the Soviet East, after the settling of most border disputes of the 1920s, republican leaders went about fostering national identity under greater oversight from centralized institutions by nationalizing regional folklore, archeology, and other forms of heritage, and by asserting party control over other forms of literary and artistic production. Kafri and Aimarov's experiences show how Soviet and foreign conceptions of nationhood informed one another in the context of the Eastern International.

These entanglements arise from the fact that many Soviet domestic policies had internationalist analogues. The First Five-Year Plan's embrace of domestic proletarianization coincided with the Comintern's new approach to the colonized and decolonizing world, adopted after Stalin's miscalculated revolutionary alliance with Chiang Kai-shek. When Chiang betrayed Stalin and massacred hundreds of communists and labor activists in Shanghai in 1927, the Comintern revisited its earlier strategy of engagement with the East. Instead of trying to forge eclectic alliances with revolutionary intellectuals, pacifists, or bourgeois anticolonial nationalists, it emphasized recruitment of people with working-class or peasant backgrounds.[17] This shift opened up new possibilities for rank-and-file cadres such as Aimarov and Kafri to come to the Soviet Union.

Yet more than proletarian class solidarity, Aimarov and Kafri cared about a notion of Arab unity, which they perceived as under siege by Jews at KUTV. As students coming from Palestine, Aimarov and Kafri undoubtedly witnessed or heard about how waves of Zionist migration expanded Zionist land holdings and about growing economic disparities between the Jewish community in Palestine (Yishuv) and the surrounding Arab lands. At KUTV they were confronted with another inequality. Jews were generally overrepresented in top-level positions in the early Soviet party and state institutions,[18] but in KUTV and in the Comintern's Near Eastern Section among the researchers (*referenty*), teachers, and administrators their numbers were especially pronounced. Many of the Jewish researchers and interviewers at KUTV, such as Kitaigorodskii, were connected to Palestine through family members who emigrated before 1917 or during the civil war when an estimated 50,000 to 200,000 Russian Jews were killed in pogroms.[19] Many had emigrated to Palestine themselves and then grown disillusioned with Zionism. They joined the communist parties of Palestine, Egypt, and Syria-Lebanon and either decided to return to Moscow or were deported there by British and French authorities. These experiences—their acquired language skills, cultural knowledge, and interest in national and colonial questions—drew these ex-Zionists to KUTV in such numbers that Comintern leader Karl Radek was purported to have wittily described it as an "educational institution at which Polish and German Jews lecture in English to Chinese students about how to make Russian-style Revolution (*o tom kak delat' revoliutsiiu po-russki*)."[20]

The other relevant entanglement of domestic and international politics had to do with the Soviet approach to nationalism, specifically the embrace of majoritarian ethno-nationalism as a key component of anticolonial nation-building. In domestic national-building, Soviet authorities encouraged *korenizatsiia* (indigenization), a policy designed to indigenize Soviet power in non-Russian areas by promoting more of the local population into state and party institutions and promoting the use of indigenous languages.[21] These policies created a way for Soviet leaders to unite people around and then pose as a defender of state-sanctioned forms of national identity. They also gave leaders of the recently delineated Soviet republics license to nationalize their republics and to assimilate populations that were newly conceptualized as minorities.[22] These processes of assimilation remained incomplete and contentious, and they bred resentments that, in some cases, simmered for decades before erupting in violence. Soviet Jews were in a particularly fraught situation because the Jewish National Region of Birobidzhan, officially carved out of the Soviet Far East in 1928, proved barely inhabitable due to its harsh climate and made little sense as a place of settlement due to its distance from the historical centers of Jewish life. Despite its messiness, however, the domestic process of nation-making through delineation and then indigenization along majoritarian ethno-nationalist lines had an international analogue. The world revolution was also delineated along national lines.

At the Sixth Congress (1928), the Comintern announced a shift in policy toward the colonized world away from a "united front" and toward a "class against class" approach. Ironically, this carried ethnic implications for the communist parties of Egypt (ECP), Syria-Lebanon (CPSL), and Palestine (PCP). As part of the new class against class emphasis, the Comintern had issued a directive to "Arabize" these communist parties, by which they meant accepting and promoting more ethnic Arabs—the native majority that constituted the proletarian and peasant class—to positions of authority. Since their formation in the 1920s, these parties had all been dominated by ethnic minorities who had been alienated from other majoritarian national movements in the region. Thus, the new directive to "Arabize" recast earlier communist leaders as advocates for "minority" rights.[23]

The ECP was the least affected by this directive due to the general disintegration of its central committee into quarrelling factions by the late 1920s.[24] But the CPSL, which had strong support among Armenians, almost split between 1931 and 1933 over the Arabization directive.[25] Part of the confusion around this shift had to do with post-Ottoman transitions and the subsequent reconfiguration of religious, national, and ethnic affiliations. As historian Usama Makdisi has observed about post-Ottoman states, the idea of *being an Arab* . . . encompassed more than a secular emphasis on material progress and national unity." It was a fact that, whether religious or not, "virtually all Arabic-speaking Christians and Jews recognized that they lived in a predominantly Arab Islamic environment."[26] The Comintern's ethicized vision of politics imposed clearer boundaries on political and social organizations accustomed to operating in a more complex conditions of communal coexistence.

For the PCP, whose leaders remained predominantly Jewish émigrés from the former Russian empire and Europe, the Comintern's orders to Arabize and distance the party from its perceived "national Jewish tendencies" and persistent "preoccupation with the Jewish community" was more difficult.[27] Most of the émigrés in the PCP's leadership could not pass for Arab Jews. Instead, Wolf Auerbach, who was born in Russia in 1890 and represented Palestine at the Sixth Congress of the Comintern in 1928, had been offsetting the party's failure to Arabize by pointing to its accomplishments in "territorializing" communism and expanding its network into neighboring Syria and Lebanon.[28] Under the new Arabization directive, it became more difficult for the PCP to distinguish between Zionism and the Yishuv in arguments about communist geopolitics. Earlier, party members could oppose Zionism while still attributing a progressive role to the Jewish community in the social and economic development of Palestine and, by extension, the spread and development of revolution in the East.[29] But with the new directive, the Comintern stipulated that anything associated with the Jewish community—including not only the dream of a national Jewish economy but also immigration and agricultural settlement—had to be perceived as counterrevolutionary. The directive essentially deprived the Jewish-majority PCP leadership of any rationale for their work in Palestine and the wider region.[30]

In the summer of 1929 the PCP was still purging itself of elements who had failed to see Arabs as "the only political force capable of producing a revolutionary situation in Palestine."[31] It was thus unprepared when in August 1929 protests erupted in Jerusalem over Jewish breaches of a 1911 status quo agreement concerning rituals at the Buraq (Wailing Wall) in Jerusalem. The protests then spread to Hebron, Jaffa, and Safad. Within one week, 133 Jews and 116 Arabs were killed and 570 injured.[32] This traumatic violence shook both communities in Palestine and galvanized concern about Zionism in the Bilad al-Sham and throughout the Muslim world.[33] In the Bilad al-Sham region Zionism came to be seen as a settler colonial project supported by Western colonialism. Palestinian and Yishuvi security stances grew tougher and Jewish and Arab separations hardened.[34]

This violence also transformed the PCP's relationship with the Comintern. Before this point the Comintern had not advocated Jewish-Arab communal confrontation and had interpreted earlier examples of ethnic strife as the inevitable consequences of British imperialist provocation. Thus the PCP had reacted in 1929 as it had earlier, by issuing calls for peace and condemning the violence as an imperialist vestige. For some of its leaders, including Joseph Berger, the violence recalled pogroms.[35] For others, it seemed like the connivance of the British and traitorous Arab leaders who were converting revolutionary anger into an anti-Jewish movement before it assumed its "inevitably anti-imperialist character." Still others interpreted the violence as rooted in an agrarian conflict caused by Zionists who had been exacerbating Bedouin poverty.[36]

From the Comintern's perspective in Moscow, interpretations of the violence in Palestine seemed to be partly inflected by experiences in the domestic East. Around that time, the Comintern's Eastern Section had just been taken over by Georgi Safarov, who had returned to Moscow after a brief period of punitive exile for supporting former chairman of the Comintern and of the Petrograd Soviet Grigory Zinoviev.[37] Safarov's appointment to this position implicitly acknowledged his expertise in Eastern affairs, acquired during the civil war in Turkestan. According to Berger, Safarov was primarily responsible for managing the Comintern's response to the Palestine situation after the 1929 violence, which was perceived at the time as a spark that might ignite a wider anti-imperialist revolt.[38] Berger attested that, in over two years of close collaborative work with Safarov at the Comintern, he never detected any anti-Semitic undertones in his arguments. Rather, he believed Safarov saw the events in Palestine through the lens of his experiences in Turkestan. There, he had observed the dynamics between local Muslims and Russian colonial settlers empowered by the imperial regime. Safarov had argued that such dynamics had to be "corrected" to ensure that socialist construction would not inadvertently replicate "decades of Russian national privilege" and "colonial bias" (*kolonizatorskii uklon*).[39] Consequently, although Slavic settlers and Cossack peasants had overwhelmingly accepted the October revolution and aided the Red Army in the civil war, they would still need to be removed in the process of decolonization. The mass expulsion that followed resulted in a decline of Kazakhstan's Russian population by 19.5 percent.[40] This deportation was officially halted in 1922[41] and later determined to have been carried out with "excessive cruelty and took on the character of revenge."[42] Safarov saw these actions as necessary anticolonial correctives.

The situation in Palestine seemed analogous to him, and likely to many of the Arab communists, both those at KUTV and in the movement generally. The presence of Jewish workers in Palestine evinced imperialist designs. When Auerbach tried to sway Safarov by describing the progressive role of Yishuv professional associations and the kibbutzim, Safarov apparently replied, "But what are they doing there in the first place? . . . Is it not clear to you that, objectively, Jewish settlement in Israel is an agent of British imperialism?"[43] Safarov then warned Auerbach about showing too many tendencies "from his previous party affiliation," referring to Auerbach's past membership in Poale-Zion, a party which had been censured by the Comintern's Second Congress for "nationalist prejudices."[44] Similar language appeared in the ECCI's resolution on the 1929 riots, which warned that the PCP had been "blinded by its conciliatory attitude to Poale-Zion" and its "tendencies of Jewish-Zionist chauvinism."[45] Even PCP slogans that promoted brotherhood between Jews and Arabs had been condemned as "aiding imperialism." Arab protagonists may have understood the 1929 demonstrations in terms of anti-imperialist struggle, but the ECCI emphasized that these demonstrations were an "Arab uprising against British Imperialism and Zionism" and "not a pogrom."[46] This formulation, which emphasized the difference between Jewish experiences in Palestine and Russia, still involved use of "domestic" models to understand the "foreign East."

Safarov's logic, and the ECCI's ruling on the events of 1929, sat uncomfortably with a number of prominent Jewish communists in Palestine and Moscow, who had been horrified by the violence and found it difficult to abandon the original pacifist line that Jews and Arabs should avoid bloodshed.[47] Just as the violence itself had raised specters of pogroms to PCP members, the ECCI's post-mortem likewise may have recalled earlier Russian imperial practices of blaming the Jews themselves for pogroms by citing their alleged exploitation of poor peasants recently freed from serfdom.[48] The ECCI's ruling in Palestine pushed many Jewish members of the PCP to break from the party and join more mainstream Zionist labor parties. Others remained without a political affiliation. A small group of PCP members left Palestine and returned to the Soviet Union, perhaps out of deep disappointment with the whole ordeal, or owing to persecution by British and French Mandate police, or perhaps on orders from Moscow.[49] In Moscow, their party experience and expertise opened doors to positions in the Comintern's Eastern Section, at KUTV, or at the new KUTV-affiliated Institute of National and Colonial Problems.[50] This same network of institutions also offered employment to Arab graduates of KUTV who remained in the USSR, illustrating the shared pathways available to those seeking to promote world anticolonial revolution by serving the Soviet state or those who simply wanted to earn a living as Marxist orientalists rather than as proletarians toiling elsewhere in the state economy.

For those who returned, the 1929 violence continued to cast a shadow over communist activities in the Arab world. Some of the exiled Jewish leaders, such as Elie Naumovich Teper (alias: Shami, later naturalized as Aleksandr Moiseevich Shami) and Nahaum Leshchinskii (alias: Nadab), continued to debate the significance of the riots on the pages of *Pravda*, *Imprecor*, *Agrarnye problemy*, and the KUTV journal *Revoliutsionnyi Vostok*.[51] Nadab and Shami's disagreements about the class character of the 1929 uprising escalated quickly, illustrating the activists' zeal as well as the high stakes of these interpretations. Nadab saw the events as a popular agrarian revolt led by the Arab national bourgeoisie that started to spread from Palestine to the adjacent Arab countries.[52] Shami thought Nadab's interpretation overestimated the revolutionary potential of the Arab national bourgeoisie with its links to foreign capital. Instead, Shami saw the events as the beginning of an anti-imperialist and antifeudal revolution led by the working class against British imperialism and the complicit Arab national bourgeoisie.[53]

By publicly advocating one or another interpretation of the class dynamics of the 1929 revolt and of the role of Ottoman "imperialist" vestiges therein, Shami and Nadab connected the debate over Palestine to other Soviet and Comintern debates unfolding in the early 1930s about the legitimacy of the Asiatic Mode of Production (AMP) model and its usefulness for understanding "oriental" societies. For Marxist orientalists, this debate was extremely significant. It meant sifting through Marx's fragmentary, unformed, and inconsistent thoughts about the "East"—which mostly characterized Asiatic societies as defined by the nationalization of land, agricultural communities, artificial irrigation, and a centralized despotic state—and deciding if any part of the canon was politically useful. Already after the 1927 setback in China, Cominternians had begun to reconsider the AMP as something potentially dangerous in the wrong hands; namely, nationalist elements who could use its emphasis on the idiosyncrasies and specificities of the Orient to insist that the teachings of Marx and Lenin did not apply there.[54] By linking the conflict in Palestine with this broader discussion of Marx's usefulness for world revolution, Shami and Nadab helped to elevate the 1929 riots in Comintern and Soviet policy circles into a major colonial crisis of global significance.

The aggressive tone of the public disagreement between Nadab and Shami was consistent with the culture of debate in early 1930s Moscow party circles. Nadab mocked Shami's expertise as an "Arabist" (*araboved*) because he knew nothing of the Ottoman-era Arab national anti-imperialist movements. "He has never heard of *al-'Ahd* [the Covenant, a secret society founded by Iraqi officers in the Ottoman military who supported the Arab Revolt during World War I and later fought for independence against Britain and France], the *Istiqlal Party* [the Arab Independence Party, founded in Damascus in 1919 which included members of *al-'Ahd* and supported the Great Syrian Revolt of 1925], or any other revolutionary organizations in Syria, Iraq, and Arabia . . . [which emerged because] Turkey had exploited the Arab provinces politically and economically by granting concessions and allowing monopolistic enterprise [to develop]."[55] Shami countered that Nadab's work relied on references to the "imperialist sellout" Najib 'Azuri.[56] He also alleged that Nadab's characterization of the Ottoman empire as "imperialist" deviated from Lenin's theory of imperialism that finance capital and political hegemony had to serve a shared interest.[57] Elsewhere, Shami mocked his

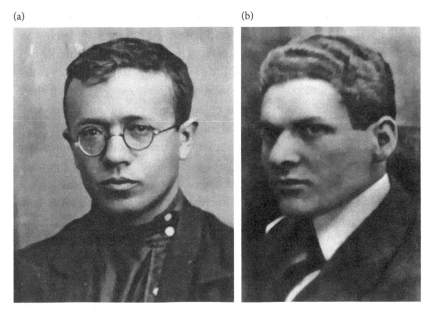

Figure 3.1 a and 3.1b Nadab and Shami. RGASPI f. 495, op. 212, d. 147, l. 4. Reprinted with permission from Marina Iur'evna Sorokina.

opponent's illiteracy (*bezgramotnost'*), ignorance (*polnoe neznanie*), pretentiousness (*s uchenym vidom znatoka*), and laziness.[58] Nadab, in turn, mocked Shami's demagoguery and overzealousness.[59]

These disrespectful exchanges in ostensibly academic publications reflected common assumptions at this time that collective forms of knowledge had to be grounded in the Marxist-Leninist canon. This grounding was unstable, however, because certain core assumptions could be critiqued and even discarded. And yet, even as they both tried to conform to the fickle Comintern line by citing "hidden resistance to Arabization" and "Zionist and imperialist influence on communists," the activists inadvertently drew attention to the fact that they had once emigrated to Palestine and, in different ways, had empathized with Jewish victims of the 1929 violence.[60] According to Nadab, Shami had described the riots as a "pogrom against Jews" and neglected "to mention the slaughter of Arabs by Zionist fascists."[61] In his defense, Shami explained that he no longer characterized the uprising as a general pogrom but did not deny "individual cases of pogroms," like the slaughter of sixty Jewish students in a Hebron school because to conceal it would be "unprincipled and cynical" (*eto tsinizm!*).[62] According to Shami,

Nadab had refused to see class struggle in the Palestinian countryside because he wanted to imagine Jewish colonialism as "an innocent lamb" that had positively helped to develop the forces of production in Palestine.[63] Since any sympathy for the Jewish community in Palestine was now deemed counterrevolutionary, both polemicists' once sympathetic expressions left them poorly positioned in a political culture that encouraged political opponents to demonize the opposition and search for an enemy within.[64]

For students of the KUTV Arab Section, the debates over the violence in Palestine offered handy pretexts to eliminate real and imagined opponents through purges.[65] The first wave of denunciations at KUTV was already underway in 1929, when the Palestinian student "Subotin" (b. 1903, Jaffa; other party names: Rauf Akhmedovich, Osman Ahmad Zaghrur, arrived at KUTV in 1927) submitted a report to the KUTV leadership calling PCP General Secretary Auerbach an "opportunist" who had fanned tensions among Palestinian workers. In the same report, Subotin pointed to a contradiction between the Comintern's insistence on Arabization and the continued presence of so many Jews in the KUTV Arab Section. These Jews were being supported for five to seven years of study, compared to Arabs who were supported for only one or two. "Where are the educated Arab workers who could lead the party? . . . Naturally our Jewish comrades are right when they say that their Arab comrades are backwards."[66] Finally, Subotin demanded that the KUTV Arab Circle leader, Avigdor (Aleks Kosoi, aka Constantine Weiss), be replaced by a Russian representative of the All-Union Communist Party. "I cannot explain this well in Russian," he concluded, but "if you want to call me, I can explain it better. In the end, you can accuse me of nationalist leanings, but the picture is clear . . . ask any of the other Arab comrades."[67]

Subotin was savvy enough to be concerned about accusations of nationalist deviation, and as he had predicted this charge was indeed leveled against him. He was also hopeful and courageous enough to try to change the system from within. In the course of the investigation by the Comintern's International Control Commission (ICC), less predictable accusations surfaced, including that he was a "pederast" and that he had composed letters to another comrade "as if he were in love with him."[68] Subotin's ICC trial concluded with a reprimand for promoting factionalism in the PCP and his expulsion from KUTV.[69] Considered too dangerous to be sent back to Palestine, he found work first as a mechanic in a Moscow factory and eventually at the Moscow Institute of Oriental Studies (MIV).[70] His initiative, however, paved the way for similar campaigns at KUTV and in the Comintern.

Another graduate, Muhamad Dwidar (b. 1901), reported that everyone at KUTV at the time was preoccupied with this issue:

> The Egyptians were the only ones [at KUTV] among whom there were no Jews, but most of the department administrators, staff, and translators were Arab Jews (al-yahud al-'arab) . . . we Egyptians joined the struggle for Arabization, but we were attacked harshly, and a trial was organized for us in the University under the pretext that were anti-Soviet and anti-Semite. . . . I was almost sure that some of the Jews were Zionist agents, but there were some Jews who truly believed and who had defended us, supported us, and were in solidarity with us.[71]

These struggles at KUTV in the early 1930s resembled contemporaneous conflicts over *korenizatsiia* (indigenization) in other Soviet institutions, especially the Soviet borderlands, where indigenization had to be balanced with the struggle against nationalist deviations. In these contexts, similar questions were raised about what to do with non-Russian national cadres who strategically invoked their ethnicity to get ahead at the expense of Russians.[72] In both cases, these struggles reflected complex layers of personal ambition, ideas about nation-building, and resentment fueled by structural inequality between different groups. Echoing Subotin and Dwidar, secretary of the Central Asian Buro Zelenskii described the situation inside the Soviet Union as follows:

> Out local [Central Asian] *intelligent* is less educated, has fewer cultural skills, and is less well prepared for work in the government apparat. He wants to get ahead. If he is a Communist, he has an advantage and this explains to a large degree the movement of the [local] intelligentsia into our Party. But if he is not a Communist—how can he move up the ladder of government service? Either he must work like a European, or he can bring up some other issue which will give him an advantage over the European. Therefore he puts forward the indigenous nationalities issue.[73]

Particularly aggressive implementations of *korenizatsiia* in Tatarstan, Kazakhstan, other eastern national republics, and in Ukraine meant that many of the minority Russian inhabitants who supported the Bolsheviks in the civil war felt betrayed. As peasants entered the labor force during the First Five-Year Plan, they took much of the ethnic conflict with them to the cities.⁷⁴ In Tashkent, *korenizatsiia* led to ethnic brawls on the floor of the labor market, a state-run job placement site.⁷⁵ In 1929, the GPU noted that "national relations are so strained that the smallest everyday incident provides misunderstandings and gives the Uzbeks cause to speak about European repression."⁷⁶ Eventually *korenizatsiia* came to be increasingly seen as strengthening both nationalism and interethnic conflict, which undermined support for the policy, and its pace slowed.⁷⁷

The Arabization of communist parties in the Near East was in many ways analogous to domestic indigenization in the Soviet borderlands. At KUTV, Arabization pitted assimilated Jewish teachers and administrators against Arabs. Most of the former were born in the Russian empire, were fluent in Russian and "Bolshevik speak," and had established relationships with higher-level Comintern and party-state authorities; the latter had difficulty expressing themselves in Russian and were likely perceived by other Comintern officials as "backward." Safarov understood the analogy. For him, a view on Zionism through the lens of the Soviet East meant supporting Arab cadres against Jewish colonizers and British colonial backers. For other officials, however, Arab students' complaints sounded more like cases of "national deviation." The KUTV purges highlighted a competition between these two different ways of relating domestic decolonization to international politics.

In 1931, Arab students made complaints against the leader of the Arab Circle, Avigdor. Such attacks on previously untouchable authorities "from below" (simultaneously encouraged, sanctioned, or provoked by trends from above) had been a core feature of what Stalin in 1929 had called "the Great Break."⁷⁸ Yet they also took place in Moscow-based international institutions. In this case, one student complained that Avigdor had threatened to toss him out of the university "like a dog" and called him a "snot-nose" (*smorkach*). Another claimed that Avigdor had accused him of showing off and "wagging a tail that he did not have."⁷⁹ Both alleged that Avigdor was leading a clandestine right-leaning Zionist faction at KUTV.⁸⁰ A third Arab student added that Avigdor may have agreed more with Shami, who had been officially reprimanded for factionalism after the debate with Nadab.⁸¹

Avigdor successfully defended himself and the other Jewish students accused of belonging to a Zionist conspiracy. Carefully outlining procedural grounds, he claimed to the ICC that he did not assign translation work to the accusers, Saburov and Sergeev, because the ECCI had already ruled that their continued presence in Moscow was detrimental to the Arab Section.

He excluded another Arab student from ECCI Eastern Secretariat meetings because they were intended for students who were graduating and leaving the USSR. As for the other Jewish students, he argued that they were learning and showed progress.[82]

The ICC not only exonerated Avigdor but also commended him for being "a strong communist who struggles for the general party line." After the trial he was sent on another Comintern assignment to Syria and Palestine. Other Jewish KUTV students were found to have committed individual mistakes and exhibited "cases of Zionist deviation," but the Arab students' claims about a wider Zionist conspiracy were found to be meritless.[83] The Arab students, the ICC concluded, were "masking" their true characters. One accuser, Zeid, had apparently concealed his class background. His father was a merchant, a fact he later claimed to have suppressed "by mistake."[84] The other accuser, Saburov, was discovered to have traveled outside Moscow without permission with three Arab comrades—Kafri, Muhamed, and Aimarov—who had all subsequently stopped attending classes in a strike against their teachers. Saburov (Taj Mir) was expelled in 1931 and exiled from Moscow, first to the North Caucasus and later to Tajikistan, where former KUTV Rector Broido served as first secretary of the Communist Party in 1934–1935 and could facilitate such transfers.[85]

Central Asia's function as a space for exiles suggested that authorities did not expect wider resistance in the region. Yet to ensure stability there, the party nevertheless signaled its unwillingness to accommodate any real or potential expressions of national dissent by refocusing the entire curricula on the glorious past of the Russian fatherland. In 1931, articles about the 1916 Central Asian Revolt that had interpreted the violence as a "nationalist" uprising directed against Russians "as an exploiting nation" were retracted for "pitting nations against each other and downplaying the shared class interests between the working masses of the Russian and Kirgiz peasantry."[86] Other historical dimensions of this complex popular rebellion across Central Asia following a wartime announcement that the tsar was revoking standing exemptions from conscription enjoyed by Central Asians were also ignored. The historical rationales for indigenization policies were thus effectively erased. Support for "defensive local nationalism" to oppose "offensive Great Power Russian nationalism" was coming to an end. By January 1934, Stalin officially announced the abandonment of the Greater Danger Principle that had stigmatized Russians as the former Great Power nationality.[87] That same year a decree by the Central Asian Bureau recommended that the idea of

Imperial Russia as "bourgeois and colonizing" be eradicated from history books.[88]

At KUTV, the Comintern's Executive Committee decided to replace Avigdor with another Jewish PCP veteran, Joseph Berger. Berger was born in Cracow, Poland, and had emigrated to Palestine in 1920 with the Zionist youth group Hashomer Hatzair (The Young Guard). In Palestine he had joined the communist movement in 1922, rose through the ranks, and went on to have an international career as a founder of communist cells in Syria and Lebanon, a Near East correspondent for the Soviet Telegraph News Agency (TASS) from 1925 to 1931,[89] and secretary for a few months of the Berlin-based League against Imperialism (LAI).[90] These positions brought him into contact with Soviet leaders Radek, Bukharin, Lev Kamenev, and Zinoviev, with whom he had developed good working relationships. He even made a favorable impression on Stalin after a meeting in March 1929, just before the August riots in Palestine.[91] His one concern before his first trip to Moscow in 1924 to negotiate the PCP's admission into the Comintern was that he had never learned Russian. But Auerbach apparently assured him that it was unnecessary if he knew German, French, and English, and especially Yiddish, which Auerbach suggested would be useful to him in the ECCI and many other Moscow circles.[92]

It is possible that the higher-level Comintern executives who recruited Berger knew little about the ethnicized struggles at KUTV. Berger recalled that when he had arrived in Moscow in 1932 and learned of his appointment as director of the Near East Department of the ECCI, Safarov cautioned him about accepting the position and warned that "it is doubtful that the Arabs will see it as a good thing for you to be in charge of their parties." Instead, he suggested that Berger take a position as head of the Comintern's Information Department (AgitProp) of all Eastern countries, including China.[93] Berger rejected Safarov's advice and took the Near East position, and the two men worked for two years in adjacent offices. "We met frequently, and had long conversations," Berger recalled. He particularly enjoyed Safarov's stories about the Bolshevik underground, his work with Lenin, and his civil war experiences. "There was only one issue we never touched upon" Berger recalled. "That was the question of the Land of Israel."[94]

When Berger assumed oversight of the KUTV Arab Section he inherited a chaotic situation. Many of the students had stopped attending class.[95] Others treated one another so rudely that their arguments escalated into physical fights.[96] At least sixteen students had to be expelled.[97] The Palestinian Ioske (real name Ahmed Ibn 'Abidin, b. 1910 in Haifa), who arrived at KUTV in August 1930, was a typical problem student.[98] Berger described him as "undisciplined," with little interest in politics, and "no backbone" (*beskhrebetnym*). By 1932, Ioske had already been suspended once from KUTV for a few months and sent to work in a factory outside Moscow.[99] This disciplinary measure seemed to have little effect. He continued to socialize with other students who had been expelled or were under observation for bad behavior;[100] he swore at Party meetings in defiance of the ideological emphasis on cultured speech;[101] and he was accused by another student of keeping foreign currency for transacting business with Tehran, presumably through other KUTV students.[102] Unhappy about infrequent bedsheet changes in the KUTV dormitory, he once asked, "What are we in, a prison?"[103]

Aimarov was another difficult case. Berger characterized him as "the seed of rotten liberalism" of the Arab group.[104] Like his friends, Aimarov started filing official complaints about being "persecuted by Zionists,"[105] accusing Berger of being a Zionist, and Berger's deputy, Mustafa (another Jewish PCP member), of being a "Trotskyite who opposed Arabization" and was "secretly pitting us [Arab students] against one another." Aimarov had boycotted an event organized by Yemeni Jewish student Simkha Tsabari (Yamina) and had thrown a chair at her Palestinian Arab boyfriend, Mukhtarov (Ridwan al-Hilu).[106]

After multiple warnings, Ioske and Aimarov were expelled from KUTV, the Komsomol, and the Party. Ioske was sent to work in a factory in Tbilisi, where his status as a foreigner without party recommendations at a time of growing xenophobia made life difficult. He complained to the Comintern that he could not find or keep employment with his only official identity document. After he returned to Moscow he claimed to have been rejected by the Eastern Section and forced to spend a few nights on the street. Eventually he found a job in a Moscow car factory through the Commissariat for Labor and was then sent to the Leningrad Oriental Institute.[107] Aimarov was sent to Rostov-on-Don along with another student, Kafri, who, according to his 1932 evaluation, was diagnosed with psychosis (*dushevno-boleznennym sostoianiem*).

108 THE EASTERN INTERNATIONAL

Figure 3.2 Ioske. RGASPI f. 495 op. 212, d. 107, l. 55.

Figure 3.3 Aimarov. RGASPI f. 495, op. 212, d. 224, l. 72.

Kafri had already been sent to work in an electrical manufacturing plant, which had apparently helped "stabilize him" and make him "understand his mistakes."[108] But by 1933 he seemed to have relapsed and needed further treatment.[109]

The behavior of these students at KUTV had as much to do with their experiences in Moscow, with its increasingly militant party culture and aura of entitlement for foreigners, as it did with the escalation of social and economic tensions in Palestine. There, indigenous Arab inhabitants, many of whom were cultivators, suffered disproportionally due to falling agricultural prices across the region. Many lost their land through foreclosure. They were also losing land to the Jews who were entering Palestine as part of the fifth aliyah (1929–1939) and bringing with them significant skills and capital. By 1931, Zionist land purchases had led to the expulsion of approximately 20,000 peasant Arab families from their lands, and over the next several years approximately 30 percent of Palestinian farmers would become landless. About 75 to 80 percent did not have enough land to support themselves. Whereas in the 1920s Zionism was a more abstract concept to many of the indigenous inhabitants of Palestine, by the 1930s it had become a tangible presence.[110] These tensions would eventually culminate in the openly anti-British and anti-Zionist Arab Revolt (1936–1939), during which the British lost control of large areas of Palestine before finally suppressing the uprising with drastic and cruel measures.[111]

In Moscow, the rulings of Comintern authorities like Safarov implicitly acknowledged some of these escalating tensions. Yet the Comintern had neither the resources to expend on supporting the anticolonial struggle abroad nor the political will to challenge Britain in Mandatory Palestine. Nor were they willing to take coercive measures to settle disputes over Palestine involving foreign students in Moscow. Aimarov and Kafri's unauthorized return from Rostov-on-Don to Moscow and their case against Berger resulted in an ICC decision to "isolate them" from other KUTV students.[112] However, a housing shortage in Moscow prevented their relocation or isolation. Before the arrival of a new cohort of Arab students, the ECCI Eastern Section chief, Lájos Magyar, had sent Aimarov to Tbilisi, but once again he returned without permission.[113] In October 1935, KUTV Foreign Section chief Fyodor Kotel'nikov complained that Aimarov and another expelled KUTV student, Rashidov (an Armenian from Syria), had appeared at his office after they had learned that the ICC had forbidden their return to their home countries. Kotel'nikov reported that they were demanding their passports, and that

Rashidov had threatened to use "all the means at his disposal," adding that he was "no stranger to repressive measures and that he was ready to face any measures brought against him by the OGPU [the Soviet secret police]."[114] Aimarov threatened to show up at Kotel'nikov's apartment and make trouble. Frustrated, Kotel'nikov reported to the ECCI Section of Cadres that the pair were treating decisions of the highest organs of the Comintern as if they were "mere papers that carried no obligation," concluding that "it is impossible to admit these people into Comintern buildings or even speak to them."[115] Caught up in the bureaucratized world of the Comintern, it was not only Bolshevik leaders who understood events abroad through the lens of Soviet domestic politics and made decisions about domestic nation-building in response to imperial collapse. Arab communists also occasionally turned their radical activist tactics and their frustration with Comintern inaction in the Arab world against hapless representatives of the Soviet state.

The lives of foreign students who had remained in Moscow by choice or by force in the second half of the 1930s converged with Soviet citizens with foreign connections more than they had earlier in the decade. In addition to rising tides of xenophobia and purges engulfing party-state institutions across the country, the lives of KUTVians were also vulnerable to specific threats to Soviet positions in various borderlands. Information intercepted by Soviet counterintelligence in the late 1920s suggested that foreign powers continued to sharpen racial, ideological, and class struggle within the Soviet Union and to "unify all Asian nations on Soviet territory against European Russia."[116] This threat, which emanated from Japan, exacerbated Stalin's concerns about capitalist encirclement of the USSR from the East (by the British in China, Afghanistan, Persia, and Turkey) as well as from the West. To help secure the Soviet far East, the Birobidzhan region near the China-Russia border was allocated as a territory for Jewish colonization in 1928.[117] However, this measure hardly allayed Stalin's fears about other potential imperialist interventions, the security threats posed by the immigration of Central Asian and Caucasian Muslims, or the potential of cross-border rebellion.[118]

Securing the Soviet borders had territorial and administrative consequences. Official "border regions" subject to heightened security measures were expanded to include all administrative regions (*raiony*) touching the Soviet border (called the primary border zone) as well as all *raiony* touching those borders (the secondary border zone).[119] This securitization of borders left students in KUTV siloed. Administratively, a 1935 All-Union Communist Party Orgburo decree isolated the KUTV foreign section, concentrated mostly in the Institute of National and Colonial Problems, from the rest of the university.[120] All foreign students were reassigned to this Institute, which was to be administratively, intellectually, and physically "quarantined" from the university.[121] They had to follow separate curricula. The foreign Easterners were taught international political economy, "imperialism and colonies," "Marxist theories of exploitation and colonial proletariat," and individual histories of national-liberation movements. The domestic Easterners focused on pre-revolutionary Russian infiltration of the East, Russian colonial occupation and plunder of former national borderlands, and struggles of future Soviet nationalities for liberation.[122] The decree also intended for them to be physically separated, but this was more difficult to implement.

Throughout the 1920s, the proportion and total number of foreign students in the university had increased. By 1930, the number of foreigners had eclipsed the number of people specializing in the domestic East, and by 1936, the foreign sector (graduates and undergraduates) comprised 60 percent of the student body.[123] This shift was driven by the existence of reliable alternative universities for domestic Easterners in Tashkent, Tbilisi, Kazan, and Alma-Ata,[124] as well as by the expansion of new communist parties admitted to the Comintern between 1928 and 1935. Because of the housing crisis in Moscow and its outskirts, students were forced to share university facilities, including a KUTV clinic, daycare, six dachas, and library. The mid-1930s directives created so much chaos that some foreign students were temporarily left without access to daycare, or they would discover that their rooms had been reassigned when they were away on political assignments. As one Institute of National-Colonial Problems official complained, "Our top secret (*zakonspirovannoe*) institution must deal with police and housing officials in courts which forces us to disclose addresses of spaces occupied by foreign students and make information available to our potential enemies."[125] By 1937, most foreign students were settled in small groups in different isolated dachas allocated to them by the Moscow Soviet and located ten to twenty miles outside of Moscow.

Soviet war scares, xenophobia, and purges shaped the experiences of the remaining foreign students at KUTV. The purges in the Comintern accelerated after the assassination of Leningrad party boss Sergei Kirov in early December 1934. The Politburo responded to the assassination by ordering all party members to identify "suspicious" or "hostile" elements in their ranks. After future state security chief Nikolai Ezhov accused Zinoviev, Kamenev, and Trotsky of direct involvement in the murder,[126] the Comintern ECCI's party organization responded with particular zeal to uncover remnants of the former "Zinoviev-Trotskyist opposition." Since Zinoviev had led the Comintern in its foundational period, he had extensive real and perceived influence. Among those purged in the direct aftermath of the Kirov affair were Eastern Section employees Georgi Safarov, who had worked closely with Zinoviev in the Leningrad Party organization, and Lájos Magyar, who had served with Safarov as the Comintern's representative in China and had tried to help him materially after Safarov's arrest.[127] As the purges reverberated through the Comintern's Eastern Section and its affiliated institutions, individuals and groups' fortunes depended on a combination of luck, proximity to power, and their ability to mobilize biographical information.

Of the old guard who once held power at KUTV, Joseph Berger was arrested in January 1935. His Comintern personal file suggested that earlier allegations against him by KUTV students were bolstered by new denunciations by a certain comrade, N. Poliani. He alleged that Berger had arrived in Palestine with the goal of purchasing land from Arabs, continued to pray to God after entering the Communist Party, impaired PCP efforts to Arabize, and allegedly almost raped a female comrade.[128] As Berger later recalled in his memoir, he was forced to sign a false confession and spent over twenty years in various Soviet labor camps before being rehabilitated in 1956 and allowed to return to Israel.[129]

The removal of KUTV and Comintern Eastern Section leadership opened up opportunities for other upwardly mobile, ambitious young communists, including a Kurdish communist from Syria, Khalid Bakdash (b. 1912 in Damascus). Bakdash was recruited into the Communist Party as a law student at Damascus University. He arrived at KUTV just as the Comintern leader Georgi Dimitrov began implementing a "renewal of cadres" strategy to make up for the decimation of ranks wrought by earlier purges. This strategy involved transferring more administrative responsibilities from Comintern authorities in Moscow to the leadership of individual communist parties.[130] Bakdash seemed like a good candidate. He showed initiative and intellectual ambitions by publishing articles in the Institute of National and Colonial Problems (NIA) journal *Revoliutsionnyi Vostok*, shortly after arriving in Moscow.

More importantly, Bakdash was savvy in navigating party bureaucracy. He clearly understood the Comintern's politics of "affirmative action," presenting himself at the Seventh Comintern Congress as an "Arab," despite being ethnically Kurdish, and listing Kurdish as one of his spoken languages.[131] While Kurdish ethnicity could have been helpful in some Soviet "affirmative action" contexts—and Soviet comrades who remembered him from later encounters always referred to him as Kurdish—this Comintern self-presentation suggests that Bakdash's ambitions in 1935 were focused on Syria, where the Comintern's directive to "Arabize" communism was operative. By staying quiet, he could continue to enjoy active support from his Kurdish constituency.[132] For an educated member of the Damascene urban milieu, comfortable with its Arabized culture, such expressions of fluidity were hardly uncommon. By contrast, Jews from the former Russian empire, even though they adopted Arabized party names such as "Shami" or "Nadab," could not pass for Arab in these contexts. Their best bet was to pass for Russian. Their limitation was an opportunity for Bakdash.

After Berger's arrest, Bakdash began to take steps to purge the remaining Comintern cadres with authority over Arab Affairs, many of whom were Jewish. On June 8, 1935, he reported to the ECCI Secretary Iosef Piatinskii (b. 1882 to a Jewish family near Vilnius, Lithuania) that a group of Jewish former members of Palestinian, Syrian-Lebanese, and Egyptian communist parties, including Nadab, Avigdor, Kuperman, Rozenberg, and Davidovich, were using the Arab research section of the NIA to "influence the work of Arab communist parties and sabotage Arabization."[133] Bakdash's harshest criticisms were reserved for Avigdor, whom he had met in Syria between 1931 and 1933. When Bakdash arrived in Moscow, Avigdor was still recognized as a leading Comintern authority on Syria, Palestine, and Egypt.[134] By 1935, he was again accused of plotting against Arabization in Palestine and against the central committee of the ECP (likely because of his association with his former father-in-law Joseph Rosenthal, who had been removed from Party leadership in 1923).[135]

This time Avigdor was expelled from the Communist Party in January and arrested in March 1936. Saadi (Najati Sidqi, PCP) and Rozenberg (SCP and PCP) recalled that in Palestine, Avigdor had agitated Arabs to organize a demonstration in the Jewish quarter of Tel Aviv during a celebration of Nabi Musa. "[Avigdor's] thinking was literally that Arab workers would go shoot at Jewish workers under leadership of Jewish communists. This would lead to pogroms," Saadi claimed.[136] The shaky logic that advocating attacks against the Jewish community in Palestine was evidence of "Zionism" went unquestioned. In the context of Comintern Eastern Section purges, "Zionist" came to function like other categories, symbols, and images that had no clear definition but could be attributed to enemies. For instance, as Getty and Naumov point out, "the vast majority of those accused and persecuted as Trotskyists had absolutely no allegiance to Trotsky or connection to any Trotskyist program."[137] The difference was that "Zionism" could only ever be attributed to Jews, and that accusations could be made based on events taking place abroad, including Palestine on the eve of the Arab Revolt.

Bakdash also testified that Avigdor was a counterrevolutionary Zionist who had contributed to the dispossession of Arab peasants and failed to differentiate among Zionism, imperialism, and the national-reformist Arab bourgeoisie.[138] Such evidence and Avigdor's good relationship with the discredited former Comintern Eastern Section chief, Magyar, was enough to send him away to a labor camp, where he died in 1938. He was posthumously rehabilitated in 1956,[139] but decades later Bakdash still described these purges as a justified struggle against Zionists trying to control Arab communist parties in the Comintern in order to sabotage Arabization. In his recollections, Bakdash continued to use "Zionist" to describe anyone of Jewish origin, real or imagined, who stood in his way. Later in life he instructed other communist parties in Iraq and Egypt to prevent Jewish communists like Henri Curriel from occupying positions in their leadership because their presence was "unnatural." He falsely accused the International Department head Boris Panomarov of being a Jew who made decisions in relation to the Syrian Communist Party "in order to spread international Zionism."[140] In short, he continued to apply these 1930s methods, including of unmasking people as Jews and crypto-Zionists, in other contexts.

Having cleared a path for himself and a handful of loyal comrades, Bakdash, despite being a minority himself, emerged as the Comintern's main representative for Arab affairs.[141] This new position gave him the power to make decisions about regional cadres. A special committee consisting of Bakdash and KUTV graduate Ridwan al-Hilu, who represented Palestine at the Comintern's Seventh Congress, reviewed all Arab communist cadres remaining in Moscow and made recommendations directly to the Eastern

Section Chief Pavel Mif.[142] For those who had been reprimanded or expelled by Berger, Avigdor, or any of the other discredited Eastern Section leaders, this review was an opportunity to clear their names and be validated for their vigilant struggle against Zionism. Thus Aimarov, who arrived for this review from Tbilisi with a recommendation from Lavrentiy Beria,[143] was initially directed to Transjordan and then, after further deliberation, to Palestine.[144] Ridwan al-Hilu, it seemed, had forgiven him for attacking him with a chair. Ioske, by contrast, was found unsuitable for work in the Middle East or for residence in Moscow and characterized as a "ruined young man."[145] He was sent to Leningrad to work at the Oriental Institute and later to the Institute of Philosophy.[146] Then, after three years of struggling with bureaucratic problems triggered by his status as a foreign citizen, he was eventually given $60 and put on a ship to Palestine.[147] Kafri was also sent to Palestine.[148] The extent of Bakdash's and al-Hilu's authority as gatekeepers was unclear because decisions about the repatriation of foreigners were also mediated by other internal security organs. For instance, Bakdash's decision to allow Hamdi Selam to return home to apply his medical and literary skills to helping the revolutionary intelligentsia was overruled.[149] But when implemented, such decisions helped Bakdash and al-Hilu surround themselves with more loyal cadres at home in Syria, Lebanon, and Palestine.

For new Arab students arriving in the late 1930s to study at the reorganized Institute for National-Colonial Problems, Soviet life seemed listless and uninspiring. Deputy Arab Section head Abdurakhman Fasliakhovich Sultanov, a Tatar Arabist graduate of MIV (1930), reported instructors' complaints that students had trouble expressing any political ideas because they had arrived illiterate or were "confused" about the new united front policy adopted at the Comintern's Seventh Congress (1935).[150] Part of the confusion may have stemmed from the fact that in September 1934 the Soviet Union had joined the League of Nations, an organization for which the Comintern was originally intended to serve as an alternative. The Soviet Union remained a permanent member of the League's Council until 1939, when it was expelled for attacking Finland. According to Sultanov, it was especially unclear to the KUTV students what the new policy meant for Palestine:[151]

> Individual comrades still make generalizations (*valiat v odnu kuchu*) about all the Jews in Palestine.... Instead of fighting the Zionist danger the struggle becomes one of Arabs against "Jews in general" (*voobshche bor'ba arabov protiv "voobshche evreev"*). I cannot say that the former leaders of the

section encouraged this spirit of bourgeois nationalism, but they did not challenge such tendencies.[152]

The NIA/KUTV organization continued to disintegrate in the bureaucratic chaos that engulfed the Comintern and other Soviet institutions responsible for connections abroad.[153] At the Ministry of Foreign Affairs the purges were so extensive they contributed to the contraction of the regime's overall international activities.[154] Overseeing the Institute of National-Colonial Problems (NIA) through this process was Fyodor Kotel'nikov, who had earlier been threatened by Aimarov and Rashidov. He had been appointed in November 1937 to wrap up loose ends and shepherd remaining KUTV properties and students to new designations.[155] Yet as of 1939, Kotel'nikov reported to Dimitrov, students remained trapped in Moscow:

> Now that the NIA is closed, the situation is more urgent. The students are going to the Comintern, writing to you and comrade Stalin, complaining about their situation, and demanding to be sent home. Some want to remain in the Institute and are demanding to be sent to work. All this undermines discipline and leads to corruption.[156]

Internal reports corroborate that aimless students did not stay at their assigned dachas but spent days wandering the streets of Moscow, going to the cinema, drinking, engaging in petty arguments, and reporting one another to the Comintern Section of Cadres. Their reports paint a picture of boredom, depression, and malaise. As one Arab student reported, his roommate Jalul (Khalil Ibrahim Doli) got so emotional that he started to cry in bed, "None of the leaders, not even Stalin or Voroshilov, would approve leading such a life of just eating and sleeping."[157]

As it became more difficult to cross the Soviet border in 1939, students marooned in the USSR had limited options.[158] Mostly they could take factory jobs. The educated minority could use their knowledge of Arabic and Arab culture to try to get positions as translators, researchers, or teachers in MIV or other orientalist institutions; or they could work for Soviet military intelligence, foreign language publishing, Moscow Radio, or the International Red Aid.[159]

The closure of KUTV and its internationally oriented research institute appear anticlimactic against a backdrop of late Stalinist terror, the Molotov-Ribbentrop Pact, and the start of World War II. The institutional confusion, loss of morale, and boredom that characterized the disintegration of this key node of the Eastern International, however, did not spell the end of the wider network. As Kotel'nikov's frustrated efforts show, its surviving students, teachers, and property would be absorbed by other institutions. At the same time, new institutions, linkages, and processes were emerging that would reconnect the two Easts and reconfigure the networks of the Eastern International from both inside and outside of the Soviet Union.

All elites, including Communists and members of the intelligentsia, were disproportionately victimized in the 1930s purges. Jews were not targeted as an ethnic group and were underrepresented in the Great Terror as a whole, compared to other nationalities targeted in the so-called national operations, such as Poles and Latvians, because at the time the Yishuv in Palestine had little international recognition or influence.[160] Thus, most Soviet Jews were not yet seen as having an alternative home and were not seen as natural targets for foreign spies or congenitally weak as loyal Soviets. The Jews in the Comintern's Eastern Section and at KUTV were different. Their knowledge and connections across the Eastern Mediterranean left them exceptionally vulnerable to this politically defined persecution, both as elites and as people in the Soviet Union with ties abroad. As Berger later wrote, most of his Jewish comrades who were recalled from Palestine to Moscow in the 1930s died in the purges.[161] In certain other contexts, low-level bureaucrats and even factory workers were also not exempt from charges of former membership in socialist Zionist groups with transregional ties to Russia, such as the Bund, Poale-Zion, and the labor group Gdud HaAvoda.[162] Felix Roziner, a nephew of a Jewish returnee from Palestine who became an English teacher at KUTV, described the 1937 "sweep of Palestinians," which led to the arrests of his mother, other family members, and "tens of workers" at one Moscow gas processing plant. When his parents made a list of former "Palestinians" and their fates, it included over sixty names.[163]

Thus, while most Soviet Jews did not suffer relative to other ethnic minorities with ethnic ties to neighboring non-Soviet peoples, those Soviet Jews with links to Palestine experienced the reverse of the so-called Piedmont Principle—the idea that it was possible to effect further influence abroad through the exploitation of cross-border ethnic ties. For those who had gone to Palestine and then returned to reinvent themselves as experts in the Near East at KUTV or in the Comintern's Near East Section, it became increasingly important to position themselves in relation to a shifting Comintern interpretation of events in Palestine. This included having to renounce their communist and socialist cousins in the Yishuv with whom they had shared experiences in the former Russian empire of struggle for access to economic opportunities, higher education, and, occasionally, pogroms. Ultimately, however, no position proved tenable.

At KUTV, Jewish instructors and administrators had absorbed anger sparked by events transpiring outside Soviet borders in Palestine that had been shaped by Ottoman, European, and ultimately Russian imperial contexts. Additionally, they were more likely targeted in connection with other accused high-ranking members of the party, government, military, academic, and the secret police with whom they may have been connected.[164] As these various contexts converged, the purges of the late 1930s eliminated most top-level Jewish activists from the party-state institutions of the Eastern International, which created openings for new mediators of Soviet power in the Arab Middle East.

In 1938, the Friendship of Peoples became the new, officially sanctioned metaphor of an imagined multinational community in the Soviet Union.[165] Its embrace and efforts to rebuild a new supranational Soviet culture brought greater acceptance of Russian nationality and its cultural supremacy. Yet it also highlighted the national cultures of various Soviet peripheries. This occurred through visits to Moscow by non-Russian national delegations and other symbolic demonstrations of friendship, such as ten-day festivals of national art.[166] By popularizing these national cultures of specific ethnic groups, first in Moscow and then throughout the USSR by radio, such festivals affirmed the unique identities of the non-Russian nations while claiming parts of their culture for the common pan-Soviet canon. This quality seemed particularly important for national cultures of the domestic East, which could help further universalize Soviet culture thanks to their historical transregional links. For instance, the 1938 jubilee celebration of the poet Nizami Ganjavi, who lived in the Seljuq empire in the twelfth century and wrote in Persian, presented him as an Azerbaijani national icon whose genius had been fostered by the unique multiculturalism of Azerbaijan's internationalist links. Incorporating him as a "national" icon into the broader Soviet canon could help Soviet internationalism transcend the East-West divide.[167]

Support for Central Asian "national" cultures likewise involved the nationalization of early Chagatai and Persianate writers and imperial histories. More sensitive was the history of Russian imperial expansion in these regions. This narrative required more complex revision, one that emphasized common elements in the histories of Russian and Central Asia peoples and promoted Stalin's "lesser evil" hypothesis that, had it not been for Russian intervention, these regions and other peripheries like Georgia and Ukraine would have been colonized by neighboring powers.[168] These revisions were reflected in new history textbooks published in the 1930s that increasingly eliminated any trace of Safarov's earlier analysis of the colonial dimensions of the conflict in Turkestan and structural continuities of imperial domination. Naturally, Safarov's work was banned after his arrest.[169] By stressing "friendship" with Russians in Soviet Central Asian and Caucasian history, official histories recast the Soviet East and its people as fully decolonized. Suppression of alternative histories made it safer for individuals from these regions to serve as Soviet mediators abroad. If they managed to survive the purges, Tatars continued to hold key diplomatic posts. They were the first Muslims to come under Russia's rule, and by the nineteenth century they were integrated into imperial power structures, occupied key positions in Russia's trade with Central Asia, and served as intermediaries for the imperial state in the steppe regions north of the Black and Caspian Seas.[170] The Tatar Abdurakhman Sultanov, who previously worked at the Institute for National-Colonial Problems, wrote for *Revoliutsionnyi Vostok,* and occasionally participated in the KUTV dramas of the 1930s, joined the Soviet Mission in Egypt in the 1943 and continued to work for Ministry of Foreign Affairs until 1948. He later transferred to the Institute of Oriental Studies of the Academy of Sciences in Moscow where after 1956 he headed the section for the study of Arab countries. For similar reasons, intermediaries willing to represent an increasingly domesticated and assimilated Soviet East in the Caucasus and Central Asia would also receive promotions and opportunities.

Soviet Central Asia continued to function as a cultural and administrative model for the foreign East in other ways as well. Arab communists on Comintern business in Moscow were explicitly directed to consider the intersection of new approaches to Comintern politics vis-à-vis the Mandate-era Arab world, and the broader relationship of nationalism and colonialism, through its lens. In 1936 the ECCI leader Dmitrii Manuil'skii sent Najati Sidqi and Khalid Bakdash to Tashkent to observe "how the Soviet Union resolves the issue of nationality."[171] According to Sidqi, this visit was supposed to resolve their dispute about Arab unity and its usefulness for anticolonial activism by studying how the USSR resolved the national question. The disagreement between Sidqi and Bakdash suggests "Arabness" remained a tenuous and potentially divisive concept. Part of the challenge, as historian Aviel Roshwald asserts, was that "the Arab nation was so broad and ill-defined that, on the one hand, it could be used as a legitimizing principle by a wide range of communities and interests that were in fact sectarian or regional in nature."[172] It is not clear what resolution Manuil'skii had in mind by sending the pair of communists to Central Asia. He certainly did not mean to point out any resemblances between Stalin's nationalities regime and the Mandate system's hybrid of Wilsonian self-determination principles with colonial practice.

Whatever the intention of the visit, Sidqi came away with a muddled account of the region's recent pass after meeting with the chairman of the Council of Peoples Commissars of the Uzbek SSR, Fayzulla Khodjaev, in Tashkent.[173] Perhaps his confusion was understandable. During this period, Khodjaev's own accounts of the revolution in which he actively participated had to transform from presenting left-leaning jadids as forerunners of the communists of the Young Bukharan Party and the Communist Party of Bukhara to presenting them as the government's opponents.[174] Yet this revised narrative about Russian power in Central Asia and the willingness to look at things "from Moscow's perspective" was echoed by other Arab communists returning from the Soviet Union. After his visit, Lebanese communist Farjalla al-Hilu published a short book about the Soviet Union, calling it "a new humanity building a new world" (*insaniyya jadida tabni 'aliman jadidan*) in which the "new person" stands "freed from all forms of social enslavement." The book included a section about Uzbekistan. This region, it argued, had been freed from the exploitation and corruption of the old Central Asian "khans [who] cooperated with Russian colonizers to suppress the toiling (*kadiha*) Islamic peoples" and were willing to use "everything for this purpose [of suppression], including religious power, even as they themselves were not pious. Attacked and debasing the pure Muslim spirit, the Emir of Bukhara had even commanded his flock to obey Nicholas II citing Qur'anic verses that obligated obedience."[175] The khans were presented as the main agents of colonialism, not the Russians—a move that intentionally erased Russia from conversations about decolonization among Arabic-speaking leftist intellectuals and from dreams of liberation on a global scale. Soviet Turkestan, the book argued, was industrializing, "weaving its own [textile] products from its cotton" and using these proceeds to "build prosperity and create national cultures."[176]

This perspective on the Soviet party-state's history in Central Asia was so powerful that it transcended Arab commitments to and disappointments with communism. In his memoirs, written long after he left the party, Sidqi described his encounters with Khodjaev and other "Eastern peoples of the Soviet Union."[177] The longevity of the "friendship of peoples" metaphor and of the "Eastern peoples" category continued to conceal certain types of history long after ideological disillusionment.

One of the tragedies for all these victims, perpetrators, and witnesses of the Soviet purges—including al-Hilu, Sidqi, Khodjaev, and Bakdash, but also Aimarov, Shami, and Nadab—is that these people who seemed genuinely invested in building a post-imperial "new world" had to do so by dividing it into ethnonational boxes. This division went beyond Soviet officials and Arab communists' mere acceptance of Mandate borders and of the borders of the new Soviet socialist republics. It involved an embrace of a majoritarian nationalist vision of politics within those borders that made certain forms of solidarity more difficult. It limited the potential of certain kinds of transregional politics possible in the 1920s by inflicting deep traumas on its various activists and protagonists.

The literary scholar Katerina Clark has argued that in the 1930s the Soviet Union sought "to define itself within the great cultural tradition of Europe, yet it was also then that an iron curtain fell more resoundingly than before, and the country became an ever more hermetic place of cultural autarky."[178] As the geopolitical borders between "domestic" and "foreign" Easts were expanded and secured, cultural autarky resulted in physical separation of the domestic and foreign sectors of KUTV and its research institute (NIA). Yet the unusual porousness of the idea of the "East" and the location of the Comintern and its "Eastern" educational institutions in Moscow meant that they remained a portal for various Eastern actors to negotiate their status as "outsiders" and "insiders" in relation to the party-state. In the process, ideas about the domestic East came to shape international relations, and international politics played out in Moscow's Party courts.

Stalin and other Moscow leaders continued to cling to the idea that the domestic East could serve as a model for the foreign East, and Comintern officials continued to selectively apply to "Eastern" foreigners domestic forms of decolonization through indigenization and affirmative action. Arabization was implemented in Arab parties, though nothing comparable was ever considered in Europe and the United States, where minorities continued to be supported as members of "oppressed" groups. This inconsistency made sense to Comintern administrators like Safarov, who interpreted violence in Palestine through the lens of the civil war in Central Asia, and his successor Manuil'skii, who sent Arab communists to Tashkent to teach them about how the Soviet Union approached the national question.

As in the domestic East, the Comintern's top-down indigenization decrees in the Arab parties aggravated tensions between minority and majority nationalities. Widespread anger and disappointment alienated the earliest and strongest bases of communist support among Jews in Palestine; Armenians in Syria and Lebanon; Jews, Armenians, and Greeks in Egypt; and the French in North Africa. The controversies in Lebanon, Egypt, and Syria, however, were less consequential for the network of the Eastern International than the one over Palestine. In Moscow, the purges were especially devastating to that network's central node—in part because of the significant presence of Russian Jews among teachers at KUTV and among Comintern bureaucrats responsible for the Near East, especially Russian Jews with various historical and familial linkages to socialist Zionism. This dynamic of Arab students lodging accusations against their Jewish teachers left Comintern authorities in a bind similar to that of Soviet domestic East administrators: they had to choose between accepting at face value Arab communists' claims about the chauvinism of their opponents, or taking their claims about Arabization as instrumental examples of "nationalist" deviation. As a dimension of foreign policy, Arabization outlived the domestic policy of indigenization for a number of reasons. The Bolsheviks were less concerned about the stability of Middle Eastern communist parties than they were about party structures in their borderlands; they were under continued pressure to behave as an anticolonial state by supporting majoritarian national liberation movements; and the purges of Jews, Armenians, and other minorities in the 1930s reconfigured communist politics and left lasting scars.[179]

By the late 1930s, Soviet Jews were no longer prominent in Communist Party's Central Committee, the Comintern, or other institutions responsible for relations with the Near East.[180] In the early 1940s, mass layoffs of

Jews with administrative positions in the cultural and propaganda organs further limited their influence, especially as members of the "Soviet intelligentsia."[181] Within the Eastern International, Arab communists, leftists, and other Soviet Easterners replaced them as mediators of the Soviet Union to the foreign East. By shifting to these other intermediaries, the Soviet "domestic East" was adapted to suit new international contexts and challenges.

4
Muslim Tradition Forbids Reciting the Qur'an While Drunk

In 1947 a group of eight Syrian and Lebanese intellectuals received an invitation from the All-Union Society for Cultural Ties Abroad, known by its Russian acronym VOKS, to visit the Soviet Union from February 17 to March 18. The VOKS invitation was unusual. From 1945 to 1951 the Soviet Union was focused on postwar reconstruction and the consequences of the 1946–1947 famine. It was a time of relative isolation. Only nineteen American groups (a total of fifty-seven delegates) visited the Soviet Union under VOKS' purview during those years. Most of them were well-known fellow travelers, like American writer John Steinbeck who toured the USSR in 1947 with photographer Robert Capa.[1] The Syrian and Lebanese intellectuals were also major cultural figures, but from states that had achieved independence just months earlier and that had been occupied by British and Free French troops until their withdrawal in April 1946. This invitation acknowledged the resilience of the Eastern International and the significance of these regions and their leftist intellectuals as mediators in the Soviet Union's continued relationship with the decolonizing world.

The group's composition indicates how postwar intellectual configurations related to earlier wartime and interwar activism. The Syrian half of the delegation was led by Damascus University historian Kamil 'Ayyad (1901–1987), founder of the Damascus-based journal *al-Thaqafa* (culture) in the 1930s and the Beirut-based periodical *al-Tali'a* (The Vanguard).[2] When the invitation was extended, he also presided over the Syrian-Soviet Friendship Committee.[3] Other invited guests included engineer Fawzi Shulaq, who had sat on the Central Committee of the Syrian Communist Party since its first post-Comintern conference in late 1943 and was part of an inner Party leadership group responsible for intellectual matters;[4] lawyer Ibrahim Hamzawi; and Syrian doctor Josef Jibran Luis.[5] The Lebanese delegation was led by architect Antun Tabit (1907–1964), who chaired the Lebanese Society of Friends of the USSR from 1946 to 1948 and had founded the Anti-Fascist League of

The Eastern International. Masha Kirasirova, Oxford University Press. © Oxford University Press 2024.
DOI: 10.1093/oso/9780197685693.003.0005

TRADITION FORBIDS RECITING QU'RAN WHILE DRUNK 125

Syria and Lebanon in 1935, together with its literary-cultural journal *al-Tariq* (The Path). Three remaining guests were all editors or regular contributors to this journal. They included novelist Ra'if Khuri (1913–1967), feminist writer Imili Faris Ibrahim, and physician-writer George Hanna (Arabic transliteration: Jurj Hanna, 1891–1969).[6] As Hanna recalled, this visit was an opportunity to join the ranks of visiting European intellectuals who had written about the Soviet Union and to describe this "new world radiating from the East" in Arabic.[7]

The group convened at a time when various ruptures across Eurasia had precipitated the end of the Versailles world order. The temporary agreements between the USSR and Nazi Germany and then between the USSR and the Allied powers had collapsed, giving way to a Cold War climate of distrust. Meanwhile, the ties between Britain and France and the bulk of their once-dependent territories were unraveling.[8] Anticolonial activism in the Mashriq (the region extending from the western border of Egypt to the eastern border of Iraq) had already won significant political concessions from Europe in

Figure 4.1 Lebanese and Syrian delegates with the Bronze Horseman statue to Peter the Great in Leningrad, 1947. From Jurj Hanna, *Ana 'a'id min Musku* (Beirut: Matabi'a al-Kashshaf, 1947), 97.

the 1930s, but in the 1940s this pressure culminated in the dissolution of the League of Nations and *de jure* independence for Lebanon, Syria, and Jordan in 1946. The partition of Palestine in 1948 would more firmly embed the Arab-Israeli conflict in postwar regional and international politics.

Throughout these transitions, the Mashriq remained of significant geostrategic interest. Great Britain maintained strong positions in Syria and Lebanon after it had helped push out the French. It concluded a new treaty of alliance with Turkey and maintained treaties with Egypt, Iraq, and Jordan. The region's proximity to newly discovered oil fields in Saudi Arabia attracted more political and financial commitments from the United States. Stalin was more interested in neighboring Iran, where he had tried and failed to maintain a military presence, and in Turkey, where he lost his bid for control of the Turkish Straits. His support for the 1948 partition of Palestine was largely motivated by a desire to undermine British positions in the region.

Postwar decolonization created political openings but Soviet support for communist networks in the region that had once connected it with Iran, the Caucasus, Moscow, and other parts of Eurasia was waning. Stalin's 1943 decision to dissolve the Comintern as a good faith gesture to the Allies before the Tehran Conference weakened connections already thrown into disarray by the 1930s purges. Remaining Moscow-based Comintern experts on the East were mostly subsumed into the newly formed International Department of the Communist Party of the Soviet Union—responsible for political connections with communist parties—and into other internationally oriented institutions responsible for information, propaganda, and cultural affairs.[9] Stalin's wartime concerns about security in Europe were evident in the 1947 creation of the Cominform to coordinate the activities of communist parties. Unlike the earlier Comintern, this new organization did not include a single non-European member.

Ironically, Stalin's waning interest in communism in the East coincided with the growth of communist activities in the Mashriq.[10] Regional communists had managed to survive the trials of the Molotov-Ribbentrop Pact, when communist parties had to follow the Soviet Union's lead in opposing the war after France and Britain declared war on Germany in September 1939 and subsequently endured the colonial powers' backlash. In reaction to this opposition, France had officially dissolved communist parties in its colonies and territories, banned Party newspapers, and arrested Party leaders. These repressions continued throughout the period of Vichy rule in France, which lasted until August 1941 in French Mandate Syria and

Lebanon.[11] In British Mandate Palestine, the predominantly Jewish members of the Communist Party found themselves in the difficult position of having to oppose the war while trying to promote the party's politics among a Jewish community that was overwhelmingly antifascist.[12] The realignment of Soviet and Allied interests against Hitler in the summer of 1941 eased these tensions. It allowed communists to reconnect with grassroots support for antifascist causes, especially among leftist intellectuals.[13] These wartime linkages reinvigorated the Soviet Union's symbolic power in the region.

As this chapter shows, Lebanese and Syrian intellectuals had to selectively ignore aspects of late 1940s Soviet politics, including the USSR's initial support for Israel, in order to revive and maintain these linkages in the postwar era. These intellectuals, both within the Soviet Union and abroad, had to make personal and political compromises to gain Soviet support for themselves as individual writers and for their collective quest for intellectual and cultural decolonization. The process helped to revive and reconfigure many of the earlier logics of the Eastern International.

Stalin's Western allies were also monitoring the growth of communism and intellectuals' interest in the Soviet Union.[14] US State Department analysts who focused on the Eastern Mediterranean seemed especially anxious about Russia's "cultural" influence among Syrians, whom they described as "intense and active psychologically."[15] European and Israeli observers of Arab communism worried about "fellow-travelers," "crypto-communists," or communist "sympathizers" among the regional intelligentsia who were reluctant to formally join the party because they held official or important positions.[16] Such reports often reduced Arab communists and non-communist leftist intellectuals to Soviet puppets. Syrian Communist Party leader Khalid Bakdash echoed a similar concern, only from the opposite perspective. The Party was having trouble building up a "proletarian mass basis," he argued in 1951, because imperialist domination, feudal tyranny, and the weakness of the local class struggle made it natural "that the noise [made by the party] should first attract [people] among the intellectuals, students, and certain enlightened workers. . . . We are in danger of regarding the noise as an end in itself."[17]

The visibility of intellectuals in late 1940s and early 1950s regional politics can be explained by the relative weakness of Syrian and Lebanese states that had just achieved independence and the domination of regional politics by a political elite composed primarily of landowning urban notables and intellectuals. Unlike the notables, the intellectuals were organized mostly around private journals, newspapers, and Marxist political circles. Their authority was based on quality of their writing and thought, erudition, courage, and, especially, practical as well as theoretical commitment to autonomous politics.[18] This autonomy is precisely what George Hanna asserted to justify his 1947 visit to the Soviet Union—a right to visit foreign countries, see conditions for himself, and independently communicate to his readers "an abstract truth free of all positive and negative propaganda."[19]

These intellectuals maintained transregional and sometimes global connections across the Middle East, Europe, Latin America, and Africa.[20] Yet their connections with the Soviet Union rarely make it into histories, apart from through individual biographies. For example, Moscow served as an intellectual home and a source of support for Husayn Muruwwa, whose influential Marxist rereading of Islamic history reflected his embrace of communism and experiences in the Soviet Union layered upon a complex integrative intellectual identity.[21] Similarly, the 1947 visit illustrates how the USSR managed to remain a potent symbol for Arab intellectuals and their publics of an alternative future built upon anti-Westernism, antifascism, respect for national differences, and anticapitalist values.

The contradictions of late Stalinism, however, continued to influence which Soviet symbols traveled and how. Soviet state power continued to propagate earlier scripts of the Eastern International. Multiple Soviet radio, press, and transregional cultural agencies restated the message that the Soviet "domestic East" had a special international role to play as a model for the "foreign East." These statements still treated the "East" mostly as an ideological abstraction that did not require interest in or knowledge about specific cultural or political conditions in the regions involved. Frequently, these statements were translated into Arabic and other languages and were reprinted in regional journals and newspapers. Yet the underlying contexts of these statements had changed to reflect the late Stalin-era cultural politics and its particular forms of xenophobia.

The new cultural doctrine developed in 1946 by Central Committee secretary Andrei Zhdanov stressed the rejection of Western culture, especially in Moscow and Leningrad, and an intensification of Russian patriotism.[22] Such anti-Westernism may have reflected officials' fears that Soviet troops returning from the frontlines in Europe had been "contaminated" by exposure to Western mores. Because of this ideological shift, the very word *patriot* in this period got conflated with the word *Russian*, and some positive expressions of non-Russian nationality fell under greater suspicion. By 1948, this cultural politics had become more explicitly anti-Semitic. Stalin had become increasingly concerned about war with the United States and the number of Soviet Jews with relatives in America who might not remain loyal to the Soviet Union in the event of a US-Soviet conflict. He was also worried by Soviet Jews' public enthusiasm over the formation of the state of Israel.[23] Reflecting these concerns, a new purge of "cosmopolitan" influences targeted Jewish institutions and individuals; the Jewish Anti-Fascist Committee was dissolved; Yiddish cultural institutions were shut down and the prominent Jewish cultural figure Solomon Mikhoels murdered; and the Politburo issued a new directive to "eliminate shortcomings in the selection and development of cadres," with special instructions to pay attention to Jewish ones. This directive was used to remove Jews from positions of power in economic, scientific, cultural, medical, educational, and political institutions and spheres in Moscow, Leningrad, and elsewhere.[24]

Suspicion toward Jews as agents of American and British imperialism made it especially difficult for them to mediate Soviet cultural or political interests in the Arab world. For instance, the Arabist Vladimir Lutskii (b. 1906 in southeastern Ukraine), who lived in Palestine from 1923 until 1926 but returned to become a leading pioneer of contemporary Arab history, was terminated from Moscow State University for "failure to demonstrate academic growth" and for making the "political mistake" of inadequately exposing the reactionary role of Zionism in Arab countries in one of his monographs. He managed to fight this decision, at great cost to his personal health, and succeeded only because his appeal happened to be made just after Stalin's death and, luckily, landed on Khrushchev's desk instead.[25]

Yet the collision of Soviet, Arab, and international contexts evident in the 1947 visit of Syrian and Lebanese intellectuals underscores the complexity and diversity of late Stalin-era official paranoia about culture and about what was appropriately Soviet and patriotic in different spaces of the USSR.[26] In the domestic East, other enigmatic purges were fueled by questions about what constituted acceptable "national" culture, which reopened debates about "nationalism" that were thought to have been resolved in the 1930s. The awkwardness and confusion that ensued during this visit had to be suppressed in order to protect the idea of the Soviet Union as a revolutionary model for a post-imperial world.

The history of cultural connections between the Eastern Mediterranean and Eurasia predates the rise of "the cultural Cold War" and are reflected in the history of the emergence of concept of culture. The seven men and one woman from Syria and Lebanon visiting the Soviet Union in 1947 all thought of themselves as intellectuals. In Arabic, the term for intellectual, *muthaqqaf*, is derived from the same root as the word for culture (*thaqafa*). Both words emerged when transformations in the world economy and Ottoman reforms extended state employment opportunities to more members of the old scholarly and bureaucratic "estate" in the second half of the nineteenth century.[27] Across the Ottoman empire, as in other parts of Asia, the concept of culture came to serve as a powerful tool to critique the anarchy and anomie of commercial society and to challenge the slavish imitation of Western civilization by recuperating an autonomous subjectivity based on indigenous tradition.[28] It described colonial cosmopolitanism, anticolonial nationalism, pan-Asianism, and anti-Western anticapitalism.

In the mid-nineteenth century, Russian Slavophile Nikolai Danilevskii similarly used culture (*kul'tura*) to articulate the autonomy of Russian values and institutions from the superficial, putatively universal judgments of Western civilization.[29] Writer Lev Tolstoy also popularized the difference between a putative traditional Russian culture and that of the Westernizers, Slavophile's opponents. Tolstoy's multiple translations into many different languages, including Arabic after 1902, helped feed a hunger among Arabic-reading intellectuals for anarchist, socialist, and anticlerical thought.[30] These conversations at the turn of the century reflected the wide-ranging search in Russia, the Mashriq, and other places for a better world, as well as the intellectual's place in it. As Syria and Lebanon fell more directly under European control, intellectuals continued to grapple with these questions and others about "useless imitation" versus "authentic invention" in the construction of national identity. They also debated the appropriate definition of the nation and its relation to other determinants of identity, such as class and colonial domination.

The presence of colonial armies and officials in civil administration only heightened the longing for cultural autonomy. These officials were often transferred in from other colonial territories, where they had imbibed the mentality of conquest, oppression, and plunder.[31] Young radicals such as Niquola Shawi from Tripoli, Lebanon—an organizer of Soviet-Arab friendship society who was instrumental in establishing its linkages with VOKS in

Moscow—was frustrated by what seemed like an erasure of the region and its culture in his school curriculum:

> The books circulating among us distanced or distorted everything related to the French Revolution and other popular uprisings against the privileges of the church and the nobility that established the foundations of the Republic.... They glorified the exploits of kings, nobles and knights of France ... moving on to contemporary marshals, generals, monks and missionaries who ... carried "civilization" and the seeds of Christian faith to Indochina and the depths of Asia. As for our history, the history of our modern country, there was no mention of it in the educational program, and there was no book. The [colonial authorities] were satisfied with sparse references to the ancient history of the East, about Phoenicians, Canaanites, Assyrians, Persians, and Pharoses, the Greeks and those who came after them in forgotten ancient times.[32]

Greater access to education deepened the desire for an alternative approach to history and culture, and for many this radicalization led to nationalist politics and political organizations.[33] For some, it led to uniformed youth organizations inspired by fascist aesthetics, hierarchical organizations, and concepts of discipline and power, such as the "Iron shirts" in Syria and the Phalanges in Lebanon. For his part, Shawi had access to materialist critiques of colonialism that had been circulating in Beirut, Cairo, Alexandria, and the Syrian diaspora since the nineteenth century and to their twentieth-century popularizers at the Armenian Evangelical College and the American University in Beirut. These materialist critiques, rearticulated by charismatic teachers in the new interwar context, led Shawi to communism.[34]

The challenges of finding employment in a French- and British-dominated Mandate economy ensured that materialist critiques continued to resonate, especially with the onset of the global economic depression in the 1930s.[35] Unprecedented labor union organization and mass protests were supported by local nationalists and communists, who had been popularizing Marxist-Leninist critiques of capitalism in published Arabic translations of *The Communist Manifesto* and other Marxist texts. KUTV graduates often framed local economic grievances in Marxist-Leninist terms, channeling critiques away from Fabian and other socialist formulations circulating around Syria and Lebanon and toward a Bolshevik frame. These graduates included Khalid Bakdash, who translated the *Manifesto*; Rashad 'Isa and

Fawzi al-Zaʿim, who played important roles in the Party newspaper, *Nidhal al-Shaʿab*; and Yusuf Khitar al-Hilu, who operated the Party's clandestine printing press in West Beirut.[36] Their publications, like Farjallah al-Hilu's 1937 booklet *New Humanity* (*al-insaniyya al-jadida*), contributed to a sense of belonging to a global community of Arab and anticapitalist activists inspired by the Soviet Union.[37]

In addition to colonial capitalism, the other nexus of global and local leftist and communist critique was fascism. Recent scholarship has highlighted diverse attitudes about fascism in the Arab world in order to question long-held assumptions about an inherent Muslim predisposition toward authoritarianism, totalitarianism, Islamo-fascism, and even anti-Semitism.[38] These works suggest that many local actors saw fascist international ambitions, especially those of Italy in the Mediterranean and Africa, as threatening. Shawi recalled one communist-led demonstration in Tripoli, Lebanon, after the 1931 execution of the Libyan resistance leader Omar Mukhtar and the commencement of Italy's punitive campaign against the Libyan population. In the crowd Shawi heard "chants against fascist Italy accompanied by denunciations of French colonialism ... [as well as] calls for Syrian unity, and complete independence."[39] The consolidation of Italian control over Libya and the 1935 attack on Abyssinia further underscored the dangers of fascist imperialism. This crisis brought anticolonial nationalist forces together with communists who shifted their emphasis to antifascism following the Comintern's embrace of the Popular Front strategy.[40]

This Popular Front coalition, which included some of the 1947 visitors, received significant organizational support from communists. Lebanese Communist Artin Maduyan recalled that during one of his visits to Moscow, the Comintern Secretary Dmitri Manuil'skii instructed him to expand the antifascist struggle in Lebanon, Syria, and Egypt, particularly the Suez Canal region.[41] Maduyan then tasked his political secretary, Niquola Shawi, with implementing these instructions. Shawi did so by commissioning his friend Salim Khayyata to write a book-length critique of fascism, which sharpened some of the points that Khayyata had made in a 1933 publication that, Maduyan said, "had great resonance with intellectuals."[42] Yusuf Khitar al-Hilu recalled other communist efforts to "establish mass organizations that could serve as tributaries of the struggle against colonialism and fascism [that] ... entered deeply into the midst of the intelligentsia (*muthaqqafin*). These [efforts] involved publishing the magazine *al-Duhur* (The Times) edited by Salim Khayyata that rallied a number of major Arab writers around it, convening a 1934 conference for non-communist intellectuals in Zahlé and publishing its records, and organizing the magazine *al-Tali'a* (The Vanguard)."[43] In their memoirs, Communists often took credit for creating such forums, yet such meetings and publications engaged a broader intellectual and political spectrum.[44] *Al-Tali'a* was published in Damascus from 1935 to 1939 and was sold across Lebanon, Syria, Iraq, Palestine, and Egypt, thus providing a platform for broad discussions of such topics as the role of the Arab writer in society.[45] Its contributors—Salim Khayyata, Michel 'Aflaq, Najati Sidqi, Ali Nasir, Fu'ad al-Shayib, and delegation members Ra'if Khuri and Kamil 'Ayyad—represented eclectic and diverse political views, as did its editorial choices. For example, a 1936 special issue was dedicated to the tenth-century Arab poet al-Mutanabbi and the recently deceased Maxim Gorky. It included an article about Gorky by 1947 delegate Ra'if Khuri, describing him as a revolutionary intellectual (*adib*) who was exiled for his convictions, continued to fight with the emerging revolutionary forces in Russia, and was a model for all oppressed people worldwide.[46]

The Lebanese and Syrian Left was further invigorated by international events. These included Mussolini's invasion of Ethiopia in October 1935, which seemed like the start of a renewed phase of Western imperialism; the election of a Popular Front government in France in May 1936, which relaxed repressive anticommunist measures in the Mandate territories; and the outbreak of the Spanish Civil War in July 1936, which created a powerful sense of transnational camaraderie among leftists worldwide.[47] In May 1939, after the victory of fascism in Spain and Hitler's annexation of Austria, the joint Lebanese-Syrian League against Nazism and Fascism ('Usbat Mukafahat al-Naziyya wa-l-Fashistiyya, henceforth the Anti-Fascist League) held its first Conference in Beirut, attracting over 200 intellectuals, members of parliament,[48] and Communist Party leaders.[49] Its founder was the Lebanese architect Antun Tabit, who would later lead the Lebanese half of the 1947 delegation to the USSR.

This anti-fascist momentum in Lebanon and Syria was stalled temporarily by the 1939 Non-Aggression Pact, as well as growing labor unrest and France's fall to Nazi Germany in 1940.[50] Anticommunist observers like Walter Laqueur saw Arab communists' ideological reversal in August 1939 as indicative of their hollow antifascist convictions.[51] Yet lack of evidence for the Vichy period, when communist activities were mostly driven underground, makes such claims difficult to prove, as do prominent exceptions such as KUTV alumnus Najati Sidqi, whose continued public commitment to antifascism led to his expulsion from the Communist Party.[52] In their memoirs, some communists explained the Molotov-Ribbentrop Pact in terms of power politics, arguing (as did Maduyan) that the Soviet Union was "pursuing a flexible and patient policy . . . in order to avoid entering the war alone and to postpone the battle as much as possible. When Hitler proposed the non-aggression treaty the Soviet Union could not reject this proposal given the conspiratorial and hostile policy of France and England towards it."[53] What is clear is that immediately after the Soviet Union entered the war on the side of the Allies, leftist intellectuals returned to their antifascist positions. The same people who in the late 1930s had contributed to *al-Tali'a* and *al-Makshuf* (The Uncovered) mobilized around a new publication of the Anti-Fascist League: *al-Tariq* (The Path).[54]

World War II was not nearly as catastrophic in Syria and Lebanon as it was in Europe and East Asia. The Middle Eastern and North African theater was ultimately peripheral but, as historian Cyrus Schayegh summarizes, "as peripheries go, it was central, to be sure. The British Suez Canal base was strategically vital, Palestine protected its northern flank, and hence, tens of thousands of troops were massed here. The Middle East and North Africa, with India, was the hinge between the war's European and Asian theaters— one the Anglo-American Allies were determined to hold."[55] Ironically, it was Britain's occupation of Lebanon and Syria from June to July 1941 that prevented the Free French troops from reasserting Mandate rule and helped Lebanese and Syrian nationalists gain conditional independence in 1943, followed by full independence in 1946.[56]

The waves of hope and disappointment generated by these developments politicized the population.[57] By the end of the war, membership in the Syrian and Lebanese communist party surged to over 10,000 members.[58] Although the surge did not lead to any electoral victories, Communist-organized rallies in anticipation of parliamentary elections in the summer of 1943 drew about 400 people in Beirut, up to 2,000 in Damascus, and upwards of 5,000 in Aleppo.[59] As part of its coverage of these events, *al-Tariq* hosted debates about the merits of parliamentary democracy and about how the ideas of liberty, equality, fraternity, and political representation could be used not only to critique Nazism and fascism internationally but also to confront antidemocratic and antiliberal forces at home.[60] It also tried to foster greater international awareness of the war fronts.[61] The journal translated and published articles about the Soviet front by prominent journalists and writers such as Ilya Ehrenburg, Boris Agapov, Yemelyan Yaroslavsky, and Konstantin Derzhavin, and included articles by Soviet writers on topics unrelated to the war.[62]

Most likely, these articles about the war and other dimensions of life in the Soviet Union were procured by *al-Tariq* either through the Anti-Fascist League or through the Society of Friends of the Soviet Union. The latter was one of a number of groups that had formed in 1941 in Syria and Lebanon to support the Soviet Union's war effort.[63] Membership in these groups overlapped. Antun Tabit, 'Umar Fakhuri, Kamil 'Ayyad, Yusuf Yazbik, Ra'if Khuri, and Wasfi al-Banni belonged to both, and many were also members in the Communist Party.[64] VOKS records indicate that the Society of Friends first made contact with Moscow in 1942 to request Soviet books and periodicals in French, English, Arabic, and Armenian.[65] VOKS was happy to oblige, sending books by political leaders such as Stalin, Molotov, Lenin, Kalinin, and Beria; articles by canonical writers such as Ehrenburg, Alexander Pushkin, and Alexander Blok; and war coverage by Platon Kerzhentsev, Boris Lavrenyov, and Vsevolod Ivanov.[66] The shipments continued even during World War II.

After the Comintern was dissolved in 1943, these "societies of friends" expanded their contacts with the Soviet Union. VOKS was well suited for this connecting role because, although it was formally a "society" (*obshchestvo*), and as such existed outside the party-state structure, in practice it worked closely with the Commissariat of Foreign Affairs (NKID) and its representatives in Soviet embassies abroad.[67] In 1944 the Society of Friends of Syria and Lebanon corresponded with the Soviet embassies in Ankara and Tehran about getting VOKS materials to host a photo exhibit, "The USSR at War." These materials were sent to Damascus and Beirut via the Soviet Embassy in Turkey.[68] In Damascus the exhibit about the wonders of Soviet industrial development and the atrocities of Hitler attracted an estimated 75,000 visitors[69] and in Beirut reportedly 65,000.[70] The Beirut opening, hosted by 'Umar Fakhuri,[71] included a surprising cross-section of elites: the Lebanese president; ministers, deputies, judges, religious officials, and members of cultural institutions; National Congress representatives; leaders of Syrian and Lebanese Communist Parties; journalists; and union leaders. In his report about this event, Shawi noted the presence of the French delegate general Mr. Chataigneaux, General Humblot, the chargé d'affaires of Egypt, the Iraqi consul, the American consul representing the American delegation in the Levant, the Iranian, Czech, and Belgian consuls, and a large number of other important foreign representatives.[72] During the war, communist intellectuals such as Fakhuri and Shawi, with VOKS' support, hosted cultural events that paved the way for more conventional diplomacy.

Within weeks of the "The USSR at War" exhibition, Soviet diplomatic missions opened in Beirut and Damascus, and Soviet diplomat and orientalist Daniel Solod was appointed plenipotentiary minister to both newly independent countries. For Syria and Lebanon, the recognition of independence by both the Soviet Union and the United States was a landmark in a long struggle for decolonization. The next major step toward independence would be the 1946 removal of British and French troops, thanks in part to Soviet advocacy at the United Nations Security Council and a Soviet offer to help with the formation of local armies.[73] The opening of diplomatic missions meant that it was no longer necessary to conduct informal cultural diplomacy through communists or neighboring countries. This layer of diplomatic connection allowed for an expansion of cultural activities. Before World War II, VOKS connections in the Mashriq were limited to answering occasional requests for copies of the VOKS bulletin from members of antifascist, communist, or friendship groups;[74] replying to genealogical inquiries from people born in Russia who had emigrated to Palestine;[75] and facilitating visa support for occasional visitors from Egypt, Yemen, Morocco, and Palestine.[76] After the wartime opening of Soviet missions in Syria and Lebanon, an increase in VOKS contacts and cultural activities reflected local enthusiasm for the Soviet Union.[77]

The expansion of demand for Soviet-supported cultural activities in Syria and Lebanon occurred during a difficult time in Soviet cultural politics. In 1946, Stalin gave his chief propagandist, Andrei Zhdanov, and his allies the go-ahead to begin an ideological crackdown that began in the realms of literature and the arts and expanded outward.[78] As head of the Agitation and Propaganda Department of the Communist Party, Zhdanov took charge of VOKS, ushering in a period when cultural relations with allies became "inept and inert" and when even diplomatic work struggled under ham-handed oversight.[79] For most of the 1930s, the vision of "common humanity" trumpeted by Maxim Gorky and the Soviet journal *International Literature* had been the voice of the transnational literary Left. But it gave way to something darker in the 1940s, and by the 1950s would seem increasingly outlandish.[80] In a sense, the USSR squandered some of the surging global antifascist sentiment that could have helped its postwar standing and cultural relations.

Despite these challenges, VOKS leadership decided to acknowledge the work of its Lebanese and Syrian antifascist leftist "friends" by inviting them in 1947 to visit the USSR. The final list of delegates was chosen by local Soviet diplomats, with input from Syrian and Lebanese communists.[81] The guests' biographies in their VOKS files show signs of an evaluation process. Potential red flags were underlined, such as the fact that Imili Faris Ibrahim was married to a businessman, and that George Hanna was suspected of supporting the British. Positive attributes, such as communist party membership, general influence, and writing talent, received check marks.[82] The biographies omitted reference to religion, an important marker of identity and social organization in Syria and Lebanon but irrelevant to their status as "Eastern" or "leftist" intellectuals. Like Comintern experts before them, postwar cultural diplomacy experts remained ignorant of this world on its own terms. Thus, they missed the fact that all the Lebanese guests were Christian. The final invitation list was approved by Mikhail Suslov, head of the CPSU's new Foreign Relations Department, highlighting the importance of these intellectuals for Soviet international ambitions.[83]

The chosen guests arrived in Moscow on February 17, and first impressions seemed positive. Kamil 'Ayyad, Fawzi Shulaq, Ibrahim Hamzawi, Josef Jibran Luis, Antun Tabit, Ra'if Khuri, Imili Faris Ibrahim, and George Hanna began with a tour of Moscow, during which their guides and French-speaking translators carefully recorded their observations, behaviors, and jokes. The guides noted who in the group was aware, or unaware, of Soviet history and works by Lenin and Stalin. They noticed Khuri's willingness to promote Soviet culture back home; he asked for permission to commission articles about Soviet life and culture for *at-Tariq* from the Lebanese representative to the USSR, Khalil Taqi al-Din (Russian: Takeddin), and the Egyptian ambassador, Mohamed Kamal al-Bindari.

After the Moscow tour, VOKS tried to accommodate their guests' specific interests by organizing smaller trips. Tabit visited the Architecture Academy; 'Ayyad explored employment opportunities at Radio Moscow and the Leningrad Oriental Institute;[84] and Imili Faris Ibrahim attempted to arrange business contracts on behalf of her husband with SovTechnoExport, where she inquired about possibilities of exporting of Soviet tractors and other agricultural machinery to Lebanon. She and Khuri also had two meetings with Solomon Lozovskii, the director of the Sovinformburo and former deputy foreign minister under Viacheslav Molotov. For Khuri and Tabit, VOKS arranged a visit to the home of Ilya Ehrenburg, where the guests sipped pepper vodka, marveled at a fireworks display, and browsed through Ehrenburg's bookshelves, where they discovered an Arabic-language translation of *Stronger than Death* (*Sil'nee smerti*) by their fellow *al-Tariq* editor Qadri Qal'aji.[85] These meetings did not raise any major concerns from the Soviet side.

VOKS officials seemed more suspicious of George Hanna. During a tour of the *Pravda* offices, Hanna learned that the printing machines had been manufactured in Britain and the United States, and apparently made a few curt statements in Arabic—the meaning of which, according to the VOKS report, "as expected, could not be understood."[86] The American origins of much of postwar Soviet machinery was a sensitive topic. When John Steinbeck made a similar observation during his 1947 tour of a famous Stalingrad tractor factory, his VOKS minders also got nervous and forbade his photographer from taking any pictures.[87] In Hanna's case, his minders' fear was compounded by their inability to understand his critique. In Baku, VOKS noted that Hanna sought out older people, especially women, and tried to speak with them in Turkish. Because Turkish and Azeri are closely related and mutually intelligible Turkic languages, Hanna was trying to get unexpurgated assessments of whether life had improved under Soviet rule or if it was better before the Revolution. According to Tabit, Hanna thought that young people raised in the Soviet system could not properly make such a judgment. As he tried to discover what the Soviet Union was actually like, he raised suspicions among his hosts and fellow delegates. To make matters worse, Hamzawi reported that the SCP leader Khalid Bakdash was also suspicious of Hanna.[88] In the final report to Suslov, Central Committee member Leonid Baranov echoed Tabit's suspicion that Hanna was "probably a British spy,"[89] an ironic evaluation of a man who would soon also be blacklisted by the US House of Representatives' Committee on Un-American Activities for activism in the Soviet-led Partisans of Peace movement and his pro-Soviet writing in *al-Tariq*.[90]

Soviet paranoia ran so high in this period that even high-ranking foreign communists could not be trusted. In his conversation with VOKS official Kisleva, Fawzi Shulaq claimed that he personally helped local diplomats draft the budget forwarded to Moscow to support the CPSL but that he wanted to increase this support.[91] Kisleva, a seasoned VOKS bureaucrat who had survived the late 1930s purges by denouncing her colleagues to the NKVD for improper behavior around foreigners, cautiously recorded in her diary that she "did not have the information to speak to Shulaq frankly about this matter." She was forced to respond with the official line that VOKS was a public organization that "did not finance the work of affiliated organizations abroad."[92] She then offered to increase non-monetary "cultural" support to the Society of Friendship, in which Shulaq also participated, by sending more films, projectors, exhibitions, and books that could be used to raise additional funds. This conversation suggests that Soviet cultural and diplomatic plenipotentiaries may have taken on some Comintern obligations after its dissolution. Meanwhile, international communists were forced to look for new ways of generating revenue by selling Soviet culture abroad.

More tensions emerged around the delegation's visit to Soviet Uzbekistan. The original itinerary proposed by VOKS was for the group to visit Georgia and Armenia. In fact, handwritten notes on the correspondence between the Soviet Mission in Lebanon, VOKS, and Suslov to plan the visit advised visiting both regions and showcasing the irrigation systems and canals in Central Asia.[93] However, when they arrived in Moscow, Hanna, Ibrahim, and Khuri refused to go to the domestic East altogether. Tabit explained this reluctance by citing Hanna's desire to shop for souvenirs, Ibrahim's interest in settling her husband's business affairs, and Khuri's interest in spending time with Ibrahim (thus alluding to their well-known affair). By way of compromise, a frustrated Tabit relayed that the group might be more interested in seeing the Muslim republics of the USSR instead of Georgia and Armenia, thus cutting the Eastern tour in half. He then forced everyone in the group to go to Tashkent and then Baku by asking VOKS to send the three contrarians back to Lebanon if they did not abide by the majority decision. He had clearly positioned himself as the group's leading intermediary, supplying VOKS with information about the other delegates' statements and reactions and assessing their trustworthiness. He seemed to embrace this role out of long-held commitments to social justice. According to his wife, since his student days he had been consumed by the search for solutions to the "problems of modern life" that could counter the French Mandate and its vestiges in Lebanese administrative, military, and cultural life. To him, friendship with the Soviet Union fed his commitments to anticolonial nationalism, patriotism, and hopes for a better world.[94] On this trip, these long-standing commitments may have helped him adjust to his hosts' expectations, including that the delegation stay together and visit the domestic East.

The group's ambivalence about visiting the Muslim Uzbekistan and Azerbaijan as opposed to the Christian Caucasus was understandable, especially considering the historical ties between Georgia, Armenia, and the Mashriq. Georgia had been the homeland of many high-level mamluks in the Ottoman administration, especially in Egypt and Iraq. Soviet Armenia had been a repatriation destination for ethnic Armenians from former Ottoman territories since the 1920s, and this flow increased after World War II.[95] Nevertheless, the earlier logic of the Eastern International prevailed, and the group was rerouted to Tashkent and Baku, the two premier showcase cities of the "Muslim" Soviet East.

In Tashkent, the delegation received a standard tour of the main textile factory, a women's school, a large collective farm, and the Academy of Sciences, where they likely learned about a newly published volume of the *History of the Peoples of Uzbekistan*.[96] Yet a deviation from the script occurred at a farewell dinner organized by the USSR Minister of Foreign Affairs for the Arab delegation and Chinese progressive writer Mao Dun, who had recently published his Chinese-language translation of Valentin Kataev's novel *Son of the Regiment* (1946).[97] According to the VOKS guide, one problem followed the other. The Uzbek hosts made toasts so distasteful that he couldn't translate them, while the other Uzbek actors, writers, and academics at the party were apparently "unable to observe basic table etiquette." At one point, the Uzbek baritone Mukhitdin Kari-Yakubov's impromptu performance of Uzbek national songs so annoyed Luis and Hamzawi that the Arab guests asked him to stop yelling. Then, when Kari-Yakubov began reciting the Qur'an in Arabic, Kamil 'Ayyad purportedly leaned over and told the VOKS guide that "according to Muslim tradition, the Qur'an should not be recited while drunk."[98]

VOKS attributed this awkwardness to the Uzbek Foreign Ministry's "failure to instruct local guests on proper etiquette."[99] Perhaps the misunderstandings had more to do with the nature of highly stressful anticosmopolitan constraints being placed on cultural figures around the USSR in this period. Singer Kari-Yakubov had been a symbol of Central Asian success within the Soviet system and was experienced in navigating the nexus of domestic-international Soviet cultural politics. He had earned the title "Kari" (Arabic: *qāri'*, meaning reader/reciter), from which he derived his stage name, for excelling in Qur'anic recitation as a child in the

Ferghana Valley in the 1890s. During World War I he had helped organize an Uzbek musical theater where he sang folk songs and performed on the dutar, a traditional long-necked two-string lute found in Iran and Central Asia.[100] After the revolution, he traveled with an Uzbek delegation to the Eleventh Congress of the Communist Party (1922) in Moscow, and there tried to enroll in the conservatory. When that plan fell through, he joined KUTV and became the director of its Uzbek circle of amateur performance. He sang

Figure 4.2 Uzbek singer Mukhitdin Kari-Yakubov and Tamara Khanum performing at an Evening of Eastern Peoples KUTV in 1924. From L. Avdeeva, *Mukhitdin Kari-Yakubov* (Tashkent: Gafur Ghulam Press, 1984), 62. Reprinted with permission of Gafur Ghulam Press.

at the KUTV "Evening of Eastern Peoples" and, like his classmates Nazim Hikmet and Najati Sidqi, worked with the experimental Soviet theater director Vsevolod Meyerhold, who later helped him enroll in the voice section of the State Institute for the Theatrical Arts.[101] By 1925, Kari-Yakubov and his wife, Tamara Khanum, an Uzbek-born ethnic Armenian dancer who was one of the first to break the Central Asian taboo against women performing on stage, had been sent to Europe to represent the USSR at the International Exhibition of Decorative Arts in Paris and at Schubert Hall in Berlin.[102]

After returning to Uzbekistan, Kari-Yakubov continued to successfully navigate the internal-external nexus of Soviet cultural politics. In accordance with domestic nation-building efforts, he founded an Uzbek Ethnographic Troupe that collected, recorded, and performed Uzbek folk songs.[103] In 1928 the troupe was shown official favor by being moved into the newly opened Uzbek State Musical Theatre in Samarkand, where they performed musicals

Figure 4.3 Poster for Kari-Yakubov's 1927 performance of Uzbek popular music in an "Ethnographic Concert" at the Uzbek State Musical Theater organized by the Commissariat of Enlightenment of the UzSSR. From the archive of Gafur Ghulam Press.

such as *Leila and Majnun, Arshin Mal Alan,* and *Farhad and Shirin,* an opera attended by the Arab delegation.[104] This timely transition from Uzbek classical and folk music to opera likely spared Kari-Yakubov during earlier repressions of "classical Uzbek" music in the 1930s.[105] His interwar success illustrates the workings of the Eastern International in the sense that Soviet imperatives to showcase domestic diversity abroad created opportunities for talented and willing representatives of the "domestic East."

In the late 1940s, however, artistic and musical spheres were once again under scrutiny. Thus 'Ayyad's characterization of Kari-Yakubov's behavior, by way of VOKS, reverberated all the way up the party's Foreign Relations structure to Mikhail Suslov.[106] It is unclear if this report had any specific consequences for the singer, but such negative attention was certainly dangerous. Later that year, a special party commission dispatched from Moscow to Uzbekistan uncovered "serious deficiencies in the work of the Uzbek Central Committee as well as the local and oblast' party organs with respect to literature and art."[107] In 1948–1949, another delegation of Moscow-based TsK VKP(b) "cultural workers" alleged that Uzbek musicians were engaged in nationalist deviation through performance of classical Central Asian music that glorified the region's "feudal past."[108] A new wave of purges in 1950–1952 targeted those suspected of "popularizing archaism," "pre-revolutionary poetry and Music," or of trying to "isolate (*zamknut'*) Uzbek culture and tear it away from the Union."[109] Significantly, the Central Committee also clarified in 1951 that its condemnation of operas, ballets, and musicals "composed on the basis of classical compositions" did not apply to the Russian classical tradition.[110] Leaders of each national republic's union of composers were expected to attend meetings in Leningrad. The goal of the meetings was clear: "Russian composers were to supervise musical composition, to assure continued literal and figurative harmony. Even notes and chords on 'national' instruments were expected to adopt European forms" by conforming to the conventions of Russian high culture.[111]

The Uzbek classical and "folk" music to which Kari-Yakubov had dedicated his life was suddenly recharacterized as bleak, dreary, archaic, and incompatible with the "spirit of the new Soviet reality."[112] A decade earlier, Persian-speaking Central Asian poets Mirzo Turson-zade had called it a travesty that party officials had labeled Shashmaqam "music composed for the Emir" and refused to support musicians who could play it. In 1939, Turson-zade and a handful of other intellectuals were able to stand their ground.[113] Similar debates in the 1950s had different results. In 1952, Kari-Yakubov was arrested for "bourgeois nationalism" and sentenced to twenty-five years in a labor camp, serving three years before his rehabilitation in 1955.[114]

The Arab delegation was certainly aware during their visit of some of repressions in the cultural sector. At the Union of Soviet Writers, Ra'if Khuri, Kamil 'Ayyad, and Antun Tabit spoke with playwrights and novelists Konstantin Simonov, Vsevolod Vishnevsky, and Leonid Leonov about the "overly narrow" definition of socialist realism as well as the official censure of satirist Mikhail Zoshchenko, which had sent a powerful message to intellectuals about conformity to the new party line.[115] They did not bring up the case of poet Anna Akhmatova, who was censured in the same 1946 statement by Zhdanov. The male-dominated world of Syrian and Lebanese intellectuals was often dismissive of exceptional female members, including Imili Faris Ibrahim. Unsubstantiated rumors circulated that it was her lover Khuri, not her, who really wrote her articles.[116] These gender dynamics might help explain why the group focused more on Zoshchenko and ignored Akhmatova, whom Zhdanov called a "half harlot, half nun" on the day she was expelled from the Writers Union.[117]

The delegates could not have foreseen the fates of Kari-Yakubov or Solomon Lozovskii, whom they met twice during their visit and who were executed in 1952 in the purge of the Jewish Anti-Fascist Committee.[118] Yet their interest in Zoshchenko, but not the anticosmopolitan forces that led to the repression of Lozovskii and especially Kari-Yakubov, helped conceal an important contradiction in late Stalinist cultural policies. During this trip and afterward, the delegates were aware of repressions of prominent intellectuals in Moscow; yet they ignored Soviet efforts to articulate a russocentric agenda in the arts by suppressing "national" deviations and molding indigenous folklore into more familiar Western forms.[119] Their compromises seemed like milder versions of those made by Soviet intellectuals. Ilya Ehrenburg, with whom Khuri and Tabit drank peppered vodka, was the only member of the Jewish Anti-Fascist Committee whom Stalin allowed to survive unscathed. Staying alive required that he ignore the repressions of many of his Jewish friends while he continued to represent the Soviet Union at international conferences.[120] It meant concealing the politics of anticosmopolitanism and its cultural implications for Jews, Central Asians, and other intellectuals that Arab intellectuals had come to admire.

Silences about Soviet treatment of cosmopolitanism and cultural nationalism were quickly filled by an onslaught of new Soviet images of Central Asia. As head of the Sovinformburo, Lozovskii had promoted images and narratives of Central Asia abroad as part of a wider cosmopolitan showcase of the superiority of "Soviet democracy" that allowed former colonized peoples to participate in the Union's governance. Under the new Zhdanov cultural doctrine of the late 1940s, the Sovinformburo shifted its coverage toward Central Asia as an alternative to Moscow- and Leningrad-based high culture of urban educated Soviet elites, for whom "Jewish and Russian [identity] were virtually interchangeable."[121] The "domestic East" came to represent a new kind of subject free of the "cosmopolitan" visual cues of the Moscow and Leningrad scene. Sovinformburo articles destined for Tehran, Beirut, Cairo, Istanbul, and Kabul more bluntly trumpeted "the advantages of the Soviet resolution of the national question in the USSR."[122] Soviet radio broadcasts destined for the Arab world described the "accomplishments" of the domestic East in abstract or numerical terms, avoiding any mention of ongoing purges or debates about the acceptable parameters of "national" cultures.[123]

Later descriptions of the Soviet Union by Syrian and Lebanese delegates also helped to marginalize the repressive nature of russocentric anticosmopolitanism. This is because Arab intellectuals faced multiple barriers to engagement with late-Stalinist russocentrism. The idea of Russians as a state-bearing people who were not entitled to their own national party organization was confusing. Not only did it baffle Soviet party officials, but it must have seemed even more illogical to anticolonial nationalists.[124] Moreover, *al-Tariq* writers credited the Soviet triumph in World War II in part to a triumph of culture against "barbarous" fascism. Ra'if Khuri described a Soviet parade of confiscated German weapons that he witnessed during his 1947 visit:

> These [confiscated] infernal weapons and those who drove them from among the colonizing invaders [were] used to occupy the house of Tolstoy in Yasnaya Poliana and to use the remains of this great immortal writer as firewood to heat water to wash their legs; these weapons ... displayed all broken like transient nothings ... mean that this state must be a true state (*watan*) of culture.[125]

For Khuri, the war against German Nazism and Italian Fascism was thus not only a struggle for territories but, as historian Götz Nordbruch argues, "for the survival of society and culture as such."[126] The main symbols of this culture were Russian classics, which made it more difficult to appreciate the russocentric dimensions of late-Stalinist cultural repressions and their complexity across the different regions of the USSR.[127] If the Soviet Union was most useful to Arab intellectuals, historian Sana Tannoury-Karam argues, as a model of a "developed, progressive, and modern East that socialism had equipped with the tools to defeat the strongest western powers," then the repressive cultural terrain of postwar Stalinism could only compromise the USSR's symbolic value.[128]

Arab intellectuals also had few useful frameworks by which to think about difference inside the USSR. For instance, in *I Return from Moscow* (*Ana 'a'id min Musku*, 1948), George Hanna—who never even wanted to go to Uzbekistan—simply ignored such differences, claiming that "everything I described about life and society in Moscow and Leningrad was found in Uzbekistan and in every republic of the Soviet Republics, a true copy of the Soviet system in all its aspects."[129] The few differences he did note were superficial. Female students wore "ethnic" (*'irqiyya*) clothes but "enjoyed the same opportunities as any Russian girl."[130] Uzbek men wore clothing similar to that of Syrian fellaheen, and houses in old Tashkent resembled those in the Syrian countryside.[131] Such descriptions of Central Asia contrast starkly with Hanna's longer and more analytical chapters about Soviet democracy and the political legitimacy conferred on a one-party regime by a party that included over 7 million members out of a population of 200 million.[132]

A third challenge may have been the absence of alternative information. As Hanna confided to his readers, "all I knew of Tashkent was that it was located in the heart of Asia and that it had once been a great civilization that lost its landmarks and became ignorant, its inhabitants became illiterate, and its civilization drew closer to the civilization of the first ages of barbarism, satisfied with slavery and not aspiring to progress and liberation."[133] This ignorance partly derived from the Soviet state's decades-long monopolization of information produced about Central Asia and its history. Indeed, the only historical narrative mentioned by Hanna was a vague description of the Uzbek opera *Biran*—which he claimed "depicted exploitation by the Tsarist regime in Uzbekistan"—a description that omitted the opera's main focus on the 1916 uprising by a union of Uzbek farmers and Russian workers.[134] If Hanna had any other observations of Tashkent, including any from Turkish or Arabic sources, they were not mentioned in his account.

A final challenge was that Lebanese and Syrian writers were clearly conscious of emerging Cold War ideological pressures, which likely made them more cautious in their published reflections about the USSR than they had been during the trip itself. In their published works Hanna, Khuri, and Tabit chose to stay within the parameters of Soviet narratives. Their choices in this regard were likely shaped as much by their ambitions to maintain access to the Soviet Union as by their previous commitments to antifascism, anticapitalism, and anticolonialism.[135]

In late 1947, engagements of Syrian and Lebanese leftists with the Soviet Union were transformed by the unexpected proclamation of Soviet support for the partition of Palestine, announced eight months after the delegation's visit. This decision and Andrei Gromyko's reasoning that it met "core national interests not only of Jews but also of Arabs" shocked Lebanese and Syrian communists, leftists, and the wider public more than the Molotov-Ribbentrop Pact.[136] Prominent communists who disagreed with the decision, such as Hashim al-Amin, Rashad 'Isa, and Qadri Qal'aji, left the party. During the war, Qal'aji had written extensively about the Soviet Union, including about Soviet nationalities policies and their misuse by "enemies of the Soviet System."[137] After 1948, in contrast, he wrote more about his disillusionment and regret over the time he spent in the party.[138] Farjallah al-Hilu, who argued that the party "should at least express disappointment with the Soviet position," was silenced.[139] For the Syrian branch of the party, this turmoil was compounded by a new wave of anticommunist repressions following the 1949 coup by Husni al-Za'im.[140]

Non-communists such as Ra'if Khuri, who had mostly been committed to Palestine since his time there in the late 1930s, also broke with his former comrades and their press. Ironically, although Khuri had never been a member of the Party, he was essentially expelled from its circles and labeled a "Titoist" by Lebanese communists, a charge echoed by the Soviet Union.[141] Throughout his estrangement, Khuri remained an important theorist of literary commitment and advocate for the importance of individual freedom.[142] This vantage point, he argued, allowed for literature critical of the state—a shift from his pre-partition admiration of the Soviet "cultural state."[143] Eventually he and former communists Imili Fais Ibrahim, Qadri Qil'aji, Maurice Kamel, and Hashim al-Amin formed a new group called the "Brothers of Omar Fakhoury" that published a weekly cultural magazine dedicated to literature, heritage, and culture.

Kamil 'Ayyad, along with Jamil Saliba and Anwar Nu'man, also protested Soviet support for the partition by dissolving the Society of Friendship with the Soviet Union on December 17, 1947. As they explained in the Damascene newspaper *Alif Ba*:

> The Society was created during conditions of the last war [and was] encouraged by the position of the Soviet Union in the Security Council on the questions of Syria and Lebanon, and Egypt. . . . The members of the Society regret and condemn the position of the Soviet Union siding with imperialists in support of the partition.[144]

Communist delegate Fawzi Shulaq tried to keep the Society alive by assuming the leadership of a competing faction, but the Lebanese government shut it down.[145] The shift in public opinion was palpable, as protestors attacked the Party's headquarters in Damascus and Beirut and the Syrian branch headquarters of the Society of Friendship.[146]

Those who wanted to maintain their relationship with the Soviet Union had to join new institutions. In 1948 the Cominform launched a Partisans of Peace movement at the International Congress of Intellectuals in Poland, which was designed to convene thinkers around commitments to universal disarmament and peace. By 1949, meetings of this group had attracted over 50,000 in Syria and over 40,000 in Lebanon, according to Soviet sources.[147] Antun Tabit re-emerged as the Lebanese spokesman at the 1949 Congress of the Partisans of Peace in Paris, voicing opposition against NATO and the dangers of the "Crescent Pact" in the Middle East—the plan by Iraqi prime minister Nuri Said to lead the Arab world after uniting Iraq with Syria, Jordan, and Lebanon.[148]

In 1950, Tabit and Hanna participated in the Partisans' Second Congress in Warsaw, where they spoke against the atomic and hydrogen bombs and reconnected with their 1947 acquaintances Ilya Ehrenburg and Mohamed Kamal al-Bindari, as well as fellow travelers W. E. B. Du Bois and Paul Robeson, both African Americans. At that congress, *al-Tariq* received the Gold Medal of Peace, the highest honor given by the World Peace Council. In 1955, Tabit and Hanna returned to Moscow as part of a Partisans of Peace delegation of Syrian artists and journalists, cohosted by the Soviet Peace Committee and VOKS, and continued to be active in the movement. After Tabit's death, his wife recalled that later in life he continued to regard the Soviet Union as "a symbol of hope for progressive humanity."[149] For him and other Arab intellectuals, the Soviet Union's ongoing support for culture and literature, including for Arab publications and writers, continued to nurture a sense of belonging and an attraction to its cultural sphere.

George Hanna was treated as a literary celebrity, perhaps even more in the Soviet Union than in Lebanon. His short stories and articles were translated into Russian, Turkmen, and Ukrainian and featured on Moscow Radio.[150] In 1954 he was invited to Moscow to participate in the Second Congress of Soviet Writers, where he and Iraqi-born Lebanese communist Husayn Muruwwa were inspired by the idea of a writer's responsibility to reveal social problems. Hanna seemed flattered to be asked to participate in a "conference of readers" that was helping Soviet literature reach its "desired humanistic goals" for which Tolstoy, Turgenev, Pushkin, Gogol, Chekhov, and Dostoevsky had all strived.[151] He clearly enjoyed the parties he attended with Muruwwa and Syrian writer Muwahab al-Kayyali, whose work was also aired on Moscow radio. Muruwwa's commitment to communism deepened in 1948 after he witnessed the discipline and integrity of Iraqi communist activists in the *wathbah* protests against the Anglo-Iraqi agreement. Many perceived this agreement as a treaty of national surrender and renewed colonial relations.[152] Hanna's second book about the Soviet Union, *In Moscow a Second Time* (*Fi musku marrah thaniyya*, 1954), described these encounters in a world in which Soviet people still saw Stalin "as a symbol of a great revival that had surprised the world." Books were still cheaper than radishes, and culture and science could not be bought as they could be in the West.[153] Perhaps, however, the currency of this world was just different. By the late 1950s, Hanna's literary celebrity in the Soviet Union was underscored by his embrace as a "representative of Lebanese literature" alongside much more famous writers such as Khalil Gibran, Amin al-Rihani, and Salma al-Sayegh. This recognition, in turn, was celebrated in Lebanese intellectual journals such as *al-Thaqafa al-Wataniyya*, as an acknowledgment of the growing political importance of Arab countries and their culture after decolonization.[154] Literary celebrity was his reward for continued collaboration.

In the late 1950s, during de-Stalinization, Hanna had new opportunities to solidify his belonging in this transregional intellectual world by rewriting the history of cultural relations between the Soviet Union and the Arab world. As head of the reconstituted Society of Cultural Relations between Lebanon and the USSR, he wrote in the Soviet Orientalist journal *Sovremennyi Vostok* that cultural ties between the USSR and the Arab world had been "virtually nonexistent" before the Twentieth Party Congress in 1956. Specifically, the Society of Friendship, founded in Lebanon by 'Umar Fakhuri, had existed "for less than two years before being closed down by the Lebanese government."[155] His new, de-Stalinized version of the past for Soviet audiences omitted references to his 1947 visit and subsequent ones in the early 1950s.[156] Writing from within the new narrative parameters of the de-Stalinizing state, perhaps he did not want to lose the sense of belonging to this world and its broader sphere of socialist humanism.[157] This required rewriting his own past to erase the inconvenient history of 1940s connections and help to clear the slate for the flourishing of Soviet contacts with the Arab world in the late 1950s.

By contrast, for Lebanese leftist audiences, these connections of the 1940s continued to be included in a wider history of local progressive struggle against fascism and colonialism and their advocacy for peace, independence, and Afro-Asian solidarity. Hanna's 1969 obituary in *al-Tariq*, written by Muhammad Dakrub, spoke openly about the 1947 trip. Yet its significance, along with that of Soviet-Arab friendship, had been reinterpreted in more nationalist terms. To do this, Dakrub quoted Hanna's article written in celebration of the fiftieth anniversary of the October Revolution, published just after the 1967 war in the November–December issue of *al-Tariq*. "For us Arabs, generations have passed and Western colonial countries play and do what they want with us. . . . If we join the Soviet Union in celebrating the golden anniversary of October, we express gratitude to a country that never missed an occasion to support us against those who try to deprive us of our rights."[158] Reflecting on the October Revolution in 1969, he felt that Beirut still had an opportunity "to discover the horizon of a bright future . . . in which colonial capital no longer governs the country's economy and its people."[159] The Lebanese Left was a diverse field that drew on multiple sources for anticolonial critique, including the European New Left and the examples of the Chinese, Algerian, Cuban, and Vietnamese revolutions. In this context it was all the more important to highlight the historical continuities of Soviet state support for Arabs, including in the 1940s.[160] This interpretation—which downplayed inconvenient moments of late Stalin-era repressions, including the Soviet Union's quasi-imperial policies in its domestic East and Soviet support for Israel—protected the USSR as a potent symbol of liberation. Such symbols of hope, and Soviet political and economic support, remained useful to communists, leftists, and anticolonial nationalists engaged in the project of "worldmaking after empire," as they faced the legacies of imperial hierarchy in their domestic politics and in the international order.[161]

Despite their erasure from official Cold War narratives, cultural encounters between the Soviet domestic and foreign Easts in the 1940s suggest that the Eastern International and its underlying assumptions about the affinity of various Easts—for the Soviets, the domestic and foreign Easts; for the Syrians and Lebanese intellectuals, of their postcolonial states and the Soviet Union as a "new world radiating from the East"—were highly resilient and adaptive. Assumptions that these regions shared a connection persisted throughout major shifts of international relations and Soviet domestic politics. These shifts included World War II, decolonization, Soviet support for the creation of the state of Israel, and the late Stalinist turn toward greater isolation, domestic russocentrism, cultural Westernization, and enigmatic repression in the Soviet cultural sphere. They withstood the independence of Syria and Lebanon and the redefinition of Central Asia from an example of the superiority of the Soviet federal "democratic" model to a symbol of a peripheral alternative to the cosmopolitan cultural subjects of Moscow and Leningrad.[162] This adaptability was aided, in part, by a limited Soviet expert knowledge about the Arab world, the whitewashing of Russia's imperial past, and the ability to abstract various fields of geography and culture as "Eastern."

The energy and compromises of leftist intellectuals in Lebanon and Syria also made this continuity possible, at least in part. Their search for a decolonized national culture, a better world, and better conditions for themselves as intellectuals continued to draw them to the USSR as an alternative to the capitalist West. At times, this attraction may have led them to imbue Soviet texts, images, and films with their own meanings.[163] Many knew enough about the USSR to translate or write articles and even produce book-length monographs about their experiences in it. The profound disappointment with the Soviet Union's support of the partition of Palestine split the ranks of the regional Arab Left, forcing some to reassess their relationship with the emerging Cold War power, at least until the Soviet Union's clear intervention on the side of Egypt during the Suez Crisis of 1956. This intervention, and the foundational relationships cultivated before 1948, may have led Ra'if Khuri to continue to hope that the Soviet Union would intervene on behalf of the Arabs in the 1967 war despite his growing alienated from organized communism.[164] Meanwhile, those leftists who chose to remain within the fold of Soviet-supported political and cultural activism had new opportunities to travel and participate in Partisans of Peace, Afro-Asian, and other literary events in Moscow, Tashkent, Baku, Cairo, and Beirut. In these spaces they rebuilt their networks around shared interests in literary commitment to social justice.[165]

Perhaps they felt, like Pan-Africanist author George Padmore, that Soviet support for anti-imperialist and antiracist struggles outweighed the system's flaws.[166] In the late 1940s and 1950s, the Soviet approach to ethnic difference contrasted with persistent racial discrimination in other parts of the British colonial empire and especially in the United States.[167] Although race was less of an explicit concern for leftist intellectuals in Syria and Lebanon, they still found comfort in belonging to "something bigger" during this unstable period of state formation, when Syrian politics was punctuated by four military coups between 1949 and 1954, and five different governments rose and fell in Iraq between 1948 and 1952. They were still flattered by the attention showered upon them in the Soviet Union, as were European intellectuals who had visited Soviet Russia in the 1920s and 1930s, and by the recognition of Arab culture in the form of Russian translations and prizes at international meetings. Perhaps they were motivated by other concerns held close to the heart.[168] The 1947 visit is just one significant example of how the powerful intellectual pull of Soviet communism continued to bring together the two Easts, and through them the politics of national and colonial problems, all the while concealing their most egregious contradictions.

5
Decolonization and the Thaw

As waves of decolonization across Africa and Asia transformed the international system, the Eastern International was once again adapted to new opportunities and challenges. The 1955 Bandung Conference, the Algerian War, and the Suez War provided new models of liberation but each highlighted the associations between revolutionary statism and Pan-Arabism. On this new terrain, decolonizing states sought to monopolize culture in the service of postcolonial nationalism that celebrated collective liberation from foreign rule.[1] In Egypt, writer Yusuf al-Siba'i presided over state efforts to achieve and maintain a state monopoly on culture and expand its influence in the Afro-Asian world. He headed such institutions as the Association of Men of Letters (founded in 1955), which operated as the Egyptian branch of the Congress of Arab Writers. He also played a leading role in the 1957 Cairo Afro-Asian conference, which drew some 500 delegates from some forty-three Asian solidarity committees, and was chosen by Nasser in 1958 to be the general secretary of Afro-Asian People's Solidarity Organization.[2] Many Arab intellectuals embraced the new Pan-Arab state as representative of the Arab cause. Supporters of Egypt and of intellectuals' responsibility to defend its postcolonial state included the 1947 VOKS visitor George Hanna. Even Ra'if Khuri, who had cautioned his readers in 1953–1954 that the Arab state might present a threat to intellectual freedom, agreed by 1957 that "if someone is an Arab, whether his specific country is Syria, Iraq, Saudi Arabia, Palestine, Jordan, or North Africa, he is obliged to love Egypt."[3]

The emergence in the 1950s of more powerful decolonizing pan-Arab states, such as Egypt, brought new challenges for the Eastern International. The fact that such states usually approached domestic communists as political opponents raised difficult questions. Pitting different factions of Soviet political and intellectual elites against one another, these questions exposed frictions between Soviet institutions designed to support the international communist movement and those designed for more conventional inter-state diplomacy.

The simultaneous expansion of global competition between the two superpowers raised the stakes for responding to such international challenges. For the United States, this expansion also meant reckoning with the contradictions between its ideology of democracy and its domestic racial politics. The Truman and Eisenhower administrations adopted a more pro–civil rights posture as part of the United States' international agenda to contain communism. These international concerns paved the way for landmark achievements of the civil rights movement such as the *Brown v. Board of Education* (1954) Supreme Court decision that outlawed school segregation and the use of federal troops to support its implementation in Little Rock, Arkansas, in 1957.[4] Such achievements were touted by US government publications abroad as evidence of "progress," even as activists such as Paul Robeson and W. E. B. Du Bois learned that McCarthyism dictated that any racial critiques of racial politics that were broadened to include the behavior of European colonial powers—America's Cold War allies—were deemed "un-American" and punished.[5]

Likewise, in the Soviet Union, competition for influence drew attention to domestic inequality. The majority of British and American journalists, academics, and politicians exploited the underdeveloped domestic East as evidence of Soviet colonial oppression of Muslims.[6] By way of exception, some French politicians and scholars in the 1940s and 1940s had considered whether the Soviet system could be adapted to assuage national aspirations and allow France to maintain control over its empire.[7] Yet such views became less popular after defeats in Algeria and Indo-China damaged French prestige. For Soviet leaders, challenging the more hostile of these 'Western' narratives meant transforming Central Asia into what historian Artemy Kalinovsky calls a "laboratory of Soviet development" and historian Paul Stronski calls a model of "how socialism could assist 'less developed' or even 'backwards' societies in advancing out of poverty and colonialism."[8] This required restructuring the relationship between Soviet leaders in Moscow and Central Asia and engaging with questions similar to those in the United States.

In these adjustments, culture became a more important tool of domestic and especially international policy than it had previously been in Soviet history. Inserting himself into the contradictory cultural politics of the Eastern International was a new Soviet intermediary. Uzbek politician Nuriddin Mukhitdinov (1917–2008) rose up the party hierarchy to become in 1957 a full member in the Moscow Politburo, the highest policymaking authority within the Soviet Union. His skillful navigation of the Soviet Eastern International as a nexus of domestic affirmative action and Soviet international ambitions allowed him to achieve a level of power unattainable for any other marginalized "minority" representing a Cold War superpower, including any Muslim from China or any African American cultural or political ambassador from the United States.[9] His role within and outside the Soviet Union was to engage the emerging decolonizing world, to use Soviet Central Asian culture to correct perceptions of Russian dominance within the Soviet Union, and to challenge Cold War–era notions that colonialism persisted in the form of socialism.

At the peak of global decolonization, from the second half of the 1950s until the early 1960s, the Soviet Union experienced what came to be called the "Thaw." This tumultuous period, named after a 1954 novella by Ilya Ehrenburg, was characterized by a loosening of cultural regulations, ideological and institutional de-Stalinization, and contacts with the outside world. In this period, Soviet power was reconfigured in relation to Central Asia and to the Arab world.

In Leningrad and Moscow, a mostly Western-oriented intelligentsia became voracious consumers of Western European and American writers, published in translation in magazines such as *Inostrannaia literatura* (*Foreign Literature*).[10] Literary scholar Rossen Djagalov observes that these intelligentsia remained decidedly less interested in texts, ideas, and cultural production from decolonizing Asia and Africa. The intelligentsia's earlier Enlightenment impulse to make culture accessible to all was replaced by a more elitist, Eurocentric conception of culture as an exclusive tradition accessible only to a chosen few. Nevertheless, Djagalov notes, *Foreign Literature* and other Soviet cultural bureaucracies continued to support Afro-Asian literature even "at the expense of reader interest."[11]

Beyond these cities, Afro-Asian "contact zones" fostered the circulation of Soviet culture in the Third World and Afro-Asian culture in the USSR through, for example, translations of texts and festivals for Afro-Asian writers and filmmakers, often organized in Central Asia.[12] Media scholar Masha Salazkina argues that these exchanges extended "affinities and intimacies across postcolonial Asia, Africa and Latin America."[13] These exchanges contributed to world-literature and world-cinema projects, as well as to Anglo-American postcolonial theory.[14] As brokers of these exchanges, Central Asian political leaders also empowered themselves to negotiate economic and cultural modernization in their republics, carving out new openings and opportunities for themselves and those whose interests they represented.[15]

The most powerful political decision maker at the time, Nikita Khrushchev, was also in many ways an antithesis of the Moscow- and Leningrad-based elites who have been the focus of scholars interested in the cultural history and politics of the Thaw. Born to illiterate peasants near the Ukrainian border, he shared the fate of many Soviet political leaders who started out as peasants or workers and then climbed the party ranks. Yet he never sought to distance himself from his roots. He withstood ridicule from Stalin for being a country bumpkin and from Western statesmen for being crude, and then succeeded in pushing from power all of his better-prepared and more high-brow colleagues.[16] This generation of former peasants who became the USSR's new political and administrative elite thought about culture in more flexible ways than did the metropolitan elites.[17]

It was Khrushchev and this new political elite that set the course of Soviet domestic and foreign cultural policy, sparking the greatest expansion yet of the Eastern International, as measured by density of contacts, linkages, and exchanges with the decolonizing Afro-Asian world. Khrushchev initiated these transformations at the Twentieth Party Congress in 1956, where he initially shifted Soviet foreign policy to embrace "peaceful coexistence" with the United States. This strategy revived and reinterpreted Lenin's earlier doctrine of peaceful coexistence between capitalism and socialism. Khrushchev's version still envisioned a global class struggle leading to an eventual disappearance of capitalism but, faced with the new threat of thermonuclear war, Khrushchev and the party spoke of a collective "mankind." Peaceful coexistence was a way of protecting mankind from destruction while diverting resources spent on the Soviet war machine to goals of domestic socialist construction.[18]

This shift inevitably raised questions. The Chinese Communist Party was reeling from Khrushchev's denunciation of Stalin's cult of personality and publicized their concerns about Soviet commitments to anti-imperialist politics in Africa and Asia.[19] China argued that Soviet revisionism would undermine national liberation movements, and representatives of Guinea, Algeria, Ghana, and Indonesia would come to agree with this argument.[20] Eventually, the Soviet Union's role as leader of the communist world would be openly challenged, first by Tito and then by Mao, to whom Stalin had conceded a kind of global "division of labor" whereby the Soviet Union would be the center of international proletarian revolution while China would promote "Eastern revolution."[21] Khrushchev's Secret Speech and his decision to dissolve the Cominform alliance of Western communist parties undermined the structure of communist internationalism. Khrushchev placed emphasis on other forms of "Eastern bloc" coherence, embodied in the Council for Mutual Economic Assistance (COMECON), established in 1949, and the Warsaw Pact, established in 1955.[22] His relationship with countries of the Afro-Asian bloc remained more haphazard and diffuse.

When Khrushchev's anti-imperialist legitimacy was challenged, he redoubled his support for revolutionary nationalism. In the late 1950s and early 1960s, this meant extending economic and political aid to such decolonizing states as India, Burma, Afghanistan, Egypt, and Syria. According to US State Department estimates, the "Middle East" received the largest amount of Soviet economic aid, followed by South Asia and Latin America, with Africa and East Asia trailing far behind. Occasionally, Khrushchev's revolutionary nationalism meant issuing nuclear threats that brought the world to the brink of war—something that he believed was ultimately impossible, given its catastrophic consequences.

Supporting revolutionary nationalist regimes like Egypt and Syria required sacrificing the interests of local communists and leftist intellectuals, who were left vulnerable to violent repressions. Within a year of the 1952 Egyptian revolution, for example, communists were pleading with Moscow for support and claiming that Nasser's regime treated communists more viciously than its predecessor.[23] During the political union of Egypt and Syria from 1958 to 1961, Nasser escalated his repressive measures, undertaking mass arrests of Egyptian and Syrian communists, disbanding the Syrian Communist Party, and closing communist and pro-communist media. At the 1959 CPSU Congress, Khrushchev called Nasser's measures "reactionary" and "naïve," but the arrests continued.[24] Within Egypt, these repressive measures made intellectuals more reluctant to contribute to the revolution.[25] As frictions between the USSR and Egypt escalated, mainly over the treatment of communists, Khrushchev was forced to choose between Egyptian communists and respect for Egypt's postcolonial sovereignty.[26] The sacrifices were often painful. In 1959, Lebanese communist Farjallah al-Hilu, who had visited the USSR and authored *A New Humanity Building a New World* (1937), was tortured to death in Syria, which was then under Nasser's control.

He had been on assignment to investigate the situation of other communists on orders of Khalid Bakdash. The decision about how to respond to such news would anticipate similar challenges presented by the leaders of Syria, Iraq, and other revolutionary postcolonial regimes.

Soviet ideologists and policymakers working with radical anti-Western regimes were under pressure. The internal debate over what to do about local communists fell roughly into two camps. The "party" position—a concern that Khrushchev's policies had unjustly abandoned local communists—had been articulated by Mikhail Suslov, Boris Ponomarev, and Rostislav Ulianovskii in the Central Committee International Department (ID), as well as by Bobojon Ghafurov, who was then in the Institute for the Study of the Peoples of Asia. The statist "non-party" position—that a country newly liberated from colonial rule could initially set its own course toward communism—was supported by the Ministry of Foreign Affairs and scholars at the Institute of World Economics and International Relations. The difference roughly correlated with the ID's and Foreign Ministry's competing styles of operation—the former through international communist parties and the latter through foreign state institutions interested in normalizing governmental relations.[27] It reprised earlier tensions between the Comintern and the Ministry of Foreign Affairs, except that in the new era of decolonization, anticommunism was no longer a purely Western or even imperialist phenomenon.[28] In practice, however, this division was not always clear.

The non-party orientation prevailed, and a new theory of "revolutionary democracy" was articulated by experts on Arab affairs such as Georgi Mirskii and, eventually, even Evgenii Primakov.[29] This new theory maintained that in underdeveloped counties, where the proletariat and the bourgeoisie were still weak, petit-bourgeois elements such as lower-ranking military officers and the intelligentsia could constitute a true "revolutionary democratic" force capable of leading their countries to socialism.[30] This theory, as Primakov put it, was meant to "bolster radical regimes in the Middle East and stop local communist parties from attacking them."[31] It emphasized statist concerns of non-capitalist development; wide-scale nationalization of the means of production, or putting the economy in state hands; and the establishment of political parties or unions under the banner of socialism. Naturally, this new approach created obstacles for local communists.[32] By 1965 the Egyptian Communist Party was persuaded to dissolve itself and tell its members to join the ruling Arab Socialist Union, while Iraqi communists were pressured in 1972 to accommodate the Ba'athist regime.[33] Syrian communist Khalid

Bakdash called the theory a "retreat bordering on revisionism."[34] Moscow's initial reactions to the Syrian Ba'athists after they seized power in March 1963 was shaped by the negative impression that they supported their Iraqi counterparts' policy of violent persecution of communists. This impression shifted, thanks to the revolutionary democracy theory and Evgenii Primakov's nuanced coverage of the Ba'ath's progressive and reactionary wings for *Pravda*.[35] Memos about the situation in Syria to Soviet leaders such as Suslov began to explain cynically that the Syrian communist party had "decided" to support the social-economic transformations.[36] In retrospect, Primakov admitted that, "although the Soviet leadership of the 1950 and 1960s was inclined to support the Arab countries' local communist parties, nothing could mask the reality that communism was a lost cause in the Middle East."[37]

Khrushchev's answer to the conflicting imperatives of perpetual peace, the historical mission of communism, and commitments to anticolonial causes was to activate the robust apparatus of cultural diplomacy.[38] The unsettling compromise of ignoring the plight of Arab communists so as not to alienate incumbent revolutionary regimes was whitewashed with exchanges of amicable official delegations, tourism, and stipends for international students to study at Soviet universities. This work was still coordinated by the Union of Soviet Societies of Friendship and Cultural Ties with Foreign Countries, with the aid of the Soviet Committee for Solidarity with Asia and Africa (SKSSAA), the International Department of the CPSU, and the Ministry of Culture. Their different programs created multiple and overlapping networks of cultural, educational, and economic exchanges that drew Arab leftists and Soviet Central Asians into foreign affairs.

Beyond the borders of the Soviet state, networks of cultural exchange that had developed in the 1940s continued to interpret and promote Soviet foreign policy. Editors and writers of Lebanese leftist publications *al-Tariq* and *al-Thaqafa al-Wataniyya* repackaged the new doctrine of Peaceful Coexistence as support for peaceful Arab independence by emphasizing the violence of interwar imperialism and of the emerging postwar neo-imperialism. New alliances such as the Baghdad Pact and the proliferation of American military bases, according to an editor of *al-Thaqafa al-Wataniyya*, required a global front of opposition.[39] Antun Tabit aligned Soviet Peaceful Coexistence with the Cairo Afro-Asian Solidarity Conference's endorsement of freedom, progress, and peace in *al-Tariq*.[40] Others emphasized the Soviet Union's record of opposing European colonial exploitation by publishing

World War I secret treaties and by "peacefully" opposing the 1955 Baghdad Pact, the 1956 Tripartite Aggression, and the Eisenhower Doctrine.

Within the Soviet Union, Uzbek politician Nuriddin Mukhitdinov also invoked the history of internationalism in his call to reimagine the new global anti-imperialist "front." At the Twenty-first Congress of the CPSU (1959) in Moscow, he spoke about "the peoples of the East forming their own front in relation to the imperialist front."[41] It echoed (almost nostalgically) Troianovskii's definition of the Eastern International as a "united anti-imperialist democratic front that could oppose the Western international of capital."[42] Mukhitdinov would often take the initiative to reconnect the domestic and foreign components of the Eastern International during this new era of global decolonization.

Khrushchev and Stalin had had different concepts of security with regard to the decolonizing world. Stalin's foreign affairs minister Maxim Litvinov once risked his career when he deplored the Kremlin's postwar "conservative" adherence to the idea of security in terms of square miles.[43] Likewise, Stalin in his last decade may have been driven by the fear of another invasion from the West, presumably by a revived Germany bent on revenge and perhaps backed by other capitalist powers.[44] To prevent this, he extended Soviet borders to the line of 1941, which meant retaining control over the Baltic states, Western Ukraine, Belorussia, and Bessarabia—all of which Russia had lost after World War I and repossessed in 1939–1941— and adding new territory in Northern Bukovina.[45] In East Asia, Soviet planners tried to regain territories and privileges lost to Japan in 1904–1905 and to secure the rule of Kim Il-sung by supporting his attack against the US-supported regime in South Korea. In southwest borderlands, the Allies eventually foiled Stalin's efforts to build up an enclave in northern Iran and acquire a controlling influence over the Turkish straits.[46] The Arab world was too remote to enter into the security calculus of defensive expansionism.[47]

Despite some continuity in Soviet foreign relations ensured by Viacheslav Molotov's return to the Foreign Ministry (foreign minister 1939–1949, 1953–1956), by the mid-1950s it was difficult to ignore transformations in global geopolitics.[48] The decline of British and French power and the growth of anti-Western sympathies throughout the remaining colonies continued unabated. Nasser's consolidation of power in Egypt suggested that Stalin was perhaps too narrowly focused on national-bourgeois movements and had failed to see that transitions to socialism could take many forms. Elsewhere in the Middle East, US military and economic interests around existing and prospective oil fields had expanded, especially since World War II had highlighted the importance of oil for powering complex weapons systems.[49] The consolidation of efforts to contain Soviet power in the Middle East and Southeast Asia with the Baghdad and Manila Pacts created new challenges and opportunities.[50]

In this competitive context, the new Soviet administration had to be proactive.[51] The 1955 Bandung Conference, which brought together leaders of twenty-nine newly sovereign Asian and African countries to celebrate the demise of formal colonialism and to commit to a joint future struggle against imperialism, seemed like a perfect opportunity. Six of the twenty-nine participants had already been driven into military-economic arrangements with the United States and Britain by concerns about domestic communist parties and pressure from Soviet interests to the north. But Sukarno, Nehru, U Nu, and Nasser denounced all alliances that divided the world into a toxic Cold War.[52] Realizing that any potential new alliances negotiated or thwarted at this meeting would have lasting consequence for Soviet influence, the Soviet government issued a public statement on Middle East security days before the meeting. This statement reminded its participants that Western interests were trying to reduce Middle Eastern states "economically, to the status of colonies or dependent territories," and that the Soviet Union at its inception had repudiated unequal tsarist treaties.[53]

Molotov tried to secure an invitation to the conference for a Soviet delegation through formal and informal diplomatic channels, including one for observer rather than participant status. He had even selected a leader of this Soviet delegation, the chairman of the Council of Ministers of the Uzbek SSR, Nuriddin Mukhitdinov. But the invitation never came. At least one factor behind this rejection had been a campaign by anti-Soviet forces, represented by the SEATO bloc nations and led by the Philippines president Carlos Romulo, to prove that the Soviet Union "was not an Asian power."[54] In any event the Soviet Union was forced to rely on others to protect its interests at Bandung, including Chinese premier Zhou Enlai.[55]

US leaders were more skeptical than Soviet ones about the political potential of Bandung. US Secretary of State John Foster Dulles described Third World neutralism as an "obsolete . . . immoral and shortsighted conception." Efforts to recognize the importance of US representation at Bandung were led by New York Congressman Adam Clayton Powell Jr., a biracial former member of the Communist Party of America who worked with the NAACP on international issues.[56] Powell actually attended the conference as a private individual in defiance of State Department efforts to discourage him. There, he was joined by a handful of other Black Americans who were inspired by its call, including the novelist Richard Wright, who described the event in his 1956 book, *The Color Curtain*, as something "extra-political, extra-social, almost extra human."[57] At the meeting Powell delivered a speech that distorted reality in what the *African American* described as a "glowing picture of the racial situation in the United States."[58] Ironically, this effort, which annoyed Black American press commentators and was dismissed as "grandstanding," was still deeply uncomfortable to the State Department because it connected US domestic race relations with race as an international issue.[59]

Mukhitdinov did not experience Bandung but nonetheless took the initiative to emphasize its importance to his superiors.[60] Like Powell, he knew how to spot an opportunity. Mukhitdinov was an ethnic Uzbek born in 1917 outside Tashkent. He studied Arabic as part of his childhood religious education, joined the Komsomol, and was one of six Uzbek youth activists selected to study in Moscow at what he referred to as the Trade-Cooperative Institute.[61] There, he witnessed the show trial of Akmal Ikramov and Fayzulla Khodjaev, two prominent leaders of the Uzbek SSR purged for their association with right-opposition leaders Alexei Rykov and Nikolai Bukharin. Seeing them stand accused of treason, nationalism, and of trying to tear Uzbekistan away from the USSR left a powerful impression on the young man.[62]

Mukhitdinov's postwar career growth was "meteoric."[63] Having only formally joined the Communist Party during the war, in 1947 he became secretary for propaganda and agitation for the Namangan regional committee; in 1948 he became first secretary of the Namangan regional committee; in 1950 he was promoted to Central Committee secretary and also to first secretary of the prestigious Tashkent party organization; by 1951 he was chairman of the Council of Ministers and secretary for propaganda of the Uzbek SSR; and by 1955 he was first secretary of the Uzbek TsK, the highest position in Uzbekistan. In 1956 he become the first Central Asian candidate member of the Presidium of the union-wide CPSU; and in 1958 he joined the CPSU Secretariat.[64] During the 1959 visit to the USSR of US statesman Averell Harriman, Khrushchev spoke of Mukhitdinov as one of his possible

Figure 5.1 Mukhitdinov (left) and Nasser (right), 1958. From Ulugbek Alisherovich Mukhitdinov's family archive.

successors for the top job of general secretary of the Soviet Union.[65] Such a rapid career trajectory suggested a highly unusual combination of luck and talent for public speaking, political networking, and ideological innovation.

Mukhitdinov later recalled how his promotions coincided with international attention on Soviet Central Asia. Like Khrushchev, who always made time to read in translation what prominent US columnists were saying about him, Mukhitdinov enjoyed PR dossiers about himself.[66] He recalled foreign newspapers around the time of his transfer to Moscow asking such questions as, "How will Mukhitdinov—an Uzbek Muslim—reconcile his national and religious convictions with Marxist atheism and proletarian internationalism?" and suggesting that "Khrushchev is toying with the exploited Soviet peoples and through Mukhitdinov wants to forge a path to former colonial countries."[67] Mukhitdinov had the political wherewithal to exploit these headlines. For instance, he accompanied visiting foreign leaders such as Nasser on their tours of Uzbekistan and then interpreted their comments back to Khrushchev. After Jawaharlal Nehru's tour of Uzbek cities in June 1955, Mukhitdinov stressed Nehru's remarks that more attention needed to be paid to the historical connections between India, Uzbekistan, and other Central Asian republics.[68]

Pointing out flaws, such as Nehru's interlocutors' ignorance of the historical friendship between India and Central Asia, played on Khrushchev's own anxiety about the Soviet Union's capacity to understand the East, which the Twentieth Party Congress would only exacerbate. Even when speaking about the domestic East, Khrushchev sometimes confused the Central Asian republics. He committed embarrassing faux pas, such as mistakenly addressing Uzbek audiences as Tajiks, and then unconvincingly trying to explain the mistake as a test of the audience's attention.[69] When it came to Arab world, Khrushchev only started to appreciate the significance of the region after Dmitri Shepilov returned from his June 1956 visit to Egypt and confirmed that Nasser was the weakest link in Dulles's plan to build an anti-Soviet pact among the Muslim states.[70]

Khrushchev blamed this ignorance on Stalin's purges and a certain historical Eurocentrism of Marxist and early Soviet elites:

> If we look at the history of the Party, all of its leaders from Plekhanov to Lenin have a European mindset, having been born and lived in Europe. The East for them was a far-away and incomprehensible place. In the first years of the Soviet power, there were some educated Asians at the center. But they were ... accused of nationalism. The second generation of representatives of our republics ... was destroyed in the 30s. Now, when the East is boiling and when our government has great authority ... we need a new Eastern politics and new experts.[71]

This diagnosis was informed by the very dichotomies that produced the limited knowledge in the first place: the conception of the world as bifurcated into "Eastern" and "Western/European" spheres, and the presumed existence of an existential gulf between West and East that Westerners could not bridge. It also reflected how much Khrushchev had come to value Mukhitdinov—as a Soviet "representative of the East," an "Asian," a "son of a Muslim," and ultimately as someone who could control, embody, and deploy these identities.[72] Khrushchev's trust in Mukhitdinov cemented their "patron and client" relationship, which protected Mukhitdinov from those who wanted to expose him as deceitful, unscrupulous, and careerist.[73]

Khrushchev rewarded Mukhitdinov with more power and responsibilities, which in turn allowed him to transform the Uzbek political scene. Perhaps Khrushchev realized that Mukhitdinov would need this authority: he was a propagandist tasked to fight the global campaign to destabilize the Soviet Union by questioning its anticolonial legitimacy. Khrushchev was concerned about Western journalists, academics, and politicians who inverted the claims of the Eastern International—that Soviet Central Asia was a domestic model of decolonization and development for the foreign East—and presented Central Asia as a cautionary tale to the foreign East.[74] He was aware that *New York Times* foreign correspondent Cyrus Leo Sulzberger likened Soviet support for linguistic and cultural policies of "national construction" in Uzbekistan, Kazakhstan, and Tajikistan to French politics in Morocco toward indigenous Arabs and Berbers.[75] Khrushchev knew of similar warnings by Harvard University historian Richard Pipes, who had visited Moscow, Tashkent, and Alma-Ata on a tour of the USSR in spring 1957 and then predicted in *Middle East Journal* that "the future of Soviet Central Asia depends on the extent to which the local population submits to the process of Russification which is actively imposed on it by the Soviet government."[76] He was also aware that British-based academic Walter Kolarz and German scholar Gerhard von Mende studied Central Asia in order to predict how the Middle East might develop under Soviet influence.[77]

These arguments supported a larger objective, articulated in the 1953 US National Security Council directive NSC-158, to fan unrest among domestic Soviet peoples by encouraging "cooperation between satellite resistance elements and nationalists in non-Russian Soviet Republics."[78] This required a response. As Khrushchev instructed Mukhitdinov, it was better "not to engage them in direct conversations," his Russian term "*slovesnye perepalki*" literally directing him to avoid "verbal skirmishes." The shifts he wanted were political and seismic. He instructed Mukhitdinov "to seriously study our history, popularize our forefathers, accomplishments, and achievements in the development of civilization in order to ... combine the national with the international."[79] This was nothing short of a request to de-Stalinize the Eastern International by correcting Stalin's "mistakes" in domestic nationalities policies, which had killed too many Central Asian communists, and in foreign policy, where Stalin had not paid enough attention to the decolonizing "Eastern" world.

Khrushchev appreciated the challenges of governing non-Russians in the Soviet borderlands. As first secretary in Ukraine (1938–1947, 1947–1949), he had led a savage war against nationalist partisans, purging political enemies and rebuilding the ruling apparatus.[80] After Stalin's death he struggled with Beria over the future of Union-wide nationalities policies.[81] By the early 1950s, frustrations with Stalin's neglect of local cadres in favor of Russians were fulminating in the Baltics, Ukraine, the Caucasus, and Central Asia. Khrushchev had argued that combating resistance only with security organs—composed overwhelmingly of Russian rather than local cadres and dependent on repression and violence—did not allow sufficient time to uncover the causes of discontent.[82] Heeding this advice, Beria coopted more local cadres into the security services, and both Khrushchev and Beria agreed that they would curb Moscow's supervisory capabilities in the republics and advocate for the indigenization of the republics' party apparatuses.[83] Khrushchev's biographer William Taubman writes that after Beria's death, "Khrushchev not only supported his nationality reforms at the time but borrowed wholesale from them."[84] Ultimately, this restructuring unleashed waves of anti-Russian sentiment.[85] When expressions of nationalism among the population and middle management in Latvia threatened a major crisis in center-periphery relations, Khrushchev finally "applied the brakes," easing the nationality reforms.[86] These oscillations between *korenizatsiia* (indigenization) and *sblizhenie* (the rapprochement of peoples), and their accompanying waves of russophobia, were more dangerous in the global Cold War climate. Threats to Soviet legitimacy as an anticolonial state surfaced with each new wave of resistance to Sovietization in Eastern Europe. After protests in Poland and Hungary, this threat to legitimacy became a crisis along the Soviet Union's western frontier.[87] Nationalism had to be managed carefully in order to avoid protests and the political fallout from having to suppress them.

Mukhitdinov was tasked with shepherding Uzbek nationalism through de-Stalinization not only because he had supported Khrushchev in his struggle against Beria but also because he had had experience navigating Uzbek national culture during the confusing and unpredictable anticosmopolitan campaigns of the early 1950s. As secretary for propaganda for the Uzbek SSR at that time, he had dealt with the VKP(b) committee that evaluated every major cultural figure in Uzbekistan to determine if his work had "distorted" national politics.[88] In his account of this period, Mukhitdinov presented himself as trying to contain these purges. He did this first by heroically challenging First Secretary Amin Niiazov, who was ready to carry out the purges, and, later, by going to Moscow to defend the rights of republican authorities to review the list of accused. In Moscow, Mukhitdinov threatened that without an additional review the general public's "national feelings might make themselves known."[89] His victory speaks to his abilities to navigate a contradictory mission. On the one hand, he presents himself as the defender of Uzbek sovereignty against the apparatus of the "quasi-imperial instrument" of the Moscow Plenipotentiary.[90] On the other hand, he boasts about how he remained friendly with this liquidated Plenipotentiary, Semen Ignatiev, who was subsequently promoted to be the minister of state security and head of Stalin's personal security.[91]

Mukhitdinov outlined his plan for a recalibrated Eastern International in a speech on the "Tasks of the Twentieth Party Congress" before a Congress of Uzbek Intelligentsia convened in Tashkent in fall 1956. This large event included over 1,000 guests from across the Eastern International, including delegations from Kazakhstan, Kyrgyzstan, Tajikistan, Turkmenia, Georgia, Azerbaijan, Armenia, Egypt, India, China, and the Democratic People's Republic of Korea.[92] It quickly became clear that the terms of public debate had loosened. Some delegates referred to the historical incorporation of Central Asia into Russia as a "conjoining" or "voluntary union." Others called it a "capture" or "conquest" and explicitly compared it to the British conquest of India.[93] Yet even in this open atmosphere, Mukhitdinov managed to shock the conference with the first public acknowledgment of prominent figures repressed during the 1930s.

The naming and rehabilitating of victims of Stalinism was already underway across the Soviet Union.[94] In preparation for making these names public in Uzbekistan, Mukhitdinov had been granted access to records in the possession of Prosecutor General Roman Rudenko. From these records he learned the extent of the coverups associated with the case against Alexei Rykov and Nikolai Bukharin, including the retroactive invention of an "anti-Soviet rightist block." This invention allowed the case against them to be extended to Central Asia's Khodjaev and Ikramov, whose trial he had witnessed as a student in Moscow.[95] Party opposition to Khodjaev's rehabilitation was particularly strong,[96] especially considering the lack of clarity on such key issues as the territorial delineation of Central Asia and jadidism, which was still considered to be a "bourgeois ideology" that "led many prominent writers and poets astray."[97] In the final version of Mukhitdinov's speech, Ikramov was the only former Uzbek leader whose name could be uttered in public, and even then only as a preliminary decision to rehabilitate "still under consideration," although in fact the issue had already been resolved. Nevertheless, the mention of Ikramov's name—and those of other officials, writers, singers, and composers who had perished in the 1930s—was a watershed. On the one hand, it allowed Mukhitdinov to capture the attention of the republican elites and encourage them to return to creative work with less fear. To do so, he met with individual returnees, including Kari-Yakubov, to discuss the future of Uzbek musical culture. On the other hand, such acts of rehabilitation allowed Mukhitdinov to target political rivals still in power who had been directly or indirectly implicated, especially around Ikramov's downfall.[98]

His revelations tried to diffuse popular anger around perceived contradictions between national and union-wide interests. While he admitted that many "suffered innocently" from "wrongful" accusations of nationalism, Mukhitdinov's two examples were light and almost comical.[99] One involved Jewish Indologist Grigoriy Bondarevsky accusing a handful of Uzbek writers of bourgeois nationalism, and even a number of Russian scholars, of "promoting local," meaning non-Russian, nationalism, and for drawing incorrect conclusions about an academic article on the "Muridism of Shamil," the early nineteenth-century leader of the Caucasian resistance against Russia. Another involved the literary journal *Zvezda Vostoka* (*Star of the East*) calling the nineteenth-century Karakalpak poet Berdakh a "reactionary" and accusing Karakaplak Soviet literature of "nationalism."[100] Both cases channeled popular anger at safe targets since one individual accused had left Central Asia and the other one was long dead. Both cases avoided engagement with systemic pressures that had pitted republican interests against union-wide ones.

It was the intelligentsia's responsibility to remain vigilant and to cultivate the right kind of nationalism. This meant continuing the struggle against "any expression of bourgeois nationalism, national exclusiveness, and localism . . . and unfounded, slanderous accusations of nationalism leveled against honest people . . . [while] assuming responsibility for the ideological upbringing of workers . . . in the spirit of Soviet patriotism and proletariat internationalism."[101] Crucially, the intelligentsia had to acknowledge that Uzbekistan was an integral part of the USSR and define its cultural revolution in terms of Soviet accomplishments: literacy rates, numbers of universities, advances in science, and industrialization undertaken with "brotherly aid" from other Soviet peoples.[102] Mukhitdinov drew on Stalin's successful tactic of disciplining the Soviet intelligentsia and students by driving them into an ideological war with the capitalist West.[103] In the new Cold War climate the intelligentsia had to counter statements made by "ideologists of imperialism," such as US Supreme Court justice William O. Douglas, who compared Uzbekistan to colonial Africa, and British *Daily Express* journalist René MacColl, who predicted the imminent disappearance of Uzbek culture.[104] Following Khrushchev's instructions, Mukhitdinov tasked the Uzbek intelligentsia with defending Uzbek accomplishments in economic and cultural development and with upholding the "sovereignty of their statehood."[105]

The dramatic expansion of educational opportunities that followed seemed like a major step toward the fulfillment of economic and nation-building goals for Central Asians and foreign Easterners alike. In Tajikistan these opportunities allowed young people to escape the closed-mindedness of the village and transform themselves into cultured urbanites who could contribute to their republic.[106] In Uzbekistan, these expansions also created what one contemporary historian called "a new people's (*narodnaia*) intelligentsia."[107] With the use of state-mandated quotas, the number of university graduates in Uzbekistan reached 2.3 million in 1959, an increase of 50 percent from the period 1952–1958; in the late 1960s that number grew to 7 million.[108] Over the same period, the number of research institutes in the Uzbek Academy of Sciences doubled, creating more opportunities for graduate research and employment.[109] Between 1960 and 1969 nine new universities were established and the state's budgeted expenses for education rose from 294 million rubles in 1960 to 693 million rubles in 1968.[110] Soviet international education expanded in the same period. The Patrice Lumumba Peoples' Friendship University, founded in 1960 for students from Third World countries, also granted thousands of scholarships to youths from Africa and Asia who otherwise would never have been able to afford university studies abroad.[111] These opportunities were all controlled by the state.

In Central Asia, as in the Arab world, most of these opportunities were in technical fields. In Uzbekistan the expansion of opportunity was especially dramatic in fields related to cotton production. After 1962, research in hydro-technology, dynamics of cotton-picking machines, and physical-mechanical properties of cotton and synthetic materials was overseen by the Gosplan's Committee (Goskomitet) for Cotton Picking in Central Asia and the Central Asian Bureau. This was a single coordinating body for Tajikistan, Turkmenistan, Kyrgyzstan, and Uzbekistan created by Khrushchev in response to growing concerns that the search for "independence" had gone too far.[112] Contemporary Soviet scholars lauded the new Central Asian "production-technical" intelligentsia.[113] This growth, however, remained uneven over the course of the 1960s and into the 1970s. While the overall number of Central Asian experts expanded, memoirs from the era suggest that the leadership of prestigious institutions such as the Central Asian Research Institute of Irrigation remained dominated by non-natives.[114]

In Nasserist Egypt, similar opportunities for education and employment in the state sector helped to involve new elites in the work of the state, which replaced earlier views of the intelligentsia as an oppositional force.[115] Professional thinkers of all sorts became increasingly dependent on state power and agendas.[116] These new Khrushchev-era educational opportunities in the Soviet Union and Arab socialist regimes continued this integration of educated elites. Enlightenment, civilization, and the cultural capital of Soviet *kul'turnost'* were made accessible to everyone, including thousands of foreigners studying in the USSR.[117] Yet these opportunities were still presented as in service of the Eastern International. The new Uzbek intelligentsia, a historian of the Uzbek Communist Party concluded, could become "an example for the brotherly parties of socialist countries, as well as for countries of Africa, Asia, and Latin America."[118]

The expansion of these opportunities was a way for Khrushchev, Mukhitdinov, and later Uzbek historians to confront their critics, including such Western scholars as Pipes, Kolarz, and, later, Alexandre Bennigsen, who claimed that in Soviet Central Asia people "of indigenous (*korennykh*) nationalities are being deprived of opportunities." Uzbek authorities offered statistics about a growing non-Russian majority in Uzbek party structures (in the Politburo and of party candidates), and the number of students "of local (*mestnykh*) nationalities," increasing in the 1960s from 60 to 78.2 percent.[119] These official accounts avoided the term "indigenization" (*korenizatsiia*) that had proven troublesome during the interwar period and in the late 1950s in the Baltics, Ukraine, and Kyrgyzstan. Yet the transformations drew on similar modes of "affirmative action."[120] For many Central Asians, Moscow's efforts to make their region an implicit showcase of Soviet modernization brought opportunities. Of course, metrics of postwar development often fell short of projected goals. As one 1966 report concludes, Tajikistan still lacked some 32,000 specialists, which meant that industrialization required importing people from other parts of the USSR or using underqualified cadres.[121] Yet they also facilitated upward mobility, participation in domestic transnational networks (beyond their own republic within the USSR), and, occasionally, international travel.[122]

Aside from the expansion of opportunities in education and employment for various "Easterners," the other key transformation of the Eastern International had to do with knowledge about the East. At the Twentieth Party Congress, Khrushchev announced the arrival of a new period in world history, predicted by Lenin, "when the peoples of the East come to play an active part in deciding the destinies of the world and become a mighty factor in international relations."[123] Echoing Khrushchev, the Armenian politician Anastas Mikoyan warned the Soviet academic establishment: "While the entire east has awakened, the Institute [of Oriental Studies] goes on dozing contentedly."[124] This had to change.

On Mukhitdinov's initiative, the TsK approved the organization of a Union-Wide Conference of Soviet Orientalists in Tashkent, held July 11–13, 1957. Mukhitdinov played the foreign policy card to overcome initial Presidium resistance to holding the conference in Tashkent, rather than Moscow or Leningrad. He claimed that Tashkent had been suggested to him by a number of foreign Asian leaders as well as communist delegates to the Nineteenth and Twentieth Congresses of the CPSU.[125] Welcoming guests from Romania, Czechoslovakia, China, the Democratic People's Republic of Korea, Mongolia, and Vietnam to Tashkent, the head of the Oriental Studies Institute, Bobojon Ghafurov, asked the Congress to put aside intra-Soviet rivalries and work together to overcome the damage inflicted by the 1930s purges. They could do this by establishing a network of oriental studies centers in domestic Eastern republics such as Azerbaijan, Georgia, and Tajikistan.[126]

Soviet officials held the view that oriental knowledge could be more useful in the global anti-imperial struggle if produced in the Soviet East, both because Easterners presumably understood other Easterners and because such knowledge was implicitly different from that produced in Russia's "European" cities.[127] Eastern origin lent scholars and scholarship a kind of authority, implied by Khrushchev's special trust in Mukhitdinov as an "Easterner" and a "son of a Muslim." Like Troianovskii, who imagined the Eurasian revolutionary networks when world revolution seemed imminent, Ghafurov proposed a network of centers that would allow "problems to be studied in corresponding regions of the country."[128] Hence, centers in Central Asia would be expected to study China, Mongolia, Afghanistan, Pakistan, and Iran, and centers in the Caucasus would study Turkey, Arab countries, and Iran (the last would be studied in both centers because of cultural affinity with Tajikistan and geographical proximity to the Caucasus). Tashkent and Baku could become centers of Turcology, while Tbilisi and Erevan could focus on Arab studies, presumably by harnessing talent from the Armenians' Arab diaspora, which could also tap into Armenian communal networks in Lebanon and Syria. This Khrushchev-era geographical distribution of intellectual and material resources resembled earlier party-state maps of the Eastern revolution. The difference was that state resources in the postwar period were greater, while the goals of the state were more modest.

In practice, these plans for cultural cooperation inevitably played into the competitive relationship between the Central Asian republics, especially Uzbekistan and Tajikistan. In December 1957, after the Congress, Khrushchev warned Mukhitdinov about the increased flow of resources to Tashkent and asked him to ensure there was more equality. "Some people are saying that Tashkent is becoming the new capital of our country. This is very dangerous. The rates of growth of Uzbekistan are so high that its neighbors are becoming jealous," he warned.[129] Ultimately, however, union-wide interests in the foreign East kept harmful tensions in check and protected valuable intermediaries like Ghafurov and Mukhitdinov. For Ghafurov, who lost his position as first secretary in 1956, it allowed him to remain involved in politics at the highest levels as head of the Oriental Studies Institute, a post he held until 1977.[130]

The continued "revival" of Soviet oriental studies entailed a split of the Institute of Asia and Africa in 1959 into two continentally focused institutes.

New research positions at each institute extended opportunities to the handful of former Comintern-era Jewish experts on the Arab world who managed to survive various repressions. Vladimir Lutskii was still training students at Moscow State University and later at the institute of Africa, publishing new books, and contributing articles about the Arab world to the *Great Soviet Encyclopedia*, which he viewed as a contribution to the "political and scientific education of the masses."[131] To some of his colleagues, his "modest" academic rank belied his academic stature.[132]

In 1961, Mukhitdinov lost his Presidium seat and his CPSU secretary post. He described this as a consequence of the conflicting pressures of indigenization and the rapprochement of peoples, and specifically related to a disagreement about nationalities policies with Suslov, Mikoyan, and Kozlov. Decades later, after the independence of Uzbekistan, he presented these men as "apologists of great power chauvinism" and himself as a martyr for Uzbek nationalism.[133] The reality, however, was far more complex.[134]

The loss of a Presidium seat could be a difficult experience. The other person removed with Mukhitdinov at the Congress attempted suicide.[135] For a while Mukhitdinov coped by working for the Central Union, overseeing all former imperial-era consumer cooperative unions while mourning the material losses of his government dacha and apartment as he relocated to a shabby two-bedroom apartment with his wife and five children. He claimed that he spent the time contemplating the fates of Khodjaev, Ikramov, and Sultan Segizbaev, who had been repressed in the 1930s, and preparing himself for worst-case scenarios.[136] Of course, these never materialized. His role as a competent mediator to the foreign East protected him after his demotion. As Chinese officials increasingly joined Western voices in characterizing the USSR as a white, colonial power that betrayed national liberation causes in Asia and Africa, Mukhitdinov's experience and talent for promoting Soviet anticolonial legitimacy became more valuable.[137] After the ascent of Leonid Brezhnev, Mukhitdinov was appointed deputy head of the State Committee for Cultural Relations with Foreign Countries (SSOD), the successor to the All-Union Society for Cultural Relations with Foreign Countries (VOKS).[138]

During the Thaw, the new challenges to Soviet anticolonial legitimacy emanating from China, added to those articulated by Western critics and unruly leaders of decolonizing revolutionary regimes, had to be taken into account in the massive expansion of Soviet cultural relations. Two weeks after the Congress of Orientalists was held in Tashkent in July 1957, cultural relations authorities were given an impossible task of trying to manage the Sixth World Congress of Youth and Students, a two-week-long carnival that was a watershed in the lives of many of its Soviet participants.[139] Hosting 34,000 foreigners—about 20 percent of whom were coming from Asian, African, and Latin American countries—put stress on all existing structures and mechanisms. This provoked the 1958 transformation of VOKS into SSOD, a more flexible structure of distinct friendship societies that focused on specific countries. The transformation had two main advantages. SSOD could better deflect accusations of inequality in relations between VOKS and Soviet sympathizers abroad, and it could serve as a magnet for popular Soviet participation in these relationships.[140]

The distribution of SSOD "friendships" incorporates a similar geographical pattern to the network of intellectual centers proposed at Tashkent, and to the earlier Eastern International nodes proposed by Troianovskii.[141] Republics were assigned "friendships" to regions with which they had real or imagined historical, linguistic, or cultural ties.

Soviet republics in Europe were assigned mostly to other parts of Europe; the southern republics of Central Asia and Caucasus were assigned mostly to neighboring India, China, and Arab countries; and the Soviet Far East was mostly assigned to regions in East Asia. China, an exception, was important enough to merit overtures of friendship from even the most distant territories of Belorussia and Ukraine. These assignments reflected a view of domestic republics as carriers of historical, national, and ethnic-cultural resources that could be allocated. Soviet officials perceived these resources as opportunities for furthering Soviet interests globally.[142] But these resources, spaces, and openings advanced changes and exchanges that moved in many directions, not all of which Soviet officials could entirely control.

The bilateral exchange agreements of the 1950s—such as the ones concluded in 1956 between the Soviet Union and Egypt, Syria, and Lebanon, and in 1959 with Iraq—stipulated exchanges in the fields of education, literature, film, art, tourism, sports, and radio.[143] On the Soviet side these exchanges were often overseen by the Ministry of Culture working together with VOKS/SSOD. Although cultural exchange were happening before these bilateral agreements were concluded, they expanded opportunities in ways that continued to be shaped by the logic of the Eastern International. Specifically, they prioritized the showcasing of the domestic East to the

Table 5.1 SSOD's friendship assignments to Soviet republics

Ukrainian SSR	China, Czechoslovakia, Romania, Bulgaria, Hungary, Poland, GDR, Albania, Italy
Belorussian SSR	China, Poland, GDR
Uzbek SSR	China, Arab East, India
Kazakh SSR	China, India, Arab East, Mongolia
Georgian SSR	China, Czechoslovakia, Italy, Greece
Azerbaijan SSR	China, Albania, Arab East, India
Lithuanian SSR	Poland, GDR
Moldavian SSR	Romania, Bulgaria
Latvian SSR	Finland
Kyrgyz SSR	China, Mongolia
Tajik SSR	China, Arab East
Turkmen SSR	Arab East
Armenian SSR	Bulgaria, Arab East
Estonian SSR	Finland
Leningrad Region	China, Finland, Sweden, Norway, England, GDR, Poland
Khabarovsk Region	China, Japan
Primorsky Region	China, Japan
Irkutsk Region	China, Japan
Stalingrad Region	Czechoslovakia, Poland, GDR, England
Buriat ASSR	Mongolia

Source: RGANI f. 89 (The Communist Party on Trial), op. 55, d. 22, l. 3

foreign East. In fact, by the early 1960s, Soviet diplomats in Syria reported that so many Central Asian artists had been sent to the Damascus International Fair that its director actually objected to the Ministry of Culture's plans to send the Uzbek women's ensemble Bahor. The festival director explicitly asked if it might be possible to send performers from one of the USSR's European regions, like the ensemble Berezka or another Russian, Ukrainian, or Moldovan troupe. His reason was that "the art of your Eastern republics is similar to Arab art, so despite the high professional level of the performers, they are less interesting to our public."[144]

It is not clear what was intended by this comment. Perhaps the Damascus Fair organizer wanted to be considered worthy of the more "international" (European) Soviet cultural diplomacy, rather than its "Eastern" version reserved for Afro-Asian nations. And Berezka had a higher profile. Between 1948 and 1965, its dancers visited 250 cities in forty-five countries, including

New York, London, Washington, Paris, Frankfurt, Madrid, and most capitals of Africa and Asia.[145] His stated preference for Berezka over Bahor suggested that the Soviet attempt to overcorrect for domestic Russian cultural dominance in international cultural relations did not always have the desired effect.

Cultural exchanges proceeded more smoothly when Soviet officials worked with old friends. For instance, in 1964 George Hanna helped organize special exhibitions in Beirut, Tripoli, and Saida in celebration of the fortieth anniversary of the Uzbek SSR.[146] After a number of Central Asian films such as *Moi Tashkent* (My Tashkent) and *Tantsuet Bahor* (Bahor is dancing) were successfully screened at the Soviet Cultural Center and other locations, the Soviet embassy in Lebanon suggested that UzSOD prepare "a new color film about the republic for the 50th anniversary of the October Revolution, like *Visit Us in Uzbekistan* (*Priezzhaite k nam v Uzbekistan*, Malik Kaiumov, 1959)."[147] Thanks to Hanna, the number of UzSOD contacts in Lebanon and neighboring counties was growing.

Uzbek cultural representatives in the Arab world could more easily represent Soviet Central Asia as a model of modernization rather than one of decolonization. This was the case at high-profile events, such as the 1957 Afro-Asian Solidarity Conference in Cairo. Here, the Soviet delegation was

Table 5.2 UzSOD correspondents by country

Country	1962	1963
Lebanon	4	37
UAR	3	29
Algeria	1	17
Tunis	2	14
Morocco	1	12
Sudan	2	9
Iraq	4	6
Kuwait	–	3
Syria	2	2
Yemen	1	1
Jordan	–	2
Libya	1	3
Aden [Federation of South Arabia]	–	1

Source: TsGA Uz f. 2661, op. 1, d. 114, ll. 64–72

headed by Uzbek writer Sharof Rashidov, who would leverage such international credentials to become the longest-serving first secretary of the Uzbek SSR (1959–1983). Other opportunities for travel and tourism opened by the Thaw also showcased Soviet modernization in the sense that its technological changes made aviation culture more widely available and generally improved mass consumption.[148] According to UzOKS, the most popular destinations for Uzbek tourists were countries in Asia and Africa.[149]

The vast majority of encounters between domestic and foreign Easterners, however, occurred within Soviet borders. As a "showcase city" for the Eastern International, Tashkent became a major draw for foreign visitors. The Uzbek branch of VOKS (after 1958 SSOD) estimated that the number of official delegations visiting the republic had increased from 1 in 1951, to 10 in 1952, to 110 in 1956, and to 210 in 1963.[150] The number of tourists increased from 156 in 1956 to 2,709 in 1963.[151] These numbers did not include foreign students, who also increasingly came to Tashkent.[152] According to Uzbek records, the majority of these visitors were from the "foreign East."[153] One typical group of visitors was a delegation of Syrian university professors, hosted by the State University in Tashkent and by representatives of the official Soviet Muslim institution, Spiritual Administration of the Muslims of Central Asia (SADUM). The professors' experiences of Central Asian culture included a performance in Khamza Theater of a play, *Algeria My Homeland*, adapted from a novel by Algerian author Mohammad Dib. After the performance, Syrian psychology professor Sami al-Drubi got up on stage to thunderous applause to express the delegation's appreciation for Soviet sympathies "for the struggle of Arab countries and for the specific struggle of Algerians against colonialism."[154]

In the fall of 1958, Tashkent also hosted two important meetings of Afro-Asian writers and filmmakers. The writers' conference turned out to be significant both for forging new Soviet-aligned South-to-South literary networks and for its contribution to the intellectual history of Anglo-American postcolonial theory.[155] The conference's attendees included veterans of earlier networks that connected Soviet Central Asia with foreign Eastern intellectuals, illustrating continuity between these phases of Stalinist and de-Stalinizing Eastern internationalism.[156] Soviet intellectuals-turned-diplomats such as Rashidov parried objections to the Soviet framing of these issues. The delegation from Egypt complained about Israel's participation, Algeria demanded recognition of the Provisional Government of the Algerian Republic, and the African Cultural Society insisted on cultural and ideological independence expressed as a demand for the USSR's nonparticipation at the conference.[157]

Smaller points of friction were handled by Uzbek translators and tourist guides, singers and artists, and even construction workers who built special cafés where local youth could commingle with foreign youth during the conference.[158] These efforts fulfilled the other mandate of UzSOD, which was to enlighten the masses and rally the public.[159] Weeks before the Afro-Asian event, radio, television, and theatrical programming educated Uzbeks with "scenes from the lives of countries of Asia and the foreign East."[160] The Deputy Minister of Culture Zuhra Rakhimovna Rakhimbabaeva commissioned a series of plays by "dramaturges of the East" along with "four or five concerts of Eastern music and dance" and a concert of "our Uzbek classical music."[161] Uzbek theaters staged plays about Algeria and India, including Sharof Rashidov's "Kashmir Song," which had been inspired by his travels to India. A journalist remarked during the Writers' Conference that Tashkent bookstores and kiosks were selling hundreds of thousands of rubles worth of books each day.[162] Over sixty years later, Tashkent residents still recalled the intensity and excitement of these high-profile events and the visits by celebrity Afro-Asian intellectuals and politicians. They dubbed the magic of this time the "spirit of Tashkent"—a play on the "Spirit of Bandung" popularized by the Bandung host Roeslan Abdulgani.[163]

Following these conferences, UzSOD channeled popular interest and enthusiasm about India, China, the Arab world, and other parts of the foreign East into other events. These included lectures about Arab politics and history, conferences about Arabic literature and translations, art exhibits, festivals of Arab film, and monthly film lectures.[164] Academics and filmmakers returning from abroad shared their experiences on the radio or television, bringing images of the Arab world into the homes of thousands of Uzbeks.[165] These stories inspired some Uzbeks to join the SOD's Society of Friendship with Arab Countries. Like Soviet people in Moscow and Leningrad, they usually participated through their workplaces.[166] The society's Presidium included republican-level ministers, secretaries of city party committees, representatives of youth organizations, the committee for protecting national monuments, academic orientalists, musicians, newspaper editors, theater directors, and one "mother of many children" (*mnogoetnaia mat'*).[167] Their reports about Uzbek-Arab solidarity activities suggest wide-ranging support and interest that enabled celebrations of independence anniversaries for

Sudan, Lebanon, and Algeria; the Yemeni Revolution; African Freedom Day; and events dedicated to solidarity with Arab independence struggles to be staged across Uzbekistan's factories, libraries, universities, collective farms, and rural lecture clubs.[168]

Discussion of such events, however, remained stilted. One reason may have been UzSOD's institutional culture. Moscow's SSOD had been reorganized partly to distance it from VOKS' image as a cover for police and intelligence networks, but the republican-level branch UzSOD in the more vulnerable southern frontier remained under tight state control. Its director was appointed from the state security organs of the NKVD, MVD, and the KGB. Sharif Shirinbaev's prior international experience included special assignments to Xinjiang (1937–1939) and to Iran (1942–1949), and just before coming to UzOKS he was the chief of the KGB (1952–1957) in Surxondaryo, a region that bordered Uzbekistan, Tajikistan, and Afghanistan.[169] Shirinbaev's first act was to purge the organization and appoint his own "loyal" officials who could better support the development of Uzbek SSR's friendships with China, India, and the Arab East.[170]

In his presence, members of the Presidium of the Uzbek Society of Friendship with Arab countries were understandably cautious. Many simply used the forum to stress their belonging to Soviet rather than Afro-Asian space, in line with Mukhitdinov's instructions to the Uzbek intelligentsia. For instance, a representative of a Khorezm regional party committee claimed, "the toilers of the Khorezm region, like all Uzbek people and all Soviet people, could understand the feelings of the peoples in Arab countries."[171] Others stressed the emotional nature of the transregional bond, or avoided history by focusing on the "culture, language, traditions, and music" that they shared with Arabs. Physicist Sadiq Azimovich Azimov made one attempt to construct a narrative without touching upon unresolved historical questions. Invoking Nasser's statements about Arab-Uzbek friendship from his May visit to Uzbekistan, Azimov stressed its pre-modern roots:

> [This friendship began] when centers of Arab learning like Baghdad, Damascus, and Cairo attracted Central Asian intellectuals such as the Ferghani mathematician, [Musa] al-Khwarizmi, and Habash [al-Hasib al-Marwazi], Abu al-Fath al-Samarqandi, and many others. . . . There were also Arab geographers who visited Bukhara and Merw from Baghdad and Damascus such as the 12th–13th century geographer Yakut [Yaqut

al-Hamawi] who used materials for his geographical dictionary from Merv (Seljuk Sultanate) and Khorezm. . . . These facts speak of the high level of culture of peoples of Central Asia and Arab countries and these peoples' contribution to the cultural ties between them.[172]

Notably, this version of a shared past was devoid of references to Central Asian mystics and religious scholars. These connections were too close to taboo histories of Islamic modernism and the legacy of the jadids. Instead, Azimov emphasized rationalist figures whose contributions to a shared golden age of Islamic history could be comfortably appropriated as a "shared heritage."

The Soviet Afro-Asian Solidarity Committee (SKSSAA) likewise struggled to articulate a basis for Central Asian solidarity with the decolonizing world.[173] Central Asian republics focused on practical matters as they discussed hosting a growing number of visitors. SKSSAA Presidium chairman Mirzo Turson-zade claimed that itineraries were too repetitive and limited, which reinforced the impression that tours were staged. Bukhara and Khiva were "not yet ready for visitors," and Samarkand was "all under restoration."[174] Georgian actor Akaki' Horava expressed his concern about potential "awkward situations" when allotted funds happened to run out "just when an international group could really use another bottle."[175] The one person on the Presidiums of both the SSOD and the SKSSAA who was able to speak about transregional connections with relative freedom was the SADUM Mufti, Ziauddin Babakhanov (mufti 1957–1982). By 1958, Babakhanov had already visited most major Arab capitals and undertaken the hajj to Mecca.[176] He had made numerous contacts with foreign Muslim leaders at the 1957 Afro-Asian Solidarity Conference, while representing the Soviet Union in Cairo alongside Uzbek writer and politician Sharof Rashidov.[177] At the Tashknet meeting of the Society of Friendship with Arab countries, he assured attendees that Islam remained a stable basis of relations between Uzbeks and Arabs.[178] Having made this statement, he retreated to the margins of the conversation. Religious contacts were an important dimension of Soviet foreign relations with the decolonizing would. But in this new world being built by Soviet anticolonial state power and by increasingly powerful secularist-nationalist pan-Arab states, religion could not be the glue of the Eastern International.

Contemporaneous de-Stalinization inside the Soviet Union and global decolonization, punctuated by the international crises of the 1956 Suez War and the ongoing struggle in Algeria, helped to deepen the association between statism and revolution and to empower Soviet and Arab states as agents of modernization and development. Newly decolonizing states reframed "the masses" as a touchstone of political authenticity and embarked on the project of liberating these masses from colonialism.[179]

To Khrushchev, these shifts seemed to herald the arrival of Lenin's predicted period of world history "when the peoples of the East come to play an active part in deciding the destinies of the whole world." The liberation of "nearly half the world's population" celebrated at Bandung, Cairo, Tashkent, and elsewhere in the Global South appeared to affirm the centrality of the October Revolution in world history.[180] Continuing to accept the basic distinction between the East and West as the starting point for his theories of politics, Khrushchev went about transforming the Soviet Union's Eastern politics by enlarging the scale of earlier connections between the domestic and foreign Easts. Thus the Soviet Union's opening to the East was more of a state-driven project than the intelligentsia-driven opening to the West in Leningrad and Moscow. But then it took on a life of its own. In Uzbekistan, UzSOD made India, China, and Arab countries more accessible and created a different and perhaps a more familiar *zagranitsa*, or "imaginary elsewhere," for Central Asians than the "imaginary West" had been for Leningrad- and Moscow-based intelligentsia elites.

In this state-led expansion, the Soviet Union's domestic East became a more important barometer of its commitment to international decolonization and anticolonial nationalism. It also became a barometer of its domestic political stability against Cold War enemies, who claimed that the Soviet Union was keeping the domestic East under colonial subjugation. These dynamics created opportunities for savvy Soviet Central Asians like Mukhitdinov and Rashidov.[181]

US and European observers tended to interpret any real or apparent failure of Central Asian leaders to become fully assimilated into a Soviet (Russian) whole as evidence of a latent and potentially separatist Central Asian Muslim nationalism. British observers found it easier to imagine multiple cultures loyal to a single state.[182] But the Thaw-era transformations made it easier for "sons of Muslims" such as Mukhitdinov to achieve the highest office—not despite his national and cultural difference, but because of it. These transformations strengthened ethnic particularism in the USSR not as a reaction against the regime but as a function of it.[183] Soviet Easterners in international forums could use their ethnic particularity to support a vision of Soviet development and, implicitly, of decolonization. Sometimes this work was done silently by non-white bodies as cultural mediators or ambassadors abroad; at other times, it was done explicitly as a defense of Soviet anticolonialism.

In this respect, the parallels with the United States are striking. Soviet Central Asians and Caucasians were comparable to Black Americans, including the Black American cultural representatives on Goodwill Ambassador tours abroad, who could use race as a marker of difference that pointed beyond to a genuinely democratic world.[184] Some resembled leaders of the US civil rights movement, who in this period were also learning how to leverage international critiques of American racism in the struggle for legal and political equality at home, and against state control of this narrative. Like Central Asia, which had been cut off from global conversations about decolonization, the Black American struggle for civil rights was also severed from anticolonialism and racism abroad by the anticommunist politics of the American Society of African Culture (ANSAC), formed in 1956 with CIA support.[185]

In the 1950s and early 1960s, the conjunction of Soviet domestic and international politics allowed Mukhitdinov and other Central Asian politicians to achieve meaningful political change. By leveraging Western and later Chinese attacks on Soviet anticolonial legitimacy, these politicians negotiated the economic and cultural modernization of their republics by claiming needed resources, expanding educational and professional opportunities, and improving the quality of everyday life in their republics relative to others. The reallocation of resources to the republics was followed by the decentralization of key all-Union structures. For instance, in an effort to gain entry into the 1958 Afro-Asian economic conference in Cairo, the Soviet Chamber of Commerce (Torgovaia Palata) had to overcome objections that it represented a European power whose capital was in European Russia. To do so, the Chamber created republican-level organizations and then had only its Central Asian and Caucasian republican branches request participation.[186] Similar reorganization occurred in the SKSSAA[187] and in the SSOD, which continuously advocated for more events in Central Asia and Transcaucasia and the recruitment of more Central Asian representatives.[188] The spatial dimensions of the Eastern International set the Soviet transformation apart from the United States, where the state used Black Americans as cultural ambassadors but never systematically attempted to showcase antiracism to visiting foreigners or its ability to transform economically depressed regions.

These transformations often came as "initiatives from below" and were only later recognized by central authorities as opportunities to "harness the potential of national and regional difference."[189] This complementarity of interests challenges earlier interpretations of these dynamics as top-down, or radiating from the center to periphery. Similarly, the SKSSAA has been characterized as an "arm" of the International Department responsible for dealing with public organizations in the Middle East and Africa.[190] Yet as one former employee of both organs recalled, Ulianovskii once told a foreign delegation that the SKSSAA was "an extension of the ID" but that everyone understood that as a means of exaggerating the importance of the SKSSAA to the foreign delegation. "There were always activities that required approval like foreign travel or delegation visits but many SKSSAA initiatives came from below," recalled Vladimir Shubin, who had worked both at the SKSSAA and the International Department of the CPSU. When pushed to characterize workflow between the organizations, he described it as conducted "*po-chelovecheski*," meaning largely based on interpersonal relations or generally humanely.[191] Similarly, Kalinovsky argues, in Tajikistan the transformations of the late 1950s and early 1960s raised expectations and gave people a greater stake in the highest-level conversations about the party-state's future.[192]

In both the US and the Soviet contexts, the severing of international and domestic politics in the early Cold War had profound implications. In the United States, the issues that Black anticolonial activists fought for in the 1940s resurfaced in the 1960s, most fundamentally, a conception of democracy that embraced political, economic, and civil rights globally, and a radical democratic critique of American foreign policy. Historical amnesia led to trivialization, exoticization, and marginalization of Africa.[193] In the USSR, the expansion of institutionalized relations with the Afro-Asian world brought Soviet intellectuals into contact with many idioms of Third World progressive nationalisms: Kemalism in Turkey, Sukarnoism in Indonesia, Peronism in Argentina, Gandhism, pan-Africanism, negritude, and pan-Arabic nationalism.[194] There were times, especially during Tashkent conferences, when these contacts seemed to offer a fleeting shared cosmopolitanism between Central Asian and Afro-Asian artists. But when the celebratory aura of Tashkent lifted, these artists struggled to articulate any historical basis for their new friendships. The Eurocentric language of secular Marxist solidarity and the narrowing parameters of Central Asian history, which increasingly elided past inequalities between the rulers and the ruled as well as earlier historical ties, stunted these connections and their potential meanings.

By 1995, even Mukhitdinov spoke of his frustrations with Soviet censorship after experiencing a relative degree of freedom in what he called his "honorable exile" (*pochetnaia ssylka*) in Syria. In Damascus, Mukhitdinov could explore new historical topics at the Arab Academy of Damascus, the national library, and other research centers and political organizations. He had accumulated a small library of books about Islamic history, Soviet nationalities, and other topics in Soviet history that were prohibited within the USSR. He had gotten hold of Trotsky's autobiography in Arabic-language translation, read articles about him from Baʻathist newspapers, and taken notes on his readings. When he tried to ship his small library home to Moscow at the end of his term, however, these materials were confiscated and, to his frustration, never returned.[195] Mukhitdinov also received an official reprimand for his apparently overly critical assessments of Soviet politics in his ambassadorial reports to the Ministry of Foreign Affairs. His only comfort in this loss of freedom was the thought that "it was not 1937."[196]

6
Scripting Central Asian Revolution for the Afro-Asian World

The acceleration of decolonization after Bandung, with twenty-five new states created between 1957 and 1962, diversified the challenges of Soviet engagement with the "East" around shared commitments of anticolonialism and anti-Westernism. The processes of postcolonial state building and associated modes of development became a focal point of Cold War competition. As future US president John F. Kennedy predicted on his campaign trail in 1960, the great struggle in foreign policy over the next decade would be a test of "which system travels better, which system solves the problems of the people of Latin America and Africa and Asia."[1]

For the Soviet model, unexpected new competitors emerged. The Chinese increasingly painted the USSR as non-revolutionary and willing to sacrifice the interests of people in Asia, Africa, and Latin America for the sake of peace—and maybe even collusion—with white, Western capitalist powers. The war of words between the USSR and China at party congresses turned into an open global competition for influence.[2] A new Non-Aligned Movement (NAM) initiated by President Josip Tito at a 1961 meeting in Belgrade further widened the arena of activism from the "Afro-Asian" bloc to all states that were not part of a Cold War military alliance and that wanted to find a political "third way."

These international challenges coincided with a narrowing of possibilities for domestic nationalism within the Soviet Union. At the Twenty-second Party Congress in 1961, the Party's ideologues decided that the search for "independence" had gone too far and produced too much instability. Khrushchev and Suslov began to consider roadblocks in the process of national consolidation and ethnohistorical advancement necessary to attain communism.[3] For example, national minorities became less visible in censuses, textbooks, maps, and academic studies such that the regions they inhabited appeared to be more ethnically consolidated and homogenous.[4] Khrushchev also revived a centralized Central Asian party bureau in 1962 and then created a Central Asian economic council in 1963 to coordinate regional development and oversee decisions taken by republican leaders. Similar structures were established for the Caucasus.[5] In the Baltic republics, nationalist unrests were violently suppressed.[6]

It was a staggering challenge to sustain the "Eastern International" as a set of connections across these new contexts in the foreign and domestic Easts. Soviet cultural diplomacy had expanded since the early 1950s, but devising fresh and compelling narratives about the Soviet Union as an anticolonial power became more difficult. This was true in part because while Khrushchev and Suslov were reigning in domestic nationalism, the international conversation was moving away from mid-1950s non-alignment and toward a more radical anti-imperialism.[7] Engagement with such trends required new stories and images. One mediator who took on the mantle of trying to defend Soviet anticolonial credentials to the satisfaction of both Soviet domestic and foreign audiences was Central Asian filmmaker Kamil Yarmatov (1903–1978). He had to accommodate conflicting political imperatives: the narrowing, empire-positive parameters of Central Asian history and the theme of revolutionary armed struggle that increasingly characterized Afro-Asian cinema. His struggles to do so illustrate an ideological (but not an institutional) end to the idea that the Soviet domestic East might serve as a model of decolonization for the foreign East. As Yarmatov's career shows, his efforts collapsed under the weight not only of ideological contradictions but also of a growing generational conflict with younger filmmakers and intellectuals interested in exploring their sense of belonging to the Soviet system (and lack thereof) through new forms and cinematic genres.

Soviet legitimacy as an anticolonial state had been challenged during the popular uprisings in Poland and Hungary (1956), and in the ruptures of Soviet influence in Yugoslavia (1956), Romania (1958–1962), and Albania (1961).[8] Yet a more consistent threat to its anticolonial legitimacy emanated from China and increased in the first half of the 1960s. Tensions between Khrushchev and Mao had been growing since the Twentieth Party Congress in 1956. There, Khrushchev had opened the floodgates for criticisms of Stalin without warning Mao and announced the policy of "peaceful coexistence" that Mao construed as a betrayal of the anti-imperialist commitments of the Sino-Soviet alliance treaty.[9] By 1960, Mao made his disagreements with

Khrushchev public on the occasion of Lenin's ninetieth birthday and subsequently initiated a propaganda campaign against the Soviet Union within and outside China.[10]

Mao's campaign politicized Khrushchev's Cold War tactical bluffs and retreats, turning his commitment to anti-imperialism into a source of vulnerability. For instance, when Khrushchev backed down from a confrontation with the United States in Berlin in 1961, Beijing immediately criticized him for being weak.[11] Khrushchev's spectacular retreat during the Cuban Missile Crisis of October 1962 further undermined his anti-imperialist credentials. Initially frustrated by the unfavorable balance of power in Southeast Asia, Khrushchev sent a delegation to Cuba led by Uzbek politician Sharof Rashidov, who had been a successful Soviet emissary at many previous Afro-Asian cultural and diplomatic events. Khrushchev offered Soviet military resources to be used to defend Cuba, but after a number of tense months he agreed to withdraw Soviet missiles in return for a US commitment not to invade Cuba and a secret concession to remove Jupiter missiles from Turkey.[12] Khrushchev's compromise seemed justified from the perspective of avoiding nuclear war and securing territories proximate to American and Soviet borders. Yet to many it appeared as another betrayal of the anticolonial struggle. Throughout the crisis, the Chinese embassy reported on the mood in Cuba and on every negative change in attitude toward the USSR.[13] Even Fidel Castro criticized the Soviet "betrayal" of the Cuban revolution.[14] After this crisis, China began to devote far more resources to its competition with the USSR.

China's efforts to undermine the USSR were especially visible in East Asia. For instance, Chinese bans against the distribution of Soviet propaganda and continuing tensions after Khrushchev's ouster paved the way for the collapse of Sino-Soviet military relations during the Vietnam War. Yet Soviet leaders' abilities to understand and respond to such events was hampered by orientalist assumptions. As historian Odd Arne Westad explains, the fact that Soviet experts had touted the People's Republic of China to the North Vietnamese and North Koreans as the near perfect application of Marxist political theory in "oriental" countries proved disastrous during and after the Sino-Soviet split. Similarly, the CPSU's continued rationalization of Hanoi's political direction during the 1964–1966 war, based on the idea that the Chinese and Vietnamese, "both being 'orientals' ... would naturally draw together in their views and policies," meant that Moscow steadily lost influence in Hanoi.[15]

International voices on decolonization repeatedly challenged the crude orientalism of Moscow's decision makers. The Algerian War, as historian Matthew Connelly has argued, shifted the discourse about colonialism and state control from its previous emphasis on power, rationality, and progress to a new more radicalized understanding of self-determination and human rights.[16] This shift was in part due to the expansion of media, especially the reach of radio and film throughout the Middle East. The FLN's Voice of Algeria and Cairo-based Voice of the Arabs allowed more people to "enter into communication with the Revolution," while new pro-FNL Egyptian films entertained wide audiences.[17] Since the Soviet Union did not have substantial interests in North Africa and was less active in Algeria, China exploited the opportunity to send more propaganda to Algiers and other parts of Africa. Here, armed struggles in the former Belgian Congo and Cameroon, and armed clashes in Angola, Mauritania, Chad, and Kenya, made the Soviet position of "peaceful coexistence" seem increasingly like a betrayal.[18]

The Soviet leadership variously attempted to defend its anticolonial credentials. For example, the Brezhnev administration sought to boost its political status vis-à-vis China by recentering the communist movement in Moscow with an international meeting of communist parties in 1965. Smaller regional preparatory meetings in Moscow and Prague of communists from Iraq, Syria, Jordan, Egypt, Lebanon, and Iran were consumed by challenges of what was widely perceived as KUTV graduate Khalid Bakdash's "Stalinist" leadership style, opposition to the participation of the Israeli Communist Party, and tensions over Arab unity and relations with the USSR.[19] Ultimately, these and other fractures, and the fact that too many communist parties were hesitant to join an effort to isolate the Chinese Communist Party, thwarted Soviet plans to hold the larger international meetings in Moscow.[20]

In parallel, China had been trying to organize a rival "Second Bandung" meeting of Afro-Asian states that would exclude the Soviet Union and all of its "non-independent" republics. Unlike the first Bandung, when Khrushchev chose not to campaign openly for Soviet attendance, the Brezhnev leadership used diplomatic pressure to get the United Arab Republic, India, Ghana, Cyprus, Iraq, Laos, Senegal, Nigeria, and others to neutralize the USSR's exclusion.[21] It also used propaganda in multiple languages, disseminated by Soviet embassies abroad, to defend "peaceful coexistence" as a policy that furthered world revolution and demonized China for "replacing proletarian internationalism with the ideology of bourgeois nationalism."[22] However, the Second Bandung was first postponed after the coup against President Ben Bella and then fell apart after the anticommunist coup in Indonesia, which cost the PRC its closest ally as it tried to build its Afro-Asian-Latin American power structure.[23]

These events internationally put more pressure on Soviet propagandists to present the USSR as an anticolonial power. This pressure did not disappear after Mao launched the Cultural Revolution in 1966 and China curtailed its international outreach.[24] For the Soviet Union, the PRC's descent into self-isolation did not produce many political opportunities. In the mid-1960s the USSR lost a number of key allies in military coups: Ben Bella and Sukarno in 1965, Ghana's Kwame Nkrumah in February 1966, allegedly with CIA support, and Modibo Keita in Mali in November 1968. That same year Moscow invaded Czechoslovakia to crush efforts to "reform" socialism, which significantly damaged the USSR's image as a power committed to international anticolonialism. Meanwhile, progress on decolonization stalled in southern parts of Africa, thanks to the determination of the Portuguese and white South Africans and Rhodesians to hold on to power.[25] In the absence of political opportunities, cultural engagement remained critical.

Soviet propagandists had to maneuver on this more complex political terrain. This meant continuing to study and predict challenges to Soviet anticolonial legitimacy in Asian, African, and Latin American countries.[26] It also meant engaging with more diverse and radical voices on issues of imperialism, colonialism, and neo-colonialism. In short, making Soviet culture seem revolutionary again required new narratives and aesthetics.

Soviet Central Asian and other non-Russian political and cultural mediators continued to speak for the Soviet Union in strategically important or sensitive contexts around the world. In Syria, where rapidly shifting interests and constituencies culminated in the rise to power of former minister of defense General Hafiz al-Assad, ambassador Nuriddin Mukhitdinov helped to ensure a stable presence for the Soviets and access to Syrian naval bases.[27] As ambassador, he felt his room for political maneuvering restricted by the Soviet decision to sever diplomatic relations with Israel after the June 1967 war. He saw this decision as shortsighted from the perspectives of politics and propaganda, mostly for the loss of the USSR's political leverage compared to the Americans, who had more options because they kept up relations "with more parties."[28] Making up for the apparent disadvantageous rigidity of Soviet foreign policy and the occasional ham-handed orientalism of Soviet leaders, Mukhitdinov used Central Asian culture to foster closeness with Syrians.

Central Asia continued to function both as a backdrop for diplomatic visits and as a projection of Soviet culture abroad. For instance, Mukhitdinov invited to Tashkent Syrian president Nureddin Atasi and members of his government visiting the Soviet Union to sign a new round of bilateral agreements.[29] There, they spent an evening with Mukhitdinov's Arabic-speaking father. "We barely used the services of the translator which made the atmosphere more informal," Mukhitdinov recalled.[30] Mukhitdinov also facilitated cultural exchanges by supporting the work of Soviet cultural diplomacy organs that continued to send films, exhibits, and other materials to the region. For example, for the fiftieth anniversary of the October Revolution, SSOD sent propaganda material for celebrations of "days and weeks of Uzbekistan" to Syria, Algeria, Morocco, Egypt, Lebanon, Libya, Iraq, Iran, Tunisia, Turkey, and Sudan.[31] Mukhitdinov also facilitated meetings for other Central Asian mediators.

In the summer of 1968 a visiting delegation led by the Uzbek film director Kamil Yarmatov arrived in Damascus. The stop was part of a wider tour of Lebanon, Syria, and Egypt to promote the upcoming Afro-Asian Film Festival in Tashkent.

Yarmatov was a talented actor, writer, and director. Like Mukhitdinov, he was a beneficiary of the Soviet affirmative action.[32] Born in 1903 in Konibodom, Tajikistan, he began working for the state in the Red Army militia, from which he was discovered as an actor for his "strikingly scenic (*stsenicheskaia*) appearance" by Uzbek intellectual and dramaturg Hamza Hakimzade Niyazi.[33] In 1924, Yarmatov was sent to study at the Moscow Institute for Railway Engineers. Here, he was again discovered, this time at a movie theater, by Vladimir Gardin, who cast him in minor roles and recommended that he study acting at a night film school named after Tchaikovsky.[34] After returning to Central Asia he continued to act occasionally in films produced at Shark Iulduzi (Star of the East) film studio in Tashkent while also working for the police. He appeared in *From under the Vaults of the Mosque* (Uzbekkino, 1927), playing a young student in a Qur'anic school who turns away from his religious teachings under the progressive influence of a Russian revolutionary worker and joins the 1916 uprising against Russian imperial power. He was even cast in the Kiev Studio production *Guest of Mecca*, in which he was asked to appear in an "abstractly 'Eastern' costume" (*uslovno "vostochnyi" kostium*) to play the role of an Eastern prince.[35] In 1928 he was sent with a group of Soviet Central Asian filmmakers to study in the State Tekhnikum for Cinematography in Moscow, the precursor of the All-Soviet Institute of Cinematography (VGIK) that would educate a generation of Afro-Asian filmmakers in the postwar era.[36]

These opportunities allowed Yarmatov to became a leading Central Asian director. By 1968 he was hosting the Afro-Asian film festival in Tashkent and traveling abroad on its behalf. In Syria he met with the minister of culture, directors of the Departments of Film and Television, the Union of Cultural Workers, leading actors, members of the arts, and journalists from two Damascene newspapers. As a result of the whirlwind of meetings, Syria agreed to enter a documentary film about truck drivers into the festival. The visit also served as an opportunity to further expand a Soviet film presence in Syria. Mukhitdinov invited Yarmatov to return to screen his films at another "Week of Soviet Films" in November or December and to think about how to further develop collaborative relations between the Soviet Union and Syria.[37]

Although Yarmatov benefited from Soviet affirmative action, he resented some aspects of it. For instance, when his group of Central Asian students arrived in Moscow to enroll in the Tekhnikum for Cinematography, most were relieved to learn that they would not have to pass the selective entrance exams. Yarmatov was told that this was because "the USSR needed cadres from this region" but "levels of knowledge in Uzbekistan were too low."[38] Too proud to tolerate such a condescending attitude, Yarmatov insisted on taking the exam for acting anyway. He speculated that his examiners, Lev Kuleshov and his wife Aleksandra Khokhlova, may have gone easy on him because they viewed Central Asia "through a certain romantic fog." They asked him to impersonate a drunk man, a task that came easily to Yarmatov, who had had some vodka with lunch before the exam to take the edge off the stressful situation.[39] Although Yarmatov's insistence on taking the test suggested an ambivalence about the imperial aspects of Soviet affirmative action, he went on to enjoy life in the capital alongside other "many-tribal" students and Moscow's celebrity orators, all of whom enabled him "to touch (*prikosnulsia k*) Russian culture, and absorb a lot from this treasure chest."[40]

Yarmatov's ambivalence was also evident in his relationship to Soviet orientalism. Like other Soviet Central Asians, he was comfortable with certain forms of self-orientalizing language. Once he refused to take part in a ballet class as part of his Moscow-based acting training because "for us Asians" it was "awkward to practice in underwear."[41] On another occasion, when boasting about a successful military maneuver in which he scared his enemy with a rumor about the Red Army's advance, he claimed that "the East is always the East," so naturally a trick used "for thousands of years in oriental literature" had worked for him.[42] These assertions of difference were common in Soviet speech.

Yarmatov also understood that his "Easternness" activated certain privileges. For example, he knew that he received the most support and attention from Soviet directors and writers who were "fond of Eastern exoticism"[43] or had a "love for the East" (*vliublennost' v Vostok*).[44] He also understood that forms of thinking about culture in more abstractly orientalist terms could be helpful for dealing with censors—and he knew to pick his battles.

Yarmatov's first directed feature (silent) film, *Emigrant* (1934), was an agitprop project that addressed the sensitive topic of emigration out of Soviet Central Asia in the late 1920s and 1930s. In these years, thousands of Tajiks, Uzbeks, and others fled Bolshevik antireligious campaigns into neighboring Afghanistan, China, Saudi Arabia, and other parts of the Middle East.[45] The movie's plot follows a young man named Kamil (played by Yarmatov himself) who was convinced by a foreign imposter and a local mullah to emigrate from the Soviet Union to the land of "holy Islam." In the film, Kamil's character vacillates, until disillusionment with life in Soviet Tajikistan finally sets in when he sees his wife taking off her veil in the company of local actresses (who look like they might be prostitutes).[46] After leaving the country for the "land of Islam," Kamil realizes that his dreams of a better life abroad were a lie. He gets severely taxed first by the Emir, then the Bey, the Imam, and the mosque, and then begins to notice the misery and poverty around him. At the end of the film, he returns to Tajikistan and kills the foreign imposter who led him astray in a dramatic fight scene in the mountains.

As an agitprop film, *Emigrant* was described as politically "relevant" (*aktual'naia*) in the sense of persuading Soviet Tajiks to remain Soviet while simultaneously drawing attention to class struggle in collective farms. As a form of propaganda, meant to convince Muslims not to undertake the needless hardships of emigration, it echoed the work of Russian imperial intermediary Ismail Gasprinskii, a Crimean Tatar intellectual who helped the Russian government appeal to Muslims not to migrate to Ottoman lands during Russia's nineteenth-century conquests.[47] These conquests, like the later Russian civil war, drove millions of Muslims out of Crimea, the Caucasus, and Central Asia into Ottoman territories, Afghanistan, and Chinese Turkestan.[48] Soviet engagement with the waves of migrants fleeing in the 1920s and 1930s drew on similar themes.[49]

Yet when the Ministry of Foreign Affairs (NKID) objected to the film referencing any specific regions of the domestic or foreign East—the "land of holy Islam" was too clearly set in Afghanistan—Yarmatov agreed to have his emigrant leave for a more abstractly "Eastern bourgeois-feudal town."[50] His acceptance of this suggestion continued with his memoirs, published in 1987, where he describes the foreign land as "Gulestan," in quotes, and "the abroad" (*za rubezh*).[51]

At the same time Yarmatov actively sought "to break through the tradition of 'orientalist' (*oriental'nykh*) films and their saccharine exoticism." To differentiate himself from other directors of Soviet and Hollywood orientalist films and depict "the real life and real people of the contemporary East," Yarmatov fought for final say on the title cards.[52] "Even mullas do not express themselves in such a grandiloquent manner," he claimed, and eventually he got the cards rewritten in more accessible language.[53]

Thanks to these compromises, *Emigrant* became the first Tajikfilm Studio production to be approved for Union-wide distribution. This historical achievement meant greater engagement with the imperial gaze. In Moscow, advertisements highlighted Yarmatov's and his film's particularity. According to one radio announcer, it was the work of a talented "young national artist" (*khudozhnik-natsional*). According to another, the film showed the "colorful and distinctive" life of "our Asian borderland" about which "we still know little."[54] Moscow audiences were invited to learn about and experience "our Soviet Asia" as a version of the imperial sublime.[55]

There were reasons why Yarmatov may not have wanted to question his good fortune. It was safer to conceptualize his memoirs as a heroic adventure tale, in which he fashioned himself as wholly unconcerned with ideology and politics and succeeding solely on the merits of his hard work, artistic talent, and good luck. In 1934 he had seen the consequences of failure when his colleague Suleyman Khodjaev's historical drama about the Jizzakh uprising, *Before Dawn* (Uzbekkino, 1934), was rejected in Moscow.[56] *Emigrant* and *Before Dawn* were completed the same year, at a time when the historiography of the tsarist empire was changing. The reclassification of tsarist conquest from a greater to a lesser evil may have shaped the decision to censor the film about the 1916 revolt. As a result, Khodjaev was arrested and imprisoned before the end of the year.[57] Meanwhile, Yarmatov's film about emigration, adapted to satisfy MID requirements, enjoyed great success.

During World War II, Yarmatov's career took another favorable turn. Thanks in part to the devastation of cadres that took place in the 1930s purges, Yarmatov was appointed head of Uzbekfilm Studio in 1941, when major Soviet film studios were evacuated from Moscow and Leningrad to Central Asia and studios in the Caucasus (Tbilisi, Baku, and Erevan) acquired new importance.[58] Although the influx of people brought new opportunities, Yarmatov complained in a moment of candor to his friend and former teacher, Lev Kuleshov, about wartime restrictions on content and being forced to film Uzbek concerts for the front, since "they asked from the top, where they treat me very well."[59] Despite the period of growth for Central Asian studios, filmmakers continued to navigate significant ideological and creative constraints. Thus, after the war ended, Yarmatov had to seek approval from a reluctant Andrei Zhdanov, Stalin's propagandist-in-chief, for his major production *Alisher Navoi* (1947), about the fifteenth-century figure appropriated in 1941 as the "father of Uzbek literature."[60] To convince Zhdanov that the undertaking was worthwhile, Yarmatov cited a

Figure 6.1 Yarmatov directing actors on the set of *Death of the Black Consul*. From Kamil Yarmatov, *Vozvraschenie* (Tashkent: Gafur Ghulam, 1987).

conservative British MP's claim before the House of Commons that there were still "half savage nomadic tribes" in Soviet Central Asia. Yarmatov argued that a film about a Central Asian renaissance would "serve modernity."[61] Like Mukhitdinov, Yarmatov got his way by successfully leveraging international relations.

Alisher Navoi proved a great success. Stalin approved it for international distribution and awarded Yarmatov the Stalin Prize.[62] Part of this success reflected Yarmatov's ability to interpret the ideological terrain of Central Asian history according to prevailing politics. The film's screenplay managed to preach the communist word with such fluency that one poet from the Union of Writers had apparently observed wryly that "all he [Navoi] now had to do was apply to join the Communist Party."[63] Beyond correctly formulating the ideological position on the national question, this art form required particularly creative historicism. It had to steer clear of evoking historical reality, which could be potentially fatal in this period of late Stalinism, while offering evidence of the ancestral character of national culture in the form of continuous lineage from an imagined, ideologically acceptable origin.[64] Yarmatov would bring this talent for blending art and propaganda to the Afro-Asian circuit of the 1950s and 1960s. Throughout this period, he continued to make successful films and accumulate prestige, becoming Peoples Artist of Uzbekistan in 1955 and Peoples Artist of the USSR in 1955.

Yarmatov's 1968 trip to Syria, Lebanon, and Egypt to promote the Afro-Asian Film Festival in Tashkent points to significant continuities in cultural diplomacy from the Khrushchev to the Brezhnev periods, and especially to film as a key new sector. The 1950s bilateral agreements to promote cultural exchanges had also included film, and the volume of Soviet films imported by Egypt, Syria, and Iraq jumped in the late 1950s and then ebbed throughout the 1960s.[65] Over 200 of these exported films were translated and dubbed into Arabic by KUTV alumnus Hamdi Seliam.[66] Significantly, all seven of the films chosen by the Ministry of Culture to be sent to the 1956 Damascus International Fair were produced in the film studios of Central Asia and the Caucasus.[67] Of the thirteen other Soviet films dubbed into Arabic for distribution in Syria and Egypt in the summer of 1956, at least half focused explicitly on the Caucasus and Central Asia.[68] In this context, film diplomacy became another way of reconnecting the domestic and foreign Easts.

Part of this connection involved importing and dubbing Arab films, such as the Egyptian revolutionary melodrama *Return My Heart* (1958, Izz al-Din Zulficar), adapted from Yusuf al-Siba'i's eponymous 1954 novel. Egyptians who grew up in the 1960s watched this film annually on television in late July, during commemorations of the Egyptian Revolution of 1952, and recalled it as the quintessential cinematic rendition of the revolution.[69] By the 1960s, Siba'i had achieved a prominent role in Egypt as Nasser's pick to run his state monopoly on culture and to promote Egypt's place in the Afro-Asian world.[70] In 1967 he became chief editor of the Afro-Asian Writers Association's *Lotus* magazine, based in Egypt but sponsored by the Soviet state.[71] Thus, Soviet support for his work facilitated Soviet-Egyptian rapprochement and demonstrated support for the wider Afro-Asian cultural field.[72]

Another aspect of these exchanges was underscored by the TsK KPSS decision to organize an international film festival of Afro-Asian countries, alongside the more high-profile Afro-Asian Writers Conference in 1958.[73] The 1958 Afro-Asian Film Festival in Tashkent, held from August 20 to September 3, convened films and filmmakers from across Soviet Central Asia and Caucasus, and from Burma, Ceylon, China, Vietnam, Ghana, India, Indonesia, Korea, Mongolia, Morocco, the United Arab Republic, Pakistan, Sudan, and Thailand.[74] It also included celebrities such as the American communist singer Paul Robeson, who recalled the event's brutal heat and clouds of flies. Robeson's biographer describes how Soviet director Vasily Katanian had found him pouring sweat "prostrate from heat and exhaustion...glumly silent." In Tashkent, Robeson also apparently had to sit in a stuffy film-festival hall watching "unbearable two-reel Indonesian films that were dubbed into Uzbek." Regaining his spirits somewhat in the cool of the evening, Robeson enjoyed an official supper and even did "a strangely quiet, simple, dignified Asian jitterbug" with one of the dancers, before coming down with a fever the next day and retiring to bed.[75] The Uzbek hosts made sure to conceal these realities, reporting to Moscow only that a festival concert by Robeson had attracted thousands of spectators.[76]

The hosting Uzbek delegation was led by Deputy Minister of Culture of the Uzbek SSR S. Muhamedov, Kamil Yarmatov, and another prominent Tashkent-based director, Latif Faiziev.[77] Yarmatov's *Ibn Sina* (1956), which tells the story of how the major polymath of the Islamic Golden Age helped battle the plague in eleventh-century Central Asia, and Latif Faiziev's *Po putevke Lenina* (*On Lenin's Pass*, 1958), about the organization of the first university in Central Asia, represented Uzbekistan at the festival.[78] Like earlier projects, Yarmatov saw *Ibn Sina* (1956) as an ideological victory. During its assessment at the Moscow Film Committee (KinoKomitet), concerns were raised about particular scenes that might jeopardize "our good relations with the Muslim East." One screenwriter seemed anxious about the depiction of the Ghaznavid ruler, Mahmud of Ghazni (971–1030), as a cruel tyrant, which could potentially offend Afghan neighbors; others worried about scenes of "historical improvisation" that showed Ghazni burning down Bukhara and another that depicted Ibn Sina in prison, writing his medical treatise between the lines of an old Qur'an.[79] The KinoKomitet had reasons to be concerned. At the 1957 Soviet film festival in Cairo, Nasser ordered the suspension of the film adaptation of Gorky's novel *Mother* (Vsevolod Pudovkin, 1926) because of its praise for a woman's rejection of religion in favor of communism and atheism.[80] Yet Yarmatov stood his ground. He argued before a panel of Soviet orientalists that Ghazni was not an "Afghan" because his father was a Turkic war prisoner of the Sogdian emperor Nuh and his mother was a "Tajik."[81] He justified his historical improvisation as within the purview of his artistic license, and the scenes of Ibn Sina writing on the pages of a Qur'an, by asserting that "if Ibn Sina was unafraid to write on the Qur'an in a pious Muslim epoch when grim religious fanatics ruled the East—why should we, as atheists today, be afraid to show it?"[82] The KinoKomitet accepted these justifications and allowed Yarmatov to screen his film at the 1958 Afro-Asian Festival. In return for this level of official trust and respect for the integrity of his work, Yarmatov defended the interests of the system that nurtured his talents and provided him with such opportunities.

At the 1958 Film Festival, Yarmatov used his talents and experience of working for different audiences to mediate the interests of Uzbekistan and, by extension, the Soviet Union, for the Afro-Asian delegates. He situated both Tashkent and the Soviet Union in the official history of the Afro-Asian cinematic cultural project. According to him this history began with the 1957 week of Afro-Asian films in Beijing, which he attended and where the idea of an international Afro-Asian film festival was first proposed. As the idea grew into an Afro-Asian cinematography network, Tashkent became a node where Mongolian and Lebanese filmmakers could make connections and where someone could be both "a Soviet person" and a "a citizen of the world." For Yarmatov, being Soviet meant representing the Soviet Union well; it meant not objecting to being introduced as "Uzbek," despite being ethnically Tajik—perhaps to avoid confusing foreigners with complexities of Soviet nationalities policies.[83] It also meant that at a festival event at the

Uzbekfilm studio, he publicly embraced the "friendship of peoples" narrative of Central Asian history and film: "Our studio is still young. It was organized in 1926, by a group of energetic young people who loved this art. But when we got together, we didn't know where to start. To our rescue came our friends, our elder brothers: the Russians."[84]

Such rhetoric reflected earlier arguments of the Eastern International, suggesting that Central Asians had finally become modern and could replace Russians as teachers of other Afro-Asian studios and filmmakers. Some of the festival's participants echoed this narrative. The Indonesian delegation declared the festival to have been carried out "in the spirit of Bandung,"[85] and an Indonesian Ministry of Information press statement marveled at the great leap forward of what he had thought were "backwards" Soviet Eastern republics. This formula seemed promising to local party elites. As the head of the Uzbek Soviet of Ministers and the Festival Organization Committee, Rasul Gulamovich Gulamov reported after the festival that the Soviet Union should expand the use of the cinema industry of Central Asia, Kazakhstan, and the Caucasus to participate in yearly festivals in Afro-Asian countries, organize film exchanges, jointly produce films, and make more documentaries about the lives of Soviet Easterners, including Muslims, among other things.[86] Unlike other parts of the postwar world where Soviet cultural diplomacy did little to adjust to or fulfill the interests of specific countries, films exported to the Middle East were meant to support the specific, if still abstract and unhelpfully orientalist, assumption that one formerly colonized Muslim region could serve as the model for another.[87]

Meanwhile, the international campaign to portray the Soviet Union as a colonial "prison of nations" was heating up.[88] Chinese pressure was strong at Afro-Asian cultural events. From the Third Afro-Asian International Festival in Indonesia in April 1964, the Soviet delegation reported that it had been treated rudely by the Festival Organizational Committee and attacked in the Indonesian press and festival publications, which it claimed were controlled by the Journalist Organization of Afro-Asian Countries, with an openly pro-Chinese orientation.[89] The Soviet Union's submissions to the festival competition—*Piatero iz Fergany* (Five from Fergana, 1963, Uzbekfilm, directed by Uldash Agzamov); *Deti Pamira* (Children of the Pamirs, 1963 Tajikfilm, directed by Vladimir Motyl); and the documentary

Vperedi more (The sea is ahead, 1963, Turkmenfilm, directed by Mei Mark Vladimirovich)—received only one out of a possible thirty-two awards. Even that one award, for cinematography in Motyl's *Deti Pamira*, had to be shared with Japan and North Korea, and the film was panned as "an insult to the Leninist idea."[90] Since the film drew on the poetic themes of Mirsaid Mirshakar, a decorated Tajik writer, politician, and member of the Tajik committee for Afro-Asian solidarity, this critique could be interpreted on multiple levels that could damage Soviet cultural outreach efforts. Another Soviet film about colonialism in Africa screened at the festival, *Zakon podlosti* (Law of villainy, Central Studio for Documentary Film, 1962), was criticized for depicting religion as tool of imperialist domination. No one defended the Soviet delegates. Even Sukarno, who was drawing closer to China at the time, set the tone with an opening speech about the anti-imperialist solidarity movement that did not mention any events hosted by the Soviet Union.[91]

Things might have gone better, the Soviet ambassador to Indonesia suggested, had the delegation arrived at least seven to ten days in advance and refrained from making embarrassing statements about Southeast Asian politics; for example, its members made unvetted pledges of support for Indonesia's claims to Northern Kalimantan, which was then in dispute with Malaysia.[92] Moreover, the ambassador advised that would have been helpful to have at least one or two delegates who spoke English. Apparently the Soviet embassy had only one available translator who knew English and Indonesian, which forced delegates to attend all events as a group, unlike the Chinese, who arrived with multiple translators and could attend multiple events simultaneously. He also recommended sending more than one actress—perhaps someone like the beautiful Zinaida Kirienko, who accompanied Sergei Gerasimov's delegation and whom Sukarno showered with personal attention. Given these setbacks, he suggested, the future of Soviet film propaganda in Indonesia and the Afro-Asian world was in films about the republics of Central Asia and Caucasus.[93] The Central Committee's Section of Ideology and Propaganda endorsed these suggestions, forming a new committee to coordinate the production of films for audiences in Asia, Africa, and Latin America.[94]

Pressure to defend Soviet anticolonial legitimacy in the developing world increased just as Moscow was tightening its political controls over the domestic East. Accompanying new centralized institutions to oversee the region's party and economic affairs was a new industry of professional historians who specialized in defending the Soviet Union against "reactionary" and "bourgeois" scholars and their libelous conspiracies.[95] This pressure meant that the topic of Russian colonialism in Central Asia remained one of the least-developed areas of research by professional historians.[96]

In this context, Yarmatov was recruited to help. In 1962 he was asked to attend a meeting with First Secretary of the Uzbek Central Committee Sharof Rashidov (first secretary 1961–1983) and Yarmatov's successor at Uzbekfilm studio Ibrahim Rahim (studio director 1960–1966). Also present at the meeting was Kamil Iashena from the Khamza dramatical theater and Uzbek novelist and playwright Nazir Safarov. Rashidov had called the group together to brainstorm about how best to commemorate the fortieth anniversary of the Uzbek republic. As a writer, politician, and organizer of Afro-Asian events in Tashkent, Rashidov understood the responsibilities of political and intellectual elites. He also appreciated stories, and he wanted a new film "about the establishment of Soviet power in Uzbekistan."[97] Reacting to Rashidov's request, Yarmatov recalled, "I felt shivers down my spine." The topic seemed "*neohvatnaya*," a term often translated as overwhelming or enormous but that literally means unembraceable. He tried to dodge the request by telling Rashidov, "I fear to even think about it after all the wonderful pictures about the revolution made by the great masters of the Soviet theater!"[98] It is possible his fear may have been real. It was a mere artistic predilection against historical-adventure films, a genre that during this decade was changing with the rise of spaghetti Westerns. It is possible the request reminded Yarmatov of his friends, enemies, and competitors who were purged for such attempts in the 1930s.[99]

As a seasoned propagandist, Yarmatov knew that the official narrative about the consolidation of Soviet power in Turkestan had undergone multiple revisions that had involved the cooperation of party officials, historians, filmmakers, and other cultural figures. He knew that in the 1930s, an earlier interpretation of the revolution as an anticolonial event that had been useful to criticize British and French colonial powers during the civil war was declared obsolete. The authorities had reclassified pre-revolutionary Russian colonialism as a "lesser evil," which implied that tsarist imperialism, though somewhat objectionable, saved non-Russian peoples from a much worse fate at the hands of Britain and other imperial powers. In the early 1950s, Russian colonialism was again reassessed. "Conquest" was bowdlerized to "annexation" and, because of the allegedly beneficial ties with Russians, came to be regarded as "progressive."[100] This second adjustment may have reflected a transition from the early Soviet propaganda of agitation and subversion to the late Soviet propaganda of integration in order to stabilize, unify, and reinforce the social body.[101] It may have reflected Stalin's "Great Retreat" to the values of tsarist Russia, including Russia's imperial "civilizing mission" for non-Russians.[102] After de-Stalinization was curtailed in the mid-1960s, official Uzbek history was once again presented as a mostly continuous stream of successes.[103] Yarmatov likely understood that this position would be difficult to square with the demands of making Soviet anticolonialism legible to decolonizing peoples.[104]

In an effort to help ease the burden of his demand, Rashidov suggested that Yarmatov take a look at Nazir Safarov's play *Dawn over Asia* (*Zaria nad Aziei*, 1948). Safarov, who was also present at the initial meeting, was a graduate of the Uzbek Institute of Marxism-Leninism who had written a number of plays about the 1916 Central Asian Revolt that party authorities had approved. *Zaria nad Aziei* presented a story about the revolutionary struggle in Turkestan between the Bolsheviks, in alliance with the heads of the railway factories, and a counterrevolutionary coalition of former imperial and new provisional government actors.

Yarmatov found the script uninspiring. "The further I read the more it spoiled my mood. . . . I didn't like the play. Definitively and completely," he confessed.[105] But Rashidov was not someone to disappoint. Having promised to consider the project, Yarmatov gathered together a group of collaborators. For two weeks Yarmatov, Safarov, and screenwriters Odel'sha Agishev and Mikhail Melkumov holed up in a dacha drinking, thinking independently and collectively, and arguing, without writing a single line. Eventually, Yarmatov remembered his civil war commander from his days of fighting in the Central Ferghana region. His name was Khamdam-Khodja Kalandarov, and he had recounted stories of how he went from robbing the rich to joining the revolution after a fateful chance meeting with "'Prunze-Aka,' which is what he called Mikhail Frunze."[106] The memory conjured an introductory scene:

> Siberia. Prison. In the inner courtyard convicts line up in robes, jumpsuits, shackles. . . . A panorama of the faces creates a visual image of tsarist Russia—a prison of peoples. . . . "Khandam Kalandarov" calls the voice of the overseer, *inorodets*, Ferghana region, twenty years for brigandage.

The overseer, who is also Muslim, then offers to reduce Kalandarov's sentence if he were to "cut off the head of a shaitan, an enemy of the white tsar," and puts him in a cell with Frunze. Frunze greets Kalandarov with "*as-Salaam-Alaikum*" and then corrects the protagonist's recitation of the Qur'an from memory, earning his respect and friendship. Later Kalandarov escapes with Frunze with help from a Bolshevik organization, and returns to his village. "Here I stopped my internal 'projector', and ran to my coauthors," recalled Yarmatov, thinking that he had found an "organizing image for the Uzbek peoples and for Turkestan." The image seemed to work because there were so few proletarians among the local population that the main drivers of the struggle for Soviet power had to be the working peasants led by the Bolsheviks and a few class-conscious workers. Yarmatov's hero would thus personify a peasant (*dekhkan*) awakened by the revolution who would "transform from a spontaneous (*stikhiinyi buntar'*) rebel into a partisan, a conscious revolutionary, and eventually a Red Army commander."[107]

With this image in mind, the group quickly wrote the screenplay. Yet when they submitted it to Rashidov, the first secretary cautioned that the colorful and attractive image of the protagonist was too overwhelming. It seemed like the socialist revolution in Turkestan was orchestrated by "spontaneous rebels.... Where are the communists? Where is the revolutionary organized working class?" Rashidov wondered, sending the group back to the drawing board.[108] The next painful round of revisions progressed from one dead end to another. The group imagined new characters:

> Bolsheviks, leaders of the revolution ... our characters all came from under our collective pen stilted, schematic, forced. Each iteration of the script was worse than the last.... We decided to go to Moscow. There we had old friends to consult and shoulders to cry on.... Another round of torment began. Scene after scene was born and met with inglorious death.[109]

The most creative, talented writers and filmmakers, it seemed, could not solve the challenge put forward by the Central Committee to produce something that would meet the contradictory domestic and foreign propaganda needs of the early 1960s—something that would display Soviet anticolonialism to the foreign East, while projecting an empire-positive integrative history of the domestic East.

When the project failed as a written narrative—the Moscow KinoKomitet collegium dismissed yet another iteration of the script—Yarmatov resorted to doing what he did best. He stood up and asked his comrades if they would be willing to let him pitch his vision for the film orally. Then he gave a performance, using his body, memory, and charisma to sell the film.

> I told them about Khamdame-hodja Kalandarov and his fate, about how he had melted in my mind and heart into this mighty figure to the point that I could no longer discern where the historical Hamdam-Hoja ended and where my creative fantasy began.... I ask you comrades, give me your trust, confirm this version [of the script] which you so rightly criticized. If you trust me, I give you my word I'll make a picture. A good one.... Otherwise we will not make it to the anniversary of the republic.[110]

Yarmatov thus persuaded the collegium to approve production of his screenplay by once again playing on deeper scripts of Soviet politics. It was important to mark the fortieth anniversary of the Uzbek Republic. Such celebrations mobilized the masses and helped mark Soviet space and time. To do this, he offered himself as an example of how history and memory could be rewritten through art.[111]

After two years of filming and editing, Yarmatov's *Buria nad Aziei* (Storm over Asia), co-written with the Uzbekfilm studio screenwriter Mikhail Melkumov, was completed in 1964.[112] As promised, Yarmatov did try to blur memory and history. The film opened with a story narrated by Uzbek Bolshevik Jamal about how he acquired the courage to speak truth to power—in this case to his captor Usup Ivantush-aka. His story takes the viewer to Petrograd, on the eve of the October Revolution, where the young man was in jail for revolutionary activities. Scenes of massive jubilant demonstrations on the streets outside evoked Sergei Eisenstein's 1928 film *October: Ten Days That Shook the World*. In his memoirs, Yarmatov recalled a special pleasure of filming massive re-enactments in "real historical places" like the Leningrad Strelka. These scenes likely reminded Yarmatov of his student days in Moscow in the late 1920s and early 1930s, when Eisenstein was his teacher and public ceremonies and re-enactments were used to convey a popular aesthetic and dramatic essence of October.[113] In the film, these celebratory masses liberate the young Central Asian man from prison and allow him to return to Central Asia carrying the spark of revolution to Ivantush-aka and his men. The ensuing recreations of massive civil war–era Turkestan battles on horseback created many possibilities for Yarmatov's actors to experience the establishment of Soviet rule in Turkestan as both a personal and foundational historical event. Like Eisenstein's *October*, Yarmatov's *Storm over Asia* sacrificed historical accuracy to ideological, aesthetic, and political aims that were shaped by multiple layers of quality control.

The film's reviews were not great. For Yarmatov, naturally, the more salient critiques were the ones he managed to overcome. When *Storm over Asia* was screened before the Khudsovet (Artists Council), it raised questions about its foreign reception, as had Yarmatov's earlier films. Some worried that the final scene might "offend the faithful abroad and at home."[114] In the scene, the basmach leader turned Red Army warrior pretends to lead Muslims in prayer as he issues instructions to his troops, who are also pretending to pray behind him. Presenting this material to the Artists' Soviet, Yarmatov once again managed to allay their suspicions about reception in the foreign East, adding in his memoir that a few years later audiences in Cairo and Damascus responded to this scene with applause.[115]

Other critiques suggest that Yarmatov may have made some compromises that he wasn't too happy about. Perhaps because he resented being forced by Rashidov and the Moscow KinoKomitet to create larger roles for Uzbek and Russian Bolshevik characters, who would guide his protagonist Iavantush, Yarmatov cast these characters in ways that minimized their significance. As film scholar Dzhura Teshabaev notes, the main Uzbek Bolshevik, Jamal, seemed to have an insignificant presence—as if he could never really lead Iavantush, with his strong common sense, tactical knowledge, and strategy.[116] Perhaps this was because Yarmatov had cast in the role Moscow mime Ruslan Akhmetov, "a good looking but dull and inert actor without many dramatic attributes." The main Russian Bolshevik character, Shchukin, also seemed poorly cast, with Anatolii Solov'ev dramatizing the character's thoughtful action, organizational talent, conviction, and strength of character as a kind of "fussy readiness."[117] Other reviewers found the dialogue weak, with Iavantush's elevated speech especially pompous and overly stylized.[118]

Despite its failures, Yarmatov's artistic blurring of memory and history made the film work in ways that other cinematic attempts to honor the occasion didn't. In Kyrgyzstan, for example, the Central Committee had commissioned a documentary historical film to celebrate the founding of the Kyrgyz Autonomous Oblast and the fortieth anniversary of Soviet rule. Filmmakers tried to show simultaneously eyewitness interviews and historical footage from the archives (e.g., photos and films), but the interviewee's stories did not match the official narrative of the building of the Kyrgyz

Republic. "Perhaps inspired by the debates of the Thaw, the interviews told the filmmakers how they had been forced into kolkhozes, about denunciations, questioning, camps, and famine. Interviewees thus spoke about many of the things that Kyrgyz intellectuals had failed to address in 1956." Consequently, the film was banned.[119] Similar accounts found by anthropologists working in the Kyrgyz SSR revealed instances of ethnic and sexual violence, persecution, and persistent resentment and distrust between settlers and native inhabitants.[120] The difficulty of working with so many painful memories of the 1916 revolt and the Sovietization of Central Asia was that they were not easily represented, on or off the screen, in a way that did not threaten or complicate Soviet anticolonial legitimacy.

Even fictionalized accounts enflamed tensions. For example, Andrei Konachalovsky's film *First Teacher* (1965) depicts a former Red Army soldier who moves to a distant Kyrgyz village to try to educate local children but meets with opposition from conservative village parents. The screenplay was based on a book by Chingiz Aitmatov, and the film received positive reviews in Moscow. But critics in the Kyrgyz SSR had a more equivocal response. A member of the older generation of writers, Aziz Saliev, was disappointed in the film's representation of the Kyrgyz people as "savages" and of the October Revolution as "if it had been forced upon the Kyrgyz people from the outside, from Russia." Pointing to the imperial dynamics of the film's positive reception in Moscow, he also warned that "we should not let Simonov or Gerasimov speak for us." The last criticism may have been a covert jab at Aitmatov, who also published his works first in Moscow to evade censorship by local party bureaucrats, and whose international acclaim by this point provoked jealousy.[121] Saliev's arguments were supported by the first secretary of Kyrgyzstan, who kept the film from being screened in the republic until September 1966, when local objections were overridden directly by Mikhail Suslov in Moscow. Yarmatov's film, albeit disappointing artistically, managed to tell a story of the Central Asian revolution and avoid scandal.

Soviet efforts to promote its ideological legitimacy as an anticolonial power helped direct more resources into the cinema industry of Central Asia and the Caucasus. These resources were directed by the cinematography subsection of the Ideological Department of the TsK KPSS, together with the Party's Central Asian Bureau (in 1962–1964), to grow film studios, movie theaters, and filmgoing culture. Delegations of TsK KPSS, TsK VLKSM (Komsomol), VTsSPS (Trade Unions), and the State Committee of Cinematography under the Council of Ministers assessed the needs of the Uzbek, Tajik, Turkmen, and Kyrgyz republics. They concluded that Republican Party organs were undervaluing cinema's role in the formation of public consciousness and underutilizing it for ideological work.[122] The delegation to Uzbekistan found a dangerous level of formalism among filmmakers, too many foreign films in movie theaters, and low average attendance in theaters—less than half the Union-wide average.[123] Rashidov closely followed the progress of Uzbek film production and consumption. He received reports from the GosKomitet of the Uzbek Council of Ministers responsible for Cinematography about new cadres at Uzbekfilm and the construction of new movie theaters,[124] especially in the Uzbek countryside where "cinefication" lagged the most.[125]

Although the unpopularity of Soviet films among Uzbek audiences, compared to Western films, raised concerns about the potential success of Soviet media abroad, another major motivation behind the "cinefication" drive was to raise revenues for the state. On average, Soviet people visited movie theaters 18.5 times per year, compared with 12 times in the United States, 7 in England, and 6 in France. By the middle of the 1960s, Soviet state revenues generated by cinemagoers were outstripped only by revenues from the sale of vodka.[126] To maintain audience interest and ticket sales, production was increased across the Soviet Union, from 133 films produced in 1963 to 167 films produced in 1965, of which 124 were non-documentary (*khudozhestvennye*) and 25 were full feature-length.[127] The number of movie theaters, or literally the theater network (*kinoset'*), expanded from 92,200 in 1963 to 147,500 in 1967. By 1968, the TsK Cultural Section reported that the USSR had the highest average attendance of film theaters in the world.[128]

Central Asia followed the trend. The number of projectors had grown between 1958 and 1966 from 78,000 to 145,000.[129] In the Samarkand region, film audiences increased between 1964 and 1965 by 1.625 million, generating an increase in ticket sales proceeds of 295,000 rubles.[130] To mark these achievements, a Festival of Central Asia and Kazakhstan Films was organized in Tashkent on April 2–3, 1966.

The cinefication drive in Uzbekistan was interrupted by a 5.1-magnitude earthquake on April 26, 1966, that left hundreds of thousands homeless and destroyed all but one of the major movie theaters. The widespread destruction, however, gave Soviet planners an opportunity to rebuild the city as the symbol of Soviet modernity in Asia that had been previously imagined but had been too constrained by history and environment to achieve.[131] In the immediate aftermath of the earthquake, Brezhnev flew to Tashkent and promised to rebuild as quickly as possible. To do so, Moscow authorized lucrative compensation to the thousands of construction engineers and other specialists from across the USSR to rebuild the city and in the process to underscore the sacred geography of the October Revolution.[132]

As Tashkent was being rebuilt, the Soviet Union's main ally in the Afro-Asian movement, Egypt, became embroiled in a regional conflict that culminated in one of the greatest challenges yet to the public perception of Soviet commitments to global decolonization. In 1966–1967, Gamal Abdel Nasser felt emboldened by the Soviet Union's more militant rhetoric and by his own advisers' overestimation of Egypt's military capacities vis-à-vis Israel.[133] On May 19, as tensions between the two states escalated, Nasser ordered UN troops to leave the Sinai, without consulting first with Moscow, and then blocked the Gulf of Aqaba to Israeli ships and other vessels carrying strategic goods to Israel. Brezhnev had made some attempts to de-escalate, warning both Nasser and Syrian president Atasi (who was visiting Moscow in May) that further steps might be used as a pretext for a war by Israel. Despite these private warnings, Moscow's public support for the war remained unequivocal.[134]

A surprise attack by Israel ended the war in six days. In its aftermath protestors at anti-Soviet demonstrations in Cairo, Beirut, Baghdad, and Khartoum sought an explanation for the Soviets' nonintervention and a dearth of more active assistance to the Arabs. Brezhnev would come to characterize the Arab actions as "surprising" and "ill-advised."[135] This was a major blow to the project of Arab nationalism and to the Soviet Union's anticolonial credentials, as Chinese and to a lesser degree Cuban and Arab voices again started to blame the USSR for the defeat, despite the Soviet provision of weapons to the Egyptian and Syrian militaries. They called for "more decisive" Soviet action and asked Moscow to end its policy of "peaceful coexistence." Moscow, in turn, lashed out against Chinese and Western "imperialists" for trying to drive a wedge between the USSR and the Arabs, though it backed away from overt confrontation. Brezhnev had issued a statement suggesting that Arab leaders had not sought Soviet involvement in the armed conflict,[136] but he also dismissed officials who had argued for a more forceful Soviet posture in the Middle East, including the allies of Alexander Shelepin. Shelepin, who headed the KGB in the mid-1960s, had implemented an aggressive strategy—approved by Khrushchev in 1961—of using the KGB to help support left-wing nationalist liberation movements in Latin America, Asia, and Africa. After 1967 he lost much of his influence, indicating Brezhnev's unwillingness to get drawn into the regional conflict and the importance of culture as a means to diffuse tensions.

To showcase how disaster might be mitigated and in a short time overcome with Soviet "brotherly" aid and cooperation, the Uzbek TsK proposed that the city of Tashkent host the 1968 International Afro-Asian Film Festival.[137] The Festival would employ cultural diplomacy and the new Tashkent setting to reconnect Soviet and Afro-Asian communities and conversations about decolonization, including among Egyptian filmmakers who, after the 1967 defeat, joined other shocked and disillusioned intellectuals in questioning Nasser's regime.[138] This questioning included a reconsideration in and through film of the country's social and political life. Some films even suggested that the people had been exploited in the name of socialism, and some were barred from distribution in Egypt. Others expressed different kinds of cynicism toward revolutionary projects.[139]

The 1968 Tashkent Afro-Asian Film Festival, whose motto was "Peace, Social Progress, and Freedom of Peoples," dwarfed the 1958 festival by several measures. Soviet investments in Central Asian development and cinematic infrastructure were considerably greater; the number of countries that had achieved political independence and could send delegations had grown from twenty in 1958 to over forty in 1968;[140] and the crowd in Tashkent was significantly more distinguished than the one in 1958.[141] In the process of decolonization, many states began to support culture, and specifically film, as part of postcolonial state building and industrial development.[142] The final list of guests, according to the Council of Ministers, was a victory over American attempts to persuade countries to boycott the festival because of the Warsaw Pact invasion of Czechoslovakia.[143] This US-led effort had been coordinated through the International Federation of Film Critics (FIPRESCI), through which lobbyists called for boycotts of the Tashkent festival at gatherings in Venice and Tunis.[144] To counter this pressure, the Organizing Committee sent delegations, such as the one headed by Yarmatov, to Japan, Algeria, Tunisia, Morocco, Pakistan, India, Syria, Lebanon, and the United Arab Republic to ensure the participation of important film stars and state representatives.[145]

These efforts paid off, allowing the Soviet Union to redeem itself on the Afro-Asian circuit after the difficult experience in Jakarta in 1964. Among the attendees of the 1968 event in Tashkent were the state secretary for information and tourism of Guinea; the deputy minister of culture of India;

the director of Beirut's Inter-Arab Center of Cinema & Television; Lucienne Khoury, the director of the Department of Film of Jordan; Ali Siam, the deputy minister of culture of Mongolia; and the director of the Committee for Cinematography in the Ministry of Culture of Tunis. Egyptian actress Magda Kamel spoke about her appreciation for Soviet efforts to strengthen peace across the world, and film critic Samir Farid said the trip "opened his eyes to a lot," including the "lies of Western propaganda about the Soviet Union."[146] As the Uzbek organizers proudly reported to the TsK KPSS, "there was not one speech or statement with anti-socialist character or statement in the spirit of Chinese propaganda."[147]

According to the TsK KPSS Section of Culture, the festival's greatest political and propagandistic significance was in strengthening "creative ties, contacts, and collaborations with cinematographers of African and Asian countries."[148] It was an opportunity to showcase the contributions to cinema on the three continents by students and graduates of Moscow's VGIK.[149] These graduates included Central Asian directors like Yarmatov but also the new generation of Arab filmmakers who had studied there on scholarships since the early 1960s. Most directors in countries like Syria, which did not have a film school in the twentieth century, had studied in Moscow, Kiev, or Prague, with some going to Cairo and Paris.[150] In this regard the festival was a kind of VGIK reunion for students who had shared an education in filmmaking and, according to one alumnus, also in "world culture, world literature, the history of photography, philosophy, the history of philosophy, epistemology, a Marxist economic history of the World, as well as Marxist ethics and aesthetics."[151]

Mingling with this core network of filmmakers were 247 official foreign guests and 226 journalists from thirty-five countries of Asia, Africa, Europe, and the Americas.[152] These guests were all introduced to Central Asian history and culture in several ways, ranging from tourist excursions around Uzbekistan to a special concert with selections of multinational films that celebrated fifty years of Soviet power. After the festival the International Federation of Film Critics (FIPRESCI) held a session on the developments of cinematography in republics of Central Asia and the Caucasus. Some of this activity was expected to generate income. The TsK anticipated it could recoup the festival's expenses through screenings of festival films around Central Asia, sometimes accompanied by the film's festival delegations. Soviet cultural bureaucracies viewed cinema—unlike literature—as a profit-making industry at home and abroad.[153] One of the key networks created at the festival was that of SovExportFilm, which linked Soviet film representatives to distribution companies across Africa and Asia.[154] This market made Tashkent disproportionately important for the international distribution of Central Asian films, as well as for commercial contacts.[155]

The headliner on the festival's opening night was Yarmatov's *Horsemen of the Revolution* (1968). This was the second installment after *Storm over Asia* in Yarmatov's revolutionary trilogy. Dedicated to the Chekists of the 1920s, it resembled its predecessor in several ways. Both films starred Shukur Burkhanov; previously cast as Iavantush, he now played Aznavurpalvan, a fighter more seasoned by the Revolution.[156] Both films dealt with betrayal and enemy spies masquerading as Red Army commanders; both opened with an execution scene; and both included protracted chase scenes on horseback as the Bolsheviks try to fulfill their mission—in this case, to intercept a secret document that could jeopardize all the revolutionaries of Turkestan before it falls into the hands of the Emir of Bukhara and the White Army. Both were examples of the wave of historical-revolutionary drama films about the Central Asian revolution that had peaked in the late 1960s and early 1970s.[157]

Yarmatov's second revolutionary film also did not win any major prizes and was ignored by critics at the festival. Dutch critic Hans Saaltink, who had initially supported the US-led boycott of Tashkent but decided to attend after the boycott failed, heard Russian cynics on his way from Moscow to Tashkent "snigger that 'the festival is one of our charity institutions'" and wonder "were the standards of filmmaking in all these countries so extremely low, or the method of selection so bad?" His list of "a few exceptions" of higher-quality films from Iran, Japan, and Algeria did not include Yarmatov's *Horsemen*.[158] It also did not include Husayn Kamal's *The Postman* (al-Bustagi 1968, based on the short story by Yahya Haqqi), about a Cairo resident appointed to supervise a post office in a small village in Upper Egypt where he suffers from ignorance, hatred, and boredom that drives him to start reading their letters, yielding insights into their innermost secrets. A Polish reviewer mentioned Yarmatov's film last in a list of "films of the Asian republics of the USSR," after two films from Georgia and one from Kyrgyzstan.[159] Swiss newspaper *La liberté* focused on Yarmatov as an actor, filmmaker, and student of Eisenstein who had achieved considerable artistic success and recognition outside the USSR. It said nothing about the film itself.[160]

Yarmatov agreed that *Horsemen* was far from his best work. In his memoirs he claimed to be happier with the third part in the revolutionary trilogy, *Smert' chernogo konsula* (The death of the black consul, 1970), evidently planned for the next Tashkent Afro-Asian Festival.[161] However, it was a totally different kind of film, Yarmatov's lavish historical melodrama *Poem of Two Hearts* (*Poema dvukh serdets*, 1966), which would go on to win an award at an international film festival in Cambodia in December 1968.[162] Ironically, *Poem of Two Hearts* began with a meditation by an artist about how his art brings him misfortune.

Once again, Yarmatov's 1968 revolutionary-historical film was only part of the show he produced in Tashkent. The filmmaker also had a talent for positioning himself at the center of political theater. His more memorable performance at a press conference of the Afro-Asian Festival was a conflation of cinematic art, memory, and history about the foundations of Soviet rule in Central Asia. The Tashkent newspaper *Pravda Vostoka* presented him as "a participant of the events shown in the film," and *Horsemen* as "a type of autobiography from the time of the establishment of Soviet power in Turkestan."[163] Ten days later, *Pravda Vostoka* ran a longer review of the film by Samarkand journalist Aleksandr Tankhel'son, who described the film as evoking nostalgia for "our youth," recalled by a "long-forgotten melody, the bitter smoke of a campfire, the face of a passerby who reminds us of an old friend." Although even Tankhel'son could not refrain from pointing out flaws and insufficient character development, he praised Yarmatov for "unfolding before us images of memories permeated by a single romantic impulse of [Yarmatov's] restless youth, which coincided with the turbulent youth of our country."[164] Calling Yarmatov a "Horseman of the Revolution," other Soviet newspapers celebrated this conflation of art, memory, and history.[165]

Some of the visiting critics also noted the nostalgic effects of Yarmatov's performance but were more skeptical about allowing his recollections to represent the Revolution. The editor of the French journal *Cinema*, Marcel Martin, raised pernicious questions the influence of the "cult of personality" on Soviet film and about generational conflict in Soviet society.[166] Late socialist culture was deeply shaped by generational conflict. For the older generation of intellectuals such as Yarmatov, Ghafur Gulom, and Tursunzade, the normalized Soviet ideological discourse still had meaning; for the younger post-Stalin generation, the liberation of Central Asia, like other ideological constructs, was increasingly becoming a set of ritualized acts and pronouncements.[167] In literature and film, this younger generation was more experimental and sought new kinds of genres and entertainment.

Years later, Yarmatov would reflect on this generational conflict in his memoirs. He described his generation as the one that actually made the revolution, which gave him a special kind of conditioning. While filming the last part of his revolutionary-historical trilogy, *Death of the Black Consul* (1970), he recalled how a general whose soldiers had been cast as extras in one of the battle scenes after a few minutes in the heat wiped his brow and neck and pitied his soldiers enduring the terrible heat and dust to re-enact the storming of the fortress of Bukhara. Yarmatov replied, "Your soldiers are twenty. I am almost seventy; moreover, they could have rested in the shade, caught their breath, but I am here from 6 A.M. to 6 P.M. for ten days almost without breaks . . . directing the assault." The general answered, "But you have the conditioning of an old soldier and an old hunter, whereas my young men have yet to be hardened (*mal'chishkam moim eshche zakaliatsia i zakaliatsia*)."[168] Although this anecdote was meant to display Yarmatov's virility in his old age, it also seemed symptomatic of the disconnect between the older generation of revolutionary idealists and the Soviet youth of the late 1960s, who had grown up with material comforts and privileges.

The growing disaffection of Soviet youth concerned ruling elites and the KGB, which reported in late 1968 on pervasive political apathy and cynicism among Soviet students after the Prague Spring earlier that year. Some explicitly wondered if similar events could happen in the USSR.[169] Mostly, however, historian Vladislav Zubok argues, "it became fashionable for Soviet intellectuals of the seventies to treat the sixties' leftist intellectuals and dissidents as naïve and irrelevant Don Quixotes. In the Brezhnev years, acting passionately and heroically became gauche and unfashionable. The notion of a vanguard was replaced by a sense of the irrelevance of any public action."[170] This alienation seemed less pronounced in Central Asia. As historian Artemy Kalinovsky claimed, literary gatherings in 1960s and 1970s Tajikistan "helped socialize students into a certain kind of intellectual life, and encouraged their self-identification as cultural leaders connected to other Soviet elites but with their own local mission."[171] They did not seem to develop as much of a "cynical brotherhood" as Russian intellectuals, especially in Leningrad.[172] Yet despite Yarmatov's best efforts to channel Eisenstein by blending re-enactments and historical improvisation, his attempt to establish a place for Soviet Central Asia in the decolonizing and increasingly radicalizing Afro-Asian world exposed an emerging generational conflict between an older generation of Central Asian intellectuals hardened by 1917 and Stalinism and a younger generation shaped by the postwar, de-Stalinizing quest for cultural renewal.[173]

For the older generation, the dramatic revolutionary spectacle and accompanying nostalgia seemed almost a reminder that they were passing from the scene. For the younger generation, the conversation about Central Asian revolution was going in new directions. By 1970, a film had captured the imaginations of Soviet audiences that would become one of the most popular movies of all time in the USSR by parodying the stock Central Asian historical-revolutionary drama. Vladimir Motyl's *White Sun of the Desert* blended comedy with revolutionary adventure while referencing American Westerns. On the surface, the film contains all the elements of the Soviet civil war mythology and cinematic convention: the heroic Russian Red Amy solider Sukhov, the evil local warlord Abdulla and his ruthless army; the "women of the East" are liberated from their husband-master and from social prejudice; Russians and Turkmens fight side by side to modernize the desert; and dramatic revolutionary violence and sacrifices result in the victory of the new order. Yet the civil war setting is more of a historical backdrop in the film. Its humor—especially Sukhov's comic efforts to re-educate Oriental women—suggests that by the late 1960s both the idea of re-education of the most "backwards" elements of society and the building of revolutionary socialist utopia had lost their urgency and became tropes that could be used dramatically or comically. The film's style and visual puns poke fun at the socialist project and the revolutionary spirit that Yarmatov was trying to revive and take seriously. Its popularity was evident in the widespread use of quotations from its script in conversations, including in Tashkent.[174]

Echoing such critiques, it was the younger directors like Ali Khamraev (b. 1937) who dared to criticize Yarmatov at meetings of the Khudsovet for not changing with the times.[175] More broadly, however, the Brezhnev-era "absence of convictions of the new Soviet person in modern life" increasingly concerned the Party's Cultural Section.[176] As part of this shift, the ideological basis of the Eastern International—the idea of a Central Asian model of development—had also turned into a joke.

In Central Asia, members of the new generation of Russophone writers were also starting to reflect more critically on their place in the Soviet cultural hierarchy and in Afro-Asian solidarity networks. Already by 1961, Kazakh writer Olzhas Suleimenov's poems subverted the Russian "big brother" narrative by portraying Muscovites as newcomers to Kazakhstan, ignorant of the language and customs of Central Asia and bedeviled by desert mirages of water and trees, wondering aloud, "How do these people live here?" The Muscovite then scolds the narrator and the nomad, compelling the Central Asian narrator to speak against his fellow Central Asian. The suggestion is that it is "the responsibility of minorities to present an acceptable version of diversity to the metropole."[177] Another Kazakh writer, Satimzhan Sanbayev, expressed longing in the late 1960s for an imagined native land and hope for authentic culture and self-identification.[178] These cultural elites were hardly dissident or oppressed. "Judging by their conduct in the run-up to the disillusion of the USSR," writes literary scholar Rossen Djagalov, "they probably never even wanted their republics to be independent, unlike their peers from the Baltics and Caucasus. . . . [Yet] the impulse that the Bolshevik revolution and the new Soviet literature had once given to anti-colonial movements and cultures worldwide came back as a form of critique of late-Soviet practices in the country's periphery."[179] With the unraveling of the previously sacrosanct narrative of the Sovietization of Central Asia, the ideological foundation of the Eastern International lost its meaning. In 1925, Stalin had articulated the idea, at KUTV, that Soviet republics could "attract the workers and peasants of the neighboring colonial and dependent countries to the liberation movement." Yarmatov's rise and decline into the category of "old-fashioned" helps pinpoint when this idea became obsolete.

The 1960s plurality of global anticolonial political agendas tested the ideological reach and influence of the Eastern International. Developments in the Middle East raised the political stakes of Soviet commitments to anticolonialism. These developments included Arab territorial and political losses in 1967—including disillusionment with Nasserism, and the displacement of Palestinian refugees, with its destabilizing regional effects in Jordan, Lebanon, and Syria; they also included state-led development projects that needed foreign financing. The simultaneous expansion of America's presence in the region; competing internationalisms promoted by the United States, China, and the Third World project; and national protest movements in Eastern Europe further challenged Soviet political legitimacy as a supporter anticolonial politics and as a model for decolonization. The offerings by the revolutionary generation of Soviet cultural figures seemed uninspired.

They moved neither international film audiences nor the new generation of Soviet intellectuals who were starting to doubt the promises of socialism.

The rigid frameworks of the Soviet Eastern International, and especially their approach to Central Asian history, made it difficult to acknowledge, let along engage with, new forms of anticolonial humanism articulated by intellectuals such as Frantz Fanon, Aimé Césaire, and Léopold Sédar Senghor, who wrote about race, otherness, and decolonization; by the European New Left; and by American civil rights activists such as Dr. Martin Luther King Jr. In 1960, the Egyptian Suhayl Idris translated into Arabic Sartre's "Colonialism Is a System," making widely available its argument that "colonialism is by definition a system of racial difference," and that "one of the functions of racism is to [make] the Algerian (who does not enjoy the same universal rights) . . . subhuman."[180] This argument established the foundations of a non-Soviet global ethics and a very different theory of belonging that made erasures visible, as opposed to their continued erasure from historical narratives.[181] Subsequent translations into Arabic of Simone de Beauvoir's 1962 book about the rape and torture of Algerian nationalist Djamila Boupacha also affirmed the extent to which struggles against colonialism and racism were intertwined and could not be reduced to dogma about class struggle or isolated cases of national liberation and "transfer of power."[182] These works, like Gillo Pontecorvo's 1966 film *The Battle of Algiers*, made clear that Marxism did not always address matters of culture, spirit, and existence.[183]

These alternatives deprived the Cold War–era Soviet state of any monopoly it may have imagined on matters of racial justice and equality. Stories and films like *Horsemen of the Revolution*, with Yarmatov embodying a Soviet approach to national and, implicitly, racial, difference, was not ideologically flexible enough to engage with these conversations. Indeed, as Yarmatov's story suggests, they had trouble formulating any coherent narrative at all about the relationship between culture and revolution. As a result, conversations about decolonization unfolding across the "domestic" and "foreign" Easts became increasingly disconnected.

The United States also responded to global challenges by redrawing and tightening the ideological lines around possible speech. Like Yarmatov, Black American performers abroad had to be careful to include enough social and political messages in their songs to elicit an audience reaction without turning their evenings into "social protests."[184] Those who drew unacceptably inconvenient connections between international and domestic politics were isolated and chastised. Both white liberal and Black establishment allies abandoned Dr. King after he linked his critique of the American capitalist economy to anti-imperialist politics, challenging the United States to address its gross disparities in wealth and condemning its intervention in Vietnam as immoral. The intellectual and political culture and the forms of institutions and alliances necessary to sustain his vision—a vibrant Black press, a vigorous labor movement, and cross-class coalitions that united liberals and the Left—had all diminished under McCarthyism.[185]

Although the story of Central Asian revolution became impossible to tell in the Soviet Union's own terms, all around it remained a dynamic terrain of contacts, exchanges, and possibilities.[186] Yarmatov tried to contribute to this conversation by following in Eisenstein's footsteps and rewriting the historical memory of the revolution. His failure to tell a persuasive story about the Soviet Union as a decolonized and anticolonial power, however, was ultimately a problem of historical narrative. "Affective affinities" that could be less rigid in their perspectives on history could better accommodate the diversity and instability of conflicting forms, values, and idioms of the late 1960s decolonizing world. The parties of the 1968 Festival, and what participants recalled as Yarmatov's charisma and air of nobility, forged connections that a stilted revolutionary-historical film never could.[187]

During the 1960s, the need for ideological statements, performances, and foundational narratives about the Soviet Union as an anticolonial state allowed some established Central Asian artists to reinvent themselves as revolutionary anticolonial heroes. Such opportunities shaped the language of propaganda in heterogeneous ways across the USSR, but still followed the logic of the "Eastern International," emphasizing connections across the domestic and foreign Easts even as conversations about global politics were being reoriented around a "North-South" axis. As they participated in these events, Soviet Central Asian mediators continued to sever Central Asia from broader conversations about cultural and intellectual decolonization, ensuring that contacts between the two Easts remain productive but superficial.

7
The Eastern International in an Age of Globalization

The erosion of narratives that explained "the Eastern International" as a relationship between the two Easts and a justification for projections of Soviet power abroad intensified in the 1970s and 1980s. On the one hand, the Eastern International framework, originally intended as an anti-imperialist front of opposition to the Western international of capital, had to confront the extraordinary transformations of global capitalism—the increase of world trade, the growth in transnational corporations, and the rise of international economic institutions such as the IMF, the World Bank, and the WTO. On the other hand, the culture of late socialism within the USSR bred deeper skepticism, if not outright cynicism, toward many Soviet ideological slogans. This cynicism increasingly extended to the Soviet model of development, including the industrialization of poorer republics and the provision of aid abroad.[1]

Some late Soviet slogans remained more meaningful than others. Significantly, the ideological commitment to "Friendship of the Peoples" as a metaphor for Soviet integration and belonging was continuously articulated in the official press right through the collapse of the USSR.[2] This slogan remained meaningful to people in the "domestic East" still trying to access Soviet state resources. It also remained meaningful to migrants from Central Asia and the Caucasus seeking economic opportunities in Moscow and Leningrad.[3] Within the Soviet Union and internationally, it continued to be invoked as an umbrella term to describe positive relations with other socialist and non-socialist partners largely because it did not require any reckoning with the historical past. Yet continued faith by many in the reality and utility of the concept of "friendship of peoples" was not enough to explain the longevity of institutions that connected the two Easts.

The Tashkent Afro-Asian Film Festival (which included Latin America after 1976) was held annually until 1988, except for 1970 due to a cholera outbreak. The festival's scale—the number of countries represented, the breadth of cinematic production, and the capacity to establish connections among filmmakers and audiences—actually increased throughout the 1970s and 1980s. As long as they didn't dwell too much on history, conversations in this cultural "contact zone" allowed Soviet filmmakers and others to participate in the Third World project by creating a "shared field of audiovisual references" and "affective solidarities."[4] In the process, they reinforced the familiar Soviet geographical division of labor. Western film industry representatives and other visitors were channeled to Moscow, whereas their African, African American, Asian, and Latin American colleagues were channeled to Tashkent (or Alma-Ata, Dushanbe, Samarkand, Bukhara, and other cities that showcased the USSR's Asian modernity).[5] Supporting the production of this Eastern contact zone was a wider network of cultural and political mediators, including a larger number of domestic Easterners in diplomatic posts in Africa and Asia. This pattern extended the earlier dynamics of the imperial and Soviet periods.[6]

Beyond Soviet borders, Soviet mediators continued to invoke connections between the foreign and domestic Easts in new contexts produced by growing commitments of the Brezhnev-Kosygin leadership in the Third World. Soviet bilateral relations with Middle Eastern states were largely built around economic development and military aid, but they still relied heavily on cultural exchanges with artists, students, and youth activists to smooth over challenges and contradictions. Cultural diplomacy remained useful for diffusing tensions. Thus, for example, after the 1967 Arab-Israeli War, the Union of Soviet Friendship Societies (SSOD) sent Baku-born academic Arabist Grigorii Sharbatov to Syria, Iraq, Lebanon, Jordan, Morocco, Tunisia, Algeria, and the Sudan to help restore faith in the Soviet Union as an ally of the Arab anti-imperialist struggle.[7]

Sharbatov was an experienced mediator. He had accompanied Nasser's 1958 delegation around the Soviet Union, and from 1959 through to the late 1970s he frequently visited Arab countries as a translator and researcher. On the 1968 trip to Lebanon and Syria, Sharbatov commemorated the fiftieth anniversary of the October Revolution with lectures about the history of Arabic study in the Soviet Union and the ways that the October Revolution "drew scholarly attention to issues of the East and to the lives of its people." His lectures broadly reviewed Soviet intellectual engagements with the Arab world—the interwar studies of history by the esteemed academician Bartol'd; the work of intelligence operative Moisei Akselrod and the Cominternians Abuziam (Auerbach) and Shami (whose Poale-Zionist origins and repressions went unmentioned); and postwar studies of American imperialism in Saudi Arabia and the Persian Gulf. He spoke about the importance of Soviet translations of Arabic literature and scientific texts by Krachkovskii, Kulthum Adeh-Vasilievna, and Hamdi; and he made sure to highlight impressive manuscript collections and Soviet scholarship conducted in the research centers of the domestic East in Tashkent, Tbilisi, Baku, Dushanbe, and Erevan.[8]

In addition to this overview, Sharbatov met with Ba'ath Central Committee member Mukhammad Said Talib. The latter had formed a new Syrian-Soviet Society of Friendship in August 1967 that erased any trace of earlier connections organized by communists and antifascist leftists. The new society leaders were all Ba'athist officials—Talib, Samukh Atiya (minister of communications), Yussuf Shakra, Hussein Audat, and Useima Malik—who portrayed the Ba'ath as representative of Syria's social structure and the country's active pursuit of development. In his final report, Sharbatov suggested that more could be done by the Soviet Embassy and Cultural Center to cultivate interest in the Soviet Union among intellectuals and youth. He proposed an expansion of academic exchanges and contacts with radio, television, film organizations, and libraries. Finally, he noted, "Syrian public expresses substantial interest in the accomplishments of Soviet national republics, especially those of Central Asia and the Caucasus." Thus, it would be important to include more propaganda materials about the experience of these republics' economies, societies, cultures, and the roles of women.[9]

Facilitating Soviet political and cultural contacts in Syria was ambassador Nuriddin Mukhitdinov, one of several Central Asian diplomats who served in important diplomatic posts in Africa and Asia in the critical last decades of the Cold War.[10] From the early days of his appointment, Mukhitdinov used his background as a Central Asian and a Muslim to further the Soviet Union's relationship with Syria and, from there, with the rest of the "Muslim world." These efforts included attempts to teach Moscow officials about the art of diplomacy. In 1968, for instance, he reported on a conversation with the Grand Mufti of Syria, Ahmad Kaftaru, who was also the head of major Naqshbandiya Sufi order, the dominant order in Central Asia. Mukhitdinov relayed Kaftaru's criticism of US recruitment of rulers of Muslim countries, the creation of new "creatures" such as the religious-political Muslim Brotherhood organization to further US interests, and Kaftaru's view that more needed to be done to expand contacts and information about the life of Soviet Muslims in Arab countries. Mukhitdinov also relayed Kaftaru's warning that Soviet representatives too readily announced that they were "atheists, godless" in Arab countries and to members of visiting Arab delegations; he advised that they find a more diplomatic form of expression.[11] As he did when he was in the Central Committee, Mukhitdinov emphasized to Moscow that his Central Asian and culturally Muslim background gave him insight for mediating Soviet interests in the foreign East.

Indeed, the logic of the Eastern International seemed ever-present in strategically significant and politically unstable contexts. During Syrian president Hafiz al-Assad's first visit to Moscow in February 1971, Mukhitdinov helped conclude a $700 million arms deal, after which Syria received an uninterrupted stream of Soviet military equipment until the late 1980s. Syria also enjoyed export opportunities as part of Soviet debt repayment plans, which propelled the development of Syria's private economic sector.[12] The Ba'ath also requested that its delegations be allowed to observe party-organization and ideological work with unions and youth organizations "in one of the regions of the Soviet Union." The Ba'ath was specifically interested in visiting an oil-producing and an agricultural region.[13] They got mostly what they wanted.

In accordance with bilateral agreements signed in 1971, the Soviet Youth Organization Committee (Komitet Molodezhnykh Organizatsii, KMO) sent delegations to participate in "weeks of friendship" in the summer of 1972 in Syria, Lebanon, and Iraq. In Damascus, the KMO delegation met with the Ba'ath Damascus City Committee and the leadership of the Union of Syrian Women. The visitors toured various factories, where they were often reminded that the Revolutionary Syrian Youth was the only officially recognized youth organization in Syria, thereby dismissing the Syrian Communist Party's youth wing that the Soviet Union had dealt with previously.[14] As a result of such commitments of "friendship" in Syria, both Intourist and Aeroflot expanded their infrastructure in the region.[15]

Reciprocating the exchange, Syrian youth were invited to Tashkent (while Iraqi Ba'athist youth were invited to Dushanbe) to meet Soviet youth and witness their accomplishments in the domestic East. In preparation for the arrival of the sixty-four-person Syrian youth delegation, which included academics, artists, peasants, and workers, the Central Committee of the Komsomol of Uzbek SSR issued special propaganda pamphlets in Arabic and French and hung colorful banners and decorations.[16] During the visit, Uzbek Komsomol members showed Syrian visitors the "local conditions of labor and leisure," picking cotton together at an Uzbek kolkhoz and extending "traditional Uzbek hospitality to the Syrians."[17] Tashkent newspapers highlighted the romance and magic of these friendly exchanges, thus masking the moment's ideological and political contradictions. These approaches differed from those of the interwar decades, when cultural and educational exchanges were geared toward producing ideologues and committed revolutionaries, but drew on similar symbols and techniques.

Similar tactics and magic in Dushanbe seemed to obscure even greater tensions with the Iraqi government, which in 1972 signed a short-lived Treaty of Friendship and Cooperation with the USSR.[18] The forty-person delegation of Iraqi youth was greeted in Dushanbe by pioneers, schoolchildren, and workers on streets decorated with flags of the USSR and Iraq.[19] The secretary of the Tajik Komsomol offered bread and salt to the Iraqi guests, which *Komsomoli Tojikiston* presented as "an ancient tradition of the Tajik people."[20] The Iraqi guests were then taken on a tour of the "historical-revolutionary places" of Dushanbe, thus making an invented "Tajik" tradition of hospitality part of the foundational Soviet revolutionary narrative.[21] Throughout the event, Tajik youth highlighted their connections to the Arabic language and Iraqi youth. They recited poetry in Arabic, which one of the Komsomol leaders cited as evidence that "our students read the work of Iraqi poets."[22] One Tajik State University student representative expressed his solidarity with the struggle against Israeli aggression.[23] Such overtures of friendship and the use of historical ties between Central Asia and the Arab world helped the Brezhnev administration maintain relations with states that were actively repressing communists (including Arab communists inside the Soviet Union), censoring Soviet publications, and burdening the Soviet Union with demands for additional economic and military aid in the name of anti-imperialism.

As in earlier periods, romanticized friendship between the domestic and foreign East was used to conceal the instabilities produced by conflicts of interest. One problem was the largest prestige project of the day, the Euphrates Dam—a massive hydroelectric station built between 1968 and 1973 with Soviet economic and technical aid that would displace 60,000 people and alter the Euphrates River's division of water between Turkey, Syria, and Iraq. Syrian reluctance to address these political conflicts before and during construction understandably raised concerns about how the Soviet Union might be perceived in the region if tensions over water access were to escalate.[24]

Another set of tensions revolved around the treatment of the Syrian Communist Party, then splitting into sections led by the long-serving Bakdash, on the one hand, and, on the other hand, the majority of the Party Politburo led by Riad Turk, who resented both Bakdash's autocratic leadership and Moscow's support for the equally autocratic Assad.[25] Anticommunist pressure was especially awkward as both the Syrian and the Iraqi embassies worked aggressively to marginalize communist students from political life in Moscow and grant more Soviet university spaces to Ba'athist students.[26] It did not help that Soviet publications were periodically and inexplicably censored in Syria. At one point, thousands of copies of the Arabic-language *Moscow News* (*Moskovskie Novosti*, *Anba Mosku*) were confiscated, for allegedly "containing articles about Iraq." The paper continued to be banned from circulation as punishment thereafter. *Novoe Vremia* and *Sovetskii Soiuz* were periodically confiscated as well.[27]

The Ba'ath Party's concern with youth was understandable. The 1968 student protests around the world, the Prague Spring, and the Cultural Revolution in China indicated that this threat was unpredictable and difficult to control. Eager to acculturate the revolutionary republic and build a more cohesive national identity, Hafiz al-Assad sought to create his own Ba'athist youth movement that could provide athletic and military training to the masses and feed an authoritative revolutionary national organization. This challenge seemed especially important to address in light of political insecurity in the region. The expulsion of the Palestinians from Jordan in 1970, the turbulence in Lebanon over the presence of Palestinian guerrillas, the killings of Israeli athletes at the Munich Olympics in 1972, and the buildup to the 1973 Arab-Israeli War generated new international and domestic tensions. These and other concerns were viewed and addressed by Soviet officials through the lens of the Eastern International. Uzbek and Tajik youth could offer hospitality as well as models of discipline and political stability.

Thanks in part to Mukhitdinov's efforts as ambassador, Soviet relations with Syria remained relatively stable. Economically, Soviet-Syrian trade rocketed during his tenure, from an annual average of $36.7 million in exports and $24.1 million in imports between 1966 and 1970 to $137.5 million in exports and $95.6 million in imports in 1975.[28] Economic cooperation continued into the 1980s and even after the Soviet collapse.[29] The fact that the Eastern International persisted as an abstract and increasingly emotive framework for connectivity after its historical narratives had become incoherent exposes it as a function of state power that depended on state capacity.

This power could be claimed or utilized by various mediators for goals that could be presented as legitimate because they supported anti-imperialism, anticolonialism, and decolonization. Although they were founded on claims about history and the need to decolonize the present, these claims about shared "Easternness" were fundamentally ahistorical and their underlying historical explanations could therefore be easily altered and then, eventually, discarded. The history of this process reflects the ongoing workings of an ostensibly post-imperial "politics of difference" within the context of a modernizing state.[30]

The fact that the Eastern International, an anti-imperialist and anticapitalist idea and political constellation, managed not only to survive the major transformations of global capitalism but also to grow with them requires explanation. As an expression of Soviet internationalism it was sustained by Soviet resources, political power, and intermediaries and, in several significant ways, by the resources of Arab intellectuals and states.

Because of the wider regional and ultimately global context of the Eastern International, the 1973 Arab-Israeli War extended its life by decades. In 1973 the Arab members of the Organization of Petroleum-Exporting Countries (OPEC) imposed an embargo against the United States in retaliation for its decision to resupply the Israeli military and to gain leverage in postwar peace negotiations. The oil embargo sparked a series of economic crises. In Europe, it interrupted a period of economic growth that began in the late 1940s, and the US GDP dropped 6 percent between 1973 and 1975.[31] The shift in the balance of power toward oil exporters split the "Arab East." On the one hand, a new oil elite emerged that included the leaders of Libya, Iraq, and other OPEC members who shared to a greater or lesser extent an "economic culture of decolonization."[32] On the other hand, other postcolonial states had to rely more on aid and debt. Their leaders had to concede that economic independence still appeared out of reach.[33]

The Soviet Union was not a member of OPEC or a party to its decision, but the oil price increase initiated an economic boom within the USSR, thanks to the fortuitous discovery and exploitation of new oil fields in Siberia.[34] Energy exports accounted for 80 percent of the USSR's hard currency earnings from 1973 to 1985, augmented by money coming in from Arab oil states that "went on military spending sprees, increasing Moscow's oil windfall."[35]

The USSR's newfound oil wealth helped the state to raise living standards, acquire consumer products and new Western technology, and sustain cultural initiatives, such as the yearly Tashkent Afro-Asian Film Festival, exchanges of delegations, and export of media about the domestic East to the foreign East. Internationally, it liberated Moscow decision makers from some of the political constraints imposed by Soviet-American détente. The new revenue could be used to extend support to Soviet-allied regimes such as the Popular Movement for the Liberation of Angola (MPLA) and, following the Soviet-Cuban victory in Angola in the spring of 1976, to intervene further in Africa in support of decolonization. Soviet support for Mengistu Haile Mariam's regime in Ethiopia with military equipment—via an air bridge that began in September 1977 and lasted for eight months at a cost of more than $1 billion—was a particularly egregious oil-revenue expenditure.[36] The cost was so enormous because the Soviet Union airlifted heavy tanks, using long-distance supply planes that could carry only a single tank at a time, so transport costs were more than five times the cost of the expensive tanks themselves. Yet this air bridge showed that Moscow could project its military power, rivaling the United States thousands of miles from its own shores.[37] It could do so while simultaneously extending aid to the Peoples' Democratic Republic of South Yemen (PDRY) and to the Dhufari rebels in Oman fighting against the British-backed Omani Sultan and his ally, the Shah of Iran. Oil wealth finally brought Moscow the influence its leadership had wanted in the Indian Ocean and the Arabian and Red Seas.[38]

While such interventions established the Soviet Union as a power capable of competing globally with the United States and China, they also raised questions about costs and benefits.[39] Spurred by the inability of Soviet advisers to influence the course of the Ethiopian revolution after military victory, a few senior experts in Moscow began critiquing the character of national-democratic revolutions. By the end of the 1970s, growing disenchantment with interventionism had spilled over into key institutions of the government such as the International Department and the KGB.[40] As International Department deputy head Karen Brutents acknowledged, "the building of socialism in the Third World had become too much of a *Soviet* project while the *local* input stayed minimal." He believed that the regimes were led by petit bourgeoisie or militarists who did not want to be taught. "The Soviet Union was encouraging—at great expense to itself—fantastic projects that bore no relation to the current stage of development of the countries."[41]

It was not only distant allies in Angola, Mozambique, Somalia, Ethiopia, South Yemen, and Afghanistan that seemed recalcitrant. In 1974, Mukhitdinov joked to his American counterpart, "It's true that Syria accepts from the Soviet Union aid, loans, student exchange, military programs—when you think of it, it accepts everything from us," and paused before adding: "Except advice."[42] Throughout the 1970s the Baʻathists continued to execute imprisoned communists, ignore requests, and neglect Soviet interests in the region. In June 1976, Syria intervened in the Lebanese Civil War in favor of the Maronite Christians against their PLO and left-wing opponents, who had been supported by the Soviet Union and had worked with contacts in the KGB.[43] Preferring an independent Lebanon to a Syrian-dominated one, Moscow curtailed its arms shipments to Syria in an effort to blackmail Hafiz al-Assad to change his policy; in response the Syrians closed the port of Tartus to Soviet use and intervened in Lebanon anyway.[44] Although Soviet military aid to Syria continued to exceed that provided to any other Third World state on any continent, Moscow was unable to keep al-Assad from acting against Soviet interests.[45] Al-Assad boycotted the Arab summit for joint economic action in November 1980, tried to dislodge Yasir Arafat from leadership of the PLO (which Moscow supported), and even went so far as to confiscate Soviet weaponry sent to the PLO via Syria in 1983.[46] Moscow was also unable to persuade Damascus to patch up relations with Baghdad or in 1984 to reopen the oil pipeline that crosses Syrian territory and links Iraqi oilfields with ports on the Mediterranean.[47] The costs of the Soviet-Syrian friendship were rising, while the apparent benefits diminished.

The complexity of deeper Soviet relations with multiple parties and their multilateral rivalries undermined the conceptual neatness of the anti-imperialist front at the heart of the "Eastern International." Soviet Arabist Evgenii Primakov recalls divisions among Soviet analysts about the rift between Arafat and Assad. Some blamed Arafat for betraying the interests of the Palestinian people by meeting with King Hussein to discuss a possible confederation after the Jordanian Army's attack on Palestinian refugee camps in September 1970, and then by visiting Cairo after the Camp David Accords. Others supported Syria's interest in controlling the Palestinian movement in order to strengthen al-Assad's hand in dealing with Americans and to oppose any settlement with Israel. Soviet General Secretary Yuri Andropov's efforts to reconcile Arafat and al-Assad collapsed under the weight of tensions within the Palestinian movement.[48]

Disappointing outcomes in Iraq, Egypt, and Syria challenged the logic of the Eastern International in other ways as well. In Iraq, Saddam Hussein's admiration for Stalin coexisted with his suspicion of Soviet policy. Shortly after coming to power in 1979, he purged those he suspected of favoring close ties with the Soviet Union, including the Iraqi ambassador to Moscow, and intensified the purge of Iraqi communists.[49] The Soviet Communist Party remained silent, not wanting to undermine Iraqi efforts to disrupt the peace process between Egypt and Israel. The Soviet regime had been losing its standing in Egypt since Nasser's death in 1970. Nasser's successor, Anwar Sadat, gradually opted for a closer relationship with the United States.[50] In 1976 he terminated the Soviet-Egyptian Friendship Treaty as part of a strategy to solicit American investment and then entered into negotiations that culminated in the 1979 Peace Treaty with Israel.[51] The sacrifices of Iraqi communists again turned out to be in vain.

The Egypt-Israel peace treaty challenged the Eastern International by undermining long-term Soviet ideological support for the idea of revolutionary anticolonial Arab nationalism and its struggle against Zionist colonialism. As Mukhitdinov discovered, Soviet leaders continued to oppose diplomacy with Israel even when it seemed to him to be a potentially pragmatic tool for improving the USSR's ability to maneuver politically in the region.[52]

Nor did it help that domestic Soviet media attacks on Zionism often did not differentiate between Zionists and Jews, which fueled the resurgence of Soviet Jewish national consciousness. The aftermath of the 1967 war bolstered this national consciousness within the USSR, as well as anti-Semitic and anti-American conspiracy theories.[53] In the 1970s, diplomatic and internal pressure to allow Soviet Jews to emigrate to Israel culminated in a mass migration of Jews from the USSR. Throughout the decade, Zionism remained second only to the United States as an active KGB target inside the USSR.[54] All these factors compounded informal and institutionalized discrimination against those who remained.[55]

Postwar Soviet state concerns about politicization of the fate of Soviet Jews limited the number of Jewish mediators representing the Soviet Union abroad, especially in the Arab world. Since the late 1930s, people from nominally Muslim and Christian backgrounds had been the preferred representatives of the USSR abroad. One high-profile exception was the single most influential mediator of postwar Soviet-Arab relations, Evgenii Primakov, who graduated from the Moscow Oriental Institute and first covered the Arab world as a journalist for the State TV and Radio Committee (Gosteleradio) and for *Pravda* in the 1950s and 1960s. Then he held administrative positions at the prestigious Institute of World Economy and International Relations (IMEMO) and directed the Institute of Oriental Studies of the Academy of Sciences after Ghafurov's death in 1977. In the late 1990s he served as prime minister of the Russian Federation.

Throughout his career, Primakov concealed his Jewish background, despite rumors that had circulated among party officials since the 1950s. He admitted to it only in 2004, claiming he had only learned about this later in life.[56] He omitted this fact from his 2009 book *Russia and the Arabs*, in which he reflected on the Jewish lobby in the United States and on his dealings with various Arab and Israeli officials. The omission seemed curious in light of certain remarks. For example, Primakov was struck by Arafat's "unmistakably Jewish appearance." When Primakov told Arafat that "he looked just the same as many Israelis," Arafat replied that it was "nothing special" and that "Palestinians and Jews are cousins."[57] The playful ease with which Primakov could make such observations about others, while concealing his own background and staying above the rumors about his "secret Jewish origin," indicates his ability to use this difference and but also to conceal and overcome it in advancing his diplomatic career. Only the combination of absolute silence about family background and the possession of personal identity documents in which one's officially nationality was registered as "Russian" enabled Soviet citizens with Jewish family backgrounds to maintain positions of authority in academic and diplomatic circles after 1967.[58] In this respect they continued the follow the pattern set earlier by Troianovskii. The exceptional nature of Primakov's story is his admission of this background.

In Moscow academic circles, where the struggle for intellectual and economic resources was intense, anti-Semitism continued to operate both informally and institutionally.[59] This can especially be seen in the field of Soviet oriental studies. According to one graduate of the Institute of Asian and African studies, Bobojon Ghafurov was known for protecting Jewish orientalists who had been hired during the expansion of Soviet area studies institutes in the late 1950s and early 1960s, and whose careers came under new pressure after the 1967 Arab-Israeli War.[60] Despite these pressures, visitors to the USSR such as Egyptian medical student Mohamed Makhzangi still noted "the number of Jews in Oriental Studies departments and in Arabic language studies in particular."[61] Such remarks suggested that the postwar domestic and international political contexts continued to marginalize Soviet citizens with Jewish backgrounds while simultaneously empowering other domestic Easterners to shape Soviet policy affecting the foreign East.

Changes in the international context eventually challenged the status of Soviet Muslims in the Eastern International as well. Perhaps no shift rattled the core assumptions of Soviet leaders and decision makers as much the 1979 Iranian Revolution and the deterioration of political order in Afghanistan. The Islamic internationalism of the Iranian Revolution defied all Soviet predictions about global politics based on the expectation of the continued rise of secular, nationalist, and leftist movements. Instead, Islamic internationalism offered an alternative anti-imperialist ideology that recentered the Third World and condemned both Cold War projects of modernization.[62] Fearing another Iranian-led or US-backed Islamist challenge to a pro-Soviet regime in Afghanistan, the emboldened Soviet government invoked the "Brezhnev doctrine." This foreign policy concept, elaborated during the 1968 invasion of Czechoslovakia, proclaimed that any threat to socialist rule in any state of the Soviet bloc in Central and Eastern Europe was a threat to them all.[63] Yet even more than in 1968, when Soviet intervention in Czechoslovakia was attacked as an expression of imperialism unbecoming of a socialist state committed to decolonization, the 1979 invasion of Afghanistan raised questions about the USSR's behavior in the so-called Third World, and especially in the Muslim world. The invasion was condemned at a meeting of thirty-five Islamic nations in January 1980. Even Arab leftists, such as members of the Marxist-Leninist Organization of Communist Action in Lebanon, started to see Marxism as a "catastrophe" and as "foreign" and then turn more toward political Islam, sometimes by way of Maoism.[64]

The war in Afghanistan reversed connections between the domestic and foreign Easts as they had been imagined and forged over the decades of the Soviet century. Part of this effort can be credited to the hardliners in the Carter and Reagan administrations who plotted about how to turn Afghanistan into a "Soviet Vietnam."[65] One of the tactics explored within the NSC and CIA was the promotion of "the ethnic consciousness of Soviet Muslims," which they intended to use to undermine the Soviet Union's domestic stability.[66] This amounted to using Soviet commitments in Afghanistan and the Middle East to target Central Asians.

The challenge of defending the USSR's damaged anticolonial credentials fell once again to Soviet Central Asians.[67] Some of this difficult work was handled by religious institutions such as the Spiritual Administration for

Muslims of Central Asia.[68] It did not always help that the Soviet civilian and military advisers in Afghanistan, many of whom were Soviet Central Asians and especially Tajiks whose language was close enough to Dari to serve as translators, saw themselves as playing a role in helping "to modernize Afghanistan and protect it from imperialists."[69] Some of the Central Asians sent to Afghanistan were unnerved by the corruption they observed in the Soviet military and intelligence operations and began asking troubling new questions about Soviet legitimacy.[70]

The longevity of Eastern International in the sense of the Brezhnev-era expansion of Soviet investment in Third World interventions had indirect costs as well. It made it difficult for the Soviet Union to support its allies in the Warsaw Pact. The 1973 oil crisis and the subsequent spike in energy costs put pressure on Eastern European industry and leaders. Polish foreign debt doubled between 1974 and 1975 to $8 billion. By the end of the 1970s it had reached $20 billion, forcing Poland to borrow from the West to satisfy consumer desires and maintain a monopoly on political power. GDR leader Erich Honecker managed to survive by re-exporting cheaper Soviet oil (at world prices) until 1981 when Brezhnev cut these deliveries. The GDR continued to fall further into debt until the Berlin Wall fell in 1989.

The Soviet Union eventually succumbed to similar pressures after the price of oil worldwide collapsed in 1986 from $27 a barrel to $10, due in part to deliberate Saudi overproduction. In 1986, for the first time in decades, the USSR ended the year with a trade deficit of $14 billion.[71] Earlier efforts in 1983 by General Secretary Yuri Andropov to accumulate a stabilization fund by increasing the export of machinery and oil products had been foiled when Soviet republics and state enterprises asked for more subsidies. Left with little choice, Mikhail Gorbachev had to cover operating expenses by raising Soviet debt to Western banks in hard currency from $27.2 billion in 1985 to $39.4 billion in 1986.[72] That same year, the catastrophe at the Chernobyl nuclear plant added an unexpected 8 billion rubles to the Soviet budget, dealing another devastating blow to the Soviet economy in addition to the damage to its international prestige and domestic legitimacy. In 1988, a disastrous Armenian earthquake cost another 12–14 billion rubles.

Under pressure from the mutually reinforcing economic challenges of low oil prices, natural disasters, Eastern European bankruptcy, and pressure from American sanctions, Gorbachev sought to reconfigure the world order based on "new political thinking." This meant first and foremost easing Cold War tensions by reaching a political understanding with the United States and Western Europe, thus reviving the détente that had broken down in the late 1970s and early 1980s. Like earlier Westernizers, Gorbachev believed that different politics—for him a "democratic socialism," greater openness about political and social issues (*glasnost'*), and economic liberalization (*perestroika*)—could help Russia join a "common European home." This "Western" orientation was shaped as much by geopolitical and economic necessity as it was by his sense of belonging to the educated class of Eurocentric Soviet intelligentsia. Although he grew up in a village in the Russian southwestern region of Stavropol Krai, he developed an early love for the Russian intellectual tradition, especially the works of radical nineteenth-century Westernizing intellectual Vissarion Belinsky. While a student at Moscow State University law school, he met his wife Raisa and developed lifelong friendships with Russia's intellectual elites from Moscow's urban milieu. Later, when moving up the Party ladder, he insisted that he "remained closer to the world of scholarship and culture" and to the "intelligentsia" than to the Communist Party and its bureaucracy.[73] All these factors shaped the orientation of his interests more towards building relations with the United States and Europe than with Asia, Africa, or Latin America.

Gorbachev's hopes to integrate Russia into a "common European home" were tested in the late 1980s but never destroyed. The toppling of communist regimes in Poland, Hungary, Czechoslovakia, and Bulgaria, which Gorbachev could not bail out due to low foreign currency reserves, diminished Soviet positions in Europe. The collapse of the Berlin Wall and the flood of hundreds of thousands of East Germans across the border made the idea of gradual Soviet integration into Europe seem untenable. As historian Vladislav Zubok explains, Gorbachev admired Lenin and understood such territorial concessions in Europe through the lens of the Brest-Litovsk Treaty, a gamble to give up a million square miles of space at the end of World War I in order to buy time to preserve the Union.[74] Yet unlike Lenin, who was surrounded by ruthless geopolitical strategists willing to fight for the survival of the revolutionary new state, Gorbachev's aversion to violence and his search for an elusive democratic consensus made it impossible to control the forces he unleashed with *glasnost'* and *perestroika*. Instead of taking repressive action, Gorbachev tolerated opposition.[75] When he did decide to use force, it was too late. For instance, his 1986 decision to replace the republican party boss of Kazakhstan, Din-Muhammed Kunayev, with an ethnic Russian from the RSFSR prompted massive protests. As a result, 2,400 students were arrested, 450 injured, and two killed—an outcome that Gorbachev deeply regretted. Similarly, his initial unwillingness to intervene in the Armenian-Azeri conflict paralyzed the local authorities. The Politburo's eventual decision to use military force in Azerbaijan to maintain state borders resulted in the deaths of over 100 people in Baku and left Gorbachev visibly aged and shaken.[76]

While the story of Soviet collapse has often been reduced to Gorbachev's interest in the West and his neglect of domestic nationalism, the unraveling of the Eastern International as a Soviet ideological and institutional project points to other challenges and scales of thinking. Before Gorbachev rose to power, the growing tolerance of political critique had created a postwar generation of Soviet Central Asian writers who, often in conversation with foreign Afro-Asian ones, felt emboldened to openly question the Soviet politics of history with respect to the domestic and foreign Easts.[77] These critiques were sharper than Yarmatov's private struggles to invent a compelling narrative.

For Kazakh Anuar Alimzhanov, this meant using "the foreign East"—for instance, narratives about British colonialism in Kenya—to point out the excesses of Soviet propaganda in Central Asia.[78] For Kazakh writer and chair of Goskino (the State Cinema Committee) Olzhas Suleimenov, it meant confronting the imagined civilizational and geographical boundary between European and Asiatic Russia as part of an elaborate polemic against linguistic and historical sciences and their "prejudicial assumptions of Eurocentrism."[79]

Suleimenov's 1975 book, *Az i ya: Kniga blagonomerennogo chitatelia* (Az i ya: The book of a well-intentioned reader), challenged multiple Soviet hierarchies by rereading the canonical twelfth-century Russian epic *Slovo o pulku Igoreve* (The song of Igor's campaign) and calling attention to its Turkic words and imagery. Since the Igor tale had acquired canonic status as a monument of Russian history and identity, Suleimenov's reinterpretation and projection of a shared Eurasian cultural space back into the prerevolutionary past transgressed a major ideological boundary between the Russian Self and Asiatic Other.[80] It was immediately perceived as a provocation by Party organs and scholars, including Dmitry Likhachev, who dismissed it as "without any sense of responsibility towards the historical facts."[81] Consequently it was withdrawn from circulation, and Suleimenov was forced to issue a public apology.

Although in speeches at later international Afro-Asian events Suleimenov would claim that his ultimate vision of the Igor tale had been one of "synthesis" and "interdependence" between Slav and Turk, his book defied the scholarly establishment and Eurocentric norms that assumed the primacy of the Russian language and Moscow's central status in Soviet academic hierarchies.[82] Suleimenov's alternative vision of Eurasianism based on an ideal of cultural reciprocity that had flourished in Eurasia's remote past undermined Stalin's assertion of the Bolshevik revolution as a starting point of the history of the liberated Soviet East. The ideal of cultural reciprocity as something that could be restored from pre-revolutionary times and explored using unconventional new methods and genres, rather than something made available to people by the Bolshevik revolution and the party-state, thwarted the binary logic of the Eastern International.

By 1980, another Kyrgyz writer, Chingiz Aitmatov, had published arguably the most famous critique of Soviet conditioning, *A Day Lasts a Thousand Years*, which contested the Eastern International from a different angle. Aitmatov's father, Torekul Aitmatov, had studied at the Communist University of Toilers of the East (KUTV) from 1921 to 1924 but was purged in 1937 for nationalism.[83] Growing up as a child of an enemy of the people shaped Aitmatov's early life and work just as much as his fluency in Russian, immersion in Russian literature, and basic acceptance of the premise that Russia and its literature could be a role model for Central Asians.[84] Perhaps for all these reasons his novel critiquing life in the Soviet Union resonated with intellectuals across its vast territory and diverse cultures. This critique is voiced angrily toward the end of the work by the protagonist named Yedigei, a Turkic railway worker and World War II veteran. It is directed at Sabitzhan, a character who received a privileged Soviet education thanks to his father's sacrifices, but who is indifferent to his father's burial and local traditions. Instead, the son blindly accepts the Soviet authorities' plans to level the ancient local cemetery and replace it with a new settlement. For this, the protagonist calls him a "*mankurt*," implicitly comparing him to a mythical slave whose memory was erased by a process of horrific torture and who consequently became completely subservient to his torturers. Drawing on Kyrgyz folklore, the statement implied that the cost of upward mobility afforded by Soviet affirmative action and education had been higher than its beneficiaries had realized. The protagonist then mourns the young men who "don't believe in God and know no prayers at all" and wonders how they might come to appreciate their innermost, secret humanity.[85] Like Suleimenov, Aitmatov was suggesting that ignorance of history was a problem that needed to be solved in order to reclaim humanity and freedom.

The questions about knowledge of history, freedom, and human dignity raised by Suleimenov and Aitmatov resonated broadly. They circulated in Central Asia and were also embraced by Western-centric readers of *samizdat* (illegally reproduced censored publications) in Moscow and Leningrad. These metropolitan readers looked down on many of the other publications of "national" or "Afro-Asian" writers, due to their abiding assumptions about the superiority of Russian and European and broader Western culture. They also disdained state-supported ideological projects that promoted Soviet legitimacy, including aid to decolonizing peoples and the top-down popularization of Afro-Asian culture inside the USSR. Suleimenov's and Aitmatov's critiques transcended this imagined West-East divide because they were challenging core claims about Soviet political legitimacy and modernity. For this reason their critiques resonated with other questions about memory, political hierarchy, and the hope kindled by Gorbachev's reforms and promises of more democratic decision-making.

These critiques also resonated with new perceptions of the failures of state-led development to compete in the provision of consumer goods with other parts of the world. Competition with Europe and the United States had been a pillar of the cultural Cold War. Yet even travel to the foreign East could show how far the USSR materially lagged behind the capitalist world. This became apparent when labor unions, under pressure to provide more opportunities for local titular nationals to travel abroad in the late 1970s and 1980s, organized trips for Central Asians to India, Pakistan, the Middle East, Africa, Cuba, and other places in the "foreign East" with strategic relevance to the regime.[86] One Tajik who had been selected for tours of Libya and Iraq was fascinated by the abundance of consumer products. In an interview with Kalinovsky he said he couldn't believe that people wouldn't take "scrap" from broken cars, not even the radios.[87] Such contacts eventually inspired Central Asian travelers and economists to question Moscow's promises of equality between Soviet peoples and regions.[88] Such questions about economic justice accentuated the relevance of literary questions about injustice in the categorization, differentiation, and interrelationships of Soviet regions.

That Central Asia's difference came to be seen in Moscow in the same period as more of a liability than an asset likely contributed to the collapse of the Soviet Union's anticolonial empire. When confronted with new political and economic pressures from the Russian-speaking industrial regions of the RSFSR, Moscow leaders channeled their grievances into populist politics.[89] Their stories about how Union authorities were "robbing Russia" by taking half of its annual taxes to subsidize the non-Russian republics of Central Asia fueled expressions of racial prejudice. This was directed mostly against migrants from the domestic East, who were called "blacksnouts" and other derogatory terms in Moscow and Leningrad.[90]

It did not help that Gorbachev, desperate to raise money for a collapsing economy and finding little success among Western creditors, sent his aide Aleksandr Yakovlev to approach potential lenders in the "foreign East," including China and the oil-rich states of the Arabian Peninsula.[91] For a generation that had grown up with the civilizing mission of the Eastern International (hard-nosed diplomats like Primakov among them), it must have been jarring to see a Soviet delegation in Kuwait in search of aid.[92]

The contraction of the Soviet Union's defense expenditures and the need for credit, as well as ideological commitments to a "common European home," prompted Gorbachev to abandon long-held foreign policy positions in the Middle East.[93] When the Iraqi army invaded Kuwait in August 1990, Gorbachev initially tried to mediate the conflict with the long-term Soviet ally, sending Primakov to Baghdad to convince Saddam Hussein to withdraw his forces from Kuwait before the US-led coalition began a ground war. Although Primakov signaled from Baghdad in February 1991 that he had reached a tentative deal with the Iraqi dictator, President George H. W. Bush seemed irritated by Gorbachev's peacemaking at America's expense and argued that Hussein was only trying to drive a wedge between the United States and the Soviet Union. Unable to change the American course, and eager to preserve détente, Gorbachev capitulated. Primakov returned from Baghdad, and a US air campaign destroyed much of Iraq's Soviet-made weaponry.[94] In another sign of good faith to the West, Gorbachev restored diplomatic relations with Israel just before his resignation on December 25, 1991. In the subsequent post-Soviet decade, Russia played virtually no active role in the Middle East and retreated from its long-held interests in Cuba and Afghanistan. Vladimir Putin would be reminded of Russia's concessions in 2003 when President George W. Bush would again ignore Russia's objections to the invasion of Iraq, evading the United Nations Security Council and Russia's veto power there.

It would take over a decade for certain features of the Soviet Eastern International to be reactivated after the Soviet collapse. The breakdown of the USSR that began in the 1980s continued into the next decade. In the March 17, 1991, Union-wide referendum, over 90 percent of the population in the Central Asian republics of Uzbekistan, Turkmenistan, Tajikistan, Kyrgyzstan, and Kazakhstan voted in favor of preserving the USSR as a federation of equal sovereign republics. By contrast, around 76 percent of voters in Russia responded favorably to Boris Yeltsin's call for a popularly elected Russian president, and results in Ukraine revealed overwhelming levels of support for Ukrainian sovereignty and a Ukrainian president.

In the aftermath of collapse, by December 1991, Yegor Gaidar, Yeltsin's prime minister and architect of Russia's shock therapy reforms, went so far as to advocate keeping the subsidized Central Asian states out of the Commonwealth of Independent States (CIS), the intergovernmental organization modeled on the British Commonwealth created to replace the USSR after its breakup. Minister of Foreign Affairs Eduard Shevardnadze also warned that Central Asia might become a geopolitical problem as "an Islamic hothouse and a playground for other great powers, including communist China."[95] It was largely thanks to Kazakhstan president Nursultan Nazarbayev that Central Asian states were allowed to join the Commonwealth and commit to a "common defense" space with Russia. Yet the economic separation still proved devastating in the short term to regional economies. The Soviet economy had been developed primarily for internal trade, so as the newly independent states sought foreign outlets for their goods, the poorer republics of Central Asia that became independent states were especially disadvantaged. Economic collapse was politically destabilizing. In Uzbekistan, President Islam Karimov managed to maintain order through violent crackdowns on Islamist opposition while reinventing himself as the new "father of the nation." The poorest republic, Tajikistan, plunged into civil war from 1992 until 1997.[96]

Then the devolution of Soviet power seemed to stabilize. The civil wars in Chechnya, Karabakh, Ingushetia, Ossetia, Abkhazia, and Adjaria that seemed symptomatic of the failures in the post-Soviet transition in the 1990s waned under Vladimir Putin's leadership.[97] In 2003, Grozny was declared by the UN to be "the most destroyed city on Earth," but by 2007 Ramzan Kadyrov ruled Chechnya and was rebuilding its infrastructure, with support from Putin. This hard-fought victory would come to symbolize Russia's ability to resolve difficult questions about border security, rights of secession, and relations with the Muslim world, including the millions of Muslims still living inside the Russian Federation.

Empowered by the victory in Chechnya, Putin openly declared at the 2007 Munich Conference on Security Policy that the unipolar world led by the United States since the early 1990s was "unacceptable." He then embarked on a course of tough advocacy and expansion of Russia's interests vis-à-vis other regional states. In 2008, Russia went to war with neighboring Georgia, a move that Russian foreign policy analyst Andranik Migranyan described as a sort of comeuppance for NATO.[98] Putin asserted Russian power in Azerbaijan and Armenia.[99] In 2016, the victory in Chechnya was referenced in a way that explicitly drew on the earlier logic of connecting the domestic and foreign Easts: the Russian Embassy of the United States tweeted images of Grozny (in the domestic East) as a model for what the nation hoped to achieve in Aleppo (in the foreign East).[100]

The Chechen model seemed to work in Syria. Putin had supported Bashar al-Assad since the 2011 start of antigovernment protests in Damascus by sending arms and by using Russia's veto power in the UN Security Council to prevent sanctions or military intervention against the Syrian government. In September 2015, a little over year after invading and annexing Crimea, Russia intervened militarily in the Syrian Civil War, mostly by providing air support and limited naval and elite ground troops. To justify the invasion that saved Bashar al-Assad from an imminent demise, Russian strategists referenced threats of destabilization in domestic Muslim regions. Like in earlier decades of the Cold War, US-based analysts wondered, "Are Russia's 20 million Muslims seething about Putin bombing Syria?"[101]

Russia's media also invoked 1980s Cold War tropes to present Assad's triumph as Russia's triumph against a unilateral US world order that had already destabilized much of the Middle East by inspiring and weakly supporting Arab activists' democratic aspirations in Egypt, Libya, Tunisia, and elsewhere. In addition to having thwarted the West, Putin could claim to have provided the Russian military with training exercises in different types of warfare—including misinformation and disinformation techniques, denial of aid and essential goods, bombardment of humanitarian and civilian infrastructure, establishment of hazardous evacuation corridors for only limited numbers of evacuees, and provocation of population displacements. Putin's sense of victory bolstered Russia's presence in the Black Sea through increased trade with Crimea. And in 2017, Russia gained a permanent military presence in the Eastern Mediterranean for at least the next forty-nine years, thereby realizing a strategic aspiration that had eluded Russian czars and Soviet leaders. In this way, al-Assad reciprocated support for Putin's military efforts. Later he also extended diplomatic recognition to Donetsk and Luhansk as independent states.

More recently, the pacification of Chechnya and Syria have proved unreliable as reference points for Russia's invasion of Ukraine in February 2022. Unlike in Chechnya—located within Russia's borders—and Syria—where the government sought Russia's intervention and the United States and Europe refrained from taking a stand—the organized opposition of the Ukrainian government and people have inspired a more critical and resonant response.

Yet some media's emphasis on the Christian and white identity of Ukrainians to stake claims to their belonging in the West or Europe has implicitly reinscribed color-coded civilizational boundaries in ways that have lent a certain credibility to Russia's anti-Westernism, especially among those who feel alienated by this civilizational and racial hierarchy. Critiques of the perceived double standard in Europe's reaction have been voiced by refugees from Syria and Afghanistan who have not experienced such welcome or support. They have also been deployed by activists in support of various pro-Palestinian causes. These grievances have been amplified by Muslim authorities within Russia, such as Kamil Samigullin, the mufti of the Republic of Tatarstan, who has argued that the West's support of Ukraine is hypocritical, given its interventions in Libya and Iraq and the treatment of Palestinians.[102] Putin's denunciations of Western imperialism to justify the war, similar to Soviet-era tactics, reflects the large spatial scales of anti-Western thinking while cynically and brutally suppressing critical reflection about its Soviet historical context.

Russia's anti-Westernism remains productive in other ways as well. The "East," which was neglected by both Gorbachev and Yeltsin, has receded as a concern in academic humanities, foreign policy, and economic aid.[103] Yet in some areas it has remained resilient. In popular culture, imagery of the "Vostok" (East) remains ubiquitous in the names of cafés, clubs, and other cultural establishments. The category evokes a certain nostalgia for late-Soviet culture and its sardonic classics such as *White Sun of the Desert*, as well as more sincere nostalgia for the Soviet Union's imperial grandeur. In these ways, the East continues to conjure a different type of cultural-political imaginary than the West. The West, by contrast, symbolized a more threatening and less accessible abroad, so it was rarely referenced in café or club names.

Other legacies of the Eastern International have been reactivated in Russia's approach to regional economic integration. Like the early Bolshevik revolutionaries and planners who had to work within parameters set by their pre-revolutionary imperial context, Russian policymakers find themselves operating within the regional constraints and endowments shaped by Soviet domestic and foreign policy.[104] Like the architects of the Eastern International, they also still rely on a Eurasian framing of politics and networks in the Eurasian Customs Union (formed in 2010) and its successor, the Eurasian Economic Union (founded 2015).[105] Such organizations are sometimes presented as an antithesis to a world order defined by Western-style liberal democracy.

By the late 1990s, a theory of Russian Eurasianism was elaborated by political strategist Aleksandr Dugin, an advocate of a vast new Russian empire and a supporter of Russia's current war in Ukraine. Dugin's neo-Eurasianism has been compared to the "classical Eurasianism" of the 1920s and 1930s that flourished in Europe's émigré communities. This comparison largely owes to Dugin's claims to represent the political-intellectual legacy of classical Eurasianists, such as Petr Savitskii and Nikolai Trubetskoi, and their primacy in post-Soviet discussions on "Eurasia." Yet, as scholar Mark Bassin points out, there are important dissonances between Dugin's ideas and the perspectives and priorities of the earlier "classical" émigré thinkers.[106] Almost every case of dissonance reveals a convergence with the early activists of the Eastern International.

While they never called themselves Eurasianists and the term "Eurasia" had not come up since Mikhail Pavlovich's 1922 article in *Novyi Vostok*, the various mediators of the Eastern International worked to project Soviet power across Eurasian space and, through it, to the world. Thus, unlike classical émigré Eurasianists for whom "Eurasia" was a distinctive geographical region and singular civilization, Pavlovich understood the framework of operations in the "East" as "the whole colonial world ... that sustained capitalist society in Europe and the United States."[107] Dugin's notion of Eurasia similarly extends to any region and peoples of the globe that is struggling against American hegemony. Like Troianovskii, who imagined the spread of world revolution to the broader East, Dugin is prepared to press the boundaries of Eurasia beyond imperial Russia, Soviet, or post-Soviet space into Europe, Central Asia, and China. He too relies on the geopolitical ideas of Rudolf Kjellén and treats competitive internationalisms and Turko-Muslim minorities as "potential ... enemies if they were to decide to no longer go along with a Russian-dominated multinational Eurasia."[108] He too promotes the assertion of Russia's power in the Muslim world via Iran. Even their institutional bases overlap. Like the "red imperialist" Mikhail Pavlovich almost a century before him, Dugin taught at the Academy of the General Staff, where he popularized ideas from his book, *The Foundations of Geopolitics: Russia's Geopolitical Future* (1997).[109] Dugin and the early Bolshevik theorists of the Eastern International share a commitment to a global perspective, but rather than a "united anti-imperialist democratic front," Dugin's project is a polycentric Eurasian New World Order built upon shared opposition to a common enemy: Atlanticism, the United States, and liberal values. All of these can be combated by subversion, destabilization, and disinformation. The new face of Russian imperialism is still anti-Western, but much less explicitly anti-imperialist.

Dugin is a relatively peripheral figure in the Putin administration, even if the August 2022 car bombing of which he was the likely target refocused some media spotlight on him as the "spiritual guide" to Russia's invasion of Ukraine.[110] Yet his ideas have broadly been used to justify Russia's claim on former Soviet republics and efforts to control the strategic space in which they are situated, including barring NATO from expansion into these technically sovereign regions.[111] His neo-Eurasianism has shaped such political organizations as the Eurasia Party, which he founded, and its less anti-Western competitor, the Eurasian Party of Russia (ERP), founded in 2001 by Abdul-Vahed Niiazov, an ethnic Russian convert to Islam who claims to be descended from the Siberian Khan Kuchum. Perhaps significantly, the two parties have received support from different critics of the late Soviet era. Niiazov's ERP has been endorsed by prominent writers Olzhas Suleimenov and Chingiz Aitmatov whom Niiazov included in the party's leadership, and it has a social base among Muslim Caucasians, Tatars, and Bashkirs; Dugin's Eurasia Party was endorsed by the Chief Mufti of Russia and head of the Central Muslim Spiritual Directorate of Russia (1992–2015), Talgat Tadzhuddin.[112] Despite the institutions' significant differences and the complex relationship of Russia's diverse Muslims to Eurasianist ideology, their anti-Western, conservative slogans allow political intermediaries to "play the card of religious (Islamic) or ethnic (Turkic) distinctiveness in the hope of securing a stable electoral niche while remaining strictly loyal to the Russian state."[113] In so doing, they positively reappraise Russia's imperial and Soviet experience, much as the Soviet domestic intermediaries did, and revive key dynamics of the Eastern International.

As long as Russia continues to exist on its former imperial territory, its leaders will have to contend with the legacies of empire, some of which have survived decades of modernizing Soviet rule. The concept of Eurasia and the notion of an "internal East" will likely continue to be useful to its leaders as a way of acknowledging the country's indeterminate geographical and cultural position and extolling its internal diversity.[114] In some scenarios it might benefit Russia's security to keep the boundary between internal and external "East" somewhat ambiguous. Thus, Putin's response to the reassertion of Taliban control in Afghanistan has been to strengthen Russia's position in Central Asia. Russia's high-profile military exercises in Tajikistan are just the beginning of a strategy to mediate a conflict involving Muslims both inside and outside Russia, the CIS, and the wider region. Uzbekistan's efforts since 2021 to promote connectivity to enhance its regional leadership vis-à-vis other Central Asian republics also revives Soviet legacies of regional leadership.[115] President Shavkat Mirziyoyev's encouragement of Central Asian cooperation in the exploitation of transboundary rivers, cross-border trade, and economic cooperation with other economies in the region, including Afghanistan, might open up certain *glasnost'*-era questions and projects. These flexible and pragmatic strategies of indirect control will continue to draw upon the toolkit of Eurasian geopolitics—which for most of the twentieth century was the Eastern International.

Conclusion

The internationalist ethos of the Soviet project may be a distant memory, as are many of the material and institutional features of the anticolonial empire. Yet the history of the Eastern International continues to set the context for post-Soviet regional politics, wider transregional connections across Eurasia, and intellectuals' conceptions of decolonization, nationalism, and the relevance of the past. Although frequently invoked, the substance of this history remains largely obscure. With the emergence of nationalisms across post-Soviet territories, many conversations about this past have devolved into competing nationalist discourses. In the 1990s and early 2000s these ideological projects led to the suspension of broader supra-national conversations about regional environmental activism, development, and historical memory that had begun during *perestroika*. The contracted frameworks of post-Soviet nationalism encouraged little interest in the transregional lives and legacies of those who mediated Soviet power and protected its anticolonial legitimacy across the "domestic" and "foreign" Easts.

Instead, post-Soviet Central Asian states have approached the construction of a national identity that, to a lesser and greater extent, applies a borrowed postcolonial frame to their past. The popularity of postcolonialism in nationalist framings is related to the theme of past suffering in public history, especially the commemoration of political repressions and other types of victimhood. These themes are least visible in the public history of Tajikistan, where Stalinist repressions are virtually absent from the National Museum of Tajikistan. As Tajik historian Muzaffar Olimov has suggested, one reason it is difficult to renounce the country's Soviet past is the legacy of the Soviet scholar and politician Bobojon Ghafurov, who is now a celebrated symbol of post-Soviet Tajik nationalism.[1] By contrast, the State Museum of the History of Uzbekistan condenses the Russian and Soviet period to one room and highlights the repressions, represented prominently by the 1930s purges and the late Soviet prosecution of Uzbek officials for corruption and the falsification of cotton production data.[2] An entire floor dedicated to independence and post-Soviet Uzbek history celebrates the break with the past in a way that frames this break as decolonization.[3] Elsewhere in Tashkent, Russian and Soviet history assume more contradictory forms. A Museum of Victims of Political Repression, which opened in 2002 and is a mandatory part of secondary school and higher education curricula, coexists with the Chapel of St. George, a monument built in 1886 and fully restored in 2020 to commemorate Russian imperial soldiers who fell during the conquest of Tashkent.[4] Kazakhstan and Kyrgyzstan both have memorials to the victims of political repression and totalitarianism and support decolonization and postcolonialism in academic settings. In Kazakhstan, postcolonialism was initially tempered by Eurasianist themes embraced by Nursultan Nazarbayev, president from 1990 to 2019. These themes—which highlighted the benefits of economic connections with China, the crucial transport of Kazakh oil to world markets via Russia's Black Sea coast, and other economic possibilities stemming from its location "at the crossroads" of Europe and Asia—have been tempered by the economic crisis that started in 2014.[5] Decolonization and memorialization of suffering are increasingly part of academic and cultural events.[6] In Kyrgyzstan, the ousting of the first post-Soviet president, Askar Akayev, coincided with brutal inter-communal clashes between Uzbek and Kyrgyz inhabitants in the city of Osh, which flowed directly from interwar Soviet decisions to embrace majoritarian ethno-nationalist politics. This violence was rooted in earlier ethno-national borders and tensions that had spilled over into the internationalist communist realm in the 1930s. In its eclectic approach to the memorialization of Soviet repressions and past suffering, the Ata-Beyit memorial complex, dedicated to the victims of Stalin's political repressions of the 1930s, is also the burial site of the victims of the 2010 violence and of the writer Chingiz Aitmatov.[7] In Turkmenistan, the nationalist identity project has an ambivalent relationship with postcoloniality, subsumed as it was in President Saparmurat Niyazov's cult of personality and his ideological conflations of precolonial Turkmen epic poetry and concepts borrowed from Soviet historiography.[8]

In all these contexts in Central Asia, the memorialization of repressions, when presented in an anticolonial vein, ignores the fact that many of the victims were loyal to the Soviet regime and at times acted as executioners themselves. In addition, there is the awkward reality that political elites reached agreements with central authorities during the Khrushchev and Brezhnev eras under which the republics received extensive autonomy in domestic affairs and significant investments in the economy in exchange for loyalty to Moscow.[9]

Putin's denunciations of Western imperialism have revived large-scale thinking about Eurasian political strategies, while his regime has been suppressing critical reflections on their past and present in increasingly cynical and brutal ways. The Russian government has outlawed civil society projects that document the history of state terror and has passed other memory laws that forbid serious discussion of the Soviet past.[10] The trauma inflicted by the Russia-Ukraine War will likely make the exploration of shared and connected histories more painful. At the same time, it highlights the significance of what is and has been repressed, including the use of repression itself as a legacy of earlier practices.

This book's reconstruction of Soviet conceptualizations of domestic and global "Eastern" politics and the lives of the intermediaries who traversed these spaces is driven not by nostalgia for the Russian/Soviet empire or its great power politics but rather by a desire to more fully elucidate the meanings of the Soviet experiment. Soviet Central Asia has been fruitfully compared with other regions of the "Muslim world."[11] Yet its function as a "domestic East" was also deeply entrenched in wider Soviet politics, economics, and culture in ways that require further consideration.

As this book has argued, a better understanding of the Soviet context and the structures of state power is crucial for challenging reinterpretations of history that apply the same postcolonial critiques to Soviet and post-Soviet entities they helped popularize abroad. A more informed interpretation would have to begin by acknowledging the role Soviet Jews, Central Asians, Arabs, and other actors from the wider socialist world in producing and circulating these ideas. Not doing so reproduces the distortions and silences of the Soviet era, ensuring that Central Asia, the Caucasus, and other regions of the USSR remain disconnected from the global histories of decolonization and postcolonial critiques they helped constitute.

Like Cold War–era accounts, post-Soviet nationalist narratives obscure the powerful and complex functions of the category "East" in the long Soviet century. They cannot account for why the strongest case for retaining the term "orientalist" was made by the Soviet delegation at the 1973 International Congress of Orientalists in Paris when a consensus was emerging in favor of dropping the label on the grounds that the profession as such had ceased to exist and that the Congress had outlived its purpose. Historian Bernard Lewis described this defense made by Bobojon Ghafurov, the director of the Institute of Oriental Studies in Moscow:

The term [orientalist], said Ghafurov, had served us well for more than a century. Why would we abandon a word that conveniently designates the work we do and that was borne with pride by our teachers and their teachers for many generations back? Ghafurov was not entirely pleased with the comment of a British delegate who praised him for his able statement of the conservative point of view.[12]

Lewis explains this unexpected convergence as a symptom of Soviet ideological bankruptcy and Ghafurov as its seemingly hapless representative caught off guard by the public airing of ideological contradiction. Yet this framing misses the utility of promoting critiques of empire without dispensing with the productive category East (*Vostok*). This category could give mediators like Ghafurov access to significant resources that could be used to secure power domestically and project it internationally.[13]

This framing also cannot explain how circulations of people and ideas across the Soviet Union's various Easts have come to shape postcolonial thought. Through careful historical reconstruction, scholar Vera Tolz was able to link Edward Said's definition of orientalism as a European system of knowledge meant to control colonial populations with Soviet definitions of orientalism (*vostokovedenie*) featured in a late Stalin-era authoritative encyclopedia.[14] Cultural studies scholars excavating connections between the Second and Third Worlds have expanded upon her findings to conclude that Soviet thought and experience contributed to contemporary Anglo-American postcolonial theory.[15] As Rossen Djagalov has argued, "postcolonial studies is itself a post-Soviet phenomenon."[16] This book speaks to these themes by historicizing the circulation of ideas about colonialism and decolonization through the work of intermediaries—including Central Asians such as Ghafurov—and by contextualizing their activities and lives in a wider domestic and global history of Soviet state power.

More broadly, this book contends that Soviet history and its Marxist geopolitics continue to shape how scholars understand postcolonial studies in hidden ways. These blind spots demonstrate the success of the Soviet Union's self-representation as an anticolonial state, especially in the Global South. The USSR's continued efforts to present itself as having overcome colonial domination helped it combat some of the challenges of decolonization experienced in other states. Yet they have also made it challenging to situate the state within the larger history of twentieth-century decolonization, though Soviet nationalities studies and the histories of specific nationalities and nationalisms have begun to illuminate the international-domestic nexus of Soviet history and its contributions to the global intellectual history of decolonization.

Beyond situating Soviet power in relation to global decolonization, this book engages with questions about what it means for states to conceal or suppress histories and ideologies of empire. The United States was also built upon a foundational myth of anti-imperialism. Throughout much of the twentieth century, and especially the Soviet era, only a few dimensions of American politics were ever acknowledged as "imperial," mostly related to discrete periods in overseas colonies and dependencies, such as military rule in the Philippines.[17] Questions about empire in the United States and efforts to describe racial segregation and political domination as global problems were often silenced as communist or un-American. This silencing was necessitated in part by the existence of a competing Soviet-backed project of supporting anticolonialism and antiracism around the world often showcased by Soviet "Eastern" intermediaries.

Other states deflect the responsibility for imperial violence differently. Britain instead emphasized liberalism and the liberal principals of freedom, individualism, and universal equality.[18] France, the Netherlands, Belgium, Portugal, and Japan have also distanced themselves from their imperial pasts using the category of "post-imperial" to address their subjects without and after empire.[19] Former colonial metropolises, where imperial differences once helped sow the seeds of Third World nationalisms, have produced flourishing cosmopolitan literary and artistic scenes, cultural hybridization and aesthetic mixings, and a playful postmodernist distance from memories of direct imperial domination.[20] Political theorists have begun to re-evaluate postcolonial cosmopolitanisms and consider how they might perpetuate relations of hierarchy and domination in the international sphere.[21] In this context, conversations about the domestic and international legacies of Soviet empire are just beginning.

For the Arab world, the collapse of the Eastern International was largely subsumed under broader reactions to the breakup of the Soviet Union, the expansion of the United States' military presence, and regional economic volatility. In 1991 the Arab Left had been reeling from disappointments in the Non-Aligned Movement (NAM) and Third World project. As historian Vijay Prashad explains, there had been no institutional incentives for the ruling classes in postcolonial states to respond to their populations' grievances and aspirations. IMF-led neoliberal development allowed states to improve their competitive position in the global economy using mechanisms that exacerbated their populations' suffering.[22] Protestors were repressed and dismissed. For the Arab Left specifically, the collapse of the Third World project had started during the 1970s, with the liberalization of Egypt's economy under Anwar Sadat, the start of the civil war in Lebanon, and the assassinations of major Left figures such as Yusuf al-Sibai and Husayn Muruwwa. The weakened and disillusioned Left subsequently went into a kind of "internal exile" or looked to religious or other sources of inspiration.[23]

Yet the collapse of the Soviet Union still felt like a loss to intellectuals who had been raised with habits, interests, and ideas imbibed from the "socialist camp."[24] Old-time Arab communists, in particular, resisted the Soviet transition to *glasnost'* and *perestroika*. Khalid Bakdash denounced Gorbachev and defended Stalin.[25] Statesmen also worried about the consequences of the transition to a US-led unipolar world. For Hafiz al-Assad it meant severing Syria's advantageous trade relations with the Soviet bloc and was a blow to his goal of attaining "strategic parity" with Israel. In 1992 he noted of the Soviet collapse that "the winners are the enemies of the Arabs."[26] As the number of Soviet military, construction, railway, irrigation, and power station experts living in Syria fell from 12,000 in its heyday to about 1,000 in 1993, the contraction of the Soviet presence affected everyone—from merchants selling sour cream beloved by Russian expats, to generals and power plant managers who struggled to find and pay for spare parts, to Russian wives of Syrian officials who lost much of their community. As one senior Damascus official half-jokingly commented, "We regret the Soviet collapse more than the Russians do."[27]

A number of Arabic novels have explored the meanings of post-Soviet exile in the sense of being severed from a shared history.[28] The specific connections between the two Easts are reimagined by Mohamed Mansi Qandil in *Qamar 'ala Samarqand* (published in Arabic in 2004 and in English translation as *Moon over Samarqand* in 2009). The novel follows an Egyptian's search in Uzbekistan for a general who befriended his father while stationed as a Soviet adviser in Egypt. Through his story it explores overlapping histories of authoritarianism and humanism grounded in a shared Islamic tradition.[29]

Moving beyond the melancholia of the Arab Left and the grand narratives of Soviet "failure" or US "triumph," this book examines Soviet-Arab linkages through the lives and fates of individuals that are always fragile and contingent relative to their local and global contexts. The experiences of Arab communists and leftists and of Soviet Jewish and Central Asian orientalists, administrators, bureaucrats, and artists illustrate the longevity and ideological resilience of the Eastern International as a concept and as a world created around it by Soviet state power and its allies. The stories of these indiviuals highlight how the internationalisms of the interwar and Cold War periods were experienced on the ground.

The Soviet context of the histories of Central Asia and the Arab Left, as well as the individual and collective experiences of the protagonists of the Eastern International, remains repressed. Inside the Soviet Union, this erasure was achieved often with the help of the repressed individuals' friends and colleagues. Since these people were dismissed in the West as "victims" or as communist "puppets," "fellow travelers," or "parlor pinks," their stories rarely received serious consideration. Nevertheless, their revolutionary and later postwar Afro-Asian networks across the Soviet Union and its "foreign" Middle East were critical to the global circulations of symbols, texts, and ideas that continue to shape understandings of this past. These networks and individuals were especially influential in the development of intellectual histories of decolonization, orientalism, and Soviet and Middle Eastern area studies in ways that scholars are just beginning to appreciate. Excavating these historical connections has made it possible to bring a Second World perspective to the Middle East and vice versa. By focusing on the people who inhabit the former Eastern International, this book attempts to integrate their lost, or rather deliberately excluded, worlds into the global history of the twentieth century.

Notes

Introduction

1. Before the revolution, the main building of KUTV belonged to the Rimsky-Korsakov noble family and was known as the "House of Famusov."
2. Hauner, *What Is Asia to US?*, 177.
3. Stalin, "The Political Tasks of the University of the Peoples of the East."
4. I borrow this phrase from Getachew, *Worldmaking after Empire*.
5. Reynolds, *Shattering Empires: The Clash and Collapse of the Ottoman and Russian Empires 1908–1918*; the term "shatter zone" is also used in Rieber, "How Persistent Are Persistent Factors?," 209.
6. On Russo-Ottoman migration see Kane, *Russian Hajj: Empire and the Pilgrimage to Mecca*; Can, *Spiritual Subjects: Central Asian Hajj at the End of Empire*; and Meyer, "Immigration"; on cultural connections see Tuna, *Imperial Russia's Muslims*; on education see Shissler, *Between Two Empires: Ahmet Ağaoğlu and the New Turkey*.
7. Martin, *Affirmative Action Empire: Nations and Nationalism in the Soviet Union*, 19.
8. Chakrabarty, *Provincializing Europe: Postcolonial Thought and Historical Difference*, 4.
9. This new ideal of governance was also captured in the eighteenth-century distinctions between the terms *russkii* and *rossiiskii*. Bassin, "Russia between Europe and Asia: The Ideological Construction of Geography," 5.
10. Sunderland, "Imperial Space: Territorial Thought and Practice in the Eighteenth Century."
11. Sunderland, "The Ministry of Asiatic Russia: The Colonial Office That Never Was but Might Have Been."
12. Martin, "The Soviet Union as Empire: Salvaging a Dubious Analytical Category"; Burbank, "Controversies over Stalinism: Searching for a Soviet Society"; Will Myer, *Islam and Colonialism: Western Perspectives on Soviet Asia*; Beissinger, "The Persisting Ambiguity of Empire."
13. Ransel, "Reflections on Transnational and World History in the USA and Its Applications," 640; Conrad, *What Is Global History*, 103; Darwin, *After Tamerlane: The Global History of Empire*; Burbank and Cooper, *Empires in World History: Power and the Politics of Difference*.
14. Bassin, "Russia between Europe and Asia: The Ideological Construction of Geography," 9.
15. Schimmelpenick van der Oye, *Toward the Rising Sun: Russian Ideologies of Empire and the Path to War with Japan*, 203–4.
16. Becker, *Russia's Protectorates in Central Asia: Bukhara and Khiva, 1865–1924*.

17. Perovic, *From Conquest to Deportation: The North Caucasus under Russian Rule*, 76; Mostashari, "Colonial Dilemmas: Russian Policies in the Muslim Caucasus."
18. Brower, *Turkestan and the Fate of the Russian Empire*, 2; Sahadeo, *Russian Colonial Society in Tashkent*; Morrison, *The Russian Conquest of Central Asia*; Khalid, "Culture and Power in Colonial Turkestan."
19. Sunderland, "The Ministry of Asiatic Russia," 139.
20. Stronski, *Tashkent: Forging a Soviet City 1930–1966*, 234–56.
21. Gilburd, *To See Paris and Die: The Soviet Lives of Western Culture*, 2, 8; David-Fox, *Showcasing the Great Experiment: Cultural Diplomacy and Western Visitors to the Soviet Union, 1921–1941*, 27.
22. Riasanovsky, *Russia and the West*; Zhuravlev does not discuss the immigration to the USSR from the East, although he admits was more extensive than immigration from the West Zhuravlev, "*Malen'kie liudi*" *i "bol'shaia istoriia": Inostrantsy moskovskogo Elektrozavoda v sovetskom obshchestve 1920-kh–1930-kh*, 29; Stern, *Western Intellectuals and the Soviet Union, 1920–40: From Red Square to the Left Bank*; this view is reproduced by scholars in the West such as English, *Russia and the Idea of the West: Gorbachev, Intellectuals & and the End of the Cold War*; Malia, *Russia under Western Eyes: From the Bronze Horseman to the Lenin Mausoleum*.
23. Yurchak, *Everything Was Forever, until It Was No More: The Last Soviet Generation*, 159.
24. Riasanovsky's book *Russia and Asia* (1960), and *Asia through Russian Eyes* (1972), generated from a conference on "Russia's impact on Asia."
25. Motadel, *Islam and Nazi Germany's War*, 8; on earlier Cold War–era destabilization efforts see Bennigsen, "Colonization and Decolonization in the Soviet Union"; Bennigsen and S. Enders Wimbush, *Muslim National Communism*; summarized in Kalinovsky, "Encouraging Resistance: Paul Henze, the Bennigsen School, and the Crisis of Détente."
26. Sunderland, "What Is Asia to Us?" 821.
27. Layton, *Russian Literature and Empire*; Ram, *The Imperial Sublime: A Russian Poetics of Empire*; Djagalov, *From Internationalism to Postcolonialism: Literature and Cinema between the Second and the Third Worlds*.
28. Scoville, "Reconsidering Nahdawi Translation"; Litvin, "Fellow Travelers? Two Arab Study Abroad Narratives of Moscow"; Litvin, "Intimate Foreign Relations: Racist Inclusion in the Soviet Dormitory Novel"; Feldman, *On the Thresholds of Eurasia*; Swanson, "'I slew my love with my own hand'"; Swanson and Gould, "The Poetics of Nahdah Multilingualism"; Hodgkin, *Red Nightingales: The Poetics of Eastern Internationalism*; Kane, Kirasirova, and Litvin, eds., *Russian-Arab Worlds*.
29. Alfred Rieber eschews "geopolitical" in favor of "geocultural" analysis of Eurasian history because, he claims, "discourses of geopolitics and civilization as applied to Eurasia have been ideologically complicit in the coming of the Cold War." Rieber, *The Struggle for the Eurasian Borderlands: From the Rise of Early Modern Empires to the End of the First World War*, 5. I try to follow this discourse in early Soviet political writing. I see echoes of it in Vladislav Zubok's "revolutionary-imperial paradigm" in Zubok, *Failed Empire: The Soviet Union in the Cold War from Stalin to Gorbachev*, x.
30. David-Fox, "Implications of Transnationalism"; Siegelbaum and Moch, "Transnationalism in One Country?"

NOTES TO PAGES 8–11   251

31. Chari and Verdery, "Thinking between the Posts: Postcolonialism, Postsocialism, and Ethnography after the Cold War," 12; on the debates between Soviet novelty and uniqueness see David-Fox, "The Soviet Order between Exceptionalism and Shared Modernity," in *Crossing Borders*.
32. These tactics have included limited cross-border military interventions, political subversions, support of separatist movements such as in interwar Afghanistan and Iran and creation of Soviet-backed autonomous republics of Azerbaijan and Kurdistan in Iran (1945–1946), support of a communist coup in Afghanistan (1978), and the military invasion that followed (1979). Hauner, *What Is Asia to Us?*, 113.
33. Hauner, *What Is Asia to Us?*, 2.
34. On *masshtabnost'* see Clark, "The Mutability of the Canon: Socialist Realism and Chingiz Aitmatov's i dol'she veka dlitsia den'," 575.
35. Troianovskii, *Vostok i revoliutsiia*, 46.
36. On Comintern's anti-imperialist networks and "hubs" see Petersson, "Hub of the Anti-Imperialist Movement"; Matera, *Black London: The Imperial Metropolis and the Decolonization in the Twentieth Century*; Goebel, *Anti-Imperial Metropolis: Interwar Paris and the Seeds of Third-World Nationalism*; Boittin, *Colonial Metropolis: The Urban Grounds of Anti-Imperialism and Feminism in Interwar Paris*.
37. Studer's terminology highlights her departure from earlier approaches to the Comintern as a hierarchical institution where the relationship between its leadership in Moscow and the national sections was one of "control." I share her perspective on this "transnational world," traversed in Akira Iriye's words by "movements and forces that . . . cut across national boundaries" but still try to illuminate the uneven workings of power. Studer, *The Transnational World of the Cominternians*, 5–6.
38. Pavlovich, "Zadachi Assotsiatsii," *Novyi Vostok* 1 (1922): 9.
39. Clark, *Eurasia without Borders: The Dream of a Leftist Literary Commons, 1919–1943*, 363.
40. Sawer, *Marxism and the Question of the Asiatic Mode of Production*.
41. On the *piatichlenka* formulation see Iolk, "AMP and the Class Struggle"; M. Godes, "The Reaffirmation of Unilinealism."
42. Erley, "The Dialectics of Nature in Kara Kum," 743.
43. Kotkin, *Stalin I: Paradoxes of Power, 1878–1928*, 532.
44. My usage of "foundation myth" and "mythology" draws on the discussion in Corney, *Telling October: Memory and the Making of the Bolshevik Revolution*, 3–4.
45. Stalin, "The Political Tasks," 135.
46. Holt, "Performing as Soviet Central Asia's Source Texts"; for "Speaking Bolshevik" see Kotkin, *Magnetic Mountain*, ch. 5.
47. Goldman, *Women, the State, and Revolution: Soviet Family Policy and Social Life, 1917–1936*; Douglas Northrop, *Veiled Empire: Gender and Power in Stalinist Central Asia*.
48. Edgar, *Intermarriage and the Friendship of Peoples: Ethnic Mixing in Soviet Central Asia*, 100.
49. Salih's *The Stillborn: Notebooks of a Woman from the Student Movement Generation in Egypt*; Hammad argues these experiences were comparable to those of women in

the US civil rights and Latin American revolutionary movements in Hammad, "Arwa Salih's The Premature."
50. Abisaab, "Gendered Expressions of Labor in the Middle East."
51. Tillett, *The Great Friendship: Soviet Historians on the Non-Russian Nationalities*.
52. Roosien, "'Not Just Tea Drinking': The Red Teahouse and the Soviet State Public in Interwar Uzbekistan."
53. The Soviet nationalities regime aimed at creating a social base for itself domestically, but when one did not exist, it demonstrated the supposed existence of such support through forms of "coerced legitimacy." The myth of self-determination was maintained by the Bolsheviks, to the extent that Lenin could talk in 1920 about ordering the Red Army "to self-determine" Georgia. Beissinger, "The Persisting Ambiguity of Empire," 162.
54. Burbank and Cooper, *Empires in World History: Power and the Politics of Difference*, 13.
55. Plummer, *Rising Wind: Black Americans and US Foreign Policy*; von Eschen, *Satchmo Blows Up the World: Jazz Ambassadors Play the Cold War*; Dudziak, *Exporting American Dreams: Thurgood Marshall's African Journey*; also Dudziak, *Cold War Civil Rights: Race and the Image of American Democracy*; Campbell, *Middle Passages: African American Journeys to Africa, 1787-2005*.
56. Von Eschen, *Race against Empire: Black Americans and Anticolonialism, 1937-1957*, ch. 5.
57. Engerman, "The Second World's Third World," 186; Westad, *Global Cold War: Third World Interventions and the Making of Our Times*.
58. See Louro et al., eds., *League against Imperialism: Lives and Afterlives*; Sune Haugbolle's and Daniela Melfa's essays in Guirguis, ed., *The Arab Lefts: Histories and Legacies, 1950s-1970s*; Haugbolle, "1967 and the New Arab Left."
59. Kalinovsky, *Laboratory of Socialist Development: Cold War Politics and Decolonization in Soviet Tajikistan*; Goff, *Nested Nationalism: Making and Unmaking Nations in the Soviet Caucasus*.
60. Tolz, *Russia's Own Orient: The Politics of Identity and Oriental Studies in the Late Imperial and Early Soviet Periods*, 20, 30.
61. Ibid., 101.
62. *Bolsh'shaia sovetskaia entsiklopediia*, 2nd ed., s.v. "Vostokovedenie."
63. Tolz, *Russia's Own Orient*, 20.
64. Djagalov, *From Internationalism to Postcolonialism*.
65. Exceptions by scholars who regularly publish in Western journals include Bobrovnikov, "Pochemu my marginaly?" Abashin, "Osobennosti rossiiskogo orientalizma"; also on reception of Said see Schimmelpennick, "The Curious Fate of Edward Said in Russia"; Djagalov, *From Internationalism to Postcolonialism*, 221.
66. Abashin, "Soviet Central Asia on the Periphery."
67. Lewis and Stolte, "Other Bandungs," 8; Lewis and Wigen, *The Myth of Continents: A Critique of Metageography*, 177-78.
68. Vasil'kov and Sorokina, *Liudi i sud'byi: biobibliograficheskii slovar' vostokovedov—zhertv politicheskogo terrora v sovetskii period (1917-1991)*; Miliband, *Vostokovedy Rossii, XX-nachalo XXI veka: bibliograficheskii slovar' v dvukh knigakh*.

NOTES TO PAGES 14-16   253

69. Most Arab communists did not leave accounts of the time they spent in the Soviet Union until the late 1960s and 1970s, when some of their memoirs came out; those are used in this book. Exceptions include a pamphlet written by Fu'ad al-Shamali when he left the party in the early 1930s and Farajallah al-Hilou's 105-page pamphlet, "A New Humanity: The Soviet Union in the 20 Years 1917–37," published to commemorate the twentieth anniversary of the Soviet Union RGASPI f. 495 (Comintern), op. 84 (Syrian Communist Party), d. 101, ll. 7–60 (Farajallah al-Hilu, al-*insaniyya al-jadida* [Beirut, Damascus, 1937]). Memoirs of prominent Arab communists, like Khaled Bakdash, usually omit their experiences in the Soviet Union, or relegate them to a kind of black hole, noting only the dates of their arrivals and departures. For more on the silences see Budeiri, "Reflections on a Silenced History."
70. Examples of such histories of radicalism in the Arab world I have begun to try to link explicitly include Khuri-Makdisi, *The Eastern Mediterranean*; Khuri-Makdisi, "Inscribing Socialism into the Nahda," Khuri-Makdisi, "Fin-de-Siècle Egypt: A Nexus for Mediterranean and Global Radical Networks"; Hamzah, *The Making of the Arab Intellectual*; Di-Capua, *No Exit*; Jens Hanssen and Max Weiss, *Arabic Thought beyond the Liberal Age*; Hanssen and Weiss, eds, *Arabic Thought against the Authoritarian Age*; Tannoury-karam, "The Making of a Leftist Milieu"; and contributions to Guirguis, ed., *Arab Lefts*.
71. Mikoulski, "The Study of Islam in Russia and the former Soviet Union"; Kappeler et al., eds., *Muslim Communities Reemerge*.
72. Chari and Verdery, "Thinking between the Posts"; Engerman, "The Second World's Third World"; Pletsch, "Three Worlds, or the Division of Social Scientific Labor, circa 1950–1975."
73. Engerman, *Know Your Enemy*, Hollinger, *Humanities and the Dynamics of Inclusion*.
74. Lockman, *Contending Visions of the Middle East: The History and Politics of Orientalism*, 121–47.
75. Moore, "Is the Post in Post-Colonial the Post in Post-Soviet?"; Kandiyoti, "How Far Do Analyses of Postcolonialism Travel?"; Kandiyoti, "Postcolonialism Compared"; Jansen, "Soviet 'Afro-Asians' in UNESCO."
76. Kris Manjapra, "Communist Internationalism and Transcolonial recognition," 159–60; Katerina Clark similarly draws on this approach for thinking about vertical and horizontal cultural production in Clark, *Eurasia*, 23.
77. Marks, *Origins of the Modern World: A Global and Environmental Narrative from the Fifteenth to the Twenty-First*, 9.
78. Notable attempts to consider the Soviet bloc as a project of globalization include Mëhilli, *From Stalin to Mao: Albania and the Socialist World*; and Sanchez-Sibony, *Red Globalization: The Political Economy of the Soviet Cold War from Stalin to Khrushchev*; on cultural integration see Clark, *Eurasia without Borders*; and Studer, *The Transnational World of the Cominternians*.
79. The global impact the Soviet history is dismissed, in the sense of being overshadowed by Wilson, in Manela, *The Wilsonian Moment: Self Determination and the International Origins of Anticolonial Nationalism*; and then by the embrace of human rights in the 1970s in Moyn, *The Last Utopia and Human Rights*.

254　NOTES TO PAGES 17–23

80. The divergence of divergence of Western and Soviet categories metageography, which poses challenges on the level of narrative, is itself a product of geopolitics. Military convenience shaped the Western delineation of Central Asia, South Asia, and the Middle East: the Allied forces established a British "Middle Eastern Command" during World War II in Cairo, Egypt, and lumped together under its umbrella the countries of the Maghreb and of Arabia proper, Iran, the Persian Gulf, Turkey, Greece, and Cyprus. In contrast, Soviet regionalization considers Central Asia (*Sredniaia Aziia*) as part of the Middle East (*Srednii Vostok*)—the middle place between the Near East (*Blizhnii Vostok*) that stretches from the Maghreb to the head of the Persian Gulf, and the Far East (*Dal'nii Vostok*), which includes regions that face the Pacific Ocean. Hence, *Srednii Vostok* would begin at the great divide between the Caucasus and the Persian Gulf, which not only separated geographically the Black and Mediterranean Seas from the Caspian Sea and the Indian Ocean but also served as the great historic divide between the former Ottoman realm and those of Iran and India. I have chosen to use the Soviet references in this book for the sake of precision. For a longer discussion see Hauner, *What Is Asia to Us?*, 72.
81. Menicucci, "The Russian Revolution and Popular Movements in Syria in the 1920s"; abu Hanna, *Tala'i' al-nahda fi Filasṭin*.
82. LeDonne, *The Russian Empire and the World: 1700–1917*, 130–54.
83. On attractiveness of communist ideas in the region see Batatu, *The Old Social Classes and the Revolutionary Movements of Iraq: A Study of Iraq's Old Landed and Commercial Classes and of Its Communists, Ba'athists, and Free Officers*, 1113; Ismael and al-Sa'id, *The Communist Movement in Egypt*, xi–xii.
84. Slezkine, *The Jewish Century*.
85. The newness of Soviet engagement with the Middle East in the postwar period is stressed in Westad, *The Global Cold War*, 39–72; Zubok, *A Failed Empire*, 109–10.
86. On alternative Asian internationalisms see Linkhoeva, *Revolution Goes East: Imperial Japan and Soviet Communism*.
87. McKeown, "Global Migration, 1846–1970," 162.
88. Djagalov, *From Internationalism to Postcolonialism*, 29.

Chapter 1

1. Trotsky, *My Life: An Attempt at an Autobiography*, 341.
2. Stites, *Revolutionary Dreams. Utopian Vision and Experimental Life in the Russian Revolution*, 37–38.
3. Jones, "The Soviet Concept of 'Limited Sovereignty' from Lenin to Gorbachev: The Brezhnev Doctrine," 7.
4. Rieber, "How Persistent Are Persistent Factors?," 214.
5. On Lenin's economic determinism and the absence of his utterance on geopolitics, see Hauner, *What Is Asia to Us?*, 206; Vigor, "The Soviet View of Geopolitics," 131–39.
6. Cited in Buck-Morss, *Dreamworld and Catastrophe: The Passing of Mass Utopia in East and West*, 28.

NOTES TO PAGES 23-26   255

7. Reynolds, *Shattering Empires: The Clash and Collapse of the Ottoman and Russian Empires 1908–1918*, 177.
8. On the civil war in the South see Kenez, *Civil War in South Russia, 1919-1920: The Defeat of the Whites*; in Turkestan, Jeff Sahadeo, *Russian Colonial Society in Tashkent, 1865-1923*, 200-3; in the Caucasus, Reynolds, *Shattering Empires*, 219-29; also Yamauchi, *The Green Crescents under the Red Tsar: Enver Pasha in Soviet Russia, 1919-1922*; in Siberia see Smele, *Civil War in Siberia: The Anti-Bolshevik Government of Admiral Kolchak, 1918-1920*; Pereira, *White Siberia: The Politics of Civil War*; on the Trans-Baikal and Mongolia see Sunderland, *The Baron's Cloak: A History of the Russian Empire in War and Revolution*.
9. Fitzpatrick, "The Civil War as a Formative Experience," 73.
10. Sunderland, *The Baron's Cloak: A History of the Russian Empire in War and Revolution*, 135.
11. His "Russian" nationality is listed in RGASPI f. 495, op. 65a, d. 2707, l. 3 (Questionnaire, February 8, 1928).
12. Conversation with Tatiana Olegovna Matroshilina, January 12, 2022.
13. By 1892, 58 percent of Odessa's population was ethnically non-Russian. Herlihy, *Odessa Recollected: The Port and the People*, 34. The official biographical data is from GARF R-7868, op. 1, d. 2985, l. 8 (Autobiography, November 16, 1935).
14. On this trend and the context of Russian émigré communities in Europe see Hillis, *Utopia's Discontents: Russian Émigrés and the Quest for Freedom, 1830s-1930s*.
15. GARF R-7868, op. 1, d. 2985, l. 8 (Troianovskii's autobiography, November 16, 1935). He mentions doing "physical and mental work" in his answer to a question about his occupation pre-1917 in RGASPI f. 495, op. 65a, d. 2707, l. 2 (Anketa, October 5, 1921).
16. As he later claimed, most of his writings from this period were confiscated and lost, except for one article about the works of the neo-Kantian philosopher Wilhelm Windelband published in the Marxist journal *Obrazovanie*. GARF R-7868, op. 1, d. 2985, ll. 8 (Troianovskii's autobiography, Nov 16, 1936).
17. He was tried in connection with the arrest of the director of the Moscow Lutheran Reform Academy, Ivan Fidler, who allowed revolutionaries to gather at the Academy.
18. GARF R-7868, op. 1, d. 2985, ll. 8 (Troianovskii's autobiography, November 16, 1936).
19. "Autobiography of Elena Troianovskaia [his wife]," from the private archive of Troianovskii's granddaughter, Tatiana Olegovna Matroshilina.
20. On imperial geopolitics see LeDonne, *The Russian Empire and the World: 1700-1917, The Geopolitics of Expansion and Containment*, 144-51; on the Army, see Marshall, *The Russian General Staff and Asia, 1800-1917*; on the Asiatic Department, see Koot, "The Asiatic Department of the Russian Foreign Ministry and the Formation of Policy toward the Non-Western World, 1881-1894."
21. Trotsky recruited tsarist officers for the Red Army, and Lenin supported staffing the new commissariats with tsarist personnel. As he once told members of the Russian Young Communist League, "We can build socialism only from the sum knowledge, organizations, and institutions, with that supply of human forces left to us from the old state." Lenin, *Collected Works*, vol. 31, 284.

256   NOTES TO PAGES 26–28

22. Vera Tolz, *Russian Academicians and the Revolution: Combining Professionalism and Politics*, 13; Knight, "Grigor'ev in Orenburg"; also Knight, "On Russian Orientalism"; Schimmelpenninck, *Russian Orientalism: Asia in the Russian Mind from Peter the Great to the Emigration*, 171–98.
23. This meeting occurred in late 1917 or early 1918. Kaganovich, *Sergei Fedorovich Ol'denburg*; Tolz, *Russian Academicians and the Revolution*, 108–22.
24. Information from the memoirs of Vladimir Bonch-Bruevich, who was present at the meeting, quoted in Shastitko, *Sobytiia i sud'by: iz istorii stanovleniia sovetskogo Vostokovedeniia*, 42; and Tamazishvilli, "Vostokovedenie v 1918," 61.
25. Tamazishvilli, "Vostokovedenie v 1918," 61.
26. Voznesenskii's letter from March 3, 1920, and Bartol'd's reply are referenced in Shastitko, *Sobytiia i sud'by*, 49; Akramov, *Bartol'd*, 68–70. On the wider hostility of the Academy toward the new regime during the civil war see Fitzpatrick, *The Cultural Front: Power and Culture in Revolutionary Russia*, 37. Ethnographers were exceptional in that they actively participated in deliberations about administrative-territorial form of the Soviet state. Hirsch, *Empire of Nations: Ethnographic Knowledge and the Making of the Soviet Union*, 7, 93.
27. Tolz, *Russian Academicians and the Revolution*; Khalid, "Russian History and the Debate over Orientalism"; Knight, "On Russian Orientalism: A Response to Adeeb Khalid"; Rodionov, "Profiles under Pressure: Orientalists in Petrograd/Leningrad."
28. Historian Sheila Fitzpatrick once compared the Narkompros to the *Zhenotdel* (the women's committee) owing to the early male Party members' notorious unwillingness to work there. Fitzpatrick, *The Commissariat of Enlightenment: Soviet Organization of Education and the Arts Is under Lunacharsky, October 1917–1921*, 19–20. At its new home, the Committee was meant to support various "cultural" projects that required language skills, such as Maksim Gorky's Catalog of World Literature project meant to include translations from the Bible, literature of China, Japan, Tibet, Mongolia, Persia, Arabs, Turkey, and others, including Indian, Egyptian, and Assyrian epics. Shastitko, *Sobytiia i sud'by*, 49–53.
29. Tamazishvilli, "Vostokovedenie v 1918," 61.
30. Ibid.
31. Shastiko, *Sobytiia i sud'byi*, 52–54; on challenges of establishing the World Literature project see Khomitsky, "World Literature, Soviet Style: A Forgotten Episode in the History of the Idea," 119–54.
32. Lunacharskii, cited in Shastitko, *Sobytiia i sud'by*, 24.
33. Bukharin, "Eastern Revolution"; Radek, "Turkey Exits the war"; Kerzhentsev, "Revolutionary Fermentation in the Balkans"; and A. Voznesenskii, "Russia and Persia" are mentioned in Gurko-Kriazhin, "10 let," *Novyi Vostok* 19 (1927), 41; Bukharin cynically claimed "if we propound the self-determination for the colonies . . . we lose nothing by it." Stalin, "Ne zabyvaite vostoka," was published anonymously in *Zhizn' natsional'nostei* 3 (November 24, 1918): 1.
34. "Meeting of Muslim Communists," *Zhizn' natsional'nostei* 2 (1918), 6; "Stalin's Speech at This Meeting of Muslim communists," *Zhizn' natsional'nostei* 3 (November 24, 1918): 2.

35. Gurko-Kriazhin, "10 let vostokovednoj mysli," *Novyi Vostok*, 42. Stalin wrote of a "bridge between the socialist West and the enslaved East . . . against world imperialism." Stalin, "Do Not Forget the East," *Zhizn' natsional'nostei* 3 (November 24, 1918): 1.
36. Hauner, *What Is Asia to Us?*, 3, 71. Stephen Kotkin, *Stalin I: Paradoxes of Power, 1878–1928*, 19; Alfred J. Rieber points to Russia's porous frontiers and multinational society as "persistent factors" that shape Russia's foreign policy from the imperial to Soviet periods. Rieber, "How Persistent Are Persistent Factors?"
37. Crews, *For Prophet and Tsar: Islam and Empire in Russia and Central Asia*.
38. Aydin, *Idea of a Muslim World*; Motadel, *Islam and Nazi Germany's War*.
39. Most immediately, the Russians were drawn in by their interests in the Balkans, and a Pan-Slavic sense of duty to Slavs who practiced Eastern Orthodox Christianity, and their network of alliances, while Ottomans were drawn in by a desire to preserve their empire against expanding British, French, and Russian economic, political, and military control. Reynolds, *Shattering Empires*; Holquist, *Making War, Forging Revolution: Russia's Continuum of Crisis, 1914–1921*; Sanborn, *Imperial Apocalypse: The Great War and the Destruction of the Russian Empire*; Aksakal, *The Ottoman Road to War in 1914: The Ottoman Empire and the First World War*.
40. Central powers had distributed the call in Tatar; see Motadel, *Islam and Nazi Germany's War*, 8.
41. Blunt, Foreword, in Rothstein, *Egypt's Ruin* (1910), xvi–xviii (English edition 1910; Russian edition 1925).
42. Pavlovich, "Velikie zheleznodorozhnye i morskie puti budushchago," 229, 234. For more on Pavlovich see Kemper, "Red Orientalism: Mikhail Pavlovich and Marxist Oriental Studies in Early Soviet Russia," 440–41.
43. Catherine the Great allocated to the college more funds and more supervisory competences. Ritchie, "The Asiatic Department," 75–161, especially 88; on the expansion of consulates see Eileen Kane, *Russian Hajj*, 34, 48, 91, 104; Rezvan, *Russian Ships in the Gulf, 1899–1903*.
44. Marshall, *The Russian General Staff in Asia, 1800–1917*, 167.
45. Troianovskii, *Siniaia kniga*, xii; on Pavlovich's work at the NKID see Kemper, "Red Orientalism," 442.
46. Troianovskii, *Siniaia kniga*, 43.
47. He published the Ministry's correspondence with the Russian Council General in Calcutta and with the office of the Governor General of Turkestan.
48. The cover page bore the title *The East in Light of Revolution* (*Vostok pri svete revoliutsii*); the title *East and Revolution* appeared on the inside cover. Troianovskii, *Vostok i revoliutsiia*, 46.
49. By the turn of the century there were around two million German-speaking Tsarist subjects and residents. Hauner, *What Is Asia to Us?*, 166; On Semyonov Tian-Shanskii see Martin, *All Possible Worlds: A History of Geographical Ideas*, 252–58.
50. As an "organism," the state had territorial and resource needs.
51. Troianovskii, *Vostok i revoliutsiia*, 12–13.

NOTES TO PAGES 32-34

52. Ibid., 42–43. Despite their contradiction with the Sunna (the body of traditional Islamic law based on the words and acts of Mohammed), Troianovskii believed these "historical and psychological factors" to have entered civil law (*pravo grazhdanstva*) and Islamic cultural practices throughout the Muslim world.
53. Rac, "Arabic Literature for the Colonizer and the Colonized: Ignaz Goldziher and Hungary's Eastern Politics (1878-1918)," 80-102.
54. Heschel, "Orientalist Triangulations: Jewish Scholarship on Islam as a Response to Christian Europe," 148.
55. On the Tatar-Bashkir Republic (1918-1919) see Schafer, "Local Politics and the Birth of the Republic of Bashkortostan, 1919-1920."
56. It did not matter that Iran was Shi'a since Troianovskii already established that Islam was malleable, since it had been observed that Sunnis had participated in religious services in Shiite mosques in Tatar cultural centers like Astrakhan, and since Muslim preachers there spoke of a single unified Islam.
57. Troianovskii, *Vostok i revoliutsiia*, 44.
58. Ibid.
59. On Seymonov see Hauner, *What Is Asia to Us?*, 152-59, 200.
60. Clark, *Eurasia*.
61. Troianovskii, *Vostok i revoliutsiia*, 47.
62. Ibid., 44. This argument echoes Sir Halford John Mackinder's heartland thesis that Central Asia was a "pivotal" part of Eurasia made in "The Geographical Pivot of History" (1904), which Hausner suggests was "smuggled in by Haushofer to Soviet Russia." Hauner, *What Is Asia to Us?*, 173.
63. "Principles of a Program of the Union of Liberation of the East," in Troianovskii, *Vostok i revoliutsiia*, 66-71.
64. Troianovskii, *Vostok i revoliutsiia*, 67-68.
65. Ibid., 69.
66. Ibid., 69.
67. Ibid., 67. His idealization of a federative structure was unusual in a context where most socialists viewed federalism as a "philistine ideal" and as "an absurdity." Slezkine, "The USSR as Communal Apartment," 217, 220. Georgi Safarov who argued that the working masses of the East were "moving towards an international federation of national Soviet republics." Safarov, *Kolonial'naia revoliutsiia: Opyt Turkestana*, 22.
68. Conrad, *Global History*, 30; Aydin, *The Politics of Anti-Westernism in Asia*; Bharucha, *Another Asia*; Clark, *Eurasia without Borders: The Dream of a Leftist Literary Commons, 1919-1943*, 10, 188-93.
69. Lewis and Wigen, *The Myth of Continents: A Critique of Metageography*, 70-71.
70. Hauner, *What Is Asia to Us?*, 77; citing Snesarev, *India kak glavnyi faktor* (1906).
71. Hauner, *What is Asia to Us?*, 176.
72. Ibid.
73. Ibid., 193.
74. This slogan was promoted by the Japanese Ajia Gi Kai (Association for the Defense of Asia), which, by 1918, had attracted influential Muslim leaders within Russia. One was the Russian-born Tatar Abdurreshid Ibrahim, who had served in the Muslim

Ecclesiastic Administration in Ufa and in 1908 visited Tokyo, which had already become a major center for Asianist publications along with Istanbul. Afterward, Ibrahim expressed fears that Asian societies and cultures might not survive because of global Westernization and Western hegemony, including inside Russia. Aydin, *The Politics of Anti-Westernism in Asia: Visions of World Order in Pan-Islamic and Pan-Asian Thought*, 84–88.

75. For instance, he criticized Japanese imperialism in Asia for "playing on the 'pan-Mongoloid' feelings of the entire yellow race." Troianovskii, *Vostok i revoliutsiia*, 21–22. On other 1920s Soviet Marxist orientalists using racial categories see Kemper, "Red Orientalism," 468.

76. On the unpopularity of Social Darwinism among socialists see Marks, *How Russia Shaped the Modern World: From Art to Anti Semitism, Ballet to Bolshevism*, 41.

77. The term "the Eastern Question" entered into wider circulation with the 1815 Congress of Vienna. On its various valiances see Yilmaz, "The Eastern Question."

78. Cited in Genis, "Odin is stolpov Komissariata: Arsenii Nikolaevich Voznesenskii (1881–1937)," 122 (fn 18), from Troianovskii, "Otvet kritiky," *Turkestanskii Kommunist* 131 (October 10, 1919); Troianovskii mentions fast sales of the full 50,000 print run and positive reviews of his book in GARF, f. R-7868, op. 1, d. 2985, l. 8 (Troianovskii's cv, November 16, 1935). One positive review was Gurko-Kriazhin in *Vestnik zhizni* 5 (1919): 100–1.

79. His meeting with Lenin took place on the recommendation of Lunacharskii. GARF f. 539, op. 4, d. 2805, l. 25 (Note from Lunacharskii to Lenin asking him to meet with Troianovskii and Gurko about the Union of Liberation of the East). Troianovskii claimed to have received Lenin's and Stalin's "moral support" in at least two autobiographies. GARF f. 7668 (TsIK's Uchenyi Komitet), op. 1, d. 2985, l. 8; and GARF f. A-539 (Commission of the Council of Ministers for Personal Pensions), op. 4, d. 2805, ll. 53–54.

80. The organization possibly took its name from the earlier imperial "Union of Liberation," a liberal political group founded in St. Petersburg in 1904 that advocated for constitutional monarchy, secret and direct vote for all Russian citizens, and the self-determination of different nationalities.

81. GARF, f. 7868, op. 1, d. 2985, l. 27 (Draft of article from *Izvestiia* 238, October 31, 1918).

82. Kamenev spoke under his pseudonym, Iu. Kamanev, under which he published *Ekonomicheskaia sistema imperializma i zadachi sotsializma* (The economic system of capitalism and the goals of socialism) (Zhizn i znanie, 1918). The speakers are listed in *Izvestiia* (no. 238), October 31, 1918, 6.

83. Gurko-Kriazhin recalled this group as "curious" and provided a list of speakers in Gurko-Kriazhin, "10 let vostokovednoj mysli," *Novyi Vostok* 19 (1927), 41; Gaidar-Khan is probably Gaidar-Khan Amuogly Tariverdiev, a participant of the Iranian revolution of 1905–1911 and the head of the Revolutionary Committee of the Republic of Gilan (1920–1921). On Haidar Khan, see Chaqueri, *The Soviet Socialist Republic of Iran, 1920–1921*, 462–63. The head of the NKID Eastern Section Arsenii Nikolaevich Voznesenskii (1881–1937) described it as spontaneous and voluntary (*samochinnyi*). Genis, "Odin iz stolpov Komissariata," 83.

84. Lunacharskii, "Soiuz ugnetennykh klassov i natsii," speech given at December 8, 1918, meeting of the Union of Liberation of the East, reprinted in *Vestnik zhiz'ni* 5 (1919): 14–16. For the location of Lunacharskii's presentation, see "Osvobozhdenie vostoka," *Izvestiia* 271 (December 11, 2018): 5.
85. Kassymbekova and Teichmann, "The Red Man's Burden: Soviet European Officials in Central Asia in the 1920s and 1930s," 163–86.
86. Fitzpatrick, *The Commissariat of Enlightenment*, 95–97.
87. Among others, Voznesenskii taught courses on China and Japan; Gukro-Kriazhin on imperialism, Troianovskii on preconditions of socialism in the East; the former imperial vice consul and first representative of the RSFSR in Tehran N. Z. Bravin (1881–1921) on Persia; S. Iusupov on Revolution and Muslims (*Musul'manstvo*); Subhi on Turkey; and Sultan-Galiev on the Caucasus. Genis, "Odin iz stolpov Komissariata," 83; also Tamazishvili, "Vladimir Aleksandrovich Gurko-Kriazhin: sud'ba bojtsa 'vostokovednogo fronta,'" 46.
88. At the Communist Academy, the courses on imperialism and foreign policy were taught by SOV member Pavlovich-Vel'tman and Karl Radek. Shapiro, "The Communist Academy," 50. At the Red Army academy, courses in "applied orientalism" were required alongside language training and other topics, like historical materialism and international law. P. A., "Vostochnyi Otdel Voennoi Akademii R.K.K. Armii i Kruzhok prakticheskogo izucheniia Vostoka pri nem," *Novyi Vostok* 1 (1922): 460–62; and Gusterin, *Vostochnyi fakul'tet Voennoi akademii*, 47.
89. Genis, "Odin iz stolpov Komissariata," 83–84; A. O. Tamazishvili, "Vladimir Aleksandrovich Gurko-Kriazhin," 46.
90. Genis, "Odin iz stolpov Komissariata," 86.
91. Reynolds, *Shattering Empires*; Suny, *The Revenge of the Past: Nationalism, Revolution, and the Collapse of the Soviet Union*, 20–83; Pipes, *The Formation of the Soviet Union: Communism and Nationalism 1917–1923*, 50–113.
92. As Reynolds argued, Lenin recognized that he had no way to reinforce the Bolsheviks of Baku. *Shattering Empires*, 209; also Suny, *The Baku Commune: Class and Nationality in the Russian Revolution, 1917–1918*.
93. Brower, *Turkestan and the Fate of the Russian Empire*, 75–87.
94. Chokabaeva et al., *The Central Asian Revolt*, 10.
95. Carrère d'Encausse, "Civil War and New Governments," 225.
96. For instance, the proposed union of Muslim-Turkic world into a Republic of Turan. Bennigsen and Wimbush, *Muslim National Communism in the Soviet Union: A Revolutionary Strategy for the Colonial World*, 66–68.
97. Khalid, *Making Uzbekistan: Nation, Empire, and Revolution in the Early USSR*, 106.
98. Lenin "To the Communists of Turkestan," delivered November 22, 1919. *Lenin's Collected Works*, 4th English ed., Progress Publishers, Moscow, 1965, vol. 30, 138; Stalin, "Our Tasks in the East," *Pravda* 48 (March 2, 1919).
99. Joseph Paliukaitis, "Turkestan i revoliutsiia Vostoka," *Zhizn' natsional'nostei* 19 (27) 1919. Paliukaitis was a graduate of the Lazarev institute who had worked at the NKID and MIV. His article in was based on a speech by Karamin, the plenipotentiary of the Commissariat of the Army.

NOTES TO PAGES 39-41   261

100. Jan M. Meijer, ed., *The Trotsky Papers*, vol. 1 (London, The Hague: Mouton, 1964), 61-67.
101. Bennigsen and Wimbush, *Muslim National Communism*, 53-58; Khalid, *Making Uzbekistan*, 101-2.
102. Elena Troianovskaia, unpublished biography from family archive.
103. Troianovskii's meeting with the Kraikom in April 9, 1919, is described in *Turkestanskii Kommunist* 26 (May 1, 1919).
104. Broido joined the civil war in Turkestan after becoming acquainted with Mikhail Frunze at the Vernii gymnasium (now Almaty), working in Bishkek, and then in revolutionary organization in Tashkent and Khiva. He headed of the Tashkent Soviet during the February Revolution in 1917, joined the Bolsheviks in 1918, and became a member of the revolutionary council of the First Red Army on the Eastern front in 1919. He served as head of the Extraordinary Commission of the RSFSR to Khorezm in April 1920. Later he joined the Narkomnats. Germanov, "Novyi dokument po istorii sovetskogo Turkestana."
105. RGASPI f. 122, op. 2, d. 11, l. 2 (on correspondence with Afghanistan); l. 3 (on medicine in India); d. 75, ll. 2-3 (correspondence from the Khorezm Republic to Moscow about Broido trying to appease [*umitvorit*] hostile Uzbeks and Turkmen).
106. Genis, "Odin is stolpov Komissariata," 122 (fn 18); citing *Turkestanskii Kommunist* 26 (May 1, 1919).
107. In 1918 the Commissariat of Internal Affairs complained that administrative power in Turkestan was "uneven." "Report of Narkomvnutdel of the Turkestan ASSR about the Situation in the Republic" (May 31, 1918). Amanzholova, *Rossiia i tsentral'naia Aziia, 1905-1925: sbornik dokumentov*, 125-26.
108. Genis, "Deportatsiia russkikh iz Turkestana v 1921 gody"; Abdurakhimova, *Kolonial'naia Sistema vlasti v Turkestane*, 119-42.
109. During a wartime food crisis this meant instituting unequal rationing regimes and raiding the Central Asian part of the city for supplies. Shahadeo, *Russian Colonial Society in Tashkent, 1865-1923*, ch. 7. On the population drop as a result of starvation, see Buttino, "Study of the Economic Crisis and Depopulation in Turkestan."
110. Elena Troianovskaia's unpublished autobiography.
111. On the formation of the Turkkomissiia see Akramov and Avliakulov, *V. I. Lenin, Turkkomissiia i ukreplenie Sovetskoi Vlasti*, 39-57.
112. Safarov, *Kolonial'naia revoliutsiia: Opyt Turkestana*, 101-2, 123.
113. Safarov criticized him for inspiring the popular slogan "Away with Commissars! (*Doloi Komissarov!*)." Ibid., 105. For Kobozev's efforts with Muslims see Khalid, *Making Uzbekistan*, 92-95.
114. Khalid, *Making Uzbekistan*, 107.
115. "From Kobozev's Recollections of Spring 1918," in Amanzholova, *Rossiia i tsentral'naia aziia*, 119-20. He is referring to the destruction of the Kokand autonomy in February 1918.
116. Two days before Kobozev's article was published, Alexei Rykov of the Revolutionary Military Council received an alarming letter from Karp Sorokin about the situation in the Turkestan party organization warning that the European part of the proletariat and party had determined that Kobozev's implementation of directives from

the center would soon lead the Soviets to give birth to a khanate. "Sorokin's letter to Kykov" (September 23, 1919), in Amanzholova, *Rossiia i tsentral'naia Aziia*, 178–79. The Muslim communists also sent a delegation to Lenin to argue—on the basis of the significance of Turkestan to Soviet Eastern policy and of the colonial nature of national relations existing there—that Turkestan should be a national republic enjoying wide ranging autonomy, including the right to conduct its own foreign policy and to print its own money. These appeals were largely overruled. The confrontation is described in Khalid, *Making Uzbekistan*, 111–15.

117. *Turkestanskii Kommunist* no. 117 (September 25, 1919); Akramov and Avliiakulov, *V. I. Lenin, Turkkomissia*, 150.
118. *Turkestanskii Kommunist* no. 117 (September 25, 1919).
119. *Turkestanskii Kommunist* no. 131 (October 16, 1919).
120. According to Adeeb Khalid, the SOV attracted many Muslims who had been active in 1917 but marginalized after the Soviet takeover. Khalid, *Making Uzbekistan*, 106.
121. Akramov and Avliakulov, *V. I. Lenin, Turkkomissia*, 47.
122. In a memo to the TsK, Elieva communicated that he and Kuibashev did not think that the Musburo could have any executive power (*nikakikh funktsii vlasti*). The challenge to the Musburo intensified with the belated arrival in February 1920 of Frunze. "From Eliava's message to the TsK RKP(b) on the autonomy of Turkestan," Amanzholova, *Rossiia i tsentral'naia Aziia, 1905–1925*, 229–30.
123. "Eliava's Report to the TsK RKP(b) from January 23, 1920," in Amanzholova, *Rossiia i tsentral'naia Aziia*, 229–30. Sahadeo argues that the Turkkomission continued Kobozev's efforts to increase local participation in the Soviet state and Communist Party but focused on other issues and empowered other allies. Sahadeo, *Russian Colonial Society in Tashkent, 1865–1923*, 214–20.
124. Ibid., 215.
125. Troianovskii's wife recalled going over to Khodjaev's house in the Old City part of Tashkent—where she spent most of the time with his young wife while the men conversed together warmly. Elena Troianovskaia's autobiography.
126. Khalid, *Making Uzbekistan*, 121.
127. These republics were unified in March 12, 1922, into a Transcaucasian Soviet Federated Socialist Republic after Stalin's personal trip to Georgia in 1921 where he "dealt with recalcitrant elements." Euduin and North, *Soviet Russia and the East*, 34.
128. The Sovinterprop's creation was announced at the Second Congress of Communist Organizations of the East in 1919. Akramov and Avliakulov, *V. I. Lenin, Turkkomissiia*, 151. It was not first created at the Baku Congress in 1920, as purported in Adibekov, Shakhnazarova, and Shirinia, *Organizatsionnaia struktura kominterna*, 27. In fact, the Tashkent branch of the Sovinterprop had sent an expedition of forty people to the Caucasus in April 1920 for the Baku Congress. RGASPI f. 61, op. 2, d. 16, l. 31 (Memo to the Polygraphic Section of the Sovinterprop, April 27, 1920).
129. Akramov and Avliakulov, *V. I. Lenin, Turkkomissiia*, 151.
130. Persits, *Vostochnye internatsionalisty*, 66.
131. Eliave made the decision to close the Union of Liberation of the East and merge it into the Sovinterprop on February 1, 1920. RGASPI f. 61, op. 2, d. 16, l. 5 (Note

to the Sovinterprop, February 1920); by May 1920 the Ispolkom of Sovinterprop ruled that the Union of Liberation of the East, which had 400 members, should be revived and asked Troianovskii to issue a new set of instructions. Genis, "Odin is stolpov Komissariata," 122 (fn 18). The members of these various organizations continued to meet through the Sovinterprop Presidium into 1921. GARF, f. 5402, op.1, d. 33, ll. 36–37 (Protocol of Sovinterprop Presidium Meeting from January 22, 1921) (Reproduced on http://islamperspectives.org/rpi/items/show/12869, last accessed October 13, 2018).

132. RGASPI f. 61, op, 2, d. 16, l. 8 (Broido to the Sovinterprop, February 6, 1920).
133. RGASPI f. 61, op. 2, d. 16, l. 44 (Memo of VTsIK Commission for Turkestan, May 3, 1920).
134. Some of these concluded with the singing of the *Internationale*. Akramov and Avliakulov, *V. I. Lenin, Turkkomissiia*, 54.
135. Before the transfer the RCP(b) monitored the Sovinterprop's relationships with the foreign sectors. RGASPI f. 61, op. 2, d. 16, l. 87 (Note from Turkkomission head Valerian Kuibashev and Upravdelami Rabinovich to Geller, head of Sovinterprop asking for a summary of its foreign activities, July 1920). On the transfer to the Turkburo see RGASPI f. 61, op. 2, d. 16, ll. 112–13 (Turkburo Directive, October 1920). On the Turkburo's structure see Kudukhov, "Organizatsionnaia struktura," 185–89.
136. RGASPI f. 61, op. 2, d. 16, ll. 112–13 (Turkburo Directive, October 1920).
137. Hirsch, *Empire*, 145–46
138. On artists Aleksandr Rodchenko and Gustav Klutsis, who worked with the Comintern and voted to affiliate the Department of Fine Arts Bureau with the Comintern's work, see Clark, *Eurasia*, 45.
139. Tamazishvili, "Vladimir Aleksandrovich Gurko-Kriazhin," 33.
140. Hirsh, *Empire of Nations*; Tolz, *Russia's Own Orients*.
141. Spector, *The Soviet Union and the Muslim World*; White, "Colonial Revolution and the Communist International," 173–93; Young, *Postcolonialism*, 10, 127–39; Prashad, *The Darker Nations*, 19–20; Petersson, *Willi Munzenberg, the League against Imperialism, and the Comintern, 1925-1933*.
142. M. N. Roy, "The Awakening of the East," *The Call* (July 15, 1920), 5.
143. Others recalled regular cheering and renditions of the *Internationale*.
144. Cited in White, "Communism and the East: The Baku Congress, 1920," 492.
145. Elena Troianovskaia's autobiography.
146. *S'ezd narodov Vostoka*, 135–36; Clark, *Eurasia without Borders*, 5.
147. *S'ezd narodov Vostoka*, 93.
148. Cited in Genis, "Odin is stolpov Komissariata," 91–92.
149. Ibid., 92.
150. Genis, *S Bukharoi nado konchat'*, 15–18; Genis, "Sovetskaia Rossiia i Gilianskaia revoliutsiia," 37–42.
151. Hauner, *What Is Asia to Us?*, 170; the popularity of German geopolitics among this group was noted by the German liaison with Radek, Oskar von Niedermayer (1885–1948?); for more on the "impact" of German geographical ideas in late

nineteenth-century Russia see Martin, *All Possible Worlds: A History of Geographical Ideas*, 248–78.
152. Genis, "Odin is stolpov Komissariata," 92.
153. Chicherin mentioned that he spoke with Menzhenskii (member of the VChK Prezidium, responsible for fighting counterrevolution) about keeping Voznesenski away from the Comintern and reassigning him to be a lecturer "in some provincial town where it will be easier to keep an eye on him. Genis, "Odin iz stolpov Komissariata," 92–93.
154. Cited in Hirst, "Transnational Anti-Imperialism and the National Forces: Soviet Diplomacy and Turkey, 1920–1923," 216.
155. "NKID to the Comintern, August 14, 1920," in Persits, *Persidskii front mirovoi revoliutsii*, 186–89.
156. Riddell, *To See the Dawn, Baku, 1920: First Congress of the Peoples of the East, The Communist International in Lenin's Time*, 203–4.
157. Next a Bukharan representative, Jabarzadeh, gave a speech in Uzbek that was omitted from the official Congress record. Riddell, *To See the Dawn*, 204.
158. Cited in Hauner, *What Is Asia to Us?*, 92.
159. RGASPI f. 544, op. 4, d. 19, ll. 20–21 (Report about BCP at 2nd Comintern Congress in Moscow about their work from September 1918–July 1920). Frunze was also aware of the extent of the robberies, destruction, and rape and issued an order to shoot anyone caught engaging in these activities on September 4, 1920. These events were reported to Lenin in October 1920. See Genis, *S Bukharoi nado konchat'*, 40–43.
160. Ibid., 204–5, 232.
161. RGASPI f. 544, op. 4, d. 19, ll. 14–19 (Report of Bukharan CP TsK delegate Mukhamadi to the Comintern, August 10, 1920); Roy recalled that a Bukharan Revolutionary Committee was set up in Tashkent under the auspices of the Comintern Turkburo to distribute such propaganda literature and posters. Roy, *Memoirs*, 449–51.
162. Genis, *S Bukharoi nado konchat'*, 10–11.
163. Becker, *Russia's Protectorates in Central Asia: Bukhara and Khiva, 1865–1924*, 227.
164. Siegelbaum, *Soviet State and Society between Revolutions, 1918–1929*, 67–126. This Anglo-Soviet agreement was followed by followed by similar agreements with Germany (May), Norway (September), Austria and Italy (December), Sweden (February 1922), and Czechoslovakia (June). Jacobson, *When the Soviet Union Entered World Politics*, 20.
165. Young, *Postcolonialism: An Historical Introduction*, 143.
166. Lenin *Works*, 1st Russian ed., Vol. 18, Part I, 299.
167. Jacobson, *When the Soviet Union Entered World Politics*, 15.
168. Persits, *Persidskii front mirovoi revoliutsii*; Chosroe Chaquerie, *The Soviet Socialist Republic of Iran*.
169. Roy, *Memoirs*, 525.
170. In October 1921, Semen Dimanshtein, who had worked in the RKP(b) Jewish section, headed the Turkestan Narkompros, and was a member of the collegium of the Narkomnats, was appointed to run the Turkburo in Bukhara. RGASPI f. 544, op. 4,

NOTES TO PAGES 50–52   265

d. 5, ll. 1–6 (Report to the Secretariat of Ispolkom of the Comintern about Turkburo's work since its reorganization in May and June, October 15, 1921).

171. Using similar state-centric logic, the BCP also emphasized the significance of Eastern Bukhara, at the nexus of three regions with particularly "fanatical" Muslim populations of Fergana, Afghanistan, and Chitral, as a potential "center" (*uzel'*) of the Muslim East. RGASPI f. 544, op. 4, d. 19, ll. 49–59 (Report of the Delegation of the 5th Meeting of the BCP by Nadjie Khusanov, undated 1920).

172. In Iran the Turkburo claimed to have maintained a network of more than 4,000 affiliates interested in receiving instructional, material, and organizational support. RGASPI f. 544, op. 4, d. 1, ll. 1–6 (Report of the Turkburo to the ECCI, October 15, 1921).

173. RGASPI f. 433, op. 4, d. 13, ll. 68–70 (Report to Comintern Ispolkom Plenipotentiary in Central Asia, from the Information Section, February 1, 1922).

174. Khalid, *Making Uzbekistan*, 115.

175. Roy was one of those offered a position in the new apparatus "so as to maintain continuity with the initial work done from Central Asia," but he refused. Roy, *Memoirs*, 525; Troianovskii was also simultaneously working for the Profintern's Eastern Section.

176. In Soviet usage, the "Near East" usually referred to Iran, Turkey, and the Arab world; the Middle East referred to India, Afghanistan, and Pakistan. RGASPI f. 495, op. 18, d. 11, ll. 3–6 (Project of Construction of the Eastern Section of the Comintern, 1920).

177. Elena Troianovskaia's autobiography.

178. GARF f. 539, op. 4, d. 2805, ll. 63–66 (Autobiography, February 25, 1934).

179. Gurko-Kriazhin was forced to sell his things after relocating from the Caucasus to Moscow to work for VNAV. Timazishvili, "Gurko-Kriazhin," 58–60; on KUTV students observing that instructors seemed "tired and harassed" see Haywood, *Black Bolshevik: Autobiography of an Afro-American Communist*, 162.

180. Elena continued to work as Kollontai's secretary and, on her own initiative, also tried to direct prostitutes working at the Lux hotel into other lines of work. Conversation with Tatiana Olegovna Matroshilina, January 12, 2022.

181. RGASPI f. f. 495, op. 154, d. 75, ll. 1–3 (Protocol of the First Meeting of the Near East Section, August 12, 1921).

182. In 1919, the ECCI had received 7,445,000 rubles from the TsK RKP; by 1922 its operational budget was set at 1.5 million, and then raised to 4.18 million in 1925, with 150,000 gold rubles set aside for the Eastern Section. Adibekov et al., *Politburo TsK RKP(b)-VKP(b) i Komintern 1919–1943 gg*, 33, 125, 286.

183. RGASPI f. 495, op. 154, d. 75, ll. 1–3 (Protocol of the First Meeting of the Near East Section, August 12, 1921).

184. RGASPI f. 495, op. 154, d. 82, ll. 1–4 (Troianovskii's Memo, June 15, 1921); the Berlin Bureau seemed especially important for anticolonial and radical groups of Korean, Chinese, Indian, Japanese, Cameroon, Egyptian, and Persian activists, among others, who received money from the Soviets through it. Manjapra, "Communist Internationalism," 166. However, Troianovskii still chose Bern.

185. By way of exception, the Comintern did use radio technology to project invitations to the Baku Congress into territories beyond those contiguous with Soviet borders, including to Iraq, Syria, Arabia, and Mesopotamia (Iraq). Yenen, "The Other Jihad," 273–93. In preparation for Baku, Karl Radek admitted to the organizing Committee that the Comintern will send "whatever information we have on the partisan struggle of Arabs in Mesopotamia," but "we know that comrades living in Baku might have only fragmentary information about it." Radek's letter to Stasova, June 6, 1920. Persits, *Persidskii front mirovoi revoliutsii: Dokumenty o sovetskom vtorzhenii v Giliane*, 104–5.
186. Gail Minault, *The Khilafat Movement: Religious Symbolism and Political Mobilization in India*.
187. RGASPI f. 495, op. 154, d. 75, l. 5 (Meeting addendum, August 12, 1921).
188. This comment was made in 1921 by Eastern Section bureaucrat S. Brike-Bestuzheva in another document prepared for the Comintern Near East Section. Kosach, "Palestinets Vol'f Averbukh," 56–104. Comintern officials seemed unaware of the jihad of Muhammad Abdullah in Somaliland (1899–1920), nor the Dinka uprising (1919) in the Sudan nor the jihad in South Darfur in the Sudan (1921).
189. On the Soviet role in these negotiations see Samuel Hirst, "Transnational Anti-Imperialism."
190. RGASPI f. 5, op. 2, d. 210, ll. 1–3 (Memo from Karakhan to Stalin about Chicherin's reports, January 3, 1923).
191. Riddell, *Proceedings of the Fourth Congress of the Communist*, 707–36.
192. Ibid., 714.
193. Ibid. On the formation of the ECP and negotiations for its admission into the Comintern, see Kosach, *Krasnyi Flag nad Blizhnim Vostokom*, 65–87; Ginat, *A History of Egyptian Communism: Jews and Their Compatriots in Quest of Revolution*, 55–101.
194. RGASPI f. 495, op. 154, d. 198, ll. 1–18 ("Theses of the Progress and Tactics of the Communist Party of Egypt," by Troianovskii).
195. These included as the aerial bombardment of rebellious rural populations in British Iraq in 1920 and the shelling of Damascus in French Syria in 1925. Michael Provence, "French Mandate Counterinsurgency and the Repression of the Great Syrian Revolt," in *The Routledge Handbook of the History of the Middle East Mandates*, ed. Cyrus Schayegh and Andrew Arsan, 136–38.
196. Slezkine, *The Jewish Century*, 187.
197. Although the Bund espoused a class-based ideology and opposed Zionism, the rise of this *Jewish* revolutionary workers' organization provided remarkable evidence of the isolation of the Jews within the national working class. Vital, *Origins of Zionism*, 312; On attrition from the Bund see Selzkine, *Jewish Century*, 148; even Stalin had weighed in on the debate to repudiate the Bund's position; in 1913 he asserted that the Jews were not a nation since they inhabited different parts of the globe and spoke different languages in a section on "The Bund, Its Nationalism, and Its Separatism," in *Marxism and the National Question* (1913).

198. On the formation of PCP see Budeiri, *The Palestine Communist Party*, 3–11; Hen-Tov, *Communism and Zionism in Palestine during the British Mandate*; Kosach, *Kommunisty Blizhnego Vostoka*, 79–80.
199. The dissolution of the Bund in 1920 seemed to Auerbach as further proof of the assimilationist platform of the Russian Communist Party's *Evsektsiia* and of the lack of Comintern interest in the Jewish proletariat. Failing to see a possible resolution of the "Jewish question" without assimilation, he immigrated to Palestine. Kosach, "Palestinets Vol'f Averbukh."
200. Negotiations over Poalei Zion's entry into the Comintern fell apart in 1922. Kosach, *Krasnyi Flag nad Blizhnim Vostokom*, 177–78.
201. Karl Radek issued directives to communists in Palestine in 1924, stating that "The future of the Party depended upon its territorialization." Laqueur, *MOPS–PCP–MAKI*, 29.
202. References to "Arabistan" or "Arabia" helped emphasize the development of a unified national movement. Kosach, "Palestinets," 70–71.
203. Ibid.; also Schayegh, *The Middle East and the Making of the Modern World*, 154; Among communists, general criticism of Zionism as an impediment to capitalism coexisted with attributions to the Jewish community in Palestine as a major progressive force in the social and especially economic development of Palestine. This attitude was known as the doctrine of "Yishuvism." Hen-Tov, *Communism and Zionism in Palestine during the British Mandate*, 114.
204. RGASPI f. 495, op. 154, d. 198, ll. 37–38 (Draft Resolution of the PCP).
205. Budeiri, *The PCP*, 12.
206. Kosach, *Kommunisty*, 155; Ismael and Ismael, *The Communist Movement in Syria and Lebanon*, 7, 230; also RGASPI f. 495, op. 84, d. 8, l. 27 (Rapport du camarade Ichtyar au Secretariat de l'Orient).
207. Dodds, *Geopolitics*, 33.
208. Milan Hauner suggests that through Haushofer the Bolsheviks even became acquainted with Mackinder's 1904 heartland thesis that the Eurasian landmass was a "geographical pivot of history" and adapted it for their own purposes. Hauner, *What Is Asia to Us?*, 170, 198.
209. Ibid., 197.
210. Ibid., 2–3, 198.
211. As E. H. Carr concluded, the international communist movement had one policy, and it was directed by the RCP(B) in accordance with Soviet national interests. Jacobson, *When the Soviet Union Entered World Politics*, 35.
212. RGASPI f. 495, op. 154, d. 128, ll. 3–4 (Notes of meeting of Near and Middle East Section, February 10, 1922). From the Caucasus, Gurko-Kriazhin complained that the dire situation of the Caucasus Bureau of Russian Telegraph Agency (KavROSTA) is threatening the existence of a "large organization working to study the East and prepare workers for the East." Tamazishvili, "Vladimir Aleksandrovich Gurko-Kriazhin," 54.
213. Osterhammel, *The Transformation of the World: A Global History of the Nineteenth Century*, 79.

268 NOTES TO PAGES 57-59

214. Charles Maier described the entire century from 1860 to 1960 as the age of territoriality in which the territorial principle was transplanted in the structure and form of states in Europe's colonies. Maier, "Consigning the Twentieth Century to History."
215. Karasar, "Chicherin on the Delimitation of Turkestan: Native Bolsheviks versus Soviet Foreign Policy. Seven Letters from the Russian Archives on Razmezhevanie," 201.
216. An account of this censorship is given in Khalid, "Turkestan v 1917–22 godakh," 191; it affected accounts by such prominent political leaders of Bolshevik administration in Central Asia as the RKP(b) Turkestan Bureau official Georgii Safarov and the Musburo representative Turar Ryskulov. On censorship of narratives about the Sovietization of Bukhara see Fedtke, "Jadids, Young Bukharans, Communists."
217. For instance, the Kazakh émigré Mustafa Chokaev invoked Egypt under British rule as a place that "seems to the Turkestanians to be far better than the present form of 'the outwardly national and inwardly proletarian' Republics of Turkestan." Chokaev, "Turkestan and the Soviet Regime," 403–20. It was challenged by the Marxist orientalists Arabist Vladimir Lutskii (1906–1962), who presented a monograph-length favorable comparison between the economies of Soviet Uzbekistan and Egypt. Lutskii, *Uzbekistan i Egipet*.
218. At VNAV, Troianovskii worked with the other Marxist Orientalists Gurko-Kriazhin, Pavlovich, Dimanshtein, Safarov, and Broido. This group of new orientalists with background in the Union of Liberation of the East, Central Asian politics, and ties to KUTV also included Avetis Sultanzade and Haidar Khan, who after 1919 were sent to Central Asia to mobilize Iranian workers in Central Asia for the ICP and organize 'Adalat conferences. Chaqueri, "Sultanzade: The Forgotten Revolutionary." Troianovskii's monograph, *Sovremennyi Egipet* (*Modern Egypt*), was published by Gosizdat in 1925. He describes his failed attempts to get reinstated in the party after being dismissed ostensibly for failing to pay party dues in GARF f. 539, op. 4, d. 2805, l. 53 (Autobiography, February 25, 1934).
219. Others receiving this information included Kuusenin, Karakhan, Orzhonikidze, Aralov, Pastukhov, Brike, and the Profintern. GARF f R-5402, op. 1, d. 79, l. 1 (Pavlovich's Report on Egypt, November 1922).
220. Troianovskii worked for Gosplan in 1923–1927; on the Gosplan institution see Martin, *All Possible Worlds: A History of Geographical Ideas*, 260–63; Alec Nove, *An Economic History of the U.S.S.R*; and on its debates with the Narkomnats, Hirsch, *Empire of Nations*, 72–80.
221. GARF f. 539, op. 4, d. 2805, l. 24 (Letter from Troianovskii to the Commission for Naznachenie of Pensions, April 12, 1947). It did not make it into the family archive either.
222. Conversation with Tatiana Matroshilina, January 12, 2022.
223. Troianovskii's self-characterization is from RGASPI f. 495, op. 65a, op. 2707, ll. 2–4 (Anketa, February 8, 1928). His name is briefly referenced in Shastitko, *Sobytiia i sud'by* (Moscow, 1985), and in Kemper, "Red Orientalism." It does not appear in the biographical dictionary of orientalists by Miliband, *Biobibliograficheskii slovar' otechestvennych vostokovedov* or in the substantial four-volume *Neizvestnye stranitsy*

otechestvennogo vostokovedeniia (Moscow: Russian Academy of Science, 1997, 2004, 2008, 2014).
224. When Pavlovich died, an entire issue of *Novyi Vostok*, 18 (1927), was dedicated to his memory, unlike Troianovskii who survived more dangerous periods of Stalinism thanks, in part, to his later obscurity
225. Conversation with Tatiana Matroshilina, January 12, 2022.

Chapter 2

1. Hamdi's landlord was characterized as "feudal" in Iosef Braginskii, "Zhiznennye paradoksy," *Narody Azii i Afriki* 4 (1964): 268–71 (269). The landlord's son, Muhammad Yakan-Pasha, was exiled for his activism. One of Hamdi's teachers had been Shaykh Safwan abu al-Fath, who in 1924 admitted to being part of a conspiracy to overthrow the government and establish a communist regime. On Safwan see Beinin and Lockman, *Workers on the Nile*, 151. Hamdi's early life and the significance of the *ABC of Communism* was described by Vitalii Naumkin in Moscow on April 27, 2013.
2. Abu-Hanna, *Mudhakkarat Najati Sidqi*, 35.
3. RGASPI f. 495, op. 85, d. 74, l. 18 (Evaluation of Hamdi Selam, February 25, 1936). By 1936, this category became more acceptable in Bolshevik parlance after Stalin had called for the creation of a new "proletarian intelligentsia." The concept was defined as an administrative and specialist group drawn from the lower classes of society, trained in Soviet Universities and giving whole-hearted allegiance to Soviet power. Fitzpatrick, *Education and Social Mobility in the Soviet Union 1921–34*, 3.
4. Abu Hanna, *Mudhakkarat Najati Sidqi*, 44. Translation from Tamari, "Najati Sadqi (1905–79): The Enigmatic Jerusalem Bolshevik," 90.
5. Kotkin, *Stalin I*, 317; Jacobson, *When the Soviet Union Entered World Politics*, 84–86; Rieber, "How Persistent Are Persistent Factors?" 219.
6. Boyce, *The Great Interwar Crisis and the Collapse of Globalization*, 9; Jacobson, *When the Soviet Union Entered World Politics*, 84–86.
7. On the collapse of the "Wilsonian moment" see Manela, *The Wilsonian Moment*, 5, 155, 184; for interpretations of the contradictory wartime agreements made between the Allies, between Sir Henry McMahon and Husayn, and the Balfour Declaration see Kedouri, *In the Anglo-Arab Labyrinth*.
8. Jacobson, *When the Soviet Union Entered World Politics*, 180.
9. Manela, *The Wilsonian Moment*.
10. Schayegh, *The Middle East and the Making of the Modern World*, 103; Samuel Dolbee, "Seferberlik and Bare Feet."
11. McKeown, "Global Migration," 162; Fahrenthold, *Between the Ottomans and the Entente*.
12. Boyce, *Great Interwar Crisis*, 83.
13. Schayegh, *The Middle East and the Making of the Modern World*, 137.

270 NOTES TO PAGES 63–64

14. Owen and Pamuk, *A History of the Middle East*, 46–47.
15. McKewon, "Global Migration, 1846–1970," 162.
16. Lohr, *Russian Citizenship: From Empire to Soviet Union*, 133–34; Felshtinsky, "The Legal Foundations of the Immigration and Emigration Policy of the USSR."
17. On civil war refugees, see Moch and Siegelbaum, *Broad Is My Native Land: Repertoires and Regimes of Migration in Russia's Twentieth Century*, 236–38.
18. Lohr, *Russian Citizenship*, 136.
19. For these NKVD estimates see ibid., 166.
20. David-Fox, *Showcasing the Great Experiment: Cultural Diplomacy and Western Visitors to the Soviet Union, 1921–1941*, 1.
21. On foreigners' attraction to the USSR, see Michael David-Fox, *Showcasing the Great Experiment*.
22. Khattar Hilu, *Awraq min Tarikhuna*, 15.
23. On imperial infrastructure connecting the Eastern Mediterranean and Europe see Khater, *Inventing Home*, 12; Kane, *Russian Hajj: Empire and the Pilgrimage to Mecca*; Can, *Spiritual Subjects*; some descriptions of KUTV student itineraries—mostly by ship from Beirut, Alexandria, of Haifa, traveling through Istanbul and then Odessa, or through Alexandria and then Marseille, and then continuing the journey by train—have been published in Abu Hanna, *Mudhakkarat Najati Sidqi*, 22–28; for Hamdi Salam's travels through Greece, see RGASPI f. 495, op. 210, d. 74, l. 17 (Spravka from March 8, 1936); and Farah, *Min al-'uthmaniyya ila al-dawla al-'ibriyya*, 82–89.
24. Abu Hanna, *Mudhakkarat Najati Sidqi*, 22.
25. RGASPI f. 532 (KUTV), op. 1, d. 115, ll. 53–54 (Petition to KUTV Rector from Sarat Chandra Roy); on trans-imperial pilgrims' expectations of beneficence see the study of their petitions in Can, *Spiritual Subjects*, ch. 4. The itineraries were so similar that some Soviet leaders even embarked on a campaign to support the mobility of foreign Hajj pilgrims in the late 1920s through Odessa by reconstructing some of the tsarist-era infrastructure also used by the Comintemians. Kane, *Russian Hajj*, ch. 5; on the centrality of this as part of the 'communist experience' see Burak Sayim, "Of transits and Transitions."
26. RGASPI f. 532, op. 1, d. 366, ll. 9–10 (Report on Arab Section, January 21, 1933).
27. A comprehensive study of KUTV remains to be undertaken. On KUTV's foundation, curriculum, and general statistics about its student body see Popov, "KUTV—Kuznitsa kadrov dlia sovetskogo Vostoka," *Revoliutsionnyi Vostok*, no. 30 (1935): 189–99; Natal'ia Timofeeva, "Kommunisticheskii universitet trudiashchikhsia Vostoka," *Narody Azii i Afriki*, no. 2 (1976): 47–57; Timofeeva, "Kommunisticheskii universitet trudiashchikhsia Vostoka—tsentr ideinoi podgotovki revoliutsionnykh kadrov" (PhD diss., Institute of Oriental Studies of the Academy of Sciences, Moscow, 1989); Djagalov, "KUTV"; transnational studies focusing on specific regions include: for Africa, see Filatova, "Introduction or Scholarship?"; Apollon Davidson, "Afrikanistika, afrikanisty i afrikantsy v Kominterne," part 1, *Vostok*, no. 6 (1995); part 2, *Vostok*, no. 2 (1996); and McClellan, "Africans and Black Americans"; for Iran, see Ravandi-Fadai, "'Red Mecca'"; for India, Gopal, *Indian Freedom-Fighters in Tashkent*; for China (KUTV was the main destination for Chinese Communists

before the opening of the Communist University for the Toilers of China in 1925), McGuire, *Red at Heart*; Wilbur and How, *Missionaries of Revolution*; and Yu, "Sun Yat-sen University in Moscow, 1925–1930"; for Japan, Koshiro, *Imperial Eclipse*; for Turkey, Meyer, "Children of Trans-Empire."

28. David-Fox, *Revolution of the Mind: Higher Learning among the Bolsheviks, 1918–1929*, 3–4.

29. Marshall, *The Russian General Staff and Asia*, 176–93.

30. After KUTV Broido, served as secretary of the TsK KP(b) Tajikistan 1933–1934; for more on his biography, see Germanov, "Novyi dokument po istorii sovetskogo Turkestana," 41–47.

31. Yagodkin, "O sektsii 'Vostoka' pri universitete imeni Sverdlova," *Zhizn' natsional'nostei* 30 (87) (October 1, 1920).

32. Broido, "KUTV," *Zhizn' natsional'nostei*, 100 (January 26, 1921): 1.

33. Polov, "KUTV," *Revoliutsionnyi Vostok* 2 (1935): 189–99 (190).

34. The most detailed description of the curriculum can be found in *Izvestiia KUTVa* (Moscow, 1921), 9–25, 61–62.

35. The Turkburo expressed optimism about KUTV's potential to solve the problem of cadres. RGASPI f. 544, op. 4, d. 1, ll. 1–6 (Report on Turkburo Activities, October 15, 1921).

36. Troianovskii mentions KUTV as a definitive solution to the cadre problem in RGASPI f. 495, op. 154, d. 75, ll. 1–3 (Protocol of the First Meeting of the Near East Section, August 12, 1921), and RGASPI f. 495, op. 154, d. 75, ll. 10–11 (Protocol of Meeting of Near and Far East Sections in Moscow on December 15, 1921). He is listed as a KUTV instructor in GARF f. 539, op. 4, d. 2805, l. 1 (Troianovskii's Personal Card of RSFSR Peoples Commissariat for Social Obespechenie).

37. Roy claimed that both Lenin and Chicherin "enthusiastically approved of the idea." Roy, *Memoirs*, 526–28; Roy and Pavlovich also spoke at the graduation ceremony of KUTV's first 1922 class. "Na prazdnike narodov vostoka," *Zhizn' natsional'nostei* 5 (1922): 13; others attribute the idea to Mikhail Pavlovich, Clark, *Eurasia*, 61.

38. Broido, "KUTV," *Zhizn' natsional'nostei* 109 (May 28, 1921): 1.

39. Burbank and Cooper, "Empires after 1919 Empires after 1919: Old, New, Transformed," 91; Ron Suny, "The Empire Strikes Out: Imperial Russia, 'National' Identity, and Theories of Empire," in *A State of Nations*.

40. Suny, *Revenge of the Past*, 89.

41. Cited in Slezkine, "The USSR as Communal Apartment," 420.

42. Significantly, Stalin's discussion of the stages of national development focused on Western and Eastern Europe, making no mention of national development in the Chinese, Iranian, or Ottoman contexts outside their experiences with imperialism. Stalin, "Report on the Tasks of the Party in the National Question, March 10, 1921," in Stalin, *Works*, vol. 5, *1921–23* (https://www.marxists.org/reference/archive/stalin/works/1921/03/08.htm).

43. At the Tenth Congress, Safarov had accepted Stalin's "corrections" on behalf of the Turkestan delegation and refocused on the need to "liberate (*raskrepostit'*) the working masses of the peoples of the East from their shell of medieval culture which

has delayed their mental and ideological development." *Protokoly Xgo Kongressa* (Moscow 1933), 184–205. Stalin continued to feel uneasy about attacking Muslim national communists directly, such that in 1923 still focused criticism on the Georgians for violating party discipline and exhibiting local chauvinism and imperialism. This precedent would give him tools in the later struggle against Muslim national communists. Bennigsen and Wimbush, *Muslim National Communism*, 81–94.

44. The policy of promoting national elites was articulated as early as 1920 but came to be more actively implemented as *korenizatsiia* in 1923. Martin, *Affirmative Action Empire*, 10, 125–81.

45. Viktorov, "KUTV," *Zhizn' natsional'nostei* 1 (1923): 261–67; summaries of these numbers are also provided in Timofeeva, "KUTV (1921–25)," 51. The predicting was that a stage of historical development would come when such differences would eventually disappear. On "ethnophilia" see Slezkine, "The USSR as a Communal Apartment," 415; Hirsch, *Empire of Nations: Ethnographic Knowledge and the Making of the Soviet Union*, 8.

46. Viktorov, "KUTV," 267. Similar groupings of nationalities into geographical regions can be found in GARF R-5402, op. 1, d. 106, l. 3 (KUTV report about students of Turkic nationalities to Mikhail Pavlovich, February 12, 1926).

47. For more on MIV see Kemper, "Red Orientalism," 460; Strel'tsov, "Vostokovedenie v MGIMO."

48. Both VNAV and MIV were led by Mikhail Pavlovich, who headed VNAV from its foundation in December 1920 and who took over the leadership of MIV in 1923 from Andrei Evgen'evich Snesarev (1865–1937). Kemper, "Red Orientalism," 460–61. Many of the teachers at KUTV wrote and edited for the Narkomnats journal *Zhizn' natsional'nostei* and the VNAV journal *Novyi Vostok*. Further evidence of their connectivity is a copy of the VNAV mission statement that was preserved in the KUTV archive. RGASPI f. 532, op. 1, d. 3, ll. 15–17 (Proekt VNAV).

49. Mikhail Pavlovich, "Zadachi Vserossiiskoi Nauchnoi Assotsiatsii Vostokovedeniia," *Novyi Vostok* 1 (1922): 3–15, here 9.

50. Ibid., 11.

51. Cited in Kemper, "Red Orientalism," 443.

52. Timofeeva, "KUTV (1921–25)," 50.

53. For a firsthand account, see Haywood, *Black Bolshevik*, 148–75; and Ani Mukherji, "'Like Another Planet,'" 120–41. Other black Americans studied at the International Lenin School. Kirschenbaum, *International Communism*, 15–51.

54. On the interpretation of "socialism in one country" as a reaction to the failed revolutions in Europe in 1917–1921 see Van Ree, "Socialism in One Country."

55. Leonid Gorizontov, "The 'Great Circle' of Interior Russia," in Burbank and Von Hagen, eds. *Russian Empire* (Bloomington: Indiana University Press, 2007), 67–93; on this border see Bassin, "Russia between Europe and Asia," 1–17.

56. Stalin, "The Political Tasks," 135.

57. On conversions of *inorodtsy*, see Geraci, *Window on the East: National and Imperial Identities in Late Tsarist Russia*, 47.

58. Stalin, "Report on National Factors in Party and State Affairs," given at the Twelfth Party Congress, April 23, 1923. Stalin, *Works*, vol. 5, (https://www.marxists.org/reference/archive/stalin/works/1923/04/17.htm, last accessed September 14, 2019). In the West, he expected that generous policies toward such nationalities as Finns, Belarusians, Ukrainians, and Romanians was thought to attract their ethnic brethren in Finland, Poland, and Romania. Martin, "The Origins of Soviet Ethnic Cleansing," 831.
59. For a summary of the arguments for the absence of consideration of local interests and the strategy of "divide and rule," see Hirsch, *Empire of Nations*, 160–61. More recently, historians of Central Asia have offered more nuanced accounts of the roles and agencies of Uzbek and Turkmen indigenous elites as well as to the significant context of regional national movements. Khalid, *Making Uzbekistan*, 13–15; Adrienne Edgar, *Tribal Nation*, 41–52.
60. Stalin, "On the Tasks." Negative coverage of Soviet policy in Central Asia by the bourgeois press had been discussed in Broido, "Nasha turkestanskaia politika i angliiskaia zhurnalistika," *Novyi Vostok* 3 (1922): 76–82.
61. Kotkin, *Stalin* I, 532.
62. In January 6, 1925, a Comintern budget committee distributed 150,000 gold rubles from its total allotted 4,180,450 gold rubles to the Eastern Section. In 1924, expenses were based on 1923, which in turn had been based on expenses in 1922. In 1923 this meant 2,196,500 gold rubles for all the international sections of the Comintern excluding its sections responsible for publications, representatives of the ECCI, transport, and other administrative affairs. In May 1924 the budget of the ECCI was increased by 112,000 rubles. *Politburo i Komintern*, 246–47, 255, 286–87.
63. In 1927, Gurko-Kriazhin criticized earlier writers, including Troianovskii, Safarov, Pavlovich, and Sultan-Zade, for trying to deal with the entire "East." He characterized their work as schematic, overstretched, and overly simplistic even if it did provide valuable agitational resources. Gurko-Kriazhin, "10 let vostokovednoi mysli," *Novyi Vostok* 19 (1927), xliv.
64. RGASPI f. 532, op. 1, d. 17, ll. 1–3 (Meeting with KUTV comrades, October 10, 1925).
65. RGASPI f. 495, op. 65a, d. 4572, l. 1 (Kuchumov's personal questionnaire for membership in the Comintern ECCI).
66. On de-peasantization as a 1920s Red Army slogan and its critiques, see von Hagen, *Soldiers in the Proletarian Dictatorship*, 235–39.
67. In making this objection, Rafes echoed the same sentiment that Lenin expressed at the end of his life, that it was an error to have imposed on foreign communist parties an organizational resolution "permeated through and through with the Russian spirit . . . it is completely incomprehensible to foreigners and they will not be satisfied to hang it in the corner like an icon and pray to it." Lenin, *Sochineniia*, v. 27 (Moscow; Patizdat, 137) cited in Riebert, "How Persistent Are Persistent Factors," 275.
68. RGASPI f. 532, op. 1, d. 17, ll. 1–3 (Meeting at KUTV, October 10, 1925).
69. On the "East" as an ideological concept see Kirasirova, "The 'East' as a Category."
70. M. Rafes, *Ocherki po istorii Bunda* (Moscow, 1923); Rafes, "Kommunisticheskii 'Bund' i evreiskie sektsii," *Zhizn' natsional'nostei* 20 (77) (1920).

71. Gitelman, *A Century of Ambivalence*, 93
72. Haywood recalled the speech became a subject of continuous discussion and study. Haywood, *Black Bolshevik*, 157.
73. McGuire, *Red at Heart: How Chinese Communists Fell in Love with the Russian Revolution*, 67, 82.
74. Ibid., 67.
75. Ibid., 67; the monastery is also discussed in Ravandi-Fadai, "Red Mecca," 721.
76. Sidqi mentions Vijaya Lakshmi Nehru Pandit, sister of Jawaharlal Nehru, as an example of someone who left quickly. Otherwise, he claims they were given the best food relative to other Soviet universities. Abu Hanna, *Mudhakkarat Najati Sidqi*, 30–31, 36–38.
77. Yu, *Universitet imeni Sun' Yatsena*, 64, 102–3, 106; Miin-ling Yu, "Sun Yat-sen," 138.
78. The KUTV domestic sector records remained inaccessible to me during the period of research.
79. Hoffman, *Peasant Metropolis: Social Identities in Moscow, 1929–1941*, ch. 5; and Colton, *Moscow: Governing the Socialist Metropolis*, ch. 3.
80. RGASPI f. 532, op. 1, d. 67, ll. 1–2 (Russian-language copy of Complaint to KUTV Rector from Carl Jones, Roy Farmer, January 28, 1928).
81. RGASPI f. 532, op. 1, d. 67, l. 9 (Students' Complaints); on Muscovites diets see Fitzpatrick, *Everyday Stalinism*, 41.
82. RGASPI f. 532, op. 1, d. 75, ll. 31–32 (Report on the Foreign Section by Comrade Frantsevich, January 19, 1929).
83. RGASPI f. 532, op. 1, d. 75, ll. 12–13 (Reactions to Frantsevich's Report, 1929).
84. One argued the foreign students should not be forced to eat foods that upset their stomachs (like buckwheat), that they needed more frequent trips to sanitariums, and that they required other medical services because they were "less adjusted to Moscow weather." Ibid.; another suggested that because some had been so badly repressed in their home countries, they needed extra rest and nutrition to regain their strength to continue the revolutionary struggle. RGASPI f. 532, op. 1, d. 115, l. 168 (KUTV report to the TsK VKP(b), September 16, 1932).
85. RGASPI f. 532, op. 1, d. 115, l. 168 (Letter to TsK from September 16, 1932, from the KUTV Deputy Rector, Foreign Sector Chief, and his Deputy). For more on Insnab, see Fitzpatrick, *Everyday Stalinism*, 56; also Scott, *Behind the Urals*, 86–87; Littlepage and Bess, *In Search of Soviet Gold*, 68.
86. The NKVD campaign to re-register all foreigners in the country is mentioned in Lohr, *Russian Citizenship*, 153–54.
87. V. S., "Vecher 'Vostochnykh narodov,'" *Zhizn' natsional'nostei* 123 (November 12, 1921): 4.
88. An estimated 200–600 students visited the club each day. T. Aleksandrov, "KUTV," *Zhizn' natsional'nostei* 135 (February 16, 1922): 2.
89. On the literary-newspaper club, see M. Charnyi, "V KUTVe: literaturno-gazetnyi kruzhok," *Zhizn' natsional'nostei* 127 (December 14, 1921): 2.
90. Students also worked with Nikolai Ekk (1902–1976), whom Meyerhold sent to KUTV to help create the student theater. Hikmet, *Vstrechi s meierkhol'dom*, 237.
91. Ibid.

92. On Meyerhold's theory of performance see McCaw, *Bakhtin and Theatre Dialogues with Stanislavski, Meyerhold and Grotowski*, 168.
93. L. Liianov, "Na prazdnike narodov Vostoka," *Zhizn' natsional'nostei* 5 (April 1, 1922): 13.
94. McGuire, *Red at Heart*, 70, 80–81.
95. He loved his new military garb because he "wanted that which occurred in Russia to happen in our countries." Hikmet, "Na sluzhbe revoliutsii," 239.
96. Abu Hanna, *Mudhakkarat Najati Sidqi*, 36. Tamari, "Najati Sidqi," 88.
97. Clark, *Eurasia without Borders*, 70.
98. Hikmet, *Life's Good Brother*, 38.
99. Martin, *Affirmative Action Empire*, 440.
100. The description resembles the symbiosis of national, imperial, and cosmopolitan elements described in Clark, *Moscow, the Fourth Rome: Stalinism, Cosmopolitanism, and the Evolution of Soviet Culture, 1931–1941*.
101. Since the opening of the Soviet and Comintern archives in the early 1990s, scholars have gained access to the largest surviving collection of communist documents from the interwar period. Historians of Arab communism, such as Girorii Kosach (writing in Russian with discrete chapters on Egypt, Palestine, Syria, and Iraq), Maher Charif (writing in Arabic about Palestine), Leon Zahavi (writing in Hebrew about Palestine), and Garay Menicucci (writing in English about Syria) have started to use these collections to write histories of Arab communist parties in particular national contexts. The empirical work done by Kosach, in particular with the personal files of KUTV Arab students, has proven to be an invaluable resource for my own archival research. Kosach, *Kommunisty Blizhnego Vostoka v SSSR 1920–30-e gody*; Kosach, *Krasnyi Flag nad Blizhnim Vostokom*; Maher Charif has published a selection of documents from the Comintern archives of the Palestinian Communist Party in Charif, *Filastin fi-l-arshif as-sirri li-l-kumintirn*. Garay Menicucci has used KUTV publications in Menicucci, "The Russian Revolution and Popular Movements in Syria"; Zahavi, *Sawiyya aw 'ala infirad*; Charif and Zahavi write on Palestine, Menicucci focuses Syria-Lebanon, and Kosach separates his books into Egyptian, Palestinian, Syrian/Lebanese, and Iraqi subsections.
102. RGASPI f. 532 (KUTV), op. 1, d. 91, l. 1 (Report on Dynamics of Nationalities at KUTV as of January 1, 1930).
103. Kirasirova, "The East," *Kritika*.
104. Ahmad, *The Young Turks*, 112–38; Schayegh, *The Middle East and the Making of the Modern World*, 132–33. Kayali, *Arabs and Young Turks: Ottomanism, Arabism, and Islamism in the Late Ottoman Empire, 1908–1918*.
105. The Arab group was referred to as a "*natsgruppa*" in RGASPI f. 532, op. 1, d. 115, l. 1 (Letter from Sector A head to Madiar, January 1, 1932). The exhibitions used by these groups resemble scaled-down versions of ethnographic exhibits of the peoples of the USSR described in Hirsch, *Empire of Nations*, ch. 5.
106. Abu Hanna, *Mudhakkarat Najati Sidqi*, 38; for more on this medium see Pristed, "Soviet Wall Newspapers."
107. Vel'tman, *Vostok v khudozhestvennoi literature*, 181–82.

108. Abu Hanna, *Mudhakkarat*, 38. The word "galiata" is usually used to describe tactless or tasteless behavior, usually not writing, so it does seem like a misusage of the term. The root of the word also originally meant the fatty residue of fermented milk, making it one many idiomatic expressions that compare people's personalities to heavy, rotting things. With thanks to Eman Morsi for these references.

109. On Sidqi's settlement in Luks, see Abu Hanna, *Mudhakkarat Najati Sidqi*, 29.

110. For Kitaigorodskii's background, including admission to the RCP (b) in 1919, see RGASPI f. 495, op. 65a, d. 816, ll. 76–77 (Anketa, 1935); he was in the Bund from 1906 to 1919, ibid., l. 75; for his recommendation to the Comintern see RGASPI f. 495, op. 65a, d. 816, l. 1 (Recommendation of Kitaigorodskii from the RKP(b) to Comintern ECCI, May 30, 1921). After eight years at the ECCI Near East Section and at the Profintern, writing articles and books about Egypt, Palestine, and Turkey, he was caught up in a plagiarism scandal and transferred out to the Red Peasant International (Krestintern) where he continued to write about the Near East. RGASPI f. 495, op. 65a, d. 816, l. 65 (Memo about Kitaigorodskii, February 9, 1920); *Bibliograficheskii slovar' otechestvennyh vostokovedov*, 555. He was the author of the book *The Struggle of Egypt for Economic Independence* (1925). At the Krestintern he continued to work as a "senior researcher" specializing in the Near East. RGASPI f. 495, op. 65a, d. 816, l. 1. 60 (Commission on Kitaigorodskii, July 25, 1929); RGASPI f. 495, op. 65a, d. 816, l. 87 (handwritten autobiography, April 22, 1935).

111. Abu Hanna, *Mudhakkarat Najati Sidqi*, 29.

112. Studer, *Transnational World of the Cominternians*, 25.

113. Halfin, *From Darkness to Light*, 212.

114. Abu-Hanna, *Mudhakkarat Najati Sidqi*, 38.

115. The concern was the alleged danger he might pose to the ECP. Kosach, *Kommunisty Blizhnego Vostoka*, 44.

116. His date of graduation is mentioned in Braginskii, "Zhiznennye paradoksy," 269.

117. RGASPI f. 495, op. 210, d. 74, l. 4 (Top Secret Memo about Hamdi Salam from August 2, 1951).

118. RGASPI f. 495, op. 210, d. 74, l. 44 (Memo by Madiar, May 28, 1930).

119. Ibid.

120. On getting reinstated in the RKP(b) see RGASPI f. 495, op. 210, d. 74, l. 4 (Top Secret Memo about Hamdi Salam from August 2, 1951); on being invited back to teach Arabic see RGASPI f. 532, op. 1, d. 125, ll. 24–34 (List of KUTV teachers on May 1, 1932).

121. Other KUTV students claimed to be backwards, and domestic Easterners who used the rhetoric of "cultural backwardness" to solicit desperately needed resources to help them and their regions catch up with more advanced nationalities. Martin, *Affirmative Action*, 126, 128; also Slezkine, *Arctic Mirrors*, ch. 7.

122. RGASPI f. 495, op. 210, d. 74, ll. 21–22 (Hamdi's statement, February 1936, in Russian).

123. RGASPI f. 495, op. 210, d. 74, l. 7 (Note from ECCI Human Resources (otdel kardov) to City Committee VKP(b) on January 17, 1937).

124. Conversation with Naumkin, April 27, 2013.

125. Braginskii, "Zhizhninnye paradoksy," 270; his work as a doctor in the camps was described by Naumkin during our conversation on April 27, 2013.
126. Kosach, *Kommunisty*, 44; also RGASPI f. 495, op. 210, d. 74, l. 18 (Hamdi's evaluation from February 25, 1936).
127. He headed the Arab section of the publishing house for literature in foreign languages in 1946–1968. "Hamdi Seliam," *Narody Azii i Afriki* 6 (1966): 199.
128. Kosach, *Kommunisty Blizhnego Vostoka*, 44–45.
129. Braginskii, "Zhizhninnye paradoksy," 270.
130. "Hamdi Selam," *Narody Azii i Afriki* 6 (1966): 199. He also translated two economic histories of Egypt by Rashid al-Barawi and Abd al-Razzak Hassan, tales by the Egyptian poet Abd al-Rahman al-Khamisi (1920–1987), and Arabic poetry for *Molodaia gvardiia*. He aided Moscow Arabists in their translations of Abd al-Rahman al-Kawakibi's treatise, "The Nature of Despotism." Braginskii, "Zhizhninnye paradoksy," 271.
131. "Hamdi Selam," *Narody Azii i Afriki* 6 (1966): 199; as the Russian Arabist Grigorii Kosach has suggested, this work on Ibn Sina in particular contributed to Soviet cultural objectives in the domestic East by "claiming Ibn Sina as part of the heritage of Soviet Central Asian peoples," Kosach, *Kommunisty*, 270–71. Hamdi Salam's transformation into a Soviet scholar of Arabic resembles earlier turn-of-the-century transformations described by Vera Tolz of native Russian Muslim informants of imperial scholars who later became scholars themselves. Tolz, *Russia's Own Orient*, 115. Not everyone in the orientalist community agreed his academic work was "significant," according to my interview with Naumkin in Moscow on April 27, 2013.
132. Another KUTV graduate who later taught Arabic at MIV and then at MGIMO was Ali Liberman (1910–1967/8). Kosach, "Palestinskii communist." The unfinished card catalogue was mentioned to me by Hamdi's Arabic language student, Naumkin, on April 27, 2013.
133. Braginskii, "Zhizhninnye paradoksy," 268.
134. Tantawi trained such Russian diplomats as the First Russian Consulate in Cairo (1835–1837) N. Mukhin and his successor, Rudolf Frähn, son of the Russian Arabist Christian Martin (Hristian Danilovich) Frähn (1782–1851), who was the person that initially recommended inviting Tantawi to Russia to the Russian Minister of Foreign Affairs.
135. Scott, *Familiar Strangers: The Georgian Diaspora and the Evolution of Soviet Empire*.
136. RGASPI f. 532, op.1, d. 46, ll. 1–11 (Evaluations of foreign students, 1927).
137. Smith, *A Road Is Made*; Brandt, *Stalin's Failure in China*.
138. Halfin, *Intimate Enemies: Demonizing the Bolshevik Opposition, 1918–1928*.
139. Abu Hanna, *Mudhakkarat Najati Sidqi*, 48.
140. For an unspecified reason, the more common translation of exploitation today, *isti'mar* (meaning colonialism and/or exploitation), is not used. Instead, this document, and many other Arabic-language texts in the Comintern archive from this period, use the term *istithmar* (which usually means investment, but occasionally also exploitation).

141. The teacher explained the origins of religion, stemming from man's natural inclination to fear physical forces, leading to paganism and the worship of idols, and finally to the idea of a monotheist God. Abu Hanna, *Mudhakkarat*, 47. In playing this role, KUTV teachers resembled the imperial-era missionaries from the Kazan Academy's Anti-Islam Division. Gerasci, *Window on the East*, 54.
142. Aleksandrov, "KUTV," *Zhizn' natsional'nostei* 3–4 (1923): 2.
143. Some KUTV instructors joined the League of the Militant Godless. Bobrovnikov, "The Contribution of Oriental Scholarship to the Soviet Anti-Islamic Discourse," *Heritage*, 66–85, esp. 70–71. On the anti-religious front and the League of the Godless (after 1929, the League of the Militant Godless), see Smolkin, *A Sacred Space Is Never Empty*, 21–56.
144. On Ikramov's religious education, see the memoirs of his son, Ikramov, *Delo moego ottsa*, 15.
145. Abu Hanna, *Mudhakkarat Najati Sidqi*, 120.
146. Khalid, *Islam after Communism: Religion and Politics in Central Asia*, 101.
147. In 1922, KUTV had 501 male and 100 female students. "V KUTVe," *Zhizn' natsional'nostei* 27 (November 26, 1921): 4. In 1923, only 15 percent of KUTV students were women (786 men and 147 women). Viktorov, "KUTV," 276. In 1925, among the 292 students in the foreign sector, 14 were women. RASPI f. 532, op. 1, d. 12, l. 25 (List of students of the foreign group, December 1, 1924).
148. KUTV officials tried to prevent foreign students from bringing their families to Moscow, or from bringing any new families acquired in Moscow back to their home countries. RGASPI f. 532, op. 1, d. 64, l. l.17–17o (Instruction from June 1928 about the arrival and departure of foreign students to KUNMZ, KUTV, KUTK, and ILS).
149. RGASPI f. 532, op. 2, d. 71. ll. 12–15 (Fadl's note to the Comintern Eastern Section, July 13, 1925).
150. RGASPI f. 532, op. 1, d. 7, l. 32 (Broido's note to TsK RKP about working with foreigners, 1924).
151. Abu Hanna, *Mudhakkarat Najati Sidqi*, 53–57.
152. Ibid., 50.
153. In particularly high-profile cases, such as when Ridwan al-Hilu left his pregnant wife in Moscow to become secretary-general of the Palestine Communist Party, the Comintern did pay child support. After Hilu's departure his wife wrote multiple letters to what she called "the Palestine Section of the Comintern." She complained that she did not have enough money to care for his child; that al-Hilu made her a promise to keep the child and wait for him for two years, but when he finally returned to attend the Seventh Comintern Congress in 1935 he showed little interest in his son and his family, who were living in terrible conditions. RGASPI f. 495, op. 212, d. 265 (Letter from N. V. [signature looks like "N. V. Pozhenkopf," but is unclear] to Palestine Section of the Comintern, November 2, 1935). An internal Comintern note was made on this letter stating that al-Hilu was working for the TsK of the PCP, and his personal file contains another Comintern memo from 1941 stating that alimony and child support were being paid to this woman by the International Red Aid. RGASPI f. 495, op. 212, d. 265, l. 2 (Memo about Ridwan al-Hilu, December 22,

1942). The most likely reason for his neglect was that Hilu had started a relationship with another KUTV graduate, Simkha Tsabari.
154. For instance, the ex-wife of the high-ranking Comintern and KTUV official Vladimir Kuchumov complained that he had apparently divorced her when she was sick, refused to pay child support, and brought another woman to live with them in the same apartment. To get reinstated in the Party, Kuchumov had only to promise to change and name a few high-ranking comrades who could confirm that he took care of his children from previous marriages. RGASPI f. 495, op. 65a, d. 4572, l. 1 (Spravka on Kuchumov); RGASPI f. 495, op. 65a, d. 4572, ll. 12–15 (Kuchumov's response to the Purge Committee, February 14, 1935).
155. In 1927 a group of female Chinese KUTV students petitioned to be transferred to KUTK because they wanted "better conditions for studying" and because their bodies were "not strong enough to make good soldiers." RGASPI f. 532, op. 1, d. 35, ll. 184–85 (Letter from Sung-Ye Jein, Men Chin-Shu, Kon Yeon-Chu, Sun-Chu-Fing, November 1, 1927).
156. RGASPI f. 495, op. 212, d. 51 (Avigdor's Personal file), ll. 6–7 (Comintern Questionnaire). Avigdor does not mention his membership in the ECP or PCP in his personal questionnaire, but he did write to the ECCI as a member of the ECP in 1922, RGASPI f. 495, op. 85, d. 12, ll. 18–19 (Avigdor's letter to the ECCI, January 17, 1922); also Batatu, *The Old Social Classes*, 381; Ismael and al-Sa'id, *The Communist Movement in Egypt 1920–88*, 29.
157. Rafes's criticism in *Zhin' natsional'nostei* that "instead of liberating the Jewish people, as the English imperialists and Zionists would claim, we get instead the blatant enslavement of Arab peasants under the yoke of Anglo-Jewish capital, along with the enslavement of the small number of Jewish workers and farmers," is referenced in Budnitskii, *Russian Jews*, 87–88. M. Troianovskii, "'Nezavisimoe' korolevstvo Egipta," *Novyi Vostok* 1 (1922): 94–103.
158. On Kosoi's first mission to Egypt and dealings with Troianovskii see Ginat, *A History of Egyptian Communism*, 45–49.
159. On Charlotte's life see Kirasirova, "An Egyptian Communist Family Romance."
160. Ginat, *A History of Egyptian Communism*, 30; Ilham Khuri-Makdisi, *Eastern Mediterranean and the Making of Global Radicalism*, 119.
161. Kirasirova, "An Egyptian Communist Family Romance," 46; on Poale Zion in Egypt see Ginat, *A History*, 36.
162. "Rapport a le Roi Fouad sur le Communisme en Egypte de le Branche Spéciale de la Police du Caire," 14–16. This report was given to me by the Egyptian scholar Albert Arie, who received it from another researcher; the archival citation is unavailable.
163. Kirasirova, "An Egyptian Communist Family Romance," 329.
164. RGASPI f. 495, op. 210, d. 51, ll. 12–13 (Shami's attestation on May 15, 1937).
165. She mentions studying "in a village with nuns" in her autobiography. RGASPI f. 495, op. 258, d. 64, ll. 9–10 (Adal Ghassub's Autobiography, May 25, 1935).
166. RGASPI f. 495, op. 258, d. 64, ll. 4–5 (Alisa Zarif's letter to the Comintern, March 12, 1936). Zarif was born in Lebanon but put her nationality (*poddanstvo*) as Syrian; see RGASPI f. 495, op. 258, d. 64, l. 1 (Personal Questionnaire, 1935). Drafts of

speeches in Arabic about the "great [October] revolution mounted on the shoulders of the workers and the peasants, and on the shoulders of their wives and children" bear marks of corrections and improvements. RGASPI f. 495, op. 258, d. 64, ll. 6–8 (Statement by Alisa Zafir). The first page of this speech bears a note, in Russian, from November 5, 1935, from Abramian asking Galdjian to have it translated.
167. RGASPI f. 495, op. 258, d. 63, ll. 20–21 (Note from Galdjian to the ECCI Section of Cadres, July 1, 1936).
168. Ibid.
169. Ibid.
170. RGASPI f. 495, op. 258, d. 63, l. 13 (ob) (Jamil's letter "To My Comrades" (in Arabic), July 2, 1936).
171. RGASPI f. 495, op. 258, d. 64, ll. 4–5; Goldman, *Women, the State and Revolution*, 331.
172. KUTV stipulated in its letters of acceptance that if any single female student were to become pregnant, she would be deemed unable to finish her studies and not be allowed to return to her country of origin. RGASPI f. 531, op. 1, d. 36, l. 127 (Letter "On acceptance of Palestinian Arabs," October 24, 1927).
173. As Thompson argues, the suppression of the revolt and resulting effeminization of male political groups by the French made the reassertion of political masculinity especially expedient. Thompson, *Colonial Citizens*, 94–100, 172, 196.
174. Significantly, I have not found any records of Muslim women studying at the KUTV Arab Section.
175. As Rafes complained to Pavlovich in a request for more information on Syria, "Leningrad, as you might guess is poor in orientalists." GARF f. R-5402, op. 1, d. 421, l. 1 (Letter from Rafes to Pavlovich, February 10, 1926).
176. Hamdi, Sidqi, but also Hikmet and wrote fiction. Hamdi's novellas, originally in Arabic, "Fellah" and "Kamera 17," were published in Russian and Ukrainian translation. Braginskii, *Hamdi*, 270. Sidqi went on to a successful career in literary criticism and broadcasting in Lebanon and Cyprus.
177. On IPPO schools see Kane, "Orthodoxy across Borders: Mapping the Institutions of the Imperial Orthodox Palestine Society," in *Russian-Arab Worlds*.
178. Laura Robson, *States of Separation*, 107–12.
179. Schayegh, *The Middle East*, 132–33.
180. In his recommendation about the party, Broido cites Safarov in *Pravda* in Broido, "Ocherednye zadachi v Turkestane," *Zhizn' natsional'nostei* 84 (September 2, 1920): 1. This interpretation of "colonialism" as negative would be challenged the next year in the same paper in Iaizim, "Kolonizatsiia v usloviiakh sovetskoi rossii," *Zhizn' natsional'nostei* 131 (January 17, 1922): 1. He argued that colonization was necessary in the interests of development of agricultural, industrial, and spiritual culture (*dukhovnaia kul'tura*). This colonization would not be one of a "ruling" people (imperialists) but a planned use of lands by the forces of the socialist federation, and first and foremost the local population. In this respect, it echoed the arguments by former Poale Zionists described in the next chapter.
181. Condee, *The Imperial Trace*, 13.

182. Mally, *Culture of the Future: The Proletkult Movement in Revolutionary Russia*; Gorsuch, *Youth in Revolutionary Russia: Enthusiasts, Bohemians, Delinquents*.
183. Franco, "Socialism Internationalism and National Classification at the Comintern Schools."

Chapter 3

1. Aimarov's real name was Tawfiq Abdel Hafiz al-Hassan, transliterated in Russian as "Tewfiiu-Abdel'-Hafikh-Gel'-Asan." RGASPI f. 532, op. 1, d. 366, l. 3 (List of students' real names); Kafri's real name was Ahmed Salim Abduhamam. RGASPI f. 532, op. 1, d. 366, ll. 1–2 (Characteristics of Arab Student Group, May 10, 1932).
2. RGASPI f. 495, op. 212, d. 224, l. 23 (Val'dman's letters to the factory head. March 17, 1933); RGASPI f. 495, op. 212, d. 224, l. 24 (Val'dman's letters Aimarov April 2, 1933).
3. RGASPI f. 495, op. 212, d. 224, ll. 25–26 (Letter from Rostselmash to KUTV, April 11, 1933). On privileges of foreign workers in the USSR, see the study of lives of German experts in Zhuravlev, "*Malen'kie liudi*" *i* "*bol'shaia istoriia*"; and also Hughes, *Inside the Enigma: British Officials in Russia, 1900–1939*.
4. RGASPI f. 495, op. 212, d. 224, l. 16 (Letter from Aimarov and Kafri, February 26, 1933).
5. RGASPI f. 495, op. 212, d. 224, l. 22 (Letter from Aimarov to Mustafa, March 9, 1933).
6. RGASPI f. 495, op. 212, d. 224, l. 34 (Memo by Mad'iar, June 1933).
7. RGASPI f. 495, op. 212, d. 224, ll. 29–33 (Notes about Party Commission Meeting on April 10, 1933).
8. On the growth of foreign visitors and the "peak tourist year of 1936," see David-Fox, *Showcasing*, 108.
9. Boyce, *The Great Interwar Crisis and the Collapse of Globalization*, 4.
10. Unemployment reached an estimated 30 percent. Thomspon, *Colonial Citizens: Republican Rights*, 156.
11. Kotkin, "Modern Times: The Soviet Union and the Interwar Conjuncture," 159.
12. Scott described his journey and experiences in Magnitogorsk in Scott, *Behind the Urals*.
13. Fitzpatrick, "Cultural Revolution in Russia 1928–32."
14. S. Popov, "KUTV—Kuznitsa kadrov dlia sovetskogo Vostoka," *Revoliutsionnyi Vostok* 30 (1935): 189–99, here 195.
15. For example, KUTV graduate Rashidov (an Armenian b. 1905 in Syria) is reported as working for the Moscow metro in RGASPI f. 495, op. 85, d. 96, l. 34 (Memo on Rashidov) and in RGASPI f. 495, op. 85, d. 52, l. 5 (Memo by a ECCI Section of Cadres Researcher).
16. On this campaign, see Slezkine, *The Jewish Century*, 249.
17. Brandt, *Stalin's Failure in China*; Smith, *A Road Is Made: Communism in Shanghai*; Kotkin, *Stalin* I, 625–30.

18. Slezkine, *The Jewish Century*, 221–26; between 1934 and 1941, Jews held 33.7 percent of the posts in the central apparatus of the People's Commissariat of Internal Affairs (NK VD), 40.5 percent of its top leadership and secretariat, and 39.6 percent in its main State Security Administration (GUGB), Zeltser, "Jews in the Upper Ranks of the NKVD," 77.
19. Budnitskii, "Jews, Pogroms, and the White Movement."
20. Iurii Borev, *Stalinada*, 68–69.
21. Martin, *The Affirmative Action Empire: Nations and Nationalism in the Soviet Union, 1923–1939*, 132–81.
22. Khalid, *Making Uzbekistan: Nation, Empire, and Revolution in the Early USSR*, 280.
23. For more on Arabization of the CPSL and the role of Armenians and the Greek Orthodox see Menicucci, "Russian Revolution," 184
24. Ginat, *A History of Egyptian Communism*, 169. Sa'id, *al Yasar al-Misri*, 230–33.
25. Al-Hilu, *Awraq min Ta'rikhuna*, 421.
26. Makdisi, *Age of Coexistence: The Ecumenical Frame and the Making of the Modern Arab World*, 121.
27. Budeiri, *The Palestine Communist Party*, 9, 12–44.
28. Ibid., 9; part of the weaking of the territorializing logic was that the CPSL was separately admitted into the Comintern at the Sixth Congress (1928). Ismael and Ismael, *The Communist Movement in Syria and Lebanon*, 15.
29. Hen-Tov, *Communism and Zionism in Palestine during the British Mandate*, 113–14.
30. Ibid., 113–16.
31. Ibid., 116.
32. For a detailed account of the violence in different cities, see Cohen, *Year Zero of the Arab-Israeli Conflict: 1929*.
33. Schayegh, *The Middle East and the Making of the Modern World*, 202.
34. Ibid., 202.
35. Joseph Berger described it both as a "pogrom" and a "general Arab uprising." Cited in Budeiri, *The Palestine Communist Party*, 20.
36. Ibid., 21–22.
37. He was exiled for supporting the Zinoviev opposition in Leningrad in part against Stalin's "socialism in one country" and in opposition to the New Economic Policy; for more on this Zinoviev opposition see Halfin, *Intimate Enemies: Demonizing the Bolshevik Opposition, 1918–1928*, 178–227.
38. Berger-Barzilai, *The Tragedy of the Soviet Revolution*, 121.
39. Safarov, *Kolonial'naia revoliutsiia: Opyt Turkestana*, 123.
40. It also resulted in the decline of the sewn area of crops by 50.6 percent. Genis, "Deportatsiia russkikh iz Turkestana," 44–58.
41. Unofficially, Russians continued to be driven off their land in both Kazakhstan and Kirgizia as late as 1927. Martin, "The Origins of Soviet Ethnic Cleansing," 827.
42. Ibid.; Genis, "Deportatsiia," 46–54.
43. Berger-Barzilai, *The Tragedy of the Soviet Revolution*, 120–22.
44. For Safarov's warning see Hen-Tov, *Communism and Zionism in Palestine during the British Mandate*, 124 (ft. 79); Poale-Zion's representative objected to the Comintern's

Second Congress determination that the party had "not yet overcome its nationalist prejudices" and therefore could not be accepted into the Third International. Riddell, *Workers of the World*, vol. 1, 333; vol. 2, 1068.

45. This resolution was passed on October 16, 1929, but published on February 6, 1930, in *Imprecor*. See Degras, *The Communist International 1919-42*, vol. 3, 80-84.
46. Hen-Tov, *Communism and Zionism in Palestine during the British Mandate*, 123 (ft. 73); on the PCP's characterization of the riots as a "pogrom" see Burdeiri, *The Palestine Communist Party*, 23, 27-30, 33.
47. Hen-Tov, *Communism and Zionism in Palestine during the British Mandate*, 120 (ft. 54).
48. Nathans, *Beyond the Pale: The Jewish Encounter with Late Imperial Russia*, 194-95.
49. Hen-Tov, *Communism and Zionism in Palestine during the British Mandate*, 151.
50. Nadab taught at KUTV in 1930-1933. RGASPI f. 495, op. 212, d. 147 (Nadab's Personal File), ll. 1-3 (Memo about Nadab from March 25, 1948). Besides KUTV, Shami also taught at the International Agrarian Institute and published articles about Palestine in its journal, *Agrarnye problemy*. Emel'ianova, "Shami," 53; The KUTV postgraduate research association for the study of National-Colonial Problems (NIANKP) was created in 1926; in 1929 it was renamed a "scientific research association" (NIA); during the KUTV partition in 1935-1937, the "association" became the Scientific Research "Institute" for National-Colonial Problems (NIINKP).
51. Shami served as a delegate to the CPSL during the Syrian Revolt of 1925-1927 and had had written extensively about Syria, Egypt, and Yemen for various Comintern publications. For more on Shami's career, see Emel'ianova, "Aleksandr Moiseevich Shami," 48-49.
52. Nadab, "Vosstanie v Palestine i Arabskoe natsional'noe dvizhenie," *Revoliutsionnyi Vostok* 8 (1930): 220-34; and Nadab, "O kriticheskikh primerakh tov. Shami," *Revoliutsionnyi Vostok* 9-10 (1930): 136-37.
53. Shami argued they would remain "the most reactionary group among all the eastern bourgeoisies." Shami, "Eshche raz k voprosu o palestinskom vosstanii (Po povodu stat'i t. Nadaba)," *Revoliutsionnyi Vostok* 9-10 (1930): 139-59.
54. M. Godes, "The Reaffirmation of Unilinealism," 103-4.
55. Nadab, "O kriticheskikh primerakh tov. Shami," *Revoliutsionnyi Vostok* 9-10 (1930): 130-38.
56. According to Shami, Najib 'Azuri's book had promised "to protect the interests of all foreigners connected with our country," something Nadab would have seen "had he bothered to read past the first page." Shami, "Eshche raz k voprosu o palestinskom vosstanii."
57. Ibid.
58. Ibid., 148.
59. Nadab, "O kriticheskikh primerakh tov. Shami," 130, 135, 137.
60. Shami, "Eshche raz k voprosu o palestinskom vosstanii," 156.
61. Nadab, "O kriticheskikh primerakh tov. Shami," 137-38.
62. Shami, "Eshche raz k voprosu o palestinskom vosstanii," 158.
63. Ibid., 151.

64. Halfin, *Intimate Enemies*.
65. In 1932, the Arab Section had 21 members, with 3 more students on the way. The next largest groups included Indians (14 students, 11 more expected), Turks (15) students, 3 more expected), Negros (12 students, 4 more expected), Indochinese (8 students, 7 more expected). The number of Arabs was surpassed only by the number of students from Outer Mongolia (200) and Tuva (180). RGASPI f. 532, op. 1, d. 115, l. 168 (Note from KUTV to TsK VKP(b), September 16, 1932).
66. RGASPI f. 495, op. 212, d. 166, l. 40 (Letter from Subotin, April 9, 1930).
67. Ibid.
68. RGASPI f. 530, op. 4, d. 48, ll. 9–11 (Closed Session of the International Control Commission on January 7, 1930).
69. The reprimand was issued on January 11, 1930; RGASPI f. 495, op. 212, d. 166, l. 37 (Note of the International Control Commission, January 22, 1936).
70. For his characterization as being too dangerous to be sent back see RGASPI f. 495, op. 212, d. 166, ll. 62–63 (Report by Salim Abbud (PCP) about Subotin, December 10, 1937); Subotin worked at MIV until 1938. RGASPI f. 495, op. 212, d. 166, l. 10 (Autobiography, April 9, 1937); l. 14 (Memo to Kotel'nikov about Subotin's translation work, December 16, 1937).
71. Rif'at al-Sa'id's interview of Muhammad Dwaidar in Cairo (January 22, 1970), in al-Sa'id, *al-Yasar al-Masri*, 228–29, 231.
72. On debates in 1927 and 1933 see Martin, *The Affirmative Action Empire*, 143, 358.
73. Cited in ibid., 143.
74. Ibid., 148.
75. Ibid., 149.
76. Ibid., 153.
77. Ibid.
78. David-Fox, *Revolution of the Mind: Higher Learning Among the Bolsheviks, 1918–1929*, 254–72.
79. RGASPI f. 495, op. 212, d. 51 (Kosoi's Personal File), l. 86 (Note to the ICC from Aliev, Aimarov, Mukhamedov, and Saburov, April 5, 1931).
80. The members of this faction they identified were: Semenova (b. 1905, in the PCP since 1925; at KUTV since 1930); Antonov, Nadab, Hasan, Gol'd (Slonil), and Yamina. Zeid claimed that Nadab had been a rightist deviationist in Palestine and that Antonov was a Trotskyist who got into KUTV under false pretenses with Auerbach's help. RGASPI f. 495, op. 212, d. 51, l. 86 (Note to the ICC from Aliev, Aimarov, Mukhamedov, and Saburov April 5, 1931). They also asserted that Avigdor maintained ties with his father-in-law, the prominent Jewish Egyptian socialist Joseph Rosenthal, who had been expelled from the ECP. On the "Rosenthal affair," see Ginat, *A History of Egyptian Communism: Jews and Their Compatriots in Quest of Revolution*, 28–42.
81. RGASPI f. 532, op. 1, d. 365, l. 18 (Conversation with Saburov, April 18, 1931).
82. For instance, he explained Semenova's outburst—she had walked out of a Party meeting claiming that "arguments among Jewish comrades should not become the asset (*dostoianie*) of Arab comrades"—as being motivated by her unhappiness at being "hit hard" for her mistakes. Semenova eventually apologized for her outburst

and was allowed to return to Palestine. RGASPI f. 532, op. 1, d. 365, l. 16 (Meeting of Vorob'ev, Surin, and Avigdor, April 14, 1931).
83. RGASPI f. 532, op. 1, d. 365, ll. 6–13 (Report on the Arab Circle, undated but submitted before April 27, 1931).
84. Ibid.
85. RGASPI f. 495, op. 212, d. 164 (Uncatalogued evaluation located in Part 2 of Saburov's personal file).
86. Chokobaeva, Drieu, and Morrison, "Introduction" to *The Central Asian Revolt of 1916*, 7.
87. Martin, *Affirmative Action*, 81.
88. Chokobaeva, Drieu, and Morrison, *The Central Asian Revolt of 1916*, 6–7.
89. Berger signed his articles in *Imprecor* and elsewhere as "J.B." or "Bob." Kosach, *Kommunisty Blizhnego Vostoka v SSSR*, 109.
90. On the League against Imperialism see Prashad, *The Darker Nations: A People's History of the Third World*, 16–31; Petersson, *Willi Munzenberg*; Petersson, "Hub of the Anti-Imperialist Movement," 58–65; Louro et al., eds., *League against Imperialism: Lives and Afterlives*.
91. A later denunciation by Poliani claimed that Berger told him that after their 1929 meeting Stalin came to see Palestine as "a country of Russia" (*Palestina—eto strana Rossii*). RGASPI f. 495 op. 212, d. 59, l. 17 (Poliani's Memo to the ECCI's Commission on Purges, September 19, 1933). N. Poliani reported that he was supposed to go as Hamdi al-Husayni translator but that Berger insisted on going instead. The meeting with Stalin is also mentioned in Berger, *Shipwreck of a Generation*, 7.
92. Berger-Barzilai, *The Tragedy of the Soviet Revolution*, 14; Berger's 1924 trip to Moscow is mentioned in RGASPI f. 495 op. 212, d. 59 (Berger's personal file) and l. 7 (Memo from March 25, 1948).
93. Berger-Barzilai, *The Tragedy of the Soviet Revolution*, 123.
94. Ibid.
95. In the first semester, 12 comrades missed 149 days, or an average of 12.5 days/person. RGASPI f. 532, op. 1, d. 365, ll. 6–13 (Report on the Arab Circle, undated but submitted before April 27, 1931).
96. In 1932, Berger's deputy Mustafa also reported that relations among the comrades were not comradely, RGASPI f. 532 (KUTV), op. 1, d. 366, ll. 4–6 (Students' evaluations December 31, 1932).
97. According to another 1935 report, at least 16 students from Egypt and Palestine had been expelled from KUTV in 1930–1935. RGASPI f. 532, op. 1, d. 215, ll. 17–21 (List of expelled foreign students between 1930–1935, February 14, 1936).
98. Abdel' Did is a rare name; it appears as "Akhmed Abdel' Did" in RGASPI f. 532, op. 1, d. 366, l. 3 (List of students' real names); but elsewhere Ioske's name is recorded as Ahmad Ion Abeddin. RGASPI f. 495, op. 212, d. 107, l. 16 (Memo about Ioske from September 3, 1938).
99. RGASPI f. 532, op. 1, d. 366, ll. 1–2 (Berger's characteristics of Arabs circle students from July 10, 1932).

100. These students included Aimarov, who supported Ioske's outbursts and Khalid, one of the four Iraqi students at KUTV. RGASPI f. 495 op. 212, d. 107, l. 16 (Secret Memo about Ioske, September 3, 1938).
101. On profanity and "cultured speech" campaigns to overcome cultural backwardness and control the disorder of popular speech see Hoffmann, *Stalinist Values: The Cultural Norms of Soviet Modernity, 1917–1941*, 42–43.
102. Ioske had been supposedly caught writing letters to relatives in Palestine asking for more foreign currency and complaining about life in the USSR. RGASPI f. 532, op. 1, d. 366, ll. 9–10 (Secret memo, January 21, 1933).
103. RGASPI f. 495 op. 212 d. 107, l. 16 (Secret Memo about Ioske, September 3, 1938).
104. RGASPI f. 532, op. 1, d. 366, ll. 4–6 (Assessments of 6th [Arab] Section, December 31, 1932).
105. RGASPI f. 532, op. 1, d. 366, ll. 9–10 (Report on Arab Students from January 21, 1933).
106. Ibid.
107. RGASPI f. 495, op. 212, d. 107, ll. 28–31 (Ioske's letter to Dimitrov on June 7, 1937).
108. RGASPI f. 532, op. 1, d. 366, ll. 1–2 (Characteristics of Arab Student Group, May 10, 1932).
109. Although factory labor had been envisioned as a means of personal fulfillment and human transformation, see Hoffman, *Stalinist Values*, 26, 30–31.
110. Gelvin, *The Israel-Palestine Conflict*, 103–6.
111. Anderson, "From Petition to Confrontation."
112. RGASPI f. 495, op. 212, d. 224, ll. 29–33 (Notes from Party Commission Meeting, April 10, 1933).
113. RGASPI f. 495, op. 212, d. 224, l. 34 (Memo from Magyar (Mad'iar) about sending Aimarov to Tbilisi, June, 1933).
114. Rashidov (real name: Mihran Masmanian, b. 1908, Syria) was an Armenian who had entered the Egyptian Communist Party in 1924 and was sent to Moscow from Egypt in 1930. In 1931, Rashidov entered the all-Union Communist Party when admission to the party was opened more widely.
115. RGASPI f. 495, op. 212, d. 224, l. 44 (Kotel'nikov's letter to Section of Cadres of ECCI Kraevskii and the Eastern Secretariat of ECCI, October 4, 1934).
116. Kotkin, *Stalin I*, 621–22.
117. Ibid., 623; the campaign to encourage settlement conducted under the slogan "To a Jewish land!," some pointed out, seemed to smack of Zionism. Gitelman, *A Century of Ambivalence: The Jews of Russia and the Soviet Union, 1881 to the Present*, 104.
118. Kotkin, *Stalin II*, 38; Martin, "The Origins of Soviet Ethnic Cleansing," 836–38.
119. Martin, "The Origins of Soviet Ethnic Cleansing," 841.
120. The NIA was created in 1927 with a foreign sector broken up into departments (*kafedry*) for the study of Turkey, Iran, and Arab countries. RGASPI f. 495, op. 20, d. 848, l. 1 (On the Reorganization of KUTV).
121. Some 500 "domestic" students were expected to remain in the KUTV. Adibekon, *Organizatsionnaia*, 207, 247. According to an NIA complaint, the Moscow city planning committee was ordered to allocate buildings for the separate NIA. Additionally, Gosplan was ordered to allocate 2 million rubles to build new spaces

outside the city, but this caused multiple problems. For instance, one allocated sanatorium was discovered to have been already rented out for ten years to the NKPS (People's Commissariat of Railways), and the dorms on Tverskaia Street were 25 percent inhabited by other people. RGASPI f. 532, op. 1, d. 212, ll. 51–55 (Memo about KUTV reorganization, unsigned, 1936).

122. Popov, "KUTV," *Revoliutsionnyi Vostok* 30 (1935): 193.
123. In 1930 the number of graduate students in the foreign and domestic sections was 27 and 21; by 1931 it was 55 and 26. Timofeeva, "KUTV," 39; citing *Revoliutsionnyi Vostok* 8 (1930): 343; for the 1936 foreign/domestic ratio, see RGASPI f. 532, op. 1, d. 212, ll. 51–55 (Memo, 1936).
124. Timofeeva, "KUTV," 40.
125. RGASPI f. 532, op. 1, d. 212, ll. 51–55 (Complaint, unsigned, 1936).
126. Chase, "Scapegoating One's Comrades," 266; the fact that Trotsky, Kamenev, and Zinoviev were Jews certainly did not go unnoticed. Goldman, *Terror and Democracy in the Age of Stalin: The Social Dynamics of Repression*, 64.
127. Magyar was arrested on December 29, 1934, a day after being expelled from the party. On November 2, 1937, the Military Board of the USSR's Supreme Court sentenced him to be shot. Ibid., 267. As historian William Chase has argued, the public scapegoating of Magyar, a Hungarian, reflected the rising tide of xenophobic fears about foreign "provocateurs," "imposters," "suspicious" residing in the USSR as political émigrés. Chase, "Scapegoating One's Comrades, 1934–1937," 271.
128. RGASPI f. 495, op. 212, d. 59, l. 17 (Poliani's Memo to the ECCI Commission on Purges, September 19, 1933).
129. He initially sentenced to five years. Then, in 1936, he was brought back to the Lubianka as a potential witness in the trial of Zinoviev and was also interrogated about what he knew about Bukharin. Berger, *Shipwreck of a Generation*, 8–9.
130. Adibekov, *Organizatsionnaia struktura kominterna, 1919–1943*, 179–80.
131. On the Comintern's Seventh Congress questionnaire, Bakdash listed his nationality as "Arab" and mentioned Kurdish only as one of his known languages. Kosach, *Kommunisty*, 190, citing RGASPI f. 495, op. 1, d. 495, ll. 14–15 (Questionnaires of delegates to the Seventh Congress of the Comintern from Communist Parties of Algeria, Egypt, Iraq, Iran, Palestine, Siam [Thailand], Syria, Tannu-Tuva, Tunisia, and Turkey). In presenting himself as a member of the "dominant" nationality, he was emulating the behavior of other Cominternians. Even Safarov, the son of an Armenian father and a Polish mother, presented himself officially as "Russian." In so doing, Bakdash's flexibility followed early Jewish communists like Trotsky who famously declared his nationality to be "Social Democrat," or Kamanev who occasionally refused to provide his ethnic information. Slezkine, *The Jewish Century*, 189, 245.
132. Significantly, this questionnaire is from 1935, before Stalin's border decrees of 1937 to secure border regions with Iran and Afghanistan by deporting of over 1,000 Kurdish families, when the Soviet government still provided for the material and cultural development of Soviet Kurds in Armenia and Azerbaijan; on Bakdash and Kurdish quarter see Fuccaro, "Ethnicity and the City: The Kurdish Quarter of Damascus between Ottoman and French Rule, c. 1724–1946," 206–24.

133. RGASPI f. 495, op. 20, d. 125, ll. 1–2 (Bakdash Report to Piatinskii, June 8, 1935). As a result, a special "Commission on the Palestine Question" was convened to consider isolating these members from their work. RGASPI f. 495, op. 14, d. 363, ll. 4–14 (Directives by the Commission on the Palestine Question, June 14, 1935).

134. Avigdor, "Uroki revoliutsionnykh boev v Palestine," *Revoliutsionnyi Vostok* 25 (1934): 67–85.

135. RGASPI f. 495, op. 212, d. 51 (Kosoi), ll. 63–64 (R. Fadl's report on Avigdor, December 1, 1935). Avigdor was accused of sabotaging Arabization (while verbally promoting it); concealing provocateurs inside the PCP including Berger, Haider, Nadab, and Haribi; not promoting a single Arab comrade and not sending any to Moscow. He did, however, send Jewish comrades who were either not accepted to or expelled from KUTV. For example, he sent a certain "Orlova" from Syria, over protests from other members of SCP. She was, apparently, an open supporter of the PCP's old regime and was weeded out (as accepted by accident, "*sluchainyi element*") in 1934. By 1936, she had been transferred to the Moscow Oriental Institute named after Narimanov. RGASPI f. 532, op. 1, d. 215, ll. 17–25 (List of KUTV students expelled in 1930–1935).

136. RGASPI f. 495, op. 212, d. 51, ll. 17–23 (Testimony of Saadi (Najati Sidqi) and Rosenberg from the secret report about Avigdor, April 14, 1936, Signed by Gald'jan). Such tactics were in fact mentioned in some PCP leaflets from 1932–1934. Laqueur, *Communism and Nationalism in the Middle East*, 88, ft. 10.

137. Even faced with what we can clearly see is a non sequitur, the regime continued to destroy "Trotskyists" who had no real-world connection to Trotskyism. Getty and Naumov, *The Road to Terror: Stalin and the Self-Destruction of the Bolsheviks, 1932–39*, 21.

138. RGASPI f. 495, op. 212, d. 51 (Kosoi), ll. 44–48 (Ramzi about Kosoi, December 5, 1935, in French).

139. Lazitch and Drachkovitch, *Biographical Dictionary of the Comintern*, 12.

140. Bakdash claimed that another Syrian communist claimed that that Panomarev's "Jewish name" was Kantarovich. Bakdash, *Khalid Bakdash yatahadath*, 70–73. CPSU International Department official Vladimir Shubin dismissed these claims as "utter nonsense," affirming that Panomarev was Russian, in an interview on September 11, 2020.

141. The nomination came from Artin Maduyan who was visiting Moscow before the Seventh Congress. Maduyan, *Hayat 'ala al-Mitras*, 222–23.

142. RGASPI f. 495, op. 154, d. 550, ll. 1–10 (Eastern Section Meeting on Arab Issues, August 31, 1935).

143. Beria was then First Secretary of the Georgian Communist Party. RGASPI f. 495, op. 212, d. 224, l. 64 (Letter from Beria in ZKK VKP(b) to VKP(b) Zakkraikom, July 29, 1936).

144. RGASPI f. 495, op. 212, d. 164, l. 7 (Memo from Ramzi and Yusef to ECCI, undated but likely from 1935).

145. On his unsuitability for travel see RGASPI f. 495, op. 212, d. 107, l. 71 (Memo from Ramzi and Yusef to the ECCI, September 16, 1935); on him being ruined see RGASPI f. 495, op. 212, d. 107, l. 16 (Secret Memo about Ioske, September 3, 1938).

146. RGASPI f. 495, op. 212, d. 107, ll. 28–31 (Ioske's letter to Dimitrov, June 7, 1937) and l. 40 (Note about al-Hilu's opinion of Ioske, signed by Galdjan, July 11, 1936).
147. Because the Comintern kept his foreign passport and he did not have Soviet citizenship, Ioske had trouble receiving his salary and academic stipends. RGASPI f. 495, op. 212, d. 107, l. 26 (Letter to TsK VKP(b), June 27, 1937). When he asked to have his passport, the ECCI determined in 1937 the ECCI that it "would not be useful to him in his work" and recommended that he apply for Soviet citizenship. RGASPI f. 495, op. 212, d. 107, l. 72 (Note to Deputy Head of the ECCI Personnel Department to the Leningrad State Institute of History and Philosophy about Ioske, March 28, 1937); on his eventual return see RGASPI f. 495, op. 212, d. 107, l. 16 (Secret Memo about Ioske, September 3, 1938); a petition by his Russian wife to join him in Haifa was denied. RGASPI f. 495, op. 212, d. 107, l. 15 (Secret letter from Kropotov and Bulychev to ECCI Moskvin, September 1, 1938).
148. RGASPI f. 495, op. 212 d. 166 (Subotin's personal file), l. 32 (Memo from Ramzi and Yussuf to Pavel Miff in the Eastern Secretariat, August 29, 1935).
149. RGASPI f. 495, op. 210, d. 74, l. 20 (Ramzi on Hamdi, February 2, 1936).
150. On illiteracy see RGASPI f. 532, op. 1, d. 372, ll. 10–15 (Resolutions after meetings of April 9 10 1937). Moscow's instructions that propaganda against French and British imperialism be softened to meet Stalin's foreign policy interest in 1934 angered some anti-imperialist activists, such as George Padamore, who also famously resigned over this shift from the American Communist Party.
151. Kosach, "Palestinskii communist 1920–1930 godov: avtobiografiia Ali Libermana."
152. RGASPI f. 532, op. 1, d. 373, ll. 1–3 ([Abdurakhman Fasliakhovich] Sultanov's report, January 22, 1938).
153. In the six months after Magyar's arrest, twenty-three members of the ECCI were punished. As a result, the party organization shrank by 2 percent (from 468 to 459 members). Chase, *Enemies within the Gates*, 100.
154. On purges of the NKID see Kocho-Williams, "The Soviet Diplomatic Corps and Stalin's Purges"; Dullin, *Hommes d'influence*.
155. RGASPI f. 532, op. 1, d. 284, l. 4 (Budget Memo by Krushkov, ECCI Secretariat).
156. RGASPI f. 532, op. 1, d. 284, l. 6 (Note from Kotel'nikov to Dimitrov, January 11, 1939)
157. RGASPI f. 532, op. 1, d. 284, l. 13 (Note from Rashad to Section of Cadres, January 17, 1939). Other students corroborated this report about the drinking, smoking, and the pointlessness of their existence to the Section of Cadres. RGASPI f. 532, op. 1, d. 284, l. 15 (Note from Karim to Section of Cadres, January 10, 1939).
158. The number of foreign visitors declined and additional controls were put on their contact with Soviet citizens. In 1937 there were approximately 13,000 foreign tourists, in 1938, only 5,000, and between 1939 and the declaration of war in 1941 fewer than 3,000. Gorsuch, *All This Is Your World*, 136.
159. Kosach, "Palestinskii communist"; Kirasirova, "From Syrian Communist to Soviet Orientalist," 145–49.
160. Slezkine adds that by early 1939, the proportion of Jews in the Gulag was about 15.7 percent lower than their share of the total Soviet population. Slezkine, *The*

Jewish Century, 273; for new work on percentages of ethnic minorities and ethnic Russians purged see Kotljarchuk and Sundström, *Ethnic and Religious Minorities*.

161. Berger-Barzalai, *Tragedy of the Soviet Revolution*, 122.
162. Although similar campaigns were waged against other non-Bolshevik parties, such as the Socialist Revolutionaries, the Mensheviks, the Ukrainian Borotbists, the Azerbaijani Mussavatists, and the Armenian Dashnaks, the particular vulnerability of the Comintern Eastern Section Jews was being seen as "Palestinian" Zionists or Bundists. Slezkine, *The Jewish Century*, 273; Viola, *Stalinist Perpetrators on Trial: Scenes from the Great Terror in Soviet Ukraine*, 26, 33.
163. Roziner, *Serebrianaia tsepochka*, 189–90; Slezkine, *The Jewish Century*, 273.
164. The percentage of Jews in the NKVD declined drastically in Ukraine and throughout the Soviet Union, from 38.54 percent in 1934 to 3.92 percent in 1939; on anti-Semitic themes in the NKVD purges see Viola, *Stalinist Perpetrators on Trial*, 21, 33.
165. Martin, *The Affirmative Action Empire*, 432.
166. Kaplan, "The Art of Nation-Building," 269–70.
167. This potential for creating a multiethnic Soviet canon went largely unrealized; Kaplan places emphasis on the institution's contributions to nation-building rather than assimilation. Kaplan, "The Art of Nation-Building," 269; Kaplan, "Comrades in Arts."
168. Tillett, *The Great Friendship: Soviet Historians on the Non-Russian Nationalities*, 43–46.
169. On January 28, 1935, the Comintern signal to "stop all advertising and sale writings Magyar and Safarov" was intercepted in London and Basel; cited in Breindel and Romerstein, *The Venona Secrets*, 318; on other intellectual consequences of Magyar's repression, including on arguments about the Asiatic Mode of Production (AMP) in China, see Fogel, "The Debates over the Asiatic Mode of Production."
170. Tatars Karim Khakimov and Nazir Bey Turyakulov who helped set up Soviet diplomatic relations with Saudi Arabia were both purged in 1938.
171. Abu Hanna, *Mudhakkarat Najati Sidqi*, 116–18. Sidqi's date is slightly off. He claims they had arrived in Tashkent in the middle of July 1936, but Bakdash mentions that the pair had already returned in an evaluation of Sidqi from June 5, 1936. RGASPI f. 495, op. 212, d. 284, ll. 24–26 (Meeting about Arab Cadres of Kraevskii, Marat, Ramzi, and Galdjan on June 5, 1936).
172. Roshwald, *Ethnic Nationalism and the Fall of Empires: Central Europe, Russia, and the Middle East, 1914–1923*, 196–97.
173. He described Khodjaev's role "before the invasion (*ijtiyah*) of Turkestan by the Red Army" as that of a "leading member of a nationalist party in Turkestan, the Jadid Party, which was also known by the name basmachi (*basmajiyya*), who were trying to liberate Turkestan and give it independence. . . . [After] the making of Turkestan into a Soviet republic based on Marxist principles, the new government clashed with the jadid movement known as the baschami. The struggle between these two forces culminated in a fierce gun battle which ended with the victory of the Russians and the local Bolsheviks." Abu Hanna, *Mudhakkarat*, 118–19.

174. Fedtke, "Jadids, Young Bukharans, Communists and the Bukharan Revolution: From an Ideological Debate in the Early Soviet Union," 483–512.
175. RGASPI f. 495, op. 84, d. 101, ll. 7–62 (Farajalla al-Hilu, *al-insaniyya al-jadida: al-ittihad al-sufiati fi 'ishrin 'amman: insaniyya jadida tabani 'aliman jadidan* [The Soviet Union in twenty years: a new humanity constructs a new world], 1937); al-Hilu, *Awraq min Tarikhuna*, 20.
176. Farjallah al-Hilu, *al-Insaniyya al-jadida*, 47–49.
177. Abu Hanna, *Mudhakkarat Najati Sidqi*, 118.
178. Clark, *Moscow, the Fourth Rome*, 145.
179. On Stalin's suspicion that indigenization was abetting the defection of national communists, concerns about Russian resentment of indigenization expressed itself within the Communist Party, and the decision to foster instead a campaign for "brotherhood of the peoples," see Martin, *Affirmative Action*, 269–71.
180. The end of appointments of Jews to the Central Committee and other Party leadership positions is documented in Iakovlev, *Gosudarstvennyi Antisemitizm v SSSR, 1938–53*.
181. Zubok, *Zhivago's Children: The Last Russian Intelligentsia*, 13.

Chapter 4

1. Magnusdottir, *Enemy Number One*, 68–69; for more on late 1940s and 1950s Soviet cultural diplomacy see Giburd, *To See Paris and Die*, 35; David-Fox, *Showcasing the Great Experiment*, 207–83.
2. *Al-Tali'a* became a pulpit for radical socialist views and a gathering place for future members of the Baath Party.
3. Moubayed, *Steel & Silk*, 528.
4. At this congress, 190 delegates represented 7,000 organized communists in Lebanon and Syria and 50 party organizations of the Communist Party. Maduyan, *Hayat 'ala al-mitras*, 463.
5. For some reason, Luis was chosen at the last minute to replace the philosopher Jamil Saliba (1902–1976), and Hamzawi to replace the Kurdish communist Khalid Katrash; the original list is found here: RGASPI f. 17, op. 128, d. 258, ll. 73–74 (Delegation chosen by the USSR Mission in Syria and Lebanon).
6. Faris Ibrahim was a feminist and likely in the women's wing of the Lebanese Communist Party since in the mid-1930s, as implied in Thompson, *Colonial Citizens*, 157, 217. For *al-Tariq* she wrote articles arguing that women deserved the vote because they worked hard for the good of the country at factory jobs and in the fields. Imili Faris Ibrahim, "Sawt al-mar'a: haquq jadida' (Women's voice: New rights)," *al-Tariq* 2, 20 (1943): 15–17.
7. Hanna, *Ana 'a'id min Musku*, 5.
8. Thomas, *Fight or Flight*.
9. Schapiro, "The International Department of the CPSU."

10. In 1947 the communist parties of Syria and Lebanon had about 18,000 members; union activity expanded to nearly 30,000 workers; Ismael and Ismael, *Communist Movement*, 38; in Egypt a 1947 consolidation of communist groups into the Democratic Movement for National Liberation (DMNL) attracted a total membership of about 2 million and maintained contacts with the colonial office of the French Communist Party. Ginat, *A History of Egyptian Communism*, 207, 255–56.
11. Communist papers such as *L'Humanité* and *Sawt al-Sh'ab* were banned in this period. Ismael and Ismael, *The Communist Movement in Syria and Lebanon*, 31; Khalid Bakdash was not arrested during this time; on Vichy repressions in Syria and Lebanon see Thompson, *Colonial Citizens*, 229–31; and Stephen Hemsley, *Syria and Lebanon under the French Mandate* (London: Oxford University Press, 1958), 293–305; on the significance of the Vichy defeat see Nordbruch, *Nazism in Syria and Lebanon*, 108.
12. Burderi, *The Palestine Communist Party*, 82–92; Heller, "The Failure of Fascism," 385.
13. On antifascism in British-controlled territories such as Iraq, Egypt, and India see Bashkin, "Iraqi Shadows"; Zachariah, "Rethinking (the Absence of) Fascism in India, 1922–45"; Gershoni and Jankowski, *Confronting Fascism in Egypt Dictatorship versus Democracy in the 1930s*.
14. Laqueur, *Communism and Nationalism*; Laqueur, *The Soviet Union and the Middle East*; Hurewitz, *Soviet-American Rivalry*; Barghoorn, *The Soviet Cultural Offensive*; and other works by Yaacov Ro'i, George Ienczowski, Wayne S. Vucinich, Ivo J. Lederer, Shimon Shamir, and Michael Confino.
15. Siegried Kracauer, "Appeals to Near and Middle East: Implications for Communications along the Soviet Periphery," May 1952 (Bureau of Applied Social Research, Columbia University, Box 22), 32. American Journalist Melvin Jonah Lasky similarly warned that the real and grave void was the failure "to win the educated and cultural classes—which, in the long run, provide moral and political leadership in the community" to the American cause. Saunders, *Cultural Cold War*, 25.
16. Laqueur, *Communism and Nationalism*, 143–49, 167; similar concerns appeared in *Regional Development for Regional Peace: A New Policy and Program to Counter the Soviet Menace in the Middle East* (Washington, DC: The Public Affairs Institute, 1957), 97–98, 107–8, 114–15; in 1953, Laqueur published a Hebrew-language book about the communist movement in Palestine under the name G. S. Yisraeli. It relied heavily on materials gathered by Sherut Yediot (SHAI), the Hagana and the Jewish Agency's information gathering and intelligence department during the British Mandate in Palestine. Musa Budeiri, "Essential Readings on the Left in Mandate Palestine," retrieved January 22, 2022.
17. Laqueur, *Communism and Nationalism in the Middle East*, 169.
18. Di-Capua, *No Exit*, 106. Some members of these landowning notables flirted with fascism, but as Erlich concludes none of them could realistically aspire to get rid of competitive politics and build a dictatorship, especially while Britain and France remained the dominant powers in the region. Erlich, "Periphery and Youth," 407.
19. Hanna, *Ana 'a'id min Musku*, 6.
20. Haugbolle, "Entanglements, Global History, and the Arab Left"; Guirguis, *The Arab Lefts*; Tannoury-Karam, "The Making of a Leftist Milieu."

21. Di-Capua, "Homeward Bound: Husayn Muruwwah's Integrative Quest for Authenticity"; Younes, "A Tale of Two Communists"; for Muruwwa's account of Moscow, see Muruwwa, *Qadaya adabiyya*, 66–85.
22. Egorov and Azadovskii, "From Anti-Westernism to Anti-Semitism."
23. Rubenstein, *Tangled Loyalties: The Life and Times of Ilya Ehrenburg*, 260.
24. Most people repressed in these ways simply lost their jobs. In some institutions, like the car factory named after Stalin, over fifty were arrested and fourteen executed when an alleged Zionist plot was discovered by the administration. *Gosudarstvennyi antisemitizm*, 358–61; Zubok, *Zhivago's Children*, 14–15; on the purge of the leadership of the Jewish region of Birobidzhan in this period see Gessen, *Where the Jews Aren't: The Sad and Absurd Story of Birobidzhan, Russia's Jewish Autonomous Region*.
25. On exile: see entry on Lutskii in *Liudi i sud'by: Biobibliograficheskii slovar' vostokovedov—zhertv politicheskogo terrora v sovetskii period (1917–1991)* (https://memory.pvost.org/pages/lutskij.html, retrieved September 1, 2022); on his 1953 struggle to keep his job see Bukhert, "V zashchity sovetskoi arabistiki."
26. On the confusion of some party officials between russocentrism as an expression of Stalinist cultural politics and Russian nationalism in this period see Brandenburger, "Stalin, the Leningrad Affair."
27. Both terms are neologisms, as Dyala Hamzah explains. With the rise of this new professional class of translators, teachers, editors, and correctors of printed books, the religious "scholar (*'alim*) and/or the man of Letters (*adib*) morphed into the journalist (*sihafi*) and/or the public writer (*kātib 'amm*)," and eventually the figure of the modern intellectual (*muthaqqaf*). Hamzah, *The Making of the Arab Intellectual*, 1; Kassab, *Contemporary Arab Thought*.
28. On the history of usage of the culture concept around the world see Sartori, *Bengal in Global Concept History*, 25–67.
29. The chronology of the *kul'tura* concept's adoption is disputed. Sartori dates Danilevskii's usage of the term to the 1860s. Sartori, *Bengal in Global Concept History*, 44; by contrast, Volkov dates its emergence in the Slavophile movement to the late 1870s. Volkov, "The Concept of Kul'turnost'," 212.
30. Margaret Litvin, "Arabic Rewritings of Tolstoy's 'Kreutzer Sonata'," EUME talk, September 2018; as Khuri Makdisi argues, his *al-Hilal* was particularly interested in his theories on the social body's corruption by wealth and, consequently, the need for wealth distribution; translations of other "radicals" like Maxim Gorky and Émile Zola were also common. Khuri-Makdisi, "Inscribing Socialism," 72, 78–81; on an account of the diffusion of Tolstoy's ideas from the Russian history field see Marks, *How Russia Shaped the Modern World*, ch. 4.
31. Shawi, *Tariqi ila al-hizb*, 147–49.
32. Ibid., 151.
33. Schumann, "Generation of Broad Expectations," 174.
34. Khuri-Makdisi, "Inscribing Socialism," 66; Shawi was inspired by older Marxist intellectual friend, Salim Khayyata, an American-born descendent of emigrants from Tripoli, a graduate of AUB and the Damascus University Faculty of Law. For Khayyata and Ra'f Khuri, curiosity about the October Revolution was sparked at AUB

by faculty like the British socialist Roger Soltau. Nordbruch, "Defending the French Revolution," 223.
35. Al-Hilu, *Awraq min Tarikhuna*, 17. The socialist state seemed also more firmly established. Even such initial skeptics as Farah Antun, who doubted the Bolshevik revolution's prospects because it had broken out in a "backwards" country like Russia rather than in West Europe, by 1922 felt more confident about its future. Sharabi, *Arab Intellectuals and the West*, 70, 86. On the union organization and labor protests in the 1930s see Thompson, *Colonial Citizens*, 157, 184–96; Laqueur, *Communism and Nationalism in the Middle East*, 141–46.
36. Maduyan, *Hayat 'ala al-Mitras*, 198, 212. Similar conversations were taking place in *L'Humanité* in France, which became a communist publication after 1920, and the Lebanese *al-insaniyya* (humanity) published in Beirut 1925 but closed down by the Mandate authorities. On *al-insaniyya* see Shawi, *Tariqi ila al-hizb*, 235.
37. This sense of belonging outside the Soviet Union was rarely expressed around ideas of "Easternness." In fact, Syrian communist Abd al-Rahman Shahbandar specified that he did not want an "Eastern Congress," to avoid the linguistic, cultural, and political complexity posed by working with "Turks, Persians, Indians, Chinese, Japanese, Mongolians, Tibetans, Russians and other innumerable peoples the East." Instead, he preferred an "Arab" Congress. RGASPI f. 532, op. 4, d. 39a, ll. 3–4 (Report from July 4, 1937, on a conversation of Hussayn Abu Shalib and Mahmud Muntasar with Syrian leader Dr. Abd al-Rahman Shahbandar, originally published *al-Balagh* on February 27, 1937).
38. Gershoni, *Arab Responses to Fascism and Nazism*; Gershoni and Jankowski, *Confronting Fascism in Egypt*, 4, 9, 13; Götz Nordbruch, *Nazism in Syria and Lebanon*, 41. On other works on fascism and antifascism in the Middle East see Heller, "The Failure of Fascism"; Erlich, "Periphery and Youth"; and Kabha, "A Bold Voice."
39. Shawi recalled that the sense of solidary with the Free Mujahidin led by Omar al-Mukhtar managed to spark protests in Egypt, Syria, Lebanon, Iraq. Shawi, *Tariqi ila al-hizb*, 227–32.
40. Götz Nordbruch, *Nazism in Syria and Lebanon*, 35. This strategy enabled local communists to forge antifascist coalitions with the national bourgeoisie and other political interest groups and to work together to counter propaganda initiated by Italians and later the Germans to portray fascism "as the liberator of Islam." Motadel, *Islam and Nazi Germany's War*, 5–6.
41. Maduyan, *Hayat 'ala al-Mitras*, 231.
42. Khayyata's 1933 book, *Hamiyat al-gharb*, described fascism as a threat to Europe and the Arab Middle East because it constituted nothing more than a distraction from the material ambitions of ruling capitalist classes; his 1935 *Al-habasha al-mazluma* described the threat in more concrete political terms. Nordbruch, *Nazism*, 35. On the political resonance of these publications, see Maduyan, *Hayat 'ala al-Mitras*, 234
43. Al-Hilu, *Awraq min Tarikhuna*, 24.
44. Nordbruch, "Defending the French Revolution during World War II: Raif Khoury and the Intellectual Challenge of Nazism in the Levant," 223.

45. On the geographical sales of *al-Tali'a*, see Karam, "The Making of a Leftist Milieu," 107 (ft. 273).
46. As Sana Tannoury Karam concludes, this "mix" characterized the convergence of *nahda* intellectual trends with socialist influences. Ibid., 106, 110–14.
47. Abu Hashah, *Najati Sidqi*, 195.
48. Nordbruch, *Nazism in Syria and Lebanon*, 69.
49. Bakdash, Farjalla al-Hilu, and Mustafa al 'Aris were present. Laqueur, *Communism and Nationalism in the Middle East*, 145.
50. On protests in Syria see Thomspon, *Colonial Citizens*, 160.
51. Although it's plausible, Laqueur offers no evidence in support or illustration of his claim that the communist party in the Levant opposed the successful invasion and overthrow of Vichy rule in Syria and Lebanon by the Allied forces in May 1941. Laqueur, *Communism and Nationalism*, 146.
52. Gershoni, "Why the Muslims Must Fight against Nazi Germany"; Sidqi later presented his expulsion as motivated, in part, by the party's objection to his reliance on Islamic texts. Abu Hanna, *Mudhakkarat Najati Sidqi*, 165–66.
53. Maduyan, *Hayat 'ala al-Mitras*, 307–8.
54. Nordbruch describes *al-Tali'a* as a "precursor" of *al-Tariq*. Nordbruch, *Nazism in Syria and Lebanon*, 114; Elsewhere, Nordbruch concludes that by the end of 1945 Ra'if Khuri had contributed to some twenty different newspapers and magazines, including *al-Tariq*. Nordbruch, "the French Revolution during World War II," 223.
55. Schayegh, *The Middle East and the Making of the Modern World*, 272–74.
56. Ibid., 274; on details of political decolonization see Khoury, *Syria and the French Mandate*; Zisser, *Lebanon: The Challenge of Independence*.
57. Thompson, *Colonial Citizens*, 232.
58. Thompson draws on Laqueur and other sources to estimate that Party membership across Syria and Lebanon rose from 2,000 in 1939 to 10,000 registered members by the war's end. Thompson, *Colonial Citizens*, 234; Walter Laqueur exaggerates the numbers, drawing upon Communist reports, claiming that the number of party members in Lebanon rose from 1,500 in 1941 to 15,000 in 1946, and in Syria from 1,500 to 8,000 during the same period. Laqueur, *Communism and Nationalism in the Middle East*, 140–53. Estimates by the US Committee on Foreign Affairs of increases were even higher, from 1,500 in 1941 to 15,000 by 1945 in Lebanon; and from 1,500 to 10,000 during the same period in Syria. "Strategy and Tactics of World Communism Committee on Foreign Relations, Supplement on the Near East" (Washington DC, 1949), 18; 10,000 SCP members in 1947 was also the estimates of the TsK RKP (b), with 65–70 intelligentsia (*chelovek-intelligenty*) members in a 800-member Damascus organization. RGASPI f. 17, op. 128, d. 389, ll. 2–27 (Report on Syria to Aleksandr Paniushkin of TsK VKP(b), May 7, 1947).
59. Maduyan describes that the number of votes received in Lebanon by Farjallah al-Hilu was "a major political victory for the party, and it caused great resonance in public opinion." Maduyan, *Hayat 'ala al-Mitras*, 370.
60. Nordbruch, *Nazism in Syria and Lebanon*, 123–24,

61. Nordbruch characterized this line of *al-Tariq* editors' argument as emphasizing that in the global confrontation it was impossible to sit idle. Nordbruch, *Nazism in Syria and Lebanon*, 114; Qadri al-Qal'aji and 'Umar Fakhuri also argued that the threat of fascism and Nazism meant the responsibility to 'take sides'. Karam, "The Making of a Leftist Milieu," 127–28.
62. Many of the articles in *al-Tariq* emphasized the domestic East. Prominent Arabist Vladimir Lutskii wrote about new histories of Kazakhstan and Isaak Vinikov about an ethnography of Arabs living in Central Asia, and coverage of Soviet nationalities policies. For example, Yaroslavsky's "Landmarks in the Life of Stalin" were published as "tufulat stalin wa-sibah" in *al-Tariq* 8 (1943): 10; Finikov, "al-'arab fi awsat Asiya," *al-Tariq* 13 (1943): 8–9.
63. Other groups included a twenty-eight-member "Russian Patriotic Group" of White Russian émigrés who began in 1941 to gather clothing, soap, and cigarettes for Red Army soldiers and send aid for Soviet war orphans via the Soviet Embassy in Tehran and the Committee for Aid to Soviet Children. It raised awareness about the war by distributing Soviet books and periodicals in Lebanese markets, organizing concerts, radio programs, and lectures, and screening films, like Sergei Eisenstein's *Alexander Nevsky*. GARF f. 5283, op. 2a, d. 50, ll. 281–84 (VOKS Report on Work in Syria and Lebanon 1942–1943); and GARF f. 5283, op. 19, d. 1. 107 (Memo about the Patriotic Russian Group in Beirut, 1943). This group had access to Soviet publications that likely arrived through the Soviet Information Bureau, a news agency founded in 1941.
64. GARF f. 5283, op. 19, d. 1, ll. 122–23 (Appel de l'association des amis de l'union soviétique en Syrie et au Liban). On Tabit's role in both societies see GARF f. 5283, op. 19, d. 1, ll. 118–20 (Sections an interview with Antoine Tabit in *La Sirie* and *l'Orian*, April 25, 1942). Fakhuri had studied law, literature, and politics in the early 1920s at the Sorbonne, where he had become attracted to leftist ideas and circles. After returning to Beirut in 1923, he was elected to the Arab Academy of Damascus in 1927, wrote for the Lebanese and Syrian press, and translated from French into Arabic the works of Gandhi, Romain Rolland, and Anatole France. Khayr al-Din Al-Zirikli, ed., *al-A'lam* [encyclopedia] (Beirut: Dar al-'Ilm li'l-Milayin, 1990); Astrid Ottosson al-Bitar, "Fakhuri, 'Umar " in *Encyclopaedia of Islam*, Third Edition, ed. Gudrun Krämer, Denis Matringe, John Nawas, and Everett Rowson (Brill Online, 2013).
65. Fifty books were sent to Syria and Lebanon in 1943. GARF f. 5283, op. 19, d. l, l. 7 (List of Books sent to Syria and Lebanon, November 17, 1943).
66. One 1944 shipment included forty-seven books in French, fifty-six in English, and three in Arabic; GARF f. 5283, op. 19, d. l, ll. 11–13 (books sent in May 31, 1944).
67. Although it remained oriented around the NKID, by the 1930s it also developed firm ties with the Comintern, the secret police (OGPU), and the Central Committee apparatus.
68. For VOKS correspondence with Fakhuri, see GARF f. 5283, op. 19, d. 1, l. 1 (Letter from VOKS to Omar Fahuri, head of Society of Friends of the Soviet Union in Syria and Lebanon from September 16, 1943).

69. The exhibit proved so popular that the Association extended it by an extra five days. GARF f. 5283, op. 19, d. 1. 60 (Letter from Syrian President of Association of Friends of the USSR, Kamal Ayad to Vladimir Kemenov [head of VOKS 1940–1948, and future Deputy Minister of Culture, 1954–1956]). On the opening in Damascus see *al-Tariq* 8 (May 8, 1944): 14–16.
70. *Al-Tariq* 4 (March 1, 1944): 11–12; evidence that reports of this publication were forwarded to VOKS headquarters can be found in GARF f. 5283, op. 2a, d. 50, ll. 285–87 (Report on VOKS activity in Syria and Lebanon, 1944).
71. Fakhuri helped organize the exhibit corresponding about its materials with the Soviet ambassador in Tehran who had previously sent materials for earlier events organized by the Lebanese-Syrian Society of Friendship, including a lecture on Normandy in Beirut, and a lecture in Damascus on the topic of "Why Arabs are Interested in the Soviet Union." The opening ceremony was held at the Beirut Grand Theatre. GARF f. 5283, op. 19, d. 1, l. 98 (Letter from Letter from The Society of Friends of the Soviet Union in Syria and Lebanon to the Soviet Ambassador in Tehran, May 14, 1943, in French) and included screenings of Soviet films and sales of the book, *Notre ami—l'Union Soviétique*, published by the Society of Friends using VOKS materials. GARF f. 5283, op. 19, d. 1, l. 61 (Telegram from Beirut to VOKS, February 20, 1944).
72. GARF f. 5283, op. 19, d. 1, l. 61 (Telegram from Niqula Shawi in Beirut to VOKS [in French], February 20, 1944). For the Western view of such soirées "at which the Communist Party invariably succeeded in producing as sponsor or guest speaker some prominent member of the government to lend prestige to the occasion," see Laqueur, *Communism and Nationalism in the Middle East*, 149; also *The Strategy and Tactics of World Communism*, Supplement on Communism in the Near East (Washington DC: US Government Printing Office), 16.
73. Ginat, "Soviet Policy towards the Arab World, 1945–48."
74. Abraham Levi from Alexandria, Egypt, asked for copies of the *VOKS Bulletin* to be sent to him, preferably in Arabic. GARF f. 5283, op. 4, d. 53, ll. 58–60 (VOKS Eastern Section researcher diary entry from February 1–28, 1929).
75. GARF f. 5283, op. 4, d. 53, ll. 22–23 and ll. 28–29 (VOKS diary entries for November 11–20 and December 11–20, 1929).
76. A Palestinian actress the VOKS bureaucrat called "Armon" asked for help to get a visa to enter the Soviet Union in 1929. GARF f. 5283, op. 4, d. 53, ll. 58–60 (VOKS Eastern Section researcher diary entry from February 1–28, 1929). Overall, the number of such interwar visitors was negligible compared with those from Europe, North America, but even East Asia and Australia. The exception that proved the rule was the visit of Hamdi al-Husseini, a prominent Palestinian nationalist activist and editor of the Jaffa-based paper *Sawt al-Haqq* who was recorded by a VOKS referent only as a certain as "Hussein . . . traveling with a German communist." GARF f. 5283, op. 4, d. 53, ll. 58–60 (VOKS Eastern Section researcher diary entry from February 1–28, 1929). VOKS' sparse correspondence with Lebanon and Syria in French was concerned with the shipment and distribution of VOKS materials in French, English, and Armenian languages among intellectuals, engineers, doctors, pharmacists,

lawyers, teachers, and architects, and the Anti-Fascist League. GARF f. 5283, op. 4, d. 240, l. 3 (Letter from Gabriel Delpine in Beirut to the Head of the Eastern Section of VOKS, June 25, 1937, in French). He sent them to the American University of Beirut library as a place that, as he stressed to VOKS, attracted not only Lebanese, but also youth from Iraq, Palestine, Transjordan, and Egypt. GARF f. 5283, op. 4, d. 240, l. 6 (Letter from Gabriel Delpine in Beirut to the Head of the Eastern Section of VOKS, September 3, 1937, in French).

77. By 1946, the VOKS chair reported that the Society maintained regular direct exchanges with fifty-four countries, in which there were a total of sixty-two Societies of Cultural Relations with 4,244 branches. VOKS corresponded regularly with 1,250 foreign institutions and 1,902 "major cultural figures." During the war, such new Societies of Friendship with the USSR formed in Palestine, Egypt, Syria, and Lebanon. RGASPI f. 17, op. 128, d. 258, l. 352 (from Kemenov at VOKS to Beria, Chief of Council of Ministers, December 6, 1946).

78. GARF f. 5284, op. 19, d. 6, l. 11 (VOKS Report titled "Activities of the Society of Friends for 1946").

79. On inept and inert cultural outreach to the socialist bloc see Babiracki, *Soviet Soft Power in Poland*. On the Zhdanov purges see Hahn, "The Fall of Zhdanov"; on impact in scientific and educational sectors, see Pollock, *Stalin and the Soviet Science Wars*.

80. Gilburd, *To See Paris and Die*, 32.

81. RGASPI f. 17, op. 128, d. 258, ll. 330–46 (VOKS final report about work with the Syrian and Lebanese delegation, April 1947).

82. The evaluations were signed by the Soviet representative to Syria and Lebanon Solod. RGASPI f. 17, op. 128, d. 258, l. 59 (Proposal from Vladimir Kemenv to Suslov, February 2, 1947). Except for Kamil 'Ayyad, Jamil Saliba, and George Hanna, other guests were described as members of the Communist Party. Ra'if Khuri who did not join the Party was called a "sympathizer." An extra check mark was placed next to Fawzi Shulaq's party experience (he had been a member of the SCP since 1937). As a consequence of this evaluation, two of the Syrian candidates were replaced for unspecified reasons. Katrash and Saliba were replaced by Dr. Josef Luis and the lawyer Ibrahim Hamzawi. RGASPI f. 17, op. 128, d. 258, ll. 330–46 (VOKS Final Report about work with the Syrian and Lebanese delegation, April 1947).

83. Suslov would succeed Zhdanov as Stalin's chief ideologist after Zhdanov's death in 1948. Suslov's approval of the list is indicated in RGASPI f. 17, op. 128, d. 258, l. 69 (Letter from VOKS to Mikhail Suslov in the Orgburo of VTsK VKP(b), February 2, 1947). The group arrived on March 18, 1947; the length of the visit, twenty-five days, was more than twice that of other 1946–1947 visits by delegations from Sweden and Norway. RGASPI f. 17, op. 128, d. 258, ll. 1–5 (List of 28 cultural delegations from Sweden in 1946); and ll. 6–8 (List of 17 cultural delegations from Norway). Prior to the approval, Suslov received memos on the situation in Syria and Lebanon that presented such leftist cultural groups as created by the Communist Party of Syria and Lebanon. RGANI f. 81 (Suslov), op. 1, d. 358 (Lebanon and Syria, 1946), ll. 32–38 (Memo about communist parties and labor unions of Syria and Lebanon). The CPSL was also credited with the creation of the Anti-Fascist League and union of democratic writers in a 1938 report to the Comintern. RGASPI f. 495, op. 84, d. 105, ll. 5–8 (Salim Aboud, "On the Situation in Syria," January 19, 1938).

84. RGASPI f. 17, op. 128, d. 258, l. 115 (Report from a diary entry of VOKS Leadership member Kisleva about her conversation with Fawzi Shulaq, head of Syrian branch of the Society of Friendship on February 22, 1947).
85. *Al-Tariq* No. 7–8 (July and August 1947), 3–10.
86. Ibid.
87. Magnusdottir, *Enemy Number One*, 68–69.
88. Khalid Bakdash had apparently summoned Tabit and Shulaq before their departure and told them that they had to be careful of George Hanna because he was "a dangerous man." RGASPI f. 17, op. 128, d. 258, ll. 330–46 (VOKS report on work with the Syrian and Lebanese delegation, April 1947).
89. RGASPI f. 17, op. 128, d. 258, ll. 347–50 (Letter from Deputy Head of the Section of TsK VKP(b) L. Baranov to TsK VKP(b) Secretary Suslov, July 2, 1947).
90. "Report on the Communist 'Peace' Offensive," Appendix XVI, 165; Laqueur, *Communism and Nationalism*, 150.
91. RGASPI f. 17, op. 128, d. 258, l. 115 (Diary entry of VOKS Leadership member Kisleva about her conversation with Fawzi Shulaq, head of Syrian branch of the Society of Friendship, February 22, 1947).
92. Ibid.
93. RGASPI f. 17, d. 128, op. 258, ll. 73–74 (List of delegation, February 1947).
94. Tabet and Tabet, *Antuan Tabet*, 7, 11–12.
95. Between 1946 and 1949, 32,238 had relocated to Soviet Armenia from Syria and Lebanon out of 89,750 from twelve different countries, with more than a third from Arab countries. Ara Sanjian, "Armenian Immigration from the Arab World to the USSR after WWII (1945–9)," in Kane, Kirasirova, and Litvin, eds., *Russian-Arab Worlds*.
96. On this work see Laruelle, *The Concept of Ethnogenesis*, 177.
97. On Mao Dun's early communist activities see Clark, *Eurasia*, 265–76; on his later participation in Tashkent-based Afro-Asian activities starting with the 1958 Afro-Asian Writers Conference see Yoon, "Our Forces Have Redoubled"; he would soon become the PRC's Minister of Culture (1949–1965).
98. Literally: "Po musul'manskomu obychaiu v p'ianom vide koran ne chitaiut." RGASPI f. 17, op. 128, d. 258, ll. 330–46 (VOKS Final Report about work with the Syrian and Lebanese delegation, April 1947).
99. Ibid.
100. Mastura Iskhakova, "Uzbekskii Shaliapin," accessed January 12, 2023, https://mytashkent.uz/2011/09/24/muxitdin-kari-yakubov-uzbekskij-shalyapin-chast-1/.
101. Meyerhold himself was purged during the late 1930s attack on leading Soviet composers. His theatre was closed in 1938, near the end of the Great Terror. He was arrested later in 1939 and probably shot in prison in 1940. Tomoff, "Uzbek Music," 216.
102. Iskhakova, "Uzbekskii Shaliapin."
103. On composers willingly taking up orientalist codes to propagate musically orientalist national traditions see Frolova-Walker, "National in Form, Socialist in Content."

104. Kari-Yakubov often performed the roles of ideological "bad guys," like of the "bey" in "The Bey and the Farmhand (*batrak*)" and the Turkestan Governor General in the first Uzbek opera, *Buran*, in 1934. Rahmanov, *Khamza i uzbekskii teatr*, 103.
105. On earlier "musical nationalism" in Uzbekistan see Kale-Lostuvali, "Varieties of Musical Nationalism."
106. RGASPI f. 17, op. 128, d. 258, ll. 347–50 (Letter from the Deputy Head of the Section of TsK VKP(b) L. Baranov to the TsK VKP(b) Orgburo Secretary Mikhail Suslov, July 2, 1947).
107. Cited in Hansen, "The Ambivalent Empire," 113; these criticisms of Uzbek theatrical and musical culture came up at an Uzbek Party congress in August 1947, just a few months after the Arab delegations' visit. They were voiced at the XIV Plenum of the TsK KP(b) Uz and published in *Qizil Uzbekiston* on August 10, 1947. Ishankhodjaeva, "Repressivnaia politika Sovetskoi vlasti," 39.
108. On Suslov's orders and Ignat'ev's reports see Tomoff, "Uzbek Music's Separate Path"; on Moscow ethnomusicologists in Uzbekistan see also Shepilov, *The Kremlin Scholar*, 97.
109. Writers criticized included: Ainbek, G. Alimov, M. Babaev, A. Karrakh, Mirtemir, Tuigun, U. Rashidov, Kh. Guliam, A. Kaiumov, and Shaikhzade. The office also criticized the journals *Shark iulduzi* and *Zvezda Vostoka* for publishing articles that are "full of the spirit of cosmopolitanism which disorganizes the readers" (*proniknutykh dukhom kosmopolitizma i dezorganizuiushchikh*). Ishankhodjaeva, "Repressivnaia politika," 39–40.
110. On style, see Tomoff, "Uzbek Music's Separate Path."
111. Sahadeo, *Voices*, 54; Igmen, *Speaking Soviet with an Accent*, 111.
112. Ishankhodjaeva, "Repressivnaia politika," 40.
113. Kalinovsky, "Opera as the Highest Stage of Socialism."
114. Kari-Yakubov was rehabilitated and released in 1955. Kari-Yakubov's arrest date was confirmed by Dr. Khasanov Bakhtier Vakhapovich, director of the Museum of Victims of Political Repression in Tashkent for this information (conversation May 5, 2019). His post-camp state is described by his family in "Uzbekskii Shaliapin," accessed May 4, 2018, http://mytashkent.uz/2011/09/24/muxitdin-kari-yakubov-uzbekskij-shalyapin-chast-2/.
115. RGASPI f. 17, op. 128, d. 258, ll. 330–46 (VOKS Final Report about work with the Syrian and Lebanese delegation, April 1947).
116. The rumors were mentioned to me by Elias Khoury on May 7, 2013. On male-dominant discourse within the labor, communist, and leftist circles see Abisaab, "Gendered Expressions of Labor in the Middle East."
117. The phrase was originally used by critic Boris Eikhenbaum and then repeated in a speech by Zhdanov in September 4, 1946. Reeder, *Anna Akhmatova*, 291–92.
118. Stalin suggested in 1948 that it was providing anti-Soviet information to the organs of foreign (Israeli) espionage agencies. On this purge in a wider context of postwar state-sponsored anti-Semitism see Rubenstein and Naumov, *Stalin's Secret Pogrom*. After Lozovskii's arrest, most of his Sovinformburo colleagues were dismissed, and

those who remained recalled that the organization lost much of its wartime energy. Nunan, "A Union Reframed," 582.
119. Tomoff, "Uzbek Music's Separate Path," 213.
120. Ehrenburg later recalled these years as "perhaps the most painful in my whole life"; Rubenstein, *Tangled Loyalties*, 253.
121. Nunan, "A Union Reframed."
122. GARF f. 8581, op. 1, d. 216, ll. 15–33 (Articles for Tehran, Beirut, Cairo, Istanbul, Addis Ababa, 1948).
123. A large majority of programming focused on the domestic East, comparing numbers of specialists trained in Uzbekistan compared to Iran, Turkey, and even France and other such cultural "accomplishments." E.g., GARF r-6903, op. 24, d. 25, ll. 1–4 (Broadcast by Professor Cherkasov, May 19, 1953).
124. Party ranks were apparently divided in the 1940s between those who used russocentric rhetoric to express a sense of Russian patriotism and those who invoked this rhetoric in support of the regime. Brandenberger, "Stalin, the Leningrad Affair," 247.
125. Ra'if Khuri, "Khitab Ra'if Khuri fi haflah jami'ia al-ta'awun al-thaqafi bayn lubnan wa-l-ittihad al-sufyati," *al-Tariq* 11–12 (November–December 1947): 113–16.
126. Nordbruch, "Defending the French Revolution," 219.
127. Instead they focused on the warm welcome received from "the Soviet people." Ra'if Khuri, *al-Tariq* 3 (March 1947): 3–5; also *al-Tariq* 7–8 (July and August 1947): 3–10 (about his meeting with Ilya Ehrenburg); *al-Tariq* 11 (November–December 1947): 113–16 (summarizing his speech before Society of Friendship on the Thirtieth Anniversary of the October Revolution); and Antoine Tabit, "shahr fi bilad al-ishtirakiyya," *al-Tariq* 4 (April 1947): 3–8.
128. Karam, "The Making of a Leftist Milieu," 23; Tillett, *Friendship of Peoples*, 84–129;
129. Hanna, *Ana 'a'id min Musku*, 106.
130. Ibid., 102.
131. Hanna deemed these differences trivial because it seemed to him like a foregone conclusion that "in twenty years, [the old city of Tashkent] will become a historical monument." Ibid., 106–7.
132. Ibid., 124.
133. Ibid., 105.
134. Ibid., 108.
135. The editors of *al-Tariq* addressed this challenge of Cold War ideological pressure directly by publishing a serialized translation into Arabic of Konstantin Simonov's *The Russian Question* (first performed as a play in 1947 and made into a film by Mikhail Romm in 1948) about an American journalist who visits the Soviet Union and grapples with editorial pressure to write a scaremongering report about Soviet expansionism. *Al-Tariq* 7–8 (July and August 1947): 85–128; the second part was published in *al-Tariq* 9 (September 1947): 47–89.
136. Gromyko's speech in the UN, November 26, 1947, in Naumkin, ed., *Blizhnevostochnyi konflikt* I, 10.

137. On Qal'aji's wartime writing see Qadri Qil'aji, "al-hayat al-qawmiyya fi al-ittihad al-sufyati," *at Tariq* 20–21 (1944): 29–32 (31).

138. This disillusionment did not mean that he was ready to join in a new consensus, like André Gide, Arthur Koestler, and Ignazio Silone. Rather, he joined forces with other exiled communists to write about culture as part of the "Brothers of Omar Fakhuri." Qal'aji, *Tajribat arabi fi al-hizb al-shuyu'i*; Karim Muruwwa, "al-muthaqqaf wa-l-thawra: haqa'iq 'an Ra'if Khuri," *al-Tariq* 1 (1989): 5–18 (17).

139. Rashad 'Isa and Meir Mus'ad expressed reservations, but al-Hilu publicly challenged Bakdash to condemn the partition plan and the decision of the Security Council at a news conference on September 1948. After that, Bakdash initiated a campaign against him; al-Hilu was kicked out of Party leadership from 1949 and 1952 and readmitted after being subjected to humiliating self-criticism. Hilu, *Awraq min Ta'rikhina*, 32–33.

140. The SCP was outlawed in December 1947; LCP in January 1948. The coup of Husni al-Za'im in Syria further intensified persecution of communists, and the center of Party activity was moved from Damascus to Beirut. Nevertheless, bilateral diplomatic relations remained stable as Syrian representative Farid Zeineddin repeatedly visited Deputy Minister of Foreign Affairs Andrei Gromyko to voice his hopes about the improvement of relations with the USSR. RGASPI f. 82 (Molotov Personal File), op. 2, d. 1307, ll. 11–12, 13 (Reports about Zeineddin's conversations with Gromyko in 1949–1950).

141. In 1950, Khuri is described a "bourgeois nationalist and agent of Tito." RGASPI f. 82 (Molotov Personal File), op. 2, d. 1307, ll. 21–23 (Report to Molotov about CPs of Syria and Lebanon, 1950); on defamation that was a typical form of punishment for an expelled communist Karim Muruwwa, "al-Muthaqqaf," 11–12; for more on Khuri's break with the party, see Yussuf Khattar Al-Hilu, "Ma'a raif khuri," *al-Tariq* (February 1989): 126–30.

142. Part of his disagreement may have been an objection to the leadership type of Bakdash. On his critiques of Marxist *iltizam* for submitting the individual to a collective order and defense of individual freedom necessary for any literary, intellectual, political, or social project see Di-Capua, *No Exit*, 89–90

143. This position made Khuri one of the first intellectuals to identify the Arab state of the 1950s as a menace to intellectual freedom rather than its guardian. Not confusing Arab nationalism, which he wholly supported, with statism, which he feared, Khuri found his inspiration in the street. Ibid., 90. By 1953 he saw fundamental conflict between literature and the state because of the pressures applied by the state and its rulers who wish to remain in power. Ra'if Khuri, "Al-Adab: Naqid al-dawla," *al-Adab* (March 1953): 5–7 (6).

144. RGASPI f. 17, op. 128, d. 611, l. 5 (Memo about the dissolution of the Society of Cultural Relations with the Soviet Union in Syria).

145. RGASPI f. 17, op. 128, d. 611, l. 7 (Memo about the Fawzi Shulaq's rebuttal).

146. In Damascus, anti-Communist demonstrations on November 29, 1947, left three communists dead and a bomb exploded in Party headquarters in Beirut. Solold's

NOTES TO PAGES 148-152   303

conversation with Prime Minister and Minister of Foreign Affairs of Syria Jamil Mardam-Bey, January 5, 7, 1948, in *Blizhnevostochnyi konflikt*, vol. 1, 22-23.
147. RGASPI f. 82, op. 2, d. 1307, ll. 21-23 (Memo on Communist Parties).
148. RGASPI f. 495, op. 232, d. 6, l. 117 (TASS excerpt from Tabit's speech, April 24, 1949); for more on the Partisans of Peace movement in Syria and Lebanon and Hanna's and Tabit's roles in it, see Kirasirova, "The Partisans of Peace in Lebanon and Syria: Towards and Intellectual and Political History of the Early 1950s Arab Left."
149. In 1958, Tabit fought against military occupation of Lebanon and for support of the Iraqi revolution of July 14, 1958. In 1962 he received the Lenin Prize for his work in strengthening peace among people, awarded to him in Moscow at an all-world Congress for Disarmament and Peace that he attended with Mikhail Naimy. Tabet and Tabet, *Antuan Tabet*, 11-14.
150. GARF f. 6903 (Radio Committee), op. 24, d. 39, ll. 43-45 (Report on May 5, 1955); ll. 127-34 (show about Hanna's story "Temple Priests," December 23, 1954).
151. Hanna, *Fi Musku marra thaniya*, 66-69.
152. Di-Capua, "Homeward Bound," 36; Frangie, "The Afterlives of Husayn Muruwwa."
153. Hanna, *Fi Musku marra thaniya*, 9, 31, 35.
154. "kutub wa-dirasat 'an biladna," *al-thaqafa al-wataniyya* 2 (1957): 62; "ihtimam mutazayyid bi-l-adab al-'arabi," *al-thaqafa al-wataniyya* 1 (1959): 88-89.
155. George Hanna, "Razvitie kul'turnykh sviazei mezhdu Livanom i Sovetskim Soiuzom," *Sovremennyi Vostok* 7 (1957): 10-12.
156. Hanna, *Shumikha v filosofii*, 4-10.
157. As Czesław Miłosz argued, by structuring society on a system of abstract thought and enabling its articulators, Soviet-style socialism made intellectuals feel like they belonged; cited in Tromly, *Making of Soviet Intelligentsia*, 8.
158. Hanna, "On the 50th Anniversary of October," *al-Tariq* 1968; Muhammad Dakrub, "With George Hanna, History of Thought and Struggle," *al-Tariq* 3-4 (1968): 3-7
159. Dakrub, "The Role of George Hanna," *al-Tariq* 2 (1969): 42-46.
160. On this new 1960s Lebanese Left and its critiques of the old pro-Soviet party's theoretical poverty and its lack of autonomy, see Bardawil, *Revolution and Disenchantment*.
161. Gretshaw, *Worldmaking after Empire*.
162. Nunan, "A Union Reframed," 556.
163. In this sense, they seemed more aware than other readers and viewers in Africa, Asia, and Latin America who, as described by Djagalov, were unable to see Soviet culture in its sequential development and for whom far more common experience was of a decontextualized arrival of Russian and Soviet texts and films. Djagalov, *From Internationalism to Postcolonialism*, 16.
164. Interview with Malekeh Khuri, July 20, 2020.
165. Despite being excommunicated by the communists, Ra'if Khuri continued to advocate for socialist realism beyond without the Soviet criteria. Di-Capua, *No Exit*, 100-2.
166. Padmore experienced his share of disappointments with organized communism since his days of lecturing about imperialism and colonialism at KUTV, especially

around the Comintern's flagging support for liberation struggles in Africa. He severed his connections with the International Trade Union Committee of Negro Workers in 1933 and was excluded from the Communist Party in 1934. Yet in the wake of the Soviet victory over fascism and the of new economic imperialism in British Africa, he seems to have reconsidered. In 1946 he concluded: "However much we may criticize the Soviet Union's sins of commission and omission, its policy towards the former colonial peoples of the far-flung tsarist empire indicates conclusively that only under a planned economy based on socialist principles is it possible to abolish, root and branch, national and racial oppression and exploitation. In the USSR there are no signs reading 'Niggers and dogs keep out.' This is why, despite its many shortcomings, the Soviet Union enjoys widespread sympathy among the colored races of the world." Padmore, *How Russia Transformed Her Colonial Empire*, x, 64–65.

167. Leys, *Color Bar in East Africa*; the contrast was clear despite racism observed by generations of African students and other racialized foreign minorities. Matusevich, "Black in the USSR."
168. The sheer breadth and diversity of the attraction of foreign intellectuals to the Soviet Union continued to ensure that Soviet communism remained a potent force of political and intellectual history in the second half of the twentieth century as it had been in its first half. David-Fox, *Showcasing the Great Experiment*, 4.

Chapter 5

1. Di-Capua, *No Exit: Arab Existentialism, Jean-Paul Sartre, and Decolonization*, 111.
2. Jacquemond, *Conscience of the Nation: Writers, State, and Society in Modern Egypt*, 19.
3. On Khuri's caution about the Arab state see Di-Capua, *No Exit*, 90, 114.
4. Dudziak, *Cold War Civil Rights: Race and the Image of American Democracy*, 27; the decision was announced months after the UN Sub-Commission on the Prevention of Discrimination and the Protection of Minorities initiated an international study of discrimination in education. Plummer, *Rising Wind*, ch. 6.
5. Robeson and Du Bois were banned from traveling internationally until a 1958 Supreme Court decision ruled that the secretary of state had no right to deny a citizen a passport because of political beliefs. Von Eschen, *Race against Empire: Black Americans and Anticolonialism, 1937–1957*, 112–21.
6. Myer, *Islam and Colonialism: Western Perspectives on Soviet Asia*, 101–24.
7. Ibid., 3, 14; Sabine Dullin and Etienne Forestier-Peyrat, "Flexible Sovereignties of the Revolutionary State: Soviet Republics Enter World Politics," *Journal of the History of International Law* (published online May 16, 2017).
8. Kalinovsky, *Laboratory of Socialist Development*, 19–42; Stronski, *Tashkent: Forging a Soviet City 1930–1966*, 234–56.

9. By engaging with the question of culture in international relations, especially in a comparative Soviet, Chinese, and US context, this story offers a new answer to this question raised in Iriya, "Culture and Power."
10. Gilburd, *To See Paris and Die*, 106–14; Yurchak, *Everything Was Forever, until It Was No More: The Last Soviet Generation*.
11. Djagalov, *From Internationalism to Postcolonialism: Literature and Cinema between the Second and the Third Worlds*, 107.
12. Ibid., ch. 3–4.
13. Salazkina, *World Socialist Cinema*, 80.
14. Djagalov, *From Internationalism to Postcolonialism*, 106–7; Tolz, "European, National, and (Anti-) Imperial," 132–33; Clark, *Eurasia without Borders*.
15. Kalinovsky, *Laboratory of Socialist Development*, 19; Stronski, *Tashkent*, 234–56.
16. Zubok and Pleshakov, *Inside the Kremlin's Cold War*, 175–77.
17. Ibid., 178, 184.
18. Gilburd, *To See Paris and Die*, 34.
19. Friedman, *Shadow Cold War: The Sino-Soviet Competition for the Third World*, 25–59.
20. Ibid., 83–84, 109, 115.
21. Chen Jian, *Mao's China*, 3.
22. Brzezinski, *The Soviet Bloc: Unity and Conflict*.
23. Rami Ginat, "Abandoned Comrades," in *Russia-Arab Worlds*.
24. Khrushchev also affirmed his commitments to support the Arab "progressive forces" in their battle with "internal reactionary forces." Roi, *From Encroachment To Involvement*, 276–80.
25. Di-Capua, *No Exit*, 129.
26. Roi, *From Encroachment*, 276–80, 296–326.
27. The non-party position as supported by the Institute of World Economics and International Relations. Eran, "Soviet Perception of Arab Communism and Its Political Role," 112–13.
28. Primakov, *Russia and the Arabs*, 59.
29. Miller, "Georgii Mirskii"; Primakov, *Russia and the Arabs*, 59.
30. Eran, "Soviet Perception of Arab Communism and its Political Role," 112; citing Mirskii, "The UAR Reforms," *New Times* 4 (January 24, 1962); and G Mirskii, "O klassovoi strukture v slaborazvitykh stranakh," MEiMO 4 (April 1962); for more on this theory see Friedman, *Shadow Cold War*, 108.
31. Primakov, *Russia and the Arabs*, 59.
32. Friedman, *Shadow Cold War*, 112.
33. Dawisha, *Soviet Foreign Policy towards Egypt*, ch. 2, 3.
34. Primakov, *Russia and the Arabs*, 60.
35. Primakov takes credit for this reassessment with his October 1965 *Pravda* article "Multi-Story Damascus" on the diversity and progressive elements within the Syrian Ba'ath Party. Primakov, *Russia and the Arabs*, 70–71.
36. On official reassessment of Syria entering a new stage of national-democratic revolution with nationalization of property and agrarian reforms, see RGANI f. 81 (Suslov's Fond), op. 1, d. 359, ll. 10–12 (Memo on the contemporary situation in the Syrian CP, 1965).

37. Primakov, *Russia and the Arabs*, 75–86.
38. Gilburd, *To See Paris*, 33; Zubok and Pleshakov, *Inside*, 185.
39. Review of *America and the Aggression Against Egypt* (Cairo, Dar al-Fikr) in *al Thaqafa al-Wataniyya* 3 (1957): 54–55.
40. "Neutrality . . . Our Hope," Tabit, "Implementing the Decisions of the Afro-Asian Solidarity Conference"; and Bakdash, "The Arab World and the October Revolution," *Al-Tariq* 1 (1958): 1–2, 4–5, 62–69; Yusuf Khattar al-Hilu, "al-'arab wa al-ittihad as-sufiyati 'ala da'a al-madi wa al-hadir," *al-Tariq* 10–11 (1957): 10–11.
41. Roi, *From Encroachment to Involvement*, 281–95.
42. On the wider context of Khrushchev-era nostalgia for 1920s internationalism see Brinkley, "The 'Withering' of the State under Khrushchev"; Gilburd, *To See Paris and Die*, 19–54.
43. He did so in a 1946 interview with the *Washington Post* journalist Richard Hottelet, which was published a few weeks after Litvinov's death, but after which Livtinov was dismissed from his post as deputy minister for foreign affairs. *Washington Post*, January 23, 1952.
44. Pechatnov and Edmondson, "The Russian Perspective," 89–90.
45. Pechatnov, "The Soviet Union and the World," 90–111.
46. On Stalin's support of Kim see Westad, *The Global Cold War*, 66; on his ideas about the southern borderlands see Goff, *Nested Nationalisms*, ch. 2.
47. Stalin, "Speech of the 19th Party Congress of the Communist Party of the Soviet Union" (October 14, 1952), accessed September 20, 2020, https://www.marxists.org/reference/archive/stalin/works/1952/10/14.htm; American aid was extended to China and North Korea, as well as French Indochina, Thailand, Burma, and the Philippines.
48. Mastny described Molotov's conduct of foreign policy as "Stalin's without Stalin." Mastny, "Soviet Foreign Policy, 1953–62," 315.
49. Painter, "Oil, Resources, and the Cold War," 486–507; Douglas Little, *American Orientalism: The United States and the Middle East since 1945*.
50. Pakistan, the Philippines, and Thailand joined SEATO, also known as the Manila Pact, and Iran, Iraq, Pakistan again, Turkey, and the United Kingdom had joined the Baghdad Pact; Jasse, "The Baghdad Pact."
51. On his 1955 tour of India, Burma, and Indonesia, Khrushchev stressed Soviet willingness to cooperate with the "national development" of nonsocialist countries in economic and military terms. Westad, *Global Cold War*, 67–68.
52. Ampiah, *The Political and Moral Imperatives of the Bandung Conference*.
53. Cited in Ramet, *Soviet-Syrian Relationship*, 15–16.
54. Such arguments rested on two premises: first that the two seats the USSR had in the UN (besides its main seat) went to its "European" republics of Ukraine and Belorussia; and second, that "Soviet Asian republics were de facto colonies and could only participate in a forum for independent sovereign states once they too became fully independent." Mukhitdinov, *Reka vremeni*, 222–23.
55. Judge and Langdon, *The Struggle against Imperialism*, 80; Nutting, *Nasser*, 101.

56. Lawrence Rushing, "The Racial Identity of Adam Clayton Powell Jr.: A Case Study in Racial Ambivalence and Redefinition," *Afro-Americans in New York Life and History* (January 1, 2010), accessed December 10, 2020, https://www.thefreelibrary.com.
57. Wright, *The Color Curtain*, 13–14; on rumors that the US government had paid the traveling expenses of other "safe" reporters such as African American journalist Carl Rowan, see Plummer, *Rising Wind*, 248–51.
58. Cited in Von Eschen, *Race against Empire*, 170–71; earlier, Powell had spoken differently about US racial bias, claiming in 1953 that the United States "is the most hated nation in the world today," and declaring that "communism must win the global cold war by default" if reform measures were not taken "immediately." Plummer, *Rising Wind*, 249.
59. Fisher, "An American Dilemma."
60. Mukhitdinov, *Reka vremeni*, 220–21.
61. Mukhitdinov, *Gody, provedennye v Kremle*, 15; anecdotally, two people who knew him described his Moscow education as him attending "a KGB school," but I have not been able to verify this assertion.
62. Both Ikramov and Khodjaev were executed in 1938. Ibid., 15–17.
63. Carlisle, "The Uzbek Power Elite," 105.
64. Ibid., 106; Mukhitdinov, *Gody, provedennye v Kremle*, 44; Mukhitdinov, *Reka vremeni*, 50.
65. *Foreign Relations of the United States, 1958–1960. Eastern Europe Region, Soviet Union, Cyprus*, Volume X, Part I, 1958/1960, 279.
66. On Khrushchev, see Fursenko and Naftali, *Khrushchev's Cold War*, 487.
67. Mukhitdinov, *Reka vremeni*, 273.
68. Ibid.
69. Ibid., 215.
70. Zubok and Pleshakov, *Inside the Kremlin's Cold War*, 190; Shepilov also conveyed to Khrushchev the trust he sensed trust and gratitude from Nasser and his ministers toward the Soviets. *Blizhnevostochnyi konflikt*, vol. 1, 436–37.
71. Mukhitdinov, *Gody, provedennye v Kremle*, 157; Mukhitdinov also describes being tasked by TsK KPSS with "handling Eastern politics (*zaimites' vostochnoi politikoi*)." Mukhitdinov, *Reka vremeni*, 302.
72. Zubkova, "Vlast' i razvitie," 4.
73. A nineteen-page handwritten letter preserved in Mukhitdinov's personal file describes him as a trickster (*plut*), deceitful (*khitrosts', listymerie*), exceptionally skilled in the art of perverting the truth (*soznatel'noe izvrashenie istiny*), power-hungry (*vlastoliubiv*), tyrannical (*tolerana*), and unscrupulous in personal matters (*v bytu ne chistoplotin*), specifically by pressuring female subordinates into compromising "cohabitation" (*sozhitel'stvo*) in exchange for positions in party-state organs (in the TsK, Orgkom, Goskomitet, and the Council of Ministers), and his retaliations for rejection. RGANI f. 3, op. 62, d. 141, ll. 3–21 (To Khrushchev from member of the party from 1941 [Ubeidokhon] Khaimove [Khalimova] . . . living in Tashkent, April 22, 1959); on their "patron-client relationship" see Carlisle, "The Uzbek Power Elite," 107.

74. Mukhitdinov, *Reka vremeni*, 165.
75. C. L. Sulzberger, "Moscow Revolutionizes Central Asia Differences Are Encouraged Deterioration Is Deliberate," *New York Times*, February 6, 1956, 22. Cyrus Sulzberger was nephew of publisher Arthur Hays Sulzberger. Some of Cyrus's colleagues have argued that he was a known CIA "asset." Carl Bernstein, "The CIA and the Media," accessed November 9, 2023, https://www.carlbernstein.com/the-cia-and-the-media-rolling-stone-10-20-1977.
76. Mukhitdinov, *Gody, provedennye v Kremle*, 207; these interviews conducted in 1953 were with subjects described as "middle aged members of the Soviet 'intelligentsia.'" Pipes, "Muslims of Soviet Central Asia."
77. Mukhitdinov, *Gody, provedennye v Kremle*, 207; Meyer, *Islam and Colonialism*, 18–19, 101–24.
78. NSC 158, "US Objectives and Actions to Exploit the Unrest in the Satellite States," June 29, 1953.
79. Mukhitdinov, *Gody, provedennye v Kremle*, 207.
80. On Khrushchev in Ukraine, see Taubman, *Khrushchev*, 179–207.
81. Loader, "Beria and Khrushchev"; Elena Zubkova, "Vlast' i razvitie."
82. Loader, "Beria and Khrushchev," 1762–64.
83. Ibid., 1766.
84. Taubman, *Khrushchev*, 249; Loader, "Beria and Khrushchev," 1788.
85. In his memoirs, Khrushchev recalled that "Beria was promoting the idea that Russian domination held sway in local areas.... [Local cadres] began thundering not only against Russians but also against national cadres who would not fight against Russian 'domination.' This happened in many Party organizations in the republics." Khrushchev, *Memoirs of Nikita Khrushchev*, 189. As Latvian propaganda chief Janis Avotins argued, "we gave them a reason to talk about the Russification of Latvia." Loader, "Beria and Khrushchev," 1775.
86. Loader, "Beria and Khrushchev," 1783.
87. Weiner, "The Empires Pay a Visit"; Hungarian protests inspired residents of western Ukraine to speak about the need to rise up against Soviet power. Wojnowski, *The Near Abroad*.
88. These "distortions" could be read from the popularization of "archaism" like "court poetry," or from attempts to "enclose (*zamknut'*) Uzbek culture and tear it away from the Union." Mukhitdinov, *Gody, provedennye v Kremle*, 48.
89. Ibid., 50–54.
90. Hansen, "Ambivalent Empire," 124.
91. From these positions he later helped organized the "Doctors' Plot." Mukhitdinov, *Reka vremeni*, 63; Hansen, "Ambivalent Empire," 110, 120–21. On Mukhitdinov's relationship with him see Mukhitdinov, *Gody, provedennye v Kremle*, 67–68.
92. Mukhitdinov, *Gody, provedennye v Kremle*, 236.
93. Ibid., 243.
94. Jones, "From the Secret Speech to the Burial of Stalin."
95. Mukhitdinov claimed to have challenged those opposing his rehabilitation, in vain, by asking how it was possible "to call these people enemies of the people, criminals, when they created Soviet power, the communist party . . . and contributed to making Uzbekistan an inseparable (*nerazryvnoi*) part of the Soviet Union?" Mukhitdinov, *Gody, provedennye v Kremle*, 213.

NOTES TO PAGES 168–170   309

96. Ibid., 213. As a result, Khodjaev was not rehabilitated until 1965. On the rehabilitation question see Hansen, "Ambivalent Empire," 222; Carlisle, "Clan and Politics in Uzbekistan," 294.
97. Mukhitdinov, *Gody, provedennye v Kremle*, 239; *Istoricheskie resheniia XX s"ezda i zadachi intelligentsia Uzbekistana*, 1956, 51; on this censorship of the "jadid" question see Tillett, *The Great Friendship*; Fedtke, "Jadids, Young Bukharans."
98. Carlisle, "Uzbek Power Elite," 107–9; Mukhitdinov was understandably more cautious about naming victims of purges in which he may have been directly implicated. For instance, with regard to 1940s and 1950s purges, he spoke of repressions of ideas, genres, or works of art, rather than of people. For instance, he rehabilitated the *makoms* (the same as Arabic *maq'am*), a popular genre of Central Asian musical drama that had been "undeservedly criticized" during his tenure. *Istoricheskie resheniia XX s"ezda KPSS i zadachi intelligentsii Uzbekistana*, 55, 62; Frolova-Walker, "National in Form, Socialist in Content."
99. Mukhitdinov cited Suleiman Azimov, former second secretary of the UzCP, who had been arrested in 1938 but survived his sentence until rehabilitation. *Istoricheskie resheniia XX s"ezda KPSS i zadachi intelligentsii Uzbekistana*, 60–61.
100. Ibid., 61.
101. Ibid., 61–62.
102. Other acknowledged aid was from oilmen from Baku and Grozny and from mining specialists from the Donbass and Kuzbass (Siberia). Ibid., 62.
103. Tromley, *Making the Soviet Intelligentsia*, 80–81; in 1925, Stalin had also called on KUTV students to join in fighting "the crusade conducted against our country by the bourgeois press"; see discussion in ch. 2.
104. *Istoricheskie resheniia XX s"ezda KPSS i zadachi intelligentsii Uzbekistana*, 7.
105. Ibid., 8.
106. Kalinovsky, *Laboratory of Socialist Development*, 53–55.
107. Nasyrkhodjaev, *Kompartiia Uzbekistana*, 10.
108. Ibid., 11.
109. There were ten research institutes in 1943 growing to twenty-eight in 1969; ibid., 19.
110. Ibid., 11.
111. Katsakioris, "The Lumumba University in Moscow"; Katsakioris, "Les étudiants de pays arabes."
112. Kalinovsky, *Laboratory of Socialist Development*, 41; Khlevniuk, *Regional'naia politika*, 484–87.
113. Nasyrkhodjaev, *Kompartiia Uzbekistana*, 17; on this new postwar Central Asian "proletarian intelligentsia" see Kalinovsky, *Laboratory of Socialist Development*, 44.
114. Obertreis, *Imperial Desert Dreams: Cotton Growing and Irrigation in Central Asia, 1860–1991*, 384.
115. Zezina, *Sovetskaia khudozhestvennaia intelligentsia i vlast' v 1950–60-e gody* (Moscow, 1999).
116. Tromply, *Making the Soviet Intelligentsia*, 5.
117. Ibid., 4–9.
118. Nasyrkhodjaev, *Kompartiia Uzbekistana*, 7

119. Ibid., 6, 13.
120. Martin, *Affirmative Action Empire*; Loader, "Beria and Khrushchev," 1790; Florin, "What Is Russia to Us?"
121. Kalinovsky, *Laboratory of Socialist Development*, 55–56.
122. Siegelbaum and Moch, "Transnationalism in One Country," 970–86.
123. Cited in Roi, *From Encroachment to Involvement*, 157.
124. Mikoyan, *Speech at the 20th Congress of the CPSU*, 36.
125. Mukhitdinov, *Gody, provedennye v Kremle*, 308–10.
126. *Materialy pervoi vsesoiuznoi nauchnoi konferentsii vostokovedov v g. Tashkente*, 35. Uzbek-Tajik competition over selective appropriations of a common past had been ongoing since the territorial divisions of 1924–1929. On Ghafurov's academic monographs about the history of the Tajik people in territories later claimed by Soviet Uzbekistan see Jansen, "Peoples' Internationalism Central Asian Modernisers"; Laruelle, "The Concept of Ethnogenesis."
127. Kalinovsky, *Laboratory of Socialist Development*, 205.
128. *Materialy pervoi vsesoiuznoi nauchnoi konferentsii vostokovedov v g. Tashkente*, 33, 35.
129. Mukhitdinov, *Reka vremeni*, 265. Ghafurov also continued to channel resources to support Tajik interests by organizing large conferences in Dushanbe. Kalinovsky, *Laboratory of Socialist Development*, 203.
130. When Ghafurov reported back to the TsK KPSS about changes to Soviet Oriental Studies in Moscow and in Central Asia in 1958, his letters were addressed to Mukhitdinov. RGANI f. 5, op. 35, d. 78, ll. 1–7 (Letter from Ghafurov in the Academy of Sciences to the Secretary of TsK KPSS Mukhitdinov, February 21, 1958).
131. Bukhter, "G. A. Neresov o V. B. Lutskii," 82; Seiranian, "V. B. Lutskii (1906–62)—uchenyi, pedagog, chelovek," 326–43.
132. Non-Jewish interwar MIV graduates who had supported Lutskii in 1953, like the South-East Asia specialist Aleksandr Guber and the Turkologist Nikolai Smirnov, had long reached the rank of "professor." Lutskii's colleagues' assessment of his academic rank of *kandidat nauk* as incommensurate with his stature is mentioned in Bukhert, "G. A. Nerserov o V. B Lutskom," 82.
133. Mukhitdinov, *Gody, provedennye v Kremle*, 5; Hansen shows that in the final version of the Congress document, Suslov's recommended language about a future "fusion" or merging (*sliianie*) of nationalities and languages was indeed replaced by a fraternal *sblizheniie* (drawing together) on the advice of Otto Kuusinen, who advised that the latter formulation would "have greater influence amongst the millions of people in Asia, Africa, and Latin America who are fighting for their national cause." Hansen, "Ambivalent Empire," 268.
134. It did not help that the Congress followed a conflict over the discovery of pervasive fraud orchestrated in Tajikistan at every level of the state bureaucracy, which Mukhitdinov had been sent to troubleshoot. Kalinovsky, *Laboratory*, 38–39. In the aftermath of the shakeup in Tajikistan, central authorities reasserted control in Central Asia through the newly formed Central Asian Bureau (1962–1964) and a "rotation of cadres principle" for officeholders that limited the tenure of elected functionaries to

avoid the "accumulation of powers in single hands." Hansen, "Ambivalent Empire," 262, 266; Mukhitdinov later learned of the role played by Rashidov in convincing Khrushchev and the Party to remove him from the Presidium. Mukhitdinov, *Reka vremeni*, 529, 549; for Mukhitdinov's role in troubleshooting contentious national disputes in Azerbaijan see Goff, *Nested Nationalisms*, 107.

135. Mukhitdinov, *Reka vremeni*, 538.
136. Ibid., 531.
137. On Western scholarship on this topic see Myer, *Islam*. On Chinese critics, Jeremy Friedman, *The Shadow Cold War*, 89.
138. Mukhitdinov, *Reka vremeni*, 567.
139. Gilburd, *To See Paris and Die*, 55.
140. Ibid., 35–42.
141. RGANI f. 89, op. 55, d. 22, ll. 1–2 (TsK Secretariat instructions on SSOD friendships, July 31, 1958).
142. Dawisha, "Soviet Cultural Relations," 428.
143. Agreements were signed with Egypt on June 22, with Syria on June 26, and with Lebanon on June 28. On the agreement with Egypt: RGALI f. 2329, op. 8, d. 323, l. 49 (Newspaper clipping from *La Bourse Egyptienne* September 1, 1956); on Syria and Lebanon: RGALI f. 2329, op. 8, d. 323, ll. 2–5 (Translations from *al-Nur* newspaper, August 21, 1956), ll. 6–11 (Translations from *Alif Ba* newspaper, August 21, 1956); and l. 29 (Arabic original).
144. Had it not been for the large Armenian colony in Syria, he added, the Armenian dance troupe would not be very successful either. RGALI f. 2329, op. 8, d. 2296, l. 11 (Note from Embassy of USSR in Syria about discussion with Faisal Daliati, director of the Damascus Fair on March 2, 1962). The name of the director Faisal Daliati is transliterated from Russian and sounds strangely un-Arabic. Perhaps he was Kurdish.
145. Between August 18 and October 8, 1966, Berezka performed in Syria, Jordan, Lebanon, Kuwait, and Iraq; earlier that year, it had also toured Alexandria, Beirut, Port Said, Morocco, and Algeria, and had performed at the Baalbek International Arts Festival. RGALI f. 2329, op. 9, d. 1280, ll. 41–47 (Nadezhdina's Interview with Iraqi newspaper, *Sawt al-Arab*, September 27, 1966).
146. TsGA Uz f. 2661, op. 1, d. 133, l. 9 (Letter from Lebanese Embassy representative Shmeliakov to Shukurova, September 25, 1964).
147. TsGA Uz f. 2661, op. 1, d. 150, l. 211 (Embassy of USSR in Lebanon to UzSOD, May 10, 1965).
148. Harris, "Dawn of the Soviet Jet Age," 591.
149. In 1963, 700 Soviet Uzbeks were able to travel abroad as part of Soviet delegations; of them, 495 (or 70.7%) went to Asia, 115 (16.4%) to countries of Africa, 113 (16.1%) to Europe, and 20 (2.8%) to the United States. Twenty-three of the delegates visited more than one continent. Another 1,093 Uzbek tourists were permitted to travel abroad in 1963, also disproportionately to Asia and Africa. TsGA Uz f. 2661, op. 1, d. 108, ll. 80–86 (Decision of Presidium of Uzbek SOD, April 1963, about work of

Uzbek Society of Friendship and Cultural Ties with Foreign Countries about work with Asia and Africa).

150. For the numbers for 1956 see TsGA Uz, f. 837, op. 38, d. 8468, ll.1–9 (Spravka about Improving the Uzbek Society of Cultural Ties with the Abroad from 1957); for numbers for 1963 see TsGA Uz f. 2574 (Shirinbaev Personal File), op. 1, d. 8a, ll. 1–3 (Foreign Relations of Uzbek SSR, 1963).

151. TsGA Uz f. 2574, op. 1, d. 8a, ll. 1–3 (Foreign Relations of Uzbek SSR, 1963); by 1965, 20,000 tourists were projected in Tashkent yearly. TsGA Uz f. 2661, op. 1, d. 66, l. 30a (Numbers of Foreign Tourists Serviced in Tashkent by Intourist, 1960); *Pravda Vostoka* reported 874 delegations in 1959 of 4,716 people and 2,268 tourists. See "Vtoroi s"ezd intelligentsii Uzbekistana," *Pravda Vostoka* (December 12, 1959), 4, cited in Stronski, *Tashkent*, 320.

152. In 1962, UzSOD was also organizing visits for over 200 foreign students from eleven countries of Africa and Asia to industrial complexes, collective farms, and arranging "meetings, conversations, and lectures about Soviet reality (*sovetskaia deistvitel'nost'*)." TsGA Uz f. 2661, op. 1, d. 108, ll. 80–86 (Decision of Presidium of Uzbek SOD about work with Asia and Africa, April 1963). Some of these foreigners included students from the University of Friendship of Peoples named after Patrice Lumumba coming for vacation. TsGA Uz f. 2661, op. 1, d. 238, ll. 64–65 (Students from Lumumba Visiting Tashkent, 1968).

153. Of the 110 delegations in 1956, 64 had come from countries of the "foreign East." TsGA Uz f. 2574, op. 1, d. 8a, ll. 1–3 (Foreign Relations of Uzbek SSR, 1963).

154. "Wa qad thaqafi suri yazur al-ittihad al-sufiyati," *Al thaqafa al-wataniyya* 7 (1957): 70.

155. Djagalov, *From Internationalism to Postcolonialism*, 31.

156. The 1958 Afro-Asian Writers Conference participants including KUTV graduate Nazim Hikmet, and returning visitors W. E. B. Du Bois and Mao Dun. Djagalov, *From Internationalism to Postcolonialism*, ch. 1 and 2.

157. For objections by the Egyptian delegation headed by Yusuf al-Sibai see RGALI f. 5, op. 36, d. 63, l. 10 (On Sibai's questions, June 1958); for the Algerians' efforts see RGALI f. 5, op. 36, d. 63, l. 9 (Members of AAWC Preparatory Committee Meeting in Moscow, June 1958); on objections of the African Cultural Society see Katsakioris, "L'union soviétique et les intellectuels africains Internationalisme."

158. TsGA Uz f. 837, op. 38, d. 8468, ll.1–9 (Memo about Improving the Uzbek Society of Cultural Ties with Foreign Countries, February 20, 1957).

159. Gilburd, *To See Paris and Die*, 36.

160. They played "Algeria My Homeland," "Daughter of the Ganges," "Kashmir Song," and others. TsGA Uz f. 837, op. 38, d. 9226, ll. 20–23 (Memo on Implementing Tsk KPUz directives for preparing for AAW Conference, June 29, 1958).

161. TsGA Uz f. 2487, op. 1, d. 109, l. 71 (Rakhimbabaeva's Speech at the Navoi Theater, June 16, 1958).

162. Mal'tsev, *Tashkentskie vstrechi*; TsGA Uz f. 837, op. 38, d. 9226, ll. 78–80 (Translation from English of "Tashkent Conference" by Ralf Parker).

163. Nasser visited Tashkent the same year, greeted in a spectacular ceremony by tens of thousands of Uzbeks. Interview with Guzal Alimova, who grew up in Tashkent, in winter 2012.
164. TsGA Uz f. 2661, op. 1, d. 150, l. 62 (Event Plans for 1965).
165. Writer Hamid Guliam spoke to radio and television audiences about his impressions of Algeria and Lebanon; Navoi Theater director Habibulla Rahmanov spoke about his trip to Tunis, Algeria, and Morocco; poet Sultan Akbari and journalist Snajar Tilla who spoke about their trips to the OAR and the Sudan. TsGA Uz f. 2661, op. 1, d. 114, ll. 64–72 (Report about expansion of Ties with Arab Countries, 1963).
166. Gilburd, *To See Paris and Die*, 36–37. Shirinbaev mentioned requests to join Society from Tashkent region kolkhozes, sovkhozes, scientific/educational institutes, public organizations, factories, the Musical Theatre named after Mukimi, and schools. Requests also came from the Bukhara Silk Spinning Factory and the Fergana Textile Factory. TsGA Uz f. 2661, op. 1, d. 52, ll. 2–29 (UzOKS Section on Friendship with Arab Countries Presidium meeting, December 19, 1958).
167. The Presidium included the Uzbek Republican Ministers of Culture, Foreign Affairs, Finance, Trade, and Construction, Chairmen of the Council of Ministers, the First Secretary of the Bukhara City Party Committee, Tashkent City Executive Committee, Secretary of the Committee of Youth Organizations (KMO), academics from the Institute of Oriental Studies, Institute of Archeology and Ethnography, the Institute of Particle Physics Research, poet Gafur Guliam, and a "mother hero," Kh. Yusupova. TsGA Uz f. 2661, op. 1, d. 52, ll. 37–40 (List of founding members of the UzSOD Society of Friendship with the Arab East, December 19, 1958); also TsGA f. 2661, op. 1, d. 46, l. 17 (UzSOD members of Presidium of the Society of Friendship with Arab Countries, December 19, 1958).
168. TsGA Uz f. 2661, op. 1, d. 114, ll. 64–72 (UzSOD Report on Ties with Arab Countries, 1964); TsGA Uz f. 2661, op. 1, d. 52, ll. 1–20 (First Meeting of the Presidium of the UzSOD Society of Friendship with Arab Countries, December 19, 1958).
169. TsGA Uz f. 2574, op. 1, d. 121, ll. 1–3 (Shirinbaev's autobiography).
170. TsGA Uz f. 2574, op. 1, d. 52, ll.1–6 (Report to TsK head Rahimbabaeva about the problem of cadres in UzOKS, December 19, 1957); the request by the Communist Party that UzSOD focus its attention and propaganda on countries in Africa and Asia was reiterated in 1963. TsGA Uz f. 2661, op. 1, d. 108, ll. 80–86 (UzSOD Presidium directive, April 1963). At this time, Chinese, Hindi, and Arabic also became priority secondary languages. They were taught in some of the Tashkent secondary schools and the Ministry of Education of Uzbekistan began preparing new textbooks. Barghoorn, *Soviet Cultural Offensive*, 173. Shirinbaev's official justification for the purge was "nepotistic relations" (*semeistvennosti i panibratskogo otnoshenia*, literally "family-like and pan-brotherly relations"), echoing earlier critiques of *semeistvennost'* (familyness) in the Uzbek party apparatus made by Stalin in 1937 and Ignat'ev in 1950. Hansen, "Ambivalent Empire," 120; Carlisle, "Clan and Politics," 271–77.

171. TsGA Uz f. 2661, op. 1, d. 52, ll. 1–20 (First Meeting of the Presidium of the Uzbek Branch of the Society for Cultural Relations with Arab Countries, December 19, 1958).
172. Ibid.; Nasser's statements about this are mentioned in Mukhitdinov, *Reka vremeni*, 211.
173. For more on the SKSSAA see Casula, "The Soviet Afro-Asian Solidarity Committee."
174. The number of monuments opened to foreigners expanded from 50 in 1953 to over 300 in 1956, with initial funding allocated for the restoration of architectural monuments, mostly in Samarkand. TsGA Uz f. 837, op. 41, d. 207, ll. 83–89 (Plans for Restoring Historical Monuments, April 2, 1965, signed by the Representative of the Commission of the Highest Council of UzSSR for Foreign Affairs). The Navoi Theater was also renovated before the 1958 Afro-Asian events. Kirasirova, "Building Anti-Colonial Utopia."
175. GARF f. 9540, op. 1, d. 2, l. 15 (From transcript of Presidium meeting on November 1, 1956).
176. He was part of a Central Asian delegation that embarked on the hajj in 1954. "Soviet Muslims in Mecca," *Moscow News* 22 (1954): 28. On Babakhanov's role in Soviet foreign affairs see Taser, *Soviet and Muslim*.
177. He attended the Afro-Asian Islamic conference in Indonesia in early 1965, as well as other such events. Friedman, *The Shadow Cold War*, 111.
178. TsGA Uz f. 2661, op. 1, d. 52, ll. 2–29 (Presidium of meeting of UzOKS section of friendship with Arab countries, December 19, 1958).
179. Di-Capua, *No Exit*, 24.
180. "Khrushchev's 'Report of the Party's Central Committee,' delivered on February 14, 1956," cited in Roi, *From Encroachment to Involvement*, 157–59.
181. Mukhitdinov's report to the Twenty-first Congress of the CPSU, from Roi, *From Encroachment*, 283.
182. Myer, *Islam and Colonialism*, 94–95.
183. Ibid., 95.
184. Von Eschen, *Satchmo Blows Up the World*, 4.
185. The ANSAC, formed after the Congress of Colored Writers and Artists in Paris. It helped silence earlier Black American anticolonial activists such as Du Bois and Robeson. Von Eschen, *Race against Empire*, 175–76, 184.
186. GARF f. 9540, op. 1, d. 60, ll. 3–17 (SKSSAA Presidium Meeting, January 8, 1960); Mikoyan suggested creating the Central Asian Chamber in Tashkent to handle Soviet representation at Afro-Asian conferences. Friedman, *Shadow*, 109.
187. GARF f. 9540, op.1, d. 80. ll. 59–60; GARF f.9540 o.1 d.109, l. 85 (SKSSAA Presidium Meeting, January 8, 1962).
188. Friedman, *The Shadow Cold War*, 110.
189. GARF f. 9540, op.1, d. 81, ll. 3–4 (Transcript of SKSSAA Presidium meeting in Moscow, May 18, 1961).
190. Casula, "Soviet Afro-Asian Solidarity," 514; Brutents, *Tridsat' let*, 375; Vasiliev, *Rossiia na blizhnem i srednem vostoke*, 238; some have pointed out that SKSSAA activities were directly overseen by Ulianovskii. Kitrinos, "The CPSU Central Committee's International Department," 184; Schapiro, "The International Department of the CPSU."

191. Shubin was responsible for African Affairs at the SKSSAA from 1969 to 1979 and worked at the Internal Department from 1982 to 1991. Conversation with Vladimir Shubin, September 11, 2020.
192. Kalinovsky, *Laboratory of Socialist Development*, 66.
193. Eschen, *Race against Empire*, 3–6, 187.
194. Djagalov, *From Internationalism to Postcolonialism*, 113–15, 143.
195. Mukhitdinov, *Reka vremeni*, 585, 620–24.
196. Ibid., 625.

Chapter 6

1. Cited in Naftali, *Khrushchev's Cold War*, 339.
2. China's campaign to replace the Soviet Union as the main inspiration for the decolonizing world was only somewhat slowed down by the Sino-Indian war of 1962, which made China's behavior seem narrow-minded and nationalistic. Westad, *Global Cold War*, 163; Friedman, *Shadow Cold War*.
3. Goff, *Nested Nationalism*, 150.
4. Goff describes how in this period researchers working on national minorities, as well as people producing censuses, maps, and textbooks strengthened their claims about smaller non-titular groups merging (*sblizhenie*) with the larger titular national ones, like the Talysh merging with the Azerbaijanis, which contributing to the erasure of minorities and their sense of alienation. Goff, *Nested Nationalism*, 161–68.
5. Kalinovsky, *Laboratory of Socialist Development*, 41.
6. Michae Loader, "A Stalinist Purge in the Khrushchev Era? The Latvian Communist Party Purge, 1959–1963."
7. For instance, the Tricontinental Conference in Havana in January 1966—where both China and the USSR were present alongside delegates from eighty-two other "non-Western" countries gathered around anticolonial and anti-imperial issues—left a massive cultural imprint even if little from it translated into political change. Young, "Disseminating the Tricontinental."
8. These challenges were sometimes accompanied by the losses of strategic military or naval positions, such as the loss of the Albanian-Soviet submarine base off the coastal city of Vlorë in the culmination of the Soviet-Albanian row. Mëhilli, *From Stalin to Mao*, 202.
9. Lüthi, *The Sino-Soviet Split*, ch. 2; Friedman, *Shadow Cold War*.
10. The outbreak of ethnic conflict in Xinjiang in 1962, with mass flight of ethnic Central Asians and Russians to the Soviet Union, further taxed relations between Beijing and Moscow, which did not disappear under the new Brezhnev administration. For more on the deterioration of relations see Lüthi, *Sino-Soviet Split*, ch. 6.
11. Fursenko and Naftali, *Khrushchev's Cold War*, 411.
12. Ibid., 434.

13. Friedman, *Shadow Cold War*, 94.
14. On Castro's critique see Fursenko and Naftali, *Khrushchev's Cold War*, 490.
15. Westad, *Global Cold War*, 184; Friedman, *Shadow Cold War*, 129–30; Radchenko, *Two Suns in the Heaven*, 141–43; Jian, *Mao's Cold War*.
16. Westad, *Global Cold War*, 105; the Soviets withheld military aid and Khrushchev actually endorsed the French offer of self-determination, explaining to de Gaulle that "he hoped the French would remain in some form in Algeria because if they left the Americans would move in and that would be worse." Connelly, *Diplomatic Revolution. Algeria's Fight for Independence and the Origins of the Post–Cold War Era*, 226–27.
17. Connelly, *Diplomatic Revolution*, 28.
18. One report claimed that an item published in Beijing was available in bookstores in Algiers five days later. Friedman, *Shadow Cold War*, 96.
19. Ibid., 126.
20. Particularly momentous were refusals of the Romanian, British, and Italian communist parties. Ibid.; the Soviet Union was able to reassert its power as leader of the international communist movement and hold a last meeting of international communist community in June 1969. Although its involvement in the developing world would increase in the 1970s in terms of resources devoted to Asia, Africa, and Latin America, its work would be more decentralized and focused on building parties and armies rather than dams and factories. Andrew and Mitrokhin, *The World Was Going Our Way*, 178.
21. Friedman, *Shadow Cold War*, 127.
22. In fall 1963, *Novosti* also launched a publication called *Questions of the World Communist Movement* in English, French, Spanish, and Russian to cover the conflict with China. Rupen, "Peking's Challenge to Moscow," 375; on Soviet embassies' anti-Chinese activities, such as seminars on the "Problems of Development of Revolution and the Struggle for Socialism in Liberated Countries" in Cairo, Algiers, and Baku, see Friedman, *Shadow Cold War*, 106–8; on other Chinese propaganda offensives see Lovell, *Maoism: A Global History*, 135–36, 146–50.
23. Friedman, *Shadow Cold War*, 145–46.
24. Ibid., 144, 150–55.
25. Ibid., 149. In 1970, NAM finally was able to arrange its third conference, in the Zambian capital Lusaka, but with much of the initial optimism gone. Westad, *Global Cold War*, 107.
26. On Soviet studies of Mao's propaganda initiatives after 1966 see RGANI f. 5, op. 60, d. 44, ll. 14–48 (Report on the Foreign Propaganda of Mao's Group to the Section of Higher Education Organizations TsK KPSS, by the Institute of Far East under the Academy of Sciences, April 30, 1968).
27. The collapse of the United Arab Republic in September 1961 was followed by a period of unstable military rule (September 1961–March 1963), then a period of rule by a right-wing Ba'ath Colonel Lu'ay al-Atasi and General Amin al-Hafiz (March 1963–February 1966); followed by a left-wing Ba'ath regime of President Nur al-Din al-Atasi and General Salah Jadid (February 1966–November 1970). Hafez al-Assad

assumed de facto power in March 1969 (before arresting the former leader Salah al-Jadid in November 1970). Ramet, *Soviet-Syrian Relationship*, 31–43.

28. Direct relations were not resumed until January 1991 (three years before the publication of his memoirs). Mukhitdinov also advised against allowing Soviet and other socialist bloc volunteers to participate in any Arab-Israeli war because it would be too "costly" and because it would mean that the Soviet Union was going to war against a state it helped to create. Mukhitdinov, *Reka vremeni*, 589–90, 597.
29. Atasi was soon deposed and imprisoned by Assad in November 1970.
30. Mukhitdinov, *Reka vremeni*, 592.
31. Materials sent included the films *When the Cranes Fly* and *13 Seagulls*, sound recordings of *Uzbekistan over 50 Years*, and a TV film about the 1966 earthquake. TsGA Uz f. 2661, op. 1, d. 226, l. 34 (Memo on activities of SSOD in Arab world, 1968).
32. On "affirmative action" in the Soviet East see Martin, *Affirmative Action Empire*, 159–77; Fitzpatrick, *Education and Social Mobility*, ch. 9.
33. Yarmatov, *Vozvrashchenie: Vospominanie*, 74.
34. Ibid., 99.
35. He later discovered during a screening of the Kiev Film that the team had already filmed many scenes with his character using another actor, such that in the end "without knowing the screenplay or role, having been paid for one episode of work, without realizing it I had played an important role—that of a prince!" Yarmatov, *Vozvrashchenie*, 110–20; for more on these early films, including in *The Jackals of Ravat* (Uzbekkino, 1927) see Drieu, *Cinema, Nation, Empire*, 68.
36. Chomentowski, "Filmmakers from Africa and the Middle East at VGIK."
37. RGALI f. 2936, op. 4, d.1927, ll. 1–7 (Yarmatov's report about trip to Lebanon, Syria and UAR).
38. Although he recalled some personal disappointment with this treatment, he allowed the VGIK director to persuade him that the need for "national cadres" and was a critical prerogative of Soviet policy. Yarmatov, *Vozvrashchenie*, 135.
39. Ibid., 136.
40. Ibid., 150.
41. Ibid., 138.
42. Ibid., 163.
43. Ibid., 129.
44. An example of someone in love with the East, Yarmatov was the screenwriter Leonid Solov'ev, author of "Tale of Naserddin." Ibid., 65.
45. Ibid., 166.
46. Ibid., 172.
47. Edward Lazzerini, "Local Accommodations and Resistance to Colonialism in Nineteenth-Century Crimea," 176–85; on his efforts to curb immigration see Meyer, "Immigration, Return, and the Politics of Citizenship."
48. Estimates for Muslim emigration from the tsarist to Ottoman empires vary from around 600,000 from the Russian Caucasus during 1855–1907, cited in Meyer, "Immigration, Return, and the Politics of Citizenship," 29, to over one million. The numerical differences are outlined in Hamed-Troyansky, "Circassian Refugees," 607 (ft. 14).

49. On migration in the interwar period, see Masden, "Beyond Bukhara."
50. Yarmatov, *Vozvrashchenie*, 180.
51. He used Samarkand as the basis for this "eastern bourgeois-feudal city." Ibid., 176 (gulestan), 186 (za rubezh).
52. Ibid., 131–32.
53. Ibid., 189.
54. Ibid., 195.
55. Ram, *The Imperial Sublime*.
56. Yarmatov describes the rejection of Khodjaev's film screened right before his own in Yarmatov, *Vozvrashchenie*, 190.
57. *Before Dawn* was classified as "an act of resistance to the ideological assimilation by Soviet and Russian hegemony and ultimately insist[ed] on how unreal any imported national enterprise is while assimilating Russian revolutionary discourse." Drieu, *Cinema, Nation, Empire*, 197–98.
58. Drieu argues that Uzbekfilm lost many of its managers to purges of nationalist groups who had been in control, and production was entirely ruined. Drieu, *Cinema, Nation, Empire*, 199; on the Caucasus see Kenez, *Cinema and Soviet Society*, 172; film historian Sergei Kapterev speculated that Yarmatov had denounced too many people in Tajikistan to return.
59. RGALI f. 2679, op. 1, d. 802, ll. 2–3 (Yarmatov's Letter to Kuleshov, July 18, 1942); one of the concerts Yarmatov filmed featured Kari-Yakubov (discussed in ch. 4). Kamil Yarmatov, "O vremeni i o sebe," *Iskusstvo kino* 10 (October 1972): 18–34, 26.
60. On the 500th anniversary jubilee of Alisher Navoi planned at an All-Union level see Khalid, *Making Uzbekistan*, 388–89.
61. Yarmatov, *Vozvrashchenie*, 232.
62. It was estimated to have been watched by over 300 million people internationally in 1949. RGALI F. 966, op. 2, d. 913, ll. 3–36 (1949 article by Minister of Cinematography Ivan Grigor'evich Bol'shakov); on prizes, see Drieu, "Alisher Navoi: prix Staline 1948."
63. Cited in Drieu, *Cinema, Nation, and Empire in Uzbekistan*, 231.
64. Ibid., 231.
65. See tables for imports of Soviet films (in kilos) in Dawisha, "Soviet Cultural Relations with Iraq, Syria, and Egypt," 431.
66. Braginskii, "Zhizhninnye paradoksy," *Narody Azii i Afriki* 4 (1964): 268–71 (270).
67. RGALI f. 2918, op. 1 d. 41, l. 69 (Letter from the Ministry of Culture to SovExportFilm director Davydov about Films for Damascus International Fair, February 21, 1956).
68. RGALI f. 2918, op. 1, d. 41, ll. 59–61 (Films recommended for the 1956 Damascus International Fair).
69. Gordon, *Revolutionary Melodrama*, 115–16.
70. On the Egyptian government's role in the expansion of the publishing field see Klein, "Egypt's Revolutionary Publishing Culture, 1952–62."
71. Halim, "Lotus, the Afro-Asian Nexus and Global South Comparatism."
72. By 1958, al-Siba'i was the first secretary-general of the newly established Higher Council for the Arts and Letters (1956) and presided over other state and quasi-state institutions, such the Association of Men of Letters (jam'iyyat al-udaba', founded in

1955), which operated as the Egyptian branch of the Congress of Arab Writers. DiCapua, *No Exit: Arab Existentialism, Jean-Paul Sartre, and Decolonization*, 113.
73. RGANI f. 5, op. 36, d. 81, ll. 66–76 (Letter from Head of Organizing Committee of Countries of Asia and Africa in Tashkent to TsK KPSS, September 15, 1958).
74. Lebanon and Iraq declined their invitations because of tense political situations, and Cambodia, Turkey, and South Africa declined because they claimed they did not have films. Iran, Malaysia, Singapore, Tunisia, and the Philippines did not answer the invitations. RGANI f. 5, op. 35, d. 81, ll. 66–76 (Report of Organizational Committee of Afro-Asian Film Festival head R. Gulamov to the TsK KPSS, September 15, 1958).
75. Duberman, *Paul Robeson*, ch. 23.
76. RGANI f. 5, op. 35, d. 81, ll. 64–65 (Information about AAFF from the Head of Section of Culture of TsK KPSS, September 8, 1958.
77. RGANI f. 5, op. 55, d. 113, ll. 77–85 (List of Afro-Asian Festival Participants).
78. Like Yarmatov, Faiziev also studied at VGIK and was a decorated artist of the UzSSR. His film *Po putevke Lenina* dealt with the organization of the first University for Central Asians, and was timely considering the growing international demand for study in the USSR.
79. Yarmatov, *Vozvrashchenie*, 263.
80. Karen Dawisha, "Soviet Cultural Relations," 432.
81. His mother was the daughter of Iranian landowner of Zabolestan in eastern Afghanistan.
82. Yarmatov, *Vozvrashchenie*, 264.
83. RGALI f. 2912, op. 1, d. 584, ll.1–56 (Uzbek Film Studio meeting of 1958 Afro-Asian Film Festival participants Transcript).
84. Ibid., l. 21.
85. RGANI f. 5, op. 35, d. 81, l. 63 (Letter from Head of Culture of TsK KPSS D. Polikarpov and Section Head A. Sazanov, August 29, 1958).
86. RGANI f. 5, op. 35, d. 81, ll. 66–76 (Report to the TsK KPSS by Afro-Asian Film Festival organizational committee leader R. Gulamov, September 15, 1958).
87. On the failure of Soviet cultural diplomats to tailor their repertoires see Applebaum, *Empire of Friends: Soviet Power and Socialist Internationalism in Cold War Czechoslovakia*.
88. Myer, *Islam and Colonialism*, 125–61.
89. The Soviet delegation included head of UzSSR Goskomitet Kino Muhamedov, Kyrgyz SSR Ministry of Culture's Film Section Chief Usubaliev; the Kazakh actress Umurzakova, editor of *Sovetskii Ekran* (Soviet Screen) Pisarevski; and SovExportFilm official Stoliarskii. RGANI f. 5, op. 55, d. 113, ll. 89-98 (Report to the TsK KPSS International and Ideological sections and to MID from the Embassy of USSR in Indonesia, June 11, 1964).
90. The delegation was also instructed to edit out a section of *Piatero iz Fergany* that showed destruction of flags with Muslim symbols, but things were so disorganized that SSOD official Deikov had to "use personal connections and influence" to edit out these scenes just minutes before screening. Ibid.
91. On Sukarno's relations with China see Liu, "Constructing a China Metaphor."

92. RGANI f. 5, op. 55, d. 113, ll. 89-98 (Report to the TsK KPSS International and Ideological sections and to Ministry of Foreign Affairs from the Embassy of USSR in Indonesia, June 11, 1964).
93. RGANI f. 5, op. 55, d. 113, ll. 99-102 (Report to TsK KPSS on Soviet film propaganda in Indonesia by Ambassador N. Mikhailov, July 5, 1964).
94. RGANI f. 5, op. 55, d. 113, l. 103 (Letter from Deputies of Ideological and International Sections A. Romanov and V. Korionov, September 6, 1964).
95. On "rebuttal writers" see the "BENNIGSEN, ALEXANDRE" entry in *Encyclopedia Iranica*. Also V. Ustinov, "Protiv fal'sifikatsii istorii Srednei Azii Kazakhstana," *Voprosy istorii* 9 (1963): 100-3.
96. Tillett, *The Great Friendship*, 105-9, 149-93; Abashin, "Soviet Central Asia on the Periphery"; Khalid, *Central Asia: A New History from the Imperial Conquests to the Present*.
97. Yarmatov, *Vozvrashchenie*, 273-74.
98. Ibid., 274.
99. Those he knew who suffered were not only the aforementioned Suleiman Khodjaev (1892-1937) but also Yarmatov's friend Nabi Ganiev, imprisoned from 1937 to 1939, whose film *Jigit* (Uzbekkino, 1936) was found "superficial" and "clumsy" by S. L. Vel'tman. S. Vel'tman, "Ob ostavanii kino v natsrespublikakh," *Revoliutsiia i natsional'nosti* 10 (1936): 75-77.
100. Tillett, *The Great Friendship*.
101. Drieu, *Cinema, Nation, and Empire*, 225.
102. Andreas Kappeler, "The Russian Empire and Its Nationalities in Post-Soviet Historiographies," 36.
103. Carlisle, "The Uzbek Power Elite," 115.
104. Some filmmakers managed to survive making films about the revolution in Central Asia, including *Rybaki arala* (1957) and *Po putevke Lenina* (1958). Yarmatov initially attempted to duck the project by reminding Rashidov of another such film, *Plamennye gody* (The flaming years, 1958, by the Alekseev brothers). Yarmatov, *Vozvrashchenie*, 274.
105. Ibid., 274.
106. Ibid., 280.
107. Ibid., 281-82.
108. Ibid., 286.
109. Ibid., 286-87.
110. Ibid., 288.
111. On history being rewritten by art, see Kane Petrone, *Life Has Become More Joyous*, 200, 150.
112. Originally the film was titled "Dawn over Asia," then "Son of the Earth." The final title of the film was one it shared with Vsevolod Pudovkin's classic dramatization of anti-imperial revolt in Central Asia, *Storm over Asia* (1928).
113. Corney, *Telling October*, 242 (ft. 123).
114. Yarmatov, *Vozvrashchenie*, 291.
115. Ibid.
116. Teshabaev, *Schast'e mastera: o tvorchestve kinorezhissera Kamila Iarmatova*, 103.

117. Ibid., 94.
118. Ibid., 103–4.
119. Florin, "What Is Russia to US?," 185.
120. The transcripts were kept in the manuscripts section of the National Academy of Sciences and remained largely inaccessible until the collapse of the Soviet Union. Chokobaeva, Drieu, and Morrison, introduction, to *The Central Asian Revolt of 1916*, 8.
121. Florin, "What Is Russia to US?," 184.
122. RGANI, f. 5, op. 55, d. 112, l. 51 (Commission's Report to the TsK, July 1, 1964). The Commission warned that in the Central Asian context, there were not enough Soviet films and too many foreign action films (*boiveki*) were screened for the rural population.
123. The average Uzbek attended the movie theater an average of 10 times per year; in the first quarter of 1963 Navoi movie theater screened Soviet films 165 times, films from other socialist countries 222 times, and films from capitalist countries 383 times. In Voton Theater only 207 of 712 screenings were of Soviet films. RGANI, f. 5, op. 55, d. 112, ll. 54–62 (Deputy head of Cinematography of TsK KPSS Ideological Section about the state of film services for the population of the Uzbek SSR, July 29, 1964).
124. Rashidov was updated on Uzbekfilm's new cadres, including eighteen graduates of Moscow's VGIK and Leningrad's Universitet Kino i Televidenia (LIKI) (University of Cinema and Television) joining in 1964, the training of 250 film technicians, and Uzbekistan's Ministry of Cinematography plans to build thirty-four new movie theaters. TsGA f. 837, op. 41, d. 303, ll. 159–60 (Letter to Head of Uz Soviet of Ministers Kurbanov, from Uzbek Ministry of Cinematography head Azizhon Kaiumov, June 3, 1965); and TsGA f. 837, op. 41, d. 303, l. 172 (Report to Uzbek Council of Ministers about increasing the "kinoset," June 8, 1965).
125. TsGA f. 837, op. 41, d. 304, l. 27 (Report about cinefication of the countryside to the Council of Ministers, July 13, 1965; TsGA f. 837, op 41, d. 304, ll. 50–52 (Report to Uzbek Council of Ministers about the cinefication of Surxondaryo Province, September 1965).
126. Prokhorov, "Springtime for Soviet Cinema re/viewing the 1960s," 8; by the late 1960s, proceeds continued to grow every year. RGANI f. 5, op. 60, d. 66, ll. 9–13 (Report to TsK KPSS from Deputy Head of Culture of TsK KPSS, V. Shauro, February 2, 1968).
127. TsGA f. 837, op. 41, d. 682, ll. 56–66 (Report to Uzbek Council of Ministers by Head of UzCinefication, August 3, 1966).
128. RGANI f. 5, op. 60, d. 66, ll. 9–13 (Report to TsK KPSS from Deputy Head of Culture of TsK KPSS, V. Shauro, February 2, 1968).
129. TsGA f. 837, op. 41, d. 682, ll. 14–23 (Memo on Cinefication to Council of Ministers of USSR, August 4, 1966).
130. TsGA f. 837, op. 41, d. 860, ll. 149–55 (Memo on Cinefication of Samarkand, 1966).
131. City planners reorganized traffic flow, built a metro, and made other changes that would, in Brezhnev's words, allow Tashkent to be reborn. Stronski, *Tashkent: Forging a Soviet City 1930–1966*, 271–72.
132. Kirasirova, "Building Anti-Colonial Utopia," 59–61.

133. Some of this rhetoric was in support of the Palestinian cause, although as Ramet argues, the Soviets had little intrinsic interest in the Palestinians and as late as August 1967 characterized the Palestinian guerrillas as having "chauvinistic tendencies." After 1967 they were concerned about the problem of Palestinian refugees more than questions of Palestinian national rights. Remet, *Soviet-Syrian Relationship*, 5.
134. Moscow signaled that any "aggression" in the Middle East would be met with "strong opposition from the Soviet Union," and increased the size of its Mediterranean fleet. On Nasser's calculations see Popp, "Stumbling Decidedly into the Six-Day War," 306.
135. Brezhnev, "On Soviet Policy Following the Israeli Aggression in the Middle East" (Speech to the Plenum of the TsK KPSS, June 20, 1967), Wilson Center Digital Archive, accessed January 14, 2023, https://digitalarchive.wilsoncenter.org/document/soviet-policy-following-israeli-aggression-middle-east.
136. Friedman, *Shadow Cold War*, 159; the Americans reacted to the statement by describing the Soviet policy in the Middle East as having a "schizophrenic appearance." "Soviet Policy and the 1967 Arab-Israeli War (March 16, 1970)," 50, accessed December 30, 2020, (https://www.cia.gov/library/readingroom/docs/caesar-50.pdf).
137. The guests visited local agricultural exhibitions, museum of literature named after Navoi, Palace of the Pioneers, Tashselmash factory, Uzbekfilm studio, an agricultural research institute, and the Tashkent textile factory, and a visit to Samarkand.
138. Djagalov and Salazkina, "Tashkent 68"; on post-1967 despair see Dawisha, *Arab Nationalism in the Twentieth Century: From Triumph to Despair*.
139. Gordon, *Revolutionary Melodrama*, 195.
140. All the original 1958 attendees were invited (and came) except for the Burmese Union, which was dissolved in 1962. On the invitations, see RGALI f. 2936, op. 4, d.1833, ll. 17–18 (Memo from A. Romanov to TsK, June 5, 1967).
141. Djagalov, *From Internationalism to Postcolonialism*, ch. 4.
142. For instance, in 1963, the Baʿathist Party Constitution's linkage of revolution with the industrialization process—including that of film as a means of establishing a robust regional sovereignty—were consolidated into the National Film Organization in 1963 under the Ministry of Culture. Dickinson, *Arab Cinema Travels: Transnational Syria, Palestine, Dubai, and Beyond*, 39.
143. On Soviet reactions to 1968 see Wojnowski, *The Near Abroad*, ch. 3.
144. RGANI f. 5, op. 60, d. 66, ll. 336–42 (Report to TsK KPSS on Film Festival by Sharof Rashidov, A. Romanov, L. Kulidjzhanov).
145. Ibid.
146. Ibid.
147. RGANI f. 5, op. 60, d. 66, ll. 343–46 (On the Afro-Asian Film Festival in Tashkent, from Deputy Heads of Culture of TsK KPSS Z. Tumanova, I. Chernozutsan, L. Larfenov to TsK KPSS, Nov 14, 1968).
148. Ibid.
149. Djagalov, *From Internationalism to Postcolonialism*, 30.
150. Dickinson, *Arab Cinema Travels*, 42.
151. VKIG alumnus Riad Shaya cited in ibid., 50.

152. RGALI f. 2936, op. 4, d. 1735, ll. 1–6 (Report from Committee for Cinematography and Cinematographers Union to the Soviet of Ministers of USSR).
153. Djagalov, *From Internationalism to Postcolonialism*, 27.
154. RGALI f. 2936, op. 4, d. 1833, ll. 19–20 (Memo from Head of Festival Organizing Committee Sarvar Azimov).
155. As Djagalov writes: "The lists of Soviet films purchased at the first festival contain Mosfilm and Lenfilm productions, but approximately half of the films come from Central Asian and Caucasian film studios, especially Uzbekfilm." Djagalov, *From Internationalism to Postcolonialism*, 156.
156. Yarmatov, *Vozvrashchenie*, 210.
157. Prusin and Zeman, "Taming Russia's Wild East," 259.
158. The festival was called "boring" in *Variety* magazine in Hans Saaltink, "Tashkent: USSR Woos Africa: First 'Fest' as Bore, Not Art," *Variety* (November 13, 1968), 13.
159. The Georgian films were *Skoro pridet vesna* and *Okhotnik iz Lalvara*, and the Kyrgyz was *Nebo nashego detstva*. RGALI f. 2936, op. 4, d. 1995, ll. 1–4 (Russian translation of "Festival' dvukh kontinentov," *Ekran*, November 12, 1968).
160. RGALI f. 2936, op. 4, d. 1994, l. 105 (Russian translation of *La liberté*, Fribourg, Switzerland, November 6, 1968).
161. Yarmatov, *Vozvrashchenie*, 210.
162. Salakina, *World Socialist Cinema*.
163. *Pravda Vostoka*, October 20, 1968, 1.
164. Aleksandr Tankhel'son, "V sadniki revoliutsii," *Pravda Vostoka*, October 30, 1968, 3.
165. RGALI f. 2679, op. 1, d. 1251, l. 55 (unspecified newspaper clipping from September 15, 1968).
166. RGANI f. 5, op. 60, d. 66, ll. 343–46 (On the Afro-Asian Film Festival in Tashkent, from Deputy Heads of Culture of TsK KPSS Z. Tumanova, I. Chernozutsan, L. Larfenov to TsK KPSS, November 14, 1968).
167. This trend was recorded in other parts of the USSR as well. A group of sociologists conducting opinion polls among young readers of *Komsomolskaia Pravda* registered a continuing decline in romanticism and idealism among this cohort, and the spread of cynical conformism. Zubok, *Zhivago's Children*, 316; Suri, *Power and Protest*, 105–14.
168. Yarmatov, *Vozvrashchenie*, 299, 333.
169. On disaffected youth in the 1960s, see Zhuk, *Rock and Roll in the Rocket City*; Americans John Scott, William Taubman, and other foreigners' observations of Soviet youth disaffection are mentioned in Zubok, *Zhivago's Children*, 317.
170. Zubok, *Zhivago's Children*, 320.
171. Kalinovsky, *Laboratory*, 58.
172. Zubok, *Zhivago's Children*, 321–22.
173. Florin, "What Is Russia to Us?"
174. Interview with Timur Kaiumov in Tashkent, November 5, 2022.
175. Ibid.

176. RGANI f. 5, op. 60, d. 66, ll. 9–13 (Report to TsK KPSS from Deputy Head of Culture of TsK KPSS, V. Shauro, February 2, 1968).
177. Caffee, "Between First, Second, and Third Worlds," 104–5.
178. Kudaibergenova, *Rewriting the Nation*, 139.
179. Djagalov, *From Internationalism to Postcolonialism*, 136.
180. The category subhuman, explains Di-Capua, "captured the complete erasure of indigenous subjectivity and any trace of its humanity . . . [with] its vexed properties of agency and responsibility indispensable if one wished to understand the dynamic world of colonial relations and the process of decolonization." Di-Capua, *No Exit*, 156.
181. Ibid., 156–57.
182. Ibid., 158–59.
183. Ibid., 163.
184. Von Eschen, *Satchmo Blows Up the World*, 226.
185. Von Eschen, *Race against Empire*, 188.
186. Djagalov and Salazkina argue that the variety and instability of hegemonies at play and a confluence of new cinematic languages at the Tashkent film festival could be seen as a contribution to an emerging new language *about* Third-World film. Djagalov and Salazkina, "Tashkent '68," 281–82.
187. This description of the festival and Yarmatov's nobility and charisma was from a conversation with Timur Kaiumov on November 5, 2022.

Chapter 7

1. Kalinovsky, *Laboratory of Socialist Development*, 219–43.
2. Brandenberger, "Global and Transnational in Form, Soviet in Content: The Changing Semantics of Internationalism in Official Soviet Discourse, 1917–1991," 579.
3. Sahadeo, *Voices from the Soviet Edge*, 4.
4. Djagalov, *From Internationalism to Postcolonialism*, 145; Salazkina, "People's War: Socialist Cinema of Armed Struggle," in *World Socialist Cinema: Alliances, Affinities and Solidarities of the Global Cold War*.
5. Djagalov and Salazkina, "Tashkent '68," 291–93.
6. The first Russian imperial consul in Jeddah was a Bashkir Shagimardan Ibragimov (1841–1892), who had taken charge of diplomacy in Turkestan under the governor generalship of Konstantin von Kaufman. Ibragimov was replaced by Russian A. D. Levitskii, who nonetheless worked closely with the Tatar Shakirdzhan Ishaev, who had also served the Russian administration in Turkestan and was posted to the Jeddah consulate in 1895 to work with Muslim pilgrims and to encourage them to come to the consulate. In the interwar period, the Soviet government opened diplomatic ties with Jeddah by sending the Tatar Muslim Karim Khakimov (1890–1938) to pick up the pieces of tsarist-era networks of networks of transport and migration, trade, and communications. In Jeddah, Khakimov worked with Nazir Tiuriakulov (1892–1937), a Kazakh from Kokand who worked in the Hijaz from 1928 to 1935; E. A. Mansanov, "Sh. M. Ibragimov—drug Ch. Valikhanova," *Vestnik Akademii Nauk Kazakhskoi SSR* 9 (1964): 53–60; Naumkin, *Nesostoiavsheesia partnerstvo*.

7. Among more general doubts, the Soviet Union's unwillingness to support Nasser militarily revived questions about Soviet commitments to Arabs and anti-imperialism and Judeo-Bolshevist tropes that linked communism and Zionism. Al-Hilu, *al-Shuyu'iyah wa-al-Sihyuniyah*.
8. The text of his speech is reproduced in Shabratov, "Khamsun 'ammam in al-dirasat al-'arabiyya fi al-ittihad al-sufiyati," *al Tariq* 1 (1968): 75–83.
9. RGANI f. 5, op. 60, f. 438, ll. 23–40 (Report on SSOD delegation to Syria and Iraq: I. Ivanov, R. Korol'kova, G. Sharbatov, April 12, 1968).
10. Besides Mukhitdinov, Tajik Jabobor Rasulov served as ambassador to Togo (1960–1961) before assuming leadership of Tajikistan. Tajik politician Mirzo Rakhmatov, who accompanied Nasser on his tour of the Soviet Union in 1958, was appointed Soviet ambassador to Yemen in 1966, and during the civil war he oversaw Soviet aid and continued to defend the Soviet Union against the charge that it oppressed Muslims. Uzbek Rafiq Nishanov helped mediate talks between India and Pakistan in Tashkent after the 1965 war, traveled to Egypt after the 1967 war to meet with senior leaders, and later served as ambassador to Sri Lanka and Jordan (appointed 1978). Uzbek Rafik Nishanov et al., *Derev'ia zeleneiut do metelei: Rafik Nishanov rasskazyvaet Marine Zavade i Iuriiu Kulikovy*. Uzbek Sarvar Azimov served as ambassador in Lebanon (1969–1974) and Pakistan (1974–1980), and chaired the Committee Solidarity of Uzbekistan with People of Asia and Africa (1984–1987). Bakhtiyor Karim, *Sarvar Azimov: sarmondoshlari hotirasida*. Kazakh Malik Fazylov was appointed ambassador to Morocco in 1983. Kalinovsky, *Laboratory of Socialist Development*, 207–8.
11. RGANI f. 5, op. 60, f. 438, ll. 104–6 (Ambassador Mukhitdinov's report on meeting with Syrian Mufti Kaftaro, October 24, 1968).
12. For more on the economic impact of agreements with the Soviet Union see Haddad, *Business Networks in Syria*, ch. 4.
13. RGANI f. 5, op. 64, d. 363, ll. 3–4 (Plan project from Baath, translated from Arabic, forwarded by Mukhitdinov to the TsK International Section on Dec 1971).
14. RGASPI f. m-3, op. 8, d. 476, ll. 3–24 (Memo from KMO about youth exchange with Syria, Lebanon, and Iraq, August 15, 1972).
15. Ibid.
16. RGASPI f. m-3, op. 8, d. 580, ll. 2–11 (Report on Second Week of Friendship between Youth of Syria and the USSR, October 23, 1973).
17. *Komsomol Uzbekistana*, September 26, 1973, 3.
18. This cooperation lasted until 1973 when the rise in oil prices created a basis for Iraq's widening economic ties with the United States and European states.
19. The delegation was led by Abdul Wahab Madjid and by 'Imad al-din al-Shaykh, director of the department of athletic preparation of youth of the Ministry of Youth in Iraq. The full list of the forty delegates' names can be found in RGASPI f. m-3, op. 8, d. 574, ll. 25–26 (Iraqi delegates to the Soviet-Iraqi Week of Friendship).
20. The tradition of welcoming people with bread and salt is common across Eurasia—in Eastern Europe (including among Slavic, Nordic, Baltic, Balkan, and Jewish peoples) and the Middle East—and was incorporated into official Soviet ceremonies, with bread and salt referred to as "traditional" symbols of friendship. *Komsomoli Tojikiston*, August 19, 1973.

21. Between these visits, delegates were expected to discuss the role of youth in various sectors, such as in scientific-technical progress, and attend parties. RGASPI f. m-3, op. 8, d. 574, ll. 17–20 (Program of Iraqi-USSR Week of Friendship, 1973); also see *Komsomoli Tojikiston*, August 26, 1973.
22. Tajik newspapers also ran poems about Iraqi-Russian friendship by the Iraqi poet Abdul Razzaq Abdul Wahid, which had been translated first from Arabic into Russian, then from Russian into Tajik. RGASPI f. m-3, op. 8, d. 574, ll. 50–54 (Speech of the Secretary TsK LKSM of Tajikistan).
23. RGASPI f. m-3, op. 8, d. 574, ll. 44–46 (Speech by students of Tajik State University to the Iraqi delegation).
24. RGANI f. 5, op. 64, d. 363 (Correspondence with Syria, January 1972–1973), ll. 25–27 (Note from Mukhitdinov to TsK KPSS, January 31, 1972).
25. Andrew and Mitrokhin, *World Was Going Our Way*, 142; Taubman, *Khrushchev: The Man and His Era*, 175, 178, 201–2, 208–10.
26. On Ba'athist pressure in Soviet embassies to accept more Ba'athist students and give them more generous stipends see RGANI f. 5, op. 64, d. 363, ll. 23–34 (From head of Cultural Ties section of MID Kapitanov's diary, January 14, 1972). On tensions between Ba'athists and Communist students in Moscow see RGASPI f. m-1, op. 46, d. 343, ll. 1–4 (Reports about Iraqi and Syrian Student Groups meetings, 1964–1965); also Katsakioris, "Les étudiants de pays arabes," 13–38.
27. RGANI f. 5, op. 64, d. 363, l. 117 (Memo on the banning of *Moskovskie Novosti* in Arabic in Syria).
28. Dickenson, *Arab Cinema Travels*, 49 (ft. 31); Karsh, *Soviet Policy towards Syria since 1970*, 54.
29. From 1979 to 1985, 28.3 percent of Syria's exports and 12.2 percent of its imports were attributed to the USSR and other European Comecon members. Ramet, *The Soviet-Syrian Relationship*, 218
30. On the "politics of difference" in imperial and post-imperial context see Burbank and Cooper, *Empires and the Politics of Difference*.
31. Charles Maier, "Malaise," in *Shock of the Global: The 1970s in Perspective*, 29.
32. Dietrich, *Oil Revolution*; Garavini, *The Rise and Fall of OPEC in the Twentieth Century*, ch. 5.
33. Adom Getachew, *Worldmaking after Empire: The Rise and Fall of Self-Determination*, 144.
34. Rogers, *The Depths of Russia: Oil, Power, and Culture after Socialism*.
35. Kotkin, *Armageddon Averted*, 12, 14; According to Rogers, Soviet oil exports ran at about 70 percent crude and 30 percent refined oil products during the late Soviet period. Rogers, *Depths of Russia*, 49.
36. On Ethiopia see Westad, *The Global Cold War*, 276; on the expansion of Soviet commitments after 1967 in the Arab world see Roi, *From Encroachment to Involvement*; Andrew and Mitrokhin, *The World Was Going Our Way*.
37. Kotkin, *Armageddon Averted*, 24; Westad, *The Global Cold War*, 207–87.
38. Dhufari insurgents in Oman drew from Palestinian *fida'iyin* and South Yemen but also from "movements ranging from the Cuban to the Vietnamese." Takriti, *Monsoon*

Revolution: Republicans, Sultans, and Empires in Oman, 1965–1976, 4, 254. On Soviet aid see Peterson, "Guerrilla Warfare and Ideological Confrontation in the Arabian Peninsula: The Rebellion in Dhufar." On Soviet access to naval facilities at Aden and Socotra see Andrew and Mitrokhin, *The World Was Going Our Way*, 214.
39. Westad, *The Global Cold War*, 279.
40. Ibid., 284.
41. Ibid., 284–85.
42. Anecdote relayed by former US ambassador to Syria Richard Murphy, referenced in Lund, "From Cold War to Civil War," 7.
43. On the KBG and the Palestinians, see Andrew and Mitrokhin, *The World Was Going Our Way*, 246–59. Soviet-Syrian talks ended badly, and Assad would have been further outraged had he known that the KBG residency in Damascus was secretly providing funds to support the Lebanese Communist Party which opposed Syrian intervention. Ibid., 206.
44. Ramet, *Soviet-Syrian Alliance*, 1.
45. Ibid.; Karsh, *The Soviet Union and Syria: The Assad Years*, 94. In October 1980, Syria signed a new twenty-year friendship treaty with the Soviet Union, and that year Syrian arms imports from the Soviet bloc exceeded $3 billion. Andrew and Mitrokhin, *The World Was Going Our Way*, 208.
46. On Soviet supply of Palestinians, see Andrew and Mitrokhin, *The World Was Going Our Way*, 246–59.
47. Ramet, *Soviet-Syrian Alliance*, 2.
48. Primakov, *Russia and the Arabs: Behind the Scenes in the Middle East from the Cold War to the Present*, 240–42.
49. In addition to the executions of Party militants, more than 10,000 persons were arrested and subjected to mental and physical torture. Andrew and Mitrokhin. *The World Was Going Our Way*, 178.
50. Primakov, *Russia and the Arabs*, 60. As Soviet foreign minister Andrei Gromyko recalled, "had [Nasser] lived a few years longer, the situation in the region might today be very different." Andrew and Mitrokhin, *The World Was Going Our Way*, 153.
51. Andrew and Mitrokhin, *The World Was Going Our Way*, 146–68.
52. Mukhitdinov, *Reka vremeni*, 590–91.
53. On the 1967 war as a catalyst of Jewish national consciousness in the Soviet Union see Gitelman, *A Century of Ambivalence*, 176–88.
54. Andrew and Mitrokhin, *The World Was Going Our Way*, 237.
55. Those who remained had to navigate workplace environments characterized by slowing down of academic hiring, increased competition over resources, and policies that limited Jewish access to elite colleges and prestigious professional positions. Slezkine, *The Jewish Century*, 335–43.
56. Primakov, *Russian Crossroads: Toward the New Millennium*, 17.
57. Primakov, *Russia and the Arabs*, 221.
58. This point was stressed to me by a number of former Soviet diplomats, all of whom have asked to remain anonymous on this matter.

NOTES TO PAGES 227-231

59. Ibid., 17; on postwar discrimination against Jews in Soviet academia see Isaakyan, "Blood and Soil of the Soviet Academy"; also Sawyer, *The Jewish Minority in the Soviet Union*.
60. Conversation with Georgy Derlugyan, September 1, 2022; on the return of Jews to the top of the Soviet professional hierarchy after Stalin's death see Slezkine, *The Jewish Century*, 229-331.
61. Makhzangi, *Memories of a Meltdown*, 97.
62. Westad, *The Global Cold War*, 295-99; Citino, "The Middle East and the Cold War"; Lesch, *1979: The Year That Shaped the Modern Middle East*.
63. Ouimet, *Rise and Fall of the Brezhnev*; on the significance of 1968 as the end of de-Stalinization see Wojnowski, *The Near Abroad*.
64. Bardawil, *Revolution and Disenchantment*, 175.
65. Westad, *Global Cold War*, 329.
66. Paul Henze's responsibilities within the NSC mapped on to a kind of inverse Eastern international, with a portfolio that included Soviet nationalities, the Horn of Africa, Greece, Turkey, and Cyprus. Kalinovsky, "Encouraging Resistance," 219-26.
67. Kalinovsky, *Laboratory of Socialist Development*, 214-18.
68. Interview with Hoji Akbar Turajonzoda, Vahdat, Tajikistan, July 20, 2011; also Tasar, "The Central Asian Muftiate in Occupied Afghanistan, 1979-1987."
69. For more on the role of Central Asians as Soviet advisers in Afghanistan, see Giustozzi and Kalinovsky, *Missionaries of Modernity*, 174-216; also Kalinovsky, *Laboratory of Socialist Development*, 215.
70. Kalinovsky, *Laboratory of Socialist Development*, 214-17.
71. Kotkin, "Kiss of Debt," 81-90.
72. Zubok, *Collapse: The Fall of the Soviet Union*, 25.
73. Taubman, *Gorbachev: His Life and Times*, 29-30, 119.
74. Zubok, *Collapse: The Fall of the Soviet Union*, 46.
75. Gorbachev allowed Baltic representatives in Moscow to denounce the "secret protocols" of the Molotov-Ribbentrop Pact of 1939 as the basis for the Soviet annexation of Lithuania, Latvia, and Estonia. He also did not respond to worker strikes in Russia and Ukraine, or to Yeltsin's efforts to channel such discontent into nationalist programs, thinking he could use Lenin's strategy of devolving some power to the republics to tame nationalism and preserve the federation. Zubok, *Collapse*, 76, 104-5.
76. Ibid., 53-54.
77. Djagalov, *From Internationalism to Postcolonialism*, 132-36; Kudaibergenova, *Rewriting the Nation in Modern Kazakh Literature*, 149-72; Caffee, "Between First, Second, and Third Worlds."
78. Djagalov, *From Internationalism to Postcolonialism*, 134.
79. Suleimenov, *Az i ya*, 200. Ram, "Imagining Eurasia: the Poetics and Ideology of Olzhas Suleimenov's Az i Ia," 289-90.
80. Kudaibergenova, *Rewriting the Nation in Modern Kazakh Literature*, 167.
81. Ram, "Imagining Eurasia: The Poetics and Ideology of Olzhas Suleimanov's Az i Ia," 295.

82. See Olzhas Suleimenov's speeches at the 1977 symposium of the Association of the Writers of African and Asian Nations in Tashkent, cited in Ram, "Imagining Eurasia," 292.
83. Khodakov, "Gnilaia politika TsK KP(b) Kirqizii," *Pravda*, September 13, 1937, 2.
84. Florin, "What Is Russia to Us?," 180.
85. The action of the novel takes place in a wider international context of the USSR and United States deciding together to create a trans-space defensive system to keep out communications from other worlds, thus reducing the whole world to the condition of *mankurt*-like slavery.
86. Some 6,762 people from the Uzbek SSR visited foreign countries in 1974 for the exclusive purpose of vacation and recreation, traveling mostly in small professional delegations with colleagues, and not families—to ensure that they returned home. For their part, tourists were interested in leisure pursuits and the consumption of foreign products, which introduced Soviet citizens to non-Soviet standards. Some would use these trips as opportunities for illicit trade. Bota Kassymbekova, "Leisure and Politics: Soviet Central Asian Tourists across the Iron Curtain," 70, 74–81.
87. Kalinovsky, *Laboratory of Socialist Development*, 211–12.
88. Ibid., 12, 219–43.
89. Zubok, *Collapse*, 102, 201.
90. Sahadeo, "Soviet 'Blacks' and Place Making in Leningrad and Moscow."
91. Gorbachev had asked the United States to help the USSR become "stronger but democratic . . . progressive, dynamic, free, and turned towards the outside world and the US." Zubok, *Collapse*, 116–19. This language made the quieter approaches to China Saudi Arabia seem the more desperate.
92. In 1991, Gorbachev sent Primakov to Saudi Arabia and the Emirates to look for funds; ibid., 338.
93. The defense budget was cut from 77.3 billion to 71 billion rubles in 1989, with estimates for 1991 of further decline to 66.5 billion. Ibid., 166. In 1990, the Ukrainian Supreme Soviet passed laws blocking conscriptions of young men from their territory or banning their deployment outside their "national" territories, and Yeltsin declared the same for Russian draftees. The Soviet army's simultaneous retreat from Central and Eastern Europe destroyed the legal and political grounds for the Soviet army's deployment. Ibid., 159.
94. Ibid., 196–97.
95. Ibid., 408.
96. Kalinovsky, *Laboratory of Socialist Development*, 241.
97. Kotkin, *Armageddon Averted*, 4.
98. Julia Ioffe, "What Putin Really Wants," *Atlantic*, January/February 2018.
99. Lieven et al., *Russia's Restless Frontier*, 171–78.
100. Kavitha Surana, "Russian Embassy: Grozny Is the 'Solution' for Aleppo," *Foreign Policy*, October 17, 2016, accessed January 20, 2022, https://foreignpolicy.com/2016/10/17/russian-embassy-grozny-is-the-solution-for-aleppo-syria-war-john-kerry/.

101. Egor Lazarev and Anna Biryukova, "Are Russia's 20 Million Muslims Seething about Putin Bombing Syria?," *Washington Post*, March 7, 2016.
102. Robert D. Crews, "Muslims Are Fighting on Both Sides of Ukraine," *Washington Post*, March 10, 2022, accessed December 24, 2022, https://www.washingtonpost.com/outlook/2022/03/10/ukraine-war-muslims-conflict-chechnya/.
103. Undeniably the contraction of Russia's international interests in the 1990s corresponded to an erosion of some of its key institutions and the physical infrastructure of the Eastern International. Media scholar Rossen Djagalov has described the dilapidated buildings of the Institute of African and Asian Countries, the Institute of Oriental Studies, and the Institute of Africa, as well as the decline of the Eastern Literature publishing house and the disappearance of other platforms devoted to non-Western culture. Djagalov, *From Internationalism to Postcolonialism*, 211. My own browsing of Moscow's bookstores between 2011 and 2014 confirms the dearth of interest in histories of decolonization and postcolonial theory; in an April 2017 meeting in Abu Dhabi, Arabist and historian Alexei Vassiliev expressed nostalgia about late Soviet Aeroflot routes to the Afro-Asian world, compared to the near absence now of flights to Africa and a contraction of its service to Asia. Interview with Alexei Vassiliev in Abu Dhabi, April 19, 2017.
104. Kramer, "The Soviet Legacy in Russian Foreign Policy," 591–92.
105. Ibid., 600; Lo, *Russia and the New World Disorder*.
106. Bassin, "Eurasianism 'Classical' and 'Neo': The Lines of Continuity."
107. Mikhail Pavlovich, "Zadachi Vserossiiskoi Nauchnoi Assotsiatsii Vostokovedeniia," *Novyi Vostok* 1 (1922): 3–15 (9).
108. Laruelle, *Russian Eurasianism: An Ideology of Empire*, 116–18.
109. Ibid., 107–44.
110. Mohammed Tawfeeq et al., "Car Bomb Kills Daughter of 'Spiritual Guide' to Putin's Ukraine Invasion," CNN, August 20, 2022, https://edition.cnn.com/2022/08/20/europe/darya-dugina-killed-car-explosion-alexander-dugin-russia-intl-hnk/index.html.
111. Lo, *Russia and the New World Disorder*, 248.
112. On the appeal of neo-Eurasianism to Muslim elites see Sibgatullina and Kemper, "The Imperial Paradox: Islamic Eurasianism in Contemporary Russia," 101–13; Shlapentokh, "Islam and Orthodox Russia," 32–33.
113. Laruelle, *Russian Eurasianism*, 150; Sibgatullina and Kemper, "The Imperial Paradox," 102.
114. Laruelle, *Russian Eurasianism*, 101.
115. Navbahor Imamova, "Uzbekistan Promotes Connectivity to Enhance its Regional Leadership," VOA, July 13, 2021, accessed July 7, 2023, https://www.voanews.com/a/south-central-asia_uzbekistan-promotes-connectivity-enhance-its-regional-leadership/6208215.html.

Conclusion

1. Muzaffar Olimov, "Discourse of Nation Building and Development in the Countries of Central Asia: The Shared and the Particular," presented at the "Social Science

NOTES TO PAGES 241–246   331

Knowledge and Development in Central Asia from Socialism through 'Transition'" Conference. Tashkent: University of World Economy and Diplomacy, June 2, 2023.
2. Mario Riccardo Cucciolla, "Legitimation through Self-Victimization: The Uzbek Cotton Affair and Its Repression Narrative (1989–1991)."
3. Hansen, "The Ambivalent Empire," 220–40; Uzbek National Museum visit on November 5, 2022.
4. On the Museum of Repression see Abashin, "Soviet Past and Memory Policy in the Countries of Central Asia," 305–6.
5. Laruelle, *Russian Eurasianism*, 171–87.
6. Kudaibergenova, "The Use and Abuse of Postcolonial Discourses in Post-independent Kazakhstan."
7. Abashin, "Soviet Past and Memory Policy in the Countries of Central Asia," 307–8.
8. Khalid, *Central Asia: A New History from Imperial Conquest to the Present*, 264–67.
9. Ibid., 312.
10. Weiss-Went, *Putin's Russia and the Falsification of History*; Weiss-Wendt and Adler, eds., *The Future of the Soviet Past: The Politics of History in Putin's Russia*.
11. These comparisons have focused on economic histories (e.g., control over *waqf* property in endowments protected under Islamic law), modernization, approaches to nationalism, race, and gender. Khalid, "Locating the (Post-) Colonial in Soviet History," 467.
12. Bernard Lewis, "The Question of Orientalism," *New York Review of Books*, June 1982, 4–5.
13. Ghafurov was never appointed ambassador to any Asian or African country, despite rumors to that effect circulating among the academic community. Nevertheless, as head of the Moscow Oriental Institute he continued to direct the intellectual efforts that informed Soviet foreign policy in Asia and Africa. As Petrosian writes: "Ghafurov knew about these rumors and once joked in conversation with me a few years afterwards that if the rumors . . . had any basis in reality, he would have visited all Asian and African countries as the Soviet ambassador." Petrosian, "Shtrikhi biografii V. G. Gafurova-vostokoveda," 43.
14. Tolz, *Russia's Own Orient*.
15. Clark, *Eurasia without Borders*, 363; Caffee, "Between First, Second, and Third Worlds: Olzhas Suleimenov and Soviet Postcolonialism, 1961–1973."
16. Djagalov, *From Internationalism*, 31.
17. In US history, since early critiques from the Left, like Howard Zinn's *A People's History of the United States*, these arguments have moved into the mainstream of American historical studies. E.g., Immerwahr, *How to Hide an Empire: A History of the Greater United States*.
18. Jeanne Morefield, *Empires without Imperialism: Anglo-American Decline and the Politics of Deflection*, 1.
19. Burkett, *Constructing Post-Imperial Britain: Britishness, "Race" and the Radical Left in the 1960s*, 1, 112.
20. Kwame Anthony Appiah, *Cosmopolitanism: Ethics in a World of Strangers*.
21. Getachew, *Worldmaking after Empire: The Rise and Fall of Self-Determination*, 32.
22. At the 1986 NAM Summit in Harare, Zimbabwe, the chair of the South Commission created to study the economic and political problems of NAM states, Tanzania's

former president Julius Nyerere, summarized this collapse in five words: "growth and hope—then disillusionment." Prashad, *Darker Nations*, 276, 278, 289.
23. Al-Sibai was killed in 1978 by Palestinian militants angered by his personal support for the peace treaty with Israel; Muruwwa was killed in Lebanon in 1987. Bardawil, *Revolution and Disenchantment*; Samer Frangie, "The Afterlives of Husayn Muruwwa," 245; Frangie, "Exiled from History: Yasin al-Hafiz's Autobiographical Preface and the Transformation of Political Critique." New work interrogating the relationships of Arab communist parties to their respective Arab states and to the USSR, and to networks as students exchanges between the "Second" and "Third" worlds, is summarized in Guirguis, "Introduction" to *The Arab Left*. Also Louro et al., eds., *League against Imperialism: Lives and Afterlives*; Di-Capua, *No Exit*; Bardawil, *Revolution and Disenchantment*; and https://www.orient-institut.org/research/current-projects/relations-in-the-ideoscape-middle-eastern-students-in-the-eastern-bloc-1950s-to-1991.
24. Al-Khafaji, "The Arab Left after Glasnost: Who's Afraid of Bureaustroika?"; Faleh A. Jabar, ed., *Post-Marxism and the Middle East*.
25. Andrew and Mitrokhin, *World Was Going Our Way*, 210; Ismael and Ismael, *Communist Movement of Syria and Lebanon*, 206–25.
26. Daniel Pipes, "Syria beyond the Peace Process," Washington Institute for Near East Policy Papers, February 1, 1996, 8.
27. Peter Ford, "Forgetting the Debt Is Nice, but Syrians Still Miss the Soviets," *Christian Science Monitor*, October 29, 1993, 9.
28. Sellman, "The Ghosts of Exilic Belonging."
29. Litvin, "Egypt's Uzbek Mirror: Muhammad Mansi Qandil's Post-Soviet Islamic Humanism."

Bibliography

Interviews

Guzal Alimova, December 3, 2012
Georgy Derlugyan, September 1, 2022
Timur Kaiumov, November 5, 2022
Elias Khoury, May 7, 2013
Malekeh Khuri, Skype, July 20, 2020
Tatiana Olegovna Matroshilina, January 12, 2022
Vitalii Naumkin, April 27, 2013
Vladimir Gennad'evich Shubin, September 11, 2020
Hoji Akbar Turajonzoda, July 20, 2011
Khasanov Bakhtier Vakhapovich, May 5, 2019
Alexei Vassiliev, April 19, 2017

Archives

Central State Archive of Uzbekistan (TsGA Uz)

f. 837 (Council of Ministers), op. 38
f. 2574 (Shirinbaev Personal File), op. 1
f. 2661 (UzSOD), op. 1

Russian State Archive of Literature and Art (RGALI)

f. 2329 (Ministry of Culture of the USSR), op. 8 (information, notices)
f. 2329, op. 9 (information, notices)
f. 2679 (Personal file of Lev Kuleshov), op. 1
f. 2912 (Editors of *Isskustvo kino*), op. 1
f. 2918 (SovExportFilms), op. 1
f. 2936 (OrgKomitet of Union of Cinematography Workers of USSR), op. 4

The Russian State Archive of Contemporary History (RGANI)

RGANI f. 3 (Politburo Presidium), op. 62
RGANI f. 5 (Central Committee), op. 35 (Ideological Section)
RGANI f. 5, op. 36
RGANI f. 5, op. 55
RGANI f. 5, op. 60
RGANI f. 5, op. 64
RGANI f. 81 (Suslov's Fond), op. 1
RGANI f. 89 (Communist Party on Trial), op. 55

The Russian State Archive of Socio-Political History (RGASPI)

RGASPI f. 17, op. 128
RGASPI f. 61 (Turkestanskoe Buro TsK RKP(b)), op. 2 (Sovinterprop)
RGASPI f. 82 (Molotov Personal File), op. 2
RGASPI f. 122 (Administration and Personal Affairs of Employees of the Central Executive Committee and Council of People's Commissars), op. 2
RGASPI f. 495 (Comintern Executive Committee), op. 20 (Secretariat of the ECCI)
RGASPI f. 495, op. 65a (Comintern Administrative Department Personal Files)
RGASPI f. 495, op. 84 (Communist Party of Syria)
RGASPI f. 495, op. 85 (Communist Party of Egypt)
RGASPI f. 495, op. 154 (Eastern Section)
RGASPI f. 495, op. 210 (Personal files of members of the Egyptian Communist Party)
RGASPI f. 495, op. 212 (Personal files of members of the Palestine Communist Palestine)
RGASPI f. 495, op. 232 (Personal files of members of the Communist Party of Lebanon)
RGASPI f. 495, op. 258 (Communist Party of Syria-Lebanon)
RGASPI f. 530 (Communist University for the Toilers of China), op. 4 (TsK VKP(b) Commission on Examining KUTK)
RGASPI f. 532 (KUTV), op 1 (Foreign Sector of KUTV Operations)
RGASPI f. 544 (Union for Propaganda and Action of the Peoples of the East), op. 4 (Turkburo)
RGASPI f. m-1 (Komsomol Central Committee), op. 46
RGASPI f. m-3 (KMO USSR Committee of Youth Organizations), op. 8 (Council for the Affairs of Foreign Students)

State Archive of Russian Federation (GARF)

GARF f. A-539 (Commission of the Council of Ministers for Personal Pensions), op. 4
GARF f. 5283 (VOKS), op. 2a
GARF f. 5283, op. 4
GARF f. 5283, op. 19
GARF f. 5402, op.1 (Sovinterprop)
GARF f. 6903 (Radio Committee), op. 24
GARF f. 7668 (TsIK's Uchenyi Komitet), op. 1
GARF f. r-7868, op. 1, d. 2985 (Troianovskii's file)
GARF f. 8581 (SovInformBuro), op. 1
GARF f. 9540 (SKSSAA), op. 1
Columbia University Bureau of Applied Social Research
Periodicals
al-Adab
Agrarnye problemy
Atlantic
The Christian Science Monitor
Ekran
Foreign Policy
Iskusstvo kino
Izvestiia
Izvestiia KUTVa
Komsomol Uzbekistana
Komsomoli Tojikiston

Moscow News
Narody Azii i Afriki
New Times
Novyi Vostok
Pravda
Pravda Vostoka
Revoliutsiia i natsional'nosti
Revoliutsionnyi Vostok
Sovremennyi Vostok
al-Tariq
al-thaqafa al-wataniyya
Turkestanskii kommunist
Variety
Vestnik Akademii Nauk Kazakhskoi SSR
Vestnik zhizni
Washington Post
Washington Institute for Near East Policy Papers
Zhizn' natsional'nostei

Secondary Sources

Abu Hanna, Hanna. *Tala'i' al-nahda fi Filasṭin: khirriju al-madaris al-Rusiyah*. Beirut: Mu'assasat al-Dirasat al-Filastiniyya, 2005.

Abu Hanna, Hanna, ed. *Mudhakkarat Najati Sidqi*. Beirut: Institute for Palestinian Studies, 2001.

Abu Hashhash, Ibrahim. *Najati Sidqi*. East Jerusalem: Passia, 1990.

Abashin, Sergei. "Osobennosti rossiiskogo orientalizma." In *Tsentral'naia Aziia v sostave Rossiiskoi imperii*, edited by D. Abashin, Iu. Arapov, and N. E. Bekmakhanova, 332–33. Moscow: Novoye literaturnoye obozreniye, 2008.

Abashin, Sergei. "Soviet Central Asia on the Periphery." *Kritika* 16, no. 2 (2015): 359–74.

Abashin, Sergei. "Soviet Past and Memory Policy in the Countries of Central Asia." In *Russland und/als Eurasien: Kulturelle Konfigurationen*, edited by Christine Engel and Birgit Menzel, 303–17. Berlin: Frank & Timme, 2018.

Abdurakhimova, Nodira, and Govkharshod K. Rustamova. *Kolonial'naia sistema vlasti v Turkestane v vtoroi polovine xix–pervoi chertverti xx vv*. Tashkent: Universitet, 1999.

Abisaab, Malek. "Gendered Expressions of Labor in the Middle East." *International Journal of Middle East Studies* 48, no. 3 (2016): 570–73.

Adibekov, G. M., K. M. Anderson, and K. K. Shirinya. *Politburo TsK RKP(b)-VKP(b) i Komintern 1919–1943 gg*. Moscow: Rosspen, 2004.

Adibekov, G., E. Shakhnazarova, and K. Shirinia. *Organizatsionnaia struktura kominterna, 1919–1943*. Moscow: Rosspen, 1997.

Ahmad, Feroz. *The Young Turks and the Ottoman Nationalities: Armenians, Greeks, Albanians, Jews, and Arabs, 1908–1918*. Salt Lake City: University of Utah Press, 2014.

Akramov, Akmal, and K. Avliakulov. *V. I. Lenin, Turkkomissiia i ukreplenie Sovetskoi Vlasti v Srednei Azii*. Tashkent: Uzbekiston, 1991.

Akramov, Nariman. *Vydaiushchiisia russkii vostokoved V. V. Bartol'd*. Dushanbe: AN Tadzhikskoi SSR, 1963.

Aksakal, Mustafa. *The Ottoman Road to War in 1914: The Ottoman Empire and the First World War*. Cambridge: Cambridge University Press, 2008.

Amanzholova, Dina, ed. *Rossiia i tsentral'naia aziia, 1905-1925: sbornik dokumentov*. Karagandy: Karagandinskii GosUniversitet im. Buketova, 2005.

Ampiah, Kweku. *The Political and Moral Imperatives of the Bandung Conference of 1955: The Reactions of the US, UK and Japan*. Leeds: Global Oriental, 2007.

Anderson, Charles. "From Petition to Confrontation: The Palestinian National Movement and the Rise of Mass Politics, 1929-1939." PhD diss., New York University, 2013.

Andrew, Christopher, and Vasili Mitrokhin. *The World Was Going Our Way: The KGB and the Battle for the Third World*. New York: Basic Books, 2006.

Ani Mukherji, S. "'Like Another Planet to the Darker Americans': Black Cultural Work in 1930s Moscow." In *Africa in Europe: Studies in Transnational Practice in the Long Twentieth Century*, edited by Eve Rosenhaft and Robbie Aitken, 120-41. Liverpool: Liverpool University Press, 2014.

Appiah, Kwame Anthony. *Cosmopolitanism: Ethics in a World of Strangers*. New York: W. W. Norton, 2006.

Applebaum, Rachel. *Empire of Friends: Soviet Power and Socialist Internationalism in Cold War Czechoslovakia*. Ithaca, NY: Cornell University Press, 2019.

Aydın, Cemil. *The Idea of the Muslim World: A Global Intellectual History*. Cambridge, MA: Harvard University Press, 2017.

Aydın, Cemil. *The Politics of Anti-Westernism in Asia: Visions of World Order in Pan-Islamic and Pan-Asian Thought*. New York: Columbia University Press, 2007.

Babiracki, Patryk. *Soviet Soft Power in Poland: Culture and the Making of Stalin's New Empire, 1943-1957*. Chapel Hill: University of North Carolina Press, 2015.

Bailey, Anne M., and Joseph R. Llobera, eds. *The Asiatic Mode of Production: Science and Politics*. London: Routledge, 1981.

Bakdash, Khalid. *Khalid Bakdash yatahadath*. Beirut: Dal al-Tali'a, 1992.

Bardawil, Fadi. *Revolution and Disenchantment: Arab Marxism and the Binds of Emancipation*. Durham, NC: Duke University Press, 2020.

Barghoorn, Frederick. *The Soviet Cultural Offensive: The Role of Cultural Diplomacy in Soviet Foreign Policy*. Princeton, NJ: Princeton University Press, 1964.

Bashkin, Orit. "Iraqi Shadows, Iraqi Lights: Anti-Fascist and Anti-Nazi Voices in Monarchic Iraq, 1932-1941." In *Arab Responses to Fascism and Nazism*, edited by Israel Gershoni, 141-68. Austin: University of Texas Press, 2014.

Bassin, Mark. "Eurasianism 'Classical' and 'Neo': The Lines of Continuity." In *Beyond the Empire: Images of Russia in the Eurasian Cultural Context*, edited by Mochizuki Tetsuo, 279-94. Sapporo: Slavic Research Center, 2008.

Bassin, Mark. "Russia between Europe and Asia: The Ideological Construction of Geography." *Slavic Review* 50, no. 1 (1991): 1-17.

Batatu, Hanna. *The Old Social Classes and the Revolutionary Movements of Iraq: A Study of Iraq's Old Landed and Commercial Classes and of Its Communists, Ba'athists, and Free Officers*. Princeton, NJ: Princeton University Press, 1978.

Beinin, Joel, and Zachary Lockman. *Workers on the Nile: Nationalism, Communism, Islam and the Egyptian Working Class, 1882-1954*. Cairo: American University in Cairo Press, 1998.

Beissinger, Mark R. "The Persisting Ambiguity of Empire." *Post-Soviet Affairs* 11, no. 2 (April-June 1995): 185-96.

Becker, Seymour. *Russia's Protectorates in Central Asia: Bukhara and Khiva, 1865–1924.* Cambridge, MA: Harvard University Press, 1968.
Bennigsen, Alexandre. "Colonization and Decolonization in the Soviet Union." *Journal of Contemporary History* 4, no. 1 (1969): 141–52.
Bennigsen, Alexandre, and S. Enders Wimbush. *Muslim National Communism in the Soviet Union: A Revolutionary Strategy for the Colonial World.* Chicago: University of Chicago Press, 1980.
Berger, Joseph. *Shipwreck of a Generation.* London: Harvil, 1971.
Berger-Barzilai, J. *The Tragedy of the Soviet Revolution.* Tel Aviv: Am Oved, 1968.
Bharucha, Rustom. *Another Asia: Rabindranath Tagore and Okakura Tenshin.* New Delhi: Oxford University Press, 2006.
Bobrovnikov, Vladimir. "Pochemu my marginaly? (Zametki na poliakh russkogo perevoda 'Orientalizma' Edvarda Saida)." *Ab Imperio* 2 (2008): 325–44.
Boehmer, Elleke. *Empire, the National, and the Postcolonial, 1890–1920: Resistance in Interaction.* Oxford: Oxford University Press, 2005.
Boittin, Jennifer. *Colonial Metropolis: The Urban Grounds of Anti-Imperialism and Feminism in Interwar Paris.* Lincoln: University of Nebraska Press, 2010.
Borev, Iuri. *Stalinada: Memuary po chuzhim vospominaniiam s istoricheskimi anekdotami i razmyshleniiami avtora.* Moscow: Olimp, 2003.
Boyce, Robert. *The Great Interwar Crisis and the Collapse of Globalization.* Basingstoke: Palgrave Macmillan, 2009.
Brandenberger, David. "Global and Transnational in Form, Soviet in Content: The Changing Semantics of Internationalism in Official Soviet Discourse, 1917–1991." *Russian Review* 80 (2021): 562–80. https://doi.org/10.1111/russ.12331.
Brandenberger, David. "Stalin, the Leningrad Affair, and the Limits of Postwar Russocentrism." *Russian Review* 63, no. 2 (2004): 241–55.
Brandt, Conrad. *Stalin's Failure in China, 1924–1927.* Cambridge, MA: Harvard University Press, 1958.
Breindel, Eric, and Herbert Romerstein. *The Venona Secrets: Exposing Soviet Espionage and America's Traitors.* Washington, DC: Regnery, 2000.
Brinkley, George. "The 'Withering' of the State under Khrushchev." *Review of Politics* 23, no. 1 (1961): 37–51.
Brower, Daniel. *Turkestan and the Fate of the Russian Empire.* New York: Routledge Curzon, 2003.
Brutents, Karen. *Tridtsat' let na staroi ploshchadi.* Moscow: Mezhdunarodnye otnosheniia, 1998.
Brzezinski, Zbigniew. *The Soviet Bloc, Unity and Conflict.* Cambridge, MA: Harvard University Press, 1960.
Buck-Morss, Susan. *Dreamworld and Catastrophe: The Passing of Mass Utopia in East and West.* Cambridge, MA: MIT Press, 2000.
Bukhert, V. G. "V zashchity sovetskoi arabistiki." *Vostochnii arkhiv* 1, no. 29 (2014): 68–75.
Budeiri, Musa. "Essential Readings on the Left in Mandate Palestine." *Jadaliyya.* https://www.jadaliyya.com/Details/41513.
Budeiri, Musa. *The Palestine Communist Party: Arab and Jew in the Struggle for Internationalism.* 2nd ed. Chicago: Haymarket, 2010.
Budeiri, Musa. "Reflections on a Silenced History: The PCP and Internationalism." *Jerusalem Quarterly* 49 (2012): 68–78.

Budnitskii, Oleg. "Jews, Pogroms, and the White Movement: A Historiographical Critique." *Kritika* 2, no. 4 (2001): 751–72.
Bukhert, V. G. "G. A. Nersesov o V. B. Lutskom i S. R. Smirnove." *Vostochnyi arkhiv* 1, no. 25 (2012): 81–86.
Bukhert, V. G. "V zashchitu sovetskoi arabistiki." *Vostochnii arkhiv* 1, no. 29 (2014): 68–75.
Burbank, Jane. "Controversies over Stalinism: Searching for a Soviet Society." *Politics and Society* 19, no. 3 (1991): 325–40.
Burbank, Jane, and Fred Cooper. "Empires after 1919: Old, New, Transformed." *International Affairs* 95, no. 1 (2019): 81–100.
Burbank, Jane, and Fred Cooper. *Empires in World History: Power and the Politics of Difference*. Princeton, NJ: Princeton University Press 2010.
Burkett, Jodi. *Constructing Post-Imperial Britain: Britishness, "Race" and the Radical Left in the 1960s*. New York: Palgrave Macmillan, 2013.
Buttino, Marco. "Study of the Economic Crisis and Depopulation in Turkestan 1917–1920." *Central Asian Survey* 9, no. 4 (January 1990): 59–74.
Caffee, Naomi. "Between First, Second, and Third Worlds: Olzhas Suleimenov and Soviet Postcolonialism, 1961–1973." *Russian Literature* 111–112 (2020): 91–118. https://doi.org/10.1016/j.ruslit.2020.03.004.
Campbell, James. *Middle Passages: African American Journeys to Africa, 1787–2005*. New York: Penguin, 2006.
Can, Lale. *Spiritual Subjects: Central Asian Hajj at the End of Empire*. Stanford, CA: Stanford University Press, 2020.
Carlisle, Donald S. "The Uzbek Power Elite: Politburo and Secretariat (1938-83)." *Central Asian Survey* 5, no. 3/4 (1986): 91–132.
Carlisle, Kathleen Bailey. "Clan and Politics in Uzbekistan." PhD diss., Boston College, 2001.
Carrère d'Encausse, Hélène. "Civil War and New Governments." In *Central Asia: 130 Years of Russian Dominance*, edited by Edward A. Allworth, 224–53. Durham, NC: Duke University Press, 1998.
Casula, Philipp. "The Soviet Afro-Asian Solidarity Committee and Soviet Perceptions of the Middle East during Late Socialism." *Cahiers du Monde russe* 59, no. 4 (2018): 499–520.
Chakrabarty, Dipesh. *Provincializing Europe: Postcolonial Thought and Historical Difference*. Princeton, NJ: Princeton University Press, 2000.
Chari, Sharad, and Katherine Verdery. "Thinking between the Posts: Postcolonialism, Postsocialism, and Ethnography after the Cold War." *Comparative Studies in Society and History* 51, no. 1 (2009): 6–34.
Charif, Maher. *Filastin fi-l-arshif as-sirri li-l-kumintirn*. Damascus: al-Mada, 2004.
Chaqueri, Cosroe. *The Soviet Socialist Republic of Iran, 1920–1921: Birth of the Trauma*. Pittsburgh: University of Pittsburgh Press, 1995.
Chaqueri, Cosroe. "Sultanzade: The Forgotten Revolutionary Theoretician of Iran: A Biographical Sketch." *Iranian Studies* 17, no. 2–3 (1984): 215–35.
Chase, William. "Scapegoating One's Comrades, 1934–1937." In *The Anatomy of Terror: Political Violence under Stalin*, edited by James Harris, 263–84. Oxford: Oxford University Press. 2013.
Chokaev, Mustafa. "Turkestan and the Soviet Regime." *Journal of Central Asian Society* 18, no. 3 (1931): 403–20.

Chokobaeva, Aminat, Cloé Drieu, and Alexander Morrison. "Editors' Introduction." In *The Central Asian Revolt of 1916: A Collapsing Empire in the Age of War and Revolution*, edited by Chokobaeva, Drieu, and Morrison, 1–26. Manchester: Manchester University Press, 2020.

Chomentowski, Gabrielle. "Filmmakers from Africa and the Middle East at VGIK during the Cold War." *Studies in Russian and Soviet Cinema* 13, no. 2 (2019): 189–98.

Citino, Nathan. "The Middle East and the Cold War." *Cold War History* 19, no. 3 (2019): 441–56.

Clark, Katerina. *Eurasia without Borders: The Dream of a Leftist Literary Commons, 1919–1943*. Cambridge, MA: Harvard University Press, 2020.

Clark, Katerina. *Moscow, the Fourth Rome: Stalinism, Cosmopolitanism, and the Evolution of Soviet Culture, 1931–41*. Cambridge, MA: Harvard University Press, 2011.

Clark, Katerina. "The Mutability of the Canon: Socialist Realism and Chingiz Aitmatov's I dol'she veka dlitsia den'." *Slavic Review* 43, no. 4 (1984): 573–87.

Cohen, Hillel. *Year Zero of the Arab-Israeli Conflict: 1929*. Waltham, MA: Brandeis University Press, 2015.

Colton, Timothy. *Moscow: Governing the Socialist Metropolis*. Cambridge, MA: Harvard University Press, 1995.

Condee, Nancy. *The Imperial Trace: Recent Russian Cinema*. New York: Oxford University Press, 2009.

Connelly, Matthew. *A Diplomatic Revolution. Algeria's Fight for Independence and the Origins of the Post–Cold War Era*. New York: Oxford University Press, 2002.

Conrad, Sebastian. *What Is Global History?* Princeton, NJ: Princeton University Press, 2016.

Corney, Frederick. *Telling October: Memory and the Making of the Bolshevik Revolution*. Ithaca, NY: Cornell University Press, 2004.

Crews, Robert. "Empire and the Confessional State: Islam and Religious Politics in Nineteenth-Century Russia." *American Historical Review* 108, no. 1 (2003): 50–83.

Crews, Robert. *For Prophet and Tsar: Islam and Empire in Russia and Central Asia*. Cambridge, MA: Harvard University Press, 2006.

Cucciolla, Mario Riccardo. "Legitimation through Self-Victimization: The Uzbek Cotton Affair and Its Repression Narrative (1989–1991)." *Cahiers du Monde russe* 58, no. 4 (2017): 639–68.

Darwin, John. *After Tamerlane: The Global History of Empire*. London: Penguin, 2007.

David-Fox, Michael. *Crossing Borders: Modernity, Ideology, and Culture in Russia and the Soviet Union*. Pittsburgh: University of Pittsburgh Press, 2015.

David-Fox, Michael. "Implications of Transnationalism." *Kritika* 12, no. 4 (2011): 885–904.

David-Fox, Michael. *Revolution of the Mind: Higher Learning among the Bolsheviks, 1918–1929*. Ithaca, NY: Cornell University Press, 1997.

David-Fox, Michael. *Showcasing the Great Experiment: Cultural Diplomacy and Western Visitors to the Soviet Union, 1921–1941*. New York: Oxford University Press, 2011.

Davidson, Apollon. "Afrikanistika, afrikanisty i afrikantsy v Kominterne." Part 1 in *Vostok* 6 (1995): 112–34; part 2 in *Vostok* 2 (1996).

Dawisha, Adeed. *Arab Nationalism in the Twentieth Century: From Triumph to Despair*. Princeton, NJ: Princeton University Press, 2003.

Dawisha, Karen. "Soviet Cultural Relations with Iraq, Syria and Egypt 1955–70." *Soviet Studies* 27, no. 3 (1975): 418–42.

Dawisha, Karen. *Soviet Foreign Policy towards Egypt*. New York: St. Martin's Press, 1979.

Degras, Jane. *The Communist International 1919–42*. Vol. 3. London: Royal Institute of International Affairs, 1964.

Di-Capua, Yoav. "Homeward Bound: Husayn Muruwwah's Integrative Quest for Authenticity." *Journal of Arabic Literature* 44, no. 1 (2013): 21–52.

Di-Capua, Yoav. *No Exit: Arab Existentialism, Jean-Paul Sartre, and Decolonization*. Chicago: University of Chicago Press, 2018.

Dickinson, Kay. *Arab Cinema Travels: Transnational Syria, Palestine, Dubai, and Beyond*. London: BFI Publishing, 2016.

Dietrich, Christopher. *Oil Revolution: Anticolonial Elites, Sovereign Rights, and the Economic Culture of Decolonization*. Cambridge: Cambridge University Press, 2017.

Djagalov, Rossen. *From Internationalism to Postcolonialism: Literature and Cinema between the Second and the Third Worlds*. Montreal: McGill-Queen's University Press, 2020.

Djagalov, Rossen. "KUTV." *Global South Studies*, August 28, 2020, https://globalsouthstudies.as.virginia.edu/key-moments/communist-university-toilers-east-kutv.

Djagalov, Rossen, and Masha Salazkina. "Tashkent '68." *Slavic Review* 75, no. 2 (2016): 279–98.

Dodds, Klaus. *Geopolitics: A Very Short Introduction*. Oxford: Oxford University Press, 2007.

Dolbee, Samuel. "Seferberlik and Bare Feet: Rural Hardship, Citied Dreams, and Social Belonging in 1920s Syria." *Jerusalem Quarterly* 51 (2012): 21–35.

Drieu, Cloé. "Alisher Navoi: prix Staline 1948. Cinéma et politique des nationalités." *Théorème* 8 (2005): 119–27.

Drieu, Cloé. *Cinema, Nation, and Empire in Uzbekistan, 1919–1937*. Translated by Adrian Morfee. Bloomington: Indiana University Press, 2018.

Duberman, Martin. *Paul Robeson: No One Can Silence Me*. New York: New Press, 1995.

Dudziak, Mary. *Cold War Civil Rights: Race and the Image of American Democracy*. Princeton, NJ: Princeton University Press, 2000.

Dudziak, Mary. *Exporting American Dreams: Thurgood Marshall's African Journey*. New York: Oxford University Press, 2008.

Dullin, Sabine. *Hommes d'influence: les ambassadeurs de Staline en Europe, 1930–1939*. Paris: Payot, 2001.

Dullin, Sabine and Etienne Forestier-Peyrat, "Flexible Sovereignties of the Revolutionary State: Soviet Republics Enter World Politics," *Journal of the History of International Law* (published online May 16, 2017).

Edgar, Adrienne. *Intermarriage and the Friendship of Peoples: Ethnic Mixing in Soviet Central Asia*. Ithaca, NY: Cornell University Press, 2022.

Edgar, Adrienne. *Tribal Nation: The Making of Soviet Turkmenistan*. Princeton, NJ: Princeton University Press, 2006.

Egorov, Boris, and Konstantin Azadovskii. "From Anti-Westernism to Anti-Semitism: Stalin and the Impact of the Anti-Cosmopolitan Campaigns on Soviet Culture." *Journal of Cold War Studies* 4, no. 1 (2002): 66–80.

Emel'ianova, Galina. "Aleksandr Moiseevich Shami." In *Neizvestnye stranitsy otechestvennogo vostokovedeniia*, edited by Vitalii Naumkin, 39–81. Moscow: Vostochnaia literatura, 1997.

Engerman, David. *Know Your Enemy: The Rise and Fall of America's Soviet Experts*. New York: Oxford University Press, 2009.

Engerman, David. "The Second World's Third World." *Kritika* 12, no. 1 (2011): 183–211.

English, Robert. *Russia and the Idea of the West: Gorbachev, Intellectuals & and the End of the Cold War*. New York: Columbia University Press, 2000.

Eran, Oded. "Soviet Perception of Arab Communism and its Political Role." In *The USSR and the Middle East*, edited by Michael Confino and Shimon Shamir, 109–21. Jerusalem: Israel University Press, 1973.

Erley, Mieka. "The Dialectics of Nature in Kara Kum." *Slavic Review* 73, no. 4 (Winter 2014): 727–50.

Erlich, Haggai. "Periphery and Youth: Fascist Italy and the Middle East." In *Fascism Outside Europe*, edited by Stein Ugelvik Larsen, 393–423. New York: Columbia University, 2002.

Eudin, Xenia Joukoff, and Robert C. North. *Soviet Russia and the East 1920–1927: A Documentary Survey*. Stanford, CA: Stanford University Press, 1964.

Fahrenthold, Stacy D. *Between the Ottomans and the Entente: The First World War in the Syrian and Lebanese Diaspora, 1908–1925*. New York: Oxford University Press, 2019.

Farah, Bulus. *Min al-'uthmaniyya ila al-dawla al-'ibriyya*. Haifa: al-Sawt, 1985.

Fedtke, Gero "Jadids, Young Bukharans, Communists and the Bukharan Revolution: From an Ideological Debate in the Early Soviet Union." In *Muslim Culture in Russia and Central Asia from the 18th to the Early 20th Centuries*, edited by Anke von Kugelgen, Michael Kemper, and Allen J. Frank, 483–512. Vol. 2. Berlin: Klaus Schwarz Verlag, 1998.

Feldman, Leah. *On the Thresholds of Eurasia*. Ithaca, NY: Cornell University Press, 2018.

Felshtinsky, Yuri. "The Legal Foundations of the Immigration and Emigration Policy of the USSR, 1917–27." *Soviet Studies* 34, no. 3 (July 1982): 327–48.

Filatova, Irina. "Introduction or Scholarship? Education of Africans at the Communist University of the Toilers of the East in the Soviet Union, 1923–37." *Paedagogica Historica* 35, no. 1 (1999): 41–66.

Fisher, Cary. "An American Dilemma: Race and Realpolitik in the American Response to the Bandung Conference 1955." In *Window on Freedom: Race, Civil Rights and Foreign Affairs, 1945–88*, edited by Brenda Gayle Plummer, 115–40. Chapel Hill: University of North Carolina Press, 2004.

Fitzpatrick, Sheila. "The Civil War as a Formative Experience." In *Bolshevik Culture: Experiment and Order in the Russian Revolution*, edited by Abbott Gleason, Peter Kenez, and Richard Stites, 57–76. Bloomington: Indiana University Press, 1985.

Fitzpatrick, Sheila. *The Commissariat of Enlightenment: Soviet Organization of Education and the Arts under Lunacharsky, October 1917–1921*. Cambridge: Cambridge University Press 1970.

Fitzpatrick, Sheila. *The Cultural Front: Power and Culture in Revolutionary Russia*. Ithaca, NY: Cornell University Press, 1992.

Fitzpatrick, Sheila. "Cultural Revolution in Russia 1928–32." *Journal of Contemporary History* 9, no. 1 (1974): 33–52.

Fitzpatrick, Sheila. *Education and Social Mobility in the Soviet Union 1921–34*. Cambridge: Cambridge University Press, 1979.

Fitzpatrick, Sheila. *Everyday Stalinism. Ordinary Life in Extraordinary Times: Soviet Russia in the 1930s*. New York: Oxford University Press, 1999.

Florin, Moritz. "What Is Russia to Us? Colonialism and Soviet Modernity in Kyrgyzstan, 1956–65." *Ab Imperio* 3 (2016): 165–89.

Fogel, Joshua. "The Debates over the Asiatic Mode of Production in Soviet Russia, China, and Japan." *American Historical Review* 93, no. 1 (1998): 56–79.

Franco, Rainer Matos. "Socialism Internationalism and National Classification at the Comintern Schools." *Ab Imperio* 3 (2021): 135–65.
Frangie, Samer. "The Afterlives of Husayn Muruwwa: The Killing of an Intellectual, 1987." In *The Arab Lefts: Histories and Legacies, 1950s–1970s*, edited by Laure Guirgis, 243–58. Edinburgh: Edinburgh University Press, 2020.
Frangie, Samer. "Exiled from History: Yasin al-Hafiz's Autobiographical Preface and the Transformation of Political Critique." *Thesis Eleven* 133, no. 1 (2016): 38–58.
Friedman, Jeremy. *Ripe for Revolution: Building Socialism in the Third World*. Cambridge, MA: Harvard University Press, 2021.
Friedman, Jeremy. *Shadow Cold War: The Sino-Soviet Competition for the Third World*. Chapel Hill: University of North Carolina Press, 2015.
Frolova-Walker, Marina. "National in Form, Socialist in Content: Musical Nation-Building in the Soviet Republics." *Journal of the American Musicological Society* 51 (Summer 1998): 331–71.
Frye, Richard. "Oriental Studies in Russia." In *Russia and Asia*, edited by Wayne Vucinich, 34–46. Stanford, CA: Hoover Institute, 1972.
Fuccaro, Nelida. "Ethnicity and the City: The Kurdish Quarter of Damascus between Ottoman and French Rule, c. 1724–1946." *Urban History* 30, no. 2 (2003): 206–24.
Fursenko, Aleksandr, and Timothy Naftali. *Khrushchev's Cold War: The Inside Story of an American Adversary*. New York: W. W. Norton, 2006.
Garavini, Giuliano. *The Rise and Fall of OPEC in the Twentieth Century*. Oxford: Oxford University Press, 2019.
Gelvin, James. *The Israel-Palestine Conflict: One Hundred Years of War*. Cambridge: Cambridge University Press, 2005.
Genis, Vladimir. "Deportatsiia russkikh iz Turkestana v 1921 gody." *Voprosy istorii* 1 (1998): 44–58.
Genis, Vladimir. "Odin iz stolpov Komissariata: Arsenii Nikolaevich Voznesenskii (1881–1937)." In *Neizvestnye stranitsy otechestvennogo vostokovedeniia*, edited by Vitalii Naumkin, 62–124. Vol. 2 of 4. Moscow: Vostochnaia literatura, 2004.
Genis, Vladimir. *S Bukharoi nado konchat'—k istorii butaforskikh revoliutsii*. Moscow: MNPI, 2001.
Genis, Vladimir. "Sovetskaia Rossiia i Gilianskaia revoliutsiia." *Aziia i Afrika segodnia* 3 (2000): 37–42.
Geraci, Robert. *Window on the East: National and Imperial Identities in Late Tsarist Russia*. Ithaca, NY: Cornell University Press, 2001.
Germanov, Valerii. "Novyi dokument po istorii sovetskogo Turkestana nachala 20-x godov." *Obshchestvennye nauki v Uzbekistane* 4 (1991): 41–47.
Gershoni, Israel. "Why the Muslims Must Fight against Nazi Germany: Muhammad Najati Sidqi's Plea." *Die Welt des Islams* 52 (2012): 471–98.
Gershoni, Israel, ed. *Arab Responses to Fascism and Nazism: Attractions and Repulsions*. Austin: University of Texas Press, 2014.
Gershoni, Israel, and James Jankowski. *Confronting Fascism in Egypt: Dictatorship versus Democracy in the 1930s*. Stanford, CA: Stanford University Press, 2009.
Gessen, Masha. *Where the Jews Aren't: The Sad and Absurd Story of Birobidzhan, Russia's Jewish Autonomous Region*. New York: Schocken, 2016.
Getachew, Adom. *Worldmaking after Empire: The Rise and Fall of Self-Determination*. Princeton, NJ: Princeton University Press, 2019.

Getty, Arch, and Oleg Naumov. *The Road to Terror: Stalin and the Self-Destruction of the Bolsheviks, 1932–39*. New Haven, CT: Yale University Press, 1999.

Gilburd, Eleonory. *To See Paris and Die: The Soviet Lives of Western Culture*. Cambridge, MA: Harvard University Press, 2018.

Gilmore, Glenda Elizabeth. *Defying Dixie: The Radical Roots of Civil Rights, 1919–1950*. New York: W. W. Norton, 2008.

Gitelman, Zvi. *A Century of Ambivalence: The Jews of Russia and the Soviet Union, 1881 to the Present*. Bloomington: Indiana University Press, 2001.

Ginat, Rami. *A History of Egyptian Communism: Jews and Their Compatriots in Quest of Revolution*. Boulder, CO: Lynne Rienner, 2011.

Ginat, Rami. "Soviet Policy towards the Arab World, 1945–48." *Middle Eastern Studies* 32, no. 4 (October 1996): 321–35.

Giustozzi, Antonio, and Artemy Kalinovsky. *Missionaries of Modernity: Advisory Missions and the Struggle for Hegemony from the 1940s to Afghanistan*. London: Hurst & Co., 2016.

Godes, M., "The Reaffirmation of Unilinealism." In *The Asiatic Mode of Production: Science and Politics*, edited by Anne Bailey and Josep Llobera, 99–105. Boston: Routledge, 1981.

Goebel, Michael. *Anti-Imperial Metropolis: Interwar Paris and the Seeds of Third-World Nationalism*. Cambridge: Cambridge University Press, 2016.

Goldman, Wendy Z. *Terror and Democracy in the Age of Stalin: The Social Dynamics of Repression*. New York: Cambridge University Press, 2007.

Goldman, Wendy Z. *Women, the State, and Revolution: Soviet Family Policy and Social Life, 1917–1936*. New York: Cambridge University Press, 1993.

Goff, Krista. *Nested Nationalism: Making and Unmaking Nations in the Soviet Caucasus*. Ithaca, NY: Cornell University Press 2020.

Gopal, Surendra. *Indian Freedom-Fighters in Tashkent, 1917–1922: Contesting Ideologies, Nationalism, Pan Islamism, and Marxism*. Kolkata: Maulana Abul Kalam Azad Institute of Asian Studies, 2002.

Gordon, Joel. *Revolutionary Melodrama: Popular Film and Civic Identity in Nasser's Egypt*. Chicago: University of Chicago Press, 2002.

Gorizontov, Leonid. "The 'Great Circle' of Interior Russia." In *Russian Empire: Space, People, Power, 1700–1930*, edited by Jane Burbank and Mark von Hagen, 67–93. Bloomington: Indiana University Press, 2007.

Gorsuch, Anne. *All This Is Your World: Soviet Tourism at Home and Abroad after Stalin*. Oxford: Oxford University Press, 2011.

Gorsuch, Anne. *Youth in Revolutionary Russia: Enthusiasts, Bohemians, Delinquents*. Bloomington: Indiana University Press, 2000.

Guirguis, Laure, ed. *The Arab Lefts: Histories and Legacies, 1950s–1970s*. Edinburgh: Edinburgh University Press, 2020.

Gusterin, Pavel. *Vostochnyi fakul'tet Voennoi akademii RKKA*. Germany: LAP Lambert Academic Publishing, 2014.

Haddad, Bassam. *Business Networks in Syria: The Political Economy of Authoritarian Resilience*. Stanford, CA: Stanford University Press, 2012.

Hahn, Werner. *Postwar Soviet Politics: The Fall of Zhdanov and the Defeat of Moderation, 1946–53*. Ithaca, NY: Cornell University Press, 1982.

Halfin, Igal. *From Darkness to Light: Class, Consciousness, and Salvation in Revolutionary Russia*. Pittsburgh: University of Pittsburgh Press, 2000.

Halfin, Igal. *Intimate Enemies: Demonizing the Bolshevik Opposition, 1918–1928*. Pittsburgh: University of Pittsburgh Press, 2007.

Halim, Hala. "Lotus, the Afro-Asian Nexus and Global South Comparatism." *Comparative Studies of South Asia, Africa, and the Middle East* 3, no. 3 (2012): 363–83.

Hamed-Troyansky, Vladimir. "Circassian Refugees and the Making of Amman, 1878–1914." *IJMES* 49, no. 4 (2017): 605–23.

Hammad, Hanan. "Arwa Salih's *The Premature*: Gendering the History of the Egyptian Left." *Arab Studies Journal* 24, no. 1 (Spring 2016): 118–42.

Hamzah, Dyala. "Introduction." In *The Making of the Arab Intellectual: Empire, Public Sphere and the Colonial Coordinates of Selfhood*, edited by Dyala Hamzah, 1–19. New York: Routledge, 2012.

Hanna, Jurj. *Ana 'a'id min Musku*. Beirut: no publisher listed, 1947.

Hanna, Jurj. *Fi musku . . . marra thaniya*. Beirut: Dar al-'ilm l-ilmalayin, 1955.

Hanna, Jurj. *Shumikha v filosofii*. Moscow: Progress Publishers, 1965.

Hansen, Claus Bech. "The Ambivalent Empire: Soviet Rule in the Uzbek Soviet Socialist Republic, 1945–1964." PhD diss., European University Institute, 2013.

Hanssen, Jens, and Max Weiss, eds. *Arabic Thought against the Authoritarian Age: Towards an Intellectual History of the Present*. Cambridge: Cambridge University Press, 2018.

Hanssen, Jens, and Max Weiss, eds. *Arabic Thought beyond the Liberal Age: Towards an Intellectual History of the Nahda*. Cambridge: Cambridge University Press, 2016.

Harris, Steven. "Dawn of the Soviet Jet Age: Aeroflot Passengers and Aviation Culture under Nikita Khrushchev." *Kritika* 21, no. 3 (2020): 591–626.

Haugbolle, Sune. "1967 and the New Arab Left." *British Journal of Middle Eastern Studies* 44, no. 4 (2017): 497–512.

Haugbolle, Sune. "Entanglements, Global History, and the Arab Left." *IJMES* 51 (2019): 301–4.

Hauner, Milan. *What Is Asia to Us? Russia's Asian Heartland Yesterday and Today*. New York: Routledge, 1992.

Haywood, Harry. *Black Bolshevik: Autobiography of an Afro-American Communist*. Chicago: Liberator Press, 1978.

Heller, Joseph. "The Failure of Fascism in Jewish Palestine, 1925–1948." In *Fascism outside Europe*, edited by Stein Ugelvik Larsen, 362–92. New York: Columbia University Press, 2002.

Hen-Tov, Jacob. *Communism and Zionism in Palestine during the British Mandate*. New Brunswick, NJ: Routledge, 2021.

Herlihy, Patricia. *Odessa Recollected: The Port and the People*. Brighton, MA: Academic Studies Press, 2018.

Heschel, Susannah. "Orientalist Triangulations: Jewish Scholarship on Islam as a Response to Christian Europe." In *The Muslim Reception of European Orientalism: Reversing the Gaze*, edited by Susannah Heschel and Umar Ryad, 147–67. London: Routledge, 2019.

Hikmet, Nazim. *Life's Good, Brother*. Translated by Mutlu Konak Blasing. New York: Persea, 2013.

Hikmet, Nazim. "Na sluzhbe revoliutsii." In *Vstrechi s Meierkhol'dom: sbornik vospominanii*, edited by L. D. Vendrovskaia, 236–45. Moscow: Vserossiiskoe Teatral'noe Obshchestvo, 1967.

Hillis, Faith. *Utopia's Discontents: Russian Émigrés and the Quest for Freedom, 1830s–1930s*. New York: Oxford University Press, 2021.

al-Hilu, Ibrahim, *al-Shuyu'iyah wa-al-Sihyuniyah walidata al-'aql al-Yahudi*. Beirut: al-Hilw, 1968.
al-Hilu, Yusuf Khattar. *Awraq min Tarikhuna*. Beirut: Dar al-Farabi, 1988.
Hirsch, Francine. *Empire of Nations: Ethnographic Knowledge and the Making of the Soviet Union*. Ithaca, NY: Cornell University Press, 2005.
Hirst, Samuel. "Transnational Anti-Imperialism and the National Forces: Soviet Diplomacy and Turkey, 1920–1923." *Comparative Studies of South Asia, Africa, and the Middle East* 33, no. 2 (2013): 214–26.
Hodgkin, Samuel. *Red Nightingales: The Poetics of Eastern Internationalism*. Cambridge: Cambridge University Press, 2023.
Hoffman, David. *Peasant Metropolis: Social Identities in Moscow, 1929–1941*. Ithaca, NY: Cornell University Press, 1994.
Hoffman, David. *Stalinist Values: The Cultural Norms of Soviet Modernity, 1917–1941*. Ithaca, NY: Cornell University Press, 2003.
Hollinger, David, ed. *The Humanities and the Dynamics of Inclusion since World War II*. Baltimore: Johns Hopkins University Press, 2006.
Holquist, Peter. *Making War, Forging Revolution: Russia's Continuum of Crisis, 1914–1921*. Cambridge, MA: Harvard University Press, 2002.
Holt, Katharine. "Performing as Soviet Central Asia's Source Texts: Lahuti and Džambul in Moscow, 1935–1936." *Cahiers d'Asie centrale* 24 (2015): 213–38.
Hughes, Michael. *Inside the Enigma: British Officials in Russia, 1900–1939*. London: Hambledon Press, 1997.
Hurewitz, J. C., ed. *Soviet-American Rivalry in the Middle East*. New York: Praeger, 1969.
Iakovlev, A. *Gosudarstvennyi antisemitizm v SSSR, 1938–53*. Moscow: Materik, 2005.
Igmen, Ali. *Speaking Soviet with an Accent: Culture and Power in Kyrgyzstan*. Pittsburgh: University of Pittsburgh Press, 2012.
Ikramov, Kamil. *Delo moego ottsa: Roman-khronika*. Moscow: Sovetskii Pisatel', 1991.
Immerwahr, Daniel. *How to Hide an Empire: A History of the Greater United States*. New York: Farrar, Straus & Giroux, 2019.
Iolk, Struve. "AMP and the Class Struggle." In *The Asiatic Mode of Production: Science and Politics*, edited by Anne Bailey and Josep Llobera, 97–98. Boston: Routledge, 1981.
Iriya, Akira. "Culture and Power: International Relations as Intercultural Relations." *Diplomatic History* 3, no. 2 (1979): 115–28.
Isaakyan, Irina L. "Blood and Soil of the Soviet Academy: Politically Institutionalized Anti-Semitism in the Moscow Academic Circles of the Brezhnev Era through the Life Stories of Russian Academic Emigrants." *Nationalities Papers* 36, no. 5 (November 2008): 833–59.
Ishankhodjaeva, Zamira Raiimovna. "Repressivnaia politika Sovetskoi vlasti i ee vozdeistvie na kul'turnuiu zhizn' Uzbekistana, 1925–1950." PhD diss., Tashkent State University, 2012.
Ismael, Tareq, and Jaqueline Ismael. *The Communist Movement in Syria and Lebanon*. Gainesville: University Press of Florida, 1998.
Ismael, Tareq, and Rif'at al-Sa'id. *The Communist Movement in Egypt 1920–88*. Syracuse, NY: Syracuse University Press, 1990.
Istoricheskie resheniia XX s'ezda KPSS i zadachi inteligentsii Uzbekistana: doklad na s'ezde inteligentsii Uzbekistana, Okt 11, 1956. Moscow: Gos. Izd-vo polit. lit., 1956.
Jabar, Faleh, ed. *Post-Marxism and the Middle East*. London: Saqi, 1997.

Jacquemond, Richard. *Conscience of the Nation: Writers, State, and Society in Modern Egypt.* Cairo: AUC Press, 2008.

Jacobson, Jon. *When the Soviet Union Entered World Politics.* Berkeley: University of California Press, 1994.

Jansen, Hanna. "Peoples' Internationalism Central Asian Modernisers, Soviet Oriental Studies and Cultural Revolution in the East (1936–1977)." PhD diss., University of Amsterdam, 2020.

Jansen, Hanna. "Soviet 'Afro-Asians' in UNESCO: Reorienting World History." *Journal of World History* 30, no. 1–2 (June 2019): 193–221.

Jasse, Richard. "The Baghdad Pact: Cold War or Colonialism." *Middle Eastern Studies* 27, no. 1 (Winter 1991): 140–56.

Jersild, Austin. *Orientalism and Empire: North Caucasus Mountain Peoples and the Georgian Frontier, 1845–1917.* Montreal: McGill-Queen's University Press, 2002.

Jian, Chen. *Mao's China and the Cold War.* Chapel Hill: University of North Carolina Press, 2001.

Jones, Polly. "From the Secret Speech to the Burial of Stalin: Real and Ideal Responses to De-Stalinization." In *The Dilemmas of De-Stalinization: Negotiating Cultural and Social Change in the Khrushchev Era*, edited by Polly Jones, 41–63. London: Routledge, 2006.

Jones, Robert A. "The Soviet Concept of 'Limited Sovereignty' from Lenin to Gorbachev: The Brezhnev Doctrine." *Studies in East European Thought* 45, no. 3 (1993): 213–14.

Judge, Edward, and John Langdon. *The Struggle against Imperialism: Anticolonialism and the Cold War.* Lanham, MD: Rowman & Littlefield, 2018.

Kabha, Mustafa. "A Bold Voice Raised above the Raging Waves: Palestinian Intellectual Najati Sidqi and His Battle with Nazi Doctrine at the Time of World War II." In *The Holocaust and the Nakba: A New Grammar of Trauma and History*, edited by Bashir Bashir and Amos Goldberg, 154–72. New York: Columbia University Press, 2019.

Kaganovich, B. S. *Sergei Fedorovich Ol'denburg: Opyt biografii.* St. Petersburg: Fenix, 2006.

Kale-Lostuvali, Elif. "Varieties of Musical Nationalism in Soviet Uzbekistan." *Central Asia Survey* 26, no. 4 (2007): 539–58.

Kalinovsky, Artemy. "Encouraging Resistance: Paul Henze, the Bennigsen School, and the Crisis of Détente." In *Reassessing Orientalism: Interlocking Orientologies in the Cold War Era*, edited by Michael Kemper and Artemy Kalinovsky, 221–42. London: Routledge, 2015.

Kalinovsky, Artemy. *Laboratory of Socialist Development: Cold War Politics and Decolonization in Soviet Tajikistan.* Ithaca, NY: Cornell University Press, 2018.

Kalinovsky, Artemy. "Opera as the Highest Stage of Socialism." *International Institute for Asian Studies*, Newsletter 74 (2016), https://www.iias.asia/the-newsletter/article/opera-highest-stage-socialism.

Kandiyoti, Deniz. "How Far Do Analyses of Postcolonialism Travel? The Case of Central Asia." In *Postsocialism: Ideas, Ideologies and Practices in Eurasia*, edited by Chris Hann, 238–57. London: Routledge, 2002.

Kandiyoti, Deniz. "Postcolonialism Compared: Potentials and Limitations in the Middle East Central Asia." *IJMES* 34 (2002): 279–97.

Kane, Eileen. *Russian Hajj: Empire and the Pilgrimage to Mecca.* Ithaca, NY: Cornell University Press, 2015.

Kane, Eileen, Masha Kirasirova, and Margaret Litvin, eds. *Russian-Arab Worlds A Documentary History.* New York: Oxford University Press, 2023.

Kaplan, Isabelle R. "The Art of Nation-Building: National Culture and Soviet Politics in Stalin-Era Azerbaijan and Other Minority Republics." PhD diss., Georgetown University, 2017.

Kaplan, Isabelle R. "Comrades in Arts: The Soviet Dekada of National Art and the Friendship of Peoples." *RUDN Journal of Russian History* 19, no. 1 (2020): 78–94.

Kappeler, Andreas. "The Russian Empire and Its Nationalities in Post-Soviet Historiographies." In *The Construction and Deconstruction of National Histories in Slavic Eurasia*, edited by Tadayuki Hayashi, 35–51. Sapporo: Slavic Research Center of Hokkaido University, 2003.

Kappeler, Andreas, Gerhard Simon, and George Brunner, eds. *Muslim Communities Reemerge: Historical Perspectives on Nationality, Politics, and Opposition in the Former Soviet Union and Yugoslavia*. Durham, NC: Duke University Press, 1994.

Karasar, Hasan Ali. "Chicherin on the Delimitation of Turkestan: Native Bolsheviks versus Soviet Foreign Policy. Seven Letters from the Russian Archives on Razmezhevanie." *Central Asian Survey* 21, no. 2 (2002): 199–209.

Karim, Bakhtiyor. *Sarvar Azimov: sarmondoshlari hotirasida*. Tashkent: Investbook, 2023.

Karsh, Efraim. *Soviet Policy towards Syria since 1970*. London: Palgrave Macmillan, 1991.

Karsh, Efraim. *The Soviet Union and Syria: The Assad Years*. London: Routledge, 1988.

Kassab, Elizabeth. *Contemporary Arab Thought: Cultural Critique in Comparative Perspectives*. New York: Columbia University Press, 2009.

Kassymbekova, Botakoz. "Leisure and Politics: Soviet Central Asian Tourists across the Iron Curtain." In *Mobilities in Socialist and Post-Socialist States: Societies on the Move*, edited by Kathy Burrell and Kathrin Hörschelmann, 62–86. London: Palgrave Macmillan, 2014.

Kassymbekova, Botakoz, and Christian Teichmann. "The Red Man's Burden: Soviet European Officials in Central Asia in the 1920s and 1930s." In *Helpless Imperialists: Imperial Failure, Fear and Radicalization*, edited by Maurus Reinkowskii and Gregor Thum, 163–86. Göttingen: Vandenhoeck & Ruprecht, 2013.

Katsakioris, Constantin. "Les étudiants de pays arabes formés en Union soviétique pendant la guerre froide, 1956–1991." *Revue européenne des migrations internationales* 32, no. 2 (2016): 13–38.

Katsakioris, Constantin. "The Lumumba University in Moscow: Higher Education for a Soviet-Third World Alliance, 1945–1991." *Journal of Global History* 14, no. 2 (2019): 281–300.

Katsakioris, Constantin. "L'union soviétique et les intellectuels africains: Internationalisme, panafricanisme et négritude pendant les années de la décolonisation, 1954–1964." *Cahiers du Monde russe* 47, no. 1–2 (2006): 15–32.

Kayali, Hasan. *Arabs and Young Turks: Ottomanism, Arabism, and Islamism in the Late Ottoman Empire, 1908–1918*. Berkeley: University of California Press, 1997.

Kedouri, Elie. *In the Anglo-Arab Labyrinth: The McMahon-Husayn Correspondence and Its Interpretations 1914–1939*. London: Routledge, 2000.

Kemper, Michael. "Red Orientalism: Mikhail Pavlovich and Marxist Oriental Studies in Early Soviet Russia." *Die Welt des Islams* 50 (2010): 472–76.

Kemper, Michael, and Gulnaz Sibgatullina. "The Imperial Paradox: Islamic Eurasianism in Contemporary Russia." In *Resignification of Borders: Eurasianism and the Russian World*, edited by Nina Friess and Konstantin Kaminskij, 97–124. Berlin: Frank und Timme, 2019.

Kenez, Peter. *Cinema and Soviet Society: From the Revolution to the Death of Stalin*. London: I. B. Tauris, 2001.

Kenez, Peter. *Civil War in South Russia, 1919–1920: The Defeat of the Whites*. Berkeley: University of California Press, 1977.

al-Khafaji, Isam. "The Arab Left after Glasnost: Who's Afraid of Bureaustroika?" *Middle East Report* 167 (1990): 30–34.

Khalid, Adeeb. *Central Asia: A New History from the Imperial Conquests to the Present*. Princeton, NJ: Princeton University Press, 2021.

Khalid, Adeeb. "Culture and Power in Colonial Turkestan." *Cahiers d'Asie centrale* 17–18 (2009): 403–36.

Khalid, Adeeb. "Introduction: Locating the (Post-) Colonial in Soviet History." *Central Asian Survey* 26, no. 4 (2007): 465–73.

Khalid, Adeeb. *Islam after Communism: Religion and Politics in Central Asia*. Berkeley: University of California Press, 2007.

Khalid, Adeeb. *Making Uzbekistan: Nation, Empire, and Revolution in the Early USSR*. Ithaca, NY: Cornell University Press, 2015.

Khalid, Adeeb. "Russian History and the Debate over Orientalism." *Kritika* 1, no. 4 (Fall 2000): 691–99.

Khalid, Adeeb. "Turkestan v 1917–22 godakh: bor'ba za vlast' na okraine Rossii." In *Tragediia velikoi derzhavy: natsional'nyi vopros i raspad Sovetskogo Soiuza*, edited by G. Sevost'ianov, 189–226. Moscow: Sotsial'no-politicheskaia mysl', 2005.

Khater, Akram Fuad. *Inventing Home: Emigration, Gender, and the Middle Class in Lebanon, 1870–1920*. Berkeley: University of California Press, 2001.

Khayyata, Salim. *Hamiyat al-gharb. Jawlat dirasiyya bayn sira' al-jama'at fi-l-'alam al-gharbi*. Beirut: Matba'at Sadir, 1933

Khayyata, Salim. *Al-habasha al-mazluma*. Beirut: Rawda al-Funun, 1935.

Khlevniuk, Oleg, ed. *Regional'naia politika N. S. Khrushcheva: TsK KPSS i mestnye partiinye komitety, 1953–1964 gg*. Moscow: ROSSPEN, 2009.

Khomitsky, Maria. "World Literature, Soviet Style: A Forgotten Episode in the History of the Idea." *Ab Imperio* 3 (2013): 119–54.

Khoury, Philip. *Syria and the French Mandate: The Politics of Arab Nationalism, 1920–1945*. Princeton, NJ: Princeton University Press, 1987.

Khrushchev, Nikita. *Memoirs of Nikita Khrushchev*, Vol. 2: *Reformer 1945–1964*. Philadelphia: Pennsylvania State University Press, 2006.

Khuri-Makdisi, Ilham. *Eastern Mediterranean and the Making of Global Radicalism, 1860–1914*. Berkeley: University of California Press, 2010.

Khuri-Makdisi, Ilham. "Fin-de-Siècle Egypt: A Nexus for Mediterranean and Global Radical Networks." In *Global Muslims in the Age of Steam and Print*, edited by James L. Gelvin and Nile Green, 78–100. Berkeley: University of California Press, 2014.

Khuri-Makdisi, Ilham. "Inscribing Socialism into the Nahda." In The Making of the Arab Intellectual: Empire, Public Sphere and the Colonial Coordinates of Selfhood, edited by Dyala Hamzah, 63–89. New York: Routledge, 2012.

Kindleberger, Charles P. *The World in Depression, 1929–1939*. Los Angeles: University of California Press, 1973.

Kirasirova, Masha. "An Egyptian Communist Family Romance: Revolution and Gender in the Transnational Life of Charlotte Rosenthal." In *The Global Impacts of Russia's Great War and Revolution*, Book 2, Part 1, edited by Choi Chatterjee et al., 309–36. Bloomington, IN: Slavica Publishers, 2019.

Kirasirova, Masha. "Building Anti-Colonial Utopia: The Politics of Space in Soviet Tashkent in the 'long 1960s'." In *The Routledge Handbook of the Global Sixties*, edited by Jian Chen, Martin Klimke, Masha Kirasirova, Mary Nolan, and Marilyn Young, 53–66. New York: Routledge, 2018.

Kirasirova, Masha. "The 'East' as a Category of Bolshevik Ideology and Comintern Administration: The Arab Section of the Communist University of the Toilers of the East." *Kritika* 18, no. 1 (2017): 7–34.

Kirasirova, Masha. "The Partisans of Peace in Lebanon and Syria: Towards and Intellectual and Political History of the Early 1950s Arab Left." *The International Journal of Middle East Studies* (2024), forthcoming.

Kirschenbaum, Lisa A. *International Communism and the Spanish Civil War: Solidarity and Suspicion*. New York: Cambridge University Press, 2015.

Kitrinos, Robert. "The CPSU Central Committee's International Department." In *Soviet Foreign Policy in a Changing World*, edited by Robbin Frederick Laird and Erik P. Hoffmann, 180–206. New York: Adeline Publishing, 1986.

Klein, Menachem. "Egypt's Revolutionary Publishing Culture, 1952–62." *Middle Eastern Studies* 39, no. 2 (2003): 149–78.

Kotljarchuk, Andrej, and Olle Sundström, eds. *Ethnic and Religious Minorities in Stalin's Soviet Union New Dimensions of Research*. Stockholm: Södertörn University, 2017.

Knight, Nathaniel. "Grigor'ev in Orenburg, 1851–1862: Russian Orientalism in the Service of Empire?" *Slavic Review* 59, no. 1 (2000): 74–100.

Knight, Nathaniel. "On Russian Orientalism: A Response to Adeeb Khalid." *Kritika* 1, no. 4 (2000): 691–715.

Kocho-Williams, Alastair. "The Soviet Diplomatic Corps and Stalin's Purges." *Slavonic and East European Review* 86, no. 1 (January 2008): 90–110.

Kolarz, Walter. "Colonialism—Theory and Practice." In *Communism and Colonialism: Essays by Walter Kolarz*, edited by George Gretton, 23 (London: Macmillan, 1964).

Koot, John. "*The Asiatic Department of the Russian Foreign Ministry and the Formation of Policy Toward the Non-western World, 1881–1894.*" PhD diss., Harvard University, 1980.

Kosach, Grigorii. *Kommunisty Blizhnego Vostoka v SSSR 1920–30-e gody*. Moscow: Russian State Humanitarian University, 2009.

Kosach, Grigorii. *Krasnyi Flag nad Blizhnim Vostokom*. Moscow: Institute of Countries of Asia and Africa, 2001.

Kosach, Grigorii. "Palestinets Vol'f Averbukh." In *Neizvestnye stranitsy otechestvennogo vostokovedeniia*, edited by Vitalii Naumkin et al., 56–104. Vol. 4. Moscow: Vostochnaia Literatura, 2014.

Kosach, Grigorii. "Palestinskii kommunist 1920–1930 godov: avtobiografiia Ali Libermana." *Oriens* 2 (2004): 128–45.

Koshiro, Yukiko. *Imperial Eclipse: Japan's Strategic Thinking about Continental Asia before August 1945*. Ithaca, NY: Cornell University Press, 2013.

Kotkin, Stephen. *Armageddon Averted: The Soviet Collapse, 1970–2000*. New York: Oxford University Press, 2001.

Kotkin, Stephen. "The Kiss of Debt: The East Bloc Goes Borrowing." In *Shock of the Global: The 1970s in Perspective*, edited by Niall Ferguson, Charles Maier, Erez Manela, and Daniel Sargent, 80–94. Cambridge, MA: Harvard University Press, 2010.

Kotkin, Stephen. *Magnetic Mountain: Stalinism as a Civilization*. Berkeley: University of California Press, 1995.

Kotkin, Stephen. "Modern Times: The Soviet Union and the Interwar Conjuncture." *Kritika* 2, no. 1 (2001): 111–64.
Kotkin, Stephen. *Stalin*, Vol. 1: *Paradoxes of Power, 1878–1928*. New York: Penguin, 2014.
Kotkin, Stephen. *Stalin*, Vol. 2: *Waiting for Hitler, 1929–1941*. New York: Penguin, 2018.
Koyagi, Mikiya. *Iran in Motion: Mobility, Space, and the Trans-Iranian Railway*. Redwood City, CA: Stanford University Press, 2021.
Kramer, Mark. "The Soviet Legacy in Russian Foreign Policy." *Political Science Quarterly* 134, no. 4 (Winter 2019–20): 585–609.
Kudaibergenova, Diana. *Rewriting the Nation in Modern Kazakh Literature*. Lanham, MD: Lexington Books, 2017.
Kudaibergenova, Diana. "The Use and Abuse of Postcolonial Discourses in Post-independent Kazakhstan." *Europe-Asia Studies* 68, no. 5 (2016): 917–35.
Kudukhov, K. "Organizatsionnaia struktura i glavnye napravleniia deiatel'nosti Turkestanskogo Biuro Kominterna v nachale 1921 g." *Pro Nunc Sovremennye politicheskie protsessy* 1, no. 10 (2011): 185–89.
Laruelle, Marlene. "The Concept of Ethnogenesis in Central Asia: Political Context and Institutional Mediators (1940–50)." *Kritika* 9 (2008): 169–88.
Laruelle, Marlene. *Russian Eurasianism: An Ideology of Empire*. Baltimore: Johns Hopkins University Press, 2008.
Laqueur, Walter. *Communism and Nationalism in the Middle East*. New York: Praeger, 1956.
Laqueur, Walter. *The Soviet Union and the Middle East*. New York: Praeger, 1959.
Laqueur, Walter [writing as G. Z. Yisraeli]. *MOPS–PCP–MAKI*. Tel Aviv: Am Oved, 1953.
Layton, Susan. *Russian Literature and Empire: Conquest of the Caucasus from Pushkin to Tolstoy*. New York: Cambridge University Press, 1994.
Lazitch, Branko, and Milorad M. Drachkovitch. *Biographical Dictionary of the Comintern*. Stanford, CA: Hoover Institution, 1986
Lazzerini, Edward. "Local Accommodations and Resistance to Colonialism in Nineteenth-Century Crimea." In *Russia's Orient: Imperial Borderlands and Peoples, 1700–1917*, edited by Daniel Brower and Edward Lazzerini, 169–87. Bloomington: Indiana University Press, 1997.
LeDonne, John. *The Russian Empire and the World: 1700–1917, The Geopolitics of Expansion and Containment*. New York: Oxford University Press, 1997.
Lenin, V. I. *Collected Works*. Vol 31. Moscow: Progress Publisher, 1966.
Lesch, David. *1979: The Year That Shaped the Modern Middle East*. Boulder, CO: Westview Press, 2001.
Lewis, Martin, and Karen Wigen. *The Myth of Continents: A Critique of Metageography*. Berkeley: University of California Press, 1997.
Lewis, Su Lin, and Carolien Stolte. "Other Bandungs: Afro-Asian Internationalisms in the Early Cold War." *Journal of World History* 30, no. 1–2 (June 2019): 1–19.
Leys, Norman. *Color Bar in East Africa*. New York: Negro Universities Press, 1970.
Lieven, Anatol, Aleksei V. Malashenko, and Dmitri Trenin, eds. *Russia's Restless Frontier: The Chechnya Factor in Post-Soviet Russia*. Washington, DC: Carnegie Endowment for International Peace, 2004.
Linkhoeva, Tatiana. *Revolution Goes East: Imperial Japan and Soviet Communism*. Ithaca, NY: Cornell University Press, 2020.
Little, Douglas. *American Orientalism: The United States and the Middle East since 1945*. Chapel Hill: University of North Carolina Press, 2003.

Littlepage, John D., with Demaree Bess. *In Search of Soviet Gold.* New York: Harcourt, Brace, 1938.

Litvin, Margaret. "Egypt's Uzbek Mirror: Muhammad Mansi Qandil's Post-Soviet Islamic Humanism." *Journal of Arabic Literature* 42, no. 2 (2011): 101–19.

Litvin, Margaret. "Fellow Travelers? Two Arab Study Abroad Narratives of Moscow." In *Illusions and Disillusionment: Travel Writing in the Modern Age,* edited by Roberta Micallef, 96–118. Cambridge, MA: ILEX/Harvard University Press, 2018.

Litvin, Margaret. "Intimate Foreign Relations: Racist Inclusion in the Soviet Dormitory Novel." *Comparative Literature* 75, no. 2 (2023): 153–71.

Liu, Hong. "Constructing a China Metaphor: Sukarno's Perception of the PRC and Indonesia's Political Transformation." *Journal of Southeast Asian Studies* 28, no. 1 (1997): 27–46.

Lo, Bobo. *Russia and the New World Disorder.* London: Chatham House, 2015.

Loader, Michael. "Beria and Khrushchev: The Power Struggle over Nationality Policy and the Case of Latvia." *Europe-Asia Studies* 68, no. 10 (2016): 1759–92.

Loader, Michael. "A Stalinist Purge in the Khrushchev Era? The Latvian Communist Party Purge, 1959–1963." *Slavonic and East European Review* 96, no 2 (2018): 244–82.

Lockman, Zachary. *Contending Visions of the Middle East: The History and Politics of Orientalism.* Cambridge: Cambridge University Press, 2004.

Lohr, Eric. *Russian Citizenship: From Empire to Soviet Union.* Cambridge, MA: Harvard University Press, 2012.

Lovell, Julia. *Maoism: A Global History.* New York: Penguin, 2019.

Louro, Michele, Carolien Stolte, Heather Streets-Salter, and Sana Tannoury-Karam, eds. *League against Imperialism: Lives and Afterlives.* Chicago: University of Chicago Press, 2020.

Lund, Aaron. "From Cold War to Civil War: 75 Years of Russian-Syrian Relations." Swedish Institute of International Affairs, 2019, https://www.ui.se/globalassets/ui.se-eng/publications/ui-publications/2019/ui-paper-no.-7-2019.pdf.

Lüthi, Lorenz. *The Sino-Soviet Split: Cold War in the Communist World.* Princeton, NJ: Princeton University Press, 2008.

Lutskii, Vladimir. *Uzbekistan i Egipet: itogi dvukh system.* Moscow: International Agrarian Institute, 1934.

Maduyan, Artin. *Hayat 'ala al-Mitras.* Beirut: Dar al-Farabi, 2011.

Magnusdottir, Rósa. *Enemy Number One: The United States of America in Soviet Ideology and Propaganda, 1945–1959.* New York: Oxford University 2019

Maier, Charles. "Consigning the Twentieth Century to History: Alternative Narratives for the Modern Era." *American Historical Review* 105, no. 3 (2000): 807–31.

Makdisi, Ussama. *Age of Coexistence: The Ecumenical Frame and the Making of the Modern Arab World.* Oakland: University of California Press, 2019.

Makhzangi, Mohamed. *Memories of a Meltdown.* Cairo: American University in Cairo Press, 2006.

Malia, Martin. *Russia under Western Eyes: From the Bronze Horseman to the Lenin Mausoleum.* Cambridge, MA: Harvard University Press, 1999.

Mally, Lynn. *Culture of the Future: The Proletkult Movement in Revolutionary Russia.* Berkeley: University of California, 1990.

Mal'tsev, Orest. *Tashkentskie vstrechi: literaturnye portrety uchastnikov Tashkentskoi konferentsii pisatelei stran Azii i Afriki.* Tashkent: Gos. izd-vo khudozh. lit-ry UzSSR, 1960.

Manela, Erez. *The Wilsonian Moment: Self-Determination and the International Origins of Anticolonial Nationalism*. New York: Oxford University Press, 2007.

Manjapra, Kris. "Communist Internationalism and Transcolonial Recognition." In *Cosmopolitan Thought Zones: South Asia and the Global Circulation of Ideas*, edited by Sugata Bose and Kris Manjapra, 159–77. Basingstoke: Palgrave Macmillan, 2010.

Marks, Robert. *The Origins of the Modern World: A Global and Environmental Narrative from the Fifteenth to the Twenty-First Century*. Lanham, MD: Rowman & Littlefield, 2015.

Marks, Stephen. *How Russia Shaped the Modern World: From Art to Anti Semitism, Ballet to Bolshevism*. Princeton, NJ: Princeton University Press, 2003.

Marshall, Alex. *The Russian General Staff and Asia, 1800–1917*. London: Routledge 2006.

Martin, Geoffrey J. *A History of Geographical Ideas*. 4th ed. New York: Oxford University Press, 2005.

Martin, Terry. *The Affirmative Action Empire: Nations and Nationalism in the Soviet Union, 1923–1939*. Ithaca, NY: Cornell University Press, 2001.

Martin, Terry. "The Origins of Soviet Ethnic Cleansing." *Journal of Modern History* 70, no. 4 (1998): 813–61.

Martin, Terry. "The Soviet Union as Empire: Salvaging a Dubious Analytical Category." *Ab Imperio* 2 (2002): 91–105.

Masden, Magnus. "Beyond Bukhara: Trade, Identity and Interregional Exchange across Asia." *History and Anthropology* 29 (2018): 84–100.

Mastny, Vojtech. "Soviet Foreign Policy, 1953–62." In *The Cambridge History of the Cold War*: Vol. 1, *Origins*, edited by Melvyn Leffler and Odd Arne Westad, 312–33. Cambridge: Cambridge University Press, 2010.

Matera, Marc. *Black London: The Imperial Metropolis and the Decolonization in the Twentieth Century*. Berkeley: University of California Press, 2015.

Matusevich, Maxim. "Black in the USSR." *Transition* 100 (2008): 56–74.

McCaw, Dick. *Bakhtin and Theatre: Dialogues with Stanislavsky, Meyerhold and Grotowski*. London: Routledge, 2016.

McClellan, Woodford. "Africans and Black Americans in the Comintern Schools, 1925–1934." *International Journal of African Historical Studies* 26, no. 2 (1993): 371–79.

McGuire, Elizabeth. *Red at Heart: How Chinese Communists Fell in Love with the Russian Revolution*. New York: Oxford University Press, 2018.

McKeown, Adam. "Global Migration, 1846–1970." *Journal of World History* 15, no. 2 (2004): 155–89.

Mëhilli, Elidor. *From Stalin to Mao: Albania and the Socialist World*. Ithaca, NY: Cornell University Press, 2017.

Meijer, Jan M., ed. *The Trotsky Papers*. Vol. 1. London: Mouton, 1964.

Menicucci, Garay. "The Russian Revolution and Popular Movements in Syria in the 1920s." PhD diss., Georgetown University, 1993.

Meyer, James. "Children of Trans-Empire: Nâzım Hikmet and the First Generation of Turkish Students at Moscow's Communist University of the East." *Journal of the Ottoman and Turkish Studies Association* 5, no. 2 (2018): 195–218.

Meyer, James H. "Immigration, Return, and the Politics of Citizenship: Russian Muslims in the Ottoman Empire, 1860–1914." *IJMES* 39 (2007): 15–32.

Mikoulski, Dimitri. "The Study of Islam in Russia and the Former Soviet Union: An Overview." In *Mapping Islamic Studies: Genealogy, Continuity and Change*, edited by Azim Nanji, 95–107. Berlin: Walter de Gruyter, 1997.

Mikoyan, Anastas. *Speech at the 20th Congress of the CPSU*. Moscow: Foreign Languages Publishing House, 1956.
Miller, Chris. "Georgii Mirskii and Soviet Theories of Authoritarian Modernization." *International History Review* 41, no. 2 (2019): 304–22.
Miliband, Sofiia. *Biobibliograficheskii slovar' otechestvennych vostokovedov s 1917 g.* Moscow: Nauka, 1995.
Miliband, Sofiia. *Vostokovedy Rossii, XX–nachalo XXI veka: bibliograficheskii slovar' v dvukh knigakh*. Moscow: Vostochnaia literatura RAN, 2008.
Minault, Gail. *The Khilafat Movement: Religious Symbolism and Political Mobilization in India*. New York: Columbia University Press, 1982.
Moch, Leslie Page, and Lewis H. Siegelbaum. *Broad Is My Native Land: Repertoires and Regimes of Migration in Russia's Twentieth Century*. Ithaca, NY: Cornell University Press, 2014.
Moore, David Chioni. "Is the Post- in Postcolonial the Post- in Post-Soviet? Toward a Global Postcolonial Critique." *PMLA* 116, no. 1 (2001): 111–28.
Morefield, Jeanne. *Empires without Imperialism: Anglo-American Decline and the Politics of Deflection*. Oxford: Oxford University Press: 2014.
Morrison, Alexander. *The Russian Conquest of Central Asia*. Cambridge: Cambridge University Press, 2020.
Mostashari, Firouzeh. "Colonial Dilemmas: Russian Policies in the Muslim Caucasus." In *Of Religion and Empire: Missions, Conversion, and Tolerance in Tsarist Russia*, edited by Robert Geraci and Michael Khodarkovsky, 229–49. Ithaca, NY: Cornell University Press, 2001.
Motadel, David. *Islam and Nazi Germany's War*. Cambridge, MA: Harvard University Press, 2014.
Moubayed, Sami. *Steel & Silk: Men and Women Who Shaped Syria, 1900-2000*. Seattle: Cune, 2006.
Moyn, Samuel. *The Last Utopia and Human Rights*. Cambridge, MA: Harvard University Press, 2013.
Mukhitdinov, Nuriddin. *Gody, provedennye v Kremle*. Tashkent: Izd-vo narodnogo naslediia im. Abduly Kadyri, 1994.
Mukhitdinov, Nuriddin. *Reka vremeni ot Stalina do Gorbacheva: Vospominanie*. Moscow: Rusti-Rosti, 1995.
Muruwwa, Husayn. *Qadaya adabiyya*. Cairo: Dar al-Fikr, 1956.
Myer, Will. *Islam and Colonialism: Western Perspectives on Soviet Asia*. London: Routledge Curzon, 2002.
Nasyrkhodjaev, Sabitkhan. *Kompartiia Uzbekistana—organizator aktivnogo uchastiia intelligentsii v sotroitel'stve kommunizma, 1959-1970*. Moscow: Moscow University Press, 1971.
Nathans, Benjamin. *Beyond the Pale: The Jewish Encounter with Late Imperial Russia*. Berkeley: University of California Press, 2002.
Naumkin, Vitalii. *Nesostoiavsheesia partnerstvo: sovetskaia diplomatiia v Saudovskoi Aravii mezhdu mirovymi voiinami*. Moscow: Aspekt Press, 2018.
Naumkin, Vitalii, ed. *Blizhnevostochnyi Konflikt, 1957-1967: Iz dokumentov Arkhiva Vneshnei Politiki Rossiiskoi Federatsii*. 2 vols. Moscow: Materik, 2003.
Nishanov, Rafik. *Derev'ia zeleneiut do metelei: Rafik Nishanov rasskazyvaet Marine Zavade i Iuriiu Kulikovy*. Moscow: Molodaia gvardia, 2012.

Nordbruch, Götz. "Defending the French Revolution during World War II: Raif Khoury and the Intellectual Challenge of Nazism in the Levant." *Mediterranean Historical Review* 21, no. 2 (2006): 219–38.

Nordbruch, Götz. *Nazism in Syria and Lebanon: The Ambivalence of the German Option, 1933–1945*. London: Routledge, 2009.

Northrop, Douglas. "Nationalizing Backwardness: Gender, Empire and Uzbek Identity." In *A State of Nations: Empire and Nation-Making in the Age of Lenin and Stalin*, edited by Ronald Suny and Terry Martin, 191–222. New York: Oxford University Press, 2001.

Northrop, Douglas. *Veiled Empire: Gender and Power in Stalinist Central Asia*. Ithaca, NY: Cornell University Press, 2004.

Nove, Alec. *An Economic History of the U.S.S.R.* Rev. ed. London: Penguin Books, 1989.

Nunan, Timothy. "A Union Reframed: Sovinformbiuro, Postwar Soviet Photography, and Visual Orders in Soviet Central Asia." *Kritika* 17, no. 3 (2016): 553–83.

Nutting, Anthony. *Nasser*. London: Constable, 1972.

Obertreis, Julia. *Imperial Desert Dreams: Cotton Growing and Irrigation in Central Asia, 1860–1991*. Germany: V&R Unipress, 2017.

Osterhammel, Jürgen. *The Transformation of the World*. Princeton, NJ: Princeton University Press, 2014.

Ouimet, Matthew. *Rise and Fall of the Brezhnev Doctrine*. Chapel Hill: University of North Carolina Press, 2003.

Padmore, George. *How Russia Transformed Her Colonial Empire*. London: Dennis Dobson, 1946.

Painter, David. "Oil, Resources, and the Cold War, 1945–1962." In *The Cambridge History of the Cold War*, vol. 1, edited by Melvyn P. Leffler and Odd Arne Westad, 486–507. Cambridge: Cambridge University Press, 2010.

Pavlovich, Mikhail. "Velikie zhelezhnodorozhnye i morskie puti budushchago." St. Petersburg: Vol'f, 1913.

Pechatnov, Vladimir. "The Soviet Union and the World, 1944–1953." In *The Cambridge History of the Cold War*, vol. 1, edited by Melvyn P. Leffler and Odd Arne Westad, 90–111. Cambridge: Cambridge University Press, 2010.

Pechatnov, Vladimir, and Earl Edmondson. "The Russian Perspective." In *Debating the Origins of the Cold War; American and Russian Perspectives*, edited by Ralph B. Levering et al., 85–177. Lanham, MD: Rowman & Littlefield, 2002.

Pereira, Norman. *White Siberia: The Politics of Civil War*. Montreal: McGill-Queen's University Press, 1995.

Perovic, Jeronim. *From Conquest to Deportation: The North Caucasus under Russian Rule*. Oxford: Oxford University Press, 2018.

Persits, M. A. *Persidskii front mirovoi revoliutsii: Dokumenty o sovetskom vtorzhenii v Gilian (1920–1921)*. Moscow: Kvadriga, 2009.

Persits, M. A. "Vostochnye internatsionalisty v Rossii i nekotorye voprosy natsional'no-osvoboditernogo dvizheniya (yuF 1918–1920)." In *Komintern i Vostok*, edited by R. A. Ulyanovskii, 53–109. Moscow: Nauka, 1969.

Peterson, John E. "Guerrilla Warfare and Ideological Confrontation in the Arabian Peninsula: The Rebellion in Dhufar." *World Affairs* 139, no. 4 (1977): 278–95.

Petersson, Fredrik. "Hub of the Anti-Imperialist Movement: The League against Imperialism and Berlin, 1927–1933." *Interventions* 1 (2014): 49–71.

Petersson, Fredrik. *Willi Munzenberg, the League against Imperialism, and the Comintern, 1925–1933*. Lewiston, NY: Edwin Mellen Press, 2013.

Petrone, Karen. *Life Has Become More Joyous, Comrades: Celebrations in the Time of Stalin.* Bloomington: Indiana University Press, 2000.
Petrosian, Iu. "Shtrikhi biografii V. G. Gafurova-vostokoveda." In *Akademik Bobojon Ghafurov: k 100-letiu so dnia rozhdenia*, edited by Ninel Ghafurova, 39–46. Moscow: Vostochnaia literatura, 2009.
Pipes, Richard. *The Formation of the Soviet Union: Communism and Nationalism 1917–1923.* Cambridge, MA: Harvard University Press, 1997.
Pipes, Richard. "Muslims of Soviet Central Asia: Trends and Prospects." *Middle East Journal* 9 (1955): 147–62.
Pletsch, Carl. "Three Worlds, or the Division of Social Scientific Labor, circa 1950–1975." *Comparative Studies in Society and History* 23, no. 4 (October 1981): 565–90.
Plummer, Brenda Gayle. *Rising Wind: Black Americans and US Foreign Policy, 1935–60.* Chapel Hill: University of North Carolina Press, 1996.
Pollock, Ethan. *Stalin and the Soviet Science Wars.* Princeton, NJ: Princeton University Press, 2006.
Popp, Roland. "Stumbling Decidedly into the Six-Day War." *Middle East Journal* 60, no. 2 (2006): 281–309.
Prashad, Vijay. *The Darker Nations: A People's History of the Third World.* New York: The New Press, 2007.
Primakov, Yevgeny. *Russia and the Arabs: Behind the Scenes in the Middle East from the Cold War to the Present.* New York: Basic Books, 2009.
Primakov, Yevgeny. *Russian Crossroads: Toward the New Millennium.* Translated by Felix Rosenthal. New Haven, CT: Yale University Press, 2004.
Pristed, Birgitte Beck. "Soviet Wall Newspapers: Social(ist) Media of an Analog Age." In *The Oxford Handbook of Communist Visual Cultures*, edited by Aga Skrodzka, Xiaoning Lu, and Katarzyna Marciniak, 110–35. Oxford: Oxford University Press, 2020.
Prokhorov, Alexander. "Springtime for Soviet Cinema Re/viewing the 1960s." Pittsburgh: Russian Film Symposium, 2001.
Protokoly Xgo Kongressa. Moscow, 1933.
Provence, Michael. "French Mandate Counterinsurgency and the Repression of the Great Syrian Revolt." In *The Routledge Handbook of the History of the Middle East Mandate*, edited by Cyrus Schayegh and Andrew Arsan, 136–52. London: Routledge, 2015.
Prusin, Alexander, and Scott Zeman. "Taming Russia's Wild East: The Central Asian Historical-Revolutionary Film as Soviet Orientalism." *Historical Journal of Film, Radio and Television* 23, no. 3 (2003): 259–70.
Qal'aji, Qadri. *Tajribat arabi fi al-hizb al-shuyu'i.* Beirut: al-Jihad Press, 1960.
Rac, Katalin. "Arabic Literature for the Colonizer and the Colonized: Ignaz Goldziher and Hungary's Eastern politics (1878–1918)." In *Muslim Reception of European Orientalism, Reversing the Gaze*, edited by Susannah Heschel and Umar Ryad, 80–102. London: Routledge, 2019.
Radchenko, Sergey. *Two Suns in the Heavens: The Sino-Soviet Struggle for Supremacy, 1962–1967.* Stanford, CA: Stanford University Press, 2009.
Rahmanov, Mamadzhan. *Khamza i uzbekskii teatr.* Tashkent: Gosizdat, 1960.
Ram, Harsha. "Imagining Eurasia: The Poetics and Ideology of Olzhas Suleimenov's Az i Ia." *Slavic Review* 60, no. 2 (2001): 289–311.
Ram, Harsha. *The Imperial Sublime: A Russian Poetics of Empire.* Madison: University of Wisconsin Press, 2003.

Ramet, Pedro. *Soviet-Syrian Relationship: Since 1955: A Troubled Alliance*. Boulder, CO: Westview Press, 1990.

Ransel, David L. "Reflections on Transnational and World History in the USA and Its Applications." *Historisk tidskrift* 127, no. 4 (2007): 625–42.

Rashidov, Sharof, ed. *Materialy pervoi vsesoiuznoi nauchnoi konferentsii vostokovedov v g. Tashkente*. Tashkent: Izdatel'stvo Akademii Nauk Uzbekskoj SSR, 1958.

Ravandi-Fadai, Lana. "'Red Mecca'—The Communist University for Laborers of the East (KUTV): Iranian Scholars and Students in Moscow in the 1920s and 1930s." *Iranian Studies* 48, no. 5 (2015): 713–27.

Razlogova, Elena. "Cinema in the Spirit of Bandung: The Afro-Asian Film Festival Circuit, 1957–1964." In *The Cultural Cold War and the Global South: Sites of Contest and Communitas*, edited by Kerry Bystrom, Monica Popescu, and Katherine Zien, 111–28. New York: Routledge, 2021.

Razlogova, Elena. "World Cinema at Soviet Festivals: Cultural Diplomacy and Personal Ties." *Studies in European Cinema* 17, no. 2 (2019): 140–54.

Reeder, Roberta. *Anna Akhmatova: Poet and Prophet*. New York: St. Martin's Press, 1994.

"Report on the Communist 'Peace' Offensive: A Campaign to Disarm and Defeat the United States." Washington, DC: US House of Representatives Committee on Un-American Activities, 1951.

Reynolds, Michael. *Shattering Empires: The Clash and Collapse of the Ottoman and Russian Empires 1908–1918*. Princeton, NJ: Princeton University Press, 2011.

Rezvan, Efim. *Russian Ships in the Gulf: The Russian General*. London: Garnett, 1993.

Riasanovsky, Nicholas V. "Asia through Russian Eyes." In *Russia and Asia*, edited by Wayne S. Vucinich, 3–29. Stanford, CA: Hoover Institution Press, 1972.

Riasanovsky, Nicholas V. "Russia and Asia: Two 19th Century Views." *California Slavic Studies* 1 (1960): 170–81.

Riasanovsky, Nicholas. *Russia and the West in the Teaching of the Slavophiles: A Study of Romantic Ideology*. Gloucester, MA: P. Smith, 1965.

Riddell, John. *Toward the United Front: Proceedings of the Fourth Congress of the Communist International, 1922*. Leiden: Brill, 2011.

Riddell, John. *Workers of the World and Oppressed Peoples, Unite: Proceedings and Documents of the Second Congress, 1920*. Vols. 1 and 2. New York: Pathfinder Press, 1991.

Riddell, John, ed. *To See the Dawn, Baku, 1920: First Congress of the Peoples of the East, The Communist International in Lenin's Time*. New York: Pathfinder, 1993.

Rieber, Alfred J. "How Persistent Are Persistent Factors?" In *Russian Foreign Policy in the Twenty-First Century and the Shadow of the Past*, edited by Robert Legvold, 205–78. New York: Columbia University Press, 2007.

Rieber, Alfred. *The Struggle for the Eurasian Borderlands: From the Rise of Early Modern Empires to the End of the First World War*. Cambridge: Cambridge University Press. 2014.

Ritchie, Galen. "The Asiatic Department during the Reign of Alexander II, 1855–1881." PhD diss., Columbia University, 1970.

Robson, Laura. *States of Separation: Transfer, Partition, and the Making of the Modern Middle East*. Oakland: University of California Press, 2017.

Rodionov, Mikhail. "Profiles under Pressure: Orientalists in Petrograd/Leningrad." In *The Heritage of Soviet Oriental Studies*, edited by Michael Kemper and Stephan Conermann, 47–57. London: Routledge, 2011.

Rogers, Douglas. *The Depths of Russia: Oil, Power, and Culture after Socialism*. Ithaca, NY: Cornell University Press, 2015.
Roosien, Claire. "'Not Just Tea Drinking': The Red Teahouse and the Soviet State Public in Interwar Uzbekistan." *Kritika* 22, no. 3 (2021): 479–510.
Roshwald, Aviel. *Ethnic Nationalism and the Fall of Empires: Central Europe, Russia, and the Middle East, 1914–1923*. London: Routledge, 2001.
Rothermund, Dietmar. *The Global Impact of the Great Depression, 1929–1939*. New York: Routledge, 1996.
Roi, Yaacov. *From Encroachment to Involvement: A Documentary Study of Soviet Policy in the Middle East, 1945–1973*. New York: Praeger Publishers, 1975.
Rotshtein, Theodore. *Egypt's Ruin, a Financial and Administrative Record*. London: A. C. Fifield, 1910.
Roy, M. N. *Memoirs*. Bombay: Allied Publishers, 1964.
Roziner, Feliks. *Serebrianaia tsepochka: sem' pokolenii odnoi sem'i*. Tel Aviv: Biblioteka Aliia, 1983.
Rubenstein, Joshua. *Tangled Loyalties: The Life and Times of Ilya Ehrenburg*. London: I. B. Tauris, 1996.
Rubenstein, Joshua, and Vladimir Naumov, eds. *Stalin's Secret Pogrom: The Postwar Inquisition of the Jewish Anti-Fascist Committee*. New Haven, CT: Yale University Press, 2005.
Rupen, Robert. "Peking's Challenge to Moscow." *The High School Journal* 47, no. 8 (1964): 369–82.
Safarov, Georgii. *Kolonial'naia revoliutsiia: Opyt Turkestana*. Oxford: Society for Central Asian Studies, 1985.
Sahadeo, Jeff. *Russian Colonial Society in Tashkent, 1865–1923*. Bloomington: Indiana University Press, 2007.
Sahadeo, Jeff. "Soviet 'Blacks' and Place Making in Leningrad and Moscow." *Slavic Review* 71, no. 2 (2012): 331–58.
Sahadeo, Jeff. *Voices from the Soviet Edge: Southern Migrants in Leningrad and Moscow*. Ithaca, NY: Cornell University Press, 2019.
al-Sa'id, Rif'at. *al-Yasar al-misri: 1925–40*. Beirut: Dal al-Tali'ah, 1972.
Salazkina, Masha. *World Socialist Cinema Alliances, Affinities, and Solidarities in the Global Cold War*. Oakland: University of California Press, 2023.
Salih, Arwa. *The Stillborn: Notebooks of a Woman from the Student Movement Generation in Egypt*. Calcutta: Seagull Books, 2017.
Sanborn, Joshua. *Imperial Apocalypse: The Great War and the Destruction of the Russian Empire*. Oxford: Oxford University Press, 2014.
Sanchez-Sibony, Oscar. *Red Globalization: The Political Economy of the Soviet Cold War from Stalin to Khrushchev*. Cambridge: Cambridge University Press, 2014.
Sartori, Andrew. *Bengal in Global Concept History: Culturalism in the Age of Capital*. Chicago: University of Chicago Press, 2009.
Saunders, Frances Stonor. *The Cultural Cold War: The CIA and the World of Arts and Letters*. New York: The New Press, 1999.
Sawer, Marian. *Marxism and the Question of the Asiatic Mode of Production*. The Hague: Martinus Nijhoff, 1977.
Sawyer, Thomas. *The Jewish Minority in the Soviet Union*. Boulder, CO: Westview Press, 1979.

Sayim, Burak. "Of Transits and Transitions: Moscow-Bound Travels of Foreign Communists as a Transformative Experience, 1919-1939." *Revolutionary Russia* 36, no. 1 (2023): 100-120.
Schapiro, Leonard. "The International Department of the CPSU: Key to Soviet Policy." *International Journal* 32, no. 1 (Winter 1976/1977): 41-55.
Schayegh, Cyrus. *The Middle East and the Making of the Modern World*. Cambridge, MA: Harvard University Press, 2017.
Schimmelpenninck van der Oye, David. "The Curious Fate of Edward Said in Russia." *Études de lettres* 2-3 (2014): 81-94.
Schimmelpenninck van der Oye, David. *Russian Orientalism: Asia in the Russian Mind from Peter the Great to the Emigration*. New Haven, CT: Yale University Press, 2010.
Schimmelpenninck van der Oye, David. *Toward the Rising Sun: Russian Ideologies of Empire and the Path to War with Japan*. DeKalb: Northern Illinois University Press, 2001.
Schumann, Christoph. "Generation of Broad Expectations: Nationalism, Education, and Autobiography in Syria and Lebanon, 1930-1958." *Die Welt des Islams* 41 (2001): 171-205.
Scott, Erik R. *Familiar Strangers: The Georgian Diaspora and the Evolution of Soviet Empire*. New York: Oxford University Press, 2016.
Scott, John. *Behind the Urals: An American Worker in Russia's City of Steel*. Bloomington: Indiana University Press, 1973.
Scoville, Spencer. "Reconsidering Nahdawi Translation: Bringing Pushkin to Palestine." *The Translator* 21, no. 2 (2015): 223-36.
Schafer, Daniel. "Local Politics and the Birth of the Republic of Bashkortostan, 1919-1920." In *A State of Nations: Empire and Nation-Making in the Age of Lenin and Stalin*, edited by Ronald Grigor Suny and Terry Martin, 165-90. New York: Oxford University Press, 2001.
Seale, Patrick. *Asad of Syria: The Struggle for the Middle East*. London: I. B. Tauris, 1988.
Seiranian, B. G. "V. B. Lutskii (1906-62)—uchenyi, pedagog, chelovek." In *Slovo ob uchieliakh: Moskovskie vostokovedy 30x-60x godov*, edited by O. Dreier, G. Tiagai, and P. Shastitko, 326-43. Moscow: Vostochnaia literatura, 1988.
Sellman, Joanna. "The Ghosts of Exilic Belonging: Mahmud al-Bayyati's Raqs 'ala al-ma': ahlam wa'rah and Post-Soviet Themes in Arabic Exile Literature." *Journal of Arabic Literature* 47 (2016): 111-37.
Shapiro, Joel. *A History of the Communist Academy, 1918-1936*. PhD diss., Columbia University, 1976.
Sharabi, Hisham. *Arab Intellectuals and the West: The Formative Years, 1875-1914*. Baltimore: Johns Hopkins University Press, 1970.
Shastitko, Petr. *Sobytiia i sud'by: iz istorii stanovleniia sovetskogo Vostokovedeniia*. Moscow: Nauka, 1985.
Shawi, Niquola. *Tariqi ila al-hizb*. Beirut: Dar al Farabi, 1984.
Shepilov, Dmitrii. *The Kremlin's Scholar: A Memoir of Soviet Politics under Stalin and Khrushchev*. Edited by Stephen V. Bittner. Translated by Anthony Austin. New Haven, CT: Yale University Press, 2007.
Shissler, Ada Holland. *Between Two Empires: Ahmet Ağaoğlu and the New Turkey*. London: I. B. Tauris 2003.
Shlapentokh, Dmitry. "Islam and Orthodox Russia." *Communist and Post-Communist Studies* 41, no. 1 (2008): 27-46.

Siegelbaum, Lewis. *Soviet State and Society between Revolutions, 1918–1929*. Cambridge: Cambridge University Press, 1992.
Siegelbaum, Lewis H., and Leslie Page Moch. "Transnationalism in One Country? Seeing and Not Seeing Cross-Border Migration within the Soviet Union." *Slavic Review* 75, no. 4 (2016): 970–86.
Slezkine, Yuri. *Arctic Mirrors: Russia and the Small Peoples of the North*. Ithaca, NY: Cornell University Press, 1994.
Slezkine, Yuri. *The Jewish Century*. Princeton, NJ: Princeton University Press, 2006.
Slezkine, Yuri. "The USSR as a Communal Apartment, or How a Socialist State Promoted Ethnic Particularism." *Slavic Review* 53, no. 2 (1994): 414–52.
Smele, Jonathan. *Civil War in Siberia: The Anti-Bolshevik Government of Admiral Kolchak, 1918–1920*. Cambridge: Cambridge University Press, 1996.
Smith, Stephen. *A Road Is Made: Communism in Shanghai, 1920–1927*. Honolulu: University of Hawai'i Press, 2000.
Smolkin, Victoria. *A Sacred Space Is Never Empty: A History of Soviet Atheism*. Princeton, NJ: Princeton University Press, 2018.
Spector, Ivar. *The Soviet Union and the Muslim World, 1917–1956*. Seattle: University of Washington Press, 1956.
Stalin, Joseph. "The Political Tasks of the University of the Peoples of the East." In *Works*. Vol. 7, 135–154. Moscow: Foreign Languages Publishing House, 1954.
Stalin, Joseph. *Works*. Vol. 5, *1921–23*. Moscow: Foreign Languages Publishing House, 1954, https://www.marxists.org/reference/archive/stalin/works/1921/03/08.htm.
Stern, Ludmila. *Western Intellectuals and the Soviet Union, 1920–40: From Red Square to the Left Bank*. Abingdon: Routledge, 2007.
Stites, Richard. *Revolutionary Dreams. Utopian Vision and Experimental Life in the Russian Revolution*. New York: Oxford University Press, 1989.
Strel'tsov, Dmitrii. "Vostokovedenie v MGIMO." *Vestnik MGIMO Universiteta* 5, no. 38 (2014): 143–50.
Stronski, Paul. *Tashkent: Forging a Soviet City 1930–1966*. Pittsburgh: University of Pittsburgh Press, 2010.
Studer, Brigitte. *The Transnational World of the Cominternians*. Basingstoke: Palgrave Macmillan, 2015.
Suleimenov, Olzhas. *Az i ya: Kniga blagonomerennogo chitatelia*. Alma-Ata: Engbek, 1975.
Sunderland, Willard. *The Baron's Cloak: A History of the Russian Empire in War and Revolution*. Ithaca, NY: Cornell University Press, 2014.
Sunderland, Willard. "Imperial Space: Territorial Thought and Practice in the Eighteenth Century." In *Russian Empire: Space, People, Power, 1700–1930*, edited by Jane Burbank and Mark von Hagen, 36–38. Bloomington: Indiana University Press, 2007.
Sunderland, Willard. "The Ministry of Asiatic Russia: The Colonial Office That Never Was but Might Have Been." *Slavic Review* 69, no. 1 (2010): 120–50.
Sunderland, Willard. "What Is Asia to Us?: Scholarship on the Tsarist 'East' since the 1990s." *Kritika* 12, no. 4 (2011): 817–33.
Suny, Ronald. *The Baku Commune, 1917–1918: Class and Nationality in the Russian Revolution*. Princeton, NJ: Princeton University Press, 1972.
Suny, Ronald. *The Revenge of the Past: Nationalism, Revolution, and the Collapse of the Soviet Union*. Stanford, CA: Stanford University Press, 1993.
Suri, Jeremi. *Power and Protest: Global Revolution and the Rise of Détente*. Cambridge, MA: Harvard University Press, 2003.

Swanson, Maria. "'I slew my love with my own hand': On Tolstoy's Influence on Mikhail Naimy and the Similarity between their Moral Concerns." *Al-'Arabiyya* 51 (2018): 69–87.
Swanson, Maria, and Rebecca Ruth Gould, "The Poetics of Nahdah Multilingualism: Recovering the Lost Russian Poetry of Mikhail Naimy." *Journal of Arabic Literature* 1–2 (2021): 179–201.
Tabet, Marie, and Jed Tabet. *Antuan Tabet*. Translated from French by L. Pirozhnikova. Moscow: Izdatel'stvo literatury po stroitel'stvu, 1968.
Takriti, Abdel Razzaq. *Monsoon Revolution: Republicans, Sultans, and Empires in Oman, 1965–1976*. Oxford: Oxford University Press, 2013.
Tamari, Salim. "Najati Sadqi (1905–79): The Enigmatic Jerusalem Bolshevik." *Journal of Palestine Studies* 32, no. 2 (2020): 79–94.
Tamazishvili, Aleksandr. "Vladimir Aleksandrovich Gurko-Kriazhin: sud'ba bojtsa 'vostokovednogo fronta.'" In *Neizvestnye stranitsy otechestvennogo vostokovedeniia*, edited by V. Naumkin, N. G. Romanova, and I. Smilianskaia, 32–128. Vol. 3 of 4. Moscow: Vostochnaia literatura, 2008.
Tamazishvili, Aleksandr. "Vostokovedenie v 1918g." *Aziia i Afrika segodnia* 11 (1993): 60–63.
Tannoury-Karam, Sana. "The Making of a Leftist Milieu: Anti-Colonialism, Anti-Fascism, and the Political Engagement of Intellectuals in Mandate Lebanon, 1920–1948." PhD diss., Northeastern University, December 2017.
Tasar, Eren. "The Central Asian Muftiate in Occupied Afghanistan, 1979–1987." *Central Asian Survey* 30, no. 2 (July 2011): 213–26.
Taubman, William. *Gorbachev: His Life and Times*. New York: W. W. Norton, 2017.
Taubman, William. *Khrushchev: The Man and His Era*. New York: W. W. Norton, 2003
Teshabaev, Dzhura. *Schast'e mastera: o tvorchestve kinorezhissera Kamila Iarmatova*. Tashkent: Izd-vo lit-ry i iskusstva im. Gafura Guliama, 1975.
Thomas, Martin. *Fight or Flight: Britain, France, and Their Roads from Empire*. Oxford: Oxford University Press, 2014.
Thompson, Elizabeth. *Colonial Citizens: Republican Rights*. New York: Columbia University Press, 2000.
Tillett, Lowell. *The Great Friendship: Soviet Historians on the Non-Russian Nationalities*. Chapel Hill: University of North Carolina Press, 1969.
Tolz, Vera. "European, National, and (Anti-) Imperial: The Formation of Academic Oriental Studies in Late Tsarist and Early Soviet Russia." *Kritika* 9, no. 1 (2008): 53–81.
Tolz, Vera. *Russian Academicians and the Revolution: Combining Professionalism and Politics*. New York: Palgrave Macmillan, 1997.
Tolz, Vera. *Russia's Own Orient: The Politics of Identity and Oriental Studies in the Late Imperial and Early Soviet Periods*. Oxford: Oxford University Press, 2011.
Tomoff, Kiril. "Uzbek Music's Separate Path: Interpreting 'Anticosmopolitanism' in Stalinist Central Asia, 1949–52." *Russian Review* 63, no. 2 (2004): 212–40.
Troianovskii, Konstantin. *Siniaia kniga: sbornik tainykh dokumentov, izvlechennykh iz arkhiva byvshego Ministerstva inostrannykh del*. Moscow, 1918.
Troianovskii, Konstantin. *Vostok i revoliutsiia: Popytka postroeniia novoi politicheskoi programmy dlia tuzemnykh stran Vostoka—Indii, Persii, Kitaia*. Petrograd: Izdatel'stvo Vserossiiskago Tsentral'nago Ispolnitel'nago Komiteta Sovetov, 1918.
Tromly, Benjamin. *Making the Soviet Intelligentsia: Universities and Intellectual Life under Stalin and Khrushchev*. Cambridge: Cambridge University Press, 2014.

Trotsky, Leon. *My Life: An Attempt at an Autobiography*. New York: Pathfinder Press, 1970.
Tuna, Mustafa. *Imperial Russia's Muslims: Islam, Empire, and European Modernity, 1788–1917*. Cambridge: Cambridge University Press 2015.
Van Ree, Erik. "Socialism in One Country: A Reassessment." *Studies in East European Thought* 50, no. 2 (June 1998): 77–117.
Vasil'ev, Alexei. *Rossiia na blizhnem i srednem vostoke. Ot messianstva k pragmatizmu.* Moscow: Nauka, 1993.
Vasil'kov, Ia. V., and M. Iu. Sorokina. *Liudi i sud'byi: biobibliograficheskii slovar' vostokovedov—zhertv politicheskogo terrora v sovetskii period (1917–1991)*. St. Petersburg: Petersburgskoe vostokovedenie, 2003.
Vel'tman, S. *Vostok v khudozhestvennoi literature*. Moscow: State Publisher, 1928.
Vigor, Peter. "The Soviet View of Geopolitics." In *On Geopolitics: Classical and Nuclear*, edited by Ciro Zoppo and Charles Zorgbibe, 131–40. The Hague: Martinus Nijhoff, 1985.
Viola, Lynne. *Stalinist Perpetrators on Trial: Scenes from the Great Terror in Soviet Ukraine*. New York: Oxford University Press, 2017.
Vital, David. *Origins of Zionism*. London: Oxford University Press, 1975.
Volkov, Vadim. "The Concept of Kul'turnost'. Notes on the Stalinist Civilizing Process." In *Stalinism. New Directions*, edited by Sheila Fitzpatrick, 210–30. London: Routledge, 2000.
Von Eschen, Penny. *Race against Empire: Black Americans and Anticolonialism, 1937–1957*. Ithaca, NY: Cornell University Press, 1997.
Von Eschen, Penny. *Satchmo Blows Up the World: Jazz Ambassadors Play the Cold War*. Cambridge, MA: Harvard University Press, 2006.
von Hagen, Mark. *Soldiers in the Proletarian Dictatorship: The Red Army and the Soviet Socialist State, 1917–1930*. Ithaca, NY: Cornell University Press, 1990.
Weiner, Amir. "The Empires Pay a Visit: Gulag Returnees, East European Rebellions, and Soviet Frontier Politics." *Journal of Modern History* 78, no. 2 (June 2006): 333–76.
Weiss-Went, Anton. *Putin's Russia and the Falsification of History*. London: Bloomsbury Academic, 2021.
Weiss-Went, Anton, and Nanci Adler, eds. *The Future of the Soviet Past. The Politics of History in Putin's Russia*. Bloomington: Indiana University Press, 2021.
Westad, Odd Arne. *The Global Cold War: Third World Interventions and the Making of Our Times*. Cambridge: Cambridge University Press, 2007.
White, Stephen. "Colonial Revolution and the Communist International, 1919–1924." *Science & Society* 40, no. 2 (Summer 1976): 173–93.
White, Stephen. "Communism and the East: The Baku Congress, 1920." *Slavic Review* 33, no. 3 (1974): 492–514.
Wilbur, Clarence Martin, and Julie Lien-ying How. *Missionaries of Revolution: Soviet Advisers and Nationalist China, 1920–1927*. Cambridge, MA: Harvard University Press, 1989.
Wojnowski, Zbigniew. *The Near Abroad: Socialist Eastern Europe and Soviet Patriotism in Ukraine, 1956–1985*. Toronto: University of Toronto Press, 2017.
Wright, Richard. *The Color Curtain: A Report on the Bandung Conference*. New York: World, 1956.
Yamauchi, Masayuki. *The Green Crescents under the Red Tsar: Enver Pasha in Soviet Russia, 1919–1922*. Tokyo: Institute for the Study of Languages and Cultures of Asia and Africa, 1991.
Yarmatov, Kamil. *Vozvrashchenie: Vospominanie*. Tashkent: Izdatel'stvo iskusstvo, 1987.

Yenen, Alp. "The Other Jihad: Enger Pasha, Bolsheviks, and Politics of Anticolonial Muslim Nationalism during the Baku Congress 1920." In *The First World War and Its Aftermath*, edited by T. G. Fraser, 273–93. London: Ginko, 2015.

Yilmaz, Huseyin. "The Eastern Question and the Ottoman Empire: The Genesis of the Near and Middle East in the Nineteenth Century." In *Is There a Middle East? The Evolution of a Geopolitical Concept*, edited by Michael E. Bonine, Abbas Amanat, and Michael Ezekiel Gasper, 11–35. Stanford, CA: Stanford University Press, 2012.

Yoon, Duncan M. "'Our Forces Have Redoubled': World Literature, Postcolonialism, and the Afro-Asian Writers' Bureau." *Cambridge Journal of Postcolonial Literary Inquiry* 2, no. 2 (2015): 233–52.

Younes, Miriam. "A Tale of Two Communists." *Arab Studies Journal* 24, no. 1 (Spring 2016): 98–116.

Young, Robert. "Disseminating the Tricontinental." In *The Routledge Handbook of the Global Sixties: Between Protest and Nation-Building*, edited by Klimke et al., 517–47. New York: Routledge, 2018.

Young, Robert. *Postcolonialism: An Historical Introduction*. Malden, MA: John Wiley, 2016.

Yu, Min-ling. "Sun Yat-sen University in Moscow, 1925–1930." PhD diss., New York University, 1995.

Yurchak, Alexei. *Everything Was Forever, until It Was No More: The Last Soviet Generation*. Princeton, NJ: Princeton University Press, 2006.

Zachariah, Benjamin. "Rethinking (the Absence of) Fascism in India, 1922–45." In *Cosmopolitan Thought Zones*, edited by Sugata Bose and Kris Manjapra, 178–212. New York: Palgrave Macmillan, 2010.

Zahavi, Leon. *Sawiyya aw 'ala infirad: al-Yahud w-al-'Arab fi Filistin Hasab Watha'iq al-Komintirn*. Jerusalem, 2009.

Zeltser, Arkadii. "Jews in the Upper Ranks of the NKVD, 1934–1941." *Jews in Russia and Eastern Europe* 1, no. 52 (2004): 64–90.

Zhuk, Sergei. *Rock and Roll in the Rocket City: The West, Identity, and Ideology in Soviet Dniepropetrovsk, 1960–1985*. Baltimore: Johns Hopkins University Press, 2010.

Zhuravlev, Sergei. *"Malen'kie liudi" i "bol'shaia istoriia": Inostrantsy moskovskogo Elektrozavoda v sovetskom obshchestve 1920-kh–1930-kh*. Moscow: Rosspen, 2000.

Zinn, Howard. *A People's History of the United States*. New York: Harper & Row, 1980.

Zisser, Eyal. *Lebanon: The Challenge of Independence*. London: I. B. Tauris, 2000.

Zubkova, E. Yu. "Vlast' i razvitie etnokonfliktnoy situatsii v SSSR 1953–1985 gody." *Otechestvennaya istoriya* 4 (2004): 3–32.

Zubok, Vladislav M. *Collapse: The Fall of the Soviet Union*. New Haven, CT: Yale University Press, 2021.

Zubok, Vladislav M. *A Failed Empire: The Soviet Union in the Cold War from Stalin to Gorbachev*. Chapel Hill: University of North Carolina Press, 2007.

Zubok, Vladislav M. *Zhivago's Children: The Last Russian Intelligentsia*. Cambridge, MA: Belknap Press of Harvard University Press, 2009.

Zubok, Vladislav M., and Constantine Pleshakov. *Inside the Kremlin's Cold War: From Stalin to Khrushchev*. Cambridge, MA: Harvard University Press, 1996.

Index

For the benefit of digital users, indexed terms that span two pages (e.g., 52–53) may, on occasion, appear on only one of those pages.

Figures and tables are indicated by an italic *f* and *t* following the page number.

ABC of Communism (Bukharin), 60
Abdul-Malik, Anwar, 13
abortion, 85–86
Academy of Sciences, 26–27, 36–38, 66, 140
"affective affinities," 216
affirmative action
    beneficiaries of, 190–91
    Comintern politics of, 113
    decolonization through, 121–22
    disadvantages of, 191
    for Soviet Central Asia, 170–71
    Soviet Eastern International as nexus of, 154–55
    for underdeveloped peoples, 87–88
    upward mobility, cost of, 232–33
"affirmative action empire," 67, 90
Afghanistan
    Communist coup, 251n.32
    Soviet Central Asians in, 228–29
    Soviet invasion of, 16, 228, 251n.32
    Soviet withdrawal from, 234
    Taliban control in, 240
    war in, 228
Africa
    China activity in, 188
    decolonizing, 155, 189
    European imperial railroad projects in, 30
    expansion of Soviet commitments in, 22
    jihads and uprisings in, 266n.188
    nationalist liberation movements in, 207–8
    students from, 169–70
    trivialization, exoticization, and marginalization of, 183–84
    Uzbek tourist trips to, 176–77
African activists, connection to anti-imperial communities, 90–91
African countries, 189
African Cultural Society, 177–78
Afro-Asian cinema, revolutionary armed struggle as theme of, 186
Afro-Asian cinematic networks, 21
Afro-Asian contact zones, 155–56
Afro-Asian cultural events, Chinese pressure at, 198–99
Afro-Asian culture, 155–56
Afro-Asian Film Festival, 217–18, 224
Afro-Asian Film Festival, 1958, 196–98
Afro-Asian Film Festival, 1968, 190, 191, 195, 208–11, 216
Afro-Asian intellectuals and politicians, 178
Afro-Asian literary events, 151–52
Afro-Asian literature, 155
Afro-Asian networks, 247
Afro-Asian world
    culture influence on, 153
    exchanges with, 156
    institutionalized relations with, 183–84
    Moscow's concerns about, 20–21
Afro-Asian writers and filmmakers, 177–78
agricultural specialists, 93
Aimarov (Tawfiq Abdel Hafiz al-Hassan)
    as difficult case, 107
    expulsion from KTUV, 92–93, 107–9
    factory assignment, 92, 93–94
    Jews, attitude toward, 94–95
    Kotel'nikov, F., confrontation with, 109–10, 116
    Palestine, return to, 7–8, 114–15
    photo, 108*f*
    Soviet Union, opportunity to come to, 94

Aitmatov, Chingiz, 205, 232–33, 239, 241–42
Aitmatov, Torekul, 232–33
Ajia Gi Kai (Association for the Defense of Asia), 258–59n.74
Akhmatova, Anna, 144
al-Amin, Hashim, 147
al-'Arabi, Husni, 53–54, 56
al-Assad, Bashar, 236–37
al-Assad, Havez, 220, 222, 225, 246
Albania, rupture of Soviet influence in, 186–87
alcohol and traditional culture, fusions of, 82
Algeria
  provisional government, 177–78
  right-wing coup in, 21
  struggle in, 181
Algerian War, 153, 188
al-Hilou, Farajallah [Farhalla al-Hilu], 120–21, 131–32, 147, 157–58, 253n.69, 295n.59
al-Hilu, Ridwan, 114–15, 278–79n.153
al-Hilu, Yusuf Khitar, 131–33
Alisher Navoi (film), 194–95
Allied Powers, 124–25
All-Russian Central Executive Committee, 35, 65
All-Russian Scientific Association of Oriental Studies (VNAV), 9, 30, 67–68
All-Soviet Institute of Cinematography (VGIK), 190–91
All-Union Communist Party, 102
All-Union structures, decentralization of, 182–83
al-Shamali, Fu'ad, 253n.69
Al-Siba'i, Yusuf, 153, 196, 245–46
alternative histories, suppression of, 119
alternative information, absence of, 146
alternative narratives, silencing of, 12, 14, 58
al-Za'im, Husni, 147
American imperialism, Jews as alleged agents of, 129
Americans, visits to Soviet Union, 124
American Society of African Culture (ANSAC), 182–83

American-style imperialism, 40–41
Americas, immigration to, 62–63
Andropov, Yuri, 225, 229
Anglo-American postcolonial theory
  exchanges contributing to, 155–56
  intellectual history of, 177–78
  Soviet thought and experience contribution to, 13–14, 244
Anglo-Iraqi agreement, 149
Anglo-Soviet Trade Agreement, 1921, 49
Angola, Soviet-Cuban victory in, 224
anticapitalism, commitment to, 146–47
anticapitalist activists, global community of, 131–32
anticapitalist values, alternative future built on, 128
anticolonial activism, 125–26
anticolonial foreign policy, 3–4
anticolonial front of world revolution, 64–65
anticolonial humanism, 215
anticolonial integration friction, 16
anticolonial internationalism, 7–8, 58–59
anticolonialism
  abroad, narratives about, 12
  commitment to, 146–47, 185
  in East, 88
  Egypt and Palestine compared, 83–84
  goals supporting, 222–23
  Soviet anticolonial and imperial politics severed from, 3
  Soviet commitments to, 214–15
  Soviet Union as symbol of, 21, 245
anticolonial liberation, 33
anticolonial movements, Soviet literary treatment of, 213–14
anticolonial nationalism, 7–8, 181
anticolonial nationalist movements, 20
anticolonial nation-building, 95
anticolonial power, myth of Soviet Union as, 3
anticolonial revolution, 28, 99
anticolonial state
  policy decisions of, 11
  Soviet Union as, 12, 14
  strengthening, 9
anticommunism, 158
anticosmopolitan campaigns, 167

INDEX

antidemocratic and antiliberal forces, confronting, 134–35
antifascism, 20, 128, 146–47
Anti-Fascist League, 133–34, 135
Anti-Fascist League of Syria and Lebanon, 124–25
anti-imperialism
　American foundational myth of, 245
　clash between differing visions of, 41–42
　goals supporting, 222–23
　shift toward emphasizing, 186
　Soviet Union as symbol of, 21
anti-imperialist communities, 90–91
anti-imperialist foreign policy, 3–4
anti-imperialist front, 42
anti-imperialist propaganda, 42
anti-imperialist state, 3–4, 14
anti-imperialist struggle
　in progress, 2
　Soviet support for, 152
anti-materialism, 20
antiracism, 245
antiracist struggle, 152
anti-religious campaigns, 82
anti-Russian sentiment, restructuring unleashing, 166
anti-Semitism
　campaign against, 94
　in late Soviet period, 227–28
　postwar rise in, 128–29
　during Russian civil war, 54
anti-Western internationalism, 8–9
anti-Westernism
　alternative future built on, 128
　commitment to, 185
　postwar rise of, 128–29
　Soviet Union as symbol of, 20
"Appeal to All Toiling Muslims of Russia and the East" (Lenin and Stalin), 27, 29
Arab activists, 131–32
Arab anti-imperialist struggle, 218
Arab communism, 14–15, 127
Arab communist parties, 275n.101
Arab communists
　agency of, 13
　Eastern International concept resilience illustrated by experiences of, 246–47
　glasnost' and *perestroika* resisted by, 246
　memoirs, 253n.69
　Moscow's perspective echoed by, 120–21
　plight of, 159
　Soviet state representatives, confrontations with, 109–10
　as Soviet Union intermediaries, 122–23
　Turkestan as training ground for, 89
Arab countries, 52–53, 181
Arab culture, 152
Arab filmmakers, 209
Arab films, importing and dubbing, 196
"Arabia," references to, 267n.202
Arabic
　early childhood education in, 20–21
　instruction in, 78, 79–80
　language and culture, 80, 116
　translations into, 61, 79–80
Arabic-language autobiographies, 78
Arabic literature, 27–28, 246
Arabic-reading intellectuals, Russian influences on, 130
Arab intellectuals
　russocentrism, barriers to engagement with, 145
　Soviet Union, perceptions of, 146
　Soviet Union as symbol for, 128
　Soviet Union significance to, 145–46, 148–49
Arab-Israeli conflict, 125–26
Arab-Israeli War, 1967, 207–8
　aftermath of, 218
　buildup to, 222
　defeat, 21, 208
　Jewish orientalists after, 227–28
　Soviet Union response to, 151–52, 189–90
Arab-Israeli War, 1973, 223
"Arabistan" (term), 267n.202
Arabization
　calls for, 96, 102
　challenges of, 96–97
　claims about, 122
　hidden resistance to, 101–2
　impact of, 96
　implementing of, 121–22
　perceived threats to, 113, 114
　struggle for, 103

Arab-Jewish brotherhood, 98–99
Arab-Jewish conflict, 97–98
Arab-Jewish relations, 99
Arab-Jewish tensions, 93–94
Arab Jews at KUTV, 103
Arab lands, 94–95
Arab left
  disillusionment of, 245–47
  histories of, 13, 14–15, 247
  Palestine partition, split over Soviet support of, 151–52
Arab Marxists, 13–14
Arab Middle East, Soviet power mediators in, 118
Arab nationalism, 21, 207–8
Arabness
  conversations about, 76
  as divisive concept, 119–20
  political ideas of, 75–76
Arab parties, 122
Arab provinces under Ottoman rule, 75–76
Arab publications and writers, 148–49
Arab radicalism, 14–15
Arab Revolt, 100–1, 109, 113–14
Arabs
  as category, 75–76
  education opportunities *versus* Jews, 102
  enemies of, 246
  families in USSR, 88
  history interpretation acknowledging role of, 243
  land losses, 109
  in Mesopotamia, 266n.185
  Soviet response to 1967 war criticized by, 207–8
  Soviet state support for, 150–51
Arab Socialist Union, 158–59
Arab solidarities, 76
Arab-Soviet ties, 22
Arab state, intellectual freedom *versus*, 302n.143
Arab states as modernization and development agents, 181
Arab students
  at Institute for National-Colonial Problems, 115
  interpretive mistakes, consequences for making, 81
  Jewish teachers, accusations against, 122
Arab territories, British and French expansion into, 19
Arab unity, 7–8, 94–95
Arab world
  Bolshevik Revolution and, 54
  Comintern politics regarding, 119–20
  Eastern International collapse impact on, 245–46
  educational opportunities in, 170
  enthusiasm about, 178–79
  fascism, attitudes concerning, 132
  interest in, 52
  Muslim visitors from, 82
  remoteness of, 160
  Soviet collapse impact on, 245–46
  Soviet knowledge, limited concerning, 151
  Soviet power reconfigured in relation to, 155
  Soviet relations with, 53, 149–50
  and Soviet Union, cultural relations with, 149–50
  term, 17
  as *terra incognita*, 52–53
  Uzbek cultural representatives in, 176–77
Arafat, Yasir, 225, 227
archaism, popularizing, 143
Armenia
  earthquake in, 229
  immigration to, 140
  Russian power asserted in post-Soviet, 236
Armenian-Azeri conflict, 230–31
Armenians, 122, 140
art
  Eastern Revolution in, 43–46, 43*f*, 44*f*, 45*f*
  in student assignments, 76
Asia
  as category, 4
  decolonizing, 155
  European imperial railroad projects in, 30
  expansion of Soviet commitments in, 22

INDEX 367

ideas of, 10
nationalist liberation movements in, 207–8
Russian overreach in, 30
Russia's geopolitical impact on, 6–7
and Soviet East, relationship between, 89
students from, 169–70
trading opportunities beyond, 62–63
Uzbek tourist trips to, 176–77
"Asia for Asians," 34–35
Asian activists, 90–91
Asian countries, 189
Asianism as movement, 19
Asian societies and cultures, threats to, 258–59n.74
Asian universalisms, 34–35
Asiatic categories, Bolshevik codifying of, 6
"Asiatic mode of production" (AMP) (concept), 10, 100
Asiatic Museum, 27–28
"Asiatic Russia" (term), 4
"Asiatic social order" (concept), 10
assimilation, processes of, 95
Atasi, Nureddin, 190, 207
atheism, 82, 232–33
"attraction," inward-focused model of, 68–69
Auerbach, Haim (Abu Za'im), 54–55, 56, 98–99, 102, 106
Austria, 133, 264n.164
autobiographies, student, 78
autonomous politics, 127–28
Avigdor (Yehiel Kosoi; Constantine Weiss)
  accusations against, 113, 114
  as Arab Circle leader, 102, 104–5
  arrest and execution, 84–85, 113–14
  Comintern, dealings with, 83
  Egypt, activities in, 83–84
  persons reprimanded or expelled by, 114–15
  replacement as Arab Circle leader, 106
  Rosenthal, C. meeting of, 84
  Turkestan as training ground for, 89
'Ayyad, Kamil
  Communist Party membership not noted for, 298n.82
  Kari-Yakubov, M.'s behavior critiqued by, 140, 143

organization memberships, 135
Society of Friendship with the Soviet Union dissolved by, 148
Soviet Union, visit to, 124–25, 137–38
after Soviet Union visit, 148
Soviet writers, contact with, 144
writings, 132–33
Azerbaijan, post-Soviet, 236
Azerbaijan, Soviet republic of, 42, 140, 230–31
Azerbaijani poets, 118
Azimov, Suleiman, 179–80
'Azuri, Najib, 100–1

Ba'athist regime, 158–59
Ba'ath Party, 222
Babakhanov, Ziauddin, 180
"backwardness, rhetoric of," 78–79, 86
Baghdad Pact, 159–61
Bakdash, Khalid, 112–13, 114–15
  Al-Hilu, F., campaign against, 302n.139
  Arab nationality assumed by, 7–8
  communist situation investigation ordered by, 157–58
  Gorbachev, M. criticized by, 246
  Hanna, G., suspicions toward, 138
  memoirs, 253n.69
  proletarian support, challenges of building cited by, 127
  "revolutionary democracy" theory criticized by, 158–59
  Stalinist leadership style, 188
  Syrian Communist Party leadership, 222
  Tashkent, visit to, 119–20
  translations done by, 131–32
  Turkestan as training ground for, 89
Baku
  Bolsheviks' tenuous grip on, 38
  Comintern message at, 47
  visits to, 107–9
Baku Congress for the Peoples of the East, 1920, 67–68
Balfour Declaration, 89–90
Bandung Conference, 1955, 153, 161, 162, 185
Baranov, Leonid, 138
Bassin, Mark, 4, 238

The Battle of Algiers (film), 215
Before Dawn (film), 193–94
Beirut, 135–36
Belgian Congo, 188
Bella, Ben, 188–89
Berezka ensemble, 174–76
Berger, Joseph
　arrest and rehabilitation, 112, 113
　Jews in purges recalled by, 117
　as KUTV Arab Section leader, 106–7
　as PCP leader, 97
　persons reprimanded or expelled by, 114–15
　Safarov, G., attitude toward, 97–98
　student complaints against, 109–10
Beria, Lavrentiy, 114–15, 166, 167
Berlin Bureau. *See* Comintern Western Bureau
Berlin Wall, collapse of, 229, 230–31
Bilad al-Sham, 62–63, 97
bilateral exchange agreements, 174–75
Biran (Uzbek opera), 146
Birobidzhan region, 95, 110
Black Americans, 182
　anticolonial activists, 183–84
　communists, 67–68
　leaders, 161–62
　performers abroad, 215–16
　visitors, 217–18
Blue Book (Siniaia kniga) (Troianovskii), 31*f*
Blunt, Wilfrid Scawen, 29
Bolshevik ideology, 71
Bolshevik Revolution
　anticolonial movements and, 213–14
　and Arab world, 54
　as global anticolonial event, 58
　historical change through, 16
　life before and after compared, 138
　spread to East, 32–33
Bolshevik revolutionary movement, Jews in, 17–18
Bolsheviks
　challenges faced by, 38
　cultural front as focus of, 64–65
　global politics as approached by, 23
　self-determination, position on, 66–67
"Bolshevik speak," 87–88, 104

Bolshevism, assimilation of Jews through, 54
borderlands, party structures in, 122
border-making, political and ideological, 88–89
borders, importance of, 9
Bosnia-Herzegovina, 32
bourgeois nationalism, struggle against, 169
bourgeois order, anticolonial critiques of, 38–39
Braginskii, Joseph, 80–81
Brest-Litovsk, Treaty of, 23–24, 57–58, 230–31
Brezhnev, Mikhail
　ascent of, 173
　communist movement recentering by, 188
　competition with West under, 6
　1967 war, response to, 207–8
　political elites under, 242
　Tashkent, visit to, 206–7
　Third World interventions under, 229
　youth disaffection during time of, 212–13
Brezhnev doctrine, 228
Britain
　France relations with, 125–26
　power, decline of, 160–61
　Soviet Union relations with, 47, 49, 53
British and French mandates
　anticolonial nationalist movements in regions under, 20
　employment, seeking under, 131–32
British empire, 53–54, 152
British imperialism, Jews as alleged agents of, 129
British imperialist provocation, 97
British Middle Eastern command, 254n.80
Broido, Grigorii
　antireligious instruction by, 82
　Hamdi, predictions concerning, 80
　at KTUV, 65–66, 70–71
　NKID Turkestan office directed by, 39–40
　Rafes, M., disagreement with, 71–72
　Sovinterprop appointments made by, 42
　student recruitment critiqued by, 83

INDEX 369

at Sverdlov University, 65
in Tajikistan, 105
Turkestan, hopes for, 89
Bronze Horseman statue, 125*f*
"build a world after empire" (term), 3
Bukhara
  "liberation" of, 48
  population, addressing, 49
  as protectorate, 5–6
  Red Army in, 48
Bukharan communist party, 49–50
Bukharan People's Soviet Republic, 41–42, 48–49
Bukharan Revolutionary Committee, 264n.161
Bukharin, Nikolai
  associations with, 162
  Berger, J. relations with, 106
  case against, 167–68
  German influences on, 31–32
  writings, 28, 60
Bund (secular Jewish party)
  dissolution of, 267n.199
  former membership in, 117
  joining, 54
  members of, 71–72
  politics of, 88
Buraq (Wailing Wall), Jerusalem, 97
Burkhanov, Shukur, 210
Bush, George H. W., 234

cadres
  creating, 65–66
  lack of, 50–51
  overlap of, 67
  preparing, 65
  recruitment of, 26–27, 42
Cameroon, 188
capitalism
  critiques of, 2–3, 131–32
  metaphors of, 16
  opposition to, 16
capitalist imperialism, collapse of, 74
capitalist West, 151–52
Carr, E. H., 267n.211
castes and estates, abolishing system of, 33
Castro, Fidel, 187
Catherine the Great, 24, 30

Caucasian Muslims, 110
Caucasians, 182
Caucasus
  attitudes concerning, 140
  autonomy, status of, 90–91
  cinema industry in, 205–6, 209–10
  dramatic depictions of colonial
    life in, 74
  historic friendship with Russians in, 119
  impressions of people from, 74–75
  liberation of Soviet, 10
  migrants from, 217
  Muslims communists in, 57–58
  oriental studies centers in, 172
  republics, assignment of, 174
  Russian conquest of, 3, 5–6
  Soviet East representatives in, 119
  territorial conquests in, 5
Central Asia. *See also* Soviet Central Asia
  autonomy, status of, 90–91
  cinema industry in, 205–6, 209–10
  civil war in, 121–22
  competing plans for, 38–39
  concerns about, 34–35
  cultural and intellectual decolonization,
    exclusion from conversations
    about, 216
  delimitation of, 68, 69, 87
  descriptions of, 146
  Eastern Mediterranean,
    connection to, 17
  educational opportunities in, 170
  events in, advocating for, 182–83
  gender and family norms in, 11
  impressions of people from, 74–75
  India ties to, 164
  information, limited about, 146
  intellectual life in, 212–13
  irrigation systems and canals in, 139–40
  as liability, 233–34, 235
  liberation of Soviet, 10
  migrants from, 217
  as model of development, 213
  narratives of, 144–45
  oriental studies centers in, 172
  as part of Middle East, 254n.80
  as pivotal point of Eurasia, 258n.62
  redefinition of, 151

Central Asia (*cont.*)
    "Red Man's Burden" in, 35–36
    Russian colonialism in, 199–200
    Russian conquest of, 3, 14
    Russian ignorance concerning, 213–14
    Russian incorporation of, 167
    Russian position, strengthening in, 240
    Russian power in, narrative
        about, 120–21
    Soviet diplomacy and culture measures
        in, 190
    Sovietization of, 21, 204–5, 213–14
    as Soviet modernization
        showcase, 170–71
    Soviet party-state's history in, 121
    Soviet power reconfigured in relation
        to, 155
    Soviet rule in, 211
    as space for exiles, 105–6
    status of, 5–6
    territorial conquests in, 5
    territorial delineation of, 167–68
    territories, redistribution of, 58
    Turkic-, Persian- and Arabic-speaking
        regions, historical connections
        to, 20–21
    Western delineation of, 254n.80
Central Asian artists, 183–84, 216
Central Asian Bureau, 49–50, 185–86,
    205–6, 310–11n.134
Central Asian communists, 165–66
Central Asian economic council, 185–86
Central Asian history
    ideological terrain of, 195
    introduction to, 209–10
    parameters of, 183–84, 186
    Soviet context of, 247
    Soviet Eastern International approach
        to, 215
Central Asian leaders, 181–82
Central Asian music, 110–11
Central Asian Muslims, 110, 181–82
Central Asian national cultures, 119
Central Asian orientalists, 246–47
Central Asian politicians, 182–83
Central Asian republics
    assignment of, 174
    competitive relationship between, 172
    confusion over, 164
    economic and cultural modernization
        of, 182–83
    India, Uzbekistan, and other, historic
        connections between, 163–64
    Turkestan refashioned into, 88–89
    visitors, 180
Central Asian Revolt, 1916, 38, 105–6
Central Asian revolution, films about,
    210, 216
Central Asians
    economic and national-building goals
        for, 169–70
    history interpretation acknowledging
        role of, 243
    modernization of, 198
    zagranitsa (imaginary elsewhere),
        familiar, creating for, 181
Central Asian states, post-Soviet,
    235, 241–42
Central Europe, Soviet retreat from, 329n.93
Central European Jews, 32
Chechnya, 235–36, 237
Chiang Kai-shek, 81, 94
Chicherin, Georgy, 47–48, 53–54, 58, 66
China
    access, increased to, 181
    anti-imperialist struggle in, 2
    antisocialist dictatorship in, 81
    Cultural Revolution, 189, 222
    dramatic depictions of colonial
        life in, 74
    economic connections with, 241–42
    enthusiasm about, 178–79
    friendship, overtures to, 174
    internationalisms promoted by, 214–15
    preconditions for revolution in, 30–31
    setback, 1927, 100
    Soviet anticolonial legitimacy challenged
        by, 173–74, 182–83, 186–87
    Soviet competition with, 21, 185, 188–
        89, 224
    Soviet response to 1967 war criticized
        by, 207–8
    Soviet revisionism, views on, 156–57
    trade in, 62–63
    Western ways and imperialism
        rejected in, 52

Chinese Communist Party, 156–57, 188
Chinese communists, 81
Christian and Jewish women's experiences compared, 86–87
Christian visitors to Soviet Union, 137
cinema industry, Soviet, 190–206
civil rights, global movement for, 183–84
civil rights movement (U.S.). *See* US civil rights movement
Clark, Katerina, 9, 121
class struggle, 81, 110
"coerced legitimacy," 252n.53
Cold War
  alliances dividing world into, 161
  climate of distrust, 124–25
  competition, 185
  Eastern Mediterranean during, 17
  Eastern Mediterranean/Eurasia connections predating, 130
  economic competition in, 233
  enemies, Soviet political stability against, 181
  ideological pressures, 146–47
  intelligentsia responsibility in, 169
  international and domestic politics severed during, 183–84
  internationalisms of, 246–47
  Soviet legitimacy, threats to during, 166
  tropes, Russian invoking of, 236–37
Cold War exceptionalism, 8
colonialism
  corrupt system of, legacies of, 86
  critiques of, 2–3, 13–14, 131
  demise of, 161
  historicizing circulation of ideas about, 244
  interpretation of, 280n.180
  khans as agents of, 120–21
  masses liberated from, 181
  socialism in contrast to, 154–55
  Soviet anticolonial and imperial politics severed from, 3
  struggle against, 132–33, 215
  as system of racial difference, 215
colonial metropolises, 245
colonial modernity, 64
colonization, arguments for, 280n.180
colonized world, policy toward, 96

The Color Curtain (Wright), 161
Cominform
  Comintern compared to, 126
  dissolution of, 156–57
  Partisans of Peace movement launched by, 148
Comintern
  Arabization, calls for, 102
  Arab world, new approaches to, 119–20
  colonized and decolonizing world, approach to, 94
  colonized world, policy toward, 96
  communist parties admitted to, 111
  Congresses, 46
  dissolution of, 126, 135–36, 138–39
  Egyptian Communist Party acceptance into, 53–54
  ethicized vision of politics, 96
  interests of, 53
  Jewish socialist network role in forging, 84
  Ministry of Foreign Affairs, tensions with, 158
  nation-state internationalism role in structuring membership in, 7–8
  opportunities provided by, 64
  organizational-propagandist efforts by, 36–38
  Popular Front strategy embraced by, 132
  priority shift, 49–50
  radio technology used by, 266n.185
  resource limitations, 109–10
  term, 64
  women not supported by, 86
  working-class and peasant people, recruitment of, 94
Comintern-affiliated parties, purges in, 14–15
Comintern Eastern Section, 49–50, 52–53, 76–77, 97–98, 99
  Jews in, 117
  purges throughout, 111–12
Comintern Executive Committee (ECCI), 43–45
Comintern Near East Section, 19, 24, 94–95
Comintern networks, expansion of, 62
Cominterns, transnational world of, 8–9

Comintern Western Bureau, 51–52
Commissariat of the Enlightenment (Narkompros), 27
Committee for the Study of Central and Eastern Asia, 27
Commonwealth of Independent States, 235
communication, nationalizing forms of, 33
communism
  Arab commitments to and disappointments with, 121
  Arabizing, 113
  attraction to, 131
  containment of, 154
  conversions to, 78
  growth of, 127
  pressures pushing young people to, 92–93
Communist Academy, 36–38, 59
Communist everyday culture, 82
Communist Manifesto, 131–32
communist parties
  Arabizing, 96
  Chinese Communist Party, attitudes toward, 188
  Comintern, requirements for joining, 58–59
communist parties in Syria and Lebanon (CPSL)
  Arabization impact on, 96
  ethnic implications for, 96
  headquarters, attacks on, 148
  Jews in, 94–95
  leaders of, 57–58
  membership, 134–35, 292n.10
  organizing, 55–56
  support for, 138–39
Communist Party of the Soviet Union, International Department, 126
Communist Party of Turkestan, 40–41
communist revolutions, failed, 42
communists
  antifascist causes supported by, 126–27, 132–33
  labor union organization and protests supported by, 131–32
  pan-Arab state policy toward domestic, 153
  Zionist and imperialist influence on, 101–2

communist studies, marginalization of, 16
communist sympathizers, European and Israeli concerns about, 127
competition, monopolies replaced by free, 33
construction workers, student contact with, 93
cosmopolitanism
  between Central Asian and Afro-Asian artists, 183–84
  Soviet treatment of, 144–45
cosmopolitan literary and artistic scenes, 245
Cossack peasants, 97–98
cotton production, 170, 241–42
Council for Mutual Economic Assistance (COMECON), 156–57
Crescent Pact, 148
cross-border military interventions, 251n.32
cross-border rebellions, potential of, 110
Cuba, Soviet withdrawal from, 234
Cuba Missile Crisis, 1962, 187
Cubans, Soviet response to 1967 war criticized by, 207–8
cultural assimilation, limits of, 71–72, 88, 89–90
cultural autonomy, 130–31
cultural backwardness, rhetoric of, 276n.121
cultural differences, 76
cultural doctrine, postwar, 128–29
cultural exchange networks, 159–60
cultural exchanges, 174–80
cultural hybridization, 245
cultural nationalism, 144–45
cultural politics, late Stalin-era, 128–29
cultural regulations, loosening of, 155
cultural repressions, 145–46, 151
Cultural Revolution (China), 189, 222
cultural sector, repressions in, 144
culture
  alternative approach to, 131
  concept, 130
  of debate, 100–1
  Eastern, abstract, 151
  Eurocentric conception of, 155
  struggle for survival of, 145–46

INDEX 373

Czechoslovakia
  Soviet invasion of, 189, 208, 228
  Soviet Union agreements with, 264n.164

Dakrub, Muhammad, 150–51
Damascus, 135–36
Danilevskii, Nikolai, 130
Darwinism, 33
Dawn over Asia (later *Storm over Asia*) (film), 201–5, 210
A Day Lasts a Thousand Years (Aitmatov), 232–33
Death of the Black Consul (film), 194f, 211, 212
decolonization
  academic and cultural events highlighting, 241–42
  acceleration of, 185
  anticommunism in era of, 158
  conversations about, disconnected, 215
  culture and film, state support in process of, 208
  expulsions in process of, 97–98
  global intellectual history of, 244–45
  goals supporting, 222–23
  historicizing circulation of ideas about, 244
  intellectual histories of, 247
  international relations shift due to, 151
  international voices on, 188
  participants in project of, 90–91
  postwar, 126
  Soviet Easterner support for, 181–82
decolonizing revolutionary regimes, Soviet anticolonial legitimacy challenged by, 173–74
decolonizing world
  accommodating, 216
  Soviet Union relationship with, 124, 180
"defensive" expansionism, 10, 160
delegations, exchanges of, 159
democracy
  political, economic, and civil rights as part of, 183–84
  racial politics *versus* ideology of, 154
  Soviet, 144–45
  Western-style liberal, 238
depression, 92–93, 131–32
de-Stalinization
  curtailing of, 200–1
  of domestic nationalities policies, 165–66
  global decolonization contemporaneous with, 181
  ideological and institutional, 155
  transregional intellectual world during, 149–50
  Uzbek nationalism, shepherding through, 167
Dimanshtein, Semen, 264–65n.170
Dimitrov, Georgi, 78–79, 112–13, 116
divorce, 83, 85–86
Djagalov, Rossen, 13–14, 155, 213–14, 244, 324n.186, 330n.103
dogola (term), 48–49
domestic and foreign Easterners
  distinction between, 73
  education and curricula compared, 82, 110–11
  encounters between, 177
  relations between, 75
domestic and foreign Easts
  blurring of, 93
  conflicts of interest between, 221
  connections, challenges of sustaining, 186, 218
  connections, expanding between, 181
  connections across, 216
  cultural encounters between, 151
  decolonization unfolding across, 215
  distinction between, 9, 88–89, 90
  entanglements of, 93–94
  geopolitical borders between, 121
  integration between, 68
  Soviet communism role in bringing together, 152
  Soviet connection between, 7–8
  Soviet politics of history, questioning regarding, 231
  Soviet power anticolonial legitimacy, protecting across, 241
domestic and international priorities, intersection of, 3–4

domestic East
  accomplishments of, 144–45
  adapting of, 122–23
  as barometer, 181
  composition of, 10
  as drain on Russian resources, 22
  emphasis placed on, 90–91
  empire-positive integrative history projected to, 202
  faux pas concerning, 164
  as foreign East model, 121–22
  Friendship of the Peoples slogan meaning in, 217
  hubs developed in, 8–9
  intermediaries representing, 119
  international relations shaped by ideas about, 121
  liberating, 66–67
  media export, 224
  as model for foreign East, 128, 174–75, 186
  as model for foreign Easterners, 20–21
  Muslim treatment in, 154
  national cultures of, 118
  people specializing in, 111
  representatives of, opportunities for, 142–43
  revolution in, 58
  Soviet Central Asia as, 243
  Sovietization of, 2
  Soviet perspectives on, 74
  Soviet political controls, tightening over, 199–200
  Soviet references to, 5–6
  wartime interest in, 296n.62
domestic Easterners
  exoticizing and feminizing, 75
  foreign student interactions with, 82
  racial prejudice against, 233–34
  role of, 13
domestic Eastern migrants, racism and resentment of, 22
domestic inequality, 154
domestic nationalism, 185
domestic socialist construction, 156
drama performances (at KUTV), 73–74, 119, 140–42

Du Bois, W. E. B., 148–49, 154, 312n.156, 314n.185
Dugin, Aleksandr, 238–39
Dwidar, Muhamad, 102–3

East
  ancient history of, 70–71
  anti-colonial revolution in, 19, 46, 57
  anti-imperialist revolution in, 19
  Asia term used interchangeably with, 4
  Bolshevik activity in, 25–26
  Bolshevik ideology relationship to, 71
  category, functions of, 243
  as category, 7, 14, 87, 90–91, 243, 244
  communism in, 126–27
  concept, 2–3
  depictions, critiques of, 76
  homogenizing assumptions about, 88
  as ideological abstraction, 128
  immigration from, 250n.22
  knowledge about, increasing, 171–72
  "living space" in, 56
  mission to liberate, 38–39
  perceptions of, 67–68, 80–81
  porousness of idea of, 121
  priority shift to, 42
  reduced emphasis on, 49–50
  revolutionary knowledge for, 61
  Soviet definition of, 9
  Soviet interest, decline in, 20
  symbolism of, 237
  term usage, 25–26
  women of, 11
  world influence predicted for, 171, 181
East, revolution in
  concept used by different groups, 57–58
  future of, 40–41
  porous space of, 87
  revolution spread to East, 24, 56–57
  Soviet institutionalization of, 80–81
  world revolution, 56
The East and Revolution (Troianovskii), 30–31, 40–41
East Asia
  China efforts to undermine Soviet Union in, 187
  territorial conquests in, 5
  in World War II, 134

Eastern Bukhara, 265n.171
Eastern culture, laboratory for, 64–65
Easterners
　as category, 29
　definition and overview of, 1–2
　Soviet orientalist attitudes toward, 80
Eastern Europe
　allies, cultural relations with, 136–37
　national protest movements in, 214–15
　Sovietization, resistance in, 166
　Soviet retreat from, 329n.93
Eastern front strategy, 26–27
Eastern intermediaries, Soviet
　anticolonialism and antiracism, global showcased by, 245
　overview of, 11–13
Eastern International networks, 61–62
Easternization *versus* Sovietization, 71
Eastern Mediterranean
　border-making in, 88–89
　Central Asia, connection to, 17
　enduring interest in, 18
　Eurasia, cultural connections with, 130
　investments in, 20–21
　migration to, 17
　Russian presence in, 236–37
　schools set up in, 88
　students from, 64
　in World War II, 20
Easternness
　privileges of, 192
　sense of belonging *versus*, 294n.37
　Soviet assumptions about, 78–79, 80
Eastern otherness, 12
Eastern peoples, 58
Eastern politics, 70, 243
Eastern Question, 34–35, 53–54
Eastern revolution
　imagining, 30–31, 52
　party-state maps of, 172
The East in the Light of Revolution (Troianovskii), 30–31, 31*f*
Easts. *See also* domestic and foreign Easts
　borders between, 10
　persistence of two, 12, 20–21
Easts, connections between
　activation of, 21
　Eastern International and, 217
　institutions involved in, 217
　more emotive, less historically grounded, facilitating of, 22
　reconnection of, 116–17
　reimagining of, 246
　superficial nature of, 216
East-West divide
　continued acceptance of, 181
　enduring nature of, 6
　Eurocentric notion of, 87–88
　as existential gulf, 164–65
　imperial period challenging of, 5
　Soviet internationalism role in transcending, 118
　Soviet orientalist view of, 80
East-West duality, conversations about, 34–35
East-West worldview, 64–65
economic determinism, 23
economic development, stages of, 10
economic hardship, internationalist solutions to problem of, 64
economic injustice, perceptions of, 233
education (term), 64–65
educational opportunities, expansion of, 169–71
Egypt
　anti-imperialist struggle in, 2
　Comintern focus on, 83–84
　economic conditions, 62–63, 245–46
　emergence of, 153
　ethnic groups in, 122
　nationalist movement in, 88–89
　references to, 17
　revolution, 1952, 157–58, 196
　Soviet Union, relations with, 53–54, 151–52
　Soviet weapons supplied to, 207–8
　strategic significance of, 52
　uprisings in, 62
Egyptian Communist Party
　acceptance into Comintern, 53–54
　dissolution of, 158–59
　divisions within, 96
　ethnic implications for, 96
　membership in, 60
　members ousted from, 84–85
　Russian Jews in, 94–95

Egyptian communists, sacrificing, 157–58
Egyptian student and Palestinian editor, dispute between, 76
Egypt-Israel peace treaty, 1979, 226
Ehrenburg, Ilya, 134–35, 137–38, 144, 148–49, 155
Eisenhower Doctrine, 159–60
Eisenstein, Sergei, 73–74, 203–4, 210–11, 212–13, 216
electrical manufacturing plant, work at, 107–9
Eliava [Elieva], Shalva, 40–42
elites
  integration into Soviet order, 170
  purges of, 117
Emigrant (film), 192–93
empire
  legacies of, 240
  promoting critiques of, 244
  Soviet Union as, 4–5, 14
  suppressing histories and ideologies of, 245
  transformation of, 3
  worldmaking after, 150–51
empires
  post-Soviet views of, 4–5
  territorializing logic of, 58–59
engineers, education and training of, 93
enlightenment (term), 64–65
Ethiopia
  Italian invasion of, 133
  Soviet military aid to, 224
ethnic conflict, *korenizatsiia* contribution to, 103–4
ethnic difference, 67, 152
ethnic groups, national cultures of, 118
ethnonational boxes, world divided into, 121
Euphrates Dam, 221
Eurasia
  Central Asia as pivotal point of, 258n.62
  concept of, 240
  Eastern Mediterranean, cultural connections with, 130
  new borders in, 23–24
  term, 67–68, 238–39
Eurasian Customs Union, 238
Eurasian dynamics, regional, 31–32
Eurasian Economic Union, 238

Eurasian geopolitics, 240
Eurasian history, analysis of, 250n.29
Eurasian New World Order, 238–39
Eurasian transcontinental bloc, 56
Eurasia Party, 239
Eurocentric assumption of world binary division, 87–88
Eurocentric conception of culture, 155
Eurocentric view of history, East-West divide and, 6
Europe
  moral authority, critiques of, 34
  Russian Jewish immigration to, 54
  security in, 126
  Soviet competition with, 233
  Soviet relations with, 229–30
  in World War II, 134
European categories, Bolshevik codifying of, 6
European imperial rule, legacy of, 34–35
European intellectuals, visits to Soviet Union, 124–25, 152
European New Left, 215
European oppression, mocking symbols of, 74
European racial categories, 34–35
exploitation (term translated), 277n.140

factories, internships in, 93
factory work, 92, 107–9
Faiziev, Latif, 196–97
Fakhuri, 'Umar, 135–36, 149–50
family, official attitudes toward, 85–86
famine, 1946–1947, 124
fascism
  Arab world attitudes concerning, 132
  critiques of, 2–3
  culture triumph against, 145
  opposition to, 16
  in Spain, 133
  struggle against, 132–33
  war against, 145–46
fascist imperialism, 132
federalism, 258n.67
film, reaching non-Western audiences through, 21
film industry, Soviet, 190–206, 208–12, 217–18

Finland, 38, 115
First Five-Year Plan, 72, 78, 93, 94
First Teacher (film), 205
folklore, indigenous, molding, 144
food access, 40
food supply chains, destruction of, 38
foreign communists, exile of, 20
foreign East
    composition of, 10
    and domestic East (*see* domestic and foreign Easts)
    domestic East as model for, 121–22, 128, 174–75, 186
    domestic East media export to, 224
    domestic models used to understand, 98–99
    revolution in, 58
    Soviet aid-seekers in, 234
    Soviet anticolonialism displayed to, 202
    Soviet Central Asia as model for, 119–20, 165
    Soviet Union intermediaries to, 122–23
    Tashkent visitors from, 177
foreign Easterners
    domestic East as model for, 20–21
    economic and national-building goals for, 169–70
foreign Eastern students, cultural Sovietization of, 83
foreigners, repatriation of, 114–15
foreign language publishing, 116
foreign rule, collective liberation from, 153
The Foundations of Geopolitics (Dugin), 238–39
France
    Britain relations with, 125–26
    communist parties dissolved by, 126–27
    fall to Nazi Germany, 133–34
    Popular Front government in, 133
    power, decline of, 160–61
French colonialism, 132
French empire, colonial brutality under, 53–54
Friendship of Peoples, 118, 121, 217
From under the Vaults of the Mosque (film), 190–91
Frunze, Mikhail, 41–42, 49, 201, 202, 261n.104, 264n.159

futurism, visual artists interested in, 45–46

"galiata" (term), 76
Ganjavi, Nizami, 118
Gasprinskii, Ismael, 192–93
gender dynamics, 144
gendered hierarchies, 86
gender norms, Soviet rule impact on, 11
generational conflict, 211–13
geography, Eastern, abstract, 151
geopolitics
    in Asia, 47
    changing global, 71
    concept of, 8
    language of, 49, 55, 56
    Marxist approach to, 10, 69
    term, 31–32
    territorial logic of, 58–59
    transformations in global, 160–61
Geopolitik (term), 56
Georgia
    neighboring power colonization, hypothetical of, 119
    in Ottoman administration, 140
    Russian war with, 236
Georgia, Soviet republic of, 42
Germany
    aggression of 1941, 56
    communist revolution, failed in, 42
    France's fall to, 133–34
    geopolitics, 263–64n.151
    intellectual culture, 31–32
    Soviet Union agreements with, 124–25, 264n.164
    Versailles Treaty, opposition to, 61–62
Ghafurov, Bobojon, 172, 327n.53
    call for undoing damage of purges, 171–72
    as intermediary, 244
    Jewish orientalists protected by, 227–28
    local communists, concern over, 158
    "orientalist" term usage defended by, 243–44
    Oriental Studies Institute headed by, 172
    as post-Soviet Tajik nationalism symbol, 241–42
Ghana, 21

Ghassub, Adal (Alice Zarif), 85–87
Gilan (Iranian province), 49–50
Glasnost', 229–31, 246
glasnost'-era questions and projects, 240
global and regional geopolitics, 8
global anticolonialism, 46, 90
global anticolonial political agendas, 214–15
global anti-imperialist "front," call to reimagine, 160
global capitalism, transformations of, 223
global decolonization
  de-Stalinization contemporaneous with, 181
  Eastern International domestic and foreign components, reconnecting during, 160
  peak of, 155
  slowing of, 21
  Soviet power in relation to, 245
global history, 247
global ideal, Soviet Union as vanguard of, 16
global integration theories, 16
global migration, 63
global politics, 23, 216
Global South, 9, 244–45
global trans-colonial solidarity, contradictions of, 58–59
godless, self-descriptions as, 219–20
Goldziher, Ignaz, 32–33
Gorbachev, Mikhail
  critics of, 246
  East neglected by, 237
  economic challenges, 229
  foreign East aid sought by, 234
  foreign policy, 234
  reforms, 229–31, 233
  Westernization under, 6
Gorky, Maxim, 27–28, 132–33, 136–37, 196–97
Gosplan (State Planning Commission), 59
Great Britain foreign policy, 126
Greater Danger Principle, 105–6
Great Game, 34
Grozny, Chechnya, 235–36
Guest of Mecca (film), 190–91
Gulag, Jews in, 289–90n.160

Gurko-Kriazhin, Vladimir, 35, 36–38, 50, 267n.212, 273n.63

Haidar Khan (Radjeb Bombi) (Gaidar-Khan Amuogky Tariverdiev), 35, 259n.83
Hamdi Salam (Muhammed Ahmed Said)
  career and professional opportunities, 79–80
  East(s), influences on life and views of, 68, 80–81
  films translated and dubbed by, 195
  as foreign exchange student, 60–61, 64
  Ghassub, A.'s position compared to that of, 86
  labor camp internment and release, 79
  return home not feasible for, 114–15
  Soviet perspectives on domestic East embraced by, 74
  system gaming by, 78–79
  worldwide anticolonialism, interest in, 63–64
  writings, 280n.176
Hamzawi, Ibrahim
  Soviet Union, visit to, 124–25, 137, 140, 298n.82
  suspicions toward G. Hanna recalled by, 138
Hanna, George [Jurj Hanna]
  Egypt supported by, 153
  exhibitions organized by, 176
  Soviet Union, 1st visit to, 124–25, 127–28, 137, 139–40, 146, 150–51
  Soviet Union, 2nd visit to, 149
  after Soviet Union visit, 148–51
  suspicions toward, 137, 138
  writings, 138, 146–47, 149–51
Hapsburg collapse, 3, 19
Hauner, Milan, 56
Haushofer, Karl, 34, 47, 56
hegemonies, variety and instability of, 324n.186
Hikmet, Nazim
  drama club led by, 73–74, 140–42
  drama performances recalled by, 74–75
  Easterners described by, 74–75
  fiction written by, 280n.176

Meyerhold, V. recruited by, 74
Soviet perspectives on domestic East embraced by, 74
Tashkent conference attended by, 312n.156
uniform worn by, 74
historical-adventure films, 200
historical memory, 7–8
history
alternative approach to, 131
challenging reinterpretations of, 243
history education, 66, 130–31
History of the Peoples of Uzbekistan, 140
Hitler, Adolf, 126–27, 133–34, 135–36
Holy Land, 17
Horsemen of the Revolution (film), 210–11, 215
Hotel Lux, 76–77
human rights, 188, 253n.79
Hungary
communist revolution, failed in, 42
protests in, 166
uprising in, 186–87
Hussein, Saddam, 226, 234

Ibn Sina (film), 196–97
Ibragimov, Bashkir Shagimardan, 324n.6
Ibrahim, Abdurreshid, 258–59n.74
Ibrahim, Imili Faris
background, 137
gender dynamics impact on, 144
Soviet Union, visit to, 124–25, 137–38, 139–40
after Soviet Union visit, 147
ideas, circulation of, 9
ideological contradiction, 244
ideological struggle, 110
Ikramov, Akmal Ikramovich, 82, 162, 167–68, 173
immigration to Soviet Union, East and West origins compared, 250n.22
imperial hierarchy, legacies of, 150–51
imperial ideology, Eurocentrism of, 5
imperial influence, Soviet leaders subject to, 4, 90
imperialism
nature of, 23
opposition to, 16
struggle against, 161
Imperialism (Lenin), 23
imperialist state, aid sought from personnel of, 255n.21
imperial legacies, 88
imperial violence, 245
India
access, increased to, 181
anti-imperialist struggle in, 2
British rule, protest against, 52
Central Asia, ties to, 163–64
concerns about, 34–35
dramatic depictions of colonial life in, 74
East-West fusion, role in facilitating, 34
enthusiasm about, 178–79
history of, 26–27
preconditions for revolution in, 30–31, 48
Russian-British competition over, 34
indigenization. *See korenizatsiia* (indigenization)
individual freedom, importance of, 147
Indonesia, right-wing coup in, 21, 188–89
industrial development, postcolonial, film industry during, 208
industrialization as connective process, 68
In Moscow a Second Time (Hanna), 149
Institute of Africa, buildings of, 330n.103
Institute of Asia and Africa, split of, 172–73
Institute of National and Colonial Problems, 99, 110–11, 115, 116
Institute of Peoples of the USSR, 59
integration, limits of, 71–72
intellectual (term in Arabic), 130
intellectual and material resources, geographical distribution of, 172
intellectual freedom, Arab state *versus*, 302n.143
intellectuals
regional politics, involvement in, 127–28
repression of, 144
Soviet collapse impact on, 246
transregional and global connections maintained by, 128

intelligentsia
   in Central Asia, 170
   creation of new, 169–70
   Gorbachev, M. admiration of, 229–30
   overview of, 61
   responsibility of, 169
   role in work of state, 170
   Western-oriented, 155, 181
"internal East," 240
international affairs, territory and culture role in, 34–35
international communism
   administration of, 88
   histories of, 14–15
international communist movement, 153, 267n.211
international communist party loyalty, 90–91
international decolonization, Soviet commitment to, 181
International Federation of Film Critics (FIPRESCI), 208, 209–10
internationalisms
   alternative, 19
   anti-Western internationalism, competition with, 8–9
   competing, 214–15, 238–39
   experience of, 246–47
international politics, 183–84
international relations
   domestic East, ideas about role in shaping, 121
   shifts of, 151
international students, stipends for, 159
inter-state diplomacy, 153
interwar period, internationalisms of, 246–47
Ioske (Ahmed Ibn 'Abidin), 107–9, 108f, 114–15
Iran
   Soviet interest in, 126
   Turkburo in, 265n.172
Iranian plateau, 32–33
Iranian Revolution, 228
Iraq
   anticolonial protests in, 52
   communist repression in, 22
   government rise and fall, repeated in, 152

   independence, fight for, 100–1
   Kuwait invaded by, 234
   Soviet relations with, 221, 226
   uprisings in, 62
Iraqi communists
   Anglo-Iraqi agreement, protests against, 149
   Ba'athist regime, pressure to accommodate, 158–59
   purge of, 226
'Isa, Rashad, 131–32, 147
Islam
   alcohol, references to, 82
   Arabic-speaking world, association with, 15
   flexible approach to, 32–33
   as religion of socialism, 82
   Uzbek-Arab relations based on, 180
Islamic modernism, taboo histories of, 180
Islamic universalism, 19
Israel
   Jewish settlement in, 98–99
   in 1967 war, 207–8
   Soviet relations with, 189–90, 193
   Soviet support for, 127
   state, creation of, 128–29, 151
Israeli athletes, killing of, 222
Italian fascism, war against, 145–46
Italy, Soviet Union agreements with, 264n.164

jadidism, 167–68, 180
Japanese imperialism, 34–35
Jerusalem, Arab-Jewish violence in, 83–84
Jewish Anti-Fascist Committee, 128–29, 144
Jewish assimilation
   debates on, 71–72
   pressure, reaction to, 55
   voluntary, 54
Jewish Bolshevik activists
   backgrounds of, 56–57
   East, involvement in, 29
   imperial Russia's Jewish Question, confrontation with, 54
Jewish colonization, 110
Jewish comrades, arrest and sentencing of, 84–85

Jewish cultural rights, debates on, 71–72
Jewish labor movement, 54
Jewish socialist networks, 84
Jewish teachers, 122
Jewish transregional family ties, 76–77
Jews
    accusations against, 122, 287n.126
    Arabization and, 113
    from former Russian empire, 89–90
    purging of, 113, 117, 118, 122, 144
jihad, 29
Jordan
    Army, 225
    independence, 125–26
    in interwar period, 17

Kafri (Ahmed Salim Abduhamam)
    expulsion from KTUV, 92, 107–9
    factory assignment, 92, 93–94
    Moscow, return to, 109–10
    sent to Palestine, 114–15
    Soviet Union, opportunity to come to, 94
    Stalin Revolution impact on, 92–93
Kalandarov, Khamdam-Khodja, 201, 202, 203
Kamal, Husayn, 210–11
Kamenev, Lev, 35
    Berger, J. relations with, 106
    book recommendations made by, 35
    Chicherin, G. instructions to, 47
    murder accusation against, 111–12
    nationality not disclosed by, 287n.131
Kari-Yakubov, Mukhitdin, 140–44, 141*f*, 142*f*, 167–68
Kataev, Valentin, 140
Kazakhstan
    cinema industry in, 209–10
    republican party boss, replacement of, 230–31
    Russian population, decline of, 97–98
Kennedy, John F., 185
Kerzhentsev, Platon
    war coverage by, 135
    writings, 28, 135
Khakimov, Karim, 290n.170, 324n.6
Khanum, Tamara, 140–42, 141*f*
Khayyata, Salim, 132–33, 293–94n.34

Khiva as protectorate, 5–6
Khodjaev, Fayzulla
    arrest, 193–94
    fate of, 173
    Sidqi, N. meeting with, 120–21
    trial of, 162, 167–68
    Troianovskii, K. friendship with, 41–42
Khorezm People's Soviet Republic, 48–49
Khrushchev, Nikita
    background, 156
    competition with West under, 6
    cotton production committee created by, 170
    Cuba policy, 187
    cultural diplomacy, 159
    East faux pas, 164
    East policy, 20–21, 181
    East role in world history predicted by, 171, 181
    foreign policy, 156–58
    Lutskii, V. termination from job appealed to, 129
    Mukhitdinov, N., relationship with, 164–66, 169, 172
    national consolidation and ethnohistorical advancement, attempts to curb, 185–86
    nationalist liberation movements, aid approved by, 207–8
    non-Russians, challenges of governing, 166
    ouster, 187
    "peaceful coexistence" policy, 186–87
    political elites under, 242
    publicity concerning, 163–64
    Secret Speech, 156–57
    security as approached by, 160
    Soviet Central Asia policy, countering criticism over, 170–71
Khudsovet (Artists Council), 204, 213
Khuri, Ra'if
    as Communist sympathizer, 298n.82
    Egypt supported by, 153
    Ehrenburg, I., contact with, 144
    1967 war, hopes concerning, 151–52
    organization memberships, 135
    Soviet Union, visit to, 124–25, 137–38, 139–40

382　INDEX

Khuri, Ra'if (*cont.*)
　after Soviet Union visit, 147
　Soviet World War II victory,
　　commentary on, 145–46
　Soviet writers, contact with, 144
　writings, 132–33, 146–47
King, Martin Luther, Jr., 215–16
Kingdom of Hijaz, 53, 62
Kirov, Sergei, assassination of, 111–12
Kitaigorodskii, Paltiel (Palia) Volkovich,
　76–77, 84–85, 94–95
Kjellén, Johan Rudolf, 31–32, 33, 238–39
Kobozev, Pyotr, 40–42
Kolarz, Walter, 165, 170–71
Konachalovsky, Andrei, 205
korenizatsiia (indigenization), 67, 95, 103
　decolonization through, 121–22
　deemphasis on, 105–6
　implementation of, 103–4
　versus schizhenia (rapprochement of
　　peoples), 166, 172–73
　term, avoidance of, 170–71
Kotel'nikov, Fyodor, 109–10, 116–17
Kuchumov, Vladimir, 70, 279n.154
Kuleshev [Kuleshov], Lev, 191, 194–95
Kurdish ethnicity, 113
Kurdish families, deportation of, 287n.132
KUTV (Communist University of the
　Toilers of the East), 232–33
　Arab-Jewish conflict at, 103, 104
　closure of, 116–17
　cultural clubs, 73–74
　cultural front, role in, 64–65
　disintegration of, 116
　domestic and foreign Easts blurred at, 93
　domestic and foreign sectors, physical
　　separation of, 121
　as "Eastern" contact zone, 89
　Eastern Mediterranean communist
　　schools compared to, 88
　establishment of, 64–65
　ethnicized struggles at, 106
　ex-Zionists at, 94–95
　geopolitics, role in changing, 71
　instructors, administrators, and staff,
　　118, 122, 140–42
　Jewish attraction to, 89–90
　Jews at, 94–95, 117
　Jews at (instructors and administrators),
　　118, 122
　as laboratory, 90
　leadership, 70–71
　nationalism and supra-national
　　belonging, conversations at, 90
　nation-building activities in, 76
　as portal of ideas about East, 20
　purges at, 104
　purpose of, 65–66
　uniforms, 74
　workers and peasants at, 68
KUTV Arab Section (Arab Circle)
　as case study, 75
　domestic and foreign Easts
　　entanglements in, 93–94
　leadership, 104–5, 107
　Palestine violence, debates on, 102
　student group photo, 77*f*
KUTV foreign section, isolation
　of, 110–11
KUTV foreign students
　Arab students, 105
　assignments, 76, 78
　attracting of, 19–20, 64, 90–91
　backgrounds, 60–61, 78
　behavior problems, 107–9
　constraints and opportunities offered
　　to, 80–82
　diversity, 1, 67, 75
　and domestic students compared, 72–
　　73, 82, 110–11
　evaluations and personal files of, 80–81
　events for, 73, 140–42
　expulsions, 92, 102–3, 105, 107–9
　female students, 83, 86
　gender breakdown, 278n.147
　group photo, 77*f*
　health and diet, 72, 274n.84
　integration into institution, 76–77
　internships, 93
　marriage and romance, 83
　Muslim background, 82
　opinion, expressing, 81–82
　privileged status of, 87–88
　school closure aftermath, 116
　Soviet Easterners, attitude toward, 89
　Sovietization of, 78

Soviet war scares, xenophobia, and purges impact on, 111–12
Stalin, J. lectures and messages to, 1, 72, 213–14
as unmarried men, 83
KUTV graduates
  Arabs, employment for, 99
  as intermediaries, 90–91
  local economic grievances as framed by, 131–32
KUTV research institute. *See* NIA (KUTV research institute)
KUTV students
  bourgeois press crusade against Russia, calls for fight against, 309n.103
  gender breakdown, 278n.147
  internships, 93
  Jewish students, 104–5
  living conditions, 72
  opportunities offered to, 87
  purge of former, 232–33
Kuwait
  Iraq invasion of, 234
  Soviet aid-seekers in, 234
Kyrgyz Republic, 204–5
Kyrgyzstan, 241–42

lands, colonization as planned use of, 280n.180
Laqueur, Walter, 133–34
Latin America, 207–8
Latin American countries, 189
Latin American revolutionary movements, women in, 251–52n.49
League against Imperialism, 88, 106
League of Nations
  categories, 58–59
  Covenant of, 52–53
  dissolution of, 125–26
  Mandate system, 62, 69
  nation-state internationalism role in structuring, 7–8
  Open Door Policy, 62–63
  Soviet Union joining of, 115
  territories, communists in, 53–54
League of the Militant Godless, 278n.143
Lebanese Civil War, 225

Lebanese intellectuals. *See* Syrian and Lebanese intellectuals
Lebanese Left, 133, 150–51
Lebanese leftists, visit to Soviet Union, 20
Lebanese literature, representatives of, 149
Lebanese Society of Friends of the USSR, 124–25
Lebanese-Syrian League against Nazism and Fascism, 133
Lebanon
  anticommunist campaign in, 148
  anti-fascist momentum in, 133–34
  Armenians in, 122
  British involvement in, 126, 134
  emigration from, 62–63
  European control over, 130
  gendered hierarchies in, 86
  history, treatment of, 130–31
  independence, 125–26, 134, 136, 151
  in interwar period, 17
  Palestinian guerrillas in, 222
  Soviet-supported cultural activities in, 136–37
  weakness of, 127–28
  in World War II, 134
Left, intellectual history of, 14–15
leftist intellectuals, return to antifascist positions, 133–34
Lefts, histories of, 14–15
Lenin, Vladimir
  aid sought by, 26–27
  birthday, occasion of, 186–87
  on bringing orientalism to the masses, 27
  on building socialism, 255n.21
  capitalism and social peaceful coexistence doctrine, 156
  on colonial country workers and peasants, 49–50
  domestic and international priorities, 3–4
  East role in world history predicted by, 171, 181
  on foreign affairs, 23
  Gorbachev, M. compared to, 230–31
  governance challenges, 25–26
  imperialism crisis imagined by, 52–53
  imperialism theory, 100–1
  Muslim leaders, dealings with, 29
  Roy, M. N., dealings with, 46, 66

Lenin, Vladimir (*cont.*)
  Russian approach to foreigners criticized by, 273n.67
  territory given up by, 23–24, 57–58
  Troianovskii, K., dealings with, 35
  Troianovskii, K. vision endorsed by, 57
  Turkestan, views on, 38–39
  writings, 27, 29, 30, 137
Leningrad, 146
Lewis, Bernard, 243–44
liberation, models of, 153
Libya, 132
literary events, Syrian and Lebanese intellectual participation in, 151–52
localism, struggle against, 169
Lozovskii, Solomon, 137–38, 144–45
Luis, Josef Jibran, 124–25, 137, 140, 298n.82
Lunacharskii, Anatolii
  as Commissar of the Enlightenment, 27, 35
  Troianovskii, K., dealings with, 35–36
Lutskii, Vladimir
  Moscow State University, position at, 172–73
  Moscow State University, termination from, 129
  professional activities, 172–73
  Uzbekistan and Egypt economies compared by, 268n.217
  writings, 296n.62

Mackinder, Sir Halford John, 34, 258n.62
Maduyan, Artin, 132–33
Magyar, Lájos, 109–10, 111–12, 114
Maier, Charles, 268n.214
majoritarian ethnonationalism, 20, 95
majoritarian national liberation movements, 122
male activists, risks and sacrifices of, 12
male-dominated Soviet project, 11
Mali, 21
Mandates, nation-making projects in, 94
Manila Pact, 160–61
Manuil'skii, Dmitri, 78–79, 119–20, 121–22, 132–33
Mao Zedong, 156–57, 186–87, 189
market competition, 40–41
Marx, Karl, 10, 87–88, 100

Marxism
  growing opposition to, 228
  limitations of, 215
Marxist culture, 89–90
Marxist geopolitics, 244–45
Marxist-Leninist canon, knowledge grounded in, 101–2
Marxist literature, 13
Marxist orientalists
  debates significant to, 100
  employment for, 99
  Soviet *versus* European rule comparisons discouraged by, 58
Marxists
  Eurocentrism of, 164
  imperialism crisis imagined by, 52–53
Marxist solidarity, Eurocentric language of, 183–84
Marxist texts, translations into Arabic, 61
Mashriq
  anticolonial activism in, 125–26
  communist activities in, 126–27
  Georgia and Armenia, ties to, 140
  geostrategic importance of, 126
  search for a better world, 130
  VOKS (All-Union Society for Cultural Ties Abroad) connections to, 136
masses, decolonizing states reframing, 181
masshtabnost' (term), 8–9
Mayakovsky, Vladimir, 72, 74
McCarthyism, 154, 215–16
Melkumov, Mikhail, 203–4
Meyerhold, Vsevolod, 73–74, 140–42
Middle East
  Central Asia as part of, 254n.80
  communism defeat in, 159
  developments in, 214–15
  films exported to, 198
  partition of, 58–59
  radio and film reach throughout, 188
  Soviet definition of, 265n.176
  Soviet economic aid to, 157
  Soviet policy in, 207–8, 234
  Soviet power, efforts to contain in, 160–61
  Soviet power mediators in, 118
  in US world order, 236–37
  Western delineation of, 254n.80
  in World War II, 134

Middle Eastern area studies, 247
Middle Eastern contexts, Soviet politics and Marxist literature in, 13
Middle Eastern politics, official interpretations of, 12
Middle Eastern studies, illuminating blind spots of, 22
Middle East Mandate territories, recession, 1930s, 92–93
Mikhoels, Solomon, 128–29
Mikoyan, Anastas, 171
Ministry of Foreign Affairs, 116, 158
minorities, reduced visibility of national, 185–86
minority and majority nationalities, tensions between, 122
missionary efforts, imperial, 68–69
missionary schools, 88
modernism, celebration of, 45–46
modernizing state, Soviet Union as, 4–5, 14
Molotov, Viacheslav, 137–38, 160–61
Molotov-Ribbentrop Pact, 116–17, 126–27, 133–34, 147, 328n.75
monetary system, collapse of, 38
Mongol peoples, 19
monopolies, abolishing, 33
Moon over Samarqand (Qandil), 246
Morocco
  anticolonial protests in, 52
  anti-imperialist struggle in, 2
Moscow
  cultural setting, diverse in, 73
  domestic Eastern migrants in, 22
  Eastern International, building from, 51–52
  foreigner experiences in, 19–20, 92–93
  housing crisis in, 111
  as hub of global anticolonial activism, 8–9
  intellectual environment, 90
  material conditions in, 72
  Near East, link to, 19
  periphery relations negotiated in, 90
  travel to, 50, 64
  visits to, 137, 146
Moscow Institute of Orientalism (MIV), 67, 119

Moscow metro, work for, 93
Moscow Radio, 116, 149
Moscow State University, medical faculty of, 78
Mother (Gorky), 196–97
Motyl, Vladimir, 198–99, 213
Mukhitdinov, Nuriddin, 161, 219–20, 226
  background, 154–55, 162
  Brezhnev, L., appointment after ascent of, 173
  in Central Asia, 190
  conference organized by, 171–72
  global anti-imperialist "front," call to reimagine, 160
  Khrushchev, N. relationship with, 20–21, 164–66, 172
  photo, 163f
  Presidium seat and CPSU secretary post, loss of, 173
  publicity concerning, 163–64
  repressions acknowledged by, 167–68
  Soviet censorship, frustrations with, 184
  Soviet Central Asia policy, countering criticism over, 170–71
  Syria involvement, 189–90, 222–23, 225
  Uzbek intelligentsia, instructions to, 169, 179
Mukhtar, Omar, 132
multinational community in Soviet Union (metaphor), 118
Munich Olympics, 1972, killing of Israeli athletes in, 222
Muruwwa, Husayn, 128, 149, 245–46, 332n.23
Musburo (Bureau of Muslim Communist Organizations of Turkestan), 40–42
Museum of Eastern Art, 27–28
Museum of Victims of Political Repression, 241–42
Muslim communists, 57–58, 261–62n.116
Muslim intermediaries, 28
Muslim Khalifat movement, 52
Muslim refugees, migrations of, 3
Muslims
  conflict, mediating, 240
  Eurasianist ideology, relationship to, 239
  Ottoman territories, migration to, 192–93

Muslims (*cont.*)
   Russia, post-Soviet relations with, 235–36
   Russian rule over, 28, 29, 119
   southern Central Asia autonomy sought by, 38–39
   Sovietization, potential to resist, 6–7
   Soviet treatment of, 154
   Thaw era opportunities for, 181–82
Muslim states, 164
Muslim-Turkic regions, independence of, 38–39
Muslim world, 29, 243
Mussolini, Benito, 133

Nadab (Nahaum Leshchinskii), 99–102, 113
Narkomnats (Commissariat of Nationalities)
   KUTV established under, 64–65
   maps produced by, 45–46
Nasser, Gamal Abdel
   appointments by, 153, 196
   Arab-Uzbek friendship, statements about, 179
   Cold War divisions denounced by, 161
   communist repression by, 157–58
   consolidation of power, 160–61
   death, 226
   defeat in Arab-Israeli War, 1967, 21
   delegation around Soviet Union, 218–19
   film censorship by, 196–97
   Mukhitdinov, N. dealings with, 163–64
   Nasserism, disillusionment with, 214–15
   1967 war launched by, 207
   photo, 163*f*
   regime, questioning of, 208
   Soviet relations with, 325n.7
   Tashkent, visit to, 313n.163
   as weak link, 164
national and colonial question, debates about, 66–67
national cultures, debates on parameters of, 144–45
national differences, respect for, 128
national elites, policy of promoting, 272n.44
national exclusiveness, struggle against, 169
national exhibition, literary exercises in, 76

national home, 94
national identity, construction of, 130, 241–42
nationalism
   conversations about, 90
   cultivating right kind of, 169
   debates about, 129
   managing, 166
   neutralizing, 3–4
   Soviet approach to, 95
nationalist deviation, 102–3, 104, 122, 143, 144
nationalist liberation movements, 207–8
nationalist parties, dissolving and incorporating, 55
national minorities, reduced visibility of, 185–86
national question, Soviet resolution of, 144–45
nation-building, 103
nationhood, 3–4, 94
nation-making, 95
nation-state internationalism, 7–8
NATO, 148, 236
Nazarbayev, Nursultan, 235, 241–42
Nazi foreign policy, 56
Nazism, war against, 145–46
Near East
   Jewish interest in, 89–90
   Moscow link to, 19
   Soviet definition of, 265n.176
   Soviet power in, 53
   term, 17
Nehru, Jawaharlal, 161, 163–64
neo-Eurasianism, 239
New Economic Policy (NEP), 60, 76–77
New Humanity Building a New World (al-Hilu), 131–32, 157–58
NIA (KUTV research institute), 113, 116, 121
NIA/KUTV organization, 116
Niiazov, Abdul-Vahed, 239
1967 war. *See* Arab-Israeli War, 1967
NKID (Commissariat of Foreign Affairs)
   Comintern *versus*, 47–48
   committees under, 27
   films reviewed by, 193
   intelligence resources of, 52
   interests of, 53

in organizational schema, 43–45
Tashkent branch, abolishing of, 49–50
VOKS work with, 135–36
NKVD (People's Commissariat of Internal Affairs)
    denunciations to, 138–39
    foreigners at KTUV under control of, 72–73
    Jews in, 290n.164
Non-Aligned Movement (NAM), 185, 245–46
non-communist leftist intellectuals, 127
"non-party" orientation, 158–59
non-Russian national cadres, 103
non-Russians, Russia's imperial civilizing mission for, 200–1
non-Russian Soviet republics, 165–66
non-Russian territories, 1
nonsocialist countries, national development of, 306n.51
non-Soviet quasi-national group, Arabs treated as, 76
North Africa
    China activity in, 188
    French in, 122
    uprisings in, 62
    in World War II, 134
North-South axis, 216
Norway, 264n.164
Nu'man, Anwar, 148

October Revolution
    anniversaries of, 73, 150–51
    geography of, 206–7
    world history, centrality in, 181
October: Ten Days That Shook the World (film), 203–4
Odessa, 24–25
OGPU (secret police), 52, 109–10
oil industry
    in Middle East, 160–61, 223
    in Soviet Union, 223–24, 229
oil revolution, 1973, 22
Ol'denburg, Sergei
    Lenin, V. dealings with, 26–28
    new government, work with, 27
On Lenin's Pass (film), 196–97
Open Door Policy, 62–63

oppressed groups, minorities supported as members of, 121–22
Organization of Petroleum-Exporting Countries (OPEC), 223
Orient, spiritual *versus* materialist West, 34
orientalism
    approach to, 66
    definition of, 13, 244
    instruction on, 70–71
    intellectual histories of, 247
    Western critiques of, 14
"orientalist" (term), 243
oriental studies, revival of Soviet, 172–73
oriental studies centers, 171–72
Oriental Studies Institute, 172
Orthodox churches, 30
Ottoman collapse, 3, 19
Ottoman empire
    Arab territories of, 51–52
    priorities of, 257n.39
    Russian empire, dealings with, 29
Ottoman oppression, mocking symbols of, 74

Padmore, George, 152
Palestine
    Arab community in, 20, 109
    Arab-Jewish conflict in/Zionist enterprise in, 83–84
    Bolshevik revolutionary movement activist ties to, 17–18
    Comintern interpretation of events in, 117–18
    communist movement, source materials on, 292n.15
    emigration to, 89–90
    Jewish immigration to, 55–56
    nationalist movement in, 88–89
    Russian Jewish immigration to, 54
    small landownership in, 81
    social and economic development of, 267n.203
    social and economic tensions in, 109
    Soviet Jews with links to, 117–18
    strategic importance of, 55
    uprisings in, 62
    in World War II, 134
    Zionist emigration to, 54

Palestine, Jewish community in (Yishuv), 101–2, 109, 113–14
  antifascism in, 126–27
  Arab community, boundaries with, 20
  and Arab lands compared, 94–95
  Auerbach, H. views on, 55
  communist support in, 122
  generalizations about, 115–16
  international recognition and influence low for, 117
  Jewish workers in, 98–99
Palestine, partition of
  Arab-Israeli conflict and, 125–26
  overview, 17
  Soviet support for, 126, 147, 151–52
Palestine Communist Party (PCP)
  Arabizing, challenges of, 96–97
  Comintern, admission into, 55–56, 106
  Comintern, relationship with, 97
  ethnic implications for, 96
  formation of, 54
  Jewish exodus from, 99
  Jewish members, wartime dilemma of, 126–27
  leadership, 55
  Poale-Zion, relations with, 98–99
  Russian Jews in, 94–95
  students sent to KUTV by, 76–77
Palestine violence, 1929
  interpretations and debates over, 97–102, 121–22
  Jewish *versus* Arab victims of, 101–2
  Stalin-Berger meeting before, 106
Palestinian cause, 322n.133
Palestinian editor and Egyptian student, dispute between, 76
Palestinian Liberation Organization (PLO), 192
Palestinian refugees
  camps, Jordanian attack on, 225
  displacement of, 214–15
Palestinians
  expulsion from Jordan, 222
  sweep of, 117
Pan-Arabism, 153
pan-Arab nationalism, 88–89
pan-Arab states, 153
pan-Islamic movements, 32–33
pan-Islamism, 34–35

pan-Mongolism, 19, 34–35
Pan-Slavs, Eurocentrism challenged by, 5
parliamentary democracy, 134–35
Partisans of Peace, 138, 148–49, 151–52
party-state, survival of, 49
patriarchal authority, negotiating forms of, 86
patriarchies, intersection of, 11
patriot (term), 128–29
Pavlovich, Mikhail
  in Baku, 47
  East as perceived by, 67–68
  "Eurasia" term used by, 238–39
  European imperial railroad projects analyzed by, 30
  Marxist orientalists led by, 59
  on studying East, 9
  Troianovskii's reports forwarded by, 59
  VNAV and MIV headed by, 272n.48
peaceful coexistence policy, 159–60, 188
  calls for end to, 207–8
  China criticism of, 186–87
  overview of, 156
peasants, recruitment of, 94
people, circulation of, 9
People's Democratic Republic of South Yemen (PDRY), 224
"peoples of the East," 9, 29
perestroika, 229–31, 241, 246
Persia
  preconditions for revolution in, 30–31
  revolutionary movements in, 32–33, 48
"personal" politics in Eastern International world, 11
Peter the Great, 4, 125*f*
Philippines, 245
piatichlenka (five stages of economic development), 10
Pipes, Richard, 165–66
Poale-Zion (Jewish labor movement)
  Comintern recognition not extended to, 55
  former membership in, 117
  former members of, 71–72, 98–99
  overview of, 54
  Palestinian section of, 54
  politics of, 88
  in United States, 83
Poem of Two Hearts (film), 211

pogroms
    action potentially leading to, 113–14
    flight from, 17
    numbers killed in, 94–95
    Palestine violence compared to, 97, 99, 101–2
    in Russian empire, 117–18
Poland
    foreign debt, 229
    protests in, 166
    uprising in, 186–87
Politburo, 47–48, 53, 69, 111–12, 128–29, 154–55, 170–71, 222
political and cultural integration, debates on, 71–72
political criticism, growing tolerance of, 231
political decolonization, acceleration of, 20–21
political elite, regional politics dominated by, 127–28
political elites, central authorities, agreements with, 242
political mobilization, 29
political repressions, commemoration of, 241–42
political subversions, 251n.32
political theater, 211
politics
    nationalist vision of, 121
    Soviet large-scale thinking about, 8–9
    territorialization of, 57–58
Pontecorvo, Gillo, 215
Popular Front
    Comintern embrace of strategy of, 132
    communist support of, 132–33
    in France, 133
Popular Movement for the Liberation of Angola (MPLA), 224
populist politics, 233–34
postcolonialism
    popularity of, 241–42
    Soviet anticolonial and imperial politics severed from, 3
    and Soviet internationalism, relationship between, 13–14
    universalizing tendencies of, challenging, 14–15
postcolonial movement, predecessor of, 9

postcolonial state building, film industry during, 208
postcolonial studies
    illuminating blind spots of, 22
    Soviet history and Marxist geopolitics influence on, 244–45
    tendencies in, 15–16
postcolonial theory, limited application of, 14
postcolonial thought, forces shaping, 244
"post-imperial" category, 245
The Postman (film), 210–11
post-Ottoman states, observations concerning, 96
post-Soviet entities, postcolonial critiques of, 243
post-Soviet exile as Arabic literature theme, 246
post-Soviet nationalist narratives, 243
post-Soviet territories, nationalisms across, 241
Powell, Adam Clayton, Jr., 161, 162
Prague Spring, 212–13, 222
pre-revolutionary poetry and music, purges of those suspected of, 143
Primakov, Evgenii, 158–59, 225
    career, 226–27
    Hussein, Saddam, negotiations with, 234
    Jewish background, 227
private property, transformation into public property, 33
production-technical intelligentsia in Central Asia, 170
progressive taxation, 33
"proletarian intelligentsia," 269n.3
proletarianization, 93–94
prominent figures, rehabilitation of, 167–68
purges
    against artists, 200
    commemoration of, 241–42
    containing, 167
    damage inflicted by, overcoming, 171–72
    against elites, 117
    impact of, 122, 126
    against Iraqi communists, 226
    of Jews, 113, 117, 118, 122, 144

purges (*cont.*)
    rationalization for, 114, 129
    silence concerning, 144–45
    against those popularizing archaism, 143
    victims, perpetrators, and witnesses of, 121
Pushkin, Alexander, 135, 149
Putin, Vladimir, 234
    figures in, 239
    foreign policy, 235–36, 239
    Russian military under, 236–37
    Western imperialism denounced by, 237, 243

Qal'aji, Qadri, 137–38, 147
Qandil, Mohamed Mansi, 246

race as international issue, 161–62
racial justice and equality, 215
racial politics, 154
racial segregation and political domination as global problems, 245
racial struggle in Soviet Union, 110
racism, 16, 215
Radek, Karl
    on Arabs in Mesopotamia, 266n.185
    Berger, J. relations with, 106
    communists in Palestine, communication with, 267n.201
    Eastern policy, 47
    on Eastern Question, 53–54
    on Eurasian transcontinental bloc, 56
    on ex-Zionists at KUTV, 94–95
    German influences on, 31–32
    on international diversity at KUTV, 94–95
    writings, 28
Rafes, Moisei, 70, 71–72, 83–84
railroads, nationalizing, 33
Rashidov (KUTV graduate), 109–10, 116, 281n.15
Rashidov, Sharof, 176–78
    Babakhanov, Z., dealings with, 180
    Cuba delegation led by, 187
    Mukhitdinov, N. removal from Presidium, role in, 310–11n.134
    opportunities for, 181
    Uzbek film industry followed by, 205–6

    Yarmatov, K., dealings with, 200, 201, 202, 204
Ratzel, Friedrich, 25, 31–32, 33, 56
Red Army
    in organizational schema, 43–45
    rape and plunder by, 48–49
    victories, 42
"Red Man's Burden," 35–36
regional communist movements, 7–8
regional environmental activism, 7–8
regional politics in Syria and Lebanon, 127–28
religion, 82
religious contacts, role in Soviet-decolonizing world relations, 180
religious diversity, 75–76
repressed or discarded historical frameworks and contingencies, 18
repression, post-Soviet as legacy, 243
Return My Heart (film), 196
revolution, statism association with, 181
revolutionary activities, cultural front of, 64–65
"revolutionary democracy" theory, 158–59
revolutionary-historical films, limitations of, 216
revolutionary nationalism, Soviet support for, 157
revolutionary spaces, geography, expanded of, 52
revolutionary statism, 153
Robeson, Paul, 148–49, 154, 196, 314n.185
Rodchenko, Aleksandr, 45*f*, 46
Romania, 186–87
Rosenthal, Charlotte, 83–85, 86–87, 89
Rosenthal, Joseph, 113
Rostsel'mash (factory), 92, 93–94
Rothstein, Theodore, 29
Roy, M. N., 42–43, 46, 47–48, 49–50, 66, 264n.161
Roziner, Felix, 117
rural societies, depression impact on, 92–93
Russia
    Caucasian resistance against, 168
    colonization as lesser evil, 200–1
    crisis, 1921 in, 53–54
    diverse populations, integration of, 45–46
    economic modernization of, 23

Eurasian location of, 67–68
Europe-Asia division of, 4
foreign policy, factors affecting, 257n.36
Islam and, 15
porous borders and multinational society, 257n.36
search for a better world, 130
tsarist, values of, 200–1
Russia (post-Soviet period), economic crisis, 241–42
Russia and the Arabs (Primakov), 227
Russian, Central Asian, Global, and Middle Eastern studies, integration of, 7
"Russian Arab" (term), 80
Russian "big brother" narrative, 213–14
Russian Civil War, 1917–1920
 anti-Semitism during, 54
 Eastern International creation during, 46
 outbreak of, 23–24
 political imagination during, 43–45
 utopian schemes vulnerable to chaos of, 56–57
Russian classical tradition, 143
Russian Communist Party (RCP), 267n.211
Russian empire
 boundaries, legacy of, 68–69
 narratives about, 11
 Ottoman empire, dealings with, 29
 priorities of, 257n.39
Russian Eurasianism, theory of, 238
Russian fatherland, glorious past of, 105–6
Russian Federation
 anti-Westernism, 237
 expansion of interests, 236–37
 internal diversity, 240
 leadership, 226–27
 Muslims in, 235–36, 239
 regional economic integration, approach to, 238
Russian Imperial College of Foreign Affairs, 30
Russian imperialism, new face of, 238–39
Russian imperial rule
 expansion, history of, 119
 Jewish Question under, 54

legacy of, 34–35
whitewashing of past, 151
Russian Jewish minority, imperial treatment of, 89–90
Russian Jews
 assimilation of, 24
 discrimination against, 18
 elimination from KUTV and Comintern, 20
 emigration to United States and Europe, 54
 killing of, 94–95
 in Palestine, 54
 socialist Zionism, ties to, 122
 in Soviet leadership, 54
Russian language training, 70
Russian Marxist culture, 89–90
Russian minority inhabitants in Soviet borderlands, 103–4
Russian patriotism, 128–29
The Russian Question (Simonov), 301n.135
Russian studies, illuminating blind spots of, 22
Russian values and institutions, 130
Russian women, foreign student relationships with, 83
Russian workers and working class in Turkestan, 40
Russia-Ukraine War, 243
russocentric agenda, Soviet pushing of, 144
russocentric anticosmopolitanism, 145
russocentrism, domestic, 151
Russo-Ottoman War, 1768–1774, 30
russophobia, 166
Rykov, Alexei, 162, 167–68, 261–62n.116

Saburov (Taj Mir), 105
Sadat, Anwar, 226, 245–46
safarbatik (term), 62–63
Safarov, Georgi, 200, 201
 Arabization, views on, 104
 arrest, 119
 Berger, J. relations with, 106
 as Comintern Eastern Section leader, 97–98
 on domestic East and Russian colonialism legacies, 66–67

Safarov, Georgi (*cont.*)
    on Eastern Question, 53–54
    Jewish presence in Palestine criticized by, 98–99
    nationality presented by, 287n.131
    Palestine tensions recognized by, 109–10
    Palestine violence as interpreted by, 121–22
    purge of, 111–12
    on Russians in Turkestan, 40
    Stalin's comments directed at, 71–72
    as Turkburo leader, 42–43
    Turkestan, hopes for, 89
    on Turkestan failures, 40–41, 50–51
Said, Edward, 13, 244
Saliba, Jamil, 148, 298n.82
Saliev, Aziz, 205
samizdat, 233
Sanbayev, Satimzhan, 213–14
Savitsky, P. N. (Petr Savitskii), 34, 238
Second International (Comintern), 54
Second World, Third World connection to, 15
self-determination, 188, 252n.53
self-orientalizing language, 78–79, 87–88
Seliam, Hamdi, 19–20, 195
sense of belonging
    in de-Stalinization era, 149–50
    Easternness *versus*, 294n.37
    Soviet Union nurturing of, 148–49
separatist movements, 251n.32
Shami (Elie (Ilya Naumovich Teper))
    (alias: Shami), 84–85, 99–102, 101*f*, 113, 218–19
Shanghai, 1927 massacre at, 81
Sharbatov, Grigorii, 218–19
Shawi, Niquola, 130–31, 132–33, 135–36
Shelepin, Alexander, 207–8
Shevardnadze, Eduard, 235
Shirinbaev, Sharif, 179
Shubin, Vladimir, 183
Shulaq, Fawzi
    background, 298n.82
    budget drafting, role in, 138–39
    Soviet Union, visit to, 124–25, 137
    after Soviet Union visit, 148
Sidqi, Najati
    career, 280n.176
    Communist Party, expulsion from, 133–34
    divorce laws, Russian explained by, 83
    "Eastern peoples" encounters described by, 121
    Hikmet, N. recalled by, 74
    KUTV living conditions recalled by, 72
    organized communism, attraction to, 19–20
    Soviet perspectives on domestic East embraced by, 74
    Tashkent, visit to, 82, 119–21
    theater director, work with, 140–42
    Trotskyism, accusation of, 81
    Turkestan as training ground for, 89
    work with Hamdi Salam, 61
    writings, 132–33
Simonov, Konstantin, 144, 205, 301n.135
skilled workers, education and training of, 93
Slavic settlers, 97–98
Slavophiles, Eurocentrism challenged by, 5
Snesarev, Andrei, 34
Social Darwinism, 34–35
socialism
    building, 255n.21
    colonialism in contrast to, 154–55
    Islam as religion of, 82
    universal culture presented by, 69
"socialism in one country" doctrine, 68, 69, 87, 88–89
socialist federation, land use by forces of, 280n.180
socialist realism, 144
socialist rituals, 82
socialist state, 294n.35
socialist utopia, 16
Socialist Zionism, 122
social justice, 151–52
social problems, writer's responsibility to reveal, 149
society, struggle for survival of, 145–46
Society of Cultural Relations between Lebanon and the USSR, 149–50
Society of Friendship with Arab Countries, 178–79
Society of Friendship with the Soviet Union, 138–39, 148, 149–50
Society of Friends of Syria and Lebanon, 135–36
Society of Friends of the Soviet Union, 135

Son of the Regiment (Kataev), 140
Sorokin, Karp, 261–62n.116
South Africans, white, 189
South Asia, 254n.80
Southeast Asia
  politics, 199
  Soviet power, efforts to contain in, 160–61
southern Central Asia, 38–39
SOV (Union for the Liberation of the East)
  activities, 36–38
  founding of, 35
  importance, downplaying of, 40–41
  membership card, 37*f*
  merging of remnants into Sovinterprop, 42
  Muslims attracted to, 262n.120
  Turkestan branch, 40
sovereignty, principle of, 68–69
SovExportFilm, 209–10
Soviet Afro-Asian Solidarity Committee (SKSSAA), 180, 182–83
Soviet and Western metageography, 254n.80
Soviet anticolonial legitimacy
  challenges to, 173–74, 182–83, 186–87, 189, 214–15
  damage to, 228–29
  efforts to defend and promote, 199–200, 205–6
  films potentially threatening, 204–5
  1967 war impact on, 207–8
  public education concerning, 200–1
Soviet-Arab friendship, 150–51
Soviet-Arab friendship society, 130–31
Soviet area studies, 247
Soviet avant-garde directors, student work with, 73–74
Soviet-backed autonomous republics, 251n.32
Soviet borderlands
  domestic indigenization in, 104
  indigenization *versus* nationalist deviation countering in, 103
  non-Russians, governing in, 166
Soviet borders
  extending, 160
  secularization of, 20
  securing, 110–11

Soviet censorship, 184
Soviet Central Asia
  as domestic East, 243
  as foreign East model, 119–20, 165
  historic friendship with Russians in, 119
  international attention on, 163–64
  Russification of, 165
  Soviet East representatives in, 119
Soviet Central Asians
  in Afghanistan, 228–29
  Black Americans, comparison to, 182
  mediators, 216
  Muslim visitors from Arab world, encounters with, 82
  as Soviet Union representatives, 12
Soviet civil war mythology, 213
Soviet collapse
  Arab world impacted by, 245–46
  Eastern International fate following, 235
  empire transformation through, 3
  Gorbachev, M.'s role in, 231
  intellectual sense of loss due to, 246
  legacy of, 3
  renegotiating terms of, 22
Soviet communism, intellectual pull of, 152
Soviet counterintelligence, 110
Soviet culture, universalizing, 118
Soviet decolonization, narratives about, 12
Soviet democracy, 144–45
Soviet development, Soviet Easterner support for, 181–82
Soviet domestic "affirmative action empire," 90
Soviet East
  anti-cosmopolitan repressions, overlooking, 20
  and Asia (other parts), relationship between, 89
  Bolshevik revolution in, 21
  field of power, 15–16
  nation-making projects in, 94
  new republics of, 68
  people from, 2
Soviet Easterners
  ethnic particularity as advantage for, 181–82
  foreign student attitudes toward, 89
  as Soviet Union intermediaries, 122–23

Soviet education, value of, 78–79
Soviet-Egyptian Friendship Treaty, 226
Soviet elites, early, Eurocentrism of, 164
Soviet empire, legacies of, 245
Soviet entities, postcolonial critiques of, 243
Soviet Far East, 174
Soviet historiography, changes in, 12
Soviet history
　global impact of, 253n.79
　imperial vestiges in, 4–5
　international-domestic nexus of, 244–45
　interpretations of, 22
　postcolonial studies influenced by, 244–45
Soviet ideology, 11, 244
Soviet intelligence gathering, 53
Soviet internationalism
　characteristics of, 8
　Eastern International as expression of, 223
　East-West divide, transcending through, 118
　and postcolonialism, relationship between, 13–14
Sovietization
　Easternization versus, 71
　Muslim potential to resist, 6–7
　process of, 70
　resistance to, 166
Soviet Jewish orientalists, 246–47
Soviet Jews
　history interpretation acknowledging role of, 243
　national consciousness, 226
　and other ethnic minorities compared, 117–18
　places of settlement for, 95
　postwar repression of, 128–29
　waning influence of, 122–23
Soviet modernization, 58
Soviet modernization theory, 16
Soviet multiethnic Eurasian state, 6–7
Soviet Muslims, 228
Soviet mythology, 10
Soviet nationalities policies, 45–46
Soviet nationalities politics, 90
Soviet nationalities regime
　contradictions of, 58–59
　social base creation as aim of, 252n.53
Soviet Orientalists, 77f
Soviet oriental studies, 10
Soviet past, laws forbidding discussion of, 243
Soviet peripheries, national cultures of, 118
Soviet politics
　in Middle Eastern context, 13
　playing on scripts of, 203
Soviet power, intermediaries of, 241
Soviet project, internationalist ethos of, 241
Soviet puppets, 127
Soviet regionalization, 254n.80
Soviet republics, SSOD friendship assignments to, 174, 175t
Soviet Russia, economic collapse of, 27–28
Soviet socialist republics, borders of, 121
Soviet state
　political objectives *versus* those of other states, 8
　revolution from perspective of, 58
Soviet state power, domestic and global history of, 244
Soviet Union
　anniversaries of rule, 204–5
　and Arab world, cultural relations with, 149–50
　attraction to, 151–52
　capitalist encirclement, fears of, 110
　as colonial "prison of nations," 198–99
　creation of, 68, 87
　culture and literature, support for, 148–49
　economic conditions, 223–24, 229–30
　economic policy, 60
　economy and institutions, collapse of, 22
　emigration from, 63
　foreign policy, 56, 159–60, 165–66, 189–90
　global campaign to destabilize, fight against, 165
　ideological borders of, 88–89
　immigration to, 63–64
　intellectuals' interest in, 127, 128
　iron curtain, 121
　isolationism, 151

League of Nations joined by, 115
Middle East policy, 161
1967 war, response to, 207–8
nostalgia for imperial grandeur, 237
opportunities to come to, 94
paranoia, 138–39
postwar reconstruction, 124
Russian dominance of, perceptions of, 154–55
as symbol of liberation, 150–51
territories, efforts to regain, 160
trips and visits to, 124–25, 127–28, 136, 152, 159 (*see also under groups, e.g.,* Syrian and Lebanese intellectuals: Soviet Union, visit to)
in World War II, 126–27, 133–34, 145–46
Soviet Union source materials
European intellectuals' writings, 124–25
exhibitions, 135–36
Syrian and Lebanese delegate writings, 145, 146–47, 151–52
Soviet Vietnam, Afghanistan as, 228
Soviet youth, disaffection of, 212–13
Soviet Youth Organization Committee, 220
Sovinformburo, 144–45
Sovinterprop (Council for International Propaganda in the East)
in Baku, 50–51
schema, 44f, 43–46
Turkestan branch, 42
Sovnarkom, 36–38, 59
spaghetti Westerns, 200
Spanish Civil War, 133
SSOD (State Committee for Cultural Relations with Foreign Countries), 173–75, 177, 179, 180
after 1967 war, 218
friendship assignments, 175t
Ministry of Culture working with, 174–75
propaganda material, 190
reorganization in, 182–83
VOKS image, distancing from, 179
Stalin, Joseph
admirers of, 226
ambiguities in message, 72
awards given by, 195

Berger, J. relations with, 106
on border between Easts, 10
bourgeois press crusade against Russia, calls for fight against, 309n.103
Chiang Kai-shek, alliance with, 94
criticisms of, 186–87
cult of personality, 156–57
death, 129, 166
defenders of, 246
domestic and international priorities, 3–4
domestic Easterner-foreigner relations prescribed by, 75
domestic nationalities policies, changing, 165–66
East, concern over threats posed by, 110
East abandoned by, 20
Eastern duality as presented by, 1–2
East importance stressed by, 28, 29
Easts as distinguished by, 9, 20–21, 68–69, 70, 90, 121–22
on Eurasian transcontinental bloc, 56
Europe security, concerns over, 126
foreign policy, 126
"Great Break," reference to, 104
Greater Danger Principle abandoned by, 105–6
"Great Retreat," 200–1
ideological crackdown, 136–37
imperialism crisis imagined by, 52–53
on Jewish nationhood, 266n.197
Khrushchev, N. ridiculed by, 156
KUTV students, address to, 1–2, 69, 213–14
"lesser evil" hypothesis, 119
Muslim leaders, dealings with, 29
Muslim national communists, struggle against, 271–72n.43
Muslim world existence, belief in, 29
nationalist separatism, method of controlling, 67
on political and cultural integration, 71–72
"proletarian intelligentsia" category created by, 269n.3
security as approached by, 160
self-determination, position on, 66–67
"socialism in one country" doctrine promoted by, 88–89

Stalin, Joseph (*cont.*)
  Soviet republic autonomy as described by, 48–49
  Troianovskii, K., dealings with, 35
  Troianovskii, K. vision endorsed by, 57
  Trotsky, L., fallout with, 81
  Turkestan, views on, 38–39
  Western allies, 127
  writings, 27, 29, 137
Stalin-era repressions, 150–51
Stalinism
  contradictions of late, 128
  filmmaking during period of, 193–94, 195
  rehabilitation of victims of, 167–68
  repressive cultural terrain of postwar, 145–46
Stalin Revolution, 92–93
state, literature critical of, 147
state as organism, 257n.50
state building, postcolonial, film industry during, 208
state power, structures of, 243
State Teknikum for Cinematography, 190–91
statism, revolution association with, 181
Steinbeck, John, 124, 138
Stender, Elena, 25
Storm over Asia (originally *Dawn over Asia*) (film), 201–5, 210
St. Petersburg
  domestic Eastern migrants in, 22
  Moscow replacement of, 90
Stronger than Death (Qa'aji), 137–38
students, proletarianization of, 93–94
Subbotin (Rauf Akhmedovich, Osman Ahmad Zaghrur), 102–3
Subhi, Mustafa, 42
subhuman as category, 215
Suez Crisis, 1956, 151–52, 153, 181
Sukarno, 161, 189, 198–99
Suleimenov, Olzhas, 213–14, 231–33, 239
Sultanov, Abdurakhman, 115, 119
Sulzberger, Cyrus Leo, 165
"superiority-inferiority complex" (term), 6
superpowers, global competition between, 154
supra-national belonging, conversations about, 90

Suslov, Mikhail, 137, 139–40, 143, 158, 159, 173, 185–86
Sverdlov University, 65
Sweden, 264n.164
Syria
  anticommunist repressions in, 22, 147
  anti-fascist momentum in, 133–34
  Armenians in, 122
  British involvement in, 126, 134
  emigration from, 62–63
  European control over, 130
  gendered hierarchies in, 86
  independence, 125–26, 134, 136, 151
  in interwar period, 17
  military coups in, 152
  nationalist movement in, 88–89
  Soviet relations with, 189–90, 222–23, 225
  Soviet-supported cultural activities in, 136–37
  Soviet weapons supplied to, 207–8
Syrian and Lebanese intellectuals
  energy and compromises of leftist, 151–52
  Soviet politics, approach to, 127
  Soviet Union, visit to, 124–26, 125*f*, 129, 130, 137–40, 145, 146–47, 152
Syrian Civil War, 236
Syrian Communist Party, 222
Syrian communists, 157–58
Syrian Left, 133
Syrian Revolt, 86
Syrians, Russian "cultural" influence among, 127
Syrian-Soviet Friendship Committee, 124–25

Tabit, Antun
  Ehrenburg, I., contact with, 144
  Hanna, G., relationship to, 138
  Soviet Union, visit to, 124–25, 133, 137–38, 139–40
  after Soviet Union visit, 148–49
  Soviet writers, contact with, 144
  writings, 146–47
Tagore, Rabindranath, 34
Tajikistan
  civil war, 235

educational opportunities in, 169–70
fraud in, 310–11n.134
public history of, 241–42
Russian military exercises in, 240
transformations, expectations raised by, 183
Tajik Komsomol, 221
Talib, Mukhammad Said, 219
Tankhel'son, Aleksandr, 211
Tashkent
 Arab communists sent to, 82, 119–22
 communications between Moscow and, 42
 conferences, 177–78
 conquest, commemoration of, 241–42
 development of, 8–9
 earthquake and rebuilding, 206–7
 information, limited about, 114–15
 korenizatsiia in, 103–4
 language instruction, 313n.170
 visits to, 107–9, 114–15, 177
Tashkent Afro-Asian Film Festival. *See* Afro-Asian Film Festival
Tatar-Bashkir Republic, 32–33
Tatars, 119
technical fields, educational opportunities in, 170
technicians, education and training of, 93
telegraphs, nationalizing, 33
territoriality, age of, 268n.214
"territorialization" as slogan, 55–56
"Thaw"
 Khrushchev, N. and, 156
 Muslims, opportunities during, 181–82
 overview of, 155
 Soviet challenges during, 173–74
 travel and tourism opportunities opened up by, 176–77
Third International (Comintern), 3–4, 40–41, 51–52, 54
Third World
 anti-imperialist ideology recentering, 228
 Brezhnev-Kosygin leadership in, 218
 countries, students from, 169–70
 nationalisms, 245
 progressive nationalisms, 183–84
 Second World connection to, 15

Soviet culture in, 155–56
Soviet invasions in, 228, 229
Third World film, emerging new language about, 324n.186
Third World project
 collapse of, 245–46
 internationalisms promoted by, 214–15
 Soviet filmmaker participation in, 217–18
Three-World ideology, 15
Tian-Shanskii, Pyotr Semyonov, 32–33
Tito, Josip, 156–57, 185
Tolstoy, Lev, 130, 145, 149
totalitarian models of Soviet state, 4–5
training ground, Turkestan as, 89
Transcaucasia, 182–83
Transcaucasian Democratic Federative Republic, 38
Transcaucasian Soviet Federated Socialist Republic, 262n.127
"transcolonial ecumene" (term), 15–16
"transnational world of the Comminternians" (term), 8–9
transregional case studies, socialist and anticolonial integration friction in, 16
transregional politics, 121
Tripartite Aggression, 1956, 159–60
Troianovskii, Elena [Helen], 40, 262n.125
 career, 59
 Moscow, arrival in, 50
 photo, 51*f*
 Switzerland, family ties in, 51–52
Troianovskii, Konstantin
 on achieving anticolonial liberation, 33
 anti-imperialist revolution, 34
 arrest and imprisonment, 25
 Avigdor dealings with, 83–84
 background, 24
 Bolshevik revolution spread as conceived by, 32–33
 career, 56–57
 Comintern's Near East Section headed by, 19, 24
 Eastern International, idea of, 8–9, 30–31, 57–58, 174
 Eastern revolution as conceived by, 30–31, 34–35, 40

Troianovskii, Konstantin (*cont.*)
  education, 24–25
  Egypt, interest in, 52, 53–54
  on Egyptian independence, 83–84
  Eurasian networks of Eastern International imagined by, 172
  India, thoughts on competition over, 34
  influences on, 31–32, 34
  Islam, approach to, 32
  Kobozev, P. criticism of, 40–42
  KUTV praised by, 66
  Lunacharskii, A. background compared to that of, 35–36
  in Moscow, 50–52
  old age and obscurity, 59
  outward-moving revolutionary signals, model of, 68–69
  on Palestine's strategic importance, 55
  photos, 26f, 51f
  scholarly pursuits, 59
  SOV founded by, 35
  as Sovinterprop publication section head, 42
  SOV membership card, 37f
  students trained by, 19–20
  Tashkent, trip to, 39–40
  Turkestan, views on, 89
  in Turkestan, 40–42
  unemployment, 59
  as visionary, 57
  world revolution in East, role in, 56, 238–39
  writings, 30–31, 31f, 40–41
Trotsky, Leon
  East significance downplayed by, 49–50
  international situation as viewed by, 38–39
  Jewish background, 54
  murder accusation against, 111–12
  nationality presented by, 287n.131
  Stalin, J., fallout with, 81
  writings, 184
Trotskyists, 113–14
tsarist conquest, reclassification of, 193–94
tsarist imperialism, defense of, 200–1
Turkburo (Turkestan Bureau of the Comintern)
  abolition of, 49–50
  failures of, 50–51
  formation of, 42–43
  nodes and connections, 43–45, 51–52
  schema, 44f, 45–46
Turkestan
  and Asia (other parts), relationship between, 89
  autonomy, question of, 57–58, 261–62n.116
  Central Asian republics, refashioning into, 88–89
  Central Asian Revolt impact on, 38
  civil war in, 88, 97–98, 261n.104
  as colonial territory, 5–6
  conflict in, colonial dimensions of, 119
  dramatic depictions of colonial life in, 74
  as East prototype, 65
  food access in, 40
  Indian revolutionaries from, 66
  industrialization of Soviet, 120–21
  Muslims, indigenous in, 20, 40–42
  Muslims communists in, 57–58
  official histories of, 12
  pacification of, 49
  Russian colonial settlers in, 20
  Russians in, 40
  socialist revolution in, 202
  Soviet rule in, 200–1, 203–4
  world-historical importance of, 89
Turkestan Commission, 40–42, 49, 57–58
Turkey
  Arab provinces exploited by, 100–1
  Soviet interest in, 126
Turkmenistan nationalist identity project in, 241–42
Turko-Muslim minorities, 238–39
Turson-zade, Mirzo, 143–44

Ukraine
  neighboring power colonization, hypothetical of, 119
  Russian invasion of, 237, 239
  Russian war in, 238
Ukrainians, Christian and white identity of, 237
Ulianovskii, Rostislav, 158, 183
underdeveloped countries, 158–59

Union of Soviet Writers, 144
United Arab Republic, collapse of, 316–17n.27
United States
  anti-imperialism, foundational myth of, 245
  Egypt, relations with, 226
  foreign policy, critique of, 183–84
  internationalisms promoted by, 214–15
  Iraq, war with, 234
  isolationist policy, 62–63
  migration to, 63–64
  military bases, 159–60
  racial discrimination in, 152, 161–62
  Russian Jewish immigration to, 54
  Soviet competition with, 224, 233
  Soviet Jews with relatives in, 128–29
  Soviet relations with, 156, 229–30
  speech, restrictions on, 215–16
United States of Asia, 33, 40–41
uprising of 1905, 25
US civil rights movement
  anticommunist politics and, 154, 182
  women in, 251–52n.49
US House Un-American Activities Committee, 138
US National Security Council directive NSC-158, 165–66
US State Department, 127
utopianism, 45–46
Uzbek-Arab relations, 180
Uzbek-Arab solidarity activities, 178–79
Uzbek culture
  attempts to "isolate," 143
  disappearance, predictions of, 169
  representatives of, 176–77
Uzbek Ethnographic Troupe, 142–43
Uzbek intelligentsia, 170, 179
Uzbekistan
  cinema industry in, 205–6
  earthquake, 1966, 206–7
  educational opportunities in, 169–70
  independence, 173
  India and Central Asian republics, historic connections between, 163–64
  leaders, 157–58
  mediating interests of, 197–98
  as part of Soviet Union, 169
  regional leadership, 240
  source materials, 140
  Soviet power established in, 200
  visits to, 139–40
Uzbek music
  classical, 178
  criticisms and repressions, 142–44
  folk and classical, 142–43
  poster, 142f
Uzbek operas, 146
Uzbek republic, anniversaries of, 200, 203
Uzbek Society of Friendship with Arab countries, 179
Uzbek writers, 168
UzSOD, 176, 178–79
  correspondents, 176t
  India, China, and Arab countries access increased by, 181
  institutional culture, 179

Versailles Treaty
  opposition to, 61–62
  Soviet Union left out of, 3–4
  world order, end of, 124–25
victimhood, commemoration of, 241–42
Vietnam War, 187, 215–16, 228
VOKS (All-Union Society for Cultural Ties Abroad)
  invitations from, 124, 137
  leadership, 136–37
  Mashriq, connections to, 136
  Ministry of Culture working with, 174–75
  Partisans of Peace, involvement with, 148–49
  police networks and state control, image as cover for, 179
  records and files, 135, 137
  Soviet-Arab friendship society linkages with, 130–31, 135–36
  Soviet Union travel arrangements, involvement in, 137–38, 139–42
  successor organization, 173–74
  suspicions of, 138
  Uzbek branch of, 177 (*see also* SSOD (State Committee for Cultural Relations with Foreign Countries))

Vostochniki (Asianists), 5
Voznesenskii, Arsenii
   NKID, work in, 27, 36–38, 47–48
   writings, 28

wall newspaper in Arabic and Russian (KUTV assignment), 76
war fronts, international awareness of, 134–35
Warsaw Pact, 156–57, 165–66
wealth disparities, 215–16
West
   imaginary, 181
   materialist *versus* spiritual Orient, 34
   Soviet anticolonial legitimacy challenged by, 182–83
   Soviet relationship with, 6
   Soviet Union as alternative to, 151–52
   Soviet Union as other, 16
   symbolism of, 237
Western and Soviet metageography, divergence of, 254n.80
Western Arabia (term), 55
Western Asia (term), 17
Western civilization
   challenging imitation of, 130
   Russian values and institutions as distinct from, 130
Western critics, Soviet anticolonial legitimacy challenged by, 173–74
Western cultural superiority, myth of, 16
Western culture, rejection of, 128–29
Western Europe, encounter with and resistance to, 15
Western hegemony, Asian societies and cultures threatened by, 258–59n.74
Western imperialism
   denunciations of, 237, 243
   renewed phase of, 133
Westernization
   Asian societies and cultures threatened by global, 258–59n.74
   cultural, 151
   era of, 6
   Soviet attitudes concerning, 6
Western orientalism, 13
Western postcolonial theory, Arab Marxists' critiques of, 13–14

What Is to Be Done? (Lenin), 30
White Sun of the Desert (film), 213, 237
Wilson, Woodrow, 40–41, 62
women
   of the East, 85, 86–87
   political activism of, 11
   as revolutionary activists, 83–87
   status of, 11, 86
women students, pregnancy among, 280n.172
working class
   peasant relations with, 68
   in Turkestan, 40
world literature, globalized system of, 9
world order, post-World War I reconfiguration of, 19
World Peace Council, 148–49
World Republic, belief in, 23
world revolution
   Bolshevik projections for, 23, 64–65
   delineation of, 95
   geopolitics and, 69
   language of, 70
   Palestine conflict and, 100
   planning for, 57–58
   promoting, 99
World War I, 3, 29
World War II
   international relations shift due to, 151
   onset of, 116–17
   Soviet film industry during, 194–95
   Soviet victory in, 145–46
worldwide discourse, geography as unified, 57–58
Wright, Richard, 161

xenophobia
   foreign students affected by, 111–12
   late Stalin-era, 128
   rising tide of, 110

Yarmatov, Kamil
   Afro-Asian Film Festival, 1968 promoted by, 208
   at Afro-Asian Film Festival, 1968, 190, 196–98, 209
   Black American performers compared to, 215–16

Bolshevik revolution narrative, attempt to craft, 21
films and film career, 192–95, 210–13
ideological contradictions, grappling with, 186, 200–5, 216, 231
memoirs, 212
national and racial justice as film themes addressed by, 215
origin and background, 190–92
photo, 194f
Soviet orientalism, relationship with, 191–92
younger critics of, 213–14
Yeltsin, Boris, 235, 329n.93
East neglected by, 237
Westernization under, 6
Yemen
as republic, 224
Soviet relations with, 53
Yiddish cultural institutions, 128–29
Yishuv. *See* Palestine, Jewish community in
"Yishuvism," doctrine of, 267n.203
Young Bukharan Committee, 41–42
youth organizations, influences on, 127–28
Yugoslavia, 186–87

zagranitsa (imaginary elsewhere), 181
Zhdanov, Andrei, 136–37, 144–45, 194–95, 298n.83
Zinoviev, Grigory, 48, 81, 97–98
Berger, J. relations with, 106
East significance downplayed by, 49–50
murder accusation against, 111–12
Zionism
disillusionment with, 94–95
as fluid category, 113–14
Jewish colonization and, 286n.117
in Palestine, 109
Russian Jew ties to, 122
Soviet media attacks on, 226
Zionist emigration to Palestine, 54, 94–95
Zoshchenko, Mikhail, 144

The manufacturer's authorised representative in the EU for product safety is Oxford University Press España S.A. of El Parque Empresarial San Fernando de Henares, Avenida de Castilla, 2 – 28830 Madrid (www.oup.es/en or product.safety@oup.com). OUP España S.A. also acts as importer into Spain of products made by the manufacturer.

Printed in the USA/Agawam, MA
April 11, 2025

885760.004